The Waite Group's
Tricks of the
HyperTalk™ Masters

R E L A T E D   T I T L E S

The Waite Group's
Tricks of the
HyperTalk™ Masters

Edited by The Waite Group

HAYDEN BOOKS

A Division of Howard W. Sams & Company
4300 West 62nd Street
Indianapolis, Indiana 46268 USA

International Standard Book Number: 0-672-48431-5
Library of Congress Catalog Card Number: 89-60592

From the Waite Group

Development Editor: *Mitchell Waite*
Content Editor: *Scott Calamar*
Technical Reviewers: *Bruce Barrett and Greg Jorgensen*

From Howard W. Sams & Company

Acquisitions Editor: *Greg Michael*
Development Editor: *James Rounds*
Production Coordinator: *Katherine Stuart Ewing*
Illustrator: *Wm. D. Basham*
Cover Illustrator: *Garry Nichols*
Cover Art Production: *Celeste Design*
Indexer: *Ted Laux*
Compositor: *Shepard Poorman Communications Corporation*

Printed in the United States of America

To my wonderful mom,
Charlotte Caroline Waite,
who gave me life,
wiped away tears,
held a tiny, trembling hand,
gave birthday parties even when I was bad,
and loved me so unconditionally.
I'll love you forever, Mom.

Mitchell Waite

Overview

Contents

Part 2   Field Tricks

2   *ScrollJump*

Jumping Through a Stack Gently
—Mitchell Waite

8   *Animated Fonts*   *187*

32,000 Graphic Layers Await You
—Mitchell Waite

Part 4 Graphics and Sound

9 *The Art of Visual Effects*

Create a Look and Feel That Dazzles
   —Jeanne A. E. DeVoto

10 *Synching Sight and Sound*

From Sound Effects to Music Videos
   —Mitchell Waite

17 *Large Stacks*

Speeding Up Large Stacks
—*Steven F. Martin*

Foreword

For some time, there has been a lack of cookbooks that really exercise Hyper-Card's HyperTalk language. When I first heard of this book, I had low expectations. Happily, I am pleased to report that *The Waite Group's Tricks of the HyperTalk Masters* lives up to its goal: It provides stacks, scripts, and techniques from some real experts.

Do these authors qualify as "masters"? They certainly do if you judge them on the quality of their work in this book. Mitch Waite and his team have assembled an impressive collection of well-tested and useful tools. *The Waite Group's Tricks of the HyperTalk Masters* contains scripts for all experience levels—from simple projects that show different ways to use scrolling list boxes to an exotic CompuServe Information Service front-end called Chauffeur. The PolyButtons stack is an impressive demonstration of just how far HyperTalk can take you without requiring an external command (XCMD). You'll appreciate the complete analysis of HyperTalk's command language, in which every statement is accompanied by speed benchmarks. You can even find a chapter on how to make your own music video with HyperCard!

Take a look at the table of contents of this book and you'll see what I mean. I think you will be using your own copy of *The Waite Group's Tricks of the HyperTalk Masters* for some time to come. I tip my hat to these talented scriptors; good work!

Steve Maller
Software Engineer
Apple Computer

Preface

When we started *Tricks of the HyperTalk Masters*, HyperCard itself was less than three months old. Although The Waite Group normally waits until a software product is well established before starting a book on it, we found that HyperTalk was too revolutionary to pass up. Here was the first easy-to-use software product to implement modern concepts of object-oriented programming, message passing, and inheritance. When coupled with its powerful graphics tools, digitized sounds, and friendly interface, this product, we knew, was going to set a new standard in programming languages, so we quickly signed contracts for *two* HyperTalk books; a tutorial-reference book and a more advanced book of tricks. Although the tutorial-reference book was fairly straightforward to write, our overriding concern at that time was that very few "masters" of HyperTalk could be found, and few tricks had yet been established. After all, it takes several months to master any computer language and then several more to come up with unique things to do with it. This meant we could either have a HyperTalk tricks book that covered surface topics but was out on the market fast (a popular strategy in the computer book publishing industry), or we could have a book that went into depth but did not come out for some time and, therefore, had a harder time finding space on the bookstore shelves. We eventually chose the latter strategy, figuring we would all feel better with a quality book, even if it had to fight its way into the stores. We asked our authors to probe, test, explore, and generally tear into HyperTalk so as to stretch its capabilities to the limit. Although we gave these masters more time than most publishers offer to complete chapters, we also demanded that they go the distance to find ways to make HyperCard and HyperTalk do things that most programmers would think were difficult or impossible.

The results, in my opinion, were worth the wait. We think that the book you are holding is one of the best examples of what a team of developers can do when highly motivated and when given a clear mandate: make a great chapter that will interest other developers. *The Waite Group's Tricks of the HyperTalk Masters* contains some of the most amazing programs and developments that have passed our way in twelve years of publishing computer books.

To further complicate the development of the book, while it was in progress, HyperTalk underwent three version changes. This caused us to revise our chapters and scripts so that they would be consistent and up-to-date. You will find that the book is compatible with the latest version of HyperCard, 1.2.2. (We suggest that you upgrade to the latest version, because its new features will make your scripting much more powerful.)

Another difference between this book and others we have done is that the entire set of scripts, icons, digitized sounds, graphics, and XCMD resources are available on disk from Heizer Software Exchange, so you don't have to type or draw anything.

If you are just starting with HyperCard, take a look at *The Waite Group's Hyper-Talk Bible*, a self-study book designed for beginning to intermediate users, which teaches programming concepts along with HyperTalk syntax.

If you want to send comments on the book or suggestions for improvements, or if you wish to contribute to our future Macintosh books, you can reach us at The Waite Group, 100 Shoreline Highway, Building A, Suite 285, Mill Valley, California, 94941, (415) 331-0575. If you have a computer and a modem, you can also reach me on the following networks.

Well: hplabs!well!mitch
AppleLink: D2097
CompuServe: 75146,3515
BIX: mwaite
MCI Mail: MITCH

Mitchell Waite

Acknowledgments

Many creative minds converged in the process of writing *The Waite Group's Tricks of the HyperTalk Masters.* First, thanks to the authors: Jeremy Ahouse, Joseph Buchanan, Jeanne DeVoto, Nick Hodge, Ted Jones, Steven Martin, Jack Smith, Andrew Stone, David Sumner, Mitchell Waite, and Mark ^Zimmermann. We are grateful to this inspired group for their energy and their enthusiasm, and for sticking with us through outlines and draft after draft of rewrites.

We also greatly appreciate the support of those at Apple Computer, especially David Szetela, Manager of Developer Services, and Peggy Redpath, Evangelist, for helping us get our titles reviewed and checked. Greg Jorgensen, of Apple Computer's Macintosh Developer Technical Support staff, spent many of his own hours poring over the manuscript, scrutinizing and improving the scripts. Bruce Barrett of Lunden and Associates did more than just review the book, he showed us numerous tricks and improvements to our scripts, especially to PolyButtons. Kay Nelson once again proved herself to be an excellent editor, especially under deadline pressure.

You'll notice that there is a companion disk package to this book that contains stacks, scripts, and the Complete HyperTalk Reference section of the book in a handy on-line form. We kindly thank Gary Wells, Jeremy Ahouse, and Bob Johnson for their valuable assistance with creation of this stack. Thanks, too, to Ray Heizer and Bryan Molyneaux at Heizer Software for nursing us along.

Our thanks to the staff and readers of *Macintosh Hands-On* magazine for providing a dialogue with readers that resulted in improved scripts and some great ideas. And to the "unsung soldiers" who took part in the evolution and preparation of this book: Eveline Frei, Ken Hulme, Jeff Baudine, Birrell Walsh, Jackie Macapanan, Roland Mailleux, Eric Azarcon, Rhett Savage, Kevin Altis, TeriAnn Wakeman, and Tom Pittman. We sincerely appreciate your efforts.

As always, we are grateful to the people at Howard W. Sams & Company. Thanks to Greg Michael, Acquisitions Editor, Hayden Books, who inspired us to take on a project of this magnitude, and to Wendy Ford for making this book and the *HyperTalk Bible* live up to our most imaginative expectations. Thanks to Kathy Ewing, whose production coordination of both HyperTalk books made these products run smoothly, even under the most pressing deadlines. Glenn Santner directed, and Garry Nichols painted, a magnificent cover that completely captured our ideas. Thanks to Jim Rounds for his support and assistance during manuscript preparation. And, of course, thanks to Damon Davis, Tom Surber, and Jim Irizarry for their hard work and support.

Trademarks

All terms mentioned in this book that are known to be trademarks or service marks are listed below. In addition, terms suspected of being trademarks or service marks have been appropriately capitalized. Howard W. Sams & Company cannot attest to the accuracy of this information. Use of a term in this book should not be regarded as affecting the validity of any trademark or service mark.

Apple, the Apple logo, HyperCard, ImageWriter, and LaserWriter are registered trademarks and Finder, HyperTalk, Macintosh, Macintosh Plus, Macintosh SE, Macintosh II, MultiFinder, and Stackware are trademarks of Apple Computer, Inc. Apple Computer, Inc. also owns the copyright to ResEdit and ResCopy.

Compuserve is a registered trademark of CompuServe Information Services, an H & R Block Company.

fEdit is a trademark of MacMaster Systems.

FONTastic Plus is a trademark of Altsys Corporation.

Icon Factory is a trademark of HyperPress Publishing Company.

IBM PS/2, OS/2, and Presentation Manager are registered trademarks of International Business Machines Corporation.

Lightspeed C is a trademark of THINK Technologies, Inc.

MacDraw and MacPaint are registered trademarks of CLARIS Corporation.

MacRecorder, HyperSound, and SoundEdit are trademarks of Farallon Computing.

Microphone is a registered trademark of Software Ventures Corporation.

MockWrite is a trademark of CE Software.

Red Ryder is a registered trademark of Freesoft Corporation.

SuperPaint is a trademark of Silicon Beach Software, Inc.

Suitcase II is a trademark of Fifth Generation Systems, Inc.

Word is a trademark of the Microsoft Corporation.

WordPerfect is a registered trademark of WordPerfect Corporation.

The Authors

Jeremy John Ahouse teaches advanced HyperCard workshops for Apple Computer to educators. A veteran programmer since the early days of the Mac, Mr. Ahouse divides his time between getting a masters degree in Mathematical Modeling in Ecology and doing consulting and development for his company, Waves. His specialty is mixing technology with ecology, particularly using computers for environmental modeling. He has degrees in Biophysics and Zoology from the University of California at Berkeley. Mr. Ahouse's talent for assembling informative yet attractive HyperCard stacks is evident in his Animation Ideas and Conservation Biology stacks. Many of those ideas can be found in his chapter. He is the author of chapter 7, "Animated Icons and Cursors."

Joseph F. Buchanan is a Senior Programmer-Analyst for the University of Utah Computer Center. He began programming with Fortran II on the Univac in the summer of 1968 at the University of Utah and joined the University's Macintosh team in early 1984. Mr. Buchanan has written several external commands (XCMDs) and the HyperCard stack "Getting the Most of the Macintosh," which gives a basic understanding of the Macintosh's operating system. His HyperAnimals stack provides a fun and educational look at using binary tree structures to simulate intelligence under HyperTalk. He is the author of chapter 13, "HyperAnimals."

Jeanne A. E. DeVoto is a Macintosh consultant with expertise in HyperCard and software technical support. She works with C, Pascal, and especially UNIX and the Mac operating system. Her largest-scale HyperCard project to date is a 2 Mbyte electronic reference manual for a major Macintosh hardware and software company. Ms. DeVoto has bachelor of science degrees in Physics and Math from Reed College in Oregon. Writing HyperCard stacks for trade shows has enabled Ms. DeVoto to explore and refine the techniques of tight scripting, user-friendly stack design, and the use of visual effects, as exemplified in her chapters on stack development and visual effects. She is the author of chapter 1, "Techniques for Stack Development," and chapter 9, "The Art of Visual Effects."

Nick Hodge is the Technical Support Manager for an Apple Dealership in Adelaide, South Australia. A Macintosh programmer since Macintoshes appeared in South Australia, and a frustrated Pascal programmer, he now finds HyperTalk a perfect way to write programs. Mr Hodge is the youngest Macintosh master in this book and has produced the largest project stack. His Chauffeur front-end consumes 106 kilobytes and its listings require 65 pages. He is the author of chapter 15, "Chauffeur."

Ted Jones is a professional programming consultant and author specializing in Microsoft BASIC and HyperTalk. He is co-author of *The Waite Group's HyperTalk Bible* and a contributor to the BMUG (Berkeley Macintosh Users Group) Newsletter. Mr. Jones has a bachelor of science in Liberal Arts from Arizona State University. Along with Mitchell Waite, Mr. Jones is the creator of PolyButtons, which expands HyperTalk by adding multiple-sided, nonrectangular buttons to the scriptor's toolbench. Mr. Jones assembled the companion stack to this book and to *The Waite Group's HyperTalk Bible*. He is the author of chapter 4, "Quick Pop-Up Fields," Chapter 14, "A Grab Bag of Utilities," and the Reference section, and the co-author of chapter 3, "Dueling Scroll," and chapter 6, "PolyButtons."

Steven F. Martin works at the Computer Science Center of Texas Instruments in Dallas, Texas, where his current work in the field of Hypermedia exposed him to using HyperCard to manage very large databases. Mr. Martin has a masters of science degree in Electrical Engineering and Computer Science from The Massachusetts Institute of Technology. His love of cinema led to an ambitious (more than 5 Mbytes) database to catalog movies and gave him many insights into speeding up large stacks. He is the author of chapter 17, "Large Stacks."

Jack A. Smith is a staff engineer for the Applied Mathematics and Process Simulation group of Central Research and Engineering at Union Carbide. He specializes in system software development for UNIX-based engineering workstations and in computational chemistry, particularly molecular modeling. He holds a master of science degree and a doctorate in Chemical Physics from the University of Florida and was a member of that University's Quantum Theory Project. His most recent work includes scientific application development on the Macintosh using C and Fortran. His Menu Fields scripts show adaptive techniques for extending HyperCard's capability of making custom menus. He is the author of chapter 5, "Menu Fields."

Andrew Stone is a Macintosh programming consultant who enlisted in the computer revolution in 1980. An architect and builder, he now develops custom software in C, Fortran, and HyperTalk for clients. Mr. Stone is the "Prime Minister" of New Mexico's largest HyperCard Special Interest Group and is a prolific scriptor. In his two chapters, he provides a battery of scripting tools that he has developed over the last year, including the QuizMaker, an invoice maker, and a stack reporter. He is the author of chapter 11, "Developer's Tool Kit," and chapter 12, "The Quiz Maker."

HOWARD W. SAMS & COMPANY

Bookmark

DEAR VALUED CUSTOMER:

Howard W. Sams & Company is dedicated to bringing you timely and authoritative books for your personal and professional library. Our goal is to provide you with excellent technical books written by the most qualified authors. You can assist us in this endeavor by checking the box next to your particular areas of interest.

We appreciate your comments and will use the information to provide you with a more comprehensive selection of titles.

Thank you,

Vice President, Book Publishing
Howard W. Sams & Company

COMPUTER TITLES:

Hardware
- ☐ Apple 140
- ☐ Macintosh 101
- ☐ Commodore 110
- ☐ IBM & Compatibles 114

Business Applications
- ☐ Word Processing J01
- ☐ Data Base J04
- ☐ Spreadsheets J02

Operating Systems
- ☐ MS-DOS K05
- ☐ OS/2 K10
- ☐ CP/M K01
- ☐ UNIX K03

Programming Languages
- ☐ C L03
- ☐ Pascal L05
- ☐ Prolog L12
- ☐ Assembly L01
- ☐ BASIC L02
- ☐ HyperTalk L14

Troubleshooting & Repair
- ☐ Computers S05
- ☐ Peripherals S10

Other
- ☐ Communications/Networking M03
- ☐ AI/Expert Systems T18

ELECTRONICS TITLES:
- ☐ Amateur Radio T01
- ☐ Audio T03
- ☐ Basic Electronics T20
- ☐ Basic Electricity T21
- ☐ Electronics Design T12
- ☐ Electronics Projects T04
- ☐ Satellites T09

- ☐ Instrumentation T05
- ☐ Digital Electronics T11

Troubleshooting & Repair
- ☐ Audio S11
- ☐ Television S04
- ☐ VCR S01
- ☐ Compact Disc S02
- ☐ Automotive S06
- ☐ Microwave Oven S03

Other interests or comments: _____

_____

_____

Name _____

Title _____

Company _____

Address _____

City _____

State/Zip _____

Daytime Telephone No. _____

A Division of Macmillan, Inc.
4300 West 62nd Street
Indianapolis, Indiana 46268

48431

Bookmark

 HOWARD W. SAMS
& COMPANY

BUSINESS REPLY CARD

FIRST CLASS   PERMIT NO. 1076   INDIANAPOLIS, IND.

POSTAGE WILL BE PAID BY ADDRESSEE

HOWARD W. SAMS & CO.
ATTN: Public Relations Department
P.O. BOX 7092
Indianapolis, IN 46209-9921

David P. Sumner is Associate Professor of Mathematics at the University of South Carolina. A contributor to dozens of journals, microcomputer magazines, and a book, he has worked extensively with almost every popular microcomputer but is now primarily involved with the Macintosh. Dr. Sumner is the developer of Supera, a popular macro program for the Tandy and NEC laptop computers, and Memory Tools, a stack that provides HyperTalk developers with 14 useful external functions, including a full-fledged 68000 disassembler. Creating that stack contributed to Dr. Sumner's expertise in external functions and commands. He is the author of chapter 18, "Extending HyperTalk with Externals."

Mitchell Waite is an experienced programmer, fluent in a variety of computer languages, including C, Pascal, BASIC, Assembly, and HyperTalk. He wrote his first computer book in 1976 and is co-author of *The Waite Group's HyperTalk Bible, C Primer Plus*, and many other titles. He also writes a column on HyperTalk for *Macintosh Hands On* magazine. Mr. Waite created PolyButtons, Dueling Scroll Fields, ScrollJump, and the music video in this book. He is especially interested in educational applications of HyperCard and multimedia. Mr. Waite is president of The Waite Group, located in Mill Valley, California, a developer of computer books. He is the author of chapter 2, "ScrollJump," chapter 8, "Animated Fonts," and chapter 10, "Synching Sight and Sound," and co-author of chapter 3, "Dueling Scroll," and chapter 6, "PolyButtons."

Mark ^Zimmermann started programming mainframe computers in 1968, moved to the Macintosh in 1984, and is a pioneer HyperTalk programmer. He has written articles for *Byte, Creative Computing, Personal Computing*, and other magazines. Mr. ^Zimmermann now works mostly in C on the Mac and on UNIX machines. His main interest is the development of "real-time, high-bandwidth, free-text information retrieval tools," including the popular TEXAS DataSpace Analysis Tool. Mr. ^Zimmermann's benchmarking stack provides valuable insights into getting the most performance from HyperTalk. This indexer/browser of large text documents can be found on CompuServe. He is the author of chapter 16, "Benchmarking Hyper-Talk."

Part

General Tips and Tricks

1 Techniques for Stack Development

Techniques for Stack Development

Jeanne A. E. DeVoto

Synopsis: If you have ever programmed in a language such as BASIC, FORTRAN, or Pascal, then HyperTalk, with its object-oriented, message-driven techniques, will strike you as very different. This chapter reveals the things that an experienced programmer wants to know: mastering messages, how handlers work, the different kinds of variables in HyperTalk (such as it), input and output, creatively using the HyperTalk containers the selection and the result. You'll find work-arounds, syntactic limitations, and scripting guidelines. The chapter also explores advanced concepts, including use of the find command, structuring data, and recursion in HyperTalk. We describe HyperTalk language style, and you'll see how to avoid hard-wired objects by writing more general scripts, how to use handlers involving me and the target, how to be mindful of your environment, how to avoid write-only code, and so on.

A complete section on HyperTalk development (producing commercial stacks) provides descriptions of tools to help your scripting, shows how to keep track of objects, and tells how to make quick changes in your stack. You'll find details on protecting stacks, including trapping of menu command, password protection, setting the user level, hiding the Message box, and using the cantModify property. There is even a Vaccine handler for preventing viruses from getting into your stack.

The chapter ends by describing the art of debugging HyperTalk code, including catching bugs before they start, the problem of script installation and the Home stack, run-time errors, and testing of HyperTalk code.

Techniques for Stack Development

Notes from the Scripting Battlefields

Since HyperCard was introduced in August 1987, many people—by some estimates, as many as 70 percent of Macintosh owners—have programmed in the HyperTalk script language. By now, many people are familiar with the basics of HyperTalk. Most of those people, however, have little previous programming experience to apply to the task of creating better code and improving their HyperTalk code's speed, efficiency, and clarity. Much of the power of HyperTalk remains untapped, simply because many HyperCard programmers are not aware of the interesting and powerful ways they can use the language.

Even amateur scriptors can write HyperTalk programs to perform almost any task; the test of the scriptor's skill is in whether those programs are efficient, easy to read, and elegant. Programming "elegance" is a difficult quality to define, but you know it when you see it. Elegant programs accomplish a great deal with seeming simplicity. They take advantage of the special features of the language in a way that is clear and easily understood.

This chapter does not attempt to explain the entire HyperTalk language, nor does it discuss basic topics such as how to edit a script or the definition of a message. Rather, it presents techniques to help stack development, ways to do new things in HyperTalk and work around its syntactic limitations, and guidelines for the perplexed on what constitutes good HyperTalk programming. This chapter is for those who already know the basics, but are looking for more.

Before you tackle the material in this chapter, you should have done some scripting and have a good grasp of HyperTalk basics. You should have familiarity with the message hierarchy, writing handlers for common system messages such as `mouseUp` and `mouseDown`, and using the Message box to send commands. If any of these terms are unfamiliar, it is probably best to read a basic HyperTalk book (such as *The Waite Group's HyperTalk Bible*) before you tackle the material in this chapter.

Perspectives on HyperTalk

Often, beginning scriptors with some exposure to a procedural language (such as Pascal or BASIC) have trouble with the object-oriented aspect of HyperTalk. This section describes typical stumbling blocks that may cause problems in your scripts and discusses ways to avoid conceptual problems that interfere with your ability to construct functional and efficient scripts.

Mastering Messages

At this point, most discussions of HyperTalk introduce a graph to show the message hierarchy. Many HyperTalk guides stress the question of whether messages should be visualized as originating at the bottom of the hierarchy and bubbling upward or originating at the top and flowing down. It's not important if you think of messages as going up or flowing down through the hierarchy. What does matter is that you have a clear idea of what happens when a message is sent along the hierarchy. In this chapter, the focus is on the order in which messages are received by HyperCard's objects, rather than the perceived direction of the messages.

Handlers

HyperTalk scripts consist of two kinds of handlers: *message handlers* and *function handlers*. When a message (such as `mouseUp`) is sent, HyperCard searches the message hierarchy to find a script that contains a handler for that particular message. If such a handler is found, the instructions in it are executed. A function call, on the other hand, searches the message hierarchy for the corresponding function handler, which computes a value and returns it to the handler that called the function.

HyperCard has many built-in functions, and the most common messages are system messages (which are sent automatically by HyperCard when the user performs certain actions such as clicking the mouse). If you want, you can write custom function handlers and custom message handlers.

Message Handlers

A message handler is analogous to a procedure in Pascal or a subroutine in BASIC. Message handlers are usually written to handle system messages (such as `mouseDown` or `openCard`) that are sent automatically when the user performs certain actions, such as clicking the mouse or going to another card. You can, however, send a custom message that invokes a custom message handler.

Suppose you designed an animation sequence that is performed when the user clicks on any of several buttons in the stack. Instead of duplicating the instructions for the animation sequence in the script of each button, you can place a custom handler called animateButtons in a central location, such as the stack's script:

```
on animateButtons
  -- your commands to animate the buttons go here
end animateButtons
```

The scripts for the individual buttons look like this:

```
on mouseUp
  animateButtons
end mouseUp
```

When one of these buttons is clicked, its mouseUp handler sends the message `animateButtons`. This message is sent through the levels of the message hierarchy until it reaches the stack level. Because the stack script contains a handler for the `animateButtons` message, the handler is executed.

The use of a custom message handler, like the use of a procedure in other languages, eliminates unnecessary duplication of code. It also makes it easier to alter and enhance your stacks. For instance, suppose you want to change the way the animation sequence works in the button animation example. You need to change only the single animateButtons handler, rather than each button's script.

Custom message handlers are also used as a shorthand for a sequence of commands. For instance, suppose you set the `lockMessages`, `lockScreen`, and `lockRecent` properties to true while a script goes to another card or stack, to save time and avoid user confusion. You can put the following handlers into the script of your stack:

```
on lockEverything
  set the lockMessages to true
  set the lockRecent to true
  lock screen
end lockEverything

on unlockEverything
  set the lockMessages to false
  set the lockRecent to false
  unlock screen
end unlockEverything
```

If these handlers are in the message hierarchy, you can set the three properties on or off with just a single line in your scripts.

Function Handlers

HyperCard has many built-in functions, some of which you may have used in your scripts. For example, `the date` is a built-in HyperTalk function that returns the current date. You can also define your own functions for special purposes.

Like a message handler, a function handler can be placed anywhere in the hierarchy beyond the calling handler. For instance, if a function is called by a handler in a card script, the function handler is found if it is in that same card's script or the background, stack, or Home stack script.

A note about function calling conventions: A built-in function is either preceded with `the` or followed by parentheses. For example, the built-in HyperTalk function that returns the date can be written in either of these two ways:

```
the date
date()
```

Functions you write, however, must be called in the second form. If the function requires any input values, they are placed in the parentheses, separated by commas.

The Message Path

Most people who have done scripting are familiar with the standard message path. For instance, the `mouseUp` message resulting from a click on a button is sent first to the button, then (if no handler for the message is found in that script) to the card, the background, the stack, the Home stack, and finally to HyperCard itself. This section describes situations where this model does not hold true: when some or all messages are not sent or the message path changes.

For example, if you click on an unlocked field, `mouseDown` and `mouseUp` messages are not sent. But if you hold down the Command key while clicking, these messages are sent to the field just as though it were locked. The text you click on is also placed in the Message box.

While any tool other than the browse tool is chosen, mouse messages and idle messages are not sent. And while the `lockMessages` property is set to true, system messages (such as open and close messages and mouse messages) are not sent. Because the `lockMessages` property is set to false by HyperCard on idle, it can only be set to true while a handler is run.

You can send a message to another stack, but you cannot send a message to an object (such as a card or button) within another stack without first going to the stack. Nor can you act on objects in another stack—you cannot set object properties, get text in fields, and so on—without going to that stack. (You can have your script lock the screen before going to another stack. This way, the user will not see that you have left the current stack.)

This brings up the topic of how the standard message path changes when a script switches to another stack. Suppose your program is in stack A, running a handler located in a card script. Normally, messages sent while the handler is running go through the usual message hierarchy. If the handler contains a command to go to another stack, however, the current stack is not the same as the stack the handler is running from. The message hierarchy expands to include the current stack. See Figure 1-1. To be exact, if a message is not intercepted in the hierarchy of stack A, it is sent next to the current card in stack B, then up through stack B's hierarchy. Only if the message is not intercepted along the way does it then go to the Home stack.

In addition to system messages sent when a user does an action, such as clicking the mouse button, HyperCard sends a message every time a command is used. *Every* HyperTalk command sends a message. For example, suppose the line `visual effect zoom open` is in your script. This command sends a `visual` message (which normally is interpreted at the HyperCard level).

This is possible because the HyperCard application itself is part of the message hierarchy. The `visual` message starts at the origin and proceeds through the hierarchy like any other message. If no handler intercepts the message, it is sent to the HyperCard object. Then, because the message is a built-in command (which is another way of saying it can be handled by the HyperCard object), it is handled at that level.

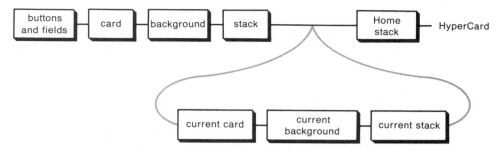

Figure 1-1. If a handler contains a command to go to another stack, the message path expands to include the current stack.

This fact has several implications. It means, for instance, that you can trap any HyperTalk command at any level and modify its function. For example, you can disable all visual effect commands in a stack by adding the following empty handler to the stack's script:

```
on visual
end visual
```

Now all `visual` commands are trapped when they reach the stack level.

Local and Global Variables

A *variable* is the name of a location that holds a value. There are two kinds of variables in HyperTalk: local variables and global variables. A local variable is temporary: it lasts only as long as the handler it is found in is executing. When the handler ends, the variable is forgotten. A global variable, on the other hand, stays around until you quit HyperCard. This means a local variable is accessible only from the handler in which it is used; a global variable can be accessed from any handler. Global variables are retained even when you move from one stack to another.

You use a local variable by putting something into it. You don't need to declare the local variable first, as you must do in other languages. HyperTalk doesn't know about the existence of the variable until you put something into it. Thus, you can read the contents of a local variable only after you have put something into it.

A global variable must be declared in every handler you use it in. For example, you might place a value in a global variable in your openStack handler, then use it later to determine some action. The two handlers might look like this:

```
on openStack
  global timeToPlay, startTime
  ask "How many minutes do you want to play?"
  put it * 60 into timeToPlay -- convert it into seconds
  put the time into startTime -- record the current time
end openStack
```

continued

```
on idle
  global timeToPlay, startTime
  if startTime + timeToPlay > the time then
    beep
    answer "Time's up!"
    quit
  end if
end idle
```

The handler stores the starting time and the amount of time the user wants to play in the global variables startTime and timeToPlay. Then, during play, the idle handler checks if the specified time has passed. If the time has passed, it quits the game.

Global variables can be declared anywhere in the handler, as long as they are declared before they are used. The convention is to place global declarations at the beginning of their handlers so that the variables are easier to find.

By the way, all variable names typed into the Message box are assumed to be global variables. Thus, you can use global variables in the Message box without a global declaration.

One disadvantage of using global variables is that they continue to use memory space because they are not forgotten when you leave the handler. This doesn't matter if you use only a few global variables to store small amounts of data. But if you use a global variable to hold a large amount of information, it will lock up a significant amount of memory. This memory is unavailable to HyperCard for other operations. Although global variables cannot be purged after they are declared (except by quitting HyperCard), they use less memory space if they contain smaller amounts of data. For instance, suppose you use several global variables in a stack to move large amounts of data. In your closeStack handler, you can remove that data and make each global variable as small as possible to free up memory:

```
on closeStack
  global customerData, officeData, callData
  put empty into customerData
  put empty into officeData
  put empty into callData
end closeStack
```

Remember, if this stack contains scripts that go to another stack and then return, the closeStack handler will be triggered. This may cause havoc if your handlers expect the global variables to contain the data that was emptied by the closeStack handler. To avoid problems like this, set the lockMessages property to true before the script goes to another stack. With the lockMessages property on, the closeStack message is not sent.

The HyperTalk Zoo

This section discusses a few special HyperTalk words. Some are functions, some are variables, and some are neither. What they have in common is that they are powerful and often misunderstood.

The *it* Variable

HyperCard has a special variable, called `it`, which is used to store the results of four commands: `answer`, `ask`, `get`, and `read`.

The `answer` command displays a dialog box with up to three buttons. The name of the button clicked by the user is placed in the `it` variable. For example, if HyperCard posts a dialog box in response to the following line:

```
answer "Do you want to play a game?" with "Yes" or ¬
"Maybe" or "No"
```

and the user clicks the Maybe button, the `it` variable contains Maybe. The next lines of the handler, then, might test the `it` variable like this:

```
if it is "Maybe" then answer "Make up your mind!" ¬
with "Yes" or "No"
if it is "No" then quit
```

The `ask` command displays a dialog box that lets the user type an answer. The answer goes into the `it` variable. (If the user clicks the Cancel button, the `it` variable is empty regardless of whether an answer was typed in.) The `get` command retrieves a value (such as the contents of a variable) and places it in the `it` variable. The `read` command is used to read data from a file. This data is placed in the `it` variable. Because the `it` variable can be changed by any of these commands, avoid keeping information in `it` any longer than necessary.

me and *the target*

The word `me` is a special object descriptor: it is the object in whose script the currently executing handler resides. The function called `the target` has no equivalent in languages such as Pascal. It is the object that first received the message now being handled.

For example, suppose you click on a button that has no mouseDown handler, but there is a mouseDown handler on the stack level. The `me` object is the stack because it contains the handler that is executing; `the target` is the button that originally received the `mouseDown` message when you clicked on it. If the object that first receives a message has a handler for that message, `me` and `the target` are the same.

One common use for `the target` function is when there is a handler for a certain message at the stack level, but the handler deals with messages only from certain objects. For instance, suppose you have a mouseUp handler at the stack level that handles only buttons and makes no sense when applied to fields or cards. You can test what kind of object was clicked on with `the target`:

```
on mouseUp
  if word 2 of the name of the target is "button" then
```

continued

```
      visual effect zoom open
      go to card the short name of the target
   else
      pass mouseUp
   end if
end mouseUp
```

Version 1.2 of HyperCard included enhancements to both the `me` descriptor and `target` function. If *me* is a field, you can use `me` to refer to the contents of that field. For example, assuming *me* is a field, the following places the first line of the field into the variable:

```
put line 1 of me into someVariable
```

The word *target* now refers to the contents of a field. If the target is a field, then

```
get the target -- places the name of the field in the it variable
get target -- places the contents of the field in the it variable
```

the selection

The selection is familiar to Macintosh users: text is selected by dragging through it (or by double-clicking on a word to select it). The current selection is reverse highlighted.

In HyperTalk, the current selection is a container and can be manipulated like any other container. You can put something into `the selection` (replacing it) or get `the selection` (enabling your script to prompt the user to select text to be manipulated).

One tricky use for `the selection` container follows. If the user clicks on a locked text field, this mouseDown handler for the field places the word the user clicked on into a variable. This enables you to implement hypertext functions in your stacks. For instance, you can go to a glossary card that gives the meaning of the word that was clicked, or you can find the next occurrence of that word in the stack. You can put the following handler into the script of any locked field:

```
on mouseDown
   lock screen
   set the lockText of the target to false
   click at the clickLoc -- double-click to select a word
   click at the clickLoc
   put the selection into myWord
   set the lockText of the target to true
   unlock screen
   -- you can now do whatever you want with the selected word
end mouseDown
```

Some actions deselect any text that is currently selected. These actions include clicking in another field, going to another card, and highlighting a button. Because highlighting a button deselects text, if one of your scripts requires the user to select some text to be worked on and then click a button, that button's `autohilite` property must be turned off.

the result

The function `the result` retrieves any error messages generated by the last `go` or `find` command. If `the result` is empty after such a command, the command was successful; if `the result` is not empty, the command failed. Here is an example of using `the result` to determine if a `find` command was successful:

```
on mouseUp
  ask "Which title do you want to find?"
  if it is not empty then findTitle it
end mouseUp

on findTitle theTitle
  global searchList
  find theTitle in background field "Book Title"
  if the result is not empty then -- means the find failed
    beep
    answer "Sorry, that title is not in this list."
    exit findTitle
  end if
  put return & background field "Title" after searchList
  -- the search list variable keeps track of which book entries
  -- each user has looked at
end findTitle
```

By first checking whether the `find` was successful, this handler avoids adding extra titles to the user's search list.

The contents of `the result` function can help your script determine if a card exists. Try going to the card; if `the result` is not empty, the `go` command failed and there is no such card.

```
on mouseDown
  go to card "Noodles"
    if the result is not empty then
      -- the card does not exist
    else
      go recent -- go back where you were
      -- the card does exist
    end if
end mouseDown
```

the

One of the most confusing points for HyperTalk beginners is the use of the word *the*. HyperTalk's syntax is fairly forgiving, and often the word `the` is optional. In a few situations, however, its use or omission will "confuse" HyperTalk. The rules for using the follow:

1. The word `the` may not be used in front of the name of an object, the name of a variable, or the name of a function that takes parameters. For example:

```
go to the first card of this stack
put "Yes" into the it
get the sin(22)
```

These lines are not legal in HyperTalk. If you use the word `the` where it doesn't belong, HyperCard generally interprets the illegal expression as the name of a stack.

2. The word `the` is necessary in front of functions that do not take a parameter and in front of properties. You may omit `the` in front of a property in a `set` command, however, because it is clear that the word refers to a property. The following lines will cause problems because they omit `the`:

```
put date into field "Current Date"
if dragspeed is not 0 then set dragspeed to 0
```

If you don't include `the` when referring to a property or function, HyperCard either interprets the word as a variable or, if there is no variable by that name, uses the word as a literal. For example, the first line places the word *date*, instead of the current date, into the field (unless *date* has been used previously as a variable, in which case it will use the contents of that variable). For Hyper-Card to recognize that you want the built-in `date` function, the line must be written either

```
put the date into card field "Current Date"
```

or

```
put date() into card field "Current Date"
```

Advanced HyperTalk Topics

This section discusses two topics of interest to advanced scriptors. The first is the use of recursion, or self-calling routines, in HyperTalk. The second is the use of chunking expressions in variables to simulate list and array data types. Some ways to use the `find` command are also explored.

Limiting the *find* Command

The simplest form of the `find` command is written like this:

```
find "thesewords"
```

This command is invoked in the same form by choosing the Find... menu item. It searches for the first card on which the specified character strings appear in card or background fields. (A string is any set of characters that doesn't include a space.) If you specify more than one string, the `find` command searches for the first card on which all the strings appear. The simplest form of the `find` command matches the string only if it appears at the beginning of a word. The `find chars` command matches the string anywhere within a word.

Although the search algorithm used by the `find` command has not been made public, it is well known that the `find` command works faster if strings consist of at least three alphanumeric characters. If your stack contains a great deal of free space, searches are somewhat slower; to speed up your finds, compact the stack often.

The `find` command can be limited to a single background field as follows:

```
find "27G" in background field "Specifications"
```

Unfortunately, although the `find` command can be limited to one background field, it cannot be limited to a single background. If you issue the preceding command and `find` is unable to locate the search string in the specified background field, it begins looking in other backgrounds for the search string. Specifically, if the background field to which the search is limited has field number X, the `find` command searches background field number X in each background.

Fortunately, there are ways around this limitation. Because the `find` command can be limited to a background field, you can make certain that field number X in all backgrounds, except the one to which you want to limit the search, is empty. In other words, in each background except the one to be searched, create a hidden, empty background field and use the Bring Closer and Send Farther commands to set the field number of each one to X.

On a successful find, you can check the card on which a match is found to see if it is in the background you are looking for.

```
on mouseUp
  ask "What do you want to find?"
  lock screen
  find it in background field "Entries"
  if the result is empty then -- means the find was successful
    if the name of this background is not "OrderEntry" ¬
    then go recent
    -- wrong background; return to the previous card you were on
  end if
  unlock screen
end mouseUp
```

You can also limit the `find` command to a single card field by first checking to see if the field contains the word you are looking for. If it does, a `find` command issued from that card will first find the word in the card field. This is useful when the user wants to locate a word in a long scrolling card field.

```
on mouseUp
  global myWord
  if card field "Noodles" contains myWord then
    lock screen
    repeat until (the name of the foundField) is ¬
    "card field" && quote & "Noodles" & quote
      find myWord
    end repeat
```

continued

```
      unlock screen
    end if
end mouseUp
```

Structuring Data

Many languages let you structure variables in special ways. For instance, in Pascal you can declare an array variable that consists of a number of items, each of which can be addressed by variable name and item number. On the surface, HyperTalk seems to lack these powerful data-structuring capabilities. You can, however, structure a single variable as a two-, three- or four-dimensional array.

You are probably familiar with the idea of *chunk expressions*, which let you deal directly with the individual lines, items, words, and characters of a field. But chunking does not apply just to fields. Information in any container, including variables, can be addressed by chunk. By using chunk expressions, you can structure a variable as a tabular array rather than a simple, one-value item.

There are several useful applications for arrays. For example, a stack that lets you play tic-tac-toe against the Macintosh might store the current state of the game board as an array:

```
on startGame
  global gameBoard
  repeat with vertical = 1 to 3
    repeat with horiz = 1 to 3
      put empty into item horiz of line vertical of gameBoard
    end repeat
  end repeat
end startGame
```

The three lines of gameBoard correspond to the rows on the tic-tac-toe board. The items of each line correspond to the three square in a row. When the user or the computer places an *X* or *O* on the board, an *X* or *O* is placed in the corresponding item and line of the gameBoard global variable. The stack can then check the gameBoard variable to see which moves are possible.

Recursion

For many scriptors, their first encounter with recursion comes when they see the dialog box in Figure 1-2.

Recursion is defined as a handler calling itself. For instance, if you have a handler for the doMenu command that itself contains a doMenu command, the command within the handler will in turn call the handler again.

```
on doMenu theItem
  if theItem is "Prev" then
    doMenu "Home" -- calls the doMenu handler again
  end if
end doMenu
```

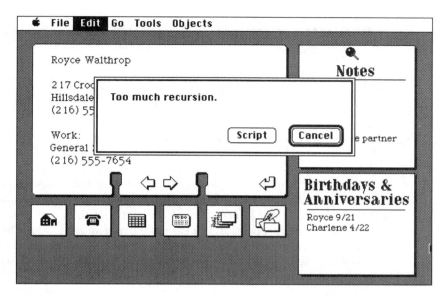

Figure 1-2. A recursion error dialog.

Recursion is a valuable tool in programming. But HyperTalk limits the number of handlers that can be waiting to complete execution at any one time, so too many levels of recursion can cause memory problems. (The limit on the number of pending handlers varies, depending on the complexity of the handler, the length of its name, and other factors. Usually, HyperTalk calls a halt when ten to twenty handlers are pending.)

You may look at a script that has caused the "Too much recursion" error and see no obvious place where you have written an accidental recursion. The reason is certain commands result in other messages being sent. One of the most common mistakes that causes the "Too much recursion" dialog to appear is in the following handler, which might be present at the stack level script:

```
on openCard
  go next card
end openCard
```

When this handler goes to the next card, the openCard message is sent. The openCard message has a handler that contains the command go next card, which results in sending an openCard message, and so on. Your script is caught in a hall of mirrors. It continues to re-run the handler until HyperCard's limit on pending message handlers is reached, at which point the handler's execution is halted and the error dialog box is posted on the screen.

One way to avoid accidental recursion is by using the send command. For example, suppose you want to intercept all visual effect commands in a stack and replace them with dissolves. (Recall from the previous discussion of messages that you can intercept any HyperTalk command by writing a handler for it.) You might do it like this:

```
on visual
  visual effect dissolve
end visual
```

This handler will involve HyperTalk in an endless recursion the first time it is called. To avoid this problem, rewrite the handler like this:

```
on visual
  send "visual effect dissolve" to HyperCard
end visual
```

This avoids the problem of recursion by sending the replacement visual effect command directly to the HyperCard object. Thus, the visual message corresponding to the command is not intercepted at the stack level.

As mentioned, recursion is a valuable programming tool. One common use of recursion in HyperCard stacks is checking a field (such as a code number) to make certain it is in the right form. This handler checks the format of a customer code in an order entry stack. If the code does not have the correct number of letters, the handler asks the user to reenter the code. The handler then calls itself to check the new code.

```
on checkCode
  if the number of chars in field "Customer Code" is not 7 then
    ask "Please type in the 7-letter customer code"
    put it into field "Customer Code"
    checkCode
  end if
end checkCode
```

The checkCode handler can be called on closeField, closeCard, or close-Stack, depending on the way data is entered into the particular stack.

Many other applications are possible for recursive techniques. A complete discussion of recursive techniques is beyond the scope of this chapter. Most general texts on programming include a discussion of recursion and its uses.

HyperTalk Language Style

Some people, particularly those who have never had to debug someone else's program code, question the importance of programming style. Some regard good, readable style as a frill, an aspect of programming that does not have much practical use.

The major reason why programming style considerations are of value is that someone, someday, may have to read your code and figure out what it does. If you have written scripts in such a way that it is easy to follow the flow of logic, they will be infinitely easier to maintain and update. Good style also tends to make your code more efficient and easier to reuse. This section presents basic principles to guide you in designing code that is easy to read and understand.

Eschew Redundant Objects

Take advantage of HyperCard's message structure in clever ways, rather than clutter your stack with extra objects. For example, many stacks have a transparent button covering an entire card that enables users to click anywhere on the screen to proceed. Because `mouseDown` and `mouseUp` messages are received by the current card, there is no need for this extra button. Put a `mouseDown` message in the card script instead. In a similar vein, remember locked fields receive `mouseDown` and `mouseUp` messages, so there is no need to cover a field with a button.

Avoid Singing a Refrain

Suppose you have a stack that uses pop-up fields on several cards. Such fields often provide additional information or caption a diagram or picture. The hidden field is made visible when the user clicks on a certain type of button.

Because all these buttons do more or less the same thing, it might be better to write a general handler in the stack script. For instance, your handler might look like this:

```
on mouseDown
  if word 2 of the name of the target is "button" then
    if the style of the target is "rectangle" then
      show card field the short name of the target
      wait until the mouseClick
      hide card field the short name of the target
    end if
  end if
end mouseDown
```

In this handler, we assume that all buttons with style "rectangle" control pop-up fields and that each of these fields has the same name as the button that controls it. This tactic saves space, but even more important, it allows you to change the operation of your pop-up fields by changing a single handler. For instance, each field is shown when its button is clicked, then hidden on the next mouse click. Suppose you want the field to appear when the cursor enters the controlling button and disappear when the cursor leaves it. It is simple to rewrite the mouseDown handler as a mouseEnter and mouseLeave handler—much simpler than rewriting all the handlers in all the pop-up buttons in your stack.

When you find you are repeating steps, think about moving the repeated part to a separate handler. This rule also applies to repetition within a handler. For example, if you perform some action on each field on a certain card, it's much easier to use a repeat loop.

Don't Be Too Specific

Think of writing every routine as though you are making a tool. The more specific the tool, the harder it is to adapt it to other purposes. If you write a handler in a general way, you can reuse the same code over and over, instead of reinventing the wheel each time your needs change a little.

For instance, suppose you have a rectangular field that contains the names of several cards, each on a separate line. You want to design a routine that will let the user click on any line and go to that card. You could write the handler for the specific conditions you need at the moment; you might use the line height of this field to determine what line has been clicked, and so forth. However, the ability to click on one line of a field and take some action based on the line's contents is very useful. It would be far better, therefore, to spend the extra time and design a general-purpose handler that can be used to solve other programming problems.

Be Mindful of the Environment

Not everyone uses the same hardware as you have. Some users have larger screens, less memory, or an earlier version of HyperCard. If your stack will be distributed to other HyperCard users, it is an essential part of testing to check the stack's operation on a variety of hardware and software setups.

If your stack uses commands specific to certain versions of HyperCard, use the version function when possible to work around the limits for older versions. At the very least, if your stack contains commands or functions specific to a later version, check the version in your openStack handler and alert users who have older versions:

```
on openStack
  if the version < 1.2 then
    answer "This stack requires HyperCard 1.2 or later."
    go Home
    exit openStack
  end if
  --- the rest of the commands for openStack
end openStack
```

Also, if you change some part of the environment (such as the userLevel), be sure to set it back where it was when you leave the stack. For instance, if you want to set the userLevel to 1 (browsing) in your stack, rather than simply change the userLevel, first save its original value. (See the section on "Setting the User Level" for an example.)

Don't Break the Flow

You can break out of a handler at any time using the exit keyword. For example, look at this mouseUp handler for a Quit button:

```
on mouseUp
  answer "Do you really want to leave the stack?" ¬
  with "Yes" or "No"
  if it is "No" then exit mouseUp -- break out of the handler
  -- do housekeeping required on leaving the stack
end mouseUp
```

You also can use `exit repeat` to break out of a repeat loop. Although these constructions can be very useful, use them with caution. Breaking out of a handler or loop makes it hard to follow the logic of the program, which makes the program harder to read or debug.

Exit constructions usually are easiest to understand when they handle an exception to the normal course of events. For instance, in the preceding example, the normal course of events is for users to confirm that they want to leave the stack. The `exit mouseUp` command is used only if a user changes his or her mind and decides not to leave after all.

Avoid Write-Only Code

When you write scripts, remember that someone—without your knowledge of what the scripts do—might need to read them. You can aid this reader in many ways: use meaningful names for variables and handlers, avoid abbreviations for HyperTalk terms such as *card* and *background*, use the names of objects where possible (rather than numbers or objects IDs), and most of all, include plentiful comments that describe what each handler does.

Pay attention to the visual clarity of your scripts, too. If you call a function, place its handler close to the handlers that call it. If you call a function or message handler that resides at a different level of the stack (for example, if you have a button that sends a message to the stack level), note the location of the destination handler in a comment. Set off comments with space. And, if a script line goes beyond the right edge of the script window, use the Option-Return character (¬) to split the line.

Some scriptors put blank lines into a long handler to distinguish between different parts of it. But blank lines slow HyperTalk's execution of a handler (see chapter 16, "Benchmarking HyperTalk"), and they may make it difficult to find the end of the handler (individual handlers are usually separated with blank lines). Also, the number of lines you can see at one time in the script editor is small, especially on a small screen. The more lines of code you can see, the easier it is to grasp the flow of a long handler.

These are commonsense observations and techniques. For more information about program style, look in basic programming textbooks (Pascal textbooks in particular tend to emphasize code readability and good design). Most discussions of programming style can be applied to all high-level languages.

Using these guidelines will help people avoid pulling out their hair in exasperation when they need to modify your scripts. And remember that months or years from now, after details have grown vague with the passage of time, you may need to rewrite your own scripts. So write well: The hair you save may be your own.

Tools for Development

Two difficulties when programming in HyperTalk are keeping tabs on objects and making quick changes to stacks. This section presents several small scripts and tricks that can make development easier.

Keeping Track of Objects

In any but the smallest stack, it's hard to remember the names and locations of all objects. In many cases, objects such as buttons and fields may get lost. (Remember the many early stacks based on the Home stack whose authors forgot to remove the transparent buttons from the Home card?)

In all versions of HyperCard, you can press the Command and Option keys to show the outlines of any visible buttons. Version 1.2 of HyperCard added new capabilities to this feature. When using the button tool, pressing the Command and Option keys shows the outlines of all buttons, visible and invisible. Pressing the Command, Option, and Shift keys shows the outlines of all visible fields. When using the field tool, holding down these three keys shows the outlines of all fields, visible and invisible.

Even with these new capabilities, you may want to keep a list of objects in your stack. The following script compiles such a list:

```
on makeAList
  lockEverything -- see handler in section on message handlers
  put the name of this stack into theObjectList
  ---- first get all the background object names ----
  repeat with b = 1 to the number of backgrounds
    go background b
    put return & the name of this background after theObjectList
    repeat with x = 1 to the number of background fields
      put return & the name of background field x after ¬
      theObjectList
    end repeat
    repeat with x = 1 to the number of background buttons
      put return & the name of background button x ¬
      after theObjectList
    end repeat
  end repeat
  ---- now get all the card object names ----
  repeat with b = 1 to the number of cards
    go card b
    put return & the name of this card after theObjectList
    repeat with x = 1 to the number of card fields
      put return & the name of card field x after theObjectList
    end repeat
    repeat with x = 1 to the number of card buttons
      put return & the name of card button x after ¬
      theObjectList
    end repeat
  end repeat
  put theObjectList into card field "list" of card 1
  unlockEverything -- see handler in section on message handlers
end makeAList
```

This handler lists all object names in use. Variations of this basic framework could list object IDs along with names or make a complete script listing.

Making Quick Changes

Often, you will want to use scripts as an aid in development. Such scripts may include locking or unlocking all fields at once, listing objects, searching through scripts, and so on.

There are some ways to make these quick changes easier. You can type single commands directly into the Message box. But the Message box (at present) can only handle one line, and many things that make development easier, such as if-then constructs and repeat loops, use more than one line.

One method is to write small, often used sequences as custom message handlers and place them in the Home stack script (so they are accessible when you work in HyperCard). You can run the handler simply by typing its name into the Message box.

If you need to invoke one of these routines often, consider putting it in a button. Then paste the button into the needed location in your stack. A button makes a convenient little container for a routine, because the button can be easily copied and pasted to the card you need it on. You can remove the button when you have finished developing the stack.

Protecting Stacks

One of the most controversial issues among HyperTalk scriptors is stack protection. The consensus seems to be that locking other scriptors out is not good when it is done to hide code—we all benefit from sharing. This sharing is one of the best things about the HyperCard community. A stack with protected scripts is less useful than the same stack with open scripts because an open stack can be customized easily to the user's needs and preferences. (If you really don't want your routine seen by anyone else, you can write it as an XCMD.)

In some situations, however, you may want to protect a stack. Several categories are: protecting inexperienced users, keeping a publicly accessible stack from being modified, and protecting personal information. For example, you might "childproof" a stack intended for very young users or protect personal financial information from being viewed by others.

This section provides techniques for protecting access to a stack and information on defeating various protection methods. Note that using other people's code in your stacks without acknowledging their contribution is not a good thing to do, even if the code is in the public domain. (If the code is copyrighted, it is illegal as well.) If you find a routine you want to use, contact the author and ask permission—most likely, he or she will be glad to give it and gratified you had the courtesy to ask. And always give credit on your stack's About card to stacks and authors that helped you, even if you didn't borrow from them directly.

Several levels and types of stack protection are discussed. Be aware that all of these can be defeated by a persistent and knowledgeable person.

Trapping Menu Commands

Because a user's selection of a menu item sends the `doMenu` message to the current card, any menu item can be trapped by a handler for the `doMenu` message. This means you can selectively disable any menu item a user might choose. For example, to let a user choose any menu item except those allowing movement within the current stack, place this handler in the stack's script:

```
on doMenu theItem
  if theItem is "First" or theItem is "Last" or theItem is ¬
  "Prev" or theItem is "Next" then
    beep
  else
    pass doMenu      ---------- VERY IMPORTANT! ----------
  end if
end doMenu
```

If you accidentally omit the `pass doMenu` line, you are in trouble: all menu items will be disabled, including their Command key equivalents. If this happens, you can type the following command if the Message box is visible (or the `blindTyping` property is set to true):

```
edit script of this stack
```

The script editor will appear, and you can then add the `pass doMenu` line.

If you are unable to type into the Message box because it is hidden and `blindTyping` is set to false, try to find a button in the stack that will take you to another stack (such as Home) or allow you to quit from HyperCard. From another stack, you can type the command

```
edit script of stack "My Stack"
```

into the Message box.

In fact, you can hide the entire menu bar (although this does not disable the Command key equivalents to the menu commands). In a script, this can be done with the `hide menubar` and `show menubar` commands. You can also press the Spacebar while holding down the Command key to toggle the menu bar on and off.

If you are trapping a menu command, it is a good idea to let the command work normally if a certain key is pressed. For instance, you could write the preceding handler like this:

```
on doMenu theItem
  if theItem is "First" or theItem is "Last" or theItem is ¬
  "Prev" or theItem is "Next" then
    if the option key is not down then
      beep
      exit doMenu
    end if
    pass doMenu      ---------- VERY IMPORTANT! ----------
```

continued

```
    end if
end doMenu
```

This version of the handler traps the four menu items Next, Prev, First, and Last, unless the Option key is being held down. This makes it easier to navigate within the stack while you are developing it.

The Protect Stack Menu Item

The Protect Stack menu item lets you set an upper limit on the user level in a stack. Because this command is not available in the shortened File menu that appears when the user level is set to 1 or 2, it is effective against users who are not very knowledgeable about HyperCard.

Pressing the Command key while pulling down the File menu, however, gives users access to the full-length File menu, even at a lower user level. Then they can set the upper limit to whatever they prefer. Many users will be aware of this trick because it is in the HyperCard *User's Manual.*

There is an additional disadvantage to using Protect Stack to set the user level. In some stacks, you may want a script to increase the user level temporarily to perform some task. For instance, you may have a script in which users create pop-up notes by clicking a button. To create the field associated with the note, you need to temporarily set the userLevel to at least level 4 (authoring). If stack protection is set lower than 4, your script cannot override the protection and set the userLevel high enough.

Password Protection

The Protect Stack command gives you the option to set a password. Users cannot access the Protect Stack dialog box without the password. You can set a password also to control access to the stack: HyperCard will not let you open the stack until you enter the password.

HyperCard version 1.01 has a serious bug in the Private Access feature of the Protect Stack dialog. Under some circumstances, the bug could prevent the stack from being reopened. To avoid this, never set Private Access on a stack that already has a password. (The bug is corrected in HyperCard version 1.1 and later versions.)

To remove password protection, you need an XCMD such as the Deprotect XCMD (available on many electronic bulletin boards). Thus, it is a little more difficult (though by no means impossible) to get around password protection. Even in the absence of an XCMD capable of removing a password, be aware that the text and scripts of a stack can still be read with a disk editing program such as fEdit or MacSnoop.

Setting the User Level

You can set the user level in an openStack handler. To be courteous, if you change the user level (or any other global setting) in your stack, save the original user level in a variable and restore it when the user leaves your stack:

```
on openStack
  global theLevel
  put the userlevel into theLevel
end openStack

on closeStack
  global theLevel
  set the userlevel to theLevel
end openStack
```

Some annoying stacks reset the user level on idle, presumably to prevent users from simply using the Message box to reset the level to their preferred one. Faced with such a stack, you may need to edit the stack script from outside the stack (using the edit script command described previously) to remove the offending command.

Hiding the Message Box

Many stack protection schemes can be thwarted if the user can type commands into the Message box (for example, the user level can be set from the Message box). Some stack authors set up elaborate tricks to make certain the Message box is inaccessible. For instance, the Message... menu item can be trapped and the blindTyping property, which allows users to type commands into the Message box even when it's hidden, can be set to false.

This type of stack protection is suitable only if you must be concerned about vandalism by knowledgeable users. One example is a demonstration stack that will be at a trade show, accessible to visitors.

Using the *cantModify* Property

Needs for stack protection often can be met by using the cantModify property introduced in version 1.2 of HyperCard. The cantModify property, when set to true, prevents users from making any changes to the stack. It is different from simply setting the userLevel to 1 (which also does not allow any changes to be made). If cantModify is true, users can still copy text and graphics from the stack. When the cantModify property is set to true, a padlock icon appears in the stack's menu bar, if the menu bar is visible.

The appeal of the cantModify property is that spectators can look at scripts, but the stack is protected. Like any HyperCard property, however, the cantModify property can be set from the Message box. If your stack is on public display and you want to keep mischievous individuals from altering the stack, put the following in the stack's script:

```
on idle
  if the cantModify is false then
    set the cantModify to true
    play "DragnetTheme" -- or any loud, attention-getting sound
```

continued

```
      answer "Please don't modify me" with "I'm sorry"
    end if
  end idle
```

You can modify this stack in spite of this idle handler. Recall that `idle` messages are sent only when the browse tool is selected. If the stack's userLevel is set to 3 (painting) or higher, you can disable the idle check simply by choosing another tool.

If all else fails, after removing the stack's password protection, you can edit the script from another stack by typing the following line into the Message box (from any stack in which you can set the userLevel to 5):

```
edit script of stack "Obnoxious Protection"
```

A Vaccine Handler

Lately there has been much talk about computer viruses, and there has even been a HyperTalk virus that modified the script of a user's Home stack. Fortunately, viruses are uncommon. More annoying than deliberate viruses are stacks that modify the script of your Home stack without notifying you. For some protection against such stacks, you may want to place this small "vaccine" handler in your Home stack:

```
on set
  if the params contains "script" then
    answer the params with "Yes" or "No"
    if it is "No" then exit set
  end if
  pass set
end set
```

This handler notifies you when a stack attempts to change a script, then asks you if you want to allow the change.

Debugging

Many times, you will find that a carefully coded script isn't doing what you expected. Such times can be very frustrating, especially when you don't know where to start looking for the problem—everything looks as though it should work. The following debugging techniques will not solve the problem, but they will help you narrow the problem area to where you know what is wrong.

A problem with your script can appear at several stages in script development. The script may fail to indent properly in the editor—a clue that something is wrong with the script's syntax. The script may indent properly but fail to run, posting an error message when you try it out. Or the script may run without generating error messages or other untoward events, but fail to produce the results you expected. At this point, it's time to get out the debugging tools.

Catching Problems Before They Start

Clearly, the best time to squash a bug is before you put it in your script. To avoid problems at the beginning, you need a clear idea of what you want to accomplish and how you are going to do it. For simple tasks, deciding on the technique you will use is easy. For more complex tasks, you need to look carefully at the task and make certain you understand it completely before you start the script editor.

One rule is to get the script working first, before you attempt any speed optimization or other "tweaking." When you understand the task and its solution completely, you will be able to change the script without causing problems.

Script Indentation Problems

HyperCard's built-in debugging tools are not as extensive as those provided with some development systems, but they can be useful. The automatic indentation built into the script editor checks some parts of the syntax. Specifically, it checks for the correct use of HyperTalk keywords. HyperTalk has thirteen keywords:

```
else
end
exit
function
global
if
next
on
pass
repeat
return
send
then
```

The most common problems that cause the script editor to fail to indent your script correctly are

➤ an on <message name> line that is not matched with a corresponding end <message name> line

➤ a pass <message name> or exit <message name> line in a handler for another message

➤ an if-then-else construction that does not contain the correct number of end ifs

➤ a repeat construction that is not matched with end repeat

If the script is indented correctly, all keywords are being used legally. It is important to remember, however, that you can write a handler that is correct from a syntactic standpoint, yet has a flaw in the logic that causes it to produce an undesired result. In other words, just because the editor formats your script correctly does not mean it will do what you want.

Some people prefer to write their own script editor because the built-in editor does not allow you to access menus and the Message box and has no search-and-replace feature. Most custom editors place the script being edited in a field. If you use such an editor, you can still take advantage of the HyperTalk editor's automatic indentation by placing the following lines in an appropriate script of your custom script editor:

```
on closeField
  set the script of this card to card field "My Script"
    -- use any handy empty script
  put the script of this card into card field "My Script"
end closeField
```

When you click outside the field (or press the Tab key), the contents of the field are placed in a script, then brought back and placed in the field. The trick is that anything placed in a script is automatically indented. This handler, then, automatically formats your script.

Runtime Errors

Most scripting problems are not apparent until you try to execute the script. At this point, the handler may fail to run completely, or it may produce a result other than the one you intended. If the script editor's indentation fails to indicate a problem, your script may be syntactically sound, but may contain a mistake that prevents the program from producing the desired result. Errors that occur while a handler is being run are called, logically enough, *runtime errors*.

If HyperCard finds a statement or instruction it can't interpret during script execution, it displays a dialog box to tell you what it can't understand. See Figure 1-3.

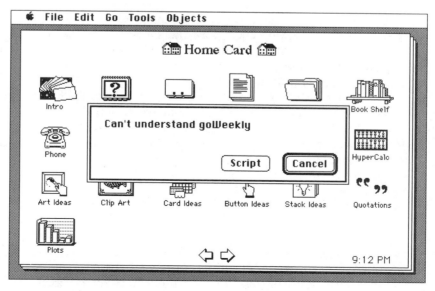

Figure 1-3. A HyperTalk "can't understand" dialog box.

If the `userlevel` property is set to 5 (scripting), a script button will be in the error dialog box. Clicking this button opens the problem script and usually puts the insertion point at the place in the script where HyperCard is having trouble. Occasionally, HyperCard is so confused that it cannot locate the problem, and it simply puts the insertion point at the beginning of the script.

The usual causes for the "can't understand" dialog box are spelling errors, using variables you haven't put a value into, and other easy-to-correct problems.

Another problem that may cause a runtime error is unlimited recursion. See the previous section on recursion for an explanation of this error and how to avoid it.

If your script keeps running and never seems to stop, you may have set up an endless loop. This usually can be traced to a problem with a repeat structure. (Remember, you can always halt any script by pressing the Command and period keys.)

A script that runs, but does not produce the desired result, is a tougher problem. One of the most useful principles for dealing with a problem of this type is "I got this far." In other words, you want to determine exactly where the script is going "off the rails." This part of debugging largely consists of looking behind the scenes to find out what your script is really doing.

You can use several methods. One of the simplest is to place a `beep` command at a strategic point in the handler. If you hear the beep, you know the handler reached the point in the script where you put the beep.

Another method uses the Message box. If a variable value is not what you expected, place this line at an opportune point in your script:

```
put myVariable
```

Such lines allow you to keep close track of the values of variables, properties, and anything else you fear might be causing problems. Remember, the whole point of debugging is to narrow the problem to where you can deal with it.

You can also use dialog boxes to announce that the script has reached a certain milestone. The advantage of using dialog boxes is each dialog must be explicitly dismissed by clicking OK before the script can continue. If you directed several messages to the Message box, on the other hand, each one would overwrite the previous one, and there might not be time to read each one. Dialog boxes are easier to use when you need to post multiple messages.

To simplify a complicated handler for debugging, you can temporarily remove some lines by changing them to comments. Suppose you have a problem with a handler that computes a name, puts it into a variable, goes to a card by that name, and collects data on the card. You can "comment out" the part of the handler that computes the name, then place a "dummy" name into the variable. This technique can help you isolate the problem.

Testing

After you think the stack is bug free, it's time to test it. You can do some testing yourself. As the writer of a program, however, you can never test it adequately—you know it too well. The ideal program is one in which no normal user action can cause an error message. But you, as the stack's designer, know it so well that you might avoid automatically any action that may cause a problem. Find at least one or two people who were not involved in the making of the stack, and invite them to do their worst.

If you plan to distribute a stack you have designed, make sure it is tested first with an unmodified copy of the HyperCard application and the Home stack, with a stock system folder. If you have customized your Home stack by adding useful message handlers and functions, stacks that call those handlers won't work with another person's Home stack. Some people also place custom resources such as icons and XCMDs in their Home stacks. These resources are likewise unavailable to other users unless you put them in the stack before you distribute it. If you use any fonts other than the standard set, place them in the stack as well. In general, any stack you distribute should be able to stand alone, without requiring special resources in the System file or the Home stack.

It is important to test common user actions for their impact on your scripts. For example, a bug is in the Home stack distributed with HyperCard 1.0.1. If you click on the Weekly button and HyperCard cannot find the DateBook stack, it presents a dialog asking you where it is. If you click Cancel instead of opening the stack, the script complains that it `can't understand goWeekly`. The goWeekly handler is in the DateBook stack; the handler is called in the Weekly button script, after the command to go to the DateBook stack. If you have not opened the DateBook stack, the HyperTalk interpreter cannot find the goWeekly handler, and therefore it presents an error message to the (understandably confused) user.

You may think some of these matters are only for serious stack developers— those who design HyperCard stacks for a living. If any of your stacks will be used by anyone else, however, you too are a HyperCard developer. You owe it to your users to be careful and attentive. The steps of design, debugging, and testing do not have to be extensive, especially for a simple stack, but they should not be omitted.

As you learn more about HyperCard and HyperTalk, share what you've learned. Join a local user group. If you have a modem, call an electronic bulletin board service to exchange news and information with other HyperCard users. The more you share your ideas, the more you will learn about HyperCard.

Part 2

Field Tricks

ScrollJump

Mitchell Waite

Synopsis: One of the first challenges a HyperTalk programmer faces is to provide a way to automatically move users from a set of general topics to a particular card or stack containing further information. The most typical way is to arrange buttons on a card in some sort of matrix, as done on the Home card. Each button is the name of an item, such as the table of contents of a book or a list of help items. Clicking a button takes the user to a card, or stack, usually with a visual effect. A return button on the card or stack gets you back to the button matrix, but what happens when you have more topics than can fit on a card?

A neat solution is to use a HyperTalk scrolling text field to hold the topics or items that would normally be on the buttons. With this type of interface, the user would scroll through the list, click an item, and in a Macintosh intuitive manner, would automatically be sent to the proper card. The only problem with this approach is that there is no mechanism in HyperCard 1.2.2 for selecting and jumping to cards: You have to brew this up yourself.

This chapter shows three different ways to accomplish the scrolling list box that jumps to a stack or card. The simplest is ScrollJump1, which uses a hidden and unhidden button to simulate the inverting selection process that happens in a normal Macintosh list box. (This is the most primitive but most realistic version.) ScrollJump2 uses a technique involving `the selection` that allows you to limit the words that cause a card jump and provides a nice way to handle HyperText applications. ScrollJump3 takes advantage of HyperCard 1.2's `select` command, which greatly simplifies the code.

ScrollJump

Jumping Through a Stack Gently

One of the first challenges facing the HyperTalk scriptor is designing a way to move from a list of items in a single card to a particular card in the stack. The HyperCard Help stack is a typical example. In the Help stack, cards are jumped to by buttons with the ID or name of the card hard-coded in the button script. For example, the first button of the index in Help reads:

```
go to card id 59622 of stack "Help"
```

The link was set up with the `Link` function in the button's dialog box. The trouble with this, however, is that every time you add a new card, you must add a new button, then link to it. A better way is to use the card's name, rather than its ID number, for identification. Suppose that the name of the card is in a list presented to the user in a text field. You can get the name when the user clicks on it with the mouse, then use the name to jump to the card. (This technique also allows you to jump to or pop up named text fields.)

This chapter goes beyond presenting a creative solution to a HyperCard challenge. It follows an evolutionary process. This is one of the few chapters to feature pre-version 1.2 scripts. Three versions of ScrollJump are presented; the differences between them show the development of the HyperTalk language from HyperCard version 1.0.1 to version 1.2.2. Follow us on our journey.

ScrollJump1

Suppose that the list or number of card names is large. You might want to present the user with a scrolling text field rather than a fixed one. The technique of jumping by name can still be applied. There are several ways to accomplish this jump by the name technique; ScrollJump1 is the most obvious way to do it.

What It Does

The ScrollJump1 script instantly jumps to any named card in the current stack when someone clicks in a list of names in a scrolling text field. When the user clicks on a name, the line appears to be autohighlighted, as shown in Figure 2-1. (This is a special feature we created by using a trick.) HyperTalk attempts to jump to the card of the same name as the line. If there is no card with that name, a message is posted for one second, a hammer sound occurs, the message is removed, and the highlight on the line is turned off.

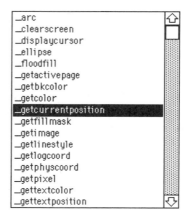

Figure 2-1.   The line in the scrolling box is highlighted using a trick.

How It Works

ScrollJump1 is simple. The first word of text on each line of the scrolling field contains the name of a card in the stack. The script calculates the number of the line containing the text clicked on, accesses the first word of that line, and uses the name as the card to jump to. The user gets the browse tool when the mouse is moved over the scrolling field. (In this script, the text field must be locked.)

The highlight over the line is *not* automatic. It comes from an invisible, transparent button, about the width of the field and as high as the text height. (Recall that objects such as buttons and fields can be visible or invisible.) When the user clicks on a line, the button is moved so that it is over the line clicked on, the button is made visible and highlighted (which makes it black), the text underneath shows through, and you get the desired effect.

Background Objects

Three objects are in the background of the card holding ScrollJump. One is a scrolling text field that contains the script and holds the names of the cards in the database. The second object is a transparent button that is the width of the scrolling box. The third is a small shadow text field containing the message: "This card is under construction." There is also a sound resource that sounds like the rim shot on a snare drum. If you don't have such a sound, you can use one of HyperTalk's built-in sounds, such as harpsichord.

The first section of the script computes the line number of the mouse click:

```
on mouseUp
  -- compute line number of the mouse click
  get item 2 of the clickloc - item 2 of the rect of me ¬
  + scroll of me
  put 1 + it div the textHeight of me into lineNum
```

In this script, `item 2 of the clickloc` is the y-coordinate of the mouse click relative to the screen. The second item of `the rect of me` is the y-coordinate of the top of the scrolling box. Note that `the rect of me` could have been written `the rect of field name`. Using the Hypertalk term `of me` saves you from having to give an absolute name because `of me` always refers to the name of the object in which the script is executing. Because the script is in the text field, `of me` is the name of the text field the user is clicking in. The third item is the number of pixels the field has scrolled from the top of the window. If you subtract the first two y-coordinates, you get the difference from the top of the scrolling window to the mouse. And if you add `scroll of me`, you get the total amount of pixels from the top of the scrolled box to your line. The entire first line starts with `get`, so the result of the calculation is placed in HyperTalk's universal holding variable `it`.

The second line of the script takes this pixel offset to the line (stored in the `it` variable) and divides by the `textHeight` property of the field (also called `me`). The `textHeight` measures the height of one line of the text in pixels. Because a line is `textHeight` pixels high, this division results in the number of the line for that number of pixels. The value of 1 is added to compensate for the fact that 0 is not a valid line, and the result is put into the `lineNum` variable.

Simulating Text Selection

The second section of the handler moves the invisible button over the line the user clicked on, then makes it visible and highlights the line. This simulates the word being selected. The cursor is set to the watch.

```
-- highlight line, use magic button
set hilite of bkgnd button "hiliter" to false
get item 2 of rect of me + lineNum * textHeight of me - scroll ¬
of me
put 1 + it - textHeight of me div 2 into v
show bkgnd button "hiliter" at item 1 of loc of ¬
bkgnd button "hiliter",v -- this lights up the button
set hilite of bkgnd button "hiliter" to true -- make button black
set the cursor to 4
-- set to watch because the search may take a while
```

First, the `hilite` of the background button is set to false in case it was true before. Recall that a `hilite` turns the button black (inverts the button). The next two lines calculate the position of the upper left corner of the button and put this value into the variable v. The line beginning show bkgnd button "hiliter" reveals the power of HyperTalk's show command. It uses the button's x-coordinate and the new y-coordinate to place the button over the field on the right line. The hilite of the button is set to true to turn it on, and the cursor is set to a watch for the upcoming delay as the search for the card is made.

Computing the Card Name

The third and final part of the script uses the do command to assemble the name of the card to search for. (There are other ways to do this). The do command will create a command such as: put line 14 of myField into cardName, which is what we want. You could use searching to strip just the first word if more text followed the name.

```
-- compute card name and go to it
do "put line " & lineNum & " of " & name of me & " ¬
into cardName"
visual effect iris open slow
go to card cardName
  if the result is not empty then
    show bkgnd field warning
    -- warning is the name of a text field containing the
    -- message: card not installed yet
    play "Drum2"
    -- put a short click sound here if you have one
    wait one seconds
    -- let user see the "card not installed" message
    hide bkgnd field warning
    hide bkgnd button "hiliter"
  end if
end mouseUp
```

The visual effect gives you a neat lens opening from the center of the screen into the card. The script tries to go to the card. If the script succeeds, it transfers control to that card and any script it may contain. The card probably contains information keyed to the original text in the line you clicked in, and there would be a way to return to the scrolling box. If the card is not found, the result is *not* empty, and an if-then statement shows the message "card not installed," waits a second (play a little sound if you like here), then puts the warning field away and hides the button.

Modifications

If you want to organize the information in the box so that each item uses two, three, four or more lines, change the statement:

```
put 1 + it div the textHeight of me into lineNum
```

to:

```
put (lineNum - 1) div <nlpi> * <nlpi> + 1 into lineNum
```

where *nlpi* is the number of lines per item. The highlight falls in the first line of the item, regardless of where you click.

The ScrollJump1 Script

The HyperTalk listing for ScrollJump1 follows. You do not need to type in the information the *DESCRIPTION* section of the script, but it can be useful.

```
-- ********* DESCRIPTION *********
-- TYPE:        Fields, jumping to cards.
-- AUTHOR:      Mitchell Waite
-- NAME:        ScrollJump1.
-- RESTRICTIONS: Cards must be in the current stack; scrolling
--               box must be locked.

-- ********* FIELD SCRIPT STARTS *********
on mouseUp
  -- compute the line number of the mouseclick
  get item 2 of the clickloc - item 2 of the rect of ¬
  me + scroll of me
  put 1 + it div the textHeight of me into lineNum

  -- highlight line, use magic button
  set hilite of bkgnd button "hiliter" to false
  get item 2 of rect of me + lineNum * textHeight of ¬
  me - scroll of me
  put 1 + it - textHeight of me div 2 into v
  show bkgnd button "hiliter" at item 1 of loc of ¬
  bkgnd button "hiliter",v -- this lights up the button
  set hilite of bkgnd button "hiliter" to true
  -- make button black
  set the cursor to 4
  -- set to watch because the search may take a while
  -- compute card name and go to it
  do "put line " & lineNum & " of " & name of me & ¬
  " into cardName"

  visual effect iris open slow
  go to card cardName
  if the result is not empty then
    show bkgnd field warning
    -- warning is the name of a text field containing the
    -- message: card not installed yet
    play "Drum2"
    -- put a short click sound here if you have one.
    wait one seconds
    -- let user see the "card not installed" message
    hide bkgnd field warning
    hide bkgnd button "hiliter"
  end if
end mouseUp
```

ScrollJump2

In ScrollJump1, you saw how you could use a button to highlight a line in a scroll field clicked on by the user, then jump to a card containing the name in the line clicked on. The technique involved putting a transparent button, with its hilite turned on, over the line of text clicked on. Dan Winkler, the developer of the HyperTalk language, has pointed out that it is often possible to rethink a handler and reduce it to a more unembroidered and elegant routine. Is there anything you can do to ScrollJump1 to reduce its intricacy?

Using *the selection*

Another way to get almost the same action as in the ScrollJump1 script is to use the HyperTalk global variable the selection. This approach, called ScrollJump2 (pretty creative, huh?), uses fewer lines of handler scripts than ScrollJump1. Furthermore, it rejects any words clicked on that are not in a specific list. Thus, you can set up a text field to contain a paragraph with certain keywords and only the keywords will be accepted (and jumped to if they are card names). The scroll box appears exactly like the one in ScrollJump1, with one exception. When the user clicks on the word, only the word is highlighted, not the entire line. See Figure 2-2. This script is easier to set up, requires less code, has fewer parts, and ignores all but the keywords you define.

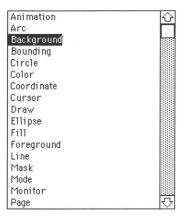

Figure 2-2.   Scrolling box with highlighted word.

What It Does

The ScrollJump2 script instantly jumps to any named card in the current stack when someone double-clicks in a list of names in a scrolling text field. When the user double-clicks on a word, the word appears to be autohighlighted (a special feature created using a trick). HyperTalk attempts to jump to the card of the same name as the word. If there is no card, a message is posted for one second, a hammer sound occurs, the message is removed, and the highlight on the line is turned off.

How It Works

There are two scripts for this version, one in the background of the stack and the other in the field itself. The initialization script is in the background and begins when the card is opened. The script reads the words in the text field and puts the first word of each line of the field in a variable array called storeNames. Each word in the array is separated by a single space in the list. The core of the script is the code

```
repeat while true
  add one to y
  get word y of bkgnd field "My Field"
  if it is not in storeNames then
    put it && "" after storeNames
  end if
  if it is lastword then exit repeat
end repeat
```

Here the script is in an infinite loop. The variable y is set to zero, so the loop adds one to y and gets word one from the list of words in the field (the word is in the universal variable it now). If you improve this part to get only the first word of each line, any text after the keyword is ignored.

The script uses an if-then statement to compare the word to the list of words stored so far in storeNames. The line of code that does this is powerful but simple: if it is not in storeNames then. The code in storeNames is doing all the searching. If the word is not in storeNames, the word is added to the last word in storeNames with the put statement. If the word is the last word in the field, an exit statement breaks out of the infinite loop and the handler ends. The variable storeNames is ready to go.

The script in the text field works like this. The script is inside a mouseUp handler, and the text field itself is locked, so when the user passes the mouse over the field, the browse tool appears. When the mouse button is pressed and released, it generates a mouseUp message, which starts the handler. The handler (which follows) first sets locktext to false, thereby unlocking the field. Then clickloc is accessed (get the clickloc), which returns the x and y locations of where the user clicked into the global variable it.

The next technique is a trick that shows off HyperTalk's skill over nonmessage driven languages such as BASIC. The two lines click at it simply simulate the mouse being double-clicked on a word in an open field. The word is selected as if you double-clicked on it, even though the field is locked when you click.

Next, the field is locked so the user cannot change its contents. Then the key line of the script that makes this all possible executes: get the selection. This places the word that was double-clicked into the universal variable it. After the word is in it, you can use the word to jump to the desired field or card.

```
set the locktext of me to false
```

continued

```
get the clickloc
click at it -- this and
click at it -- this simulates a double-click on the word
set the locktext of me to true
get the selection
```

The only difference between the third and final part of this script and ScrollJump1 is that the button used in ScrollJump1 to highlight the line is not necessary.

The ScrollJump2 Script

The HyperTalk listing for ScrollJump2 follows. (See ScrollJump1 for allowing the program to scroll by more than one line at a time.) You do not need to type the information in the *DESCRIPTION* section, but it can be useful.

```
-- ****************** DESCRIPTION **************************
-- TYPE:         Fields, jumping to cards
-- AUTHOR:       Mitchell Waite
-- NAME:         ScrollJump2
-- RESTRICTIONS: Cards must be in the current stack; scrolling
--               text field must be locked.

-- ********** BACKGROUND SCRIPT STARTS **********
on OpenBackground
  -- this script reads in the first word of each line of text in
  -- the background field "My Field" and puts it into a variable
  -- called storeNames. The field script uses this to find out if
  -- the name is acceptable and in the list.

  global storeNames, lastword

  put empty into storeNames -- read the names in text field
  get last word of bkgnd field "My Field"
  put it into lastword
  put zero into y
  set cursor to 4 -- be nice and give them the watch
  repeat while true
    add one to y
    get word y of bkgnd field "My Field"
    if it is not in StoreNames then
      put it && "" after StoreNames
    end if
    if it is lastword then exit repeat
  end repeat
end OpenBackground

-- ********** FIELD SCRIPT STARTS **********
on mouseUp
  -- this is the workhorse script that gets the name clicked on
  global storenames
  set the locktext of me to false
```

continued

```
      get the clickloc
      click at it -- this and
      click at it -- this simulates a double-click on the word
      set the locktext of me to true

      get the selection
      -- put it into msg
      if storenames contains it then
        visual effect iris open slow
        go to card it
        if the result is not empty then
          show bkgnd field warning
          play "Drum2"
          -- substitute "boing" here if no drum sound
          wait one seconds
          hide bkgnd field warning
        end if
      end if
end mouseUp
```

ScrollJump3, Version 1.2 Features

ScrollJump3 takes our streamlining process one giant step further by using Hyper-Card's 1.2 `select` command. Recall that ScrollJump2 used the container `the selection` to improve on ScrollJump1. But we had to simulate the action that put text into `the selection`. That was the purpose of the double-click operation in the script of ScrollJump2. With the `select` command, you can select any character, word, or line of the contents of a text field. We can use `select line` to highlight a single line of text in our scrolling box. By also using the `top of me` feature of HyperCard version 1.2 +, ScrollJump3 takes much less code than our first two examples. It also does not include the `global storenames` background script of ScrollJump2.

Using *select* and *top of me*

The `select` command reduces the six-line `line highlight` handler of ScrollJump1 to just one line:

```
select line lineNum of me
```

This shortcut bypasses the invisible button technique devised for ScrollJump1 and the simulated double-click of ScrollJump2. By using the `top of me` property to compute the number of the selected line, we eliminate the need to use `the rect`, which makes ScrollJump3 even shorter.

Because ScrollJump3 doesn't share the `global storenames` background script of ScrollJump2, it does not filter unwanted words. You can easily add this feature if you want.

A Caveat

Note that when select line operates, it starts inverting at the beginning of the line and ends at the end of the text. A real scroll list box highlights to the extreme right side of the box. Thus, this is not a "regulation" scroll box and is more like ScrollJump2. ScrollJump1 is still the only one that does a regulation select. As shown in Figure 2-3, the highlight does not extend across the entire scroll box, as in a regulation scroll box.

Figure 2-3.   ScrollJump3 uses *select line.*

The ScrollJump3 Script

Here is the script for the locked scrollable field. ScrollJump3 highlights the clicked line and goes to the card with the matching name. It displays an error if the card is not found.

```
--   ******************* DESCRIPTION *************************
-- TYPE:         Fields, Jumping to Cards.
-- AUTHORS:      Mitchell Waite, Bruce Barrett
-- NAME:         ScrollJump3.
-- RESTRICTIONS: Requires HyperCard version 1.2 or greater.
-- LOCATIONS:    Put the main script in the field, no script
                 in button.
--   ***************** FIELD SCRIPT STARTS ******************

on mouseUp
  -- compute line number clicked
  get item 2 of the clickloc - top of me + scroll of me
  put 1 + it div the textHeight of me into lineNum

  -- highlight the text in the line
  select line LineNum of me
```

continued

```
      -- save the text in the cardName variable
      put the selection into cardName

      set the cursor to watch -- this may take a while

      visual effect iris open slow
      go to card cardName
      if the result is not empty then
        show bkgnd field warning
        play "Drum2"
        wait one second
        hide bkgnd field warning
      end if
end mouseUp
```

Dueling Scroll

Mitchell Waite and Ted Jones

Synopsis: A weakness in HyperCard is its inability to have multiple fonts and styles in a single text field. You must choose a single font type, size, and attributes and this makes your text boxes look plain and boring.

This chapter reveals a neat set of scripts that allows you to join two or more separate scrolling fields into one continuously operating field. These fields can contain text and/or graphics. The separate scrolling fields can have different fonts and styles, and still scroll in sync—there are no "catching up" effects that are typical of nonsyncing approaches.

Dueling Scroll is particularly interesting in that it shows how to use existing HyperCard parts to sit on top of normal parts and "trap" mouseDowns so that you, rather than HyperCard, can direct what happens. The chapter also shows the technique for making custom icons so that HyperCard accurately simulates a real scrolling box.

Chapter 3

Dueling Scroll

Synchronizing Multiple Scrolling Fields

A surprising HyperCard shortcoming you can correct with some creative scripting is the lack of a mechanism for synchronizing multiple fields so they scroll at the same time. With such a mechanism, you could use different styles and point sizes in the fields to create list boxes and use them in many different ways.

Synchronized Scrolling

In Dueling Scroll, you can synchronize two or more scrolling fields so they operate like one smooth scrolling box. (Dueling is a play on words, like dueling banjos.) You can mix fonts and styles and even add graphics to your scroll boxes so they are more dramatic and useful. (Figures 3-1 through 3-4 were made with the Dueling Scroll script.)

Figure 3-1 shows two fields of the same font and size. The one on the left is bold. The one on the right is plain; it is the box for displaying author biographies.

```
┌──────────────────┬──────────────────────────────┬─┐
│ Mitchell D. Waite │ The Waite Group, Inc         │⬆│
│                   │ 100 Shoreline Hwy, Suite 285 │▓│
│                   │ Mill Valley, CA, 94965       │▓│
│                   │ (415) 331-0575               │▓│
│                   │ Compuserve: 74146,3515       │▓│
│                   │ BIX: mwaite                  │▓│
│                   │ uucp: hplabs!well!mitch      │▓│
│                   │                              │▓│
│                   │ Mr. Waite is President of The Waite │▓│
│                   │ Group, a computer book publisher with │▓│
│                   │ over 70 titles in print.     │▓│
│                   │                              │▓│
│ Ted Jones         │ Jones Consulting             │▓│
│                   │ 100 Shoreline Hwy, Suite 285 │▓│
│                   │ Mill Valley, CA, 94965       │▓│
│                   │ (415) 331-0575               │⬇│
└──────────────────┴──────────────────────────────┴─┘
```

Figure 3-1. Dueling Scroll for author biographies. Because both fields are the same font size (10-point Geneva and the default 13-point line height), items align easily.

Because the two fields use the same font size, it is easy to line up the text entered in the fields. Another consequence of using the same size font is that you can vary the number of lines between items. When the font size is different, you have to be careful about alignment.

Figure 3-2 shows a Dueling Scroll for an alphabetical index of HyperTalk keywords. It uses 12-point bold Geneva font on the left to make the letters A through Z stand out. A smaller 9-point plain Geneva font is used on the right field, which contains the list of items. The line height of the left field has to be 15-point for the fields to align properly.

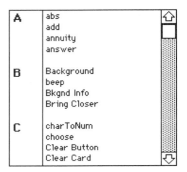

Figure 3-2.   This example of Dueling Scroll uses 12-point Geneva bold with a 15-point line height on the left and 9-point plain Geneva with a default 12-point line height on the right.

Figure 3-3 shows a Dueling Scroll used as a table of contents for a book. The left field holds the chapter names and is 18-point Dallas with a 24-point line height. (The Dallas font is available from Dubl-Click Software, 18201 Gresham Street, Northridge, California 91325.) The field on the right is 9-point Geneva on a 15-point line height.

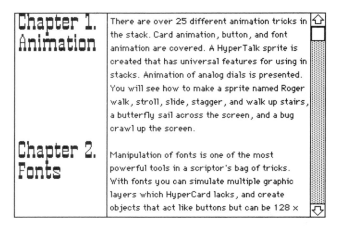

Figure 3-3.   This example is 18-point Dallas on a 24-point line height and 9-point Geneva on a 15-point line height.

Figure 3-4 shows how you can mix graphics with a Dueling Scroll to produce such objects as scrolling list boxes with illustrated glossaries. The part identifier object could be on the left or right. (One advantage of using this method for doing a glossary is you can limit a find to the header field and avoid incidental instances of the find text in other fields). Dueling Scroll is pure HyperTalk and quite short.

Figure 3-4. This example uses a font containing custom bit maps. It shows how Dueling Scroll can be used to illustrate text with objects. On the left is a custom 18-point Monaco font with a 33-point line height. On the right is a 12-point Geneva font on a 16-point line height.

Where Dueling Scroll Lives

The version of Dueling Scroll presented here resides in the card layer. Each card expects one Dueling Scroll, but you can easily modify it for multiple independent scrolling. Besides the card script, each Dueling Scroll needs two scrolling fields and four buttons. All these parts contain short scripts.

For suggestions on turning this into a background application that would appear on every card with a given background, see "Modifications."

Authentic Macintosh-Like Scrolling

Some nice touches to Dueling Scroll make it superior to most attempts at synchronized scrolling. The two fields move at the same time, so there is no delay for one to catch up with the other. Further, the way the scroll buttons (arrows) work is visually identical to the standard Macintosh scrolling arrangement. For example, a normal HyperCard button used as an up arrow highlights its entire rectangle when pressed, but an authentic Macintosh scroll arrow highlights only the arrow portion inside the box. Dueling Scroll uses custom button icons made with ResEdit that work like Macintosh scroll arrows.

Scrolling Without XCMDs

Dueling Scroll uses no XCMDs or XFCNs. This makes it possible for anyone to type and run the script immediately. The technique and algorithm are self-documented, so you control how it works. When we first looked at making this in pure HyperTalk, HyperCard did not seem fast enough to scroll like real scroll bars. But a trick solved that problem.

Scrolling two scroll fields is slower than scrolling one. Thus, the script is designed so that when you press the mouse button on one of the scroll arrows, the field scrolls three lines at a time instead of one. This greatly speeds up the operation and makes it acceptable on the slower Macintosh Plus. You can easily change the script to allow two, four, five, or more lines to be scrolled at a time, which speeds it more.

A Caveat

Our first version of Dueling Scroll was based on HyperCard 1.0.1. Because of a feature (that some might call a bug), our thumb button worked like a real scroll button. Our script allowed the user to drag a transparent button over the real thumb, and for some weird reason the Macintosh would move the actual thumb underneath our button. We could capture the mouseDown and manipulate the scroll of the field, and HyperCard would take care of moving the thumb under it (we still had to move our transparent button). Now a real Macintosh thumb when dragged gives you an outline of the thumb, then it moves the real thumb to where you let go of it. Our pre-1.2 version looked just the same; you saw the outline of the thumb move, not the thumb itself. In a sense, a trick allowed our script to hijack the regulation thumb so it looked like we were controlling it.

With version 1.2 of HyperCard, this feature disappeared. So we had to replace our transparent button with a rectangular opaque button. Instead of seeing the outline of the thumb move, you see a complete white thumb move. The regular white thumb still follows it. You could create a custom button or font to replace the normal thumb with a simulated rectangle. For people still using version 1.0.1 or 1.1, we have included the older handler so you can use it, too.

Our Secret Revealed

Dueling Scroll consists of a collection of fields, buttons, and scripts that mate two distinct scrolling text fields so they operate as one entity. Scripts in the card layer determine the maximum distance the text can be scrolled and the ratio of that distance to the distance the thumb can travel down the scroll bar. The scripts also store relevant values into global variables.

Scripts in buttons that cover the usual scroll bar translate mouse clicks on the right-hand field's scroll bar into scroll commands for both fields. We use a pseudo thumb button placed over the regular thumb, and drag the button up and down with the mouse cursor. We then calculate the scroll values for both fields based on where the thumb button ends up. The relationship of our buttons to the scroll bar is illustrated in Figure 3-5.

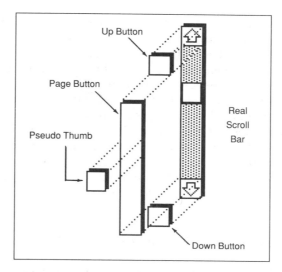

Figure 3-5. This shows how we place our own buttons, pseudo thumbs, and so on over the normal HyperCard parts and hijack mouse messages to them so our scripts can control the scrolling.

Matching Sides

Planning is required to match the two side-by-side scroll fields. Corresponding sections of both fields must be the same height in pixels for the text to move synchronously. As a result, you have to experiment (or calculate) to find the right combination of `textHeights` and lines per section. Combinations that work well include three 16-pixel lines in the left scroll field with four 12-pixel lines in the right scroll field (the rule is 3 * 16 = 4 * 12), or four 15-pixel lines with five 12-pixel lines, or four 18-pixel lines with six 12-pixel lines. These sections always scroll together because the same number of pixels per section are in each field. Another consideration is the total height of both fields (from the top of the field to the bottom) in pixels must be the same. If you meet these requirement for identical sections and have the same number of sections in both fields, you should have no problem. You may have to experiment with the line height of the fields to get them to align. Switch to the field tool and use the lines in the field as guides. At least two should line up. Click on the field and use the Command-T keys to quickly get to the information dialog for the font.

How Dueling Scroll Works

The key to our approach is that we hijack the user's attempt to use the real scroll bar by placing our own button above it (a transparent button in the pre-1.2 version, a rectangle in the 1.2 version). A mouse click or press on either the up arrow or the down arrow activates a handler in our button that scrolls both fields. A `mouseDown` on the thumb is trapped by a handler in our pseudo thumb, sitting above it. Likewise, a click in the gray area of the scroll bar is captured by a handler in our page button, which covers the entire length of the gray area.

When you open a card containing a Dueling Scroll field, a handler in the card picks up an `openCard` message that analyzes the contents of the key field (`textHeight`, number of lines, and length in pixels of the entire field) and stores this information in global variables. Custom button scripts for our scroll bar use these later. Besides the top (`y1`), bottom (`y2`), and horizontal (`x2`) location values for our thumb button, we also get the number of pixels to a line (`inc`), the number of lines (`numLines`), the current line (`lineCount`), the number of lines to a page (`page`), and the ratio between a scroll in a normal scroll field and the vertical movement of the pseudo thumb on the scroll bar (`ratio`).

Calculating the Scrolling Distance

The following script fragment calculates the thumb button coordinates. The x-coordinate is calculated by subtracting 9 (half the width of the thumb plus the right border of the scroll bar) from the right side of the right field. The top y-coordinate is calculated by adding 24 (half the height of the thumb plus the height of the arrow box) to the top y-coordinate of the left field (both fields are actually the same). The bottom y-coordinate is calculated by subtracting 24 from the bottom y-coordinate.

```
put the right of card field "right" - 9 into x2
   -- thumb x-coordinate
put the top of card field "left"  + 24 into y1
   -- thumb top y-coordinate
put the bottom of card field "left"  - 24 into y2
   -- thumb bottom y-coordinate
```

Subtracting the top y-coordinate from the bottom y-coordinate gives the distance the thumb can traverse on the scroll bar in pixels. This distance is stored as `elevHeight`. To find the height of the scroll field, you could subtract the bottom y-coordinate of the field from the top y-coordinate. But you already have `elevHeight`, and you know the distance is 24 pixels above and below it (48 pixels total). So you can simply add 48 to `elevHeight`. Dividing the height of the field by the number of pixels to a line (`inc`) gives you the number of lines to a page.

```
put y2 - y1 into elevHeight
   -- distance thumb can traverse
put trunc((elevHeight + 48)/ inc) into page
   -- number of lines to a page
```

This is straightforward, except for one glitch. Setting the scroll of a field places the specified scroll value at the *top of the display.* If you set the scroll of a field to the bottom pixel of the text in that field, you display a lot of blank lines. To avoid this, we subtract the number of lines that can show at one time (`page`) from the actual number of lines in the field, then put this adjusted figure into the variable `numLines`.

To prevent the last line of the field from scrolling to the top of the display, we reduce `numlines` by the number of lines in `page`. Multiplying the adjusted `numlines` by `inc` gives the scrolling length of the field in pixels. Dividing the distance the text can scroll (`temp1`) by the distance the thumb can move (`elevHeight`) gives the `ratio` of these two distances.

```
subtract page from numlines
put (numlines * inc) into temp1 -- total pixels in field
put temp1 / elevHeight into ratio -- ratio of field to scroll bar
```

The Buttons That Make It Work

Four card buttons contain scripts that operate Dueling Scroll. They use the following simple formulas to translate the following: scroll values to the vertical button location, the line count to scroll values, and scroll values to the line count:

```
(fieldScroll / ratio) + y1 = buttonYloc
lineCount * inc = fieldScroll
fieldScroll / inc = lineCount
```

The up arrow and down arrow buttons each contain two handlers. These handlers scroll the two fields one line at a time for a mouse click or three lines at a time for a mouse press. The examples that follow are from the up button script, but the other script is almost identical.

The mouseDown handler first gives the user some visual feedback by setting either the `hilite` of the button to true or the icon of the button to a custom black arrow (see "Making the Perfect Scroll Bar" in this chapter). Then `lineCount` is reduced by one, and if `lineCount` is below zero, it is brought back to zero. The display is frozen with `lock screen`. Next, the new `lineScroll` value is calculated:

```
put trunc(lineCount * inc) into lineScroll
  -- translate count to scroll
```

The fields are scrolled and the new display is revealed by unlocking the screen. At this point, the handler tests to see if the mouse is still down. If it is, a second handler, which handles multiline scrolls, is invoked. If the mouse is not down, the new pseudo thumb location is calculated as follows and the handler ends.

```
set the loc of card button "thumb" to x2,trunc(lineScroll/ratio+y1)
```

The fastScrollMess handler works the same as the mouseDown handler, with the following exceptions. The fastScrollMess handler scrolls three lines at a time and repeats until the mouse button is no longer down. At this point, the program returns to the mouseDown handler to reposition the pseudo thumb before that handler also ends.

The Ghost Feature

The pseudo thumb button handler in the pre-1.2 version is remarkable because of the ghost feature mentioned previously. If you press the mouse button when the cursor is over the scroll thumb, the handler in this button picks up the `mouseDown` message, freezes the screen with `lock screen`, and hides both the thumb button and the page button (the page button covers the gray area on the scroll bar). Then it clicks twice at the `clickLoc`, which passes to HyperCard the `mouseDown` it missed because the button trapped it. Script flow freezes at this point (this was a surprise to us) until HyperCard drags the ghost thumb and scrolls the right-hand field according to the new real thumb location. Now, with the screen still frozen, the handler takes back control from HyperCard (it's similar to using an XCMD) and extracts the new scroll value of the right field, which it passes to the left field.

```
click at the clickloc
click at the clickloc
-- program flow holds here until HyperCard finishes scrolling
put the scroll of card field "right" into lineScroll
  -- capture scroll value
set the scroll of card field "left" to lineScroll
  -- pass on to other field
```

Finally, the new location of the pseudo thumb and the new `lineCount` are calculated, both hidden buttons are shown, and the screen is unfrozen when the handler ends.

The post-1.2 thumb control handler is more conventional. It uses a `repeat` loop to let the thumb button follow the mouse cursor up and down the scroll elevator.

```
repeat while the mouse is down
  put item 2 of the mouseLoc into newY
  if newY < y1 then put y1 into newY
  else if newy > y2 then put y2 into newy
  set the loc of button thumb to x2,newy
end repeat
```

When the mouse button is released, the remainder of the handler converts the vertical position of the thumb button to a scroll value for the two fields. The fields are scrolled and the new value of `lineCount` is calculated.

```
-- calculate the scroll value
put trunc((newy-y1)*ratio) into lineScroll
-- scroll both fields
set scroll of card field "right" to lineScroll
set style of button "thumb" to transparent
set the scroll of card field "left" to lineScroll
-- translate into lineCount
put trunc( lineScroll / inc) into lineCount
```

The final button is the page button, which covers the gray part of the scroll bar. The mouseDown handler in this button determines if a click is above or below the thumb. It then freezes the screen, either adds a full page to `lineCount` or subtracts a full page from `lineCount`, and uses `lineCount` to calculate the new `lineScroll`.

```
put trunc(lineCount * inc) into lineScroll -- calculate scroll
```

The new pseudo thumb location is then calculated from `lineScroll`, as before, and the screen is unfrozen.

Making the Perfect Scroll Bar

For the two up and down scroll arrows to highlight correctly, with only the arrow and not the whole rectangle turned black, you need two special icons in the stack resource fork. The icons aren't essential, but they will make the finished product look better. If you don't want to work with icons, simply set the `hilite` of each button to true at the beginning of each upArrow and downArrow handler and to false at the end. You will have an almost perfect imitation of a standard Macintosh down and up scroll control.

To make your icons, first copy the stack and then launch ResEdit (available through APDA). Find the window representing the disk that holds your stack (you may have to move other windows out of the way) and double-click on the stack name. You probably will be told the document doesn't have a resource fork (the place Macintosh resources such as icons, alert boxes, and sounds are kept). Then you will be asked if you want to create one. You do, so choose New from the File menu and select Icon as the resource type in the dialog box. Now choose New again and you are given an empty window in which to design your icon. Click and drag in the window (the left area works like Fat Bits) until you locate the top and left sides of the work area. Copy the icon design in Figure 3-6 into the window, deleting the dotted guidelines when you are finished.

When you have it exactly as shown in Figure 3-6, write down the icon ID number that appears in the menu bar and click the go away box to close the window.

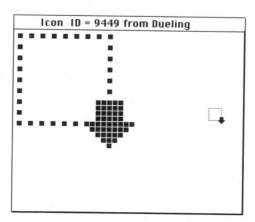

Figure 3-6. With ResEdit, you can make your own scroll arrow.

To make the up arrow icon, find your icon in the Icons window and select it by clicking once. Then choose Duplicate in the Edit menu, double-click on the duplicate, use the outer edges of the icon as guidelines for icon number two, and write down the resource number. Finally, choose Quit from the File menu, approve the saving of changes to the document, and you are finished creating the custom up and down arrow icons. Now they should be stored in the resource fork of the stack that will hold Dueling Scroll Fields. Make sure that you use these icons for the up and down arrow buttons that we place over the normal HyperCard up and down arrows on the scroll field.

Modifications

An obvious modification to Dueling Scroll is to put it in the background so that it appears on multiple cards. All this requires is that you move the card script into the background (or stack), move the fields and buttons into the background, add `bkgnd` to each button reference, and delete `card` from each field reference.

As the scripts stand, the scroll global variables are only updated on `openCard`. A useful addition is an Edit On/Edit Off button that could be either a card or a background button depending on where you decide to put your fields. Edit On would set `lockText` to false for both fields so you could edit them. Edit Off would set `lockText` back to true and send an `openCard` message to the card (or the background if you make the preceding modification) to update all the global variable values.

The Dueling Scroll Script

Here is the complete script for Dueling Scroll.

```
-- *********************** Description **********************
-- TYPE:        Field, sets up Dueling Scroll
-- SCRIPT LOC:  Card, background, or stack and 4 card buttons
-- AUTHOR:      Mitchell Waite and Ted Jones
-- RESTRICTIONS: Both fields must be the same length in pixels
-- and corresponding sections in the two fields must also be
-- the same length in pixels.
-- ****************** CARD SCRIPT STARTS *******************
on OpenCard
-- This script measures the upper and lower boundaries of the
-- scrolling window, the text height of the second field, and a
-- few other global variables. The constants represent the
-- offset size for the buttons.
  global numlines, lineCount, x2, y1, y2, inc, ratio, page
  set cursor to watch
  lock screen -- freeze the screen
  set the scroll of card "left" to 0
     -- scroll both fields to the top
  set the scroll of card "right" to 0
```

continued

```
   put 0 into lineCount -- count matches scroll position
   put textHeight of card "left" into inc -- pixels per line
   put the number of lines of card "left" into numlines
   put the right of card field "right" - 9 into x2
      -- thumb x-coordinate
   put the top of card field "left" + 24 into y1
      -- thumb top y-coordinate
   put the bottom of card field "left"  - 24 into y2
      -- thumb bottom y-coordinate
   set the loc of button "thumb" to x2,y1
      -- thumb matches scroll position
   put y2 - y1 into elevHeight -- distance thumb can traverse
   put trunc((elevHeight + 48)/ inc) into page
      -- number of lines to a page
   -- the following makes the last line of the scroll display at
   -- the bottom rather than the top
   subtract page from numlines
   put (numlines * inc) into temp1 -- total pixels in field
   put temp1 / elevHeight into ratio
      -- ratio of field to scroll bar
end OpenCard


-- *********** upArrow CARD BUTTON SCRIPT STARTS ************
on mouseDown
   global lineCount, inc, lineScroll, y1, x2, ratio
      -- if you didn't make an up icon, set autoHilite to true
      -- ******* In the following line, replace <ID#> with
      -- ******* the ID number of your black up arrow icon
   set the icon of button "UpArrow" to <ID#>
   subtract one from lineCount
      -- lineCount holds the number of the line
   put max(0,lineCount) into lineCount
     -- top scroll stop
   lock screen
   put trunc(lineCount * inc) into lineScroll
     -- translate count to scroll
   set the scroll of card field "left" to lineScroll
     -- scroll fields
   set the scroll of card field "right" to lineScroll
   -- the following translates scroll to thumb y loc and
   -- positions the thumb
   unlock screen
   if the mouse is down then fastScrollMess
     -- fast scroll if a press
   -- if you didn't make an up icon, set autoHilite to false
   set the loc of card button "thumb" to ¬
   x2,trunc((lineScroll/ratio)+y1)
   set the icon of button "upArrow" to 0 -- clears black arrow
end mouseDown


on fastScrollMess
  global lineCount, inc, lineScroll, y1, x2, ratio
  repeat while the mouse is down -- loops until mouse is up
    subtract three from lineCount -- scrolls in 3 line jumps
    put max(0,lineCount) into lineCount
    lock screen
```

continued

```
      put trunc(lineCount * inc) into lineScroll
      set the scroll of card field "left" to lineScroll
      set the scroll of card field "right" to lineScroll
      unlock screen
   end repeat
end fastScrollMess

-- ********** downArrow CARD BUTTON SCRIPT STARTS *************
on mouseDown -- see upArrow for notes
   global lineCount, inc, lineScroll, numlines, y1, x2, ratio
   -- if you didn't make an up icon, set autoHilite to true
   -- ******* In the following line, replace <ID#> with
   -- ******* the ID number of your black down arrow icon
   set icon of button "downArrow" to <ID#>
   add one to lineCount
   put min(numlines,lineCount) into lineCount
   lock screen
   put trunc(lineCount * inc) into lineScroll
   set the scroll of card field "left" to lineScroll
   set the scroll of card field "right" to lineScroll
   unlock screen
   if the mouse is down then fastScrollMess
   -- if you didn't make an up icon, set autoHilite to true
   set the loc of card button "thumb" to ¬
   x2,trunc((lineScroll/ratio)+y1)
   set icon of button "downArrow" to 0
end mouseDown

on fastScrollMess
   global lineCount, inc, lineScroll, numlines, y1, x2, ratio
   repeat while the mouse is down
      add three to lineCount
      put min(numlines,lineCount) into lineCount
      lock screen
      put trunc(lineCount * inc) into lineScroll
      set the scroll of card field "left" to lineScroll
      set the scroll of card field "right" to lineScroll
      unlock screen
   end repeat
end fastScrollMess

-- *********** thumb CARD BUTTON SCRIPT STARTS ***************
on mouseDown
   global y1,y2, ratio, inc, lineCount, x2
   set style of button "thumb" to rectangle
   repeat while the mouse is down
      put item 2 of the mouseLoc into newY
      if newY < y1 then put y1 into newY
      else if newy > y2 then put y2 into newy
      set the loc of button thumb to x2,newy
   end repeat
   lock screen
   -- calculate the scroll value
   put trunc((newy-y1)*ratio) into lineScroll
   -- scroll both fields
   set scroll of card field "right" to lineScroll
```

continued

```
    set style of button "thumb" to transparent
    set scroll of card field "left" to lineScroll
    -- translate into lineCount
    put trunc( lineScroll / inc) into lineCount
end mouseDown


--  *********** page CARD BUTTON SCRIPT STARTS **************
on mouseDown
  global lineCount, inc, ratio, y1, x2, numlines, page
  -- above or below "thumb"?
  if the mouseV < item 2 of the loc of button "thumb" then
    -- above thumb
    subtract page from lineCount
    put max(0,lineCount) into lineCount
      -- top elevator stop
    lock screen
    put trunc(lineCount * inc) into lineScroll
      -- calculate scroll
    set the scroll of card field "left" to lineScroll
      -- scroll fields
    set the scroll of card field "right" to lineScroll
    -- the following calculates the new y coordinate and
    -- positions the thumb
    set the loc of card button "thumb" to ¬
    x2,trunc((lineScroll/ratio)+y1)
    unlock screen -- show changes
  else -- below thumb
    add page to lineCount
    put min(numlines,lineCount) into lineCount
      -- bottom stop
    lock screen
    put trunc(lineCount * inc) into lineScroll
    set the scroll of card field "left" to lineScroll
    set the scroll of card field "right" to lineScroll
    set the loc of card button "thumb" to ¬
    x2,trunc((lineScroll/ratio)+y1)
    unlock screen
  end if
end mouseDown
---------------------------------------------------------------


-- The following is a replacement script for the thumb script
-- and should be used ONLY if you are running a pre-1.2
-- version of HyperCard. Note: 1.2-dependent commands in
-- preceding script must be changed.


-- ******* Pre-1.2 thumb CARD BUTTON SCRIPT STARTS *********
on mouseDown
  -- an even better handler that works only on pre-1.2
  -- versions of HyperCard
  global y1, ratio, inc, lineCount, x2
  set lockScreen to true
  hide button "thumb"
    -- hide the buttons so real scroll can take over
  hide button "page" -- hide page button also
  click at the clickLoc
```

continued

```
      click at the clickLoc
         -- I don't know why you need 2 but it works
      -- program flow holds here until HyperCard finishes scrolling
      -- the following captures scroll value
      put the scroll of card field "right" into lineScroll
      -- the following passes it to other field
      set the scroll of card field "left" to lineScroll
      -- the following line translates lineScroll into
      -- a thumb coordinate
      set loc of button "thumb" to x2,trunc( lineScroll /ratio) + y1
      show button "thumb" -- put buttons back up
      show button "page"
      -- translate into lineCount
      put trunc( lineScroll / inc) into lineCount
   end mouseDown
```

Chapter 4

Quick Pop-Up Fields

Ted Jones

Synopsis: The *Hyper* in HyperCard refers to the ability to create "hypertext"— cards with hidden fields that become visible when certain words in the text are clicked with the mouse. These hidden fields are called *pop-up fields* for short because they seem to appear from no where over the text you are reading. They allow a layered system of information so that people can explore data according to their own desires, instead of following the linear course of traditional reading systems.

With pop-ups so useful in HyperCard, you might think they come built-in, but that is not the case. Instead, Hypercard provides the tools for making pop-ups, but it's up to the scriptor to create them. Although this is not difficult, subtle problems can arise. For example, pop-ups are triggered by buttons that overlap words or locations. If these words are too close, the buttons overlap and this can prevent the pop-ups from operating correctly. Further, if the fields overlap, it may be difficult to read the one that is covered.

This chapter shows how to create a script that makes pop-up fields automatically wherever you want them. All you have to do is type the word `pop-up` in the Message box and click the location at which you wish the pop-up to be built. The script then makes an auto-positioning, pop-up field, complete with the triggering and hide buttons already installed.

Quick Pop-Up Fields

HyperText Pop-Ups with a Twist

HyperCard gives you the ability to create fields that pop up when the user clicks on a specified screen location (above a word or over a portion of a picture). But having to stop each time you need to make a pop-up field is distracting, time consuming, and repetitious. If you have to go through all the steps of making buttons and fields, changing their properties, and writing scripts for them, you wouldn't get anything else done or you would stop making pop-up fields.

Leaving Notes Automatically

What you need is a way to automatically create a pop-up field when you want to leave a note to yourself or provide information to the users of your stacks. You should be able to press a few keys and have the field appear on the screen, together with the button that displays it and another one to hide it. Well, now you can do just that. Figure 4-1 shows an empty PopUp field with the button that popped it below and a little button to hide it in its bottom right corner.

Overlaps and Auto-Sending

The little Hide button was added as a friendly way to close the field, but it presented one of two unexpected problems in this script. The problem shows up when you make a second PopUp button at the same screen location occupied by the Hide button. The second button is higher than the previously created Hide button. Thus, the `mouseUp` message generated by a mouse button click at that location is always intercepted by the PopUp button so that the PopUp field cannot be closed. The script avoids this problem by looking for Hide buttons every time it creates a PopUp button. If it finds one, the script pushes the PopUp button back (with the Send Farther menu command) until it is behind the Hide button.

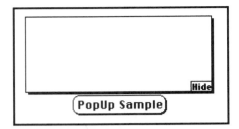

Figure 4-1. An empty PopUp field. Usually, such a field contains information about something displayed on the screen.

Auto-Positioning

The second unexpected problem involves positioning the field (and Hide button) at the edges of the screen. The script checks if the PopUp field would extend off the screen if placed in its default position (directly above the PopUp button). If so, the script finds a more visible place for it.

Figure 4-2 shows a PopUp field created by a transparent button over the words below the field (the button is highlighted to make it visible).

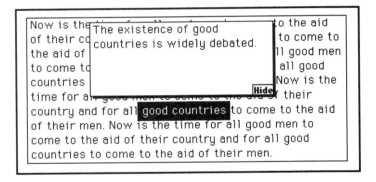

Figure 4-2. This PopUp field is created by a transparent button.

These are examples of Quick PopUp fields. As you can see, the button that triggers this field can be either a visible, round rectangle style of button or a transparent style of button. With the script that created these pop-up fields safely in your Home stack, you can quickly and easily leave a trail of notes wherever you go in your stacks.

What It Does

Quick PopUp Fields can be invoked at any time simply by typing **popup** in the Message box, placing the mouse cursor where you want the new button, and pressing the Return key. See Figure 4-3.

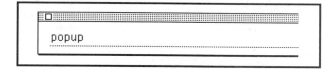

Figure 4-3. You can invoke Quick PopUp Fields by typing popup in the Message box.

The popup handler displays the watch cursor, then shows an answer box that lets the user choose the style of button to be created. See Figure 4-4.

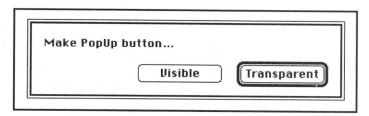

Figure 4-4. The answer box lets you choose the style of pop-up button.

The center of the new button is located at the mouse location, and the button is the autohighlighting type. If Visible is selected, the user is asked to supply a name for the button in an ask box, as shown in Figure 4-5. Transparent buttons do not require a name because they are invisible coverings over text or graphic cues behind text on the screen.

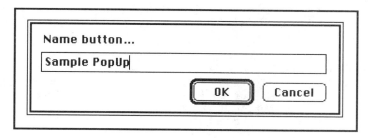

Figure 4-5. Now you can name the new button.

After making the button that causes the field to pop up, the script creates a shadow field for text. A small button is provided to hide the field when the user is finished looking at it. Finally, the handler places the insertion cursor into the new field so you can immediately type your note before hiding the field and going on to other things. The PopUp button can be in any part of the card, and there can be many PopUp buttons on the same card. Because background fields and buttons can be concealed by card fields, all these objects are made as card objects so that they are in front of other screen elements.

How It Works

Quick PopUp Fields consists of a single handler located in the stack script of your Home stack. (The handler could be placed at a lower level—in the stack or background script, for example). The popup handler is activated when the popup message reaches it from the Message box. In the preliminary section of the handler, the location of the mouse cursor and the previous user level are saved, the cursor is changed to the watch, and the screen is locked.

The next section of the handler creates the PopUp button, positions it, and sets the other button properties according to your decisions. After you create the button, the script looks for any Hide buttons (we cover these in a moment) that might occupy the same area of the screen. If it finds one, the new button is pushed behind the Hide button so that it won't prevent the Hide button of other PopUp fields from working. (Hide buttons are usually hidden so they do not interfere with PopUp buttons.)

The next section of the handler makes the field. The trick is to place the field so it is near the button, but still on the screen. If the button is near the edge of the screen, the field location is moved so that the whole field is visible.

Next, a Hide button is created to let you hide the field when you have finished reading it. The Hide button is placed in the bottom right corner of the field and given a script that hides the field and itself.

Finally, the PopUp button is given a script, the tool and userLevel are restored to normal, and the insertion point is placed in the field so the user can immediately enter text.

Making a Button

The first big job is creating the button that pops up the PopUp field. The section of the script that does this job looks like this:

```
-- create PopUp button
doMenu "New Button" -- create a new button
put the id of button the number of card buttons into popUpButton
set the loc of button id popUpButton to mouseTemp
-- position button
answer "Make PopUp button..." with "Visible" or "Transparent"
if it is "Visible" then
  Ask "Name button..."
  if it is empty then
    select card button id popUpButton
    doMenu "Clear Button"
    choose browse tool
    exit to hypercard -- End script on Cancel
  else
    set the name of button id popUpButton to it
  end if
else
  set the style of button id popUpButton to transparent
  set the showName of button id popUpButton to false
```

continued

```
   -- don't show name
end if
set the autoHilite of button id popUpButton to true
set the cursor to watch
```

The script first selects the New Button menu option to create a new button and stores the ID number of this button in the variable `popUpButton`. Then the button is relocated so it is centered at the mouse location (saved in `mouseTemp`), and the user is asked if the button should be visible or transparent. If visible is chosen, the user is asked to name the button. Choosing OK when the name field is empty or choosing Cancel both return `empty` in the `it` variable, which deletes the new button and ends the script. If anything but `empty` is returned in the `it` variable, the script sets the name of the button to that name.

If the user wants a transparent button, the handler changes the button's `style` and `showName` properties. The cursor is again set to the watch at the end of the `if-then` structure.

Now that you have a PopUp button, the next job is to make sure it does not overlay a previous Hide button. New buttons are above preexisting buttons and get any mouse messages before lower buttons. Thus, if your new PopUp button is over a Hide button, it is impossible to hide the field it is associated with. The next section of the script makes sure this does not occur:

```
-- get sides of PopUp rect
put left of button id popUpButton into popLeft
put top of button id popUpButton into popTop
put right of button id popUpButton into popRight
put bottom of button id popUpButton into popBottom

-- make sure the new "PopUp" button doesn't cover a ¬
"Hide" button
repeat with n = 1 to the number of card buttons
   -- for all card buttons
   if the short name of card button n is "Hide" then
      -- Ignore if not Hide. Otherwise get sides of Hide rect.
      put the left of card button n into hideLeft
      put the top of card button n into hideTop
      put the right of card button n into hideRight
      put the bottom of card button n into hideBottom
      -- Does "Hide" overlap "PopUp"?

      if ((hideLeft > popLeft and hideLeft < popRight) or ¬
      (hideRight > popLeft and hideRight < popRight)) and ¬
      ((hideTop > popTop and hideTop < popBottom) or ¬
      (hideBottom > popTop and hideBottom < popBottom)) then
         get the id of card button n
         -- send "PopUp" button farther until it is behind "Hide"
         repeat until the number of button id it > the number ¬
         of button id popUpButton
           doMenu "Send Farther"
         end repeat
      end if
   end if
end repeat
```

The first step is to put all four sides of the PopUp button's rectangle into variables: `popLeft`, `popTop`, `popRight`, and `popBottom`. Next is a `repeat` loop that looks through all the card buttons. If the short name of a card button is Hide, the sides of that button's rectangle are put into the variables `hideLeft`, `hideTop`, `hideRight`, and `hideBottom`. The handler then checks if both a horizontal and a vertical side of Hide is inside the area occupied by the PopUp.

If the Hide button does overlap the PopUp button, the handler uses the Send Farther menu option to push the PopUp button back until the Hide button is above it. After the Hide button is on top, where it can get a `mouseUp` message, the `repeat` loop ends.

Making a Field

Now you are ready to create the text field that will pop up. The new field is created by using the menu simulation command `doMenu`. The field's ID number is retrieved and saved in the variable `popUpField`. The `style` of the field is set to shadow. Next the handler checks if the top of the PopUp button rectangle is too close to the top of the screen. (You need to leave room there for the field.) If there is vertical space, the field is located directly above (but not covering) the button. If there isn't enough room above the button, the field is placed directly below the button. Here is the section of the script that checks this:

```
-- Create PopUp field
doMenu "New Field"
put the id of card field the number of card fields into popUpfield
set the style of card field id popUpfield to shadow
put the screenRectinto screenVar
if popTop > item 2 of screenVar then
-- if room put field above the button
  set the loc of card field id popUpfield to item 1 of ¬
  the loc of button id popUpButton, (item 2 of the rect ¬
  of card button id popUpButton) - 44
else -- if not room put field below the button
  set the loc of card field id popUpfield to item 1 of ¬
  the loc of button id popUpButton, item 4 of the rect ¬
  of card button id popUpButton + 43
end if
```

There follows another check to make sure there is horizontal space at the left side of the button to display the field. If there isn't enough room, the location of the text field is shifted right so that it will fit on the screen. If the left side is okay, the right side is checked in the same way and the location is adjusted if necessary.

Making the Hide Button

The final object to create is the Hide button for the PopUp field. The ID number of this button is stored in the `hideButton` variable, the name of the button is set to

Hide, and its `style` is changed to rectangle. To make the button as small as possible, the `textSize` for its name is set to 9-point Geneva. The button is placed at the bottom right corner of the field it hides. The button is placed by setting its `rectangle` property with the following statement:

```
set the rect of button id hideButton to the right ¬
of card field id popUpfield - 25, ¬
the bottom of card field id popUpfield - 14, ¬
the right of card field id popUpfield - 2, ¬
the bottom of card field id popUpfield - 2
```

Now that all the objects have been created, the scripts that operate the PopUp and Hide buttons must be loaded into their respective objects using the `set` command and the `script` property of the buttons. You use `set script` to replace the previous script of an object with a script you have constructed in a container or expression. The Hide button script consists of a mouseUp handler that freezes the screen, hides itself, and hides the field. To identify the button and field to hide, the ID number of each object is placed in the script from the expression. Here is the statement that creates the Hide button's script:

```
-- Load script into "Hide" button
set script of button id hideButton to "on mouseUp" & return & ¬
"lock screen" & return & "hide button id " & ¬
hideButton & return & "hide card field id " & popUpfield & ¬
return & "end mouseUp"
```

The result of this statement is a script in the Hide button that looks like this:

```
on mouseUp
  lock screen
  hide me
  hide card field id 2
end mouseUp
```

The ID number will vary. The PopUp button script is the same, except it shows objects instead of hides objects.

Next you restore the `userLevel` and the browse tool and unfreeze the screen. Finally, you place the insertion point in the new pop-up field by typing a tab to the first field, then moving to the last field by sending a Shift-Tab with the `type` command.

```
choose browse tool
set the userLevel to UseLev
unlock screen
select text of card field id popUp field
```

The PopUp field is now ready to receive a note that the Hide button will hide and the PopUp button will show again.

Caveats

For the PopUp button, Quick PopUp Fields uses the default button size, which may not be the perfect size for all applications. Although you could build into the script some button controls that would let you resize the button, HyperCard's button relocating and resizing controls are so simple that this probably would be a waste of time and code. The same is true for the PopUp field, which is set to the new field default size. The default size is large enough for a short note, but if you must have more room or you want to place the field in another area of the card, simply choose the field tool, drag the field where you want it, then choose the button tool and reposition the Hide button.

Avoid moving the Hide button because there can be problems when a Hide button is behind a PopUp button—you can't hide the field. The script looks out for that possibility, so it can only happen if you move the fields and buttons yourself.

Also remember that although you can place a PopUp button over text, the button will not move automatically if the text is altered and will not scroll with a scrolling field. HyperCard versions 1.0.1 through 1.2.1 lack sticky buttons that can follow text. If you avoid putting PopUp buttons over scrolling fields or unlocked text fields, you will avoid these problems.

Modifications

As mentioned in the preceding section, you can add your own PopUp button resizing and relocating controls to Quick PopUp Fields. You also can alter the default properties of the PopUp button and PopUp field. For instance, you could make the field larger and reduce its textSize to give more room for notes, or you could make it a scrolling field.

To make Quick PopUp Fields "friendlier," add an answer box telling the user to click where the button should go. This could get annoying after a while, so you might want to include an Option key override.

The Quick PopUp Fields Script

```
-- *********************** DESCRIPTION *********************
-- TYPE:         Field tricks
-- AUTHOR:       Ted Jones
-- NAME:         Quick PopUp Fields
-- LOCATIONS:    Home stack script, card buttons
-- RESTRICTIONS: Can't be used with scrolling fields. Risky
--               with unlocked fields.

-- ******************** SCRIPT STARTS HERE *****************
-- One handler activated by typing "popup" in the Message box.
-- This script works with HyperCard 1.2 and should work
-- with any later versions of the application.
-------------------------------------------------------------
```

continued

```
on popup
  put the mouseLoc into mouseTemp -- the mouse position
  set the cursor to watch -- shows watch cursor
  lock screen -- freezes the screen
  put the userLevel into UseLev
  set the userLevel to 5

  -- create PopUp button
  doMenu "New Button" -- create a new button
  put the id of button the number of card buttons into ¬
  popUpButton
  set the loc of button id popUpButton to mouseTemp
  -- position button
  answer "Make PopUp button..." with "Visible" or "Transparent"
  if it is "Visible" then
    Ask "Name button..."
    if it is empty then
      click at loc of button id popUpButton
      doMenu "Clear Button"
      choose browse tool
      exit to hypercard -- End script on Cancel
    else
      set the name of button id popUpButton to it
    end if
  else
    set the style of button id popUpButton to transparent
    set the showName of button id popUpButton to false
    -- don't show name
  end if
  set the autoHilite of button id popUpButton to true
  set the cursor to watch

  -- get sides of PopUp rect
  put the left of button id popUpButton into popLeft
  put the top of button id popUpButton into popTop
  put the right of button id popUpButton into popRight
  put the bottom of button id popUpButton into popBottom

  -- make sure new "PopUp" button doesn't cover a "Hide" button
  repeat with n is 1 to the number of card buttons
    -- for all card buttons
    if the short name of card button n is "Hide" then
    -- Ignore if not Hide. Otherwise get sides of Hide rect.
      put the left of card button n into hideLeft
      put the top of card button n into hideTop
      put the right of card button n into hideRight
      put the bottom of card button n into hideBottom
      -- Does "Hide" overlap "PopUp"?

      if ((hideLeft > popLeft and hideLeft < popRight) or ¬
      (hideRight > popLeft and hideRight < popRight)) and ¬
      ((hideTop > popTop and hideTop < popBottom) or ¬
      (hideBottom > popTop and hideBottom < popBottom)) then
        get the id of card button n
        -- send "PopUp" button farther until it
```

continued

```
          -- is behind "Hide"
          repeat until the number of button id it > the ¬
          number of button id popUpButton
            doMenu "Send Farther"
          end repeat
        end if
      end if
  end repeat


-- Create PopUp field
doMenu "New Field"
put the id of card field the number of card fields into popUpfield
set the style of card field id popUpfield to shadow
put the screenRect into screenVar
if popTop > item 2 of screenVar then
-- if room put field above the button
  set the loc of card field id popUpfield to item 1 of ¬
  the loc of button id popUpButton, (item 2 of the rect ¬
  of card button id popUpButton) - 44
else -- if not room put field below the button
  set the loc of card field id popUpfield to item 1 of ¬
  the loc of button id popUpButton, item 4 of the rect ¬
  of card button id popUpButton + 43
end if
-- make sure field doesn't overlap the sides of the screen
if popLeft < item 1 of screenVar then
  set the loc of card field id popUpfield to 110,¬
  item 2 of the loc of card field id popUpField
else
  if popRight > item 3 of screenVar then set the loc of ¬
  card field id popUpfield to 400,item 2 of the loc of ¬
  card field id popUpField
end if


-- Create a "Hide" button
doMenu "New Button"
put the id of button the number of card buttons into hideButton
set the name of button id hideButton to "Hide"
set the style of button id hideButton to rectangle
set the autoHilite of button id hideButton to true
set the textSize of button id hideButton to 9
set the rect of button id hideButton to ¬
the right of card field id popUpfield - 25, ¬
the bottom of card field id popUpfield - 14, ¬
the right of card field id popUpfield - 2, ¬
the bottom of card field id popUpfield - 2


-- Load script into "Hide" button
set script of button id hideButton to "on mouseUp" & return & ¬
"lock screen" & return & "hide button id " & ¬
hideButton & return & "hide card field id " & popUpfield & ¬
return & "end mouseUp"


-- Load Script into "PopUp" button
set script of button id popUpButton to "on mouseUp" & return & ¬
"lock screen" & return & "show card field id "& ¬
```

continued

```
     popUpfield & return & "show button id " & hideButton & ¬
     return & "end mouseUp"
     -- return screen to normal, then unfreeze
     choose browse tool
     set the userLevel to UseLev
     unlock screen
     select text of card field id popUp field
     beep
end popup
```

Menu Fields

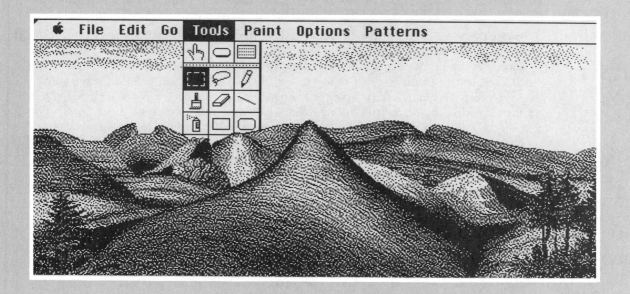

Jack A. Smith

Synopsis: A cornerstone of Macintosh applications are menus: on-screen, pull-down, selection devices that allow users to choose from a list. Menus have come a long way since the Macintosh was introduced—from simple pull-downs that are located in the Menu bar at the top of the screen and use only the Chicago font to sophisticated pop-ups that can appear anywhere on the screen, can be dragged to a new location, made to stick to a particular spot, contain any font, and can even be edited. The most modern menus have submenus that appear to the left or right of the main menu. Unfortunately, Hypercard has no built-in menu commands, so you must resort to sophisticated XCMDs or XFCNs to create these tools.

This chapter shows how to create custom menus that are fixed, scrollable, self-adjusting, user-editable, draggable, auto pop-up, temporarily sticky, and even have pop-down submenus and Menu bars that can be torn off. These menu fields use absolutely no XCMDs or XFCNs and work on any Macintosh. The chapter reveals many different selection techniques, including command-clicking, single-clicking, Tab-Enter, and combinations of all three. You will find a wealth of educational material that will greatly increase your knowledge of HyperTalk and your ability to write powerful scripts. There is even a complete replacement for the Macintosh desktop that uses HyperCard and menu fields.

Menu Fields

Draggable, Tear-Off, Auto-Positioning Menus

HyperCard, with its authoring tools and scripting language, has indeed made the Macintosh programmable by "the rest of us. " Even the simplest Macintosh program, however, usually contains a programming construct called an *event loop*, which handles menu selection events. Therefore, it seems ironic that menus are not provided as HyperCard objects and that there is no case structure in HyperTalk to help implement them.

To help fill this void, this chapter presents examples of how you can use normal text fields as menus that can be fixed, scrolled, self-adjusted, edited by users, dragged, automatically popped up, and temporarily "sticky. " Text can even be used as menu bars with pop-down submenus that can be "torn off. " Several selection techniques are demonstrated for both locked and unlocked fields, including command-clicking, single-clicking, double-clicking, a Tab-Enter technique, and variations on all of these.

This chapter moves quickly to cover many tricks. The fields and their scripts do not use any XCMDs or XFCNs. The scripts are written entirely in HyperTalk and for the most part consist of simple handlers that can be mixed to suit your needs. It should be noted, however, that many HyperCard version 1.2 features are used. Most of the handlers can be made generic enough to be moved up to the higher level card, background, and stack scripts. Many of these same techniques can also be applied to hypertext-like navigation in regular text.

Command-Clicking to Put Text in the Message Box

The field to the left in Figure 5-1 is a normal text field containing single-word items separated by carriage returns. It is shown with a shadow style, but it could be in any style, including scrolling. It can be either locked or unlocked. Let's suppose that it is a card field, visible and unlocked. To make this field act like a menu, you will use the Command-click technique normally used with the find command, and add a handler to the field script to override the default action normally taken by HyperCard. First, we define a few terms, then review the Command-click technique used with the find command.

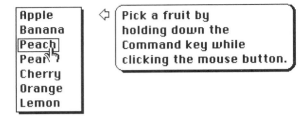

Figure 5-1.   You can use Command-click in a normal text field
to select items from a menu.

The term *outline* denotes the rectangular box used with the Command-click
selection. The term *highlight* refers to the usual reverse video effect used in selecting
text during a click-and-drag or double-click operation. Unfortunately, the word *selection* is also used to refer to the actual menu item chosen, whether the choice is
made by outlining, highlighting, or pointing and clicking with no visual effect.

The term *Command-click* refers to the user action of holding down the Command key while clicking the mouse button when the cursor is positioned over an
object. Outside a text field, this only has the effect of setting the function `commandKey`
to down, in addition to sending the usual `mouseDown`, `mouseStillDown`, and `mouseUp`
messages to the appropriate object. In a text field, however, Command-click is always
trapped first by HyperCard, and the assumption is that the user is using the `find`
command. When the Command key is held down over an unlocked text field, the
cursor changes from the I-beam to the pointing finger, as though the field is locked.
When the mouse is first pressed down over a word (with the Command key still
down), the word under the click is outlined in a rectangular box (not reversed like a
regular text selection). At the same time, the outlined word also replaces any selection in the Message box or the entire contents of the Message box if no selection is
present. If the `find` command has been previously selected from the Go menu, the
Message box looks similar to Figure 5-2, and the selection in quotation marks is
replaced by whatever is outlined in the text by the Command-click. In this example,
`Apple` would be replaced by `Peach`.

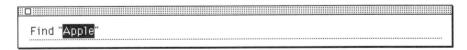

Figure 5-2.   If the *find* command has been selected, the Command-click
method replaces the word in quotation marks in the Message box.

In addition, if the mouse is dragged horizontally across the field while the
button is still down, the outlined text extends to include additional whole words
(partial words are not outlined). Multiple words are treated as one selection if they
are separated by Option-spaces instead of regular spaces. When the mouse button is
finally released (`mouseUp`), the Message box contains all the text outlined at the time
the mouse button was released. At this point, you could press the Return key to
execute the altered `find` command. The `find` command would search forward in

the stack looking for the first occurrence of the quoted text and go to that card. Before we begin to use this technique, a few observations are worth noting.

First, during a Command-click operation, no mouseDown event is posted when the mouse click occurs (in other words, no message is sent to the field or any other higher level object). Second, mouseStillDown events are posted while the mouse is still down during a drag operation (to extend the outlined selection). Only a maximum number of mouseStillDown events appear to be posted, however, even though the outlining operation continues. Third, an outlining operation will not extend beyond the initial line. And, as with a normal text selection, the anchor point cannot be changed from the initial click location. Last, and most important, a mouseUp event is posted when the mouse button is actually released, whether the field is locked or not. There is one subtle exception to the preceding. If the initial click location is not exactly within a word (such as in the white space at the end of a line), the highlighting operation is canceled without any opportunity to extend it, and an immediate mouseUp event is posted, even though the mouse may actually still be down. With all this in mind, let's see how to use this technique.

The trick is to let the Command-click put text into the Message box (and also force a mouseUp message in an unlocked field) and to use a mouseUp handler in the field script to do something with it. For this to work properly, text cannot be currently selected in the Message box. Put the following mouseUp handler in the field's script to capture the outlined text and perform some menu-like action with it:

```
on mouseUp
  get message -- puts message contents into variable it
  if it is not EMPTY then
    put "You picked a" && it
    -- do what you want with "it"
    -- For example,
    -- put myPrefix & it & mySuffix into it, and/or
    -- get myFunction(it), and
    -- put it [into>before>after myContainer]
    -- open it [with myApplication]
    -- find it [in field myField [of stack myStack]]
    -- write it to myFile
    -- go to stack it
    -- go to card it [of stack myStack]
    -- doMenu it
    -- do it
  end if
end mouseUp
```

You might want to do other things in this handler, but for the moment we will keep it simple. The key statement in this handler is the get message, which puts the contents of the Message box into the it variable. In this example, you echo it back in a message saying "You picked...", but you can do whatever you want with it. (See the handler's comments for some examples.) As an aid in controlling selection content, remember that multiple words can be treated as one word if they are separated by Option-spaces instead of regular spaces.

Remember also that this technique can be used on either locked or unlocked fields and thus does not affect normal user editing of the field. There are a few other advantages of this technique over many of the others that will be described. One is the capability to force the selection to be whole words (or word phrases with words separated by Option-spaces) and limited to a single line. Another is the ability to extend the technique into a more ambitious hypertext navigation technique (we discuss this later). And most importantly, this technique is extremely easy to implement.

One drawback, however, is the user has to use the Command key, which is not the usual way to select from a menu. The next example shows how the Command-click technique can be automated for locked fields so that the Command key does not need to be held down when selecting an item.

Single-Clicking to Simulate Command-Clicking

This menu field example automates the Command-click technique of the preceding example. An item is selected by a single click of the mouse, without having to hold down the Command key. This technique only works on a locked field, so the field must be unlocked temporarily to edit it.

Unlike an unlocked field where no mouseUp, mouseStillDown, or mouseUp events are posted (except when the Command key is down), a mouseDown event is posted for a mouse click in a locked field. This is used by many menu techniques. Most such techniques, including some in this chapter, temporarily and automatically unlock the field to do their work, then relock it. This example uses a different approach. The mouseDown is transformed into a Command-click, simulating the previous technique. The mouseUp handler, then, still takes care of determining the menu selection.

The following mouseDown handler placed in the field script simulates a Command-click:

```
on mouseDown
  global inCommandMode
  -- initialize global variable first time through
  if inCommandMode is EMPTY then put FALSE into inCommandMode
  -- ignore second mouseDown event from simulated Command-click
  if not inCommandMode then
    put TRUE into inCommandMode
    -- simulate a Command-click
    click at the clickLoc with commandKey
    put FALSE into inCommandMode
  end if
end mouseDown
```

The key statement here is click at the clickLoc with commandKey, which does almost the same thing as when a user clicks the mouse with the Command key down. The sequence of events that takes place contains a few surprises, but a detailed description is beyond the scope of this chapter. The important thing to note is that this results in another mouseDown event and mouseUp event, in addition to the ones generated by the user. The global variable inCommandMode differentiates between these simulated events and the ones generated by the user. Without this distinction and an explicit test for it, a recursion error would occur. That is, mouseDown would call `mouseDown`, which would call `mouseDown`, and so on. The mouseUp handler needs to be modified as follows:

```
on mouseUp
  global inCommandMode
  -- ignore first mouseUp event from simulated Command-click
  if not inCommandMode then
    get message
    if it is not EMPTY then
      put "You picked" && it -- Do your thing here
    end if
  end if
end mouseUp
```

One remaining drawback with this and the preceding example is the appearance of the Message box during the Command-click. This can be avoided by temporarily relocating the message window off the screen. (See the section "Putting It All Together" in this chapter.)

Before describing other aspects of implementing menus, the next few examples present more techniques for selecting the menu item. Each has its own advantages and disadvantages, and this is by no means an exhaustive treatment. You can implement many of these techniques at the same time on the same field. For example, a simulated Command-click can be used for menu selection in a field while it is locked. But a regular Command-click can be used for selection while the field is unlocked for user editing, without having to lock it first.

Or the user may want to be able to use either the mouse or the keyboard to make a selection. (See "Using Tab-Enter to Simulate Menu Selection" in this chapter.)

Double-Clicking to Simulate Menu Selection

One alternative to the two preceding techniques for simulating a menu selection is to use a double-click. This technique works only on unlocked fields, as shown in Figure 5-3. It involves using the mouseWithin handler to look constantly for a non-empty selection made by double-clicking (or by clicking-and-dragging) on a word in the unlocked text. Put the following two handlers in the field script:

```
on mouseEnter
  if the selection is not EMPTY then
    click at the mouseLoc
  end if
end mouseEnter

on mouseWithin
  if the selection is not EMPTY then
    put "You picked" && the selection -- Do your thing here
    select before text of me
  end if
end mouseWithin
```

Figure 5-3.   You can also double-click on an unlocked field to
simulate menu selection.

The important thing here is the `if the selection is not EMPTY` statement in the
mouseWithin handler. The line `click at the mouseLoc` in the mouseEnter handler is
used to void any selection that may be present before entering the field. (Remember
the selection is a global container.) The `select before text of me` in the
mouseWithin handler is used to void the selection just made, in case multiple selections will be made before leaving the field.

Although this technique works on unlocked fields, editing the field is severely
hampered because this technique cannot distinguish between a selection generated
by dragging the mouse with the button down and one generated by a double-click.
(You would have to tie a Macintosh user's hands to keep him or her from selecting
text while editing.)

Selecting with the *selectedLine* Feature

Another alternative for simulating a menu selection is to use a new HyperCard
version 1.2 feature, called the `selectedLine`. Like the simulated Command-click
technique, this is a single-click technique for locked fields. Although this technique
requires that the field be locked, the trick (as mentioned previously) is that the field
is temporarily unlocked by the script to do the selection. The selection must also be
an entire line, but for menus this is usually desirable.

Putting the following mouseDown and mouseUp handlers into the field script
will do the trick:

```
on mouseDown
  set lockText of me to FALSE
  click at the clickLoc
  select the selectedLine
  set lockText of me to TRUE
end mouseDown

on mouseUp
  put "You picked" && the selection -- Do your thing here
end mouseUp
```

The important lines here are the "click at the clickLoc" and "select the selected-
Line" in the mouseDown handler. The first passes the user click on the locked text
to the unlocked text. The latter selects the entire line containing the insertion bar

that was just clicked. (The `selectedLine` refers to the line containing the insertion bar whether there is any selection or not.) Notice that this technique, and all the others covered here, are between the mouseDown and mouseUp handlers. It could be in the mouseDown handler (as it often is elsewhere), but most actions in the Macintosh world take place on the `mouseUp`, with only intermediate feedback on the `mouseDown`. This also gives the user an opportunity to change his or her mind by dragging the mouse outside the field before letting up. (Thus, no `mouseUp` is sent to the field, although it is sent to the card and on up the hierarchy until it is caught.)

A similar technique is to simulate a double-click with the following handlers:

```
on mouseDown
  set lockText of me to FALSE
  click at the clickLoc
  click at the clickLoc
  set lockText of me to TRUE
end mouseDown

on mouseUp
  put "You picked" && the selection -- Do your thing here
end mouseUp
```

It would be better to call this one a selectedWord Menu Field because only a single word on the line is selected and there is no opportunity to extend it (except to use Option-spaces in the text, as mentioned previously with the Command-click technique). This technique is more useful in a hypertext situation to select specific words rather than whole lines or menu items that may contain more than one word (for example, Page Setup . . .).

This technique works much like the simulated Command-click technique. The main difference is the way the text is highlighted. The simulated Command-click gives the most accurate feedback (that is, only whole words are outlined and only whole words are selected). In a hypertext situation, you probably would want to use some sort of magic character (for example, *) to discern indexed words, both as a cue for the user and as a means of checking it in a script. The advantage of using this technique in a hypertext situation, instead of the usual hidden buttons, is that the hyper word or hyper phrase doesn't have to remain in a fixed position. This allows text to be edited or scrolled without changing the links. The disadvantage is building the links initially. Linking buttons is simple. You don't need to be concerned with what is under a button, and a button doesn't even have to be associated with words or phrases of text. And there lies the problem—they don't necessarily "stick" to what they are intended to be associated with. The simulated Command-click technique, on the other hand, must rely on the use of the `find` command or some kind of indexing scheme to perform a link.

Using Tab-Enter to Simulate Menu Selection

The final example of an alternative selection technique uses the Enter key to select the first line containing the selection (or the line containing the insertion bar if there is no selection). The Tab key is used to move through the menu, highlighting successive lines of the field in a wraparound fashion and in either direction. (Shift-Tab moves in the reverse direction.) The Enter key is then pressed to make the selection. This technique uses the version 1.2 enterInField message to constantly look for the Enter key and the tabKey message to trap the Tab key. It works only on unlocked fields, but it can be combined easily with any of the other techniques to handle the locked state. It is a particularly useful technique for keyboard intensive applications where using the mouse might be inconvenient. Like the selectedLine technique, however, it does not distinguish between a line with an actual selection and a line with the insertion bar in it. Nor does it know if the Tab key or the mouse makes (highlights) the selection. The two handlers needed for the field script are

```
on enterInField
  select the selectedLine
  put "You picked" && the selection -- Do your thing here
end enterInField


on tabKey
  -- select first or last line if none selected
  if the selection is EMPTY then
    if the selectedLine is EMPTY then
      if the shiftKey is DOWN then
        select last line of target
      else
        select first line of target
      end if
    else
      select the selectedLine
    end if
  else
    put the selectedLine into nextLine
    if the shiftKey is DOWN then
      if word 2 of nextLine <= 1 then
        put number of lines of target into word 2 of nextLine
      else
        subtract 1 from word 2 of nextLine
      end if
    else
      if word 2 of nextLine >= number of lines of target then
        put 1 into word 2 of nextLine
      else
        add 1 to word 2 of nextLine
      end if
    end if
    select nextLine
  end if
end tabKey
```

The enterInField handler is straightforward. (The use of the selectedLine was discussed in the previous example.) The tabKey handler needs some explanation. The idea is simple, but preselection, end-wraparound, and using Shift-Tab to reverse direction make it look complicated. It uses two version 1.2 features we have covered, the selectedLine and the select command. The trick here is realizing that the selectedLine and the argument to the select command are more than just line numbers. They are a line expression that means something like "line n of background field myfield." The second word of this line expression is the line number, which is incremented with the add command to reference the next line (or decremented with the subtract command for the previous line) before selecting. This tabKey handler is generic enough to be placed at a higher level such as the stack script or even the Home stack.

When the mouse is used, automatic highlighting (that is, highlighting the line containing the last mouse click) can be done by adding the following mouseWithin handler:

```
on mouseWithin
  -- select first line if none already selected
  if the selectedLine is EMPTY then select before text of me
  select the selectedLine
end mouseWithin
```

A simple variation on this technique is to use a returnInField handler instead of enterInField. Another variation is to put the selection in a separate global variable and use a button script to perform the action. In the latter variation, it is important to use a separate global variable because the click on a button (with autoHilite) will void the selection. Combining these two variations produces something similar to a Standard File dialog.

Creating User-Editable Menu Fields

Because some techniques discussed so far work only with locked fields, it would be nice to have an easy way for the user to lock and unlock a field for editing without going through the Tools or Objects menus. You could set up a button to act as a lock and unlock toggle, but a simpler way is to let the Option key serve as an unlocking mechanism. The following mouseWithin handler checks for the Option key and toggles in and out of edit mode.

```
on mouseWithin
  global saveStyle
  if the optionKey is DOWN and the commandKey is not DOWN then
    if lockText of target is TRUE then
      set lockText of target to FALSE
      put style of target into saveStyle
      set style of target to SCROLLING
    else
      set lockText of target to TRUE
      if saveStyle is not EMPTY then
        set style of target to saveStyle
      end if
      adjustMenu
    end if
  end if
end mouseWithin
```

When switching the field to edit mode (unlocked), the field's style is changed to scrolling style, if it's not already in that style, for more flexible editing. This is particularly useful for adding entries to a menu. It helps in this case if the field is initially wide enough to allow room for the scroll bar without obscuring text or forcing text to wrap. After editing, the field height is readjusted with `adjustMenu`. (See the next section, which describes self-adjusting menu fields.)

The use of the Option key is not perhaps the best choice because it limits the use of Option-space and Option-Return, which are useful in creating multiword and multiline menu items. But using the Control key is more limited and requires a different (and obscure) approach, and the Command key is used already for many things. Care must also be taken not to trap the Shift-Option-Command combination used for peeking at fields in version 1.2.

Creating Self-Adjusting Menu Fields

The next example demonstrates a simple pop-up menu effect. The purpose of this example, however, is to show a technique whereby a field can adjust its size and style according to its current contents. Pop-up menus are more fully addressed in following examples. The menu in this example automatically adjusts to its full size when the mouse enters the field and shrinks to a single line when the mouse leaves, as shown in Figure 5-4.

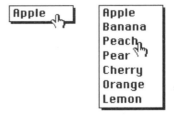

Figure 5-4. The self-adjusting pop-up menu field expands when the mouse enters the field and shrinks to a single line when the mouse leaves.

If the menu is too long to fit entirely within the card, the style is automatically changed to scrolling. The selection technique can be any of the ones previously discussed. Just add the following handlers to the field script of any of the previous examples:

```
on mouseEnter
  adjustMenu
end mouseEnter

on adjustMenu maxLines
  lock screen -- hide all movements until done
  -- determine the number of lines in the menu
  put number of lines of target into numLines
```

continued

```
    if maxLines is not EMPTY and numLines > maxLines then
      put maxLines into numLines
    else if numLines < 1 then
      put 1 into numLines
    end if
    -- determine the height of the menu in pixels
    put numLines * (textHeight of target) + 5 into pixelsNeeded
    -- determine the space left on the card in pixels
    put (bottom of card window) - (top of target) into pixelsLeft
    put top of target into savedTop -- save for resetting
    if pixelsNeeded < pixelsLeft then
      set height of target to pixelsNeeded
      if style of target is "scrolling" then
        set style of target to "rectangle"
      end if
    else
      set height of target to pixelsLeft
      set style of target to "scrolling"
    end if
    set top of target to savedTop -- reset top
    unlock screen -- now show it
end adjustMenu

on mouseLeave
  adjustMenu 1
end mouseLeave
```

The adjustMenu handler adjusts the height and style of a menu field based on an optional passed parameter, the number of lines in the menu, the `textHeight`, and the number of pixels remaining on the card. This handler uses the `set height` and `set top` features of version 1.2, rather than recalculate the rectangle's coordinates. The `set height` preserves the center location of the field. But for menus it is more appropriate to preserve the top, so the original value is saved and restored.

The value of this handler becomes more apparent in the remaining examples, where menus pop up or are moved somewhere other than their original location. It also is useful for menus whose contents are determined dynamically (such as an automatic card index). This handler is best placed at a high level, such as the stack script. When the handler adjusts a field that is not the current target (that is, not itself), however, you must use a `send...to` command, with the intended target as a parameter.

Creating Pop-Up Menu Fields and Buttons

The preceding example demonstrated a simple pop-up menu technique, but the intent was to present the adjustMenu handler, which can be used by other menu types. The next example presents a more elaborate approach to pop-up menus. This technique uses a field and button combination. Positioning the mouse over the button, without clicking, causes an associated menu field to automatically pop up underneath the button. See Figure 5-5. The menu field automatically disappears when an item is selected (by any selection method previously discussed) or when the mouse leaves the field and button area (defined by their combined rectangles).

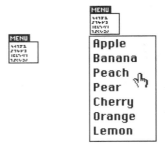

Figure 5-5. This pop-up menu field and button combination pops up a menu when the mouse enters the button.

This technique works best when the field and button share a common identifier (that is, share the same short name). In this example, we assume the name is the same for both, although you never need to explicitly refer to the actual name. The following handlers are used in the button script:

```
on mouseEnter
  global menuName
  put short name of me into menuName
  set top of card field menuName to bottom of me
  set left of card field menuName to left of me
  show card field menuName
end mouseEnter

on mouseLeave
  global menuName
  if the mouseLoc is not within rect of card field menuName then
    hide card field menuName
  end if
end mouseLeave
```

And this mouseLeave handler is added to the field script:

```
on mouseLeave
  global menuName
  if the mouseLoc is not within the rect of card button menuName then
    hide me
  end if
end mouseLeave
```

The button's mouseEnter handler sets the global variable **menuName** to the short name of itself, and the short name of the associated field is assumed to be the same (the short name does not contain the object type). Then the handler automatically positions the associated menu field directly beneath the button. (Any position is acceptable, provided the button and field rectangles overlap or have a common edge so the mouse can move from one to the other without leaving their combined rectangular areas.)

After the field is properly positioned, it is made visible. The button's mouseLeave handler checks if the mouse actually enters the field; if not, it hides the field again. Note the use of `within`, a version 1.2 feature.

After the mouse is in the field, that field's menu selection technique takes over. (See "Putting It All Together" for a complete example using a specific selection technique.) Upon leaving the field, the field's mouseLeave handler checks if the mouse has returned to the button; otherwise, the field is hidden. This latter check prevents the field from flashing as the mouse crosses the common boundary.

The menu icon used for the button can be copied from the Developer's Stack using that stack's ResCopy utility. (The Developer's Stack, by Steve Drazga of Art, Inc., is a must for any stack developer. It is available from many sources, such as Genie and CompuServe.) Any icon will do—in fact, the button does not have to be in an icon style. The next example, however, requires an icon for the button (actually, the icon ID) to denote the menu's "stickiness."

Creating Sticky Menu Fields and Buttons

This example is an extension of the previous pop-up technique. When the user clicks on the associated button, the button's icon is changed to a pin (see Figure 5-6) and the menu field remains shown (sticky). The field remains showing no matter where the mouse moves until the button is clicked again, which changes the icon back to the original menu icon and hides the field again when the mouse leaves. This technique uses the style of the field and the icon ID of its associated button to denote the menu's stickiness.

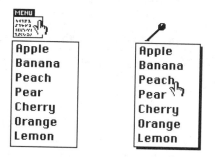

Figure 5-6. With the sticky pop-up menu field and button, the button icon changes to a pin, denoting stickiness.

The following modified mouseLeave handler and new mouseUp handler are needed in the button script:

```
on mouseLeave
  global menuName
  if the mouseLoc is not within rect of card field menuName ¬
  and not sticky(menuName) then
    hide card field menuName
  end if
end mouseLeave

on mouseUp
  global menuName
  if sticky(menuName) then
    makeUnSticky menuName
  else
    makeSticky menuName
  end if
end mouseUp
```

The only change to the mouseLeave handler is to check if the field is sticky before hiding it. The stickiness is toggled by the new mouseUp handler. The stickiness is set and unset by the following two handlers, which are good candidates for the stack script:

```
on makeSticky menuName
  global pinIconID
  if the style of card field menuName is not scrolling then
    set style of card field menuName to "shadow"
    set icon of card button menuName to "Pin"
  end if
  put icon of card button menuName into pinIconID
  set hilite of card button menuName to FALSE
  set autoHilite of card button menuName to FALSE
  show card field menuName
end makeSticky

on makeUnSticky menuName
if the style of card field menuName is not scrolling then
  set style of card field menuName to "rectangle"
 end if
  set icon of card button menuName to "Menu"
  set hilite of card button menuName to FALSE
  set autoHilite of card button menuName to TRUE
  hide card field menuName
end makeUnSticky
```

A field is made sticky by changing the icon of its associated button to a pin. The style of the field is changed to shadow. After the icon is set, the icon ID is put into a global variable for later testing. (You can set the icon of a button by name, but you can't get the name of an icon). The highlighting changes are only aesthetic.

To make the field unsticky, the button's icon is set back to the menu icon. The style of the field is set back to rectangle; this style change is also aesthetic. The field is checked to see if it is a scrolling field before changing it.

The stickiness of the field is tested by checking the icon ID of the associated button. It is best to put the following function in the stack script:

```
function sticky menuName
  global pinIconID
  return icon of card button menuName is pinIconID
end sticky
```

The mouseLeave handler of the field script also needs to be modified to check for the field's own stickiness:

```
on mouseLeave
  global menuName
  if the mouseLoc is not within the rect of card button ¬
  menuName and not sticky(menuName) then
    hide me
  end if
end mouseLeave
```

The stickiness could be denoted by global flags, but they have to be unique for each field. Because they would be less generic, it would be harder to move the handlers up the message hierarchy. An existing field or button property seemed the best way to denote this attribute. The style of the field was one consideration, but it hampered the use of scrolling fields. The button's icon seemed the best choice because it is user definable. The pin icon can be created using ResEdit in the stack itself. Of course, any icon pair will do. One drawback to using the icon to denote stickiness is that you must use the ID, not its name, for testing its identity.

Creating Draggable Menu Fields and Buttons

The next example is a further modification of the sticky pop-up menu that is moved about by just clicking and dragging the button. The associated field automatically follows the button. Add these handlers to the button script of the preceding example:

```
on mouseDown
  global moving
  put FALSE into moving
  wait 15
end mouseDown

on mouseStillDown
  global moving
  set loc of me to the mouseLoc
  put TRUE into moving
end mouseStillDown
```

The mouseUp handler in the button script should be modified as follows:

```
on mouseUp
  global menuName,moving
  if moving then
```

continued

```
      mouseEnter
      exit mouseUp
    else if sticky(menuName) then
      makeUnSticky menuName
    else
      makeSticky menuName
    end if
end mouseUp
```

The global variable moving is set to false when the mouse is first pressed (mouseDown). After 15 ticks (a fourth of a second), if the mouse is still down (mouse-StillDown), moving is set to true and the button is moved to the current mouse location (the mouseLoc). When the mouse is finally released (mouseUp), a check is made to see if the button was moving. If so, a mouseEnter is posted to force a reshow (and repositioning) of the associated field, and the usual toggle of the stickiness is skipped. No changes are needed in the associated field script.

Putting It All Together

The following scripts represent a culmination of most of the techniques discussed so far. These are all the handlers needed to set up a pop-up menu that is stickable, draggable, editable, and self-adjusting, using the simulated Command-click in the locked state and the manual Command-click or Tab-Enter technique in the unlocked (editable) state for menu selection. Most of the handlers are more modular, and the bulk of the work is moved up to the stack script for more generality. Most of the complexity is the result of the combination of many techniques in one menu.

The Stack Script

Let's first look at the handlers moved up to the stack script. Most are pulled out of the handlers we have just finished discussing, only their names are changed. The first one, commandClick, is from the mouseDown handler of the simulated Command-click menu. The message window is temporarily hidden to keep it from popping up during the Command-click-drag.

```
on commandClick
  global inCommandMode,saveMsgLoc
  if inCommandMode is EMPTY then put FALSE into inCommandMode
  -- ignore the mouseDown from the simulated Command-click
  if not inCommandMode then
    -- simulate a Command-click
    put EMPTY into message -- in case selection is present
    -- hide the message window (offscreen)
    put topLeft of message window into saveMsgLoc
    set topLeft of message window to bottomRight of ¬
    the screenRect
    put TRUE into inCommandMode
```

continued

```
    click at the clickLoc with commandKey
    put FALSE into inCommandMode
  end if
end commandClick
```

This next one, clickedItem, is from the mouseUp handler of the same menu. Note that it is changed to a function that returns the outlined text put into the Message box. It also complains when an empty selection is made, and tries to make up for the fact that only a maximum number of `mouseStillDown` events are posted by the simulated Command-click. The message window location is also restored, although it is kept hidden.

```
function clickedItem
  global inCommandMode,saveMsgLoc
  -- ignore first mouseUp event from the simulated Command-click
  if not inCommandMode then
    -- restore location of the message window, but keep hidden
    hide message window
    set topLeft of message window to saveMsgLoc
    get message
    if it is EMPTY and the mouse is not DOWN then
      put "*** Selection was empty, try again ***"
      wait 60
    end if
    -- force mouseStillDown events while mouse is down
    repeat while the mouse is DOWN
    mouseStillDown
    end repeat
    return it
  end if
  return EMPTY
end clickedItem
```

The next three deal with the `mouseEnter`, `mouseWithin`, and `mouseLeave` events, respectively, for fields used as menus. It is much easier to make a change here once than to change every field script.

```
on enterMenuField
  global inCommandMode,menuName
  put FALSE into inCommandMode
  put the short name of target into menuName
end enterMenuField

on inMenuField
  if the optionKey is DOWN and the commandKey is not DOWN then
    toggleEditMode
  end if
end inMenuField

on leaveMenuField
  global inCommandMode,menuName
  if the mouseLoc is not within the rect of card button ¬
  menuName and not sticky(menuName) then
```

continued

```
      hide target
    end if
  put FALSE into inCommandMode
end leaveMenuField
```

The following toggleEditMode handler is isolated from the mouseWithin handler and is used to toggle in and out of user edit mode (the save style part is removed).

```
on toggleEditMode
  if lockText of target is TRUE then
    set lockText of target to FALSE
    set style of target to "scrolling"
  else
    set lockText of target to TRUE
    adjustMenu
  end if
end toggleEditMode
```

For the corresponding events in the button, we have the following handlers:

```
on enterMenuButton
  global menuName
  put short name of target into menuName
  set top of card field menuName to bottom of target
  set left of card field menuName to left of target
  send adjustMenu to card field menuName
  show card field menuName
end enterMenuButton

on inMenuButton
  -- (reserved for future use)
end inMenuButton

on leaveMenuButton
  global menuName
  if the mouseLoc is not within rect of card field menuName ¬
  and not sticky(menuName) then
    hide card field menuName
  end if
end leaveMenuButton
```

The menu drag option is taken care of with the following handlers. The last one is a function that returns an indication of whether the button was moved. (If the button was moved, the icon ID isn't toggled.)

```
on beginMove
  global moving
  put FALSE into moving
  wait 15
end beginMove

on moveMenu
```

continued

```
    global moving
    set loc of target to the mouseLoc
    put TRUE into moving
end moveMenu
function endOfMove
    global moving
    if moving then
      enterMenuButton
      put FALSE into moving
      return TRUE
    else
      return FALSE
    end if
end endOfMove
```

The adjustMenu handler is the same as before. The selectNextLine handler is the tabKey handler of the Tab-Enter menu technique.

```
on adjustMenu maxLines
    set lockScreen to TRUE -- hide all movements until done
    -- determine number of lines in menu
    put number of lines of target into numLines
    if maxLines is not EMPTY and numLines > maxLines then
      put maxLines into numLines
    else if numLines < 1 then
      put 1 into numLines
    end if
    -- determine height of menu in pixels
    put numLines * (textHeight of target) + 5 into pixelsNeeded
    -- determine space left on card in pixels
    put (bottom of card window) - (top of target) into pixelsLeft
    put top of target into savedTop  -- save for resetting
    if pixelsNeeded < pixelsLeft then
      set height of target to pixelsNeeded
      if style of target is "scrolling" then
        set style of target to "rectangle"
      end if
    else
      set height of target to pixelsLeft
      set style of target to "scrolling"
    end if
    set top of target to savedTop -- reset top
    set lockScreen to FALSE -- now show it
end adjustMenu


on selectNextLine
    -- select the first or last line if selection is empty
    if the selection is EMPTY then
      if the selectedLine is EMPTY then
        if the shiftKey is DOWN then
          select last line of target
        else
          select first line of target
        end if
      else
```

continued

```
        select the selectedLine
      end if
    else
      put the selectedLine into nextLine
      if the shiftKey is DOWN then -- reverse direction
        if word 2 of nextLine <= 1 then
          put number of lines of target into word 2 of nextLine
        else
          subtract 1 from word 2 of nextLine
        end if
      else -- forward direction
        if word 2 of nextLine >= number of lines of target then
          put 1 into word 2 of nextLine
        else
          add 1 to word 2 of nextLine
        end if
      end if
      select nextLine -- hilite the line
    end if
end selectNextLine
```

These next four handle sticky menus. They are the same as before, except the last one, which is from the button's mouseUp handler for toggling the stickiness.

```
function sticky menuName
  global pinIconID
  if menuName is not EMPTY and pinIconID is not EMPTY then
    if icon of card button menuName is pinIconID and ¬
    visible of card field menuName is TRUE then
      return TRUE
    else
      return FALSE
    end if
  else
    if style of card field menuName is "shadow" and ¬
    visible of card field menuName is TRUE then
      return TRUE
    else
      return FALSE
    end if
  end if
end sticky

on makeSticky menuName
  global pinIconID
  if style of card field menuName is not "scrolling" then
    set style of card field menuName to "shadow"
  end if
  if menuName is not EMPTY then
    set icon of card button menuName to "Pin"
    put icon of card button menuName into pinIconID
    set hilite of card button menuName to FALSE
    set autoHilite of card button menuName to FALSE
  end if
  show card field menuName
end makeSticky
```

continued

```
on makeUnSticky menuName
  if style of card field menuName is not "scrolling" then
    set style of card field menuName to "rectangle"
  end if
  if menuName is not EMPTY then
    set icon of card button menuName to "Menu"
    set hilite of card button menuName to FALSE
    set autoHilite of card button menuName to TRUE
  end if
  hide card field menuName
end makeUnSticky

on toggleSticky
  global menuName
  if sticky(menuName) then
    makeUnSticky menuName
  else
    makeSticky menuName
  end if
end toggleSticky
```

The Field Script

Now for the field part of our feature-packed pop-up menu. Note how simple it becomes when most of the work is moved up to the stack script. The menu action has been put into a new handler called doSomethingWith.

```
on mouseDown
  commandClick -- simulated Command-click
end mouseDown

on mouseEnter
  enterMenuField
end mouseEnter

on mouseWithin
  inMenuField
end mouseWithin

on enterInField
  select the selectedLine
  doSomethingWith the selection -- Enter key option (edit mode)
end enterInField

on tabKey
  selectNextLine -- Tab key option (edit mode)
end tabKey

on mouseUp
  get clickedItem() -- Return selection & put into variable it
  doSomethingWith it
```

continued

```
      leaveMenuField
end mouseUp

on doSomethingWith menuItem
   if menuItem is not EMPTY then
      put "You picked a" && menuItem -- do your thing here
   end if
end doSomethingWith

on mouseLeave
   leaveMenuField
end mouseLeave

on closeField
   leaveMenuField
   set lockText of me to TRUE -- lock if left in edit mode
end closeField
```

For the button part, we have the following button script:

```
on mouseEnter
   enterMenuButton
end mouseEnter

on mouseDown
   beginMove
end mouseDown

on mouseStillDown
   moveMenu -- Drag option
end mouseStillDown

on mouseUp
   if NOT endOfMove() then
      toggleSticky -- Sticky option
   end if
end mouseUp

on mouseLeave
   leaveMenuButton
end mouseLeave
```

Creating Menu Bar Fields

Now you understand pop-up menu fields. These next few examples simulate the pull-down menus of a normal Macintosh desktop. In this first example, you use the simulated double-click selection technique to replace the menu bar at the top of the card with a simulated menu bar based on a menu field. See Figure 5-7.

The job of the menu bar is to position and pop down other menus (which are presented next). For this to work, the regular menu bar must be hidden (with hide menuBar). For a more dramatic effect, you can make the background of the card gray with a filled rectangle to look like the Macintosh desktop. For a 9-inch screen (for

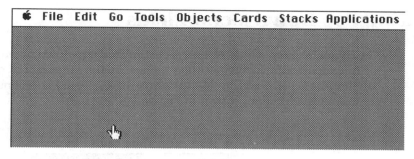

Figure 5-7. With the tricks in this chapter, you can simulate
a desktop menu bar.

example, on a Macintosh Plus or Macintosh SE), the simulated menu bar replaces the usual menu bar. On a Macintosh with a larger monitor (for example, a Macintosh II or a Radius TPD), the effect is a desktop within a window, retaining the usual menu bar.

The following are the mouseDown and mouseUp handlers for the menuBar field:

```
on mouseDown
  set the lockText of me to FALSE
  click at the clickLoc
  click at the clickLoc
  set the lockText of me to TRUE
end mouseDown

on mouseUp
  get the selection
  if it is not EMPTY then
    if it contains "" then
      -- the apple is Shift-Option-K
      set top of card field appleMenu to bottom of me
      set left of card field appleMenu to left of me
      show card field appleMenu
    else
      put it & "Menu" into menu
      set top of card field menu to bottom of me
      put trunc((width of card field menu)/4) into qtrWidth
      put the clickH - qtrWidth into leftSide
      set left of card field menu to leftSide
      show card field menu
    end if
  end if
end mouseUp
```

The only thing new is the positioning of the pop-down menus relative to the menuBar field. The appleMenu is handled separately for two reasons. First, the name of the menu cannot be derived directly from the Apple logo character. Second, the position of the appleMenu is bound by the left edge, whereas the other menus are positioned (horizontally, that is) according to the click location and a quarter of the pop-down menu's width. The field positioning uses version 1.2 features. See the next discussion for more details on the pop-down menu.

Creating Pop-Down Menu Fields

The HyperDesktop contains several customized pop-down menu fields. There is one for each item in the menu bar (their names are the same as the corresponding menu bar item name suffixed by Menu). Some have related submenus. This section discusses one such menu, shown in Figure 5-8.

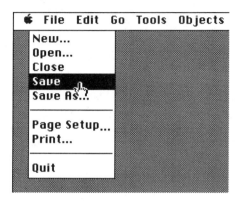

Figure 5-8.   A pop-down menu is similar to a sticky pop-up menu.

For variety, we use a `selectedLine` menu. It is similar to the sticky pop-up menu, but it is tied to the menuBar field instead of a button. We describe dragging the menu next (or "tearing off" the menu bar in this case).

The following handlers are from the fileMenu field script:

```
on mouseDown
  set lockText of me to FALSE
  click at the clickLoc
  select the selectedLine
  set lockText of me to TRUE
end mouseUp

on mouseUp
  get the selection
  if it is not EMPTY then
    put "Do menu item" && it
    doMenu it
    hide me
  end if
end mouseUp

on mouseLeave
  hide me
end mouseLeave

on closeField
  hide me
end closeField
```

Creating Tear-Off Menu Fields

Tear-off menus are an extension of pop-down menus that you tear off from the menu bar. See Figure 5-9. This technique borrows many ideas from draggable, sticky pop-up menus.

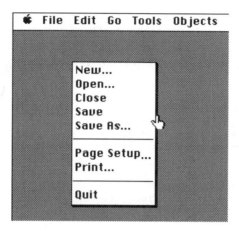

Figure 5-9. A tear-off menu allows the user to move a pop-down menu from the menu bar.

Before we can implement draggable menus, the menu field needs to trap `mouseStillDown` events. The field must remain locked to do this. The simulated Command-click technique meets this criteria; we use this technique, rather than the selectedLine technique just used in the simple pop-down menu. The mouseDown handler simply becomes:

```
on mouseDown
  commandClick
end mouseDown
```

Besides being draggable, a tear-off menu must also be made "sticky" after it is torn away from the menuBar field. We'll get back to how to make the menus sticky shortly. Meanwhile, the mouseUp handler must check for this as follows:

```
on mouseUp
  get clickedItem()
  if it is not EMPTY then
    doMenu it
    if not sticky() then hide me
  end if
end mouseUp
```

Likewise, the mouseLeave and closeField handlers should check for stickiness:

```
on mouseLeave
  if not sticky() then hide me
end mouseLeave

on closeField
  if not sticky() then hide me
end closeField
```

Furthermore, to make sure that the menu is initially sticky and to provide a means to "put away" a torn-off menu, the field script of the menuBar field needs to send a makeUnSticky message to the appropriate menu field. This is accomplished by the following modified mouseUp handler for the menuBar field script:

```
on mouseUp
  get the selection
  if it is not EMPTY then
    if it contains "" then -- the apple is Shift-Option-K
      put "appleMenu" into menuName
      put left of me into leftSide
    else
      put it & "Menu" into menuName
      put trunc((width of card field menuName)/4) into qtrWidth
      put the clickH - qtrWidth into leftSide
    end if
    set left of card field menuName to leftSide
    set top of card field menuName to bottom of me
    send makeUnSticky to card field menuName
    show card field menuName
  end if
end mouseUp
```

To enable dragging, put the following handlers in the field script:

```
on mouseStillDown
  get word 2 of name of target
  if it is "field" then
    if the mouseLoc is not within the rect of target then
      dragMenu
      makeSticky
    end if
  end if
end mouseStillDown

on dragMenu
  if the mouseV < top of target then
    set top of target to the mouseV
  else if the mouseV > bottom of target then
    set bottom of target to the mouseV
  else if the mouseH < left of target then
    set left of target to the mouseH
  else if the mouseH > right of target then
    set right of target to the mouseH
  end if
end dragMenu
```

Dragging takes effect when the mouse leaves the rectangle of the field while the mouse button is still down (on `mouseStillDown`). To drag the menu, you use the same technique as that used to drag the button in the pop-up menu in a previous example.

The dragMenu handler is restricted to dragging in only one of four directions at a time, depending on which edge the mouse leaves the rectangle from. The user "grabs" an edge of the field's rectangle and drags the menu in a direction perpendicular to the edge. Note that putting these in a higher level script would make all subordinate locked fields (which can trap `mouseStillDown` events) draggable. Even the menu bar could be made draggable, taking the pop-down menus with it. To be more selective, a field naming convention should be used to discern which fields are draggable. Even buttons could become draggable in such a scheme, by allowing the second word of the target to be `button` as well as `field` (note that `dragMenu` does not discriminate between objects).

After a menu is torn off the menu bar, it remains on the desktop, like the sticky pop-up menu already discussed. It remains until the item is selected again from the menu bar. (We have no close box yet, but this would be fairly easy to simulate with a button of style checkbox.) The notion of stickiness must now be modified to recognize menu fields that do not have associated buttons to denote their stickiness. The three "sticky" handlers can be modified to use the field's style as an indication of their own stickiness, if no argument is passed to the handler. Here are modified versions of these handlers:

```
function sticky buttonName
  global menuName,menuType,pinIconID
  put buttonName into menuName
  if menuType is "combination" and ¬
  buttonName is not EMPTY and pinIconID is not EMPTY then
    if icon of card button menuName is pinIconID and ¬
    visible of card field menuName is TRUE then
      return TRUE
    else
      return FALSE
    end if
  else
    put EMPTY into pinIconID
    put short name of target into menuName
    if style of card field menuName is "shadow" and ¬
    visible of card field menuName is TRUE then
      return TRUE
    else
      return FALSE
    end if
  end if
end sticky


on makeSticky buttonName
  global menuName,menuType,pinIconID
  put buttonName into menuName
  if buttonName is not EMPTY then
    put "combination" into menuType
```

continued

```
        set icon of card button menuName to "Pin"
        put icon of card button menuName into pinIconID
        set hilite of card button menuName to FALSE
        set autoHilite of card button menuName to FALSE
      else
        put "fieldOnly" into menuType
        put EMPTY into pinIconID
        put short name of target into menuName
      end if
      if style of card field menuName is not "scrolling" then
        set style of card field menuName to "shadow"
      end if
      show card field menuName
    end makeSticky

    on makeUnSticky buttonName
      global menuName,menuType,pinIconID
      put buttonName into menuName
      if menuType is "combination" and ¬
      buttonName is not EMPTY and pinIconID is not EMPTY then
        set icon of card button menuName to "Menu"
        set hilite of card button menuName to FALSE
        set autoHilite of card button menuName to TRUE
      else
        put EMPTY into pinIconID
        put short name of target into menuName
      end if
      if style of card field menuName is not "scrolling" then
        set style of card field menuName to "rectangle"
      end if
      hide card field menuName
    end makeUnSticky
```

The HyperDesktop

The following scripts represent a prototype for a simulated desktop using Hyper-Card. The purpose is to give you some ideas about various kinds of menus that can be used from a custom menu bar. These menus are pop-down menus, and all can be torn off the menu bar. Some menus have cascading submenus. Each demonstrates a different kind of action, such as launching applications, editing documents with a word processor, and going to a specific card. For simplicity, we assume that these menus are not user-editable and do not need adjusting. (See "Putting It All Together" in this chapter for how to add these features.)

The Stack Script

```
on doubleClick
  set lockText of target to FALSE
  click at the clickLoc
  click at the clickLoc
```

continued

```
      set lockText of target to TRUE
    end doubleClick


on commandClick
  global inCommandMode, saveMsgLoc
  if inCommandMode is EMPTY then put FALSE into inCommandMode
  -- ignore the mouseDown from the simulated commandClick
  if not inCommandMode then
    -- simulate a commandClick
    put EMPTY into message -- in case selection is present
    -- hide the message window (off screen)
    put loc of message window into saveMsgLoc
    set loc of message window to 500,500
    put TRUE into inCommandMode
    click at the clickLoc with commandKey
    put FALSE into inCommandMode
  end if
end commandClick


function clickedItem
  global inCommandMode, saveMsgLoc
  -- ignore first mouseUp event from the simulated Command-click
  if not inCommandMode then
    -- restore loc of the message window, but keep hidden
    hide message window
    set loc of message window to saveMsgLoc
    get message
    if it is EMPTY and the mouse is not DOWN then
      put "*** Selection was empty, Try again ***"
      wait 60
    end if
    -- force mouseStillDown events while mouse is down
    repeat while the mouse is DOWN
      send mouseStillDown to target
    end repeat
    return it
  end if
  return EMPTY
end clickedItem


on dragMenu
  if the mouseV < top of target then
    set top of target to the mouseV
  else if the mouseV > bottom of target then
    set bottom of target to the mouseV
  else if the mouseH < left of target then
    set left of target to the mouseH
  else if the mouseH > right of target then
    set right of target to the mouseH
  end if
end dragMenu


function sticky buttonName
  global menuName,menuType,pinIconID
  put buttonName into menuName
  if menuType is "combination" and ¬
```

continued

```
          buttonName is not EMPTY and pinIconID is not EMPTY then
            if icon of card button menuName is pinIconID and ¬
            visible of card field menuName is TRUE then
              return TRUE
            else
              return FALSE
            end if
          else
            put EMPTY into pinIconID
            put short name of target into menuName
            if style of card field menuName is "shadow" and ¬
            visible of card field menuName is TRUE then
              return TRUE
            else
              return FALSE
            end if
          end if
        end sticky


        on makeSticky buttonName
          global menuName,menuType,pinIconID
          put buttonName into menuName
          if buttonName is not EMPTY then
            put "combination" into menuType
            set icon of card button menuName to "Pin"
            put icon of card button menuName into pinIconID
            set hilite of card button menuName to FALSE
            set autoHilite of card button menuName to FALSE
          else
            put "fieldOnly" into menuType
            put EMPTY into pinIconID
            put short name of target into menuName
          end if
          if style of card field menuName is not "scrolling" then
            set style of card field menuName to "shadow"
          end if
          show card field menuName
        end makeSticky


        on makeUnSticky buttonName
          global menuName,menuType,pinIconID
          put buttonName into menuName
          if menuType is "combination" and ¬
          buttonName is not EMPTY and pinIconID is not EMPTY then
            set icon of card button menuName to "Menu"
            set hilite of card button menuName to FALSE
            set autoHilite of card button menuName to TRUE
          else
            put EMPTY into pinIconID
            put short name of target into menuName
          end if
          if style of card field menuName is not "scrolling" then
            set style of card field menuName to "rectangle"
          end if
          hide card field menuName
        end makeUnSticky
```

The Card Script

```
on openCard
  hide menuBar
  set left of card field menuBar to 0
  set top of card field menuBar to 0
  genCardIndex
end openCard

on genCardIndex
  -- generate card index for cardsMenu field
  push card
  set lockScreen to TRUE
  set lockMessages to TRUE
  put EMPTY into cardIndex
  repeat with i=1 to number of cards
    go to card i
    get short name of this card
    put it & return after cardIndex
  end repeat
  pop card
  put cardIndex into card field cardsMenu
  set lockMessages to FALSE
  set lockScreen to FALSE
end genCardIndex

on closeCard
  show menuBar
end closeCard

on mouseStillDown
  global menuMoved
  get word 2 of name of target
  if it is "field" then
    if the mouseLoc is not within the rect of target then
      dragMenu
      put TRUE into menuMoved
      makeSticky
    end if
  end if
end mouseStillDown
```

The Field Scripts

```
-- card field "menuBar" --

on mouseDown
  doubleClick
end mouseDown

on mouseUp
  get selectedItem()
  if it is not EMPTY then
```

continued

```
      if it contains "" then
        -- the apple is Shift-Option-K
        put "appleMenu" into menuName
        put left of card field appleMenu into leftside
      else
        put it & "Menu" into menuName
        put trunc((width of card field menuName)/4) into qtrWidth
        put the clickH - qtrWidth into leftSide
      end if
      set top of card field menuName to bottom of me
      set left of card field menuName to leftSide of me
      send makeUnSticky to card field menuName
      show card field menuName
  end if
end mouseUp


-- card field "appleMenu" --

on mouseDown
  commandClick
end mouseDown

on mouseUp
  get clickedItem()
  if it is not EMPTY then
    closeField
    doMenu it -- execute the Desk Accessory
  end if
end mouseUp

on mouseLeave
  if not sticky() then hide me
end mouseLeave

on closeField
  if not sticky () then hide me
end closeField
```

We assume all the remaining field scripts contain the same mouseDown, mouseLeave, and closeField handlers as the appleMenu field script. We concentrate on the action taken on the mouseUp event.

The next three menus do their regular menu counterpart by issuing a doMenu with the clickedItem(). One advantage of this simple pass-through idea is only those items put in your menu are available to the user.

```
-- card field "fileMenu" --

on mouseUp
  get clickedItem()
  if it is not EMPTY then
    doMenu it
  end if
end mouseUp
```

continued

```
-- card field "editMenu" --

on mouseUp
  get clickedItem()
  if it is not EMPTY then
    doMenu it
  end if
end mouseUp

-- card field "goMenu" --

on mouseUp
  get clickedItem()
  if it is not EMPTY then
    doMenu it
  end if
end mouseUp
```

The tool menu basically becomes a word menu instead of an icon menu. This provides the user with a selective subset of tools, without changing the userLevel. Alternatively, the mouseDown message could bring up the real tool window directly.

```
-- card field "toolsMenu" --

on mouseUp
  get clickedItem()
  if it is not EMPTY then
    show tool window
    do "choose" && it && "tool"
    hide tool window
  end if
end mouseUP
```

The objects menu does a pass-through to its regular menu counterpart, but this can be a selective subset.

```
-- card field "objectsMenu" --

on mouseUp
  get clickedItem()
  if it is not EMPTY then
    doMenu it
  end if
end mouseUp
```

The contents of the next menu were created on the openCard event. This menu provides an index to all cards in the stack. Selecting a card ID in the menu takes you to that card.

```
-- card field "cardsMenu" --

on mouseUp
  get clickedItem()
```

continued

```
      if it is not EMPTY then
        go to card it
      end if
  end mouseUp
```

The following menu presents a list of stacks for the user to go to directly, without having to use the Open Stack... dialog of the File menu.

```
-- card field "stacksMenu" --
on mouseUp
  get clickedItem()
  if it is not EMPTY then
    go to stack it
  end if
end mouseUp
```

The next menu presents a list of applications for the user to go to directly, without having to issue the open command in the Message box. Selecting an application name in this menu brings up a cascading submenu with a list of documents to choose from for that particular application. After you select a document, it is opened with the application chosen. Only a MacDraw II document menu is shown here.

```
-- card field "applicationsMenu" --

on mouseUp
  get clickedItem()
  if it is not EMPTY then
    put it & "Menu" into menuName -- e.g., macdrawMenu
    set top of card field menuName to the clickV - 3 -- submenu
    set left of card field menuName to the clickH - 12
    show card field menuName
  end if
end mouseUp
```

```
-- card field "macdrawMenu" --

on mouseUp
  get clickedItem()
  if it is not EMPTY then
    open it with "MacDraw II"
  end if
end mouseUp
```

The last menu presents a list of documents for the user to edit with a default word processing program (or any application), without having to first choose that application from the application menu. In this example, we assume the application is Microsoft Word.

```
-- card field "documentsMenu" --

on mouseUp
```

continued

```
    get clickedItem()
    if it is not EMPTY then
      open it with "Microsoft Word 3.01"
    end if
end mouseUp
```

That's it for HyperDesktop for now. A challenging project is to complete the desktop by including application and folder icons, a trash can, disk icons, and the various functions the Finder provides for these objects.

Part 3

Button, Font, and Cursor Tricks

PolyButtons

Mitchell Waite and Ted Jones

Synopsis: How many times have you wanted to cover a complex, irregular shape with a button? HyperCard only allows rectangular buttons with four sides, so you must resort to the complicated process of using several buttons like tiles to completely cover the shape. Then, you must write scripts that fit in each button and also handle the buttons that overlap each other. This is a particularly tricky problem when you have a stack that contains maps, anatomy, or complex parts that you wish to be identified with pop-up fields. Often you must resort to forcing the user to click only in the middle of your object—not very user friendly.

PolyButtons solves the problem by allowing simple multisided buttons to be drawn over any shape. These buttons are created with a special drawing tool that you use like the familiar MacPaint polygon tool. PolyButtons is a script that can reside in the card, background, or Home stack. It's activated by typing `poly` in the Message box. Buttons made with the script respond very quickly to a click and are extremely accurate. The techniques used come from computer graphics and employ a popular "crossing" algorithm.

PolyButtons

Creating Nonrectangular Buttons

Because buttons in HyperCard are rectangular, it can be hard to use them to cover complex graphic objects with precision. The degree of difficulty depends on the shape of the object. Covering something simple with many rectangular areas, like the calculator in Figure 6-1, is easy. But covering something with many irregular shapes, such as the map of the United States, can be a pain.

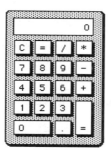 

Figure 6-1. It's easy to make buttons that cover rectangular objects, but it's hard to make buttons for irregular objects.

When an object is irregular, slanted, elliptical, or a complex polygon, the only way to simulate a single button over it is to create a series of rectangular buttons and lay them down on the surface like tiles that overlap. You put the same handler in each button so that pressing any button does what you want: goes to a card, opens a field, plays a tune, and so on. Until now, this is what scriptors have done.

PolyButtons to the Rescue

The PolyButtons script changes this rectangular button bummer. It allows you to create buttons with multiple sides (polygons) using a special button-maker drawing tool that works like the polygon tool in HyperCard's paint layer. The entire script resides in the Home stack's stack script, so it is accessible from any card in any stack.

You can have any number of polybuttons on a card, and each one can react to a mouse click inside its polygon.

With PolyButtons you can draw freehand or trace objects in either the card or background graphic layer. If you keep your original graphic in the background, you can erase the shapes PolyButtons draws without disturbing the original graphic (an answer box asks if you want to do this). You can even choose an invisible drawing mode if you don't want to interfere with existing card graphics.

Using PolyButtons: Step by Step

When you have a graphic to trace or a shape in mind, enter `poly` into the Message box and press the Return key. The answer box in Figure 6-2 is displayed, asking if you want to draw visible lines or invisible lines.

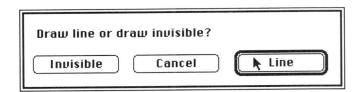

Figure 6-2.   You can choose visible or invisible lines when you
draw with PolyButtons.

If you choose Line, a solid crosshair cursor is displayed, as shown in Figure 6-3.

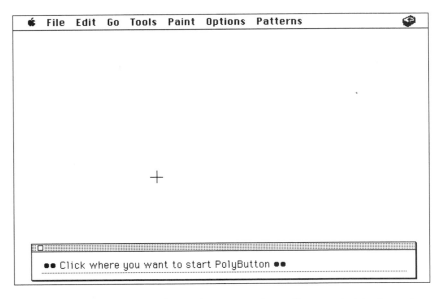

Figure 6-3.   Starting your shape: the Message box tells you what to do next.

If you choose Invisible, the screen displays a crosshair cursor made up of dashed lines. In either case, the Message box tells you what to do next.

Use the drawing cursor as you would the HyperCard polygon tool to click at the corners of the shape. Automatically, lines are drawn connecting the corners. Keep clicking until the shape is almost completed, like the shape in Figure 6-4.

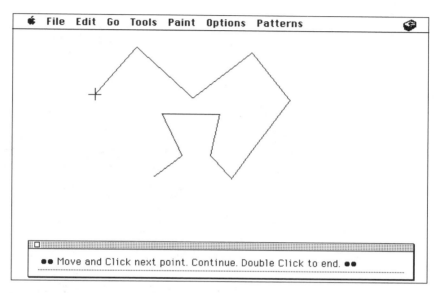

Figure 6-4. To finish your shape, double-click on the end point. A line will connect the last point to the starting point.

If you are outlining a graphic, surround it with straight line segments that approximate its shape. (By using small line segments you can approximate a very complex shape). You can cover the shape with many sides, but the speed of the script slows as the number of sides grows. About thirty sides is a practical upper limit (approximately a 2-second delay on a Macintosh SE), but it really depends on what your user can tolerate.

The next step is to double-click the mouse button on the end point. This automatically connects the last point to the first point, completing the shape. See Figure 6-5.

As soon as the shape is finished, an ask box is displayed asking you to name or cancel the shape. The name should help you remember what the shape does. Don't use the same button name for more than one polybutton on the same card. If you type in a name, as shown in Figure 6-6, and click OK, the shape is named and its location stored.

After the button is named, an answer box is displayed, letting you clear the area of the card's graphic layer in which the shape was drawn. Thus, you can outline a rough shape over a graphic, then clear the outline to remove the evidence.

Next, the script editor is opened so you can type in what you want the shape to

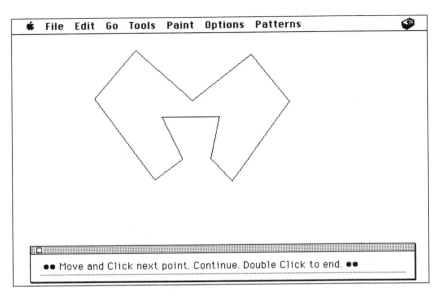

Figure 6-5.   When you connect the last points, you've completed the shape.

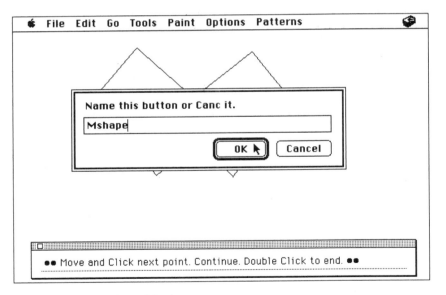

Figure 6-6.   Give the polybutton a name.

do when it is clicked in. Suppose that you entered the following in the doIt handler:

```
put "Inside Button Shape Mshape" into message box
```

See Figure 6-7.

Now PolyButtons does some processing. The Message box indicates when PolyButtons is finished, then suggests you click inside and outside the shape. When the click is inside the shape, you get a message in the Message box identifying the

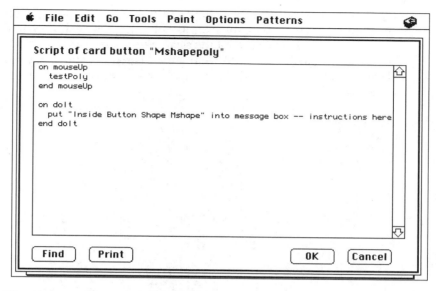

Figure 6-7.   The script of the new shape button.

button (the message you put in the doIt handler). See Figure 6-8. If you click outside the shape, nothing happens, as with any other button.

If you choose the button tool (or press Option-Command in HyperCard version 1.2 +), you will see the shape framed in a button. Note that clicking inside the button but outside the shape does not execute the doIt handler.

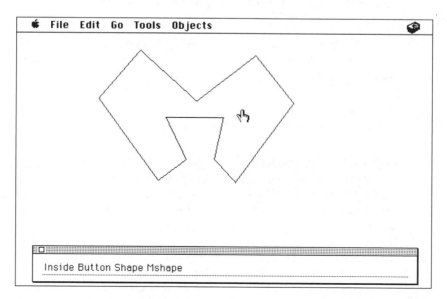

Figure 6-8.   PolyButtons tells you in the Message box when you have clicked inside the shape and gives the name of the button you assigned to the shape.

You can cover multiple shapes in the same manner, giving each button a distinct name. If you make a mistake, just click the Cancel button in the naming ask box and start over. Don't interrupt the script with Command-. (period) while it is running because this will cause confusion later. Figure 6-9 shows a sample of the western United States used for the demonstration. You can find maps like this on CompuServe.

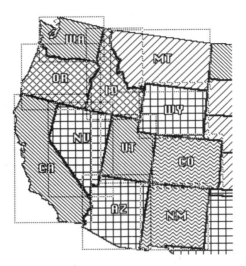

Figure 6-9.   Map of the western states to cover with polybuttons. Although the entire button rectangle is outlined, only the points inside the defined shape register as "inside" the button.

The PolyButtons script can tell which shape you clicked in even when several polybuttons overlap at that point. If the shapes within the buttons overlap, the top shape wins, as with any other button.

Overview of PolyButtons

Before we describe the script in detail, we'll give you a helicopter ride over its general structure. The PolyButtons script is a collection of handlers placed in the Home stack's stack script. When you type poly into the Message box, you are executing a user-defined command that sets the ball rolling. Because our scripts are in the Home stack, you can send the poly message whenever that Home stack is the current Home stack—which means whenever selecting Home in the Go menu takes you to that Home stack (as opposed to any other Home stacks you may have). This means you can create a polybutton on any card of any stack.

The main poly handler does some housekeeping and finds out what kind of line you will be drawing (visible or invisible). Then it starts collecting the corner coordinates and drawing lines between them. When it detects the double-click that ends the shape, it draws the last line and asks for a shape name. A button is created that frames the shape. The suffix *poly* is added to the name the user provided so that the polybutton can be differentiated from other buttons. Then the script builds a little script and inserts it into the button. This button script does two things. First, it starts the process of determining if a click in the button is also a click in the shape. Second, it determines if the click is inside not just the button cap but also the shape.

After the button is created, the Home script calculates the number of points in the shape and analyzes the lines between them. The results of this analysis, together with the number of points and the coordinates of the points, are stored in a hidden field. This field is associated with the button by the suffix *arrays*. For example, if the user enters *myButton* as the name of the shape, the actual name is *myButtonpoly* and the name of the related field is *myButtonpolyarrays*.

If the user doesn't name the shape, the shape is removed and all the information is forgotten. This is the end of the creation phase. Next, we describe the detection handlers.

Inside the PolyButtons: Searching for the Real Click

When you click on a polybutton, a message is sent to another handler in the Home script. This message starts the execution of a chain of handlers that compare the location of the click to each of the lines making up the shape. If the script determines that the click was inside the shape, a message is sent back to the button that executes the handler that performs the button's job. If the click was not in the shape, the click location is compared to the locations of the other polybuttons on the card. If the click is also inside another polybutton, that button's shape is checked in the same way that the shape of the button that originally received the message was checked. This process continues until the shape the click was inside of is found or there are no more polybuttons to check.

If you want to delete a button, finding the hidden field associated with each polybutton can be tricky. We have included a shape-deleting feature that removes a button for you. To delete a button, just click on the button while the Option key is pressed.

A special feature allows you to make each line segment of a polybutton sequentially painted in the foreground and background pattern so you can see its outline clearly. We call this "pseudo-marching ants" to contrast it with the normal dotted lines that appear around a button when it is normally selected with the button tool. You have the options of either deleting the button or outlining it on the screen with pseudo-marching ants.

Some routines used for this were used for finding a shape clicked in, so you can find a shape even if it is overlapped by other polybuttons. Each time the script finds a shape that was clicked in, the button containing that shape gets the pseudo-marching ants treatment and you are asked to confirm that this is the polybutton you want to delete. If you tell the script to keep looking, it will find any other shapes that overlap the top one. You can go deeper and deeper into any overlapping shapes on the card.

The Magic Crossings Algorithm

PolyButtons works by taking advantage of a simple rule. Draw any closed shape made of line segments on a piece of paper. Make it complicated. Now select any point inside the shape and draw a vertical line from that point to the top of the paper. Count how many times your line crosses the edge of the shape. Now repeat the same process, but choose a point outside the shape. Draw the line so it passes through the shape and count how many times it crosses.

You should find the following to be true:

▶ If a point is outside the shape, the number of crossings is an even number.
▶ If a point is inside the shape, the number of crossings is an odd number.

Figure 6-10 shows this graphically. You don't have to use vertical lines like we did; any straight line will do.

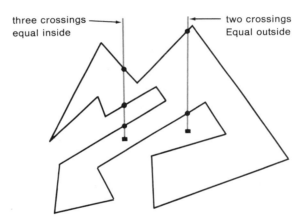

three crossings ——— equal inside

two crossings ——— Equal outside

Figure 6-10.   The crossings algorithm tells if a point is inside or outside a closed shape.

You can skip the next few paragraphs if you are not a math nut. But if you want to understand how PolyButtons uses the crossings algorithm, or if you want to modify its actions, you will have to subject yourself to some high school algebra.

When you draw the outline of a shape with PolyButtons, the script saves into variables the x-coordinate and y-coordinate of every point you click on. These click points are called the *vertices* of the shape. After they are gathered, we calculate two important mathematical entities for each line segment that makes the shape: the slope of each line (*m*) and its y-intercept (*b*). We don't need to do this calculation at this point, but it will speed up processing later because HyperCard is slow at these types of calculations. (This is called trading creation time for processing time.) The slope of a line is the angle it makes and how steep it is. It is represented by the formula

$$\text{slope} = \frac{\text{rise}}{\text{run}}$$

where *rise* is the change in *y* a line makes (delta *y*) and *run* is the change in *x* a line makes (delta x). If we call the beginning of a line x_i,y_i and the end of the line x_{i+1},y_{i+1}, we can define the slope like this:

$$m_i = \frac{(y_i - y_{i+1})}{(x_i - x_{i+1})}$$

Thus, for every vertex, we can create a slope (the beginning of each line gets an associated slope, so the first point gets the first slope and the point just *before* the last point gets the last slope). This formula is easy to represent in HyperTalk.

Next, we calculate the y-intercept for each line segment (b). The y-intercept is the point where the line crosses the y-axis (where x is equal to zero). The formula for b is derived from the general equation for the slope of a line:

$$y_i = m_i x_i + b_i$$

This reads: y is equal to the slope of the line times the x-coordinate, plus the value b. Solving for b we get:

$$b_i = y_i - m_i x_i$$

Plugging in the formula for the slope, we have:

$$b_i = \frac{y_i - (y_i - y_{i+1})}{(x_i - x_{i+1})x_i}$$

Now if we solve for b_i, we get the following formula:

$$b_i = \frac{(x_i y_{i+1} - x_{i+1} y_i)}{(x_i - x_{i+1})}$$

This can be converted easily to HyperTalk. The `xarray` variable holds the x values, the `yarray` variable holds the y-coordinates, `marray` holds the slope values, and `barray` holds the y-intercepts. So when we write:

$$y_{i+1}$$

in an algebra formula, it is spoken in HyperTalk as: "item i + 1 of yarray."

The handler for implementing the creation and setup of these array-holding variables (after the user has entered all the points) looks like this:

```
repeat with i = 1 to points -- for number of points
  -- find the slope (m) of each line segment and store it

 put ((item i+1 of yarray) - (item i of yarray)) ¬
  / ((item i+1 of xarray) - (item i of xarray)) ¬
  & ", " after marray

  -- find the y-intercept (b) of each line segment and store it
 put ((item i of xarray * item i+1 of yarray) ¬
  - (item i+1 of xarray * item i of yarray)) ¬
```

continued

```
      / (item i of xarray - item i+1 of xarray) ¬
      & ", " after barray
end repeat
```

The Trick

Now that we have set up the arrays and coordinates, we need to find if a line drawn from our point has crossed the line segment. To do this, we need to compare our point to every line segment. First we see if our point is inside a vertical strip that represents the extremes of the line segment. We compare the x value of our point with the x values of the endpoints of each line segment. If this test is true and our point is inside this strip, we find the y-intersection of our line with the line segment. If the y-coordinate of that intersection is greater than our point, our point must be under the line segment and there is no crossing. On the other hand, if our point's y-coordinate is above the y-coordinate of the line segment, our point has crossed the line and is above it.

The script must test each line segment to see if the point is above or below it. The script must also keep track of the number of times the test shows a crossing. After testing all segments, the value of the crossings will be even or odd, which tells us if the point is inside or outside the shape.

The handler that does the checking is polyButTest. One of the first things polyButTest does is execute another user-defined command named unload. The unload handler uses five put statements to read into HyperTalk variables the field values we stored previously:

```
on unload name -- PolyButtons Home script user command
   -- get arrays from field
   global xarray,yarray,marray,barray,points
   put line 1 of card field name into xarray
   put line 2 of card field name into yarray
   put line 3 of card field name into marray
   put line 4 of card field name into barray
   put line 5 of card field name into points
end unload
```

The name of the field is passed as a parameter of the message from polyBut-Test. Next, we get the point the user has clicked on and store the horizontal (x) coordinate and the vertical (y) coordinate in separate variables:

```
put the clickH into px
   -- store the click's x-coordinate
put the clickV into py
   -- store the click's y-coordinate
put zero into crossings -- make sure it starts at 0
```

The main event is a repeat loop that repeats from 1 to the number of vertices in the shape (which was stored in points). We think the first statement is a won-drous feature that makes up for all of HyperTalk's shortcomings.

Notice that we never said what would happen if the point was on a vertical line. Well, if we calculated the slope and the run was 0 and HyperTalk divided delta y by 0, the result would be infinity. This is an illegal operation in most languages. But HyperTalk comes up with the value INF or − INF, which is stored automatically as the value in the arrays. Also, HyperTalk considers 0 divided by 0 to be the value NAN(004) (don't ask why), and this is stored in the array if we have a line segment of zero length (which is possible if the user clicks on the same location twice). So all we need is an if-then statement that looks for these strings in the arrays and skip over them:

```
repeat with i = 1 to points
-- skip if a vertical line or a point
  if (item i of marray contains "INF") ¬
  or (item i of marray contains "NAN(004)") then next repeat
```

Now we are ready to see if our click point px,py is in the same vertical strip the line is in. This test uses the HyperTalk min and max functions:

```
-- skip if to the right of the line
if px >= max(item i of xarray,item i+1 of xarray) then next repeat
-- skip if to the left of the line
if px < min(item i of xarray,item i+1 of xarray) then next repeat
```

We use ⟩ = in the first test for px and just ⟨ in the second test for py because of a slight bug in our algorithm. You need to be sure if the cursor is exactly under a point at the minimum or maximum of the line that the same line isn't counted twice. The px >= makes sure that if the cursor is under the maximum of the line segment, it doesn't get counted as a crossing; if it's under the minimum, it does get counted as a crossing. If the loop is still not exited at this point, it is in the vertical strip and the actual test for a crossing is made. Next comes the main crossings test:

```
  -- check for a crossing
  if (item i of marray * px + item i of barray) ¬
  > py then put crossings+1 into crossings
end repeat
```

Now that we have the number of crossings for this shape, we need to see if they indicate that the point is inside or outside the shape. This is done by performing the operation crossings mod 2. If the result is 0, crossings is an even number and the point is outside. If the result is not 0 (in this case it would have to be 1), crossings is odd and the point is inside the shape.

And that does it. Almost. Recall this script has to work with multiple shapes. Another user-defined command, secondWave, looks for clicks inside polybuttons other than the top button. We explain this handler in a moment.

Wheels Within Wheels

We've presented an overview of PolyButtons, the principles it is based on, and its essential code segments. Now we go back and look at its basics—the scripting techniques that allow it to do so much.

The Creation

When the user-defined `poly` command is executed in the Message box, the `poly` message is sent up the hierarchy to the Home script, where it is handled. The poly handler starts by declaring global variables and asking for more information from the user about how the shape will be drawn. If visible lines are selected, the line tool is used to draw the shapes. If invisible lines are desired, the select tool is chosen to give the cursor an appropriate appearance (clicking with the select tool doesn't do anything). As a precaution, the `clearArrays` user command is executed to clear any values remaining from a prior use of this handler. The `lineSize` and `pattern` properties are then set and the `wait until the mouse is down` statement suspends program flow until the user clicks at the starting point of the polygon. The script repeats the trapped click to place the first point on the screen.

Another user-defined command, `addPoint`, is executed next. The addPoint handler stores information about the point clicked on. The coordinates of the click are accessed from the global variable `where` and split into two other variables `xarray` and `yarray`. The coordinates are stored in a comma-delimited format so they can be retrieved as items. The number of points is stored in the variable `points`. After this handler is run, program flow returns to the poly handler.

```
on addPoint -- PolyButtons Home script user command
-- adds a new point
  global where,xarray,yarray,points
  add 1 to points -- increment points
  put points into pt -- pass value to shorter variable
  put item 1 of where into item pt of xarray
  put item 2 of where into item pt of yarray
  -- draw new side from last point to new point
  if pt > 1 then drag from item pt-1 of xarray, item pt-1 of ¬
  yarray to item pt of xarray, item pt of yarray with optionKey
end addPoint
```

The main `repeat` loop of the poly handler follows this first pass through the addPoint handler. The variable `bailout` is used as a flag to signal when it is time to break the loop. Thus, the last thing we do before entering the loop is put `false` into `bailout`.

```
put false into bailOut -- when true the following loop ends
repeat forever -- main shape-building loop
  if the mouseClick then
    put the mouseLoc into where -- save the coordinates
```

continued

```
      repeat 10 -- prepare to exit on a double-click
        if the mouseClick and (points > 1) then put true ¬
        into bailOut
end repeat
```

This loop waits for the mouse button to be pressed, then starts a complex of nested if-then and repeat control structures. First, the location of the click is stored in where, as before, and another repeat structure checks for double-clicks. If you find you can't double-click fast enough to end the shape, increase the number of repeats of this inner repeat loop. If the script allows too much time between clicks, decrease the number of repeats.

If a double-click is detected, true is put into bailout and the first part of the next if-then structure is executed—but let's cover the other case first.

```
if bailOut is true then -- if finished, connect to starting point
  put item 1 of xArray into item 1 of where
  put item 1 of yArray into item 2 of where
  addPoint -- user command to save coordinates
  exit repeat -- break the loop
else addPoint -- add a point
end if
end repeat
```

If bailout is still false, the addPoint command is executed again and the loop goes back to waiting for the mouse button to be pressed.

When bailout is finally set to true, the mouse click location in where is replaced with the location of the first click so that the shape will be closed perfectly. This means you can double-click anywhere on the screen and still get a closed shape. The addPoint command is executed one last time, and the loop is broken with an exit command.

An ask command then asks the user to name the polybutton. If the result is Cancel or empty, the shape is aborted. The if-then structure for this task redraws the shape in white to erase it, then clears the global variables with the clearArrays command before exiting the entire handler.

The next section of the handler makes a button to frame the shape, sets the button's name to the user-entered name plus *poly*, and loads two handlers into the script of the new button. The mouseUp handler connects to the detection handlers (which we cover next) to determine if a click in the button is also a click inside the shape. The doIt handler contains the statements executed if the click is inside the shape. Only an outline is provided, so the user has to add code to make the polybutton do something.

```
-- create a button to contain shape --
set cursor to watch
choose button tool
drag from min(xarray),min(yarray) to max(xarray),max(yarray) ¬
with commandKey -- make and size button
put it & "poly" into nameVar -- add suffix to user-supplied name
-- name button
set the name of card button the number of card buttons to nameVar
```

continued

```
-- build script to operate new button
put "on mouseUp" & return & "send testPoly" into tempScript
put return & "end mouseUp" & return & return after tempScript
put "on doIt" & return & "-- instructions here" after tempScript
put return & "end doIt" after tempScript

-- load script into button
set script of card button nameVar to tempScript
```

Before the poly handler ends, the `initial` command (which calculates the slope and y-intercept) is executed, a new field is created, all the information about the shape is put in the field, and the field is hidden.

The user then has the opportunity to clear the area of the card's graphic layer occupied by the new button. To do this, the script executes the user command `clearOutline`, which selects the screen area of the button and clears it.

Next, global variables are cleared with `clearArrays` and the browse tool is chosen. Finally, the script editor is opened for the new button so the user can immediately type statements for the doIt handler.

The Detection

We've already covered the most important parts of the script—those that determine whether a click is inside or outside a shape. But there is still more to describe—the overall structure of the detection script.

Most of the work is done in the polyButTest and secondWave handlers, with the unload and clearArrays handlers called as needed. At the close of the first pass through the polyButTest handler, the point has either been determined to be outside the shape or inside the shape. If it is inside, a `doIt` message is sent back to the button. If the click is outside, the secondWave handler looks for other polybuttons the click could be inside. If it finds one, it calls the polyButTest handler; if it doesn't, the script ends. If another polybutton is tested in polyButTest and the point is outside the shape again, a new exit from polyButTest is provided that avoids a potentially recursive situation.

The detection process begins with the simple mouseUp handler we previously inserted into the button:

```
on mouseUp
  testPoly
end mouseUp
```

The `testPoly` user command quickly loads values into global variables for use in other handlers. The name of the button clicked on goes into `targBut`, `false` is put into `flag`, and if the Option key is down, 1 is placed in `signal`. Both `flag` and `signal` are used as flags, as you will soon see.

```
on testPoly -- PolyButtons Home script
  -- responds to button click
  global targBut,flag,signal
```

continued

```
      put the short name of target into targBut
      if the optionKey is down then put 1 into signal
      put false into flag
      polyButTest
end testPoly
```

After the polyButTest handler has created its global variables, it retrieves the shape data from the hidden field by executing the unload user command. Then it performs the tests detailed previously. If the shape fails the test (crossings mod 2 = 0), the value of flag is examined. The global variable flag is set to true in the handler for the user command secondWave. This way, if flag turns out to be true, we avoid executing secondWave again, which would result in recursion. Because HyperTalk allows only ten levels of recursion, it would break. To avoid this, the script simply exits the handler and program flow goes right back to secondWave. If flag is false, it is safe to execute secondWave, and we do so.

```
-- test the results --
if crossings mod 2 = 0 then
   if flag is true then
      exit polyButTest -- goes to secondWave, avoids recursion
   end if
   secondWave
   -- button script user command tests for overlapping buttons
else -- inside feedback
```

If the shape passed the test, we examine the value of signal. The value 1 was put in signal in the testPoly handler if the Option key was down. If the value of signal is 1 now, the user is given the choice of deleting the polybutton or showing (outlining with pseudo-marching ants) the polybutton. If signal is anything else, the clearArrays handler is executed and the doIt user message is sent to the polybutton that passed the test. Because program flow returns to PolyButTest after the doIt handler finishes, an exit to HyperCard command follows to prevent program flow from returning to the handlers that preceded polyButTest.

Now let's return to the cases that fail the test. The secondWave handler is primarily a large repeat loop that checks every card button to see first if it is a polybutton and second if the mouse click was inside it. To avoid double-checking the button originally checked, that button is explicitly ruled out. Note that our flag is set to true to indicate we've been here.

```
on secondWave -- PolyButtons Home script user command
   -- checks for overlapping buttons
   global targBut,flag,px,py -- see polyButTest
   put true into flag -- changed from false in original button
   -- look at all card buttons
   repeat with n = 1 to the number of card buttons
      -- skip the original button
      if the short name of card button n is targBut then ¬
      next repeat
      -- skip buttons without poly suffix
      if not (the short name of card button n contains "poly")
      then next repeat
```

HyperCard version 1.2 provides an easy method to get the boundaries of the button under consideration.

```
-- get boundaries of button
-- if the point is inside the boundaries
if px,py is within the rect of card button n then
  put targBut into reserve -- store original button name
  -- put name of new button to test into targBut
  put the short name of card button n into targBut
  polyButTest -- home script user command (note that
  -- polyButTest called this handler, so the script is
  -- getting recursive here)
```

If a polybutton passes this test, the name of the original target for the mouseUp message that started all this, which is still in the global variable targBut, is put into the variable reserve for safekeeping and the name of the new candidate is put into targBut. At this point, the script is on the brink of recursion by executing the command (polyButTest) that executed the secondWave command we are now executing. As shown, the script doesn't quite cross the line into serious recursion because if the new candidate fails the polyButTest, control returns to the next line with an exit command rather than another secondWave command.

If the new candidate does fail, we shuffle the original polybutton name in reserve back into targBut and look at the next button. If we didn't restore targBut, we could easily check that button more than once.

```
      put reserve into targBut -- restore original button name
      -- because the new button failed and the original could
      -- have a higher relative number and would get tested twice
    end if
  end repeat
  clearArrays
  exit to HyperCard
end secondWave
```

If all card buttons have been tested and all fail, the clearArrays handler is executed to clear the global variables. The handler ends with an exit to HyperCard statement.

Modifications

Here are some ideas for additions to PolyButtons:

- ▶ Show the outline of all shapes, like when you press Option-Command
- ▶ Show the contents of a shape's associated field that contains the shape's array values (for easy debugging)
- ▶ Add an option for increasing the line thickness and pattern of the drawing tool
- ▶ Modify the abort and delete button routines so they are not destructive to card graphics

The PolyButtons Script

What follows is the HyperTalk listing for PolyButtons. The handlers are listed in alphabetical order. There are three keyboard message handlers: enterKey, returnKey, and tabKey. The remaining eleven handlers are for user commands: addPoint, clearArrays, clearOutline, dump, initial, outline, poly, polyButTest, secondWave, testPoly, and unload.

```
-- ********************* DESCRIPTION *************************
-- TYPE:        Buttons Tricks
-- AUTHORS:     Mitchell Waite and Ted Jones
-- NAME:        PolyButtons
-- RESTRICTIONS: Can't duplicate polybutton names on a card.
-- LOCATIONS:   Card, background, stack, or Home stack
-- ***************** BUTTON SCRIPT STARTS ********************
on addPoint -- PolyButtons Home script user command
  -- adds a new point
  global where,xarray,yarray,points
  add 1 to points -- increment points
  put points into pt -- pass value to shorter variable
  put item 1 of where into item pt of xarray
  put item 2 of where into item pt of yarray
  -- draw new side from last point to new point
  if pt > 1 then drag from item pt-1 of xarray, item pt-1 of ¬
  yarray to item pt of xarray, item pt of yarray with optionKey
end addPoint

on clearArrays -- PolyButtons button script user command
  -- clears arrays
  global where,xarray,yarray,marray,barray,points
  put empty into xarray
  put empty into yarray
  put empty into marray
  put empty into barray
  put empty into points
end clearArrays

on clearOutline nVar -- PolyButtons Home script user command
  -- erases shape outline
  choose select tool
  put rect of button nVar into dragArea
  drag from item 1 of dragArea - 1, item 2 of dragArea - 1 ¬
  to item 3 of dragArea, item 4 of dragArea
  doMenu "Clear Picture"
end clearOutline

on dump -- PolyButtons Home script user command
  -- sets up for deleting a button
  -- Copyright 1988 The Waite Group, Inc.
  global signal,targBut
  put 2 into signal -- changed from 1 in original button
  select button targBut--choose button tool
  -- click at the clickLoc
  put "•• Hit Enter to remove, Tab to spare it, Return to try again ••"
```

continued

```
      exit to HyperCard
   end dump

   on enterKey -- PolyButtons Home script
      -- delete button
      global signal,targBut,name -- see polyButTest
      if signal is 2 then -- signal value set in dump user command
         put "•• Please stand by ••" into message box
         lock screen
         put 0 into signal -- clear this flag
         -- clear graphic (leaves only background)
         -- COMMENT NEXT LINE IF CARD GRAPHIC SHOULDN'T BE DISTURBED
         clearOutline targBut -- Home script user command
         choose button tool
         click at loc of button targBut
         doMenu "Clear Button" -- clear button
         show card field name
         choose field tool
         click at loc of card field name
         doMenu "Clear Field" -- clear field

         -- option to redraw card graphic --
         unlock screen
         answer "Redraw all shape outlines in card layer?" with ¬
         "Yes" or "No"
         if it is "Yes" then outlines -- Home script user command
         choose browse tool
         put "•• Click Mouse inside and outside of shape. ••" into msg
      else -- Never mind
         pass enterKey
      end if
   end enterKey

   on initial -- PolyButtons Home script user command
      -- Calculates the slope and y-intercept for each point
      -- Puts the value in an array. If there is a slope of infinity,
      -- HyperTalk puts " INF" OR " -INF" into the value
      -- (note the space). Sometimes, however, the space is left out.
      global points, xarray, yarray, marray, barray
      repeat with i = 1 to points -- points times
      set cursor to busy
         -- find the slope (m) of each line segment and store it
         put ((item i+1 of yarray) - (item i of yarray)) ¬
         / ((item i+1 of xarray) - (item i of xarray)) ¬
         & ", " after marray

         -- find and store the y-intercept (b) of each line segment
         put ((item i of xarray * item i+1 of yarray) ¬
         - (item i+1 of xarray * item i of yarray)) ¬
         / (item i of xarray - item i+1 of xarray) ¬
         & ", " after barray

      end repeat
   end initial

   on outlines -- PolyButtons Home script user command
      -- draws outlines for all polybuts
```

continued

```
      global p,xarray,yarray,marray,barray,points
      -- for all card fields
      repeat with p = 1 to the number of card fields
      set cursor to busy
        -- skip if name doesn't have suffix
        if not (the short name of card button p contains "poly") ¬
        then next repeat
        unload p -- card script user command
        set lineSize to 1
        choose line tool
        set pattern to 9
        repeat with n = 1 to (points - 1)
          -- draw lines between points
          drag from item n of xarray,item n of yarray to item ¬
          n + 1 of xarray,item n + 1 of yarray with optionKey
        end repeat
      end repeat
    end outlines


    on poly -- PolyButtons Home script user command
      -- create a new polybutton
      global xarray -- x-coordinates for all points in shape
      global yarray -- y-coordinates for all points in shape
      global barray -- y-intercepts for all points in shape
      global marray -- slope of all sides of shape
      global points -- number of points in shape
      global where -- mouseClick location
      -- local variables
      -- bailOut -- if true, repeat loop ends
      -- nameVar -- contains the name of an object
      -- tempScript -- contains script while under construction
      -- draw actual line or don't disturb graphics?
      answer "Draw line or draw invisible?" with "Invisible" or ¬
      "Cancel" or "Line"
      if it is "Cancel" then
        exit poly
      else if it is "Invisible" then
        choose select tool -- no line to disturb graphics
      else -- draw a line
        choose line tool -- paint tool with an appropriate cursor
      end if

      clearArrays -- user command
      put "•• Click where you want to start PolyButton. ••" into msg
      set lineSize to 1
      set pattern to 12 -- gray
      click at 0,0 -- shows correct cursor
      wait until the mouse is down
        -- to make up for first click of button
      put the mouseLoc into where -- save the coordinate
      click at where -- draws starting point
      addPoint -- user command to store coordinates
      put "Move and Click next point. Continue. Double Click to end."

      -- shape building --
      put false into bailOut -- when true, the following loop ends
```

continued

```
repeat forever -- main shape building loop
  if the mouseClick then
    put the mouseLoc into where -- save the coordinates
    repeat 10 -- prepare to exit on a double-click
      if the mouseClick and (points > 1) then put true ¬
      into bailOut
    end repeat
    if bailOut is true then
    -- if finished, connect to starting point
      put item 1 of xArray into item 1 of where
      put item 1 of yArray into item 2 of where
      addPoint -- user comment to save coordinates
      exit repeat -- break the loop
    else addPoint -- add a point
  end if
end repeat

-- name the shape or cancel it --
ask "Name this button or Canc it."
set cursor to watch
put "•• Please stand by ••" into message box
lock screen

-- abort shape --
if it is empty then -- if cancel or empty name
  set pattern to 1 -- white
  repeat with n = 1 to points - 1 -- erase outline
    drag from item n of xarray,item n of yarray to item n+1 ¬
    of xarray,item n+1 of yarray with optionKey
  end repeat
  clearArrays -- empty arrays
  put "•• Enter "poly" to try again. ••"
  choose browse tool -- return to normal mode
  reset paint -- restore default settings
  exit poly -- end script
end if

-- create a button to contain shape --
set cursor to watch
choose button tool
drag from min(xarray),min(yarray) to ¬
max(xarray),max(yarray) with commandKey
-- make and size button
put it & "poly" into nameVar
-- add suffix to user-supplied name
-- name button
set the name of card button the number of card buttons ¬
to nameVar
-- build script to operate new button
put "on mouseUp" & return & "testPoly" into tempScript
put return & "end mouseUp" & return & return after tempScript
put "on doIt" & return & "-- instructions here" after tempScript
put return & "end doIt" after tempScript

-- load script into button
set script of card button nameVar to tempScript
```

continued

```
-- what the script looks like --
-- on mouseUp
--    testPoly
-- end mouseUp
--
-- on doIt
--  -- instructions here
-- end doIt


-- calculate values and store in field --
subtract 1 from points
initial -- user command to calculate the slope and y-intercept
-- create field to contain array data
doMenu "New Field"
put xarray into line 1 of card field the number of card fields
put yarray into line 2 of card field the number of card fields
put marray into line 3 of card field the number of card fields
put barray into line 4 of card field the number of card fields
put points into line 5 of card field the number of card fields
-- name field with the name of the button plus a suffix
set the name of card field the number of card fields to ¬
nameVar & "arrays"
-- hide field
hide card field the number of card fields


-- option to clear card graphic --
answer "Clear shape outline in card layer?" with "Yes" or "No"
-- clear graphic (leaves only background)
if it is "Yes" then clearOutline nameVar
  -- user command in Home script
clearArrays -- user command in button script
choose browse tool -- return to normal mode
put "•• Click Mouse inside and outside of shape. ••" into msg
edit script of button the number of buttons
end poly

on polyButTest -- PolyButtons Home script user command
  -- Called by a polybutton or secondWave. Tests for
  -- inside/outside and lets user highlight or delete button.
  set cursor to watch
  global targBut -- short name of button in question
  global flag -- false first time, set to true in secondWave
  global px -- click x-coordinate
  global py -- click y-coordinate
  global name -- targBut plus arrays suffix
  global signal -- set to 1 if option key pressed with click
  global points -- number of points in shape
  global marray -- slopes of all points
  global barray -- y-intercepts of all points
  global xarray -- x-coordinates of all points
  global yarray -- y-coordinates of all points
  -- local variables --
  -- crossings
    -- number of times vertical line from click crosses line
  put targBut & "arrays" into name
  unload name
```

continued

```
            -- Home script user command; pulls arrays out of field

      -- check for inside shape
      -- if no shape, look for overlap with user command
      if points is empty then secondWave
      put the clickH into px
         -- store the click's x-coordinate
      put the clickV into py
         -- store the click's y-coordinate
      put zero into crossings -- make sure starts at 0
      -- test to see if the point is below each line
      repeat with i = 1 to points
         -- skip if a vertical line or a point
         if (item i of marray contains "INF") ¬
         or (item i of marray contains "NAN(004)") then next
repeat
         -- skip if to the right of the line
         if px >= max(item i of xarray,item i+1 of xarray) ¬
         then next repeat
         -- skip if to the left of the line
         if px < min(item i of xarray,item i+1 of xarray) ¬
         then next repeat
         -- check for a crossing
         if (item i of marray * px + item i of barray) ¬
         > py then put crossings+1 into crossings
         put i & "," & item i of marray & "," & px & "," & item i ¬
         of barray & "," & (item i of marray * px + ¬
         item i of barray) into disp

      end repeat

      -- test the results
      if crossings mod 2 = 0 then
        if flag is true then
          exit polyButTest -- goes to secondWave; avoids recursion
        end if
        secondWave
          -- button script user command tests for overlapping buttons
      else -- inside feedback

        -- Option/click choices
        if signal = 1 or signal = 2 then -- looking at top button?
          answer "Do you want to..." with "Delete" or "Show" ¬
          or "Cancel"
          if it is "Cancel" then exit to HyperCard -- end script
          if it is "Delete" then -- delete button
            dump
              -- button script user command sets up for button delete
          else -- show outline of button
            set lineSize to 1
            choose line tool
            put "•• Press Option to stop ••" into message box
            repeat until the optionKey is down
              -- alternate drawing with white and black lines
              if the pattern is 12 then set pattern to 22 else set ¬
              pattern to 12
              repeat with n = 1 to points -- draw shape
```

continued

```
              drag from item n of xarray,item n of yarray to item ¬
              n + 1 of xarray,item n + 1 of yarray with optionKey
          end repeat
        end repeat
        -- option to clear card graphic
        answer "Clear shape outline in card layer?" with ¬
        "Yes" or "No"
        -- clear graphic (leaves only background)
        if it is "Yes" then
          clearOutline targBut -- user command in Home script
        else -- card outline necessary
          set pattern to 9
          repeat with n = 1 to points
            drag from item n of xarray,item n of yarray to item ¬
            n + 1 of xarray,item n + 1 of yarray with optionKey
          end repeat
        end if
        choose browse tool
        reset paint
        put "•• Click Mouse inside and outside of shape. ••" into msg
        put 0 into signal
        exit to HyperCard
      end if
    end if

    clearArrays
    send doIt to button targBut -- activates handler in button
    -- Button action is in the doIt handler.
    -- The button handler should look like the following:

    -- on doIt
    --    <statement>
    --    <statement>
    -- end doIt

    exit to HyperCard -- ends routine
  end if
end polyButTest

on returnKey -- PolyButtons Home script user command
  -- for deleting overlapping shapes
  global signal -- see polyButTest
  if signal is 1 or signal is 2 then
    -- only in context of polyButTest
    secondWave -- try again
    put "•• Click Mouse inside and outside of shape. ••" into msg
    choose browse tool
    put 0 into signal
  else
    pass returnKey
  end if
end returnKey

on secondWave -- PolyButtons  Home script user command
  -- checks for overlapping buttons
  global targBut,flag,px,py -- see polyButTest
  put true into flag -- changed from false in original button
```

continued

```
        -- look at all card buttons --
      repeat with n = 1 to the number of card buttons
        -- skip the original button
        if the short name of card button n is targBut then next
repeat
        -- skip buttons without poly suffix
        if not (the short name of card button n contains "poly")
        then next repeat
        -- get boundaries of button
        -- if the point is inside the boundaries
        if px,py is within the rect of card button n then
          put targBut into reserve -- store original button name
          -- put name of new button to test into targBut
          put the short name of card button n into targBut
          polyButTest -- Home script user command (note that
        -- polyButTest called this handler, so the script is
            -- getting recursive here)
          put reserve into targBut -- restore original button name
            -- because new button failed and the original could have
            -- a higher relative number and would get tested twice
        end if
      end repeat
      clearArrays
      exit to HyperCard
    end secondWave

    on tabKey -- PolyButtons Home script
      -- exits delete mode started in dump
      global signal
      if signal > 0 then
        -- check the flag and restore things to normal
        put "•• Click Mouse inside and outside of shape. ••" into msg
        choose browse tool
        put 0 into signal
      else -- not in delete mode
        pass tabKey
      end if
    end tabKey

    on testPoly -- PolyButtons Home script
      -- responds to button click
      global targBut,flag,signal
      put the short name of target into targBut
      if the optionKey is down then put 1 into signal
      put false into flag
     polyButTest
    end testPoly

    on unload name -- PolyButtons Home script user command
      -- get arrays from field
      global xarray,yarray,marray,barray,points
      put line 1 of card field name into xarray
      put line 2 of card field name into yarray
      put line 3 of card field name into marray
      put line 4 of card field name into barray
      put line 5 of card field name into points
    end unload
```

Animated Icons
and Cursors

Jeremy John Ahouse

Synopsis: One of the more exciting uses of HyperCard is animation—creating images that move in predetermined ways according to your scripts. You can use animation to enhance the opening card of your stack, to attract attention to a particular place on the screen, or to create special visual effects.

Unfortunately, the techniques for doing animations are not that obvious. This chapter shows every trick for animating icons. You will see how to make buttons and icons run, jump, switch, fly, crawl, spin, and otherwise wander across your screen. Learn how to cycle through icons, how to make "sprites" (intelligent objects that move according to your scripts), correct location strategies, and how to add sound to icons.

The chapter also covers creating custom cursors so that when the user passes the mouse over certain objects, its indicator changes to whatever shape you wish. For example, when the mouse passes over certain areas corresponding to special information, the cursor can change to a question mark. The chapter contains dozens of practical examples that you can use to make your stacks more powerful, useful, and fun, including balls that bounce, books pages that turn, feet that walk, snakes that crawl, and much more.

Chapter 7

Animated Icons and Cursors

Seamless Animation with Icons and Cursors

This chapter describes techniques for animating icons, timing those animations, using icons as cursors, changing cursors, and animating cursor-like icons. These animation techniques will liven up your stacks. They get the user's attention and can convey useful information. You will find uses for animated and changing cursors and icons whose goal is communication as well as playfulness. This preamble is offered because like many facets of HyperCard, animation is addictive. Be fore-warned.

Animation has three primary advantages. First, it gives the user feedback from your stack. Second, more information can be conveyed with animated icons than with static icons. And third, animations of this kind form part of your arsenal of special effects in HyperCard.

Animated cursors and icons are not presently part of the standard Apple inter-face. When you use them, you are extending the interface. Thus, try to do so judi-ciously. Animated sequences can convey information. They can also make the metaphors you use in your stacks more real. When you decide to use animated icons, think about the symbols in your stack and try to be consistent. For example, if you take over the cursor whenever the user is over a hot spot, do this throughout the stack. When you animate an icon, you make it more real, more of an object on the screen. Take advantage of this to reinforce the main components of your stack. Remember, if everything is animated, nothing stands out as particularly memorable. All of this can be summed up by the phrase, "have a reason." Try to have a reason when you choose any design element in you stack.

What Are Icons?

Icons are small pictures that fit into an area of 32x32 pixels. See Figure 7-1. You see icons in every phase of using the Macintosh. The Macintosh uses icons to represent actions or objects. For example, the left and right arrows in HyperCard are icons representing actions. On the Finder desktop, icons represent documents and appli-cations. (Icons in the Finder are actually ICN# resources and have a mask as well as an icon.) In HyperCard, icons represent actions. Examples are left and right arrows and sort stack options.

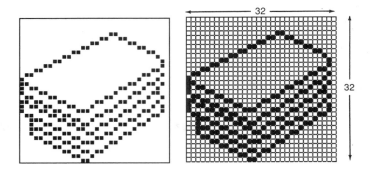

Figure 7-1.   An icon in HyperCard is 32x32 pixels.

Most icons in HyperCard don't move. You can add information to icons that represent actions by moving them around the screen and changing them. For example, an icon can change from a hand, signaling stop, to a man running, signaling go.

How Are Icons Used in HyperCard?

In HyperCard, icons can be associated with any button. This is accomplished by clicking Icon... in the Button Info dialog, as shown in Figure 7-2. It is then a straightforward matter to choose the icon.

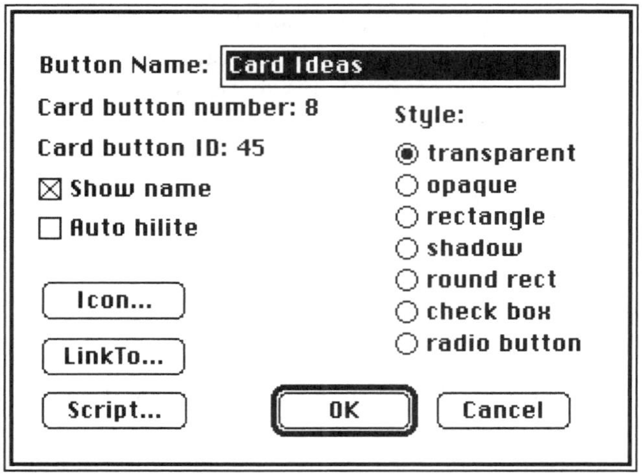

Figure 7-2.   The standard Button Info box in HyperCard.

You can select an icon from the dialog shown in Figure 7-3. When you select an icon, its ID number and name, if it has one, are shown at the top of the window. In Figure 7-3, icon ID 1012 is named Return Arrow. This dialog shows all icons available in a given stack. Any icon in the resource fork of your stack, the Home stack, or the HyperCard application is available and appears in this dialog. This is important to remember because if you distribute a stack that uses icon animations, other users probably won't have your custom icons in their Home stack or their HyperCard application. Make sure the icons your stacks use are in the resource fork of your stack.

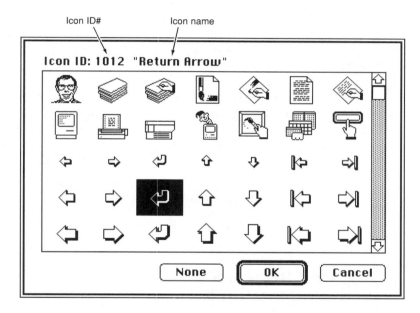

Figure 7-3.   Choose an icon from the Icon Picker dialog box.

You can change the icon associated with a button or change a button's location from within a script. You use these two HyperCard features in most of the scripts that follow.

The *set* Command

The HyperTalk `set` command sets the property of an object. The icon a button shows is one of the properties of a button, so the `set` command can be used to change that icon. The following script fragment allows you to change a button's icon:

```
set icon of [card|background] button <button
name|button id> to <icon name|icon id>
```

An Example Using *set*

Following is an icon example using set. This example uses icons you already have in HyperCard, so you can begin experimenting with icons before you learn to make your own. Most examples in this chapter do not use the icons that come with Hyper-Card.

Make a card button named my test button and choose any icon for it. Remember that the icon name identifies a 32x32 pixel image and a button name identifies a HyperCard button.

Put this script into your button:

```
on mouseUp
  set icon of card button "my test button" to "HyperCard"
end mouseUp
```

This script changes the icon assigned to the button my test button to the HyperCard icon. See Figure 7-4. This is not interesting, but it is the first step in toggling an icon.

Figure 7-4.   The icon you chose is changed to the HyperCard stack icon.

Toggling Between Icons and Changing Button Names

Now make another new button. Name it whatever you like and choose an icon for it. Make sure to choose Show name from the Button dialog when you make the button.

Put this script into your button, then click the button a few times:

```
on mouseUp
  if the icon of me = 1000 then
    set icon of me to "HyperCard"
    set the name of me to "HyperCard Icon"
  else
    set icon of me to "Stack"
    set name of me to "Stack Icon"
  end if
end mouseUp
```

This script toggles between two icons, the HyperCard application icon and the HyperCard stack icon, as shown in Figure 7-5. It also changes the name of the button. A button name, like a button icon, is a property of an object. You can use the set command to change this property.

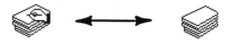

Figure 7-5. The script toggles between these two icons.

The script begins by asking for the icon ID number of the icon presently showing. It uses `me` to refer to the button itself. You can use `me` to refer to a container when the script that uses this word is in the container itself. (There is a longer discussion about `me` and `the target` later in this chapter.) The syntax `the icon of me` evaluates to an icon ID number. Based on that result, the script changes the icon to either the Hypercard application icon or the HyperCard stack icon.

Cycling Through Icons

The following script cycles through a number of icons, shown in Figure 7-6. It uses HyperCard's `send` command. You can send messages to any object in HyperCard. In this case, you use the ID number of the icon as a message and send it back to the button. This number is then trapped by one of the handlers and an action is taken.

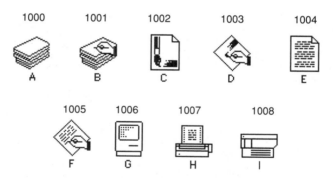

Figure 7-6. These icons, which correspond to ID numbers 1000 through 1008, are in the resource forks of the Home stack and the HyperCard application.

To use this script, make a new button, name it A, show the name, and choose the HyperCard stack icon for it. Then place this script in the button:

```
on mouseUp
  send icon of me to me -- "the icon of me" part of the statement
  -- evaluates to a number; this number becomes the message
end mouseUp

on 1000
  set icon of me to 1001
```

continued

```
      set name of me to "B"
  end 1000

on 1001
  set icon of me to 1002
  set name of me to "C"
end 1001

on 1002
  set icon of me to 1003
  set name of me to "D"
end 1002

on 1003
  set icon of me to 1004
  set name of me to "E"
end 1003

on 1004
  set icon of me to 1005
  set name of me to "F"
end 1004

on 1005
  set icon of me to 1006
  set name of me to "G"
end 1005

on 1006
  set icon of me to 1007
  set name of me to "H"
end 1006

on 1007
  set icon of me to 1008
  set name of me to "I"
end 1007

on 1008
  set icon of me to 1000
  set name of me to "A"
end 1008
```

When you click on the button, the script cycles through the eight icons. The name under the icon changes from A to B to C up to I. The technique of sending the icon ID number as a handler is one way to cycle through the icons. You can also use a series of `if-then-else` statements:

```
on mouseUp
  if the icon of me is 1000 then
     set the icon of me to 1001
     set name of me to "B"
  else if the icon of me is 1001 then
     set the icon of me to 1002
     set name of me to "C"
```

continued

```
      else if the icon of me is 1002 then
         set the icon of me to 1003
         set name of me to "D"
         -- and so on
      else if the icon of me is 1008 then
         set the icon of me to 1001
         set name of me to "A"
      end if
end mouseUp
```

The decision of which approach to use is partially aesthetic and partially dependent upon the task you are trying to accomplish.

A quick warning about changing the name of an icon from inside a script. Changing the names of icons within a script can generate free space in your stack, so be prepared to compact your stack regularly. (See chapter 17, "Large Stacks.")

Other Toggle Animations

The scripts so far use icons that come with HyperCard. The next example uses icons that you have to either make or import from another stack. Both of these techniques are discussed later in the chapter.

The best place to find examples of these toggle icon animations (and others) is in Robertson Smith's Stack Starter, which is available from many user groups. Figure 7-7 shows you a switch that can be toggled using the same technique that was used to change icons in the preceding script.

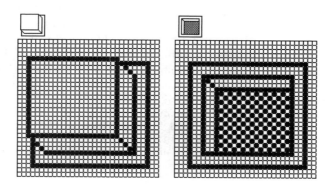

Figure 7-7.   An example of button icons that can be toggled.

To use the following script, import these icons into your script. Then find their ID numbers. (Remember, you can find the icon ID number and name from the Icon Picker dialog box by clicking on the icon.) You can use the same format used previously to toggle back and forth.

This script adds a click sound with the `play` command. It also shows you where to add the rest of the script to make the button functional. If you don't have a sound resource that sounds like a click, replace the `play "click"` line with `play "harpsichord"` or one of the other sounds that comes with HyperCard.

```
on mouseUp
  if the icon of me = <first icon's ID number> then
    play "click"
    set icon of me to <name|ID number>
    -- put script here for tasks associated with
    -- this position of the switch
  else
    play "click"
    set icon of me to <name|ID number>
    -- put script here for tasks associated with
    -- this position of the switch
  end if
end mouseUp
```

With this script, you can add toggle switches. These are particularly useful if you want to present users with a control panel that allows them to configure your stack. At this point, you should be able to use the `set` command and toggle a button through a number of icons. The next section introduces multiple icon animations (animations that use more than two images), then describes how to make your own icons and import them to your stack.

Basic Animation

This section introduces multiframe animations. Multiframe icon animations are extensions of the kinds of scripts you have already seen. By using several icons, you can get smooth animations. You can switch several icons in a row by using the `set icon` command repeatedly. This section uses a `repeat` loop to change the icons.

In the following example, you use five icons, shown in Figure 7-8. They are named world 1, world 2, world 3, world 4, and world 5. These names are not arbitrary. They all contain a number, and the script builds the names by incrementing a number in a `repeat` loop. The script cycles through these icons several times.

```
on mouseUp
  repeat 3 times -- you cycle through all of them 3 times
    repeat with n = 1 to 5 -- go from world 1 to world 5
      put "world" && n into whichicon
      set icon of me to whichicon
    end repeat
    repeat with n = 5 down to 1
      put "world" && n into whichicon
      set icon of me to whichicon
    end repeat
  end repeat
end mouseUp
```

Figure 7-8.   The icons for this multiframe animation are named
world 1, world 2, and so on up to world 5.

This example shows you the value of a naming convention when cycling through frames of animation. It is much quicker to use a `repeat` loop to generate the next frame than it is to list all the names explicitly. You can use `repeat` loops when the names of your icons are identical except for a number somewhere in the name. In the preceding script, the icon names are built in the `repeat` loop by combining the word `world` with the number stored in the variable n. (Remember that `&&` combines two strings with a space between them.) This combination is placed in the variable `whichicon`. You will see this approach in other scripts. The section describing how to make icons also explains how to rename and renumber them.

Because HyperCard uses numbers to represent icon IDs, your icon names should not consist of only digits (numbers). If they do and you write a script such as `set icon of card button 1 to 100`, HyperCard may get "confused."

You have covered the basics of using the `set icon` syntax. The next section shows you how to move icons around the screen. Then you will combine these two approaches. Also, a more object-oriented approach to the animation of icons is described.

Moving Buttons from a Script

A HyperCard card is 512 pixels wide and 342 pixels long, as shown in Figure 7-9. Every point on the screen can be described by a pair of numbers corresponding to the horizontal and vertical components. For example, 256,171 is the point at the center of the screen. The syntax is

```
show [card|background] button at <location>
```

where *location* is a pair of numbers, separated by a comma, corresponding to the center of the button. These numbers must be integers.

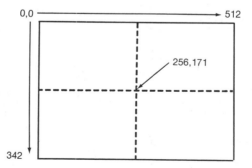

Figure 7-9. The HyperCard coordinate system starts in the upper left corner of a card and extends for 342 pixels horizontally and 512 pixels vertically.

To move a button around the screen, use a script like the following:

```
on mouseUp
  put the location of me into where
  put (10 + item 1 of where) mod 512 into item 1 of where
  show me at where
end mouseUp
```

This script moves the button across the screen 10 pixels at a time. By using `mod` 512 you make sure if the icon gets too close to the edge of the card, it doesn't "fall off." Considerations like this are important if you plan to use your stack on any of the large screen Macintosh models.

If you ever lose an icon you are working with, you can retrieve it by typing the following into the Message box:

```
show <name of your button> at 256,171
```

Using this `show <button> at <location>` approach, you can move icons all over the screen. By combining the `set` and `show` commands, you can do most of the icon animations in this chapter.

Now you know how to change icons and how to move them. The examples at the end of this chapter use these two abilities extensively. If you already know how to make icons and want to look at more icon animation examples, you can skip to the examples section.

Moving with the *mouseLoc*

This section explains one use of the `show` command. Its syntax is

```
show [card|bg] button <ID|name> at the mouseLoc
```

This allows the icon to follow the cursor all over the screen. See Figure 7-10.

Figure 7-10.   Because you haven't hidden the mouse cursor, the button icon follows the browse hand around the card.

Try this script:

```
on mouseEnter
  repeat until the mouse is down
    show [card|bg] button <ID|name> at the mouseLoc
  end repeat
end mouseEnter
```

Your button should follow the browse cursor around the screen. The `repeat` loop is necessary so that the button continuously follows the cursor. If you didn't include the loop, the script would only be executed once, on `mouseEnter`. By checking to see if the mouse is down at the beginning of the loop, the user has a way of getting out of the loop.

When a user interacts with HyperCard as a script is continuously executing, you have to provide a way out. In this example, the way out is the mouseDown event. If you don't include some way to end the script, the user will be forced to use Command-period to abort the script.

You return to cursor-like icons after the cursor section of this chapter.

The *target* and *me* with Buttons

When you are using me, target, and the target with fields in HyperCard versions 1.2.1 and later, you can access either the name of the field or its contents. When you are dealing with buttons, target and me refer to the name of the button. For operations on fields, you can use "me" as a container. In earlier versions of HyperCard, "me" referred to the object, not to its contents. For example:

```
get the name of me
  -- returns the name of the object
put "Apples" into me
  -- puts "Apples" in the container referred to by me
put "Apples" into line 2 of me
  -- puts Apples into the 2d line of text held by the container
put me into myHolder
  -- puts the contents of me into another container
```

You can use the target to refer to the object and target to refer to its contents. In earlier versions of HyperCard, the target referred to the object, but not its contents. For example:

```
put the target
  -- puts the name of the object that originally received
  -- a message into the Message box
put target into myHolder
  -- puts contents of a field into a variable called myHolder
put "Apples" into target
  -- puts "Apples" into the field represented by the target
```

One final note: put value of the target is the same as put target.

The Hierarchy, *me, the target,* and *send*

The HyperCard message hierarchy from card buttons and card fields to the background, stack, Home stack, and finally HyperCard itself is very flexible. But be wary of sending ambiguous messages. Putting me in a button script or a field script works because there is no question about which object is being referred to. The variable me can be used when a script is in the button itself. If you are going to use this script higher in the hierarchy, you have to identify the button explicitly by name or ID or use the target function. See Figure 7-11.

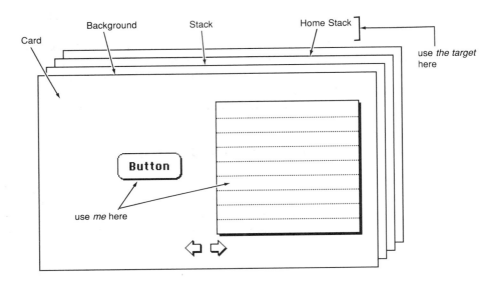

Figure 7-11.   Use **me** to refer to an object when the script is located directly in that object; otherwise, use **the target**.

Here is an example using **the target**. When a button or locked field is clicked, its name is stored in **the target** variable. This variable holds the full name of the most recently clicked object. If you want to control animation from a handler in the card, rather than the button itself, use a handler like this:

```
set icon of the target to <icon ID|icon name>
```

or

```
show the target at <newLocation>
```

where *newLocation* is a variable containing the new x,y coordinates.

The first of these checks **the target** for the name of the button, then changes its icon to the one specified by the script. The second checks **the target** and moves the button whose name was in **the target**.

A different way to control animation from scripts that are not in the buttons themselves is to send a message to a particular object in the HyperCard hierarchy. In this way, you can place your script in a button but still access it from the card, the background, or stack objects.

```
send mouseUp to card button <ID|name>
```

This line of HyperTalk sends the **mouseUp** message to a particular button. The button then responds as if it had been clicked on.

When you use radio buttons, only one button in the group should be highlighted at any one time. To manage these groups of buttons, you can use the send command in the following way.

Make a group of buttons, as shown in Figure 7-12. Name them Radio 1, Radio 2, and Radio 3. Choose radio button as the style and check the Show name box in the Button dialog when you make them.

◉ **Radio 1**

○ **Radio 2**

○ **Radio 3**

Figure 7-12. The three radio buttons you need to create for the example.

Put this script into each button in your group:

```
on mouseUp
  lock screen
    -- so it looks as if all the highlighting happens at once
  repeat with n = 1 to 3  -- because there are three buttons
    put "Radio" && n into whichone
      -- building the names of the buttons
    send buttonOFF to card btn whichone
      -- turn off the highlights
  end repeat
  buttonON  -- turn just this one on
  unlock screen  -- back to normal
end mouseUp

on buttonON
  set hilite of me to true
end buttonON

on buttonOFF
  set hilite of me to false
end buttonOFF
```

Now these radio buttons are linked. They follow the interface convention of only allowing one button of a group to be highlighted at any one time. This script can be used in any number of radio buttons. Just make sure you have a naming convention that builds the names of all the buttons in the repeat loop. You won't always have the luxury of naming your buttons with digits in the name. In this case, send the buttonOff message explicitly to all buttons that should receive it.

Script Location Strategies

Where you place scripts is mostly up to you. When you debug scripts, one strategy is to place the scripts within buttons and fields. When you want to use these scripts more universally, you can move them to cards, to backgrounds, and higher in the hierarchy. Usually, you gain speed by putting handlers in the buttons themselves and save space by not repeating scripts and by putting them as far up in the hierarchy as possible. This is a dilemma. If you are interested in fast stacks and don't worry about how much room they use, you may want to repeat many handlers in each button or field that uses them. On the other hand, if space is a concern and you want a more object-oriented message-passing approach to your stacks, use the handlers as far up in the hierarchy as possible. It is a trade-off. I prefer to have few local scripts and to do most of the work as high up in the hierarchy as possible. The examples in this chapter focus on scripts contained in buttons. This was done primarily for clarity; you can move most of these scripts to more accessible locations in the card, background, or stack script.

Controlling the Timing of Animation

Now that you know how to switch and move icons, let's discuss timing. It is important to remember there are at least four platforms that can run HyperCard: the Macintosh Plus, SE, II, and IIx. You probably want your icons to act similarly across all four machines, but each machine operates at a different speed. One way to get similar responses is to use the `wait` command in HyperCard. The command `wait #`, where # is an integer, stops execution of the script for a certain number of ticks. A tick is roughly a sixtieth of a second. (There are 60.15 ticks per second.) You can also ask HyperCard to wait for a number of seconds (for example, `wait 3 seconds`) but it is unlikely you will want or need to slow a Macintosh II quite that much. So, the first step to controlling the speed of animation should include a short wait just before you change the icon.

The first question is: how long do I wait? A wait of 15 ticks (`wait 15`) slows a Macintosh II to the speed of a Macintosh Plus. However, this approach works best if there are few lines to execute. The more lines the Macintosh II interprets and executes, the more it can outdistance a Macintosh Plus. To tackle this situation, you have to wait different amounts of time on a Macintosh Plus, SE, or II. How long you should make the script wait depends on the length of the script associated with the task, how many times in the execution of a script you call the `wait` command, and the clock speed of the Macintosh in use.

If you declare and set the global variable `waitTime` when the stack is first opened, you can control all wait messages in a stack by finding the type of computer used and putting a special value into `waitTime`. Here is a way to determine the numbers that must be put into the variable `waitTime` using HyperTalk. Put this handler into your stack script:

```
on openStack
  global waitTime
  put 0 into counter
  put the ticks into start
  repeat 60
    put 1 + counter into counter
  end repeat
  put the ticks into finish
  put round(9000/(finish - start)^2) into waitTime
end openStack
```

This script puts a much shorter wait into the `waitTime` variable on CPUs that took longer to calculate the `repeat` loop. This script should return a value of about 1 for a Macintosh Plus and a value of 17 for a Macintosh II. The value of 9000 (in the script) is an estimate that has worked for the author.

Because there are basically two kinds of Macintoshes—those with a 68000 CPU and those with a 68020 CPU—you can do the following:

```
on openStack
  global speedy
  put the ticks into start
  repeat with n = 1 to 60
    put n into counter
  end repeat
  put the ticks into finish
  if(finish - start) < 40 then
    put true into speedy
  else
    put false into speedy
  end if
  -- other openStack handlers
end openStack
```

Now you can use the following line in any animation script in your stack:

```
if speedy then wait 15 ticks
  -- remember to declare speedy as a global
```

When you are using a fast CPU, the variable `speedy` evaluates to true. Thus, the script halts for 40 ticks.

Disk Access

The first time HyperCard needs to play a sound or display an icon, it reads it from the disk. Hard disks are much faster than floppies, and you will probably see performance drop as you run a stack from floppies.

One way to overcome this problem is to lock the screen as you show all frames of your animation. This forces HyperCard to read them from the disk and store them in memory. Then you can unlock the screen and go ahead with the animation. This is true for both card-to-card animations and icon animations. (See chapter 17, "Large Stacks.")

Even with these approaches, nothing is quite as good as sitting in front of different machines and testing your stacks meticulously.

Including Sounds

You can control animation icons in concert with sounds using the `play` command. In this case, you can time your icon animation by checking to see if a particular sound is finished playing. HyperCard puts the name of the sound currently playing into the property the sound and the string done into it when the sound has finished playing. The following example shows you how to use this property with an icon switching to a new value:

```
if the sound is "done" then set icon of card btn A to 2341
```

This is a number of sounds played one after the other:

```
play "rolling wave 1"
play "rolling wave 2"
play "crashing wave"
play "whale"
play "rolling wave 3"
```

You can change icons in the following way:

```
if the sound is "rolling wave 1" then set icon of me to "Wave 1"
if the sound is "rolling wave 2" then set icon of me to "Wave 2"
if the sound is "crashing wave" then set icon of me to "Crashing"
if the sound is "whale" then set icon of me to "Whale fin"
if the sound is "rolling wave 3" then set icon of me to "Wave 1"
if the sound is "done" then set icon of me to "Calm sea"
```

The icons necessary for this script are shown in Figure 7-13.

Figure 7-13.   The rolling wave icons, which should look something like this, can be cycled through many times while the sound of a crashing wave is played.

Sometimes, HyperCard plays a sound and you want your icons to be animated while the sound is playing. This happens in the walking snake example later in this chapter. Take advantage of the feature that HyperCard continues to execute scripts after it starts to play a sound. In this case, you have to time the animation with the ticks again. For example, if you know the length of a musical passage, you can allow the script to proceed only after a certain amount of time has elapsed since the sound started. This script fragment shows you how to halt execution of a multiframe animation until sufficient time has passed.

```
put the ticks into initial
repeat with n = 1 to 10
  set icon to "Name" && n
  -- other actions in this handler
  wait until the ticks - initial is > 34
end repeat
```

This example is another way to accommodate different CPU speeds and different length scripts, because you are waiting a predetermined time before initiating an action. One of the biggest issues with sound is disk access time. For this reason, use short sounds (3 to 5 seconds or less) and check to see which sound is playing at any one time to coordinate your animation. For more on using sound in your stacks, see chapter 10.

Sprites

Sprites are little pieces of animation that you can tell to go somewhere. In the tradition of object-oriented programming, they "know" what to do. This is possible because HyperTalk can pass parameters to functions and commands that you define.

To use the following example, begin by making three icons and naming them dancer 1, dancer 2, and dancer 3. See Figure 7-14.

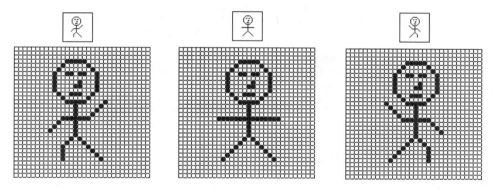

Figure 7-14.   If you aren't careful about centering the dancer icon, the motion will be jerky.

Make a button that shows icon dancer 1 but does not show its name. Then put this script into the card, background, or stack:

```
on dancing horizontal,vertical
  repeat with n = 1 to 3
    set icon of the target to "dancer" && n
    show the target at horizontal,vertical
  end repeat
end dancing
```

This is a HyperTalk function. We will invoke it from a button and pass it the location where we want to move the dancer.

Put this script into the dancer button:

```
on mouseUp
  put the mouseH into H
  put the mouseV into V
  repeat 6 times
    add 5 to H
    add 5 to V
    dancing H,V
```

continued

```
    end repeat
end mouseUp
```

This script in the button dances the icon diagonally down and to the right. You can use the same `dancing` command from any button script—you only have to pass the horizontal and vertical parameters.

In the following script, the dancer dances in a different direction, depending on where you click.

```
on mouseUp
  put item 1 of loc of me into horizLoc
  put item 2 of loc of me into vertLoc
  put the loc of me into newLoc
  put item 1 of newLoc into H
  put item 2 of newLoc into V
  if clickH <= horizLoc and clickV < vertLoc then
    put -5 into n
    put -5 into m
  else if clickH > horizLoc and clickV < vertLoc then
    put 5 into n
    put -5 into m
  else if clickH > horizLoc and clickV >= vertLoc then
    put 5 into n
    put 5 into m
  else if clickH <= horizLoc and clickV >= vertLoc then
    put -5 into n
    put 5 into m
  end if
  repeat 3 times
    add n to H
    add m to V
    dancing H,V
  end repeat
end mouseUp
```

Clicking on the dancer's upper left causes the dancer to dance in that direction. The same is true for the other three quadrants.

You often will want to pass a series of locations to the sprite. You may want the animation incremented only one frame each time it is called. To do this, the button needs to "remember" what which icon was showing the last time it was called. One way to do this is to use a global variable that you increment each time the animation is used:

```
on Dancing horizontal,vertical
  global stance
  if stance is empty put 1 into stance -- before anything is
  -- put into a HyperTalk global it is "empty"
  if stance > 3 then put 1 into stance
  set icon of the target to "dancer" && stance
  put stance + 1 into stance
  show the target at horizontal,vertical
end Dancing
```

Alternatively you could use the following;

```
on Dancing horizontal,vertical
   global stance
   if stance is empty put 1 into stance
   set icon of the target to "dancer" && stance
   put ((stance + 1) mod 2) + 1 into stance
   show the target at horizontal,vertical
end Dancing
```

The global variable stores the position of the dancer between the times the handler is called. Now the script can be called from any part of the object hierarchy. Every time a new coordinate is passed to this handler, the animation is incremented by one frame and shown at that location. The "Script Examples" section offers a number of examples that use commands you write yourself.

Making Icons

Icons are resources. Resources are an integral part of Macintosh programming. They are the bits and pieces that a Macintosh program needs to accomplish a job. Many of the parts of the Macintosh user interface are stored as resources. Dialog boxes, icons, and cursors are resources. Even the code that forms the basis of a program is stored in resources. This section concentrates on manipulating resources associated with icons. (See chapter 18 for more information about resources.)

Icons are stored in the resource fork of your stack, the Home stack, or Hyper-Card itself. To make your own icons or any of the ones in this chapter, you need to use a program that allows you to manufacture icons.

The most basic approach to making your own icons is to use the Apple utility application called ResEdit. This developer's tool is officially available from APDA and ships with many of the languages for the Macintosh. With ResEdit, you can (among other things) open the resource fork of any application or stack and examine or make new icons and cursors. To use ResEdit, double-click on the stack whose resources you want to see. This was done in Figure 7-15 to the stack Animation ideas v1.11. Double-clicking on ICON brings up the icons that are part of this stack.

You can then double-click on a particular icon to edit it or click on it once to select it and choose Get info... from the File menu to change the name and ID number of the icon. It is important not to choose an ID number that is already used by another icon. To avoid this, start with a large number, such as 2200, and number the icons sequentially. You can always renumber or rename an icon if there are conflicts. By using the Copy, Cut, and Paste commands from the Edit menu you can copy and move icons between stacks. The easiest way to move icons after they are made, however, is to use Steve Maller's XCMD called ResCopy. Like ResEdit, you can get this XCMD from most user groups or bulletin board services. It has a font/DA mover front end and is very easy to use.

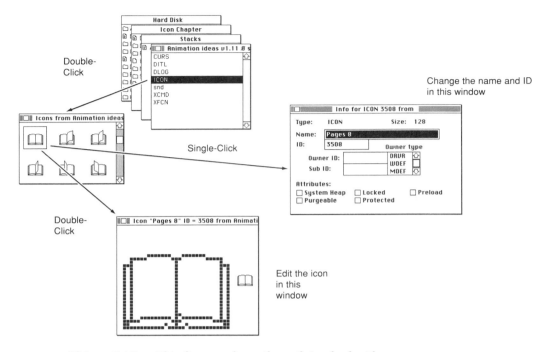

Figure 7-15. This diagram shows the path involved with editing an icon in ResEdit.

The desk accessory Icon Maker is available as shareware from many user groups. With this program, you can make icons in a graphics program, such as MacPaint, then capture the icons and save them to your stack.

A number of freeware stacks are full of icons available for your use. Robertson Smith's Stack Starter, available from ComputerWare and many user groups, has to be mentioned in this context. Even though it is not solely an icon stack, it shows you many possibilities for icons and icon animation. You can also use commercial programs, such as Icon Factory, to make, edit, and move icons.

Cursors

Now we move to cursors. Cursors, like icons, are resources and can be changed from a script. You need to learn about a few additional features, however, before you start changing cursors. Look at Figure 7-16, which shows HyperCard's standard cursors.

The beach ball cursor is in the Home stack, the browse hand is in the Hyper-Card application, and the watch, plus, crosshatch, and I-beam are in the system. All are available to you in HyperCard. You can store the cursors you make in your own stack, the Home stack, or your copy of the HyperCard application. Usually, it is best to put cursors into the resource fork of your own stack so that they are available when you give copies of your stack to others.

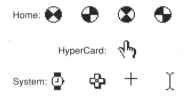

Figure 7-16.   The six standard HyperCard cursor icons: the beach ball, browse hand, watch, plus, crosshatch, and I-beam.

Differences Between Cursors and Icons

Cursors are part of the graphic interface of the Macintosh. They convey information. They are the mouse's representation on the screen. The browse hand is the primary way users interact with your HyperCard stack. It is a constant reminder that there are areas of the screen that could be pressed. The watch, on the other hand, is shown when you want the user to wait until a task is done. You can convey useful information about actions that are taking place by switching cursors.

Cursors and icons have several differences. Cursors are 16 pixels square; icons are 32 pixels square. Cursors have a mask and a hot point associated with them. These are discussed in the section on making your own cursors. The biggest difference between cursors and icons in HyperCard from a scripting point of view is that cursors require constant attention in your script. This is discussed next.

Cursor Switching

To change a cursor, you use the same set command you used to change icons:

```
set cursor to watch
```

With HyperCard version 1.2, you can refer to cursors by name or ID number, just as you do with icons. If you are using an older version of HyperCard, you have to refer to cursors by ID number. The set command is straightforward. There is a problem, however, when the handler containing the set cursor line is finished: the cursor changes to a browse hand. The only way to stop the cursor from switching back to a browse hand is to keep HyperTalk busy with a handler. One of the easiest ways to do this is to put the set cursor command into a repeat loop:

```
repeat forever
  set cursor to plus
  if the mouse is down then exit repeat
end repeat
```

There is an important drawback to this approach. Because HyperCard is executing a script, it no longer passes mouse clicks or acts upon keypresses. Your script must test for all relevant events and leave the `repeat` loop, if appropriate, to take care of the actions the user is requesting.

When you take over the cursor, you are responsible for tracking the user. Usually, this isn't difficult. Remember to give users an obvious way out of `repeat` loops, and trap all important keyboard commands and mouse clicks.

Taking over the cursor is becoming an important scriptor's tool. Just keep watching the user and you will have a useful new device.

The Hot Browse Hand

One of the perennial problems of HyperCard stacks is that a new user does not know where to click. One way to deal with this problem is to take over the cursor when the browse hand is over a button. To do this, you have to make a new cursor. Figure 7-17 shows several "hot" cursors.

Figure 7-17.   Of these hot cursors, my favorites are the mouse and the hand with the bull's-eye.

After you make the cursors, place this script into the stack script:

```
on mouseEnter
  setCursor
end mouseEnter

on mouseWithin
  setCursor
end mouseWithin

on setCursor
  if (word 2 of the name of the target) = "button" then
  -- Is it a button?
    put rect of target into shape
    repeat until the mouseLoc is not within shape
      set cursor to "hot hand"
      if the mouse is down then
        play "click"
        click at the mouseloc
        exit repeat
    else if the commandKey is down then exit setCursor
      end if
    end repeat
```

continued

```
    end if
end setcursor
```

This script switches to your hot cursor when the browse hand is over a button. This way, users know when they are over an area that is clickable. Remember to disable areas that are hot but don't do anything when clicked (for example, locked text fields).

This script is contingent on the `mouseEnter` and `mouseWithin` messages getting to the stack script. Therefore, if any buttons you use to activate the hot cursor contain a mouseEnter or mouseWithin handler, you have to pass the message up the object hierarchy. Do this by using the syntax

```
on mouseEnter
  -- various things you want done
  pass mouseEnter
end mouseEnter
```

If you don't explicitly pass the message from a handler that responds to it, the message will end at this point. This is the way you can disable the hot cursor. To disable a field or button, use the following:

```
on mouseEnter
end mouseEnter
on mouseWithin
end mouseWithin
```

When you take over a cursor like this, you have to check at least the basics, mouse clicks and the Command key. This was done in the previous script by placing an `if-then-else` within the `repeat` loop and checking explicitly for the Command keystroke (`if the commandKey is down`). You may also want to check for left and right arrows.

Hot Cursors in a Scrolling Field

In the preceding script, you only made sure that buttons responded to mouse clicks. But sometimes fields have to be hot too. For example, consider a browse-only stack that allows the user to click on any word for a hypertext link. You would want to leave the scroll bar free. The following stack script does this. Use it the way you did the preceding one. This time, however, you get the target size and subtract the part of it that is the scroll bar.

```
on setcursor
  put rect of target into shape
    -- this gives us H1, V1, H2 and V2 of the target we are in
  if the style of target is "scrolling"
    -- don't interfere with the scroll bar
  then
    put item 3 of shape into width
    put width - 15 into item 3 of shape
```

continued

```
      end if
      repeat until the mouseLoc is not within shape
        set cursor to "hand hot"

        if the mouse is down then
          play "click"
          click at the mouseloc
          exit repeat
        end if
      end repeat
    end setcursor
```

This script only invokes the hot cursor when the cursor is inside the scrolling field and not on the scroll bar. This makes scrolling less cumbersome. As it is, there is standard user interface feedback when a cursor is over a scrolling field: the browse hand turns into an arrow.

Making Cursors

Like icons, cursors are resources. And ResEdit, in addition to its use with icons, is a good way to make, move, rename, and renumber cursors. Unlike icons, cursors have a mask. Figure 7-18 shows a typical cursor and its mask.

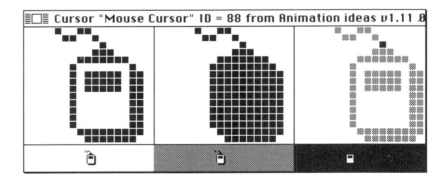

Figure 7-18.   A cursor and its mask as seen in ResEdit.

The mask allows the cursor to have opaque and transparent parts. For example, you might want a cursor that is a ring. With the appropriate mask, you can have a ring with a hole through the middle. You can also use the mask to make the cursor stand out against a dark background, as shown in Figure 7-19.

To make a new cursor, open the cursor resource of a stack that contains some cursors. Or you can copy a cursor from HyperCard, paste it into the stack's resource fork, then rename it from the Get info... dialog box. To edit the cursor, double-click on its image. You can then edit the cursor one pixel at a time.

After you have made your cursor using ResEdit, you can try it out while in ResEdit by choosing the appropriate menu. The menu is shown in Figure 7-20.

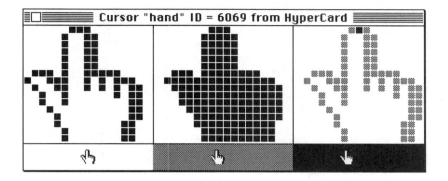

Figure 7-19. Using a mask, the hand (which would otherwise fill with the background pattern) stands out against a black or grey background.

Figure 7-20. When you edit a cursor or its mask, you will see a new menu in ResEdit. This menu lets you try out your cursor.

As was the case with icons, Steve Maller's ResCopy stack is by far the best way to move these resources after you have made them. With the ResCopy stack, you can rename, renumber, and try out the cursors that you move into your stack.

You can make icons act like cursors by showing them at the `mouseLoc` (the mouse location). This allows you to have bigger cursors and combine the animation techniques you learned with cursor actions. The advantage is you have 32x32 pixels to work with. The disadvantage is you have to do all the checking associated with `repeat` loops.

This script takes one more step in icon animation. You generate an icon that is animated (flies) and acts like a cursor. First, make a set of four icons like the ones in Figure 7-21.

After you have made the four bird icons and imported them into your stack, make a card button, called bird, and type this script into it:

```
on Freebird
  repeat
    set cursor to none
```

continued

```
repeat with j= 1 to 4
  put "wings" && j into whichicon
  set icon of me to whichicon
  show me at the mouseloc
  if the commandkey is down then exit Freebird
  if the top of me < 13 then exit to HyperCard
  if the mouse is down
  then
    hide me
    click at the clickloc
    exit Freebird
  end if
  wait 3
end repeat
end repeat
end FreeBird
```

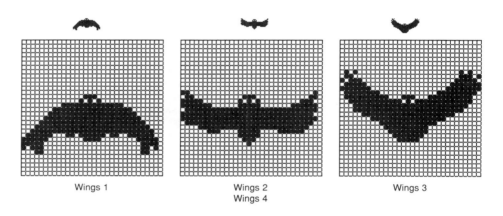

Wings 1

Wings 2
Wings 4

Wings 3

Figure 7-21. To make the bird fly, create four icons (wings 2 and wings 4 are identical).

This handler flaps the bird's wings and shows the bird at the mouse location. It can also trap for the Command key being down, mouse clicks, and any movement into the menu bar on a Macintosh Plus or SE. To activate it, you need the following script in the card:

```
on idle
  send Freebird to card btn "bird"
end idle

on openCard
  send Freebird to card btn "bird"
end openCard
```

This approach to crossing the border between icons and cursors won't work in all situations. Still, it gives you a chance to extend the interactions users can have with your stacks.

Script Examples

The following section introduces many different examples and contexts for using icons that change and move and shows many different scripting approaches. There are six long examples and a section on attention-getting buttons. These examples reinforce many of the ideas presented in this chapter. They can be used as attention-getting devices, the basis for games, or to tell stories. They are meant mostly to inspire you and give you a set of foundations to alter as needed.

Walking

In the Walking script, you can click anywhere on the screen and a pair of feet walk deliberately toward that spot. This is accomplished by using eight icons, two for each direction. These are shown in Figure 7-22.

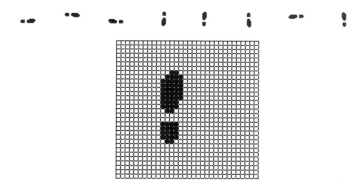

Figure 7-22. These icons are named for the direction they are heading and which foot they represent. For example, the enlarged one is left foot up.

The icons are named left foot left, right foot right, left foot up, and so on. This script is passed a list that consists of a beginning point and an end point. It then uses a standard step size and calculates the number of steps required to get from one point to the other. It then "walks" the appropriate number of steps across and down or across and up. These steps are combined with the sound of feet walking to enhance the effect.

```
on mouseUp
  put the loc of card button "left shoe" into stepper
  put "," after stepper
  put the clickloc after stepper
  walking stepper
end mouseUp

on walking where
  global waitTime
```

continued

```
-- First you extract the contents of the parameter for walking.
-- You could pass the parameters individually, but this way
-- you can build the origination and destination easily and
-- pass it to the "walking" command.
put item 1 of where into h1
put item 2 of where into v1
put item 3 of where into h2
put item 4 of where into v2

-- this initializes the stepsize and pause
put 20 into pause
put 23 into stepsize

-- this decides how many steps we'll take
put abs(trunc((h1-h2)/(2*stepsize))) into n
put abs(trunc((v1-v2)/(2*stepsize))) into m

-- this does the actual walking
-- this is the horizontal walking
-- first we check the direction
if h1 > h2
then
  put -stepsize into stepsize
  put "left" into direction
else
  put "right" into direction
end if

-- this sets the shoe's icons
set icon of card button "left shoe" to "left foot," && ¬
direction
set icon of card button "right shoe" to "right foot," && ¬
direction

-- then we walk
repeat n times
  add stepsize to h1
  show card button "right shoe" at h1,v1
  play "step"
  wait until the sound is "done"
  hide card button "left shoe"
  wait waitTime
  add stepsize to h1
  show card button "left shoe" at h1,v1
  play "step"
  wait until the sound is "done"
  hide card button "right shoe"
  wait waitTime
end repeat

-- this is the vertical walking
-- first we check the direction
put 23 into stepsize -- reset stepsize

if v1 > v2  then
  put -stepsize into stepsize
  put "up" into direction
```

continued

```
    else
      put "down" into direction
    end if


    -- this sets the shoe's icons
    set icon of card button "left shoe" to "left foot," && ¬
    direction
    set icon of card button "right shoe" to "right foot," && ¬
    direction


    repeat m times
      add stepsize to v1
      show card button "right shoe" at h1,v1
      play "step"
      wait until the sound is "done"
      hide card button "left shoe"
      wait pause
      add stepsize to v1
      show card button "left shoe" at h1,v1
      play "step"
      wait until the sound is "done"
      hide card button "right shoe"
      wait pause
    end repeat
    show card button "left shoe" at h1,v1
    show card button "right shoe" at h1,v1
    play "step"
    wait until the sound is "done"
end walking
```

Snake

The Snake script has several handlers. One of them—slithering horizontal,vertical—moves the snake to the position in the parameters horizontal and vertical and increments the animation by one frame. The handler named leave uses the first handler and plays a short song as the snake moves across the screen. The mouseUp handler resets the icon, plays several sounds that are different each time you click on the snake button, and uses the leave handler to move the snake off the screen. The sounds are digitized and represent the snake getting more and more agitated. The mouseDown handler changes the icon; this gives the impression that the snake is wiggling to move out of the way. The icons, named snakeR1 to snakeR6, are shown in Figure 7-23.

Figure 7-23. The six snake icons. Name them, from left to right, snakeR1 to snakeR6.

```
on mouseUp
  global times
  if times is empty then put 1 into times
  if times = 5 then put 1 into times
  if times = 1 then play "Hey"
  if times = 2 then play "Watch it"
  if times = 3 then play "Cut it out"
  if times = 4
  then
    play "that's it"
    leave
  end if
  add 1 to times
  set icon of me to "snakeR2"
end mouseUp


on mouseDown
  set icon of me to "snakeR1"
end mouseDown


on slithering horizontal,vertical
  global slither, snake, i
  if i = 6 then put 3 into i
  put "snakeR" & i into position
  set icon of snake to position
  show snake at horizontal,vertical
  add 1 to i
end slithering


on leave
  global snake, i
  put 3 into i
  put name of me into snake
  put the loc of me into location
  put item 1 of location into a
  put item 2 of location into b
  repeat 2 times
    play "bass guitar short" c3s s g3s c4s s g3s s a3e ¬
    a3e g2e a2e b2e
  end repeat
  play "bass guitar short" d3s s a3s d4s s a3s s b3e b3e ¬
  a2e b2e c3e
  play "bass guitar short" c3s s g3s c4s s g3s s a3e a3e ¬
  g2e a2e b2e
  play "bass guitar long" c3w
  repeat 30 times
    set cursor to none
    add 12 to a
    slithering a,b
    wait 1
  end repeat
  hide me
  wait 2 seconds
  show me at location
end leave
```

Helicopter

The Helicopter example shows how users can manipulate your animations. A helicopter is flown around the screen. The helicopter handler shows the helicopter at the mouse location and keeps the rotor spinning. Two buttons and one field are associated with this handler. The card buttons are called helicopter and I want to fly it. The card field, called A message, is filled with different messages to the user. Make five icons like the ones shown in Figure 7-24.

Figure 7-24.   These five helicopters form the basis of the animation. They can easily become part of a game.

Put the following handler in the card script:

```
on openCard
  send compfly to card btn "helicopter"
end openCard
```

Place the following handler in the I want to fly it card button:

```
on mouseUp
  fly
end mouseUp
```

Place these handlers in the Helicopter card button:

```
on fly
  put "Click the mouse to stop flying." ¬
  into card field "A message"
  hide card button "I want to fly it."
  repeat
    set cursor to none
    helicopter
    if the mouse is down
    then
      answer "Do you want to keep flying?" with yes or no
      if it is "no"
      then
        show card button "I want to fly it."
        put empty into card field "A message"
        send compfly to card btn "helicopter"
        exit fly
      end if
    end if
  end repeat
end fly
```

continued

```
on mouseEnter
  fly
end mouseenter

on helicopter
  repeat with j= 1 to 5
    put "Heli" && j into whichicon
    set icon of me to whichicon
    show me at the mouseloc
  end repeat
end helicopter

on compfly
  put "The helicopter is flying on its own." into ¬
  card field "message"
  repeat
    repeat with j= 1 to 5
      put "Heli" && j into whichicon
      set icon of me to whichicon
      if the mouse is down then
        put empty into card field "message"
        click at the clickloc
        exit compfly
      end if
      if the commandkey is down then exit compfly
    end repeat
  end repeat
end compfly
```

Strawberries

The following scripts combine changing icons with changing cursors. In the Straw-berries script, the user picks strawberries off the bush and moves them to another part of the screen. Figure 7-25 shows a large diagram of the strawberry icon and the original strawberry layout.

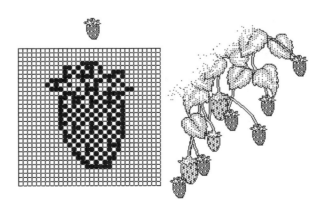

Figure 7-25. The strawberries should begin on a vine. To use the reset scripts, you need to make two identical icons.

Two icons are used. They are identical, except their ID numbers are 7831 and 7832. This allows you to differentiate between berries on the bush and those in other places. This is used to your advantage by the resetberries handler. Six card buttons are transparent buttons with berry 7832 as their icon.

```
on mouseEnter
  if icon of me is 7832 then
    put "show" &&  name of me && "at" && loc of me & ¬
    return after card field "locations"
    put "set icon of" && name of me && "to 7832" & ¬
    return after card field "reset icons"
    set icon of me to 7831
  end if
  repeat
    set cursor to 22
    show me at the mouseloc
    if the mouse is down then
      show me at the clickloc
      exit repeat
    end if
  end repeat
end mouseenter
```

The resetberries handler fills two invisible card fields, named locations and reset icons, to keep track of where the berries came from and where they need to be returned.

```
on resetberries
  repeat with n = 1 to 6
    do line n of card field "locations"
    if line n of card field "locations" is empty then
      exit repeat
    end if
  end repeat
  repeat with n = 1 to 6
    do line n of card field "reset icons"
    if line n of card field "reset icons" is empty then
      exit repeat
    end if
  end repeat
  put empty into card field "locations"
  put empty into card field "reset icons"
end resetberries

on closecard
  resetberries
end closecard
```

Bouncing Ball

The Bouncing Ball example is a ball that can be picked up and dropped anywhere on the screen. It bounces for a while, then stops. A formula computes the distance the ball should move each time through the `repeat` loop. By incrementing the distance geometrically, you mimic the impression of a ball falling. To get the special effect of the ball being squeezed on impact, you have to make the three icons shown in Figure 7-26.

Figure 7-26.   When the ball hits the floor, the script cycles through these icons.

```
on mouseEnter
  repeat
  set cursor to 22 -- an open hand cursor
  show me at the mouseloc -- drag the ball around
    if the mouse is down then
        set cursor to none -- hide cursor
      dropBall
      exit repeat
    end if
  end repeat
end mouseEnter

on dropBall
  global distance, floor, gravity, bounce
  -- "global" so you can set these variables elsewhere
  put 330 into floor
  put 1.2 into gravity
  put 1.3 into bounce
  put 4 into distance
  put item 1 of loc of me into h
  put item 2 of loc of me into v
  repeat
    repeat
      show me at h,v
      put distance^(gravity) into distance
      put round(v + distance) into v
      if v > floor then
        put floor into v
        exit repeat
      end if
    end repeat
    show me at h,v

    repeat with k = 1 to 3
      set icon of me to "ball" && k
    end repeat

    repeat with k = 2 down to 1
      set icon of me to "ball" && k
    end repeat
```

continued

```
      put distance/bounce into distance
      repeat
        put v into temp
        put distance^(1/gravity) into distance
        put round(v - distance) into v
        show me at h,v
        if abs(v - floor) < 10 then
          set icon of me to "ball 1"
          put floor into v
          show me at h,v
          exit dropBall
        end if
        if temp - v < 10 then
          exit repeat
        end if
      end repeat
  end repeat
end dropBall
```

Book in the Wind

The next animation is particularly useful if you want to reinforce the idea of pages turning as someone moves through your stack. Figure 7-27 shows the icons you have to create for this sequence.

Figure 7-27.   These eight icons create smooth animation. They are named pages 1, pages 2, and so on up to pages 8.

The script is set up so that if you click on the right-hand page, the animation flips the right-hand page. If you click on the left side, the left-hand page is flipped.

```
on mouseUp
  if item 1 of the clickloc < (item 1 of the loc of me) then
    repeat with n = 1 to 8
      set icon of me to "pages" && n
      wait 2
    end repeat
  else
    repeat with n = 8 down to 1
      set icon of me to "pages" && n
      wait 2
    end repeat
  end if
end mouseUp
```

The script puts the letters of the alphabet into a field below the icon of the flipping pages. You can tailor this animation to any use, even just going to the next or previous page.

To use this script, you need access to the eight book icons. After you make the icons, make a new button. Name it any uppercase letter *A* through *Z*. Put this script into the button:

```
on mouseUp
  global Number
  put the ChartoNum of the short name of me into Number
  if item 1 of the clickloc < (item 1 of the loc of me) then
    repeat with n = 1 to 8
      set icon of me to "pages" && n
      wait 2
    end repeat
    put -1 + Number into Number
  else
    repeat with n = 8 down to 1
      set icon of me to "pages" && n
      wait 2
    end repeat
    put 1 + Number into Number
  end if
  if Number < 65 then put 90 into number
  -- resetting the values
  if number > 90 then put 65 into number -- just in case
  put NumtoChar of Number into what
  set name of me to what
end mouseUp
```

This script takes advantage of the character-number conversion functions, charToNum and numToChar. Using these functions you can get the ASCII value of a character. After you have that number, you can manipulate the number and then turn it back into a character. The checking for out-of-bounds numbers may seem excessive, but you never know what someone will try to do to your stacks.

Attention-Getting Buttons

One of the best ways to use the techniques in this chapter is to get the user's attention. When you offer stacks to those who haven't worked with Macintosh computers or HyperCard, one problem is that it isn't always obvious where to click or what to do next. This section offers several attention-getting animations.

Flashing Star

You may want to call attention to a number of buttons on a card. One way to do this is to flash a star icon on all areas available for the user to click. Figure 7-28 offers some possible icons.

Figure 7-28.   You can use these four icons for the flashing star effect.

In this script, we assume you want to show the icon on every button of a background:

```
on star
  put number of buttons on this background into max
  repeat with n = 1 to max
    show card button "star" at loc of bg btn n
  end repeat
  hide cd btn "star"
end star
```

A more likely scenario is flashing the star across all the buttons until the user clicks on one. To accomplish this, put the following script in the card script:

```
on openCard
  put number of buttons on this bg into btnnumber
  send flashingstar btnnumber to card btn "star"
end openCard
```

Then put this script in the star card button:

```
on flashingstar max
  repeat
    show me at loc of bg button random(max)
  end repeat
end flashingstar
```

This second approach shows the star button randomly on background buttons. You can use this same approach for card buttons; just remember to bring the star icon to the front (Shift-Command- + accomplishes this easily).

Bullets

The following bullets work well in front of text. You might trigger them when you open a card. Figure 7-29 shows the five bullets used in this example.

Figure 7-29.   These bullets are named bullet 1 through bullet 5.

Put this script into the bullet:

```
on Fade
  repeat with n = 1 to 5
    put "bullet" && n into whichone
    set icon of me to whichone
    wait 3
  end repeat
  repeat with n = 5 downto 1
    put "bullet" && n into whichone
    set icon of me to whichone
    wait 3
  end repeat
end Fade
```

Then place the following in the card script:

```
on openCard
  send Fade to card button <the name of your bullet button>
end openCard
```

These fading bullets work well if you have a number of important points you want to highlight: you can trigger them one after another.

Arrows

Arrows are a wonderful set of icons for moving around the screen. They are not very flashy by themselves, but they are packaged with HyperCard. One use for moving arrows is to show the user directions on a map.

By showing an arrow icon at locations along the path of the map and switching it for left and right turns, you can trace any path across the screen. Figure 7-30 shows arrows being dragged along a line.

Figure 7-30.   By just dragging an arrow icon around the screen, you can trace a simple path.

Following are some script fragments that will help you build your own script. We assume the button is a card button and that you have named it arrow.

If you want to move the arrow from left to right:

```
repeat 10
  show card button "arrow" at x,y
  add 5 to x
end repeat
```

When you turn a corner, you will want to use a bent arrow. The ones that come with HyperCard are carriage return arrows. Using these as a basis, it is easy to make a set of arrows that turn left and right, and up and down, from any direction. See Figure 7-31. To change these icons, use the set command.

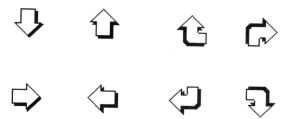

Figure 7-31. One of the first projects you may want to undertake when making your own icons is to make arrows that turn in all four directions. These can be used to direct someone's attention to any part of the screen.

Finally, you may want to leave a trail of grey arrows that show the path you want the user to take. To do this, it is convenient to make a second set of arrows that are grey. You can then use the `hide` and `show` commands to leave a trail of arrows.

Final Word

Animation with cursors and icons opens a new avenue for communication with the users of your stacks. Your stacks become alive, as phones ring off the hook, maps show where to go next, actions are reinforced by objects moving in predictable ways, and new information-filled cursors help stack users find their way around. Animation has great potential for attracting people who are unfamiliar with the Macintosh or HyperCard. It allows them to get a foothold quickly and learn the symbols you use in your stacks. For all these reasons and because it is fun, we encourage you to bring animated icons to your stack and hope the scripts in this chapter help build a foundation.

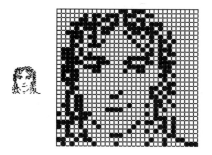

Figure 7-32. The author—A self portrait.

Animated Fonts

Mitchell Waite

Synopsis: Although icons are a great way to do animation in HyperCard, few developers know that fonts can provide even more flexibility for animation. It is possible to install custom images up to 254 x 127 pixels in each letter of the character set of a font and then use all the built-in HyperTalk commands and functions for manipulating characters to control these images.

This chapter shows how to make butterflies that sail across the screen, rabbits that hop, and guns that shoot bullets. You'll learn a primary advantage of fonts over card graphics—how to get over 32,000 graphic layers so you can have your images move behind and in front of other objects. This chapter reveals tricks for making transparent fonts opaque, ways to make animation movies, and much more. Flipping cards and icons are compared to fonts for speed, and using the Cairo font for special images is explored. Details are revealed for using font editors and for inserting images into a stack so that HyperCard can access them. Finally, a complete sprite-oriented script is presented that allows your font images to move on predetermined paths, with specific velocities, accelerations, and even allows the addition of sounds.

Animated Fonts

32,000 Graphic Layers Await You

Animation means to present images that give the impression of movement. The movement can be a static object with moving parts, such as a person standing still while juggling grapefruits, or the movement can encompass a moving object, such as a lemon pie sailing through the air. You can combine both techniques to produce a moving object that changes shape as it moves, glides, or bounces across the screen.

Our Journey

This chapter is divided into two sections. The first explores how fonts are used to produce arcade-quality animation with HyperTalk. You see how to use the graphic characters built into every Macintosh and the techniques for font animation using put and get in fields. Some simple sprite-oriented functions for manipulating font images and a sprite language are developed. In the second section, you create custom fonts with the font editor and expand the power of the sprite function data structure to include rotation of character frames, start and ending positions, and velocity and direction commands. Beware: by the end of this chapter, your Hyper-Talk stacks may appear to be full of graphic objects hopping, skipping, flittering, crawling, and sailing across the screen in unpredictable ways.

Card-Flipping Animations

The most obvious way to do animation in HyperTalk is to rapidly flip through cards, each of which contains a graphic frame of the multicard animation movie. Clip art animations are available from companies such as MacroMind. The main advantage of card flipping is that the entire card area can contain graphics. This large area allows any kind of graphic action or effect to be simulated . . . if you have the time to draw lots of details. (Other forms of HyperCard animation limit the area where you can draw to a small square.)

The main disadvantage of card flipping is that it requires the tedious creation of successive frames of graphics. It is also slow and better suited to a slide-show type of animation that can be non-fluid. Furthermore, the most visually exciting animations make many changes between frames. This usually requires precise alignment between successive images, and HyperCard has only minimal cut-and-paste tools to make this registration creation process easy.

A not so obvious advantage to using cards for animations is that card pixels are compressed by a special algorithm so that they don't require as much memory as a noncompressed graphic. You will see that storing images in fonts gives you advantages over card flipping, but does not have this compression ability.

For simple animations that involve only a few frames (5 to 25) and for animations with elaborate differences between successive images (for example, a slide show), card flipping is a good choice. HyperCard's built-in visual effects are designed for this type of card-flipping animation. Look at the Cowboy animation in chapter 10, "Synching Sight and Sound," to see how this is done.

Icon Animations

You can also do animation with buttons by using custom icons in a 32 x 32 bit image to make up the frames of the animation. Because HyperCard's active card area is the entire screen, 512 x 343 pixels, the small image area of a button limits its use to small objects (about a half-inch square on a Macintosh screen).

You can group collections of icons to make a larger object so that the buttons become 32 x 32 pixel tiles, but this is tedious because you have to visualize your image in tiles instead of as a whole. You also must purchase a special *icon editor* to make custom icons. You can edit icons with Apple's ResEdit program, available from APDA. ResCopy, a stack-based external command (XCMD), lets you move and view icons from stack to stack, but it can't edit icons. Commercial, HyperCard-stack-based, icon editor products, such as Icon Factory from HyperPress, are on the market. Some free public domain icon creators allow you to use a paint program to make the icon and then attach it to your stack. A useful desk accessory is Icon Maker, also available on CompuServe. With Icon Maker, you can copy an icon from any paint program, choose its resource ID number, then save it in any program, such as your stack. Take a look at chapter 7, "Animated Icons and Cursors," for what you can do with buttons for animation.

Font Animations

After cards and buttons, a third way to do animation in HyperCard is with font characters. To animate with font characters, you must use another utility tool, a *font editor*. You use this editor to open, copy, and modify Macintosh font resources. Like icon resources, font resources can be attached to your stack, card, Home stack, or even HyperCard itself. (Attaching font resources to HyperCard is not recommended by Apple. Also, there is some talk that the Home stack is not a good place to store a stack's resources because if you want to share your stack with others, you must also supply them with your Home stack. One suggestion is to create a special "resource" stack and have it in the search path before the Home stack. Its only job would be to hold global resources for your stack application.) Many commercial font editing tools are available, including Fontastic Plus, a powerful program for editing and viewing the characteristics of fonts. Use Apple's ResEdit to edit fonts, but exercise caution: it is a crude tool compared to a custom font utility and is more suited to minor changes. It is almost useless on large images. With the ResCopy XCMD, you can move fonts between stacks and applications, but you can't edit them.

Font/DA Mover is an application from Apple for moving fonts and desk accessories from one application to another or from Apple's font "suitcase" format to an application and back. Thus, you can use Font/DA Mover to move fonts created with Fontastic into stacks. You have to hold the Option key when you click on the Open button in Font/DA Mover; otherwise, Macintosh documents won't show up. Fontastic Plus does not allow you to move fonts into documents because it can generally mess up printing, but this does not apply to HyperCard stacks.

About Fonts

Fonts are nothing more than collections of pixels. The pixels are stored as bit maps, with each pixel in the map represented as a single bit in an on or off condition. When a single bit is turned on, the pixel becomes white. When it is off, the pixel is black. The fonts are stored in disk file resources and loaded into memory when needed.

The font organizes pixels into groups that have been assigned to a particular character in the standard set of letters and symbols that make up the Macintosh character set. Each letter and character has its own bit map. The Macintosh set has 256 characters, many of which are accessible with the Option and Shift keys. The 256 bit maps in a font share common traits: a common maximum height (the font height) and a common design element, such as Geneva compared to Chicago. The font design may be with or without serifs and is usually optimized for a certain look: the Chicago font was designed for easy reading and short commands; Monaco is a typewriter-like font. The width of individual characters in the various fonts may vary because most are proportionately spaced fonts. Monaco and Courier are monospaced fonts (all characters are the same width).

Fonts, like icons and sounds, are stored as resources. They can be stored in the System file, in an application, or in a stack. When a font is requested, the Macintosh looks for it in the stack (if in HyperCard) or in the application, then finally in the System file itself. Fonts can be resized by algorithms in the Macintosh. But when these algorithms are used, the spacing of the pixels is no longer proportional and the pixels have a "spattered paint" look to them.

A *font family* is a collection of sizes of font resources for a particular font. Associated with each font resource is a *fond* resource. This is a special resource that describes the overall characteristics of the font family.

There is a lot to know about fonts and how they work. To learn more about fonts, buy a commercial program that has an excellent manual. Also see *Inside Macintosh, Volumes I through V.*

If you are designing a Postscript font, things are more complex. These fonts are not bit maps and are resized using mathematical algorithms by the PostScript interpreter built into the LaserWriter printer—with fantastic results.

Fonts for Animation: Frame Holders

As we said, a font is nothing more than a "holder" of bit maps. Each of the 256 characters of the Apple character set (keyboard and Option keys included) has its own bit map in the font that is displayed automatically when you enter a character code into a field or type it with the paint tools. For example, suppose that you type the letter *a* in the field with the font called myFont. Macintosh looks at the position *a* always occupies in myFont, finds the bit map for the letter *a* in that font, and displays that in the field.

With a font editor, you can replace the letter with a custom bit map made in MacPaint or a similar paint program. It could look like an *a* or it could look like a banana; the Macintosh doesn't know the difference. And because the font can be a custom one that you add to HyperCard, you don't mess up the existing fonts.

Think of each character of a font as a pointer to a movie frame. There are 256 frames, each corresponding to a character in the Macintosh character set. If the animation is run at 24 frames per second, using all 256 characters corresponds to about 10 seconds of a movie. Although this doesn't seem like much, this number can be adequate with the creative use of repeating patterns.

Using a commercial font editor, you can open a font resource such as Geneva, change its name to something like myGeneva, alter its specifications so it is a different size, and add your own paint images. You would then idr Font/DA Mover to attach the new font resource to your stack. Then you start your stack, create a field, open its font information box, and change the font to the name of your new font resource, myGeneva. Now, typing a character corresponding to an image in your new font inserts that image in the field. Figure 8-1 shows a screen dump of some images in a custom font for *The Waite Group's Tricks of the HyperTalk Masters* stack. You also can store very small images in the stack, as you will see in the next section.

The Macintosh has limits to the size of the font it can hold in a bit map (127 bits tall and 254 bits wide). Because that is much larger than an icon, you can control larger images. It is like having 32 icon tiles connected in a 4 x 8 icon pattern, as shown in Figure 8-2.

You can also group fonts by joining adjacent transparent fields, thus making a larger picture. As shown in Figure 8-3, this can increase your field image to 254 x 254 pixels, which is about half the card area. Four characters would fill the screen.

32,000 Virtual Graphic Layers

There are trade-offs to using fonts for holding bit maps. The main one is that pixels in fonts are not compressed like card graphics in HyperCard, so they can increase the size of your stacks drastically.

A benefit to using fonts this way is that you get an equivalent theoretical maximum of more than 32,000 graphic layers. (The value is from the *Apple Scripting Guide*.) Contrast this with the two layers of card graphics. Another benefit of using fonts and fields for animation is that you can use HyperTalk's commands for making fields visible and invisible (show and hide). Visual effects, though slow, can be used on these virtual graphics.

In Figure 8-4, the font holds a large bit map that we used when experimenting with the opening screen of *The Waite Group's Tricks of the HyperTalk Masters* stack. An advantage of having custom images in the font instead of on the card is that you can easily hide and show them regardless of the card location. This makes visual effects easier to control. Also, because of the 32,000 virtual graphic layers, you can show and hide many different-sized graphic images on the same card with visual effects.

Figure 8-1. Several large objects stored in the custom font characters 0 through 6.

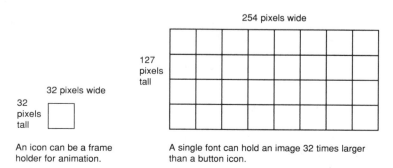

Figure 8-2. A font can hold an image 127 pixels tall and 254 pixels wide.

254 pixels wide

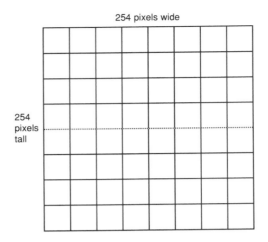

254
pixels
tall

Figure 8-3.   Combining two characters of a field for a larger image.

One drawback is that if you try to print these fields on a LaserWriter, the original character is substituted from the built-in fonts, assuming you have Substitute Fonts enabled. If you turn this off, the actual bit map image will be printed.

Figure 8-4.   This example was made using two characters in a font set 127 points tall. The entire image was scanned with the Apple Scanner, divided in half with SuperPaint, and installed in the font with Fontastic Plus.

Another advantage of using fonts to hold images is that you can eliminate "dummy" graphic cards (which do nothing) in your stack. For example, often, when you browse through a stack, you will find a "dead" card that serves no purpose other than to display graphics when the stack starts. If you are a developer moving tricks between stacks, this can cause problems because every time you manually go to the stack, the opening script will try to go to the dummy card. So you have to build code to avoid that. Second, when you use bit maps, getting an opening graphic on one card to register with the background on another card is difficult. You can't move your image around as easily as you can move a button or a field holding a graphic. See Table 8-1 for a comparison of the use of fonts, icons, and cards for animation.

Table 8-1.   Comparing Icons, Fonts, and Cards for Animation

Technique	Icons	Fonts	Cards
Easy for users to copy to their stacks	Yes	Yes	No[a]
You can create "frames" from character arrays	No	Yes	No
Requires a font editor such as Fontastic Plus for customizing	No	Yes	No
Requires ResEdit, ResCopy, or Icon Factory for customizing	Yes	No	No
Fastest technique for flipping frames	2d	1st	3d
Provides holder for images so arrays actually contain graphics	No	Yes	No
Many subtle advantages due to mapping of characters and images	No	Yes	No
All commands and functions available for frames of animation also available for images	No[b]	Yes	No
Visual effects can be used for enhancement	No	Yes	Yes
Most efficient storage	2d	3d	1st
Almost unlimited layers of graphic images	Yes	Yes	No

[a]Moving cards from one stack to another is tricky because you also take the card's background with it, which you may not want.
[b]Although you can build similar frame techniques using buttons and cards, much of Hyper-Talk's string syntax (such as *line*, *word*, and *character*) is lost.

Flipping Fonts Versus Flipping Icons

One of the more relevant points for HyperTalk scriptors when comparing the use of icons versus fonts for animation (flipping frames in particular) is that fonts can be flipped faster than icons. For example, using the techniques in chapter 16, "Benchmarking HyperTalk," setting the icon of a button takes 11.5 ms on an accelerated SE, but putting a character into a field takes only 8.2 ms on the same SE. Thus, it can be 30 percent faster to use fonts instead of icons for image flipping.

In both these tests, the identifier for the button and field was a cardinal number (for example, `cd btn 2` and `cd fld 2`). When the reference to the object is by name instead of number or ID, the processing times become more equal and approach 12 ms per operation. A stock Macintosh SE is about half as fast as the speeds in Table 8-2, so it takes about 16 ms per changing frame.

What is the end effect of these times? For non-flickering animation, you need about 1/20 of a second between frames, which means you have 50 ms per frame switch before flicker is visible. After a frame switch from HyperTalk, you have about 50 ms minus 16 ms, or 34 ms, to process coordinates and so on before you have to switch another frame of the animation.

Table 8-2.   Speed of Changing Custom Fonts Versus Icons

Command	Milliseconds per Operation
set icon of cd btn	11.5
put char into cd fld	8.2
put 1 char	6.5
put into	6.4
put before	7.2
words in	16.9
offset	14.6

Note: Speeds are on a Macintosh SE with a Radius 16 MHz accelerator. A stock SE is about half as fast.

Subtle Advantages of Fonts as Images

When you use fonts as images, all of HyperTalk's commands for manipulating characters are available for manipulating your images. You can use `put` to make the image appear anywhere in a field. You can use the `before` and `after` optional modifiers to manipulate and display individual images stored in the field.

You can use expressions such as `the number of chars in fld Rabbit` to find how many images are in the field. You can use expressions such as `put last char of cd fld Rabbit before first char of cd fld Rabbit` to move images. Try that with icons! You will see other advantages when the scripts are described.

Gallery Animation with Fonts

Let's learn how the simplest font animation can be accomplished without using any custom fonts. We are going to do something a little different here. Instead of dumping the ultimate elegant script on you all at once, we are going to start with a simple script that does bare minimum font movement. We will build functions that handle the tasks needed for font animation. To add more features to our animation, we will build up the function with more capability. Thus, while you learn about animation, you will learn about script development. Along the path, you will see decisions based on design criteria, such as making all handlers as general and generic as possible so they can be shared and placed in a higher object hierarchy.

The Shift-Option- ˜ Special Character

The simple way to do font animation is to take advantage of the many built-in special graphic characters in the various fonts of the Macintosh. Each font has a special graphic character assigned to the font location for the combination Option, Shift, and Tilde (˜) keys. The key combination can be typed between quotation marks in a HyperTalk command, or you can use the `numToChar(217)` function to access the Option-Shift-Tilde character.

Table 8-3 shows some of these special characters in various point sizes for the Geneva and Monaco fonts. If you are writing stacks, Geneva, Chicago, and Monaco are the only fonts you can be sure are on every Macintosh. You can't expect a full complement of font sizes for these fonts either. Because 9-, 10-, and 12-point Geneva are required for the operating system, these are the safest group to use.

Table 8-3.   Special Characters and Font Sizes in Geneva and Monaco[a]

Point Size	Geneva	Monaco
9	⌨	≡
10	💻	
12	🐇	♪
14	⌂	
18	🐑	
24	🐇	
36	🐑	
48	🐇	

[a]All use numtochar(217) for the character.

If a character in a different font size is required, the best solution is to copy that point size into your stack with ResCopy or ResEdit. Then all copies made with your stack will have the desired font.

Another set of graphic characters, shown in Table 8-4, is available in the Chicago font. These are not as useful for animation because they are limited to items with special meanings, such as Command key symbols or the Macintosh apple, but you can use these symbols for indicating keys in help cards.

The graphic characters available in location 217 (the Option-Shift-Tilde character) can serve in many different applications. (For a complete discussion of using the ASCII and optional characters, see *The Waite Group's HyperTalk Bible.*) Here are a few ideas.

The Geneva rabbits and sheep work well in games in which you move an animal. You also can use the sheep to indicate a gentle version of something and the rabbit to indicate speed. For example, when the rabbit moves or jumps up, this could indicate a high-speed mode. The small picture of a Macintosh in the 10-point Geneva

Table 8-4. **Special Characters in Chicago Font**

How to Access	Character	Description
numtochar(17)	⌘	command cloverleaf
numtochar(18)	✓	check mark
numtochar(19)	◆	diamond
numtochar(20)	🍎	apple with bite

font size could be used in games of chance that keep score with objects instead of numbers. Or use it to form the bars of a graph. The raven could be used with something musical, such as the sound of a bell ringing or when you quote from Edgar Allen Poe's poem "Nevermore." The Monaco font has a candle and a hatch mark in the 12-point and 9-point sizes, respectively.

Gallery Font: Rotating the Rabbit

The first trick in this chapter involves graphic character 217 in 12-point Geneva, the rabbit. We will develop a script that moves the rabbit across the screen horizontally, as in a shooting gallery. This could be the basis of a game, or it could be used to attract someone to your opening card. Figure 8-5 shows the card for this trick, taken from the Tricks stack.

For this example, we need to fill a horizontal field with several rabbit characters, each separated by several spaces. Because the rabbits face left, we write a script that places the first character in the field after the last character of the field. Then we delete the first character, which effectively makes all characters (rabbits and spaces) shift to the left. With four spaces between every rabbit, each time a space character is deleted the rabbits move in increments of a single 12-point Geneva space (which is thin). When a rabbit character is actually moved, however, the entire group jerks a bit because the rabbit is wider than the space, but it is hardly noticeable.

The following script accomplishes the shift left movement. It forms the basis of our entire animation routine.

```
repeat until the mouseClick
  put first char of cd fld fld_name ¬
  after cd fld fld_name
  delete first char of cd fld fld_name
end repeat
```

The first statement inside the `repeat` loop puts the first character of the card field called fld_name behind the last character of the same field. The second statement deletes the first character of the field. We use the `mouseClick` to signal the end of the loop because it is simple. Note that the use of the underscore character is nonstandard, but legal.

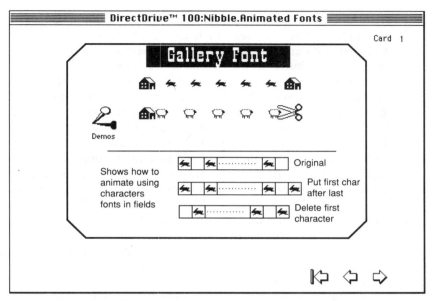

Figure 8-5. The Gallery Font trick uses graphic characters built into every Macintosh.

But how do we fill the card field with the correct number of special rabbit characters and spaces? In keeping with the rules of trying to generalize scripts, the goal is to write a handler that we can use to set up any of the various characters, in different fonts, at different locations, and with different field widths. Such a handler allows us to stretch the field to span the whole card and adjusts the number of characters to fill it with. This is best implemented as a HyperTalk handler with parameters.

Create a handler called `set_gallery` to set up the fonts as follows:

```
on set_gallery char_n, fld_name, fnt_name, fnt_size, n_spaces
  put empty into cd fld fld_name
  set the textfont of cd fld fld_name to fnt_name
  set the textsize of cd fld fld_name to fnt_size
  put the width of cd fld fld_name into w
  put trunc( w / fnt_size / 2 ) + 1 into numchars
  -- make blank part -- customized for each font and char
  repeat with i = 1 to n_spaces
    put space after blank
  end repeat
  -- fill up the field now (field can be any width)
  repeat with i = 1 to numchars
    put char_n & blank after cd fld fld_name
  end repeat
end set_gallery
```

To call the handler, you would have this line in the script:

```
set_gallery numtochar(217), Gallery, Geneva, 12, 4
```

This function sends the special character you want to use (in this example, number 217) to the actual `set_gallery` handler, along with the field name (in this example, Gallery), the name of the font (here, Geneva), the font size (12), and the number of spaces to put between the special characters.

The `set_gallery` handler first puts `empty` into the card field to clear it of any previous characters. Then it uses `set` commands to set the `textfont` and `textsize` properties of the field as specified by the parameters it was called with.

The next group of statements compute how many characters to put in the field based on the field's width in pixels and the average width of a space for the font in use. Unfortunately, this formula is not completely accurate because the fonts are proportional, which means the width in pixels for each character is not constant. The formula is a good first approximation, however, and works for our range of fonts.

The first `repeat` loop builds the intervening blank spaces, and the last `repeat` loop fills the field with the actual rabbit characters. You may have to adjust this routine for other font sizes.

You now have enough information to build the complete rabbit script:

```
on mouseUp
  set_gallery numtochar(217), Gallery, Geneva, 12, 4
    -- set up the field
  move gallery -- move the chars
end mouseUp

on move fld_name -- this moves the characters
  repeat until the mouseClick
    put first char of cd fld fld_name ¬
    after cd fld fld_name
    delete first char of cd fld fld_name
  end repeat
end move

on set_gallery char_n, fld_name, fnt_name, fnt_size, n_spaces
  put empty into cd fld fld_name
  set the textfont of cd fld fld_name to fnt_name
  set the textsize of cd fld fld_name to fnt_size
  put the width of cd fld fld_name into w
  put trunc( w / fnt_size / 2 ) + 1 into numchars
  -- make blank part -- customized for each font and char
  repeat with i = 1 to n_spaces
    put space after blank
  end repeat
  -- fill up the field now (field can be any width)
  repeat with i = 1 to numchars
    put char_n & blank after cd fld fld_name
  end repeat
end set_gallery
```

Expanding Rabbits to Sheep

Suppose that you want to add another animal, such as the sheep, moving in the opposite direction of the rabbits? Because our custom handler is set up to allow you

to change the font size easily, you can generate a sheep by simply changing the `fnt_`
`size` parameter passed to `set_gallery` to 18 points. The handler automatically calculates the correct number of sheep. Reduce the number of spaces for the sheep
because they are bigger characters than the 12-point rabbit font.

The sheep are facing right, so they should move to the right. Because the
movement of the rabbits is controlled by a custom handler, it is easy to add a few
statements to the `repeat` loop so that it handles moving right to left, as well as left to
right. In fact, by creating a new parameter for the `move` handler, you can move
characters in two fields; one set that moves to the right and one set that moves to the
left. We create two parameters for the `move` routine. The `fld_name2` parameter
holds the name of an optional second field you want to animate. The `direction`
parameter holds the direction you want to move the images in either field: left, right,
or both. Here is the modified handler:

```
on move fld_name, fld_name2, direction
  -- this moves the characters
  if direction = "left" then
    repeat until the mouseClick
      put first char of cd fld fld_name after cd fld fld_name
      delete first char of cd fld fld_name
    end repeat
  end if

  if direction = "right" then
    repeat until the mouseClick
      put last char of cd fld fld_name before cd fld fld_name
      delete last char of cd fld fld_name
    end repeat
  end if

  if direction = "both" then
    repeat until the mouseClick
      put first char of cd fld fld_name after cd fld fld_name
      delete first char of cd fld fld_name

      put last char of cd fld fld_name2 before cd fld fld_name2
      delete last char of cd fld fld_name2
    end repeat
  end if
end move
```

To move the sheep to the right, for example, you would call the handler like
this:

```
set_gallery numtochar(217), gallery2, Geneva, 18, 3
move gallery2, 0,"right"
```

The `if-then` statements are triggered by the `right` parameter. Thus, the `re-`
`peat` inside the second `if-then` operates until the user clicks. This `repeat` loop, the
opposite of the one that moves the images to the left, shows how easy it is to manipulate fonts.

The complete script for moving the rabbits, then the sheep, then both the rabbits and the sheep from the same button follows:

```
on mouseUp
  -- This shows off font animation and reveals how to use
  -- functions effectively.
  -- Set up rabbits pointing left
  -- The following function sends a char to animate (217), the
  -- name of the field containing it (gallery), the font type
  -- (Geneva), the font size (12), and the number of spaces
  -- between the animated character (4)

  set the name of me to "Demo Sheep" -- change button's name
  set the hilite of me to true
  -- set up the field details
  set_gallery numtochar(217), gallery, Geneva, 12, 4
  move gallery, 0,"left" -- call the main move loop

  set the name of me to Rabbits/Sheep
  set_gallery numtochar(217), gallery2, Geneva, 18, 3
  move gallery2, 0,"right"

  set the name of me to "Stop Demo"
  set_gallery numtochar(217), gallery2, Geneva, 18, 3
  move gallery, gallery2, "both"
  set the hilite of me to false
  set the name of me to "Demo Rabbits" -- change button's name
end mouseUp

on move fld_name, fld_name2, direction
  -- this moves the characters
  if direction = "left" then
    repeat until the mouseClick
      put first char of cd fld fld_name after cd fld fld_name
      delete first char of cd fld fld_name
    end repeat
  end if

  if direction = "right" then
    repeat until the mouseClick
      put last char of cd fld fld_name before cd fld fld_name
      delete last char of cd fld fld_name
    end repeat
    -- wait until the mouseclick -- lets you watch movement
  end if

  if direction = "both" then
    repeat until the mouseClick
      put first char of cd fld fld_name after cd fld fld_name
      delete first char of cd fld fld_name

      put last char of cd fld fld_name2 ¬
      before cd fld fld_name2
```

continued

```
            delete last char of cd fld fld_name2
        end repeat
    end if
end move


on set_gallery char_n, fld_name, fnt_name, fnt_size, n_spaces
    put empty into cd fld fld_name
    set the textfont of cd fld fld_name to fnt_name
    set the textsize of cd fld fld_name to fnt_size
    put the width of cd fld fld_name into w
    put trunc( w / fnt_size / 2 ) + 1 into numchars
    -- make blank part -- customized for each font and char
    repeat with i = 1 to n_spaces
      put space after blank
    end repeat
    -- fill up the field now (field can be any width)
    repeat with i = 1 to numchars
      put char_n & blank after cd fld fld_name
    end repeat
end set_gallery
```

Using the Cairo Font

Two other sources of font images are the Cairo and Mobile fonts, developed by Apple as part of the standard font families. Unfortunately, because Apple's System code uses a lot of disk space, little room is left for numerous fonts. Thus, Apple has not been providing the Cairo font or other fancy fonts in releases of its System software. If you can locate the Cairo font, you are in luck because it is loaded with images and can be installed easily in your stack.

You can use the Key Caps desk accessory to examine any font installed in your System. In Figure 8-6, the Key Caps desk accessory was used to present the images for the keys of the Cairo font in its regular and shifted conditions. As you can see, some images are similar to those in the Art Ideas stack provided with HyperCard, except they are stored in a font instead of a paint layer. These images work well for games, indicators, screen presentations, and so on. For example, a field button could be marked with a turtle (for slow) or a musical note (to indicate a sound). There are images of furniture for designing a floor plan, electronic symbols for making schematics, and many more. Note that fields must be locked to work like buttons (the field's locktext property must be true).

Improving the Gallery Game

Any good gallery game must have a way to shoot or knock down the moving targets. One idea is to use the pistol in character *K* of the Cairo font. Bullets can be constructed by using the Option-8 bullet character from the 10-point Geneva font. See Figure 8-7. (You can shoot the bullets by showing and hiding the field they are in. Imagine doing this with buttons.)

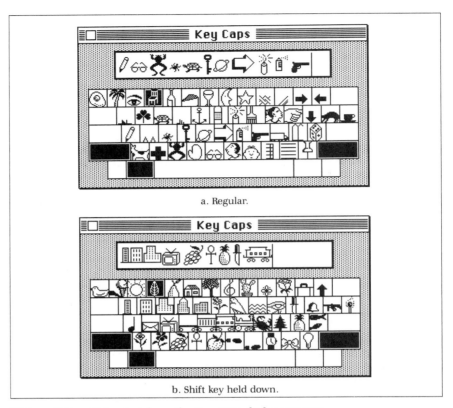

Figure 8-6.   Cairo font from the Key Caps desk accessory.

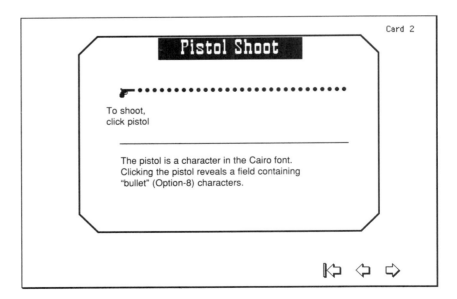

Figure 8-7.   Cairo font for the pistol is character *K*. The dark circles are the
Option-8 bullet character in 10-point Geneva.

Recall that the font of a button can be set (it is a property). Thus, you could make a button with the pistol image, if the pistol is available in the font. If you would rather use a button to hold the font image, use a statement such as:

```
set the textfont of button "name" to myBigMonaco
```

Use `textsize` to set the height of the font, and you have a button containing a special font image. In other words, the button's name would be *K*, which would show up as the pistol in the button.

Create a new field, set its name to bullet, set its style to transparent, set its font to 10-point Geneva, and drag it so it looks like the bullet field in Figure 8-7. Now put alternating Option-8 characters and space characters (Option-8, space, Option-8, space, and so on) into the field until it is full.

Next, create another new field, set its style to transparent, and set its font to 18-point Cairo. Put a *K* pistol character into it. Drag the transparent field to the left of the bullets, as shown in Figure 8-7.

Now set the `locktext` of the field from its information box. Enter the following script into the pistol field:

```
on mouseDown
   show cd fld bullet
   wait 5 ticks -- controls how long bullets are shown
   hide cd fld bullet
   -- your script can continue to do things here while the
   -- sound is running
end mouseDown
```

The script runs each time you click on the pistol. The card field containing the bullets is shown, HyperCard waits ⁵⁄₆₀ second, and the field is hidden. This gives the effect of the bullets emerging from the end of the gun. If you would like to synchronize sound with the bullets, see chapter 10, "Synching Sight and Sound."

Independent Movement

In the gallery game, you probably want the movement of the rabbits and sheep to be independent of the firing of the pistol. A button or card script could start the gallery. Then, when the pistol is fired by a `mouseDown`, the bullets are shown. You could make the pistol follow the mouse and make the starting location of the bullets dependent on where the pistol was clicked.

One more thing. You may have wondered how to get a pistol that is pointing to the right to shoot projectiles at objects moving horizontally above it. Try creating a vertical strip so the animals move up and down. (Hint: you might have to put a return character after each animal.)

You can do many other tricks with the Cairo font. How about a spider that pops into view if you set a dangerous preference or just as a cute technique in a game? You could put the spider from the Cairo font in a field. A single hanging string web could be made from several standard | characters in a long vertical field. If the line height of the field is made small enough, the bars will overlap, giving you a MacPaint-like line that you can pop up with the convenience of a field. Don't forget that you can also change the style of font images. You can have outlined rabbits, underlined sheep, bold pineapples, and even italic light bulbs.

Creating and Using Custom Fonts for Animation

You can broaden your abilities as a stack developer by using custom fonts. Custom (or homemade) fonts can be up to 127 points tall and 254 points wide and can contain any standard MacPaint image. The use of fonts for animation poses some interesting problems. First, to simulate movement, you must present alternate images to the viewer and each must blend into the next. Second, the most useful font is one that you cannot only use for frames, but also move around on the screen while flipping fonts to simulate flight, walking, and so on.

One of the first problems for the animator is finding a source of animation clip art. The best we have found is Clip Animation from MacroMind (1028 West Wolfram, Chicago, Illinois, 60657), who also make VideoWorks. We adapted the graphics for this chapter from some of that clip art. Unfortunately, animation clip art is not as available as static clip art. And HyperCard has no built-in animation clip art. Keep your animations simple or find an artist because making animation frames is tedious and difficult. For our first example, we borrowed the butterfly.

Using Font Resources

To begin creating custom fonts, you need a font editor. We chose the Fontastic Plus editor (from Altsys, 720 Avenue F, Suite 108, Plano, Texas, 75074), which has most of the features you need. Although we assume you understand the basic technology of fonts, we review some basics. Read the manual that comes with Fontastic Plus because it is a concise overview of font metrics.

Recall that fonts are resources that can be "attached" to a stack, an application (not recommended), for example, HyperCard, or part of your System file. Fonts also can be stored in special font files maintained by desk accessories such as SuitCase II (from Fifth Generation Systems, Inc., 11200 Industriplex Boulevard, Baton Rouge, Louisiana, 70809). These off-load the System file and provide easier font management for the user. Regardless of the font's location, the font editor opens up the font into a MacPaint-like interface, where each letter can be examined, changed, scaled, and so on. Fonts can also be copied, moved, and manipulated between Macintosh files.

When you first open the font editor, a window is displayed with a scrolling list box like the one in Figure 8-8. You can see the various font resources that are available, an example of images from the font, and the overall characteristics of the font. In this example, the selected font is one we created called myBigMonaco. It has a point size of 18 points (this appears in the text information box in HyperCard and other programs). The font's ID number is 210 and its size is 9090 bytes. (All fonts have a unique ID between 0 and 511.) The images of the men are characters that have been substituted for the letters *a* through *k* of this particular font.

The details of the font, including its name,
point size, ID number, and size.

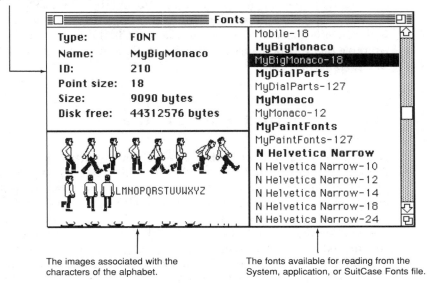

The images associated with the
characters of the alphabet.

The fonts available for reading from the
System, application, or SuitCase Fonts file.

Figure 8-8. The Fonts window for the font editor shows the
custom font myBigMonaco.

Creating a Custom Font

To create a custom font, you could modify a standard system font that HyperCard
and other programs use, but this is not a good idea. Another program may depend
on the letters supplied with the font, and substituting different images for these
could make the application not work. The solution is to copy an existing font to a
new font file, give it a unique name, modify it, then attach it to the stack or application. Because the search path for a font is always from document to application to
System, your custom font will be found immediately inside your stack. Note that
your font won't be seen by other stacks unless you attach it to the Home card
(frowned upon but sometimes necessary), the HyperCard application (thought police from Apple will put a mental pox on you for this), or the System itself. You also
could ask the user to install the font in the System.

Because we needed a monospaced font, we simply copied the normal Monaco
font to make the new myBigMonaco font. You could use proportional fonts as well.
We choose monospace because it allows easier HyperTalk calculations regarding
font locations on the screen. After the font was copied, it had a new fond and font
resource. Recall that the fond is the resource that holds the metrics for the font
family. The fond resource contains information common to all point sizes, including
metrics such as kerning tables for letter pairs. We had to be sure the fond resource
was properly copied to the stack after the font was saved.

The font resource contains the height of the entire font, among other things.
We changed this to 18 points so we could add larger images than the 12-point font
allows. The actual images, however, were larger than 18 points. Vertical and horizon-

tal "bounding boxes" are around each character, and these can be stretched. Thus, we can add larger images easily by just moving these boxes. In addition, you can set the ascent and descent positions for the font regardless of the size of the font. Ascent is the height above a baseline, and descent is the height below the baseline. Our example has a 24-point ascent, a 20-point descent, and 1-point leading. This resulted in a 45-point tall image.

Working with Custom Fonts

To work with the contents of your font, you need to open the font resource file. Double-click on the file name, and a scrolling box containing font images is displayed, as shown in Figure 8-9. This window allows you to view the entire set of characters in the font. Characters are identified in a rectangle; above each is the code for the keys to press. In this program, *O* is the Option key, *S* is the Shift key, and *C* is the Command key. In Figure 8-9, different parts of a butterfly image have been substituted for the characters Option-j, Option-\, Shift-Option-\, and Option-; in our custom font. These obscure characters were chosen so that standard (non-Option-Shift) characters could still be used.

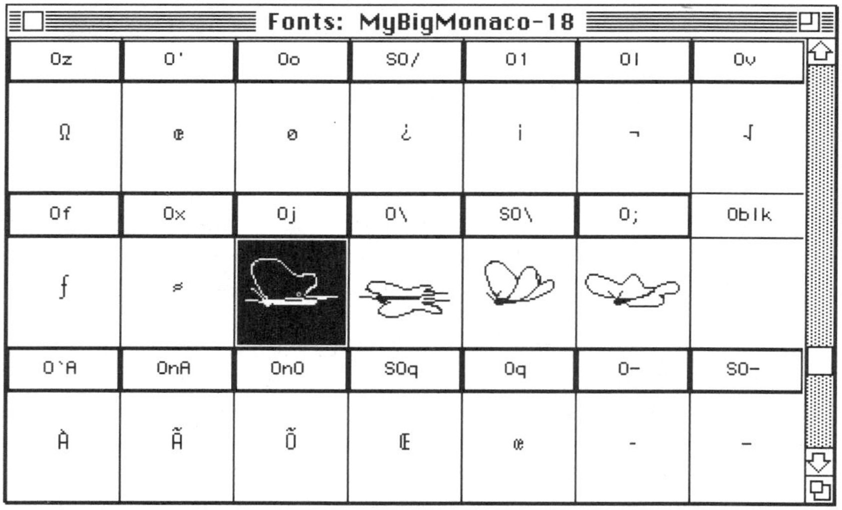

Figure 8-9.   In the window for viewing the *Fonts: myBigMonaco-18* font, you can see the images assigned to each character of the font.

Inserting the Image in the Font

The first step is to move the clip art image into your font. Open the paint document containing the clip art image. Select it with the selection rectangle tool and copy it to the clipboard. If you hold down the Option key when you select the paint object, you will lasso the object and just select the outer boundaries of the object to the clipboard.

Now open the font editor, select your new font (still empty), locate the character in it to install the image on the clipboard, and open that character in the font editor paint tool, as shown in Figure 8-10.

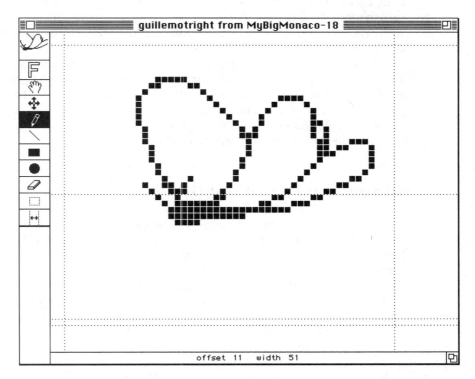

Figure 8-10. The butterfly font image opened in the paint program section of the font editor. The name of the character in which the butterfly is installed is guillmotright.

Now do a paste (Command-V). The character in the font is replaced by the image on the clipboard. Resize the window to get a good view of the image. The two parameters at the bottom of the screen are important: *offset* is the space before the character, measured from the vertical origin line to the first pixel in the shape, and *width* is the distance between the vertical boundaries of the character.

The position of the image in this window affects how the character overlaps other characters. This overlap isn't needed for the butterfly example because you usually won't move the font inside the field. Instead, you will move the font through frames. Thus, alternate images must be aligned relative to each other (so that, for example, the butterfly head is in the same position in each image). You must make sure the boundary boxes are equal in width in each character and that the characters make a natural transition when overlapped. A big screen is an important tool for effectively using fonts.

Move the Fonts to Your Stack

Save the font after the images are installed in it. Next, use a tool such as Font/DA Mover or ResCopy to move the font and font resource to the stack in which you want to place the font. In Font/DA Mover, hold down the Option key when you click Open to get a list of all files with font resources, including your stacks. Open the stack you want to move the font into, then open the font resource you made and copy it to your stack. This step is necessary because you can't use Fontastic to open and work on the font directly in the HyperCard stack.

Now that the font is installed in the stack, open the stack and create a new field. Set the font of the field to the custom font's name (it should appear in the font scrolling window of the information box for the field). Switch to the browse tool and type the character for the image into the field (Shift-Option-\ in our example). The butterfly image should appear. Resize the field so it just surrounds the image, set the field to transparent, and you are ready for animation.

Adding Sprites to the Game

Now that the characters are stored in the font, you are ready to write scripts to manipulate them. In the last gallery script, you began to build a HyperTalk function that would make it easier to move the objects stored in fonts. We'll expand that routine to provide even more flexibility.

First, you need to modify the set _gallery routine, which sets the characteristics for the field containing the objects. You won't be rotating multiple characters through the field, but you need to make sure the field has the proper `textHeight` for the objects. Add the following routine to the set _gallery script after the line `set the textsize of cd fld fld_name to fnt size`:

```
-- don't set up field for multiple chars if myBigMonaco
  if fnt_name = "myBigMonaco" then
    if fld_name = "Butterfly" then
      set the textHeight of cd fld fld_name to 34
    end if
    exit set_gallery
  end if
```

If the name of the font is myBigMonaco, the routine checks if the name of the field is Butterfly. If that is true, you do *not* call this routine to set up the gallery; thus, you set the `textHeight` of the butterfly field to 34 points and exit set _gallery. The extended `textHeight` is needed because the object is larger than the 18 points we use for the rabbits and sheep game.

Sprites are "intelligent" graphic objects in video games. In the `move` function for the gallery game, you already can specify the name of the field containing the image, the name of a second field to move (if any), and the direction to move the characters in those fields (left or right).

We only need to add the capability to specify the characters that the sprite will cycle through, in this case the butterfly characters. This is the beauty of a function:

you can easily graft new parameters, then use them in handlers later. For the butter-fly animation, you need to tell the routine the location of the butterfly characters in the font (of the 255 characters) and to cycle through them on the screen. Thus, you need to tell the handler which character to start with and end with.

We use the feature of HyperTalk string variables to act like arrays to store the characters for our sprite. A string variable called rotchars serves as an array for the images. The array acts like a set of pointers to the custom font. The numToChar() function, which converts a number to a character, is used to store the correct char-acter in the array. Add these lines right after the set gallery handler at the begin-ning of the program:

```
-- set up the number of chars into rotchars for the butterfly
-- use this order of output so it looks right
put numtochar(198) into char 1 of rotchars -- up wings fast
put numtochar(199) into char 2 of rotchars -- down wings fast
put numtochar(200) into char 3 of rotchars -- up wings slow
put numtochar(201) into char 4 of rotchars -- down wings slow
```

We obtained the character codes by setting the font editor's display to show decimal codes.

Now you need a way to use this information in the move function. The following routine replaces the one in the beginning of the older move routine:

```
on move fld_name, fld_name2, dir, rotchars, fromchar, tochar, ¬
   speed, startx, starty, xvel, yvel, ¬
   xmax, ymax, xmin, ymin, ¬
   xrand, yrand
```

We added several parameters to move after the dir parameter. A new direction called rotate is defined in the if statement. The move is called with dir set to rotate, as in move Butterfly, 0, "rotate"... A handler starting with if dir = "ro-tate" traps this word and executes the special rotating animation.

The rotchars parameter is the array of image pointers. The fromchar and tochar specify what images or the rotchars array to cycle through. If we call move with move Butterfly, 0, "rotate", rotchars, 3, 4..., move will cycle through the slower moving butterfly characters.

With the speed parameter, you can tell HyperCard how fast to move the image. The startx and starty parameters identify where to start the image on the screen's x-y plane. The xvel and yvel parameters are the velocity to move the sprite object and are usually small integers. The sign of these parameters tells which direction to move the object.

The xmax, ymax, xmin, and ymin parameters tell where to "clip" the image. In this demonstration, when the sprite reaches any of these boundaries it is recycled to the beginning xstart and ystart locations. Finally, the xrand and yrand parameters represent the amount of vertical or horizontal randomness you want to add to the sprite's normal trajectory. These give a little jitter to the movement of the butterfly, thereby making it more lifelike.

The HyperTalk code that implements these new parameters goes right after the preceding on move statement:

```
put fromchar into i
if dir = "rotate" then
  repeat until the mouseClick
    put char i of rotchars into cd fld fld_name
    if speed = "fast" then
      wait 3 ticks
    else
      wait 12 ticks
    end if
    add 1 to i
    if i > tochar then put fromchar into i
    -- the following moves the objects based on incoming
    -- sprite parameters

    get the loc of cd fld fld_name
    if item 1 of it < xmin then put xmax into item 1 of it
    if item 2 of it < ymin then put ymax into item 2 of it
    put (item 1 of it) + xvel into item 1 of it
    put (item 2 of it) + (yvel - random(yrand)) into item 2 of it
    set the loc of cd fld fld_name to it
  end repeat
  set the loc of cd fld fld_name to startx, starty
end if
```

As you can see, there is very little to the code for moving the butterfly. The `if-then` statement at the beginning looks for the word *rotate*. If it is found, the code begins. A large `repeat` loop moves the butterfly through successive frames while moving it in the screen's x-y plane. The mouse click ends the routine. Each time the loop cycles, the statement `put char i of rotchars into cd fld fld_name` moves the next image into the sprite field.

The next `if-then` statement checks for the speed parameter and uses it to control how many ticks to wait between images. The next `if-then` statement checks the `tochar` and resets if past it.

The statements beginning with `get the loc of cd fld fld_name` check the location of the field on the screen and adjust it for each new cycle. In this example, we used only the random effect on the `yvel` variable so the butterfly would jitter up and down. When the mouse click occurs, the routine ends and the image is set to the starting point.

Now you are ready to animate. The `set_gallery` and `move` routines need to be called with the new parameters. Here is the complete code for the new demonstration:

```
on mouseUp
  set name of me to "Faster" -- change the button's name
  set hilite of me to true
  set_gallery 0, Butterfly, "myBigMonaco", 18, 0

  -- set up the number of chars into rotchars
  -- use this order of output so it looks right
  put numtochar(198) into char 1 of rotchars
  put numtochar(199) into char 2 of rotchars
  put numtochar(200) into char 3 of rotchars
  put numtochar(201) into char 4 of rotchars
```

continued

```
-- The move routine must be passed the char numbers in rotchars
-- of the special fonts and the positions you want to rotate.
-- First we show the low-speed butterfly, then one that
-- is moving fast.
move Butterfly, 0,"rotate", rotchars, 3, 4, "slow",¬
323, 63, -20, 20, ¬
512, 342, 0, 0, ¬
0, 40

-- this is the faster butteryfly
set the name of me to "End Demo"
move Butterfly, 0,"rotate", rotchars, 1, 2, "fast",¬
323, 63, -20, 20, ¬
512, 342, 0, 0, ¬
0, 40

set the name of me to "Demo"
set the hilite of me to false
end mouseUp
```

There are three calls to the move routine. The name of the button we use to start the demo is changed each time it is clicked. The new name of the button tells us the next demo that will be run. The Option-Return character (¬) makes the parameters of the sprite easy to read and modify.

The Opaque Problem and Solution

When you run this demo and the object passes over a graphic background, the background shows though the object because the field is transparent. Any pixels not filled in (white) are like transparent paint. We want the pixels to be white paint. Note also that the object passes under some objects and over others because it is a field with a layer.

The Move Closer and Send Farther commands can change the field layer. The transparent problem is tougher to solve in this version of HyperCard. One creative solution is to invert the images before they are stored in the font. Make all white pixels black and make black pixels white. Then change the field in which the objects are displayed to outline style. This inverts the previously inverted image, changing everything that was white to black and everything that was black to white. At the same time, it eliminates the transparent effect. The technique is tricky on small objects. A simple inversion often does not appear right when outlined, and you will have to touch up the objects in a paint program.

The complete code for the butterfly sprite follows:

```
on mouseUp
  set name of me to "Faster" -- change button's name
  set hilite of me to true
  set_gallery 0, Butterfly, "myBigMonaco", 18, 0
```

continued

```
-- set up the number of chars into rotchars if used
-- use this order of output so it looks right
put numtochar(198) into char 1 of rotchars
put numtochar(199) into char 2 of rotchars
put numtochar(200) into char 3 of rotchars
put numtochar(201) into char 4 of rotchars
put numtochar(182) into char 5 of rotchars
  -- opaque up wings slow
put numtochar(183) into char 6 of rotchars
  -- opaque down wings slow

-- The move routine must be passed the char numbers in rotchars
-- of the special fonts and the positions you want to rotate.
-- First we show the low-speed butterfly, then one that
-- is moving fast.

move Butterfly, 0,"rotate", rotchars, 3, 4, "slow",¬
323, 63, -20, 20, ¬
512, 342, 0, 0, ¬
0, 40

-- this is the faster butteryfly
set the name of me to "Opaque"
move Butterfly, 0,"rotate", rotchars, 1, 2, "fast",¬
323, 63, -20, 20, ¬
512, 342, 0, 0, ¬
0, 40

-- this is the opaque butterfly
set the name of me to "Stop"
set the textstyle of cd fld Butterfly to outline
move Butterfly, 0,"rotate", rotchars, 5, 6, "fast",¬
323, 63, -20, 20, ¬
512, 342, 0, 0, ¬
0, 40

set the textstyle of cd fld Butterfly to plain
set the name of me to "Demo"
set the hilite of me to false
end mouseUp

on move fld_name, fld_name2, dir, rotchars, fromchar, tochar, ¬
  speed, startx, starty, xvel, yvel, ¬
  xmax, ymax, xmin, ymin, ¬
  xrand, yrand

  put fromchar into i
  if dir = "rotate" then
    repeat until the mouseClick
      put char i of rotchars into cd fld fld_name
      if speed = "fast" then
        wait 3 ticks
      else
        wait 12 ticks
      end if
```

continued

```
      add 1 to i
      if i > tochar then put fromchar into i
   -- the following moves the objects based on incoming
   -- sprite parameters

      get the loc of cd fld fld_name
      if item 1 of it < xmin then put xmax into item 1 of it
      if item 2 of it < ymin then put ymax into item 2 of it
      put (item 1 of it) + xvel into item 1 of it
      put (item 2 of it) + (yvel - random(yrand)) into item 2¬
      of it
      set the loc of cd fld fld_name to it
    end repeat
    set the loc of cd fld fld_name to startx, starty
  end if

  if dir = "left" then
    repeat until the mouseClick
      put first char of cd fld fld_name ¬
      after cd fld fld_name
      delete first char of cd fld fld_name
    end repeat
  end if

  if dir = "right" then
    repeat until the mouseClick
      put last char of cd fld fld_name ¬
      before cd fld fld_name
      delete last char of cd fld fld_name
    end repeat
    --wait until the mouseclick -- lets you watch movement
  end if

  if dir = "both" then
    repeat until the mouseClick
      put first char of cd fld fld_name ¬
      after cd fld fld_name
      delete first char of cd fld fld_name

      put last char of cd fld fld_name2 ¬
      before cd fld fld_name2
      delete last char of cd fld fld_name2
    end repeat
  end if
end move

on set_gallery char_n, fld_name, fnt_name, fnt_size, n_spaces
  put empty into blank
  put empty into cd fld fld_name
  set textfont of cd fld fld_name to fnt_name
  set textsize of cd fld fld_name to fnt_size
  -- don't set up field for multiple chars if myBigMonaco
  if fnt_name = "myBigMonaco" then
    if fld_name = "Butterfly" then
      set the textHeight of cd fld fld_name to 34
    end if
```

continued

```
    exit set_gallery
  end if
  put the width of cd fld fld_name into w
  put trunc( w / fnt_size / 2 ) + 1 into numchars
  -- make blank part -- customized for each font and char
  repeat with i = 1 to n_spaces
    put space after blank
  end repeat
  -- fill the field now (field can be any width)
  repeat with i = 1 to numchars
    put char_n & blank after cd fld fld_name
  end repeat
end set_gallery
```

Figure 8-11 shows the layout of the card for the butterfly font animation trick. The custom resources in this stack include the Dallas 18-point font for the title of the trick, the myBigMonaco 18-point font for the butterfly, the Cairo 18-point font for the pistol, a custom nail icon for the demo button, and custom icons for the house and scissors in the font movie trick card.

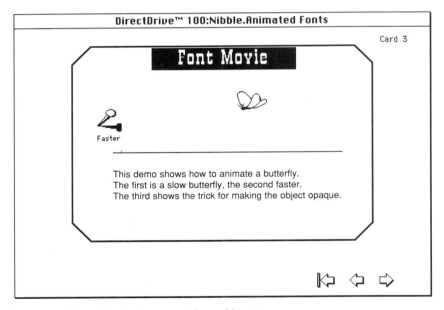

Figure 8-11.   The font movie trick card layout.

Graphics and Sound

The Art of Visual Effects

Jeanne A. E. DeVoto

Synopsis: Attracting and holding attention is a measure of the effectiveness of a stack. Although HyperCard provides numerous visual effects for grabbing attention, many developers are unclear about how best to utilize these effects. Indeed, too many effects, like too many fonts, can ruin a stack.

This chapter was written to help developers create and use graphic effects to make stacks more interesting and attractive. First, it reviews the fundamentals of the visual effect commands, from dissolves to venetian blinds. A special script is presented that serves as an on-line reminder of the visual effect syntax, so you don't have to constantly refer to the manual for the correct spelling. Traps encountered when using effects are covered, including using them with color displays.

The second part of this chapter reveals little-known tricks of visual effects, including trapping system messages, navigation, detouring, entering and exiting visual effects, changing the zoom point, emulating other communication forms, making a shutter slide show, and using visual effects and animation.

Chapter 9

The Art of Visual Effects

Create a Look and Feel That Dazzles

$\mathbf{A}$s with many forms of communication, the effectiveness of a HyperCard stack depends largely on how it presents information to the eye of the user. The appearance of a stack—its look and feel—is important in ensuring that the stack can attract and hold attention, if it is easy to learn about and use, and if the information it presents remains in the mind of the user.

This chapter is devoted to a single HyperTalk command—the `visual effect` command—and its many options. Like the special effects in movies and television, HyperCard's visual effects can direct the viewer's attention to important information, amuse, and fool the eye. When used with skill and attention, this single command gives style as well as substance to the stacks you design.

A visual effect is a visible transition from one card's image to another card's image. If you simply tell HyperCard to go to another card, either from a script or by choosing one of the items in the Go menu, the image of the destination card almost instantly replaces the image of the card previously displayed. This sharp transition is called a *cut* in movie and television production. Often, this is the most suitable way to move from card to card. It is simple and not overly distracting.

However, in some stacks, you want a different type of transition. For example, transitions can provoke the user's interest and attention, soften the edges of a switch and make it less abrupt and jarring, or achieve special effects (such as in animation). This is where visual effects become invaluable.

When used appropriately, visual effects are part of a subtle language of hints to the user about what is happening during navigation from card to card. In large or complicated stacks, a user can get lost easily. Even in small stacks, the user can quickly become disoriented if there are no visual clues to indicate the direction or, even worse, if those clues are contradictory. Care must be taken to choose effects that are appropriate as well as attention-getting.

Visual Effect Basics

Because you can design entire stacks without visual effects, many experienced HyperTalk scriptors are still unfamiliar with the `visual effect` command and the best ways to use it. Others have used a few basic visual effects in their stacks, but want to explore further possibilities, such as combining visual effects. (Adding visual effects to an existing stack is a common place for beginners to start learning about how HyperTalk works.)

A complete description of the `visual effect` command and its many options is in this chapter. The question of where to use which visual effects is discussed. Several scripts are presented, including one that lets you quickly test visual effects. You will find information about the `unlock screen with visual effect` command and about variations such as chaining a series of visual effects in sequence.

This chapter is for fairly experienced HyperCard users who have done at least a little HyperTalk scripting. You should be familiar with the basics of using Hyper-Talk, the `go` command, and the use of the Message box.

How Visual Effects Work

You can add a visual effect to any card transition by placing the following command in a handler, before any card transition command:

```
visual effect <name of effect>
```

The word `effect` is optional. (You can add other optional parameters, such as speed, to a visual effect. These are described later in the chapter.)

The specified visual effect is not executed as soon as it is declared in the script. Rather, it is stored to be used in the next card transition commanded from the handler. The most common command to go from one card to another within a script is, of course, the `go` command. The `find` and `pop card` commands also are card transitions and can be used with a visual effect.

The `visual effect` command requires two lines of code: one line to declare the visual effect and one line to go to a card. This means that visual effects cannot be used from the Message box because the Message box can only execute a single line of HyperTalk code.

You can place other command lines between the visual effect command and the card transition command. But if the handler ends before any card transition, the visual effect is ignored because all visual effect commands are forgotten when HyperCard receives an `idle` message. (The `idle` message is sent continuously when HyperCard is not executing a handler.)

When you use the `visual effect` command in a script, first you see the image of the starting card. Then the transition visual effect appears, which may mix parts of both images. Finally, when the transition is complete, the screen holds the image of the destination card. Because `go to this card` is a legal HyperTalk command, the starting card may be the same as the destination card. In this case, most of the visual effects cannot be detected on the screen. (It's hard to notice transitions from one image to an identical image.) There are nine visual effects: dissolve, zoom, iris, scroll, wipe, barn door, checkerboard, venetian blinds, and plain (no effect at all).

Dissolve

The *dissolve* effect uses successive patterns of scattered pixels from the original image to replace pixels from the destination image, continuing with denser and denser patterns until the original image is gone. The effect is that of the original image gradually dissolving into the destination image. See Figure 9-1.

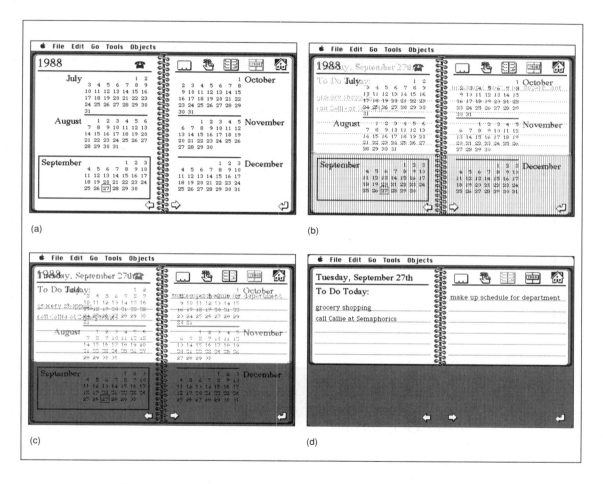

Figure 9-1. The dissolve effect alters only that part of the screen that differs between the original card and the destination image.

The dissolve effect changes only the part of the screen that differs between the original image and the destination image. For example, if you dissolve from a card that contains a small graphic on a white background to a similar card, the white background common to both cards is not affected by the dissolve. A corollary of this is that if a stack includes a dissolve from one card to an identical card, you will not see the dissolve because the original image is identical to the destination image.

Zoom Open and Close

The *zoom* effect must be used with the direction open or close. (You can also use out instead of open or in instead of close.) The zoom open effect creates the same expanding rectangles effect as seen in the Finder when you double-click a document or application to open it. The zoom close effect is the same as the contracting rectangles you see when you quit from an application and return to the Finder. The zoom open effect is centered on the last point that was clicked, as shown in Figure 9-2. (Later in this chapter, you'll see a trick to make the zoom open start from a point you select rather than from the point the user clicked on.) The zoom close effect always zooms to the center of the destination image, regardless of the last point the user clicked on.

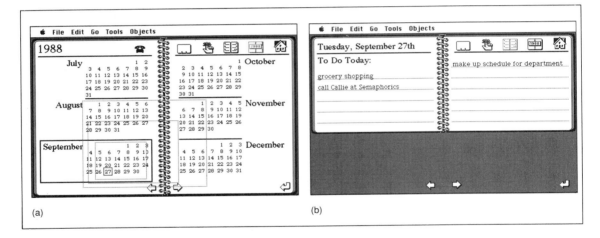

Figure 9-2. The zoom open effect starts at the point the user last clicked on.

HyperCard creates the zoom open effect by drawing a series of expanding rectangles over the image of the original card, then switching to the destination image. In the zoom close effect, HyperCard first switches to the destination image, then draws zooming rectangles over it. A zoom is an abrupt transition because there is a fast cut at the end of the zoom. There is no gradual mixing of the two images, as there is when you use the dissolve effect. Also, a zoom followed by a transition to an identical card can be seen on the screen, unlike a dissolve.

The zoom effect provides a clue about the direction of the movement, rather than a softening of the transition. Zoom open usually indicates that the user is moving into a deeper, more specific area of the stack or opening a part of the stack to look at the contents. You can think of zoom open as magnifying a small part of the card. Zoom close usually signals the user that he or she is moving back out to a previous or more general level of the stack, closing part of the stack, or moving from a detailed view to an overall view.

Iris Open and Close

There is an effect used in film called *iris* that is very similar to the HyperCard visual effect *iris open*. It shows a round lens gradually opening from a point in the center of the original image, through which the destination image can be seen. The lens opening increases until the destination image replaces the original image. See Figure 9-3. The iris close effect is similar to iris open, except the lens starts at the edges and gradually closes to a point at the center of the card.

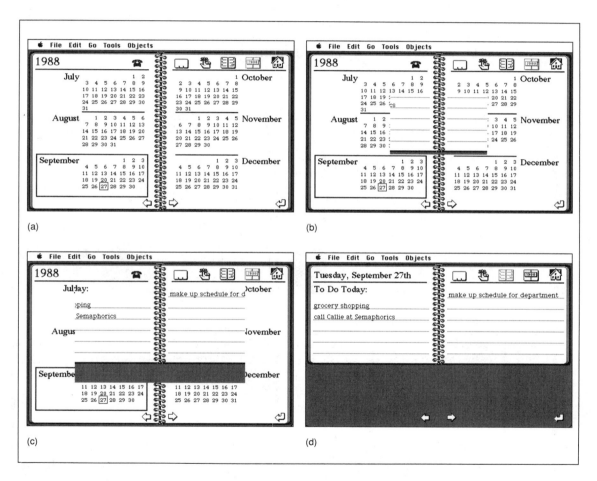

Figure 9-3. The iris open effect opens from the center of the screen to the edges.

The lens shape of the iris open effect is rectangular, instead of round (as it is in the film effect). To be exact, it follows the contour of the HyperCard window.

The iris effect is similar to the zoom effect. Like zoom, iris signals movement to a deeper area of the stack (iris open) or back out to a more general area (iris close).

Unlike the zoom effect, however, the iris displays part of both images on the screen at the same time. Thus, iris is a softer, more gradual effect than zoom. This also means an iris (like a dissolve) from one card to an identical image won't be visible. The iris open effect also differs from zoom open in that it always starts from the center of the card, rather than from the last point the user clicked on.

Scroll Left, Scroll Right, Scroll Up, and Scroll Down

As shown in Figure 9-4, the *scroll* visual effect moves the destination image across the original image in the indicated direction: left, right, up, or down. It looks as though you are sliding the new image into place over the old one or removing one card from a deck and slipping it onto the top of the deck.

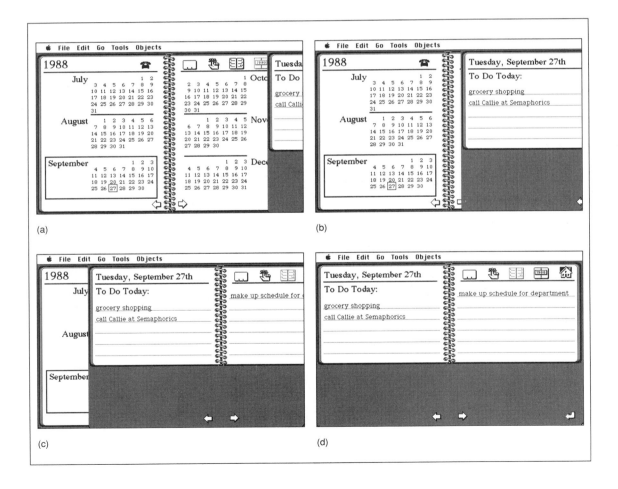

Figure 9-4.   The scroll visual effect slides the destination card over the card you started from.

A scroll is a sharp-edged transition, though not as abrupt as a transition that uses no visual effect. The scroll right and scroll left variations can indicate sequential movement through a stack. Scroll up and scroll down can be used to introduce an entirely new topic or indicate a nonsequential jump to a different part of the stack. The scroll effect is also useful when you want to create specific special effects, such as a simulation of a slide show.

Because the leading edge of a scrolling card is shown moving across the original image, scrolls appear cleaner if the edge is visually distinct in some way. For example, if the original image is mainly white and the destination image is mainly black, the edge shows clearly as it scrolls across the screen. Another way to make a clean edge is to put a border on the destination card.

Wipe Left, Wipe Right, Wipe Up, and Wipe Down

The *wipe* visual effect is similar to the scroll effect. Like scroll, the wipe effect moves the destination image into place over the original image in the indicated direction: left, right, up, or down. Instead of the destination image sliding over the original image, however, the wipe action follows an imaginary vertical or horizontal line moving across the screen in the indicated direction. See Figure 9-5. Where the line passes, it leaves behind the image of the destination card, erasing the original one.

Several other ways to think of the wipe effect may help in visualizing its action. For example, you can imagine that the wipe operates by laying one edge of the destination card against the corresponding edge of the current image and gradually unrolling it, pressing it down into place over the original image. Or imagine that the original image is being rolled up toward the edge to reveal the destination image lying underneath it.

Like the dissolve and iris effects, the wipe effect alters only whatever portion of the screen changes from the original image to the destination image.

Wipe and scroll are very similar effects and are often used for the same purposes. The major difference between wipe and scroll is that the scroll effect appears to move the destination card into place over the source card, but the wipe effect gradually replaces the source image with the destination image while not moving either image. For this reason, wipe is a somewhat softer effect than scroll.

Barn Door Open and Barn Door Close

The *barn door* effect is a type of double wipe. Barn door open wipes from the center of the screen outward to the left and right edges. Barn door close wipes from the edges to the center. The effect is like pulling a pair of sliding doors open or closed.

Like dissolve, iris, and wipe, the barn door effect alters only that part of the screen that differs between the original image and the destination image. The effect of a door opening is particularly pronounced if the destination image is very different than the original image.

The barn door open effect can be used like an iris open to indicate that the user is moving deeper into the stack's contents. The barn door close effect is used for the opposite movement—outward to a more general layer. The barn door effect is also used when the stack designer wants to show that the user is taking a "side trip" (for

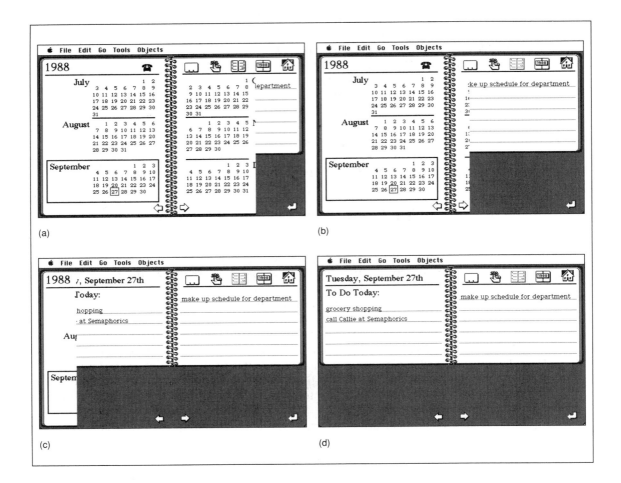

Figure 9-5. The wipe left effect replaces the image along an imaginary vertical line that moves from right to left across the screen.

example, to a help section). Barn door is especially effective when the stack's graphic design includes a clear division down the center of the card, for example, when the background graphic is a picture of an open book. See Figure 9-6.

Checkerboard

The *checkerboard* effect divides the card into a grid of squares (sixteen squares horizontally by nine squares vertically). First, all odd squares are replaced by the corresponding parts of the destination image. Then all even squares are replaced. If you look at the individual squares during the checkerboard effect, you will see that each square is replaced with a wipe type of effect from top to bottom.

The checkerboard effect, like dissolve, iris, and wipe, does not change any area that doesn't differ between the original image and the destination image. Checker-

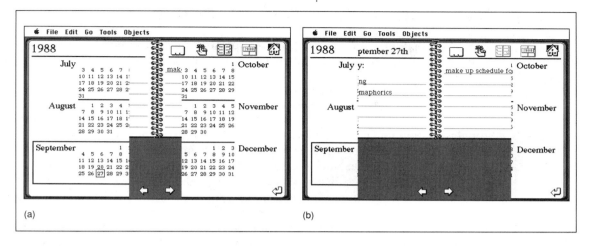

Figure 9-6.   The barn door open and close effects work especially well on horizontally symmetrical layouts like this one.

board generally looks best when the original image is very different from the destination image.

Venetian Blinds

The *venetian blinds* effect divides the card into nine horizontal strips and replaces all the strips at once, from the top of each strip down. If you look closely during a venetian blinds effect, you will see that each strip is replaced with a wipe, like in the checkerboard effect. The venetian blinds effect, like the checkerboard effect, works best if the original and destination images are very different.

The checkerboard and venetian blinds visual effects are not used in stack design as often as the other effects because they are too flashy to be appropriate in most situations. There are special circumstances where you may want to use one or both. For example, suppose that you are designing a promotional stack that will be used in a public place, such as a sales floor. Such a stack should include striking effects that are visible from a distance to attract users. The venetian blinds effect is also good to use when you want to indicate that the user is now looking "behind the scenes" of a stack. It also can be used to animate card-to-card transitions where you want a continuous "rolling" effect. The venetian blinds and checkerboard effects are obvious and unusual. Although they are too distracting and garish for many applications, they certainly catch the user's attention and can be used when that feature is needed.

Plain

The *plain* visual effect means to use no visual effect. You simply cut directly to the destination image, as though no visual effect command had been given. You might wonder when you would use this effect. The plain visual effect can be used to cut directly to a destination image other than the final destination card.

Speed and Destination Image Options

With any visual effect command, you can specify a destination image and speed. A visual effect command that includes a destination image and speed is written like this:

```
visual effect <name of effect> <speed> to <destination image>
```

Both destination image and speed are optional: you can include a destination image, a speed, both, or neither with any visual effect command.

For the destination image, you can specify one of five images: black, gray, white, card, and inverse. Black, white, and gray are self-explanatory. Card is the image of the destination card; if you haven't specified a destination image, card is used. Inverse is the black-to-white reverse of the destination card.

If the destination image is anything other than card, the effect is performed from the original image to the destination image, then there is a cut directly to the card. Suppose that the following lines are in a handler:

```
visual effect dissolve to gray
go to card "Next Topic"
```

When the handler is executed, the original card dissolves to solid gray. When the dissolve is finished, there is a cut to the Next Topic card. This cut at the end of the visual effect can give an undesired abruptness to the transition that uses an intermediate image. One way to avoid this abruptness is discussed in the section on chaining visual effects.

In addition to selecting a destination image, you can vary the speed of a visual effect. Any visual effect can take place at one of five speeds: very slowly, slowly, normal, fast, and very fast. (Slowly can be abbreviated as slow.) If you don't specify a speed, the normal speed is used. There is no visible difference between the fast and very fast speeds except on a Macintosh II or an accelerated Macintosh SE.

With some visual effects (for example, scroll and zoom), the transition is displayed in stages or steps, not continuously. At normal speed, this isn't apparent. At a very slow speed, however, some effects look jerky. This bumpy effect can be interesting, and you may want to use it sometimes. Usually, though, you will choose a normal, fast, or slow speed. Table 9-1 summarizes HyperCard's visual effects, and Table 9-2 lists the optional modifications you can make to each visual effect.

Table 9-1.   HyperCard's Visual Effects

Visual Effect	Direction
dissolve	
zoom	open (out), close (in)
iris	open, close
scroll	left, right, up, down
wipe	left, right, up, down
venetian blinds	
checkerboard	

Table 9-1. (cont.)

Visual Effect	Direction
barn door	open, close
plain	

Note: The speed and destination parameters are optional.

Table 9-2. Optional Parameters for Visual Effects

Speed	Destination
very fast	to card
fast	to white
normal	to gray
slow (slowly)	to black
very slow (very slowly)	to inverse

You will probably use the dissolve, zoom, and iris visual effects more often than the others. These three are the more subtle of HyperCard's visual effects. They are also easily understood because they correspond to actions already familiar to the user, through experience with the Macintosh interface (as in the zoom effect) or knowledge of the visual language of film and television.

A Demonstration Script for Visual Effects

As mentioned, the `visual effect` command has no visible result when simply typed into the Message box. For you to see a visual effect, HyperCard must receive a command that results in a card transfer before the next `idle` message is generated. (Recall that `idle` messages are sent continuously, when a command is not executing.)

Sometimes, you may be undecided about which visual effect to use. You may want to see several possibilities, without typing each into a script in turn. With the following custom message handler, you can demonstrate quickly any visual effect by typing the effect's name into the Message box:

```
on doVisual theEffect
  do "visual effect" && (theEffect)
    -- parentheses mean "the value of"
  go to next card
end doVisual
```

After you've typed this handler into your stack's script, type the following line into the Message box:

```
doVisual "zoom open"
```

You will see the zoom open visual effect, followed by a transfer to the next card. Notice that you must enclose the name of the visual effect in quotation marks. (Strictly speaking, this is necessary only when the effect consists of more than one word, such as "dissolve to inverse".) The quotation marks tell HyperCard that it should treat the name of the effect as a single term in the doVisual command.

If you would like this capability whenever you work on a stack, type the doVisual handler into the script of your Home stack.

Remember that only the contents of the card window are affected by visual effects. Any floating windoids (such as the Message box) remain unaffected. If you want to see what the visual effect looks like without the Message box cluttering the screen, make certain the global blindTyping property is set to true. You can set blindTyping to true on the Preferences card of the Home stack if the userLevel is set to 5. You can also set it in a script with the line

```
set blindTyping to true
```

If the blindTyping property is true, any text you type is entered into the Message box, whether or not the box is visible on the screen. Type the doVisual command, then close the Message box and press the Return key. Because blindTyping is on, the Message box receives the keypress, prompting it to execute the doVisual command.

A Reminder Script for the *visual effect* Command

While you are developing a stack and choosing visual effects, you may want a quick reminder of the available visual effects, the options for each, and their syntax. The following handler provides this information:

```
on remindVisual theEffect
  if theEffect is "dissolve" then ¬
  put "dissolve [<speed>] [to <destination image>]"
  else if theEffect is "zoom" then ¬
  put "zoom open|close [<speed>] [to <destination image>]"
  else if theEffect is "iris" then ¬
  put "iris open|close [<speed>] [to <destination image>]"
  else if theEffect is "scroll" then ¬
  put "scroll left|right|up|down [<speed>] ¬
  [to <destination image>]"
  else if theEffect is "wipe" then ¬
  put "wipe left|right|up|down [<speed>] [to <destination image>]"
  else if theEffect is "barn door" then ¬
  put "barn door open|close [<speed>] [to <destination image>]"
  else if theEffect contains "venetian" then ¬
  put "venetian blinds [<speed>] [to <destination image>]"
  else if theEffect is "checkerboard" then ¬
  put "checkerboard [<speed>] [to <destination image>]"
  else if theEffect is "plain" then ¬
  put "plain [<speed>] [to <destination image>]"
  else if theEffect contains "destination" then ¬
```

continued

```
   put "destination images: card, inverse, gray, black, ¬
   or white"
   else if theEffect is "speed" then put ¬
   "speeds: very fast, fast, normal, slow[ly], very slow[ly]"
   else
     put "visual effects: dissolve, zoom, iris, scroll, ¬
     wipe, barn door..."
     wait until the mouseClick
     put "...barn door, checkerboard, venetian blinds, plain."
   end if
end remindVisual
```

If you type this handler into your stack's script, then type `remindVisual` along with the name of the visual effect into the Message box, the syntax and variations for that effect will appear in the Message box. For example, if you want to be reminded of the variations of the barn door effect, type this into the Message box:

```
remindVisual "barn door"
```

The following line appears in the Message box:

```
barn door open|close [<speed>] [to <destination image>]
```

Following the usual conventions for HyperTalk command descriptions, a vertical line (|) indicates a choice between two or more alternatives, and optional parts of the command are enclosed in square brackets.

If, instead of specifying a visual effect, you type `remindVisual speed` or `remindVisual "destination image"` into the Message box, the handler displays all possible values for these optional parameters. If you type `remindVisual` with no additional arguments, or if the remindVisual handler doesn't recognize the visual effect you specify, all available visual effects are listed. (Because there is not enough room in the Message box for the names of all nine visual effects, the remindVisual handler lists them in two sets.) You can then ask for a reminder about a particular effect.

Chaining Visual Effects

To obtain certain special effects, you may want to execute two or more visual effects in sequence during a single card transition. You can chain several visual effects by simply declaring them in the handler in the order that you want them to appear during the card transition.

For example, suppose that you have a button that takes the user from a card containing a large graphic on a white background to another card containing mostly text. You may want the graphics card to dissolve to a completely white background (using the optional destination image of the `visual effect` command). Then, instead of an abrupt cut at the end of the dissolve, do another dissolve from the all-white image to the destination card. This combination makes the transition look as though the card is fading slowly and reappearing in a new form. The handler for such an effect is

```
on mouseUp
  visual effect dissolve to white
  visual effect dissolve to card
  go to card "Text Field"
end mouseUp
```

The to card in the second line of the handler is optional because card is the default destination image. It is included here for clarity.

Recall that visual effects you declare are not executed at once. Instead, they are stored to be used at the next card transition. This means you cannot halt a series of visual effects in the middle of the sequence. In this sense, issuing several visual effect commands and then triggering them with a card transition command is analogous to loading a pinball machine with several pinballs: after the lever has been pulled and the balls have been released, they cannot be recalled individually.

You may want to use the doVisual script to see how multiple chained effects look. Here is an enhanced version that lets you try out several effects chained together:

```
on doVisual theEffect
  repeat with x = 1 to the number of items in theEffect
    visual effect (item x of theEffect)
  end repeat
  go to next card
end doVisual
```

To use this command with one visual effect, type the doVisual command into the Message box as discussed. To use multiple visual effects, separate the effect names with commas and enclose the list of effects with quotation marks:

```
doVisual "dissolve to white,dissolve to card"
```

The capability to layer multiple effects gives you versatility in choosing effects for your stacks. For example, you can use a double dissolve like the one discussed to visually soften a transition. You can also use multiple visual effects such as those in the following combination to sharpen a transition, making it more noticeable:

```
visual effect dissolve fast to inverse
visual effect dissolve fast to card
```

Here are a few other interesting combinations. For a quick and fairly sharp transition, try this combination:

```
visual effect plain to white
visual effect plain to card
```

This works well with cards that contain a lot of information on a white background. Try it with other destination images for different effects.

As noted, the zoom effect is abrupt because it ends with a sharp cut. The iris effect is softer, but it always opens from the center of the screen rather than from the point the user clicked on. To soften a zoom open transition while retaining the visual association to the point the user clicked on, try this combination:

```
visual effect zoom open to gray -- or white or black
visual effect iris open fast to card
```

The destination image for the zoom open command should use whatever color is predominant on the card.

Many combinations give the impression of closing the original card, then opening the destination card. For example, you might use the iris effect:

```
visual effect iris close to black
visual effect iris open to card
```

The first card closes to a blank background, from which the destination card then opens. This combination is especially effective when moving between stacks or when entering a new area of a stack.

Although it is tempting to take maximum advantage of the many possibilities offered by chaining visual effects, use caution when choosing to use a multiple effect. Because multiple effects take longer to execute than a single effect, it is usually not a good idea to use them when the user may be irritated by a slightly slower response. And, although you can chain any number of visual effect commands, you seldom will want to chain more than two effects.

Partly because of reduced speed, multiple effects increase the psychological distance the user feels between the original card and the destination card. Use effects when you want to cue the user that a large "distance" is being traversed.

As a final flourish to the doVisual handler, you can add an optional card destination. In the following handler, you can specify the name of the card you want to go to after the visual effect, as well as the effect(s) you want to see. (If you don't specify any card, it just goes to the next card in the stack.) This additional capability can be useful for fine-tuning effects between two specific cards.

```
on doVisual theEffect, theCard
  repeat with x = 1 to the number of items in theEffect
    visual effect (item x of theEffect)
  end repeat
  if theCard is empty then
    go to next card
  else
    go to card theCard
  end if
end doVisual
```

To use this form of the doVisual command with a card parameter, type the card's name or ID after the visual effect(s). Here are some examples:

```
doVisual "dissolve to gray, dissolve to card","Glossary Card"
doVisual "zoom open","ID 67802"
```

Note that you must enclose the card name in quotation marks if the name contains a space.

The *unlock screen with visual effect* Command

One more method for achieving visual effects is the unlock screen with visual effect command, which was introduced in HyperCard version 1.2. This command is used with the lock screen command, also introduced in version 1.2. (For more on these two commands, see chapter 17, "Large Stacks.") Recall that while the screen is locked, any changes to the appearance of the current card, such as changes in the position of fields or buttons, are not shown. These changes appear only when the screen is unlocked.

This command lets you do a few things that are not possible using HyperTalk's original visual effect command. For example, suppose that your stack contains a button that shows, when clicked, a hidden field. You want to give the effect of the field dissolving into the rest of the card. Because go to this card is a legal HyperTalk command, it seems this handler should achieve the desired effect:

```
on mouseUp
  visual effect dissolve
  show card field "Notes"
  go to this card
end mouseUp
```

There is a problem, however, because visual effects do not take place until the card transition is made. If you first set up the visual effect, then show the field, then go to this card, as in the preceding handler, the field appears before the visual effect action takes place. But if you set up the visual effect, go to the card, then show the field, the field will suddenly appear. In both cases, the dissolve effect is not seen because the original image is identical to the destination image.

The root of the problem is that the visual effect command is not actually executed until the card transition takes place. Thus, it is impossible to change the screen during a visual effect. Using the lock screen and unlock screen with visual effect command avoid this problem by changing the card's appearance while the screen is locked and then employ a visual effect in the transition from the original image to the changed image. For example, to obtain the "dissolving field" effect, use the following handler:

```
on mouseUp
  lock screen
  show card field "Notes"
  unlock screen with visual effect dissolve
end mouseUp
```

You will notice from this handler that no card transition is required for the unlock screen with visual effect command to take effect. Unlike the visual effect command, this command is executed immediately rather than stored for later use. Be aware that unless the lock screen command is used prior to the unlock screen with visual effect, the latter will have no effect.

There are some limitations of the unlock screen with visual effect command. Because the visual effect is executed immediately, you cannot chain multiple effects with this command. Also, because the lock screen and unlock screen with visual effect commands were introduced with HyperCard version 1.2, using them in script will cause problems for users who have an earlier version of HyperCard. If HyperCard versions 1.0.1 and 1.1 encounter these commands in a script, they cannot recognize them as valid HyperTalk commands and present an error message to the user. If your stack might be used with older versions of HyperCard, check for the version in your script and don't use these commands if the version cannot handle them properly. To test the version of HyperCard being used, you might modify the preceding handler like this:

```
on mouseDown
  if the version >= 1.2 then -- this version has command
    lock screen
    show card field "Notes"
    unlock screen with visual effect dissolve
  else
    show card field "Notes"
      -- this version doesn't, so skip effect
  end if
end mouseDown
```

This handler does one of two things, depending on the version of HyperCard being used. If the version is 1.2 or later (a version that contains the lock screen and unlock screen with visual effect commands), the handler displays the visual effect. If an older version of HyperCard is used, the handler simply shows the field with no visual effect. This makes your stack compatible with all versions of HyperCard while allowing you to use the new features of later versions.

Visual Effect Traps

The following sections describe limitations to the visual effect command and situations in which visual effects won't work.

Handlers

As mentioned, a visual effect is executed on the next card transition, and if HyperCard issues an idle message before the next card transition, any visual effects are lost. (Recall that HyperCard issues idle messages continuously whenever no handler is executing.)

This does not necessarily mean visual effects are lost when you exit the handler in which they were declared. As long as HyperCard is continuously executing some handler, no idle messages are sent and any visual effects are retained for the next card transition. This is true even if the card transition command takes place in a different handler than the handler containing the visual effect command. For example, consider this script portion, which consists of two handlers:

```
on mouseDown
  visual effect iris open
  if field "Daily Notes" contains "afternoon" then
    go to card "Appointments"
  else
    cleanUp
  end if
end mouseDown

on cleanUp
  put empty into field "Daily Notes"
  go to next card
end cleanUp
```

If the field doesn't contain the word `afternoon`, HyperCard enters another handler—the cleanUp handler—before the next card transition. HyperCard immediately begins executing the cleanUp handler as soon as it exits the mouseUp handler, with no intervening idle period. Therefore, the iris open effect declared in the mouseUp handler is retained and used with the `go to next card` transition command of the cleanUp handler.

The continuous execution of handlers makes it possible to chain visual effects declared in different handlers. For example, suppose that your stack script contains the following handler:

```
on go
  visual effect dissolve -- add a dissolve effect, then
  pass go -- let the transition proceed normally
end go
```

This handler intercepts any `go` commands issued from within the stack and adds a dissolve to those card transitions. Now suppose that a button in the stack has the following script:

```
on mouseUp
  visual effect dissolve to black
  go to next card
end mouseUp
```

What happens when a user clicks on this button? The `mouseUp` message is sent, and a dissolve to black effect is stored for later use. Then a `go` command is given. But the transition does not take place at once because there is a go handler in the stack's script. This handler is executed, adding a dissolve effect to the dissolve to black that is already stored. Finally, the command `pass go` is encountered. This triggers the actual card transition, and the two visual effects are executed in order. The effect of the two handlers is equivalent to the effect of a single mouseUp handler that contains both visual effects:

```
on mouseUp
  visual effect dissolve to black
  visual effect dissolve
```

continued

```
   go to next card
end mouseUp
```

This capability is used rarely. But you may find it useful in some stack design problems. For example, you can use a generic effect (such as dissolve) for all card transitions and modify it with a different intermediate image for special transitions. Note that this technique can produce unexpected results in your stack.

The Message Box

Visual effects don't affect the Message box or other windoids (such as the tools or patterns windoid). Because the presence of the Message box may detract from the impact of your visual effects, you may want your script to hide it.

It is best to check if the Message box is visible before hiding it. Then restore the Message box to its original state after the visual effect is finished. In this way, you won't annoy users who want to use the Message box. For example, the following handler first stores the state of the Message box. It hides the Message box during the visual effect, then shows it again if it was visible before the handler started.

```
on mouseUp
  put the visible of the message box into messageVis
  hide the message box
  visual effect dissolve to black
  visual effect dissolve to card
  go to stack "My Appointments"
  set the visible of the message box to messageVis
end mouseUp
```

Color Displays

On a Macintosh II displaying color or grayscale, HyperCard will not display any visual effects; they are ignored. But even on a color display, you can use the Control Panel desk accessory to change the current number of colors to 2. You will then have a black-and-white display, on which visual effects can be seen. Unfortunately, there is no easy way to determine from within a script if a color display is being used.

You can work around this problem with the following technique. Because Macintosh II screens are larger than the standard 512 x 342 pixels of the original Macintosh screen (which is also the size of the HyperCard main window) and because HyperCard automatically centers its window on the screen, you can tell if your stack is running on a large screen by checking the location of the card window. If the `loc of card window` (the location of the upper left corner) is 0,0 (the upper left corner of the screen), you can be fairly certain that HyperCard is running on a Macintosh Plus or Macintosh SE. If the location is some other value, your script can display a dialog box asking the user to make sure the Macintosh is set to black and white before continuing.

```
on openStack
  if the loc of card window is "0,0" then
    answer "Make sure the monitor is set for 2 colors."
  end if
end openStack
```

This work-around does not distinguish between a color screen and a large black-and-white screen such as the expansion displays for the Macintosh Plus and Macintosh SE. Users with these displays may be confused by a message that refers to color. Also, because a script can change the location of the HyperCard window, a stack that was running previously may have moved the card window.

The HyperCard Tools

Visual effects are ignored by HyperCard when you are using any tool other than the browse tool.

HyperDA

The HyperDA desk accessory does not support several HyperTalk commands, including the `visual effect` command. If your stack might be used under HyperDA or on a color Macintosh II, environments in which visual effects cannot be seen, consider whether the stack still works well without visual effects. Fortunately, you do not need to go through the entire stack and eliminate all the visual effects to test this. If you want to see what the stack looks like without visual effects, temporarily lock out the `visual effect` command by placing an empty handler for the `visual effect` command in the stack script:

```
on visual
end visual
```

This empty handler intercepts all `visual effect` commands that originate in the stack, preventing their execution. Then you can navigate through the stack and observe whether the lack of visual effects makes the stack difficult to use and understand. You may want to modify the stack to give additional navigational hints that do not depend on the presence of visual effects.

Time

How much time does it take to do a visual effect? A complicated sequence of effects may be so lengthy that it annoys the user, especially if the sequence is encountered on every movement from card to card. Save time-consuming effects for infrequent transitions (for example, transitions made when the stack is first opened) and for stacks where the user has leisure time to enjoy your art.

Visual Effect Tricks

This section contains hints on the most effective use of the `visual effect` command in designing your stacks and special tricks you can do with visual effects. This section also discusses ways you can use visual effects to make your stacks more polished, professional, and easy to use.

Choosing the Right Visual Effects

Many beginning desktop publishers yield to the temptation to use all those
ful new fonts, styles, and sizes to the fullest. Consequently, they go over
including a profusion of different fonts and styles in their newsletters and
brochures. Eventually, most people realize that layouts with only a few fonts and
styles are more effective. Like fonts in a newsletter, visual effects in HyperCard are
easy to misuse or overuse. Use visual effects with care and restraint if you don't want
them to look garish and amateurish.

Subtlety is the crucial aspect you need to learn to master visual effects. Resist
the temptation to use too many effects just because the capability is there. Some
stacks achieve enormous visual impact using few or no visual effects. In film, notice
the prevalence of straight cuts that go directly to a new scene—special effects are
reserved for special moments in the film. Sometimes, you will deliberately set out to
capture the user's attention with visual effects. But in most cases, if the visual effect
calls attention to itself rather than to the information you are trying to highlight, it is
too obtrusive and should be toned down or removed.

Consistency in your use of visual effects is also important. Visual effects in your
stacks provide important cues to the user. If you don't choose visual effects carefully,
users may be disoriented or confused by mixed messages. Consistency provides a
familiar framework that lets the user navigate with confidence.

A few simple rules will help keep your visual effects consistent:

- Keep your visual effects uniform. For example, if you have a table of contents with a button to go to each chapter, use the same visual effect for
  each button.
- Match the effect with the navigational logic of what is happening. For instance, use zoom in or iris open to show that the user is penetrating to a
  more specific area of the stack.
- If you use a visual effect to indicate the direction the user is going in the
  stack, match it with the opposite effect when the user returns. For example, if you use the barn door open visual effect when the user enters a
  help section, use the barn door close effect when the user exits the help
  section.
- Match common symbols with specific visual effects. For example, if you use
  a scroll visual effect for the left arrow and right arrow buttons in one area
  of the stack, use that effect everywhere you use left arrow and right arrow
  buttons.

You also need to pay attention to the amount and type of *visual impact*. Sometimes you want the visual effect to be almost unnoticeable; other times, it's important that the visual effect be clearly noticeable. The type of effect, the variations
(speed and destination image), and the context (psychological and visual) help determine what kind of impact an effect has.

Visual effects that gradually replace part of the card image, such as dissolves,
wipes, and irises, work best when either the whole card changes or a small part
changes. For example, suppose that a clip art stack presents each piece of art in an
identical frame. You might use a dissolve between cards to give the impression that
the frame remains solid while the graphic dissolves into another graphic.

When most but not all of the card changes, it can give an unpleasant or unfin-
ished look. In these cases, you might want to use a visual effect that shows movement
of the card, such as a scroll. Another way to increase contrast between almost identical images is to use an intermediate destination image:

```
visual effect wipe right to gray
visual effect wipe right to card
```

The closer the intermediate image is to the card images, the subtler the intermediate
transition will be.

If you are in doubt about the right visual effects to use and need a place to
start, look at other stacks that use visual effects. Determine which effects you like
and don't like and, more importantly, why. Do you enjoy a certain effect when it's
used in some contexts, but hate it in others? Remember that effects that draw your
attention aren't necessarily the best: many visual effects work best when the effect is
subtle. If a particular stack is easy to use and navigate in, check out its visual effects.

Trapping System Messages

This section presents several ways to make your stack more inviting and elegant by
adding visual effects to actions such as opening and closing the stack. Although
these are small things, their cumulative impact is to give your stacks a more polished
and professional look.

Entering the Stack

The entrance to a stack is a good place for visual effects. A startup screen on the first
card can display information about your stack, then dissolve to the main area of the
stack. When the stack is first opened, you certainly have the user's attention. This is
a good place to show off a time-consuming visual effect, because it only happens
once rather than every time the user tries to get more information.

```
on openStack
  visual effect dissolve to gray
  visual effect dissolve to card
  go to card "Main Index"
end openStack
```

A striking effect can be used with an all-black first card:

```
on openStack
  visual effect barn door open
  go to card "Main Index"
end openStack
```

The openStack message is sent when the user returns from another application
after having launched the application within HyperCard, as well as when the stack is
first opened. Therefore, you may prefer to put the opening sequence in the script of
the first card if your stack launches applications. If you do this, put a comment in

the stack's openStack handler explaining that the code for the startup sequence is in the script of the first card.

Navigating Through the Stack

Visual effects are often placed in standard navigation buttons. But remember that the user can also use keyboard commands to navigate from a menu, even if the menu bar is hidden. Therefore, you may want to trap these other card transitions to add a visual effect. The following handler adds an appropriate scroll visual effect when the user goes to the previous or next card using the Go menu. Note: the doMenu message is sent when Command-key equivalents for menu items are used, as well as when the user selects a new item with the mouse.

```
on doMenu theItem
   if theItem is "Prev" then visual effect scroll right
   if theItem is "Next" then visual effect scroll left
   pass doMenu
end doMenu
```

The following handler adds a dissolve effect to every card transition done from within the stack, including those from preprogrammed buttons:

```
on go
   visual effect dissolve
   pass go
end go
```

Detouring into Another Stack

When the user goes to another stack, you may want a time-consuming effect to indicate that the distance to another stack is longer than a simple card transition within the stack. The following handler uses the iris visual effect to give the impression that the previous stack is closing and the new one is opening:

```
on doMenu theItem
   if theItem is "Home" or theItem is "Open..." then
     visual effect iris close to black
     visual effect iris open to card
   end if
   pass doMenu -- This line is VERY important!
end doMenu
```

You can similarly trap the help message that is sent when the user chooses the Help menu item in order to add a special visual effect.

Exiting the Stack

When the user exits the stack, you may want to use a visual effect to make a distinct break between the HyperCard environment and the Finder. This handler dissolves to the gray color of the desktop:

```
on Quit
  hide message box
  visual effect iris close
  go to card "Gray Card" -- an all-gray card
end Quit
```

You must go to a card for a visual effect to be visible, because a visual effect takes place only on a card transition. You may want to use your startup screen card if it is appropriate for the end of the stack. If you modify a stack designed by someone else, remember to check for existing handlers for these messages before you add your own.

Changing the Zoom Point

Recall that the zoom open effect zooms from the point the user last clicked on. Most often, you will use the zoom open visual effect in the mouseDown or mouseUp handler of a button. And you will want to zoom from the button's location, which is the last point the user clicked on. Zooming from the last point the user clicked on maintains consistency with the zooming action of the Finder.

Sometimes, however, you may zoom from another point. Use the `click` command within your handler to cause the effect to zoom from a point you select.

For example, suppose your stack contains a map of the world with a list of most continents as buttons, as in Figure 9-7. (You might do this rather than simply labeling the map if, for example, you are designing an educational stack to teach children the names of the continents.) When the user clicks on a continent name, you might want to center the zoom open effect on the corresponding part of the map, rather than on the

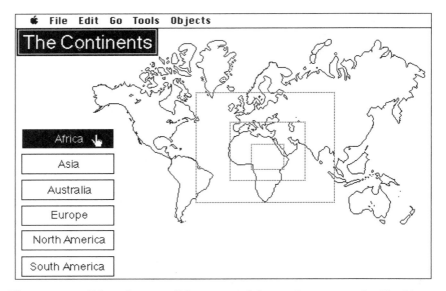

Figure 9-7.   When the user clicks on one of the continent names beside this map, the card zooms in to a more detailed map of that continent.

label that the user clicked. This sets a visual correspondence between the large map of the world and a more detailed map invoked by the click.

The following handler could be placed in the button for Africa:

```
on mouseUp
  click at 300,200
  visual effect zoom open
  go to card "Africa Map"
end mouseUp
```

One problem with this approach is the possibility of conflicting messages. For example, if there is a button with a mouseDown or mouseUp handler at the point 300,200 in the preceding example, the handler will be triggered by the `click` command.

Emulating Other Communication Forms

Visual effects let you give the impression of many other forms of communication. You can also incorporate sound to improve the presentation. It is important to choose compatible and well-integrated sounds, visual effects, and screen designs. A few examples that may be useful for presenting information follow.

Shutter Slide Show

To present a series of images like a slide show, use two wipe visual effects:

```
on mouseUp
  visual effect scroll left to black
  visual effect scroll right to card
  go to next card
end mouseUp
```

This resembles a shutter sliding into place over a slide and then moving back to reveal the next slide. This type of technique helps your audience associate a stack with a form of communication already familiar to them. For example, you might use this slide show format to present a series of graphs in a prepared presentation, then answer questions while referring to the rest of the stack.

Combining the scroll effect with a digitized "clunking" sound may enhance the slide show illusion:

```
on mouseUp
  play "clunk" -- digitized sound placed in stack
  visual effect scroll left to black
  play "clunk"
  visual effect scroll right to card
  go to next card
end mouseUp
```

Book Pages

Another way to present information, especially text, is in the pages of an electronic "book." Figure 9-8 shows an example.

Figure 9-8. You might use this type of layout for a children's stack.

There is a square transparent button covering the flap at the corner of the page. This button works like the flap in the Notebook desk accessory. Clicking in the lower right half of the square takes you to the next page; clicking in the upper left half takes you to the previous page.

```
on mouseDown
  play "click" tempo 180 c5e c6 -- click is a digitized sound
  -- x-coordinate of the click with respect to the button
  if ((item 1 of the clickLoc) - (item 1 of the rect of the target)) ¬
  < ((item 4 of the rect of the target) - (item 2 of the clickLoc))
  -- y-coordinate of the click with respect to the button
  then
    visual effect wipe left to card
    go previous card
  else
    visual effect wipe right to card
    go next card
  end if
end mouseDown
```

Because the background is common to both cards, it is unaffected by the wipe.

When you are considering using fancy effects like these, ask yourself if the effect is appropriate. The information and the way you present it should match. If you use an unsuitable effect because you want to impress viewers or capture their attention, the clash between the information and the presentation will probably distract your audience from the ideas you're trying to convey.

Visual Effects and Animation

One use for visual effects, particularly in stacks for public display, is to enhance animation techniques. If part of your stack uses movements from card to card—for example, a transparent button to zoom in on one section of a diagram—you can use a dissolve to smooth the effect. Another example is the use of effects such as venetian blinds to capture attention at a show or anyplace where you want people to walk up and take notice.

The following handler waits until the stack has been idle for 60 seconds, then begins an animation sequence using the venetian blinds effect. The script is especially suitable for demonstration stacks at trade shows and on sales floors because, if no one is using the stack, it is still visually active and attracts attention.

This handler works by keeping track of the mouse. Every two minutes, the idle handler checks the mouse position. If it is the same as the position 120 seconds ago, the stack is considered to be idle and the animation sequence starts. If the mouse is in a different position, the clock is reset and the position is checked again in another two minutes.

```
on idle
  global lastTimeChecked, lastMouseLoc
  if the seconds - lastTimeChecked < 120 then exit idle
    -- we only want to check every 2 minutes
  put the seconds into lastTimeChecked -- reset the clock
  if the mouseLoc = lastMouseLoc then -- idling routine
    repeat until the mouseLoc ≠ lastMouseLoc or the mouseClick
      visual effect venetian blinds to black
      visual effect venetian blinds to card
      go to next card
    end repeat
  end if
  put the mouseLoc into lastMouseLoc
  go to first card
end idle
```

The following lines are also required in the openStack handler to set the global variables to their initial values:

```
on openStack
  global lastTimeChecked, lastMouseLoc
  put the seconds into lastTimeChecked
  put the mouseLoc into lastMouseLoc
end openStack
```

Fooling the Eye with Visual Effects

Visual effects can be used to make two cards appear as one. For example, using the wipe effect, you can use two cards as a single paint canvas. One way to implement this type of function is to place one transparent button at the lower border of the top card and another at the upper border of the bottom card. When the mouse enters one of these border areas, the other card is brought into view.

Visual effects can also give the impression that one card is really two. As mentioned, `go to this card` is a legal HyperTalk command that triggers any waiting visual effects because it is a card transition command. This capability is useful to obtain certain effects.

For example, you can click a button to zoom open a pop-up field:

```
on mouseDown
  visual effect zoom open
  go to this card
  show card field "Notes"
end mouseDown
```

Unlike the dissolve effect described previously, the `unlock screen with visual effect` command is not needed for this. To understand the reason, recall that dissolve affects only those parts of the card that are different from the original image. This was the source of the sequence problem described in the section on `unlock screen with visual effect`. The zoom effect, however, draws on the original card rather than relies on the difference between the original and destination image. Thus, the effect appears even if the original image is identical to the destination image.

As another example, suppose that you are designing a HyperCard stack that is a replacement for the Finder. You want to emulate the Finder's actions on opening a document or application: when the icon is double-clicked, a zooming rectangles effect appears as the document is opened. The following handler provides this action:

```
on mouseDown
  global myTicks
  if the ticks - myTicks > 120 then -- if the click is soon
  -- enough
    put the ticks into myTicks -- after the last click, the user
    exit mouseDown -- has double-clicked
  else
    visual effect zoom open
    go to this card -- without a go, the effect won't be seen
    open "MacWrite"
  end if
end mouseDown
```

Remember, visual effects can give the user valuable clues for navigation, get the user's attention, and enhance the smooth operation and professional look of the stacks you design. If used inappropriately or too frequently, however, they can make a mess of the stack. When used carefully, visual effects are among the most powerful and aesthetically rewarding of HyperCard's capabilities.

Synching Sight and Sound

Mitchell Waite

Synopsis: HyperCard is the first software product that allows anyone who can cut and paste to create high-tech sound presentations, such as music videos, animations that involve sound effects, and more. All that is needed is a sound editor program and a source of sound effects. However, because HyperCard uses digitized sounds that consume large amounts of memory, problems can arise.

This chapter shows how to import sounds, convert them to resources, attach them to your stack, and combine them with graphics to make HyperTalk audio and visual projects. You'll learn tricks to avoid huge sound files, creative uses of the `play` statement, and how to make your own music videos. The chapter also reveals how to synchronize sound so that your graphics don't get ahead or behind the sound effects.

A technique called *double-buffering* is presented to show how to avoid the scratchy sounds that arise when sounds are broken up by too little memory or slow floppy disks.

Synching Sight and Sound

From Sound Effects to Music Videos

If there were any doubts that the sound features of the Macintosh are better than any other personal computer, HyperCard just ended them. With the help of a sound tool such as MacRecorder and the SoundEdit program, HyperCard stores and plays digital sounds. Further, with careful scripting, you can combine sound with animation to create music videos for high-tech presentations or entertainment. Subtle problems arise, however, when you use sounds with HyperCard.

This chapter shows you how to import sound, convert it to a resource, attach it to your HyperTalk stacks, and combine it with graphics to make HyperTalk audio and visual projects. We show you how to avoid huge sound files by using the play statement creatively and how to make music videos. Because of the demands that sounds place on the Macintosh's memory, music videos are difficult to write. And on a floppy-based Macintosh, the sound can end up broken and scratchy. A neat trick uses *double buffering* to avoid these sound breakups and provide high-quality sound and graphics.

We assume you know how the play statement works. For more information on that statement, and basic music and sound theory, see *The Waite Group's HyperTalk Bible*.

Importing Sound into HyperTalk

To use music and voice with HyperCard, you need additional tools and software. The sounds are entered into the Macintosh using third-party sound recording software. You also need a sound source, which can be a tape recorder, a CD (compact disk) player, or, for live recording, a microphone.

Digitization of the *voice* Parameter

The syntax of the play statement is

```
play "voice" [tempo] "notes"
```

The `voice` parameter is a digitized sound effect stored in your stack as a Macintosh *sound resource*. Digitization, or sampling, is the technique used with CDs (compact disks). The original waveform is sampled many times per second. For each sample, the amplitude of the sound wave is converted into a digital value, recorded, and stored, producing a file of digital numbers. When the numbers in the file are used to move the speaker, you hear a close imitation of the original waveform.

Any digitized sound has two characteristics: the frequency at which it is sampled and the precision with which the sound amplitude is recorded. The best quality sound that the Macintosh can store is at 22,000 samples per second (22 KHz). Each stored number has a precision of one part in 256. Sound stored at 22 KHz requires a precision of 8 bits, or a single byte of memory, per sample. Thus, each sampled sound requires 22,000 bytes for each second of sound. A digital audio compact disc samples at 44 KHz and uses 16 bits of precision; thus, it requires 176,000 bytes for each record of sound, or four times the storage of the Macintosh sound format.

Because each sound consumes 22K bytes per second, HyperTalk has only three voices. An 800K-byte 3.5-inch disk can hold only 36 seconds of sound in this format. Figure on sharing that space with your stack, and you can see why Apple is pushing the CD ROM. A CD can hold 500M bytes; thus, it can hold 500,000K/22K, or 23,000 seconds, which is over 38 minutes of sound. Apple and Farallon have developed a new sound format that is eight times more compact than the 22K format. This should encourage developers to use more sounds with their stacks.

Other problems with HyperCard sound have to do with the access time of the SCSI (small computer system interface) device. If it is a floppy or CD ROM, problems arise because of the time required to access these devices.

The digitized voice forms the texture of the sound that is played. The actual file is stored in the resource fork as type `"snd "` (you can examine these sounds with ResEdit). In default mode, when you `play` the `"snd "` voice without parameters, the voice is played back exactly as it was digitized and stored. If you specify a note after the voice, the voice is played in that note. Specify several notes and you can play a tune in that particular voice. The tempo can be used to speed or slow the voice.

Recall that a voice is an audio waveform converted to digital data and stored in an invisible file. The voice can be anything: a sneeze, a dog's bark, a train whistle, the clapping of an audience, a baby's crying, a car horn honking. In HyperTalk, the frequency and duration of that audio waveform is controlled by the actual notes fed to the `play` statement. Thus, you can play songs made up of the strangest voices you want. If you think the Chipmunks singing Three Blind Mice is impressive, wait till you hear HyperCard play Beethoven in the sound of pig squeals and chain saws.

Sound Recording Hardware and Software

Figure 10-1 shows a typical commercial HyperCard recording device (other devices are coming on the market). In this product, the tape recorder or CD player is plugged into the line input of the recording interface. The output of the interface is plugged into the modem or printer port of a Macintosh. The device has a built-in microphone for live recordings and a volume control.

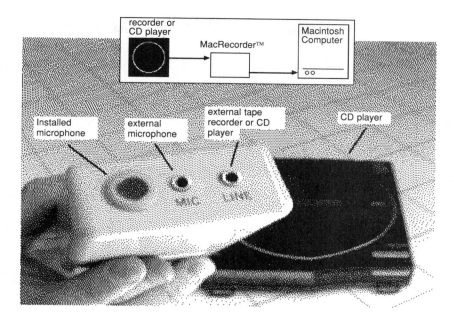

Figure 10-1. A typical HyperCard sound recorder: MacRecorder.

The recording interface contains electronics for converting the incoming microphone or external audio input into a signal of the correct proportions for the Macintosh modem or printer port. The bulk of the signal processing occurs in the software that comes with the recording hardware package. This package has two software programs: a HyperCard stack recorder called HyperSound and a more sophisticated standalone application called SoundEdit.

HyperSound is a HyperCard stack that performs and looks like a real tape recorder, except it saves sounds in a digitized format suitable for installing in your stacks. HyperSound is foolproof to use. If you only need to record a few sounds, and don't need to do much tweaking, it will probably be adequate.

SoundEdit is an extensive, standalone Macintosh sound editing program (not a stack). With SoundEdit and the microphone or line input, you can record and mix sounds, view recorded sounds, customize sounds, add special effects and cut and paste waveforms. Like HyperSound, SoundEdit allows you to save your sounds as resources in HyperCard stacks. Unlike HyperSound, SoundEdit opens existing sound resources in stacks. You can record passages just as if you were recording on a real tape recorder. You can play back your recordings, name them, control the volume, and so on. Think of SoundEdit as a word processor of sounds.

SoundEdit has its own storage format, and each sound you create with it can be stored in its own document. You can't see these sounds with ResEdit because they are not stored as Macintosh "snd" resources. You can use SoundEdit to view "snd" resources and SoundEdit can save sounds in the "snd" format, however. While you are working with sounds—and before they are stored in the stack—keep them in SoundEdit format for convenience.

Opening HyperCard's Sound Resources

With SoundEdit, you can see what HyperCard's built-in sound resources look like. You can open an "snd " resource from SoundEdit by clicking on the Resource button, as shown in Figure 10-2.

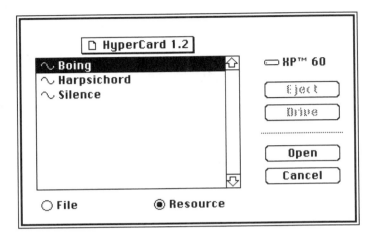

Figure 10-2.   Opening HyperCard's built-in sound resources.

We'll look at the harpsichord sound resource. First select the application that contains the sound resource to examine; in this case, it is HyperCard 1.2 (the application itself). The ~ symbols tell you that it is an "snd " resource. Now double-click on this item. You get the result shown in Figure 10-3. The top panel is the default view when you open a sound. In the lower panel, we have made the display show lines instead of dots. Note how the harpsichord sound contains distinct overtones and harmonics and has a fast attack (the sound wave rises quickly to its maximum value) and a slow decay (much of the waveform is decreasing in value). All these aural qualities can be viewed from SoundEdit. The waveform itself can be modified using the cursor as a pen, redrawing the dots that the waveform is made of. Changing the shape changes the sound. Menus provide further means for control; indeed, you have many of the same controls provided by a $30,000 sound recording studio.

For example, you can enlarge the sound waveform as shown in Figure 10-4. With this resolution, you can control individual cycles of the sound, which means you can remove clicks and scratches (using cut and paste), insert subliminal messages, and create other bizarre effects. SoundEdit and products like it have a variety of special effects that can be applied to the sampled sound.

Each waveform has its own characteristic features. Figure 10-5 shows two views of the boing sound.

With SoundEdit, you can do the following to existing sounds:

▶ amplify existing sounds to increase volume or improve the signal-to-noise ratio

▶ play a sound backwards

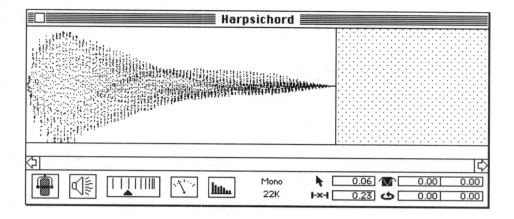

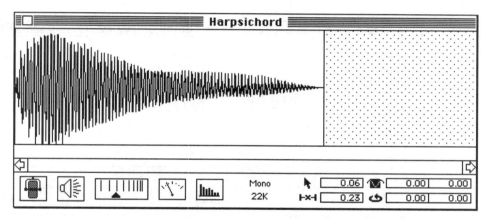

Figure 10-3. Two views of the harpsichord sound effect.

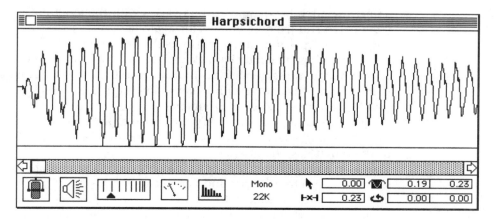

Figure 10-4. Enlargement of the beginning of the harpsichord sound.

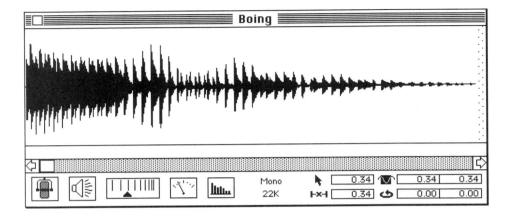

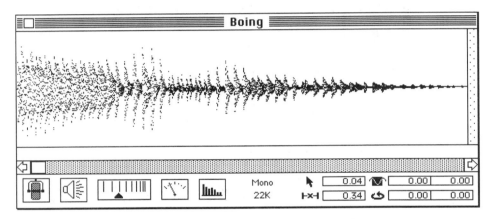

Figure 10-5.   Two views of the boing sound.

▷ adjust the pitch by an amount that varies with the length of the sound (bender) to add tremolo effects, for example

▷ add echo to the sound and control its duration and strength

▷ add an envelope to control attack and decay, to add vibrato effects, or to use with tone and noise generators to make bursts of tones and noise

▷ digitally filter the sound with a parametric equalizer, which is a tone control that lets you alter bands of frequencies

▷ flange the sound, that is, modify the phase of the sound to make it appear that the sound source is moving. The sound of a jet taking off is an example of noise that has been flanged.

▷ slowly interchange two separately recorded channels (ping-pong) so the sound appears to move around your head

▷ add any amount of silence to a sound

▷ smooth any waveform to remove harsh edges, clicks, and pops. This is essentially a low-pass filter, which passes only low frequencies.

Recording a Short Sound

Let us apply some of these techniques by recording a sound and storing it in a stack. We will use SoundEdit to capture the sound, and we will load it into our Sound stack to play with it.

Create a stack called Sound. Make a new card and name it MusicVideo. (We add a button to the card later.) For the example, we will sing the first few words of a song and record them with SoundEdit.

First, connect the MacRecorder hardware to the Macintosh, install the SoundEdit software, and start the program.

In SoundEdit, set the sound format to sample and record the sound at 22K bytes per second. Test the sound level by clicking on the meter icon and singing into the microphone. The waves should just clip at maximum voice level. You may have to adjust the volume settings to get everything smooth.

Click on the microphone icon and sing a few bars of a popular song for about 6 seconds or less. We sang "I left my heart in San Francisco." Click anywhere when you are done. You should now have a sound waveform similar to the one in Figure 10-6. You can drag the cursor through part of the song, as we have done with the word *heart* in our sound waveform, and select the echo special effect from SoundEdit's menu (not shown in the figure). Then drag through another portion and select the flanger effect. Play the new waveform by clicking on the speaker icon.

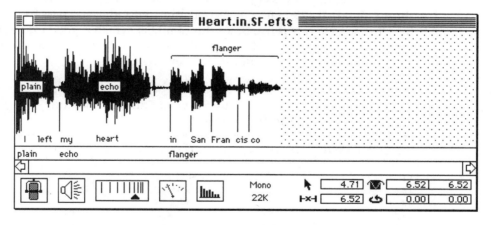

Figure 10-6.   Three special effects applied to a recording. Note the sound uses 6.52 seconds of sound, which translates to approximately 150K bytes of sound.

Amazingly, the song sounds good even though the singer has a crummy voice! If you have *The Waite Group's Tricks of the HyperTalk Masters* stack, you can appreciate this wonderful tool and hear the crooner yourself.

Save the new sound effect as a SoundEdit document so that you can play with it later. Then do a Save As and specify that the sound be saved as an **"snd"** resource. SoundEdit requests that you open the target file to attach the **"snd"** resource to, then it presents a scrolling list box. Select your Sound stack, check OK, and the new sound resource is saved inside your stack. Be careful and write down the name of the sound resource. We call our song "heart."

Exit SoundEdit, open your Sound stack, go to the first card, and add a new button called heart. Insert the following handler in the button and click on the button:

```
on mouseUp
  play "heart"
end mouseUp
```

When you click on the button, you'll hear the complete song you recorded previously.

Although the software gives a good view of the amplitude waveforms generated by your sounds, it does not give any more information. The real-time spectrum analysis portion of SoundEdit does not allow viewing the results of special sound effects. You can watch it operate only as input is being recorded.

Memory Requirements for Audio Sampling

Although we have discussed only 22K bytes per second sound, the Macintosh can actually play back sound in several storage capacities, or densities, as shown in Table 10-1. Each density trades bytes of storage for the upper frequency response of the stored sound. At 22K bytes per second of stored audio, you pass frequencies up to 10 KHz (the sample rate is two times this number), which is good for the finest sounds. You can hear a pin drop at this capacity. But, as we saw, an 800K Macintosh disk can only hold 36 seconds of audio at this density.

Table 10-1.   Formats for Storing Sampled Sound on the   Macintosh

Sampling Mode	Rate	Frequency	Memory	800K Equals
x1	22K	0-10 KHz	22K	36 seconds
x2	11K	0-5 KHz	11K	72 seconds
x3	7.3K	0-3.5 KHz	7.3K	110 seconds
x4	5.5K	0-2.5 KHz	5.5K	145 seconds
Compressed	22K	0-10 KHz	2.7K	5 minutes[a]

[a]This mode is not available with HyperCard 1.1 and 1.2, but may be available in 2.0.

The next sound format uses half the number of bytes, 11K per second, but only passes frequencies up to 5 KHz. For all but the most stringent applications, 11K per second is acceptable and is the most popular format. This density gives 72 seconds on an 800K disk. The next rate samples at 7.3K bytes per second, and cuts off the upper end at 3.5 KHz per second.

This format is adequate for speech driven stacks, and will give the same quality audio as a typical U.S. phone system. You get 110 seconds of continuous speech on an

800K floppy. If you store several short words, each about 2 seconds long (such as *press continue* or *enter the password*), this is probably the ideal rate because you can store up to 55 different speech messages on an 800K floppy. This would make a nice online help system.

A fourth sampling rate uses only 5.5K bytes per second, and cuts the upper frequency to 2.5 KHz. This is CB radio quality and is fine for industrial applications when the external noise level is high. At this density, 145 seconds of audio fit on an 800K disk.

Farallon offers a special nonstandard (non-Apple created) compressed format that samples at 22K bytes per second but uses only 2.7K bytes per second of memory. You can get 5 minutes of high-quality sound on an 800K disk with this format, which gives a 300-word vocabulary for the help system example.

Recording Special Sound Effects

There are various sources for special sound effects that you can put in your stacks. One of the best, from Bainbridge Records, is a three-volume CD set. Its advertising claims it contains "The Most Current and Authentic Living Sound Effects." Its subtitle asserts it is a complete production library for radio and television stations, home movie, home video, industrial presentations, parties, audio visual productions, and more.

Bainbridge permits non-profit uses of these sound effects but any commercial use requires a separate license.

Synching Sight and Sound

Playing a digitized sound is satisfying. But without card movement or other Hyper-Talk functions, it is no more exciting than playing a record or tape. We need to combine the playing of sounds with the movement of graphics on the screen. The most basic approach to animation is to flip through a sequence of cards with different graphic images, using the `go next card` statement. Other graphic effects—such as simulation with paint tools, animated fonts, and animated icons—can be synchronized to music and sound. Because these are covered in other chapters, we focus on synching sounds with card-based animation.

Shootout at the OK or Cancel Corral

We solved the most difficult part of creating a sight and sound animation by using clip animation from MacroMind. Figure 10-7 shows the two cowboy figures we used from the clip art animation package. A card was made for each stage of the shootout, giving us seven cards. The last cowboy is used twice, in both the first and last cards.

Copy the black cowboy from the clip art document to the clipboard using a paint program (or enter the paint mode of HyperCard and use Import Paint), then

Make sure feet match up between frames.

Arm moves up quickly on recoil.

Ready for more.

a. Winning cowboy.

Ready on the draw,

but not quick enough.

Move body back a pixel per frame on impact.

Pause and let gun fall.

On fall, match up location of right foot.

b. Losing cowboy.

Figure 10-7. The seven poses of the shootout. The Shootout script from the Tricks of the HyperTalk Masters stack combines imported sounds with card dissolve animation.

paste it on the first card in the stack. Then paste the white cowboy on that same card, positioning him so he looks correct. Next, create a new card in HyperCard (with Command-n) and repeat the process for the next stage of the draw.

To align the remaining cowboys on subsequent cards, use the following technique. After making the second card, copy the second black cowboy from the paint document using the lasso so he has marching ants around his body. Now, go to the first card in the stack and paste him on top of the first cowboy. Do not click yet. With the marching ants still around the second black cowboy, position the cowboy so his left boot is aligned over the boot of the first black cowboy on the card. Now do a cut (Command-x). This copies the second black cowboy back to the clipboard, *but now in the correct position,* and ensures that he doesn't end up on the wrong card. Now make a new card right after the first and do a paste—the second black cowboy will be placed on the card in the correct position. Repeat this for the entire set of images of the shootout. You can use the arrow keys or Command-2 and Command-3 to move through the cards and simulate the gun fight.

Adding Sound

Now you need to coordinate a sound with the animation. For our Shootout, we used three digital sounds available on CompuServe: *crunch, gunshot,* and *Uuh.* The crunch sound is a very short sound of a muffled pistol being fired and has a lot of white noise. The gunshot sound is a long sound of what seems like several shots being fired. The Uuh sound is the sound of a person expelling air as if hit in the stomach.

With these sounds in your stack, how can you can write a script that plays the right sound at the right card? You cannot just play the sound when you want it to happen in the card. The cards would flip quickly while the sounds continue to play. The problem is that HyperTalk treats `play` commands like any other commands: it queues them and moves to the next command. Card movements are dependent on their position in the script, and if you want card movement and sound to happen at the same time, you need to play some tricks on HyperCard.

Basically, because the card movement is so fast compared to the sounds, we need to make the cards come in sync with the sounds. In the Shootout card animation, we want our script to show the first two cards with no sound, then we want the sound to start. It is not until the third card that the gun is fully drawn by the black cowboy. This is where we want to synchronize the first gun sound, the crunch sound. On the fourth, fifth, and sixth card, the white cowboy is firing his gun; thus, we will make the second gunshot occur when the fifth card is shown. Finally, it is not until the sixth and seventh card that black cowboy dies and falls on the tarmac; the sixth card is when we want the Uuh sound to begin.

As we said, the problem is that if the cards are simply sequenced with the `go next card` command, all the cards will be displayed rapidly while the sound is still playing. The sound takes between ½ and 1 second, while many cards move in a second. We need to delay the cards so that the sound does not get ahead of the display. A HyperTalk visual effect is a good way to do this. By adding a dissolve between cards, the cards won't get too far ahead of the sounds. At the same time, the blending between cards is improved if you use the dissolve visual effect. You could use `wait 30 ticks` if you didn't want the visual effect between the cards.

Make a background button, call it ShootOut, and put the following script into it:

```
on mouseUp
  lock screen
  push card
  go next
  unlock screen with visual effect dissolve very fast
  go next
  visual effect dissolve very fast
  play "crunch"
  play "gunshot"
  play "Uuh"
  repeat 4 times
    visual effect dissolve very fast
    go next
  end repeat
  wait 2 seconds
  lock screen
  pop card
  unlock screen with zoom out
end mouseUp
```

We experimented with the position of these sounds. The script begins showing the first two cards with a dissolve visual effect. Because the sounds were so much longer than the number of card images, the sounds could be queued immediately with three successive `play` commands. After the first three cards are displayed, a `repeat` loop cycles though the remaining four cards. A visual effect inside the loop slows the card transitions so that they do not get ahead of the sounds. Finally, the screen is locked, and the script returns to the first card.

The trouble with this approach is that we are trying to synchronize the cards with the sounds by trial and error. There is a better way, as you will see in the next example.

Creating a Music Video and Better Synching

A music video on the Macintosh is a short 10 to 30 second series of digitized images and animation, perhaps combined with a song or a custom synthesized piece. The idea is to rival the videos on MTV and VH-1 (television channels that show videos of rock and roll songs).

As shown in the previous example, the Macintosh can play digitized audio with reasonable quality at 22K bytes per second. If you will be distributing custom sound on a standard Apple 800K 3.5-inch disk, even at the lower but still acceptable quality of 11K bytes per second, you can only store about 72 seconds of sound. Because most popular songs use at least 180 seconds, you've got a problem. If you know your presentation hardware will always be a hard disk Macintosh system, you can consider increasing the allowable storage and distributing the music on multiple 800K floppies that are loaded onto the hard disk before running the stack.

There is another problem. Digitized sound on the Macintosh can only run from a SCSI device, such as a floppy disk or hard disk. On a hard disk system, access time is so fast that the SCSI doesn't create a problem. On a floppy disk, though, sounds that cause fetches to the disk may create scratchy and broken patches in the sound that is playing during the disk activity. These problems—caused by the slow response time of the floppy—can be prevented. It is difficult to handle long (greater than 30 seconds) music-based stacks running from a floppy disk on a 1M byte Macintosh Plus, even using the paged techniques explained next. The only solution may be to run such stacks from a hard disk.

Another problem when running long sounds is that digitized sounds must be loaded into RAM before they are played. Consequently, they also consume large quantities of RAM memory. When you have a Macintosh SE with 4M bytes of RAM storage, this is not much of a problem. But on a Macintosh Plus with only 1M byte of RAM—with HyperCard using 750K, or roughly 75 percent, of that RAM—little room remains for the digitized audio waveform. When a long song is played on such machines, the sound stops while the next voice is read from the disk.

Double Buffering to Prevent Sound Break Up

There is a trick to get around this problem: make sure your sounds are always stored in RAM before they are played. If the sound resource is still on the disk when

HyperTalk is ready to play it, the disk accesses will break up the sound while it is played. If the sound is in RAM when it is ready to be played, it won't be disturbed by disk activity.

Normally, when HyperTalk encounters `play` commands, it attempts to queue all of them in RAM. Because of the limited amount of available RAM, HyperTalk fills what it can and leaves the rest on the disk. Double buffering, or "paged" playing of music, is a method of controlling the way sounds are queued and played from a script. It can eliminate sound break up due to insufficient memory on a hard disk system.

To apply double buffering, you must keep your digitized sounds short. Sounds on a Macintosh Plus should be between 4 and 8 seconds and should use the 11K bytes per second format. This means your recording segments should be between 44K and 88K bytes. The lower the figure, the better. If possible, try to cut all sounds to 44K. There will probably always be enough memory on a 1M byte Macintosh Plus to hold two of these strips at the same time, but no more. Also, by breaking longer sounds into 4 to 8 second segments, you can play long audio passages that are coordinated with your stacks.

In double buffering, the first and second sounds are executed with `play` statements. The trick is to then use the statement: `wait until the sound is "done" or the sound = "teach.1"`. Note that `done` is a predefined literal, not a constant, so the quotes must be used. This statement waits either for the current sound playing to be done or for the teach.1 sound to be completed before it executes the `play` statement for the third passage. Thus, the third passage of sound is loaded only when the first sound strip has finished and while the second passage is being played. In other words, the `wait` statement prevents the third sound from queuing up, so only one strip is playing when one strip is loading.

Likewise, the `play` statement for the fourth sound passage is executed (and consequently loaded into memory) when the second sound passage has finished and while the third passage is being played. This approach allows only one sound to be loading while another is being played, thus ensuring that the sound is always playing from memory and is not broken by disk activity. Another way to look at this is that there is a smooth in-memory seam between each sound: when one sound finishes, the next sound is in memory. This technique does not work under Multifinder because you cannot control the independent time slicing that occurs.

To create the music video, use the 11K per second storage density and find a section of music under 72 seconds long so you can fit it on an 800K disk. Record this sound with SoundEdit. Then examine it to find logical points for dividing it in sections between 4 and 8 seconds long. These divisions should be where delays will have a minor effect on how the sound is perceived. Figure 10-8 is a SoundEdit waveform showing how we divided a song into four parts. The total use in bytes for this section of music is 283K, which is well within the limits.

Install the sections of music into the Sound stack and name each with some simple number scheme so you don't lose track. Our example used a few lines from the CSNY song "Teach Your Children" by Graham Nash. We broke it into four parts, called teach.1, teach.2, teach.3, and teach.4. The biggest part is 88K bytes, and the smallest is 44K bytes.

Go to the first card of your Sound stack and add a new button called Teach. Create some cards and graphics to accompany the song. In our example, we created four card graphics, as shown in Figure 10-9. Each graphic was put in the center of a different card in the Sound stack, so there are four cards.

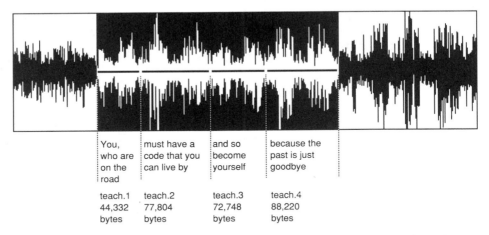

| You, who are on the road | must have a code that you can live by | and so become yourself | because the past is just goodbye |
| teach.1 44,332 bytes | teach.2 77,804 bytes | teach.3 72,748 bytes | teach.4 88,220 bytes |

Figure 10-8.   Dividing the song for the music video into four parts with similar cutting rates.

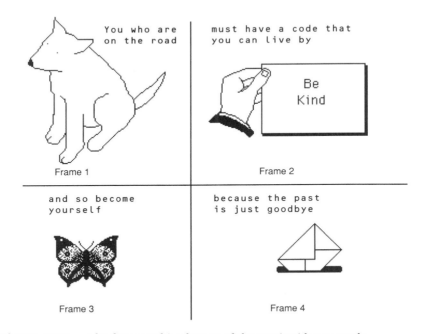

Figure 10-9.   The four graphics frames of the music video example.

Put the following handler into the Teach button you just created:

```
on mouseUp
  play "teach.1" -- you who are on the road
```

continued

```
   move
   -- queue the next sound
   play "teach.2" -- must have a code that you can live by
   wait until the sound is "done" or the sound = "teach.1"
   play "teach.3" -- and so become yourself
   wait until the sound is "done" or the sound = "teach.2"
   move
   play "teach.4" -- because the past is just a goodbye
   wait until the sound is "done" or the sound = "teach.3"
   move
   wait until the sound is "done" or the sound = "teach.4"
   move
end mouseUp

on move
   visual effect dissolve slow
   go to next card
end move
```

When you click on the Teach button, the entire 25 seconds of the song plays and the cards dissolve without a single scratch or breaking up of the sound (provided you are running the script from a hard disk). The button script uses a custom command called `move`, which executes a dissolve effect and a `go to next card`.

The first two sounds of the song are queued immediately. The statement `wait until the sound is "done" or the sound = "teach.1"` is how you tell when to load the third sound. The `wait` and `move` statements are interspersed to make the dissolves occur at the correct point in the sound.

After you have installed a sound resource, check that the stack size is what you expected. While cutting and pasting sound sections, it is easy to accidentally store 11K bytes per second sounds as 22K bytes per second documents. Add all your sound resources in bytes and make sure the final stack is not unexpectedly large.

One caveat: There is a limit to the amount of sound resources the Macintosh will queue and play before sounds start to break up. It seems like memory becomes too fragmented to handle more than about 30 seconds of continuous sound.

Go Forth and Make Videos

Many more techniques can be used with HyperCard's digitized sound. We hope Bill Atkinson will have improved HyperCard's sound system by the time we revise this book. Perhaps we'll see a 10-to-1 compression ratio, envelope modulation, true frequency tuning, tremolo, and other special effects. But for now, even with its limited `play` statement, HyperCard is still the best choice for mixing sound with graphics.

Part

Tools and Utilities

Developer's Tool Kit

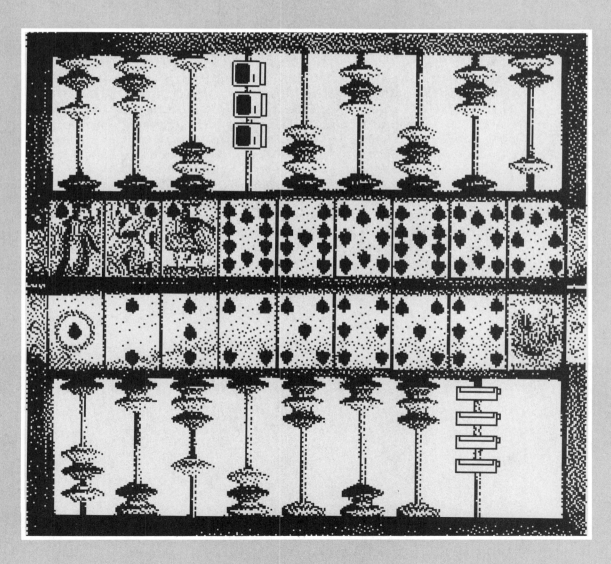

Andrew Stone

Synopsis: HyperCard developers are constantly looking for ways to more efficiently do their scripting and to reduce the time spent on repetitive tasks. This chapter presents a collection of modular scripting tools that you can install in your Home stack so that they are available from any stack you are working on.

A MakeRadios script creates groups of radio buttons with special built-in scripts that automatically coordinate the buttons' highlighting and unhighliting. Buttons can be created in vertical or horizontal columns, and names can be easily changed without affecting the inner workings of the button scripts.

A MakeIndex script goes through your entire stack and places the name of each card in a scrolling field. Then, use ScrollJump handler from Chapter 5 to access these cards from one master index. A FieldSort script presents a simple sorting algorithm that sorts your master index, or the contents of any field, alphabetically. A CreateLink tool makes a button that links to any card in any stack; a `seek` function allows rapid tranversal of a stack in either direction. There are also scripts for setting up the function keys of your keyboard and a complex invoice maker stack that provides a simple spreadsheet with automated data entry. Finally, a powerful stack reporter produces text fields that contain the scripts in all objects of your stack and helps you produce a map of your stack's listings.

Developer's Tool Kit

Utilities and Scripts for Better Scripting

This chapter contains a collection of HyperTalk *tools*, modular sections of scripting that reside in your Home stack. From your Home stack, tools can be reached from any card or stack due to the inheritance structure of HyperTalk. Usually, tools are for only your use, but you could also put them in the stack script of stacks you distribute. By taking advantage of user-defined functions and procedures— tools— you greatly enhance the power of HyperCard.

The first tool in this chapter, the MakeRadios script, creates groups of radio buttons with special scripts that automatically coordinate the buttons' highlighting and unhighlighting. You can have vertical or horizontal button groupings. You can edit a button's name—without rewriting the code—because the scripts are not contingent on the names of the buttons.

The next section describes two tools that can be used together: MakeIndex and FieldSort. With MakeIndex, you can name each card of a stack and list it in a scrolling field. Then you can access each card from one master index with the ScrollJump handler (see chapter 5). The FieldSort function is a HyperTalk sorting algorithm that sorts the lines of your index, or any field, alphabetically.

Next, the CreateLink tool creates a new button in your Home stack, on the first card of the stack, or on any other card you specify, and links the specified card to the card from which you called the script. The Seek function is also included. It allows rapid traversal of the stack in either direction, depending on whether the mouse is in the right or left half of the card window. With the Seek function, you can create links dynamically.

The Function Key script can cut the development time of many stacks: it programs the Apple extended keyboard function keys with all the standard HyperTalk multiple button or mouse click commands.

The chapter has three more complex tools. The first tool, the Invoice Maker, is actually the core of a stack. The Invoice Maker—using very few lines of code—is a simple spreadsheet and automated data entry. It can be used in billing or retail sales.

The Stack Reporter is a card that installs itself into any stack and produces text files of any combination of the card, button, field, background, or stack script. This script was developed to automate the production of listings in this author's chapters, thus guaranteeing that the book contains the most recent scripts.

Finally, the Fortune for HyperCard tool displays a random quotation, quip, or joke from a database. It includes a lesson on variable parameter lists and an algorithm for dynamic field sizing based on the amount of text in the field.

MakeRadios

Radio buttons are a powerful tool for storing global information. You use radio buttons to make an exclusive choice; if more than one button needs to be highlighted at a time, use separate groups of buttons or use checkbox buttons. In the next chapter, four groups of radio buttons on the Preferences card hold the value of four global containers.

Programming radio buttons is dull because of the repetitive nature of the scripts required to highlight a button and unhighlight the rest of the group. Enter the MakeRadios tool! After you place this tool in your Home stack script, you will be littering your stacks with groups of radio buttons.

How It Works

The MakeRadios script first asks how many buttons will be in the group and stores your answer in howmany. It then asks if you want vertical or horizontal alignment—a strip of five buttons across or up to eight down (see Figure 11-1). The script places this answer in the alignment container. The handler then asks for the location of the first button, from which it calculates the positions of the remaining buttons:

```
-- Get the location of first button
answer "Click at the center of first button's location"
wait until the mouse is down
put the clickH into hloc
put the clickV into vloc
```

You have to create all of the buttons first to obtain the ID numbers for the insertion of scripts. The buttons are created in a repeat loop indexed by *i*, and the ID number of the button is stored in the *i*th item of the variable theIDs.

```
-- Create, set, and locate the buttons; get their ID number
repeat with i = 1 to howmany
  domenu "New Button"
  set name of btn "New Button" to "unnamed" && i
  put the id of btn tempName into item i of theIDs
  put "unnamed" && i into tempName
  set style of btn tempName to radioButton
```

The location of the new button is determined by the following script portion:

```
if alignment is "Vertical" then
  set the loc of btn tempName to hloc,vloc + (i - 1) * 35
else set the loc of btn tempName to hloc + (i - 1) * 102,vloc
```

```
┌─────────────────────────────────────────────────────────┐
│              RELAX!:Tricks: Tool Tricks                   │
├─────────────────────────────────────────────────────────┤
│                                                           │
│              ┌─────────────────────────┐                  │
│              │       MakeRadios        │                  │
│              └─────────────────────────┘                  │
│   ○ unnamed 1                                             │
│                                                           │
│   ○ unnamed 2                                             │
│                                                           │
│   ○ unnamed 3                                             │
│                                                           │
│   ◉ unnamed 4          ◉ Green    ○ Blue      ○ Red       │
│                                                           │
│   ○ unnamed 5                                             │
│                                                           │
│   ○ unnamed 6                                             │
│                                                           │
│   ○ unnamed 7                                             │
│   ┌──┐  ┌─────────────────┐ ┌──────────┐ ┌──────────────┐ │
│   │↵ │  │ Clear Demo Btns │ │Show Help │ │Demo MakeRadioS│ │
│   └──┘  └─────────────────┘ └──────────┘ └──────────────┘ │
└─────────────────────────────────────────────────────────┘
```

Figure 11-1. With the MakeRadios tool, you can make radio buttons easily.

The location of the first button is `hloc,vloc` (where you clicked) because *(i − 1) * 35 = 0*. With vertical alignment, each subsequent button is placed 35 pixels below the preceding button. After the buttons are created, the handler enters a loop to install the code in each button. The scripts refer to the buttons' IDs; therefore, changing a button's name will not affect the performance of the button's code.

Inserting the Scripts of the New Buttons

The second part of the MakeRadios tool contains a nested `repeat` loop. The first few lines of the outer `repeat` loop insert the code to turn on the highlight of the button:

```
-- Install script into each of the new buttons
repeat with i = 1 to howMany
  put "on mouseUp" & return into newScript
  put "--insert globals and assignments here" & return after newScript
  put "set the hilite of me to true" & return after newScript
```

Note that you still need to add the code to modify the global variable. For example, if you are setting the state of a global variable named `UseEffects`, you would add this to the radio button that makes the global container true:

```
global UseEffects -- a global boolean variable
put true into UseEffects
```

Then, you would add the following to the button that sets the global container to false:

```
global UseEffects -- a global boolean variable
put false into UseEffects
```

The next part of MakeRadios is the inner `repeat` loop, which installs the appropriate script for each button. First you check to see if `j = i` (the script is at the ID number of the button you just set to true). If so, the script returns to the top of the loop and skips this iteration to avoid turning the button off again.

```
repeat with j = 1 to howmany
if j = i then next repeat -- don't turn it off
  -- Now toggle off the others
  put "set the hilite of btn ID " & item j of theIDs && "to ¬
  false" & return after newScript
end repeat
```

After creating the buttons, the script stores each new ID number in the next item of the `theIDs` container. In the following, the *j*th item of `theIDs` is retrieved, then that ID number is inserted in the script. The outer loop finishes by setting the script of the *i*th button to `newScript` and choosing the browse tool:

```
    put "end mouseup" & return after newScript
    set the script of btn ID item i of theIDs to newScript
  end repeat

  choose browse tool
end MakeRadios
```

A Script to Clear Groups of Buttons

After you have typed in the MakeRadios tool, you should test it. The following script is handy for deleting groups of buttons that you have created using the MakeRadios script:

```
on clearRadios
  choose btn tool
  -- Not so obvious logic trick: disappearing numbers
  repeat with num = the number of btns down to 1
    if "un" is in the short name of btn num then -- "unnamed"
      click at the loc of btn num
      domenu "Clear Button"
    end if
  end repeat
  choose browse tool
end clearRadios
```

Note that a "down to" construction is used with the `repeat` loop. First we tried the standard `repeat with i = 1 to the number of buttons`. But after deleting four buttons, the program displayed the error message `Can't Find Btn Number 5`. HyperCard changed the number of buttons while the loop was in action, shifting buttons 5, 6, and 7 to numbers 1, 2, and 3. If you need stability in a name, use the ID number, which is guaranteed to be unique. Here, the "down to" construction solves the problem.

```
--**********************Description**************************
-- TYPE:        Tool, handler
-- AUTHOR:      Andrew C. Stone
-- NAME:        MakeRadios
-- LOCATION:    Home stack script


--********************Script Starts**************************
on makeRadios
  ask "How many radio buttons do you want in this group?"
  if it is empty then exit makeRadios
  put it into howMany

  answer "Horizontal or vertical spacing?" with "Horizontal" or ¬
  "Vertical"
  if it is empty then exit makeRadios
  put it into alignment

  if howmany > 8 then answer "Come on, get real!"
  if howmany > 5 and alignment = "Horizontal" then
    answer "Only 5 buttons fit horizontally. Ok?" with ¬
    "Ok" or "Cancel"
    if it is "cancel" then exit MakeRadios
    else put 5 into howMany
  end if

  -- Get the location of the first button
  answer "Click at the center of first button's location"
  wait until the mouse is down
  put item 1 of the clickloc into hloc
  put item 2 of the clickloc into vloc

  -- Create, set, and locate the buttons; get their ID number
  repeat with i = 1 to howmany
    domenu "New Button"
    set name of btn "New Button" to "unnamed" && i
    put the id of  btn tempName into item i of theIDs
    put "unnamed" && i into tempName
    set style of btn tempName to radioButton

    if alignment is "Vertical" then
      set the loc of btn tempName to hloc,vloc + (i-1) * 35
      else set the loc of btn tempName to hloc + (i-1) * 102,vloc
  end repeat

  -- Set the script of each to make them work
  repeat with i = 1 to howMany
    put "on mouseUp" & return into newScript
    put "--insert globals and assignments here" & return ¬
    after newScript
    put "set the hilite of me to true" & return after newScript
```

continued

```
        -- Now toggle off the others
        repeat with j = 1 to howmany
          if j = i then next repeat -- don't turn it off
          put "set the hilite of btn ID " & item j of theIDs && ¬
          "to false" & return after newScript
        end repeat

        put "end mouseup" & return after newScript
        set the script of btn ID item i of theIDs to newScript
      end repeat
      choose browse tool
    end MakeRadios
```

MakeIndex and FieldSort

MakeIndex and FieldSort are two useful tools that can be used together. FieldSort sorts the lines of a field alphabetically. MakeIndex compiles a list of card names in the stack into the card field named index. This is useful, for example, when you want the program to jump to certain cards from a list of card names. The index card field uses the ScrollJump script (see chapter 2) and thus acts as a de facto link to each card in the stack.

To compile its list, MakeIndex goes through the stack and puts the name of each card in the variable theName. If the name is not filled in, you can name the card as the list is compiled. MakeIndex checks if *ID* is in the short name of the card, in which case the card is unnamed. With this script, you can create an index in an existing stack, but it is better to name the cards when they are being created. Following the listing of MakeIndex is an on NewCard handler that asks you to name the card during its creation, then places the new card's name in the index list.

```
--*************** Automatic Index Routines *********************
--********************* Description **************************
-- TYPE:       Index creation and autolinking scripts
-- AUTHOR:     Andrew C. Stone
-- NAME:       MakeIndex, FieldSort(<container>)
-- LOCATIONS:  Card, background, or Stack

--********************** MakeIndex ***************************
-- This routine gets the name of each card and puts each card
-- name in a scrolling card field named index on a card named
-- index.  Then you are asked if you want the names sorted.  If
-- so, function FieldSort is called.

on MakeIndex
  put empty into cd fld index of cd index -- flush old info
  repeat with i = 1 to the number of cards
    set the cursor to busy -- beachball
    put the short name of card i into thename -- get latest name

    -- Make sure card has a decent name
    if "Id" is in thename then
```

continued

```
      ask "This card needs a descriptive name:"
      if it is empty then exit MakeIndex
      set the name of this card to it
      put it into thename
    end if

    put thename & return after cd fld index of cd index
    -- add card to index
  end repeat
  go to card index

  -- If requested, sort lines with fieldSort function
  answer "Do you want the card names sorted?" with "Ok" or "no"
  if it is "Ok" then
    put fieldSort(cd fld index) into cd fld index of cd index
  end if
end MakeIndex

--******************** newcard handler *************************
-- Traps newcard and allows automatic naming and indexing of
-- new card

on newcard
  ask "What is the name of the new card?"
  if it is empty then -- return control to user
    exit newcard
  else
    set the name of this card to it -- auto naming of card
    visual iris close
    go card "index" -- add it to index
    put return & it after cd fld "index" of card "index"

    -- If requested, sort lines with fieldSort function
    answer "Do you want the card names sorted?" with "Ok" or "no"
    if it is "Ok" then
      put fieldSort(cd fld index) into cd fld index
    end if
    answer "Go Back Now?" with "Ok" or "Cancel"
    if it is "Ok" then go back
  end if
end newcard
```

The last section of MakeIndex and the newcard handler processes the unorganized contents of the newly formed field with the line-sorting function, FieldSort.

The syntax for using FieldSort is

```
put FieldSort(<container>) into <container>
```

FieldSort is a selection sort that is fine for a hundred lines or so. A more efficient sort might be a shell sort if you are sorting thousands of lines. This implementation only swaps one line per iteration because it uses an index to the alphabetically lowest line. For example:

```
put FieldSort(cd fld index) into cd fld index
```

First, FieldSort removes all blank lines from the field identifier `theField` by checking if each line is empty:

```
function FieldSort theField
  -- first strip all blank lines
  put return & return into crcr
  get theField
  repeat
    put offset(crcr,it) into p
    if p = 0 then exit repeat
    delete char p of it
  end repeat
  put it into theField
```

After the blank lines are deleted, the nested `repeat` loops continue to find the smallest line and move it to the front of the container. In HyperTalk, smallest means lowest ASCII value. `LeastLineNum` is initialized to `primary`, the first unsorted line (it increases by 1 each pass through the outer loop). In the inner loop, the script compares each current line with `LeastLineNum` and changes `leastLineNum` to the current line if `current` is alphabetically less than `leastLineNum`:

```
repeat with primary = 1 to the number of lines in theField - 1
  put primary into leastLineNum
  repeat with current = primary + 1 to the number of lines ¬
  in theField
    if line current of theField < line leastLineNum of ¬
    theField then
      put current into leastLineNum
    end if
  end repeat
```

If `leastLineNum` is not the first line, the script swaps them:

```
if leastLineNum > primary then -- it was out of order
  put line primary  of theField into temp -- so swap lines
  put line leastLineNum of theField into line primary of theField
  put temp into line leastLineNum of theField
end if
```

At the end, FieldSort returns the sorted field. Note that it would be easy to modify this function to sort in descending order by replacing the < (less than) operators with > (greater than) operators. In the listing in the next chapter, a modified FieldSort sorts by last name. Translated into HyperTalk, it sorts by the last word of first item.

```
--******************** function FieldSort ********************
-- A selection sort of the lines of a field
-- Usage:  put FieldSort(<container>) into <container>
-- By Andrew Stone

function FieldSort theField
  -- first strip all blank lines
```

continued

```
put return & return into crcr
get theField
repeat
  put offset(crcr,it) into p
  if p = 0 then exit repeat
  delete char p of it
end repeat
put it into theField

repeat with primary = 1 to the number of lines in theField - 1
  put primary into leastLineNum
  repeat with current = primary + 1 to the number of lines ¬
  in theField
    if line current of theField < line leastLineNum of ¬
    theField then
      put current into leastLineNum
    end if
  end repeat

  if leastLineNum > primary then -- it was out of order
    put line primary of theField into temp -- so swap lines
    put line leastLineNum of theField into line primary ¬
    of theField
    put temp into line leastLineNum of theField
  end if
end repeat
return theField -- return the sorted field
end fieldSort
```

CreateLink and the *Seek* Function

One of the most common things you will do as a scriptor or author is move between cards. For example, suppose that a card is buried deep in a stack. The most effective way to get to that card is to type

```
go card <cardName>
```

where *cardName* is the name of the card.

But often you do not know the name of your card or where it is in the stack (if, for example, you sorted the stack). You are relegated to pressing Command-3 over and over to move forward one card. That can wear out your finger and your patience.

Here is a neat card-scanning tool to place in your Home stack. When you move the cursor to the right of the card window and press Option-Shift, the on idle handler automatically moves forward through the stack. Move the cursor to the left side of the screen to go back. Press Command-Shift-Option to move quickly through the stack. When you find your card, release the keys. This seeking script follows:

```
on idle
  if the optionkey is down and the shiftkey is down then --
    repeat until the optionkey is up
```

continued

```
        if item 1 of the mouseloc > 256 then
        -- right side of window
          visual scroll left
          go next card
          if the commandkey is down then
            wait 3
          else
            wait 1 sec
          end if
        else -- left side of window
          visual scroll right
          go prev card
          if the commandkey is down then
            wait 3
          else
            wait 1 sec
          end if
        end if
      end repeat
    end if
end idle
```

CreateLink performs three basic functions:

▷ links the Home stack to the card you call CreateLink from
▷ links the first card to the card you called CreateLink from
▷ links the card you are on to any other card in the stack

These links are established with the Seek function, a modification of the previous on idle handler. The CreateLink tool creates a linked button in one step instead of the sequence: go to the card requiring a button, create a new button, link, set the icon, go back.

The Seek function turns the mousedown into a stack traversal tool. You can flip through cards as long as the mouse is still down, going to the next card if the cursor is in the right half of the screen or the previous card if the cursor is in the left half of the card window.

If the Command key is pressed, the traversal happens at breakneck speed. You can return to a card by moving the cursor to the other side of the card window while the mouse is still down. When you release the button, Seek puts the name of the card you were on into a variable that it returns, then pops back to the card you are creating a button on. This is dynamic linking at its apex.

The code is divided into the three types of links. Three is the magic number of forks because up to three answers are supported in the answer command. Sections of code are basically the same, with some variation. The icons are different if they represent a stack or a card; select the icons that meet your needs.

The syntax for setting the icon is

```
set icon of button "New Button" to <xxxx>
```

where *xxxx* is the ID number of the icon. You can get the number of each icon through the icon dialog of the button information menu item. Creating new icons is easy in ResEdit: check my freeware stack The Mayan Icons—they were doing it years ago.

The third branch of logic, which creates a link from the calling card to any other card, uses the Seek function:

```
else
  answer "To link this card with another,hold mousedown" ¬
  with "Cancel" or "Ok"
  if it is "Cancel" then exit createLink
  else
    wait until the mouse is down -- to let them get started
    put seek() into linkcard
    doMenu "New Button"
```

With wait until the mouse is down, the user can click Ok, move to the right or left of the card window, then hold the mouse button down to start cruising:

```
function Seek
  push card -- we will be back
  repeat until the mouse is up -- keep looping
    if the mouseH > 256 then -- reevaluate which way
      visual scroll left
      go next card
      if the shiftkey is down then -- speed it up
        wait 3
      else
        wait 1 sec -- seems about right
      end if
```

Because the mouseH is reevaluated each pass through the loop, you can switch directions in midstream.

The following is at the end of the function:

```
  put the short name of this card into theName
  pop card
  return theName
end Seek
```

This is where you modify the code if you want the seek function to return another value. For example, to get the script of the card where you end the search, you would use:

```
put the script of this card into theScript
return theScript
```

The visual effects of scroll left for go next card and scroll right for go prev card give a sense of equilibrium in an on-the-fly stack traversal.

```
--******************** Description **************************
-- TYPE:        Tool script
-- AUTHOR:      Andrew C. Stone
-- NAME:        createLink
-- LOCATION:    Home stack script


********************Tool Script Starts************************
on createLink
  answer "Create a button in home or first card or to other?" ¬
  with "Other" or "First Card" or "Home"
  if it is "Home" then
    put the name of this stack into stackName
    go Home
    createButton stackName,1000
  else if it is "First Card" then
    put the name of this card into cardname
    go first card
    createButton cardName,20186
  else
    answer "To link this card with another, hold mousedown" ¬
    with "Cancel" or "Ok"
    if it is "Cancel" then exit createLink
    else
      wait until the mouse is down -- to let them get started
      put seek() into linkcard
      createButton linkcard,20186
    end if
  end if
  put "Move button to desired location, then press Command-Tab"
end createLink

on createButton newName,iconNum
  lock screen
  doMenu "New Button"
  set rect of button "New Button" to 200,200,312,250
  set icon of button "New Button" to iconNum
  set style of button "new button" to transparent

  -- This inserts the script in new button
  put "on mouseUp" & return & ¬
  "go to "  & newName  & return & ¬
  "end mouseUp" into theScript
  set script of button "new button" to theScript

  set name of button "new button" to newName
  unlock screen
end createButton

-- Seek: a tool for stack transversal and card selection
function Seek
  push card
  repeat until the mouse is  up
    if the mouseH > 256 then
      visual scroll left
      go next card
      if the commandkey is down then
```

continued

```
        wait 3
      else
        wait 1 sec
      end if
    else
      visual scroll right
      go prev card
      if the commandKey is down then
        wait 3
      else
        wait 1 sec
      end if
    end if
  end repeat
  put the short name of this card into theName
  pop card
  return theName
end Seek
```

Function Key Script

For those of you lucky enough to have the Apple extended keyboard or the DataDesk keyboard, the following simple script will help shorten development time. This tool traps the pressed Function key and determines which one it is. (The HyperTalk functionKey function returns the number of the pressed Function key.) If the script does not handle the pressed key, the functionKey message is passed explicitly at the end of the script pass function. F1, F2, F,3 and F4 remain as the undo, cut, copy, and paste functions.

The browse tool, button tool, and field tool are grouped in the F5, F6, and F7 locations, respectively. The keys that edit the scripts of the card, the background, and the stack are in the F9, F10, and F11 spots.

Press F8 (the select tool), Command-A (select all), Command-I (invert screen picture), and Command-L (randomly lighten the picture) and you have created a star-filled card in four chords.

Use Function key 12 when you create a button in the wrong layer: a card button when you wanted a background button or vice versa. Because Hypertalk returns the number of the pressed Function key, the following script segment shows how to provide this functionality if the script is passed 12 in the whichKey parameter:

```
if whichKey is 12 then
  domenu "Cut Button"
  domenu "Background"
  domenu "Paste Button"
else
```

The same tact can be taken with a field-switching script. Because doMenu "Background" is a toggle, it does not matter whether you want to move a button from the card layer to the background layer or the other way around.

Function key 13 demonstrates that you can do just about anything, no matter how useless!

```
--******************* Description ****************************
-- TYPE:        Assigns HyperCard functions to functionKeys
-- AUTHOR:      Andrew C. Stone
-- NAME:        Function key script
-- LOCATION:    Home stack script

********************* Tool Script Starts *********************
on functionkey whichKey
-- The function key pressed sends a number as a parameter;
-- this is placed in "whichKey"
  if whichKey is 5 then
    choose browse tool
  else if whichKey is 6 then
    choose button tool
  else if whichKey is 7 then
    choose field tool
  else if whichKey is 8 then
    choose select tool
  else if whichKey is 9 then -- these three edit the scripts
    edit script of card
  else if whichKey is 10 then
    edit script of background
  else if whichKey is 11 then
    edit script of stack
  else if whichKey is 12 then
-- when button created in wrong layer
    domenu "Cut Button"
    domenu "Background"
    domenu "Paste Button"
  else if whichKey is 13 then -- to show you can do anything
    domenu "New Background"
    choose select tool
    domenu "Select All"
    domenu "Invert"
    domenu "Lighten"
    flash 3
    domenu "Delete Card"
    go prev card
  else
    pass functionkey -- be a good citizen
  end if
end functionkey
```

Invoice Maker

This section demonstrates how to create spreadsheet functions such as calculate and database-linked data entry techniques that look up prices and code numbers. The amount of code is minuscule: approximately 45 lines of HyperTalk for a stack that automatically searches for an inventory item's full name, then fills out its code number and price, replaces its abbreviated name with its full name, totals each line, subtotals all the lines, adds the tax, and produces a final total on an invoice.

This stack can be created with HyperCard versions 1.2 and above. It requires just two cards with different backgrounds; the Prices card of the Prices background

(Figure 11-2) and the Template card of the Invoices background (Figure 11-3). Figure 11-4 shows a sample invoice.

A welcome card is the first card of the stack and the first card of the Prices background. See Figure 11-5. It has the standard go home and Find buttons and Show Help, a button-field combination produced with the CreatePopUp handler

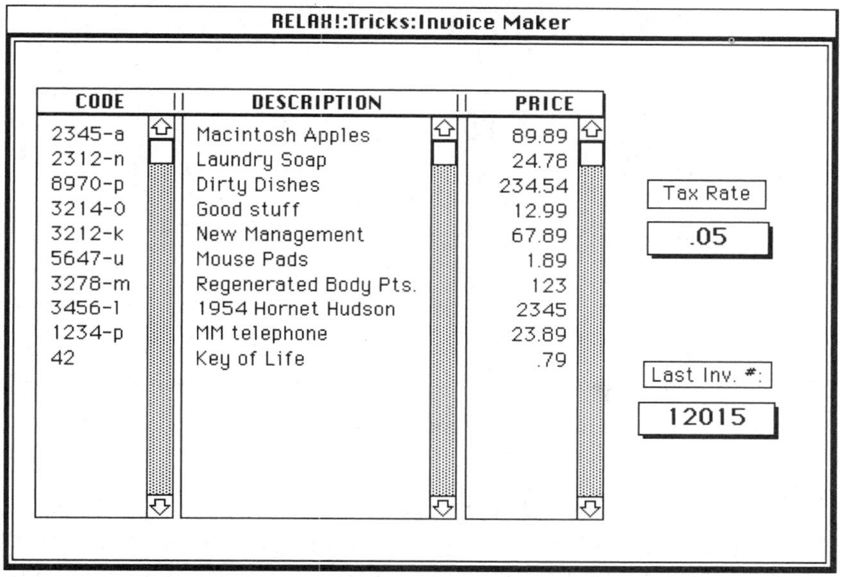

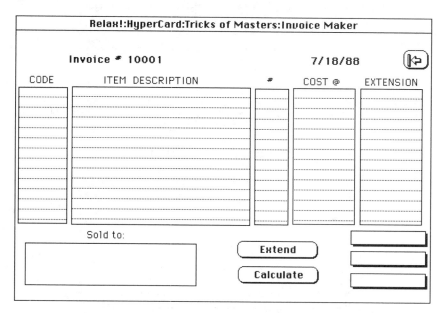

Figure 11-2.   The Prices card in the Invoice Maker stack.

Figure 11-3.   The Invoice template contains all of its objects in the background layer.

```
                RELAX!:Tricks:Invoice Maker

    Invoice # 10001                          7/18/88

   CODE          ITEM DESCRIPTION        QTY.  COST EACH  EXTENSION
  2345-a │ Macintosh Apples               3       89.89     269.67
  5647-u │ Mouse Pads                     5        1.89       9.45
  2312-n │ Laundry Soap                   2       24.78      49.56
     42  │ Key of Life                    3         .79       2.37
  8970-p │ Dirty Dishes                   1      234.54     234.54
  3212-k │ New Management                 8       67.89     543.12
  3456-1 │ 1954 Hornet Hudson             3        2345    7035.00
  1234-p │ MM telephone                   5       23.89     119.45
  3278-m │ Regenerated Body Pts.          2         123     246.00
  3214-0 │ Good stuff                     3       12.99      38.97




                                               ┌──────────────┐
                                               │     8548.13  │
                                               └──────────────┘
                    ┌──────────────────────┐   ┌──────────────┐
          Sold to:  │ Guillermo Gates      │   │      427.41  │
                    │ Look and Feel Avenue  │   └──────────────┘
                    │ Sueme, New Mexico 87049│  ┌──────────────┐
                    └──────────────────────┘   │ $  8975.54   │
                                               └──────────────┘
```

Figure 11-4.   The sample invoice, ready to be printed.

(presented previously). The script in the Price Database button is simply `go next card`, and the New Invoice button's script is `doMenu "New Card"`. The `doMenu "New Card"` is trapped at the stack script level, where a custom doMenu handler is called. The script moves to the last card of the Invoices background, then passes the doMenu message. This assures that the invoices are in sequential order.

Figure 11-5.   This card welcomes the user to the Invoice Maker stack.

The newcard handler enters today's date, automatically increments the global `lastInvNum` variable, and puts this number into the Invoice # field of the newly created card. For a more thorough discussion of the doMenu New Card and on newcard handlers, see the "Changing Modes" section in chapter 12.

Prices Card

The Prices card (Figure 11-2) has five named fields: three similar scrolling fields and the tax rate and LastInvoiceNum fields, where globals are stored when the program is not running. The scrolling fields are the same length and `textsize`. They are named Code, ItemDescription, and Prices. (The middle field can't be named Item because `item` is a reserved word.) The fields scroll together.

The following is in each field's script:

```
on mousewithin
  put the scroll of me into thescroll
  doscroll thescroll
end mousewithin
```

The following is in the card's script:

```
on doscroll thescroll
  lock screen
  repeat with i = 1 to 3
    set the scroll of card field i to thescroll
  end repeat
  unlock screen
end doscroll
```

Look at chapter 3 for other ideas on simultaneously scrolling fields. Be sure to order the fields correctly with the Send Farther menu command if you have created other, non-scrolling fields between creation of the scrolling fields. You enter your code numbers, prices, and the full name of the item into this database card.

Invoices Template Card

In the Template card (Figure 11-3) of the Invoices background, all objects are in the background layer. At the top are two transparent fields, InvoiceNum and date, which are filled automatically on newcard. The main five fields are code, ItemName, number, costEach, and extension. Below the extension field are the subtotal, tax, and total fields.

Two background buttons are on the card. The Extend button looks up the name of the product and fills in the price, code, and full name. The Calculate button multiplies the number of items times the unit cost, adds these extensions, calculates the subtotal and tax, and displays the total. The Extend and Calculate buttons simply call handlers of the same names which reside in the background script. They could be transparent buttons over obvious places, such as the column heading Extension and the total field.

How It Works

How do these scripts work? The calculate script loops through each line that contains a number of items and multiplies the number of items times the unit cost. The script first sets the `numberformat` to 0.00, which makes dollars and cents. These numbers are subtotaled, taxed, and totaled in twelve lines:

```
repeat with i = 1 to the number of lines in fld number
  put line i of fld number into foo
  put (foo * line i of fld costeach) into line i of fld extension
end repeat

put 0 into bar
repeat with i = 1 to the number of lines in fld extension
  add line i of fld extension to bar
end repeat
put bar into field subtotal
put bar * taxrate into thetax
put thetax into field tax
put "$ " & bar + theTax into field total
```

The ExtendPrices script is also simple. It looks up the full name, price, and code number of the inventory item. It uses a function from HyperCard version 1.2 and greater, the `foundline`. This function returns the line number of the container in which the item was found. After you have the line number, you can obtain the correct data from the three data fields and fill in the information on the Invoice card. The following is in a loop for each line:

```
repeat with i = 1 to the number of lines in field itemName
  put line i of field itemName into theItem
  push card
  go card prices
  find theItem -- in cd field itemDescription
  if "Prices" is not in the short name of this card then
    pop card
    next repeat
  end if
put word 2 of the foundline into lineNumber
```

The script checks if the short name of the card (the actual name) is Prices. If it is not, the information was not found and the script goes to the next line.

The `foundline` function returns an expression such as Line 6 of Field ID 3. Word 2 of the `foundline` is the line number where the information was found; this is placed in the `lineNumber` container:

```
put word 2 of the foundline into lineNumber
```

Now you can use `lineNumber` as an index into each of the information fields, then transfer their data to the Invoice card through the temporary variables `theCode`, `theItem`, and `thePrice`:

```
-- extract info from the correct line number of each field
put line linenumber of cd fld code into theCode
put line linenumber of cd fld itemDescription into theItem
put line linenumber of cd fld prices into thePrice
  pop card -- go back to the invoice card
  -- fill in data in correct place
  put thePrice into line i of fld costeach
  put theItem into line i of fld itemName
  put theCode into line i of fld code
end repeat
```

Modifications and Enhancements

This section describes several suggestions for enhancing the stack. First, you could add a field named InventoryRemaining on the Prices card. The Calculate script would attempt to subtract the number requested from the amount in InventoryRemaining. If InventoryRemaining was less than zero, a message would be displayed. Otherwise, Calculate would subtract the number requested from InventoryRemaining. On openstack, you could traverse this field with a loop; if the number was low, you could display a reorder dialog.

You could also implement a client base. When you enter a name in the sold to field, the program would search the database for the person's name. If the name was found, the program would fill out the field. Otherwise, a new client card would be created, you would fill it out, and the information would be transferred to the Invoice card.

You could add a printing routine to print your logo on the top of the page and the invoice on the bottom of the page. First, you could hide any unsightly buttons, such as the Return button, in the doMenu which handler of the stack script:

```
else if which is "Print Card" then -- Command-P
  hide bg btn "return"
  hide bg btn "Calculate"
  hide bg btn "Extend"
  push card -- hold on to it
  go card "Groovy Logo"
  open printing
  print this card
  pop card
  print this card
  close printing
  show bg btn "return"
  show bg btn "Calculate"
  show bg btn "Extend"
else
```

You could add a discount line between subtotal and tax on the Invoice card. Finally, you could use the on closefield handler to add format error checking to the fields.

```
--******************* Description ****************************
-- TYPE:         Calculation script
-- AUTHOR:       Andrew C. Stone
-- NAME:         Calculate
-- LOCATION:     Background script


--*************** Calculation Script Starts ********************
on calculate
  global taxrate
  set the numberformat to "0.00"
  repeat with i = 1 to the number of lines in fld number
    put line i of fld number into foo
    put (foo * line i of fld costeach) into line i of ¬
    fld extension
  end repeat
  put 0 into bar
  repeat with i = 1 to the number of lines in fld extension
add line i of fld extension to bar
  end repeat
  put bar into field subtotal
  put bar * taxrate into thetax
  put thetax into field tax
  put "$ "  & bar + theTax into field total
end calculate


--******************* Description ****************************
-- TYPE:         extendPrices scripts
-- LOCATION:     Background script
-- AUTHOR:       Andrew C. Stone
-- NAME:         extendPrices


--************************* Script Starts *********************
on extendPrices
  lock screen
  repeat with i = 1 to the number of lines in field itemName
  put line i of field itemName into theItem
  push card
  go card prices
  find theItem -- in cd field itemDescription
  if "Prices" is not in the short name of this card then
    pop card
    next repeat
  end if
  put word 2 of the foundline into lineNumber
  put line linenumber of cd fld code into theCode
  put line linenumber of cd fld itemDescription into theItem
  put line linenumber of cd fld prices into thePrice
  pop card
  put thePrice into line i of fld costeach
  put theItem into line i of fld itemName
  put theCode into line i of fld code
  end repeat
  unlock screen
end extendPrices
```

Stack Reporter

The Stack Reporter tool was created to develop the listings for this author's chapters and is full of minifunctions that can be called in any combination to collect a stack's scripts. It is a self-contained card that installs itself at the end of any stack. The Stack Reporter card, shown in Figure 11-6, contains one scrolling card field (named info) and many buttons that begin with the word *Display*.

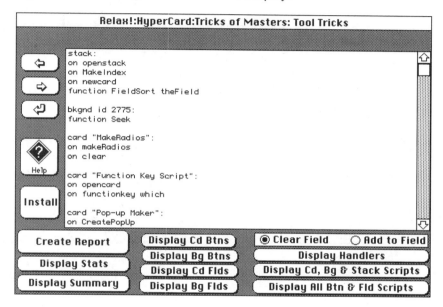

Figure 11-6. With the Stack Reporter card, you can view scripts and stack attributes as well as create reports.

The Stack Reporter is a twofold tool: you can use it to view scripts and stack attributes in the info field, and you can use it to create text file dumps of this information. To do this with a minimum of repeated code, the scripts are written as a series of functions that can be called by each other or by another script.

Figure 11-7 shows the logic layout of the Stack Reporter's buttons and handlers. The card buttons contain little code. They just clear the info field if the `clearField` global variable is true and call the name of the function. For example, the Display All Btn & Fld Scripts button contains the following:

```
put objectScripts() into cd fld "info"
```

You will notice that functions call functions that call functions and so on. Modularity is the hallmark of modifiable code. Avoid the inherent tendency towards "spaghetti" code in HyperTalk. Be a master, modularize.

Note the radio button pair Clear Field and Add to Field on the Stack Reporter card. This is where you alter the `clearField` global boolean variable, which is originally reset on opencard:

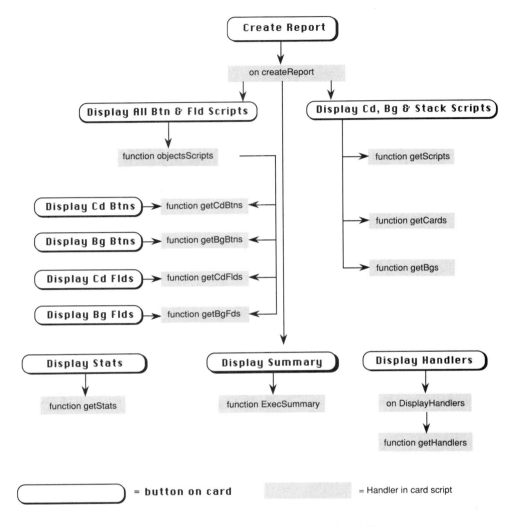

Figure 11-7. The Stack Reporter's buttons and handlers follow this logic layout.

```
on opencard
  global clearField
  -- Do you want the info field cleared after each get operation?
  put the hilite of btn "Clear Field" into clearfield
end opencard
```

The only operation that ignores the `clearField` boolean is Create Report. If you are dumping the entire stack to the scrolling field so that you can then write the stack to a text file, you probably will exceed the 30,000 character capacity of that field and the script will fail. It is best to write to the file after each major chunk of information is extracted.

Create Report starts with a three-way tree that determines the type of report requested:

```
on createReport
  -- find out which objects to dump to a text file
  answer "Summary (no scripts), All Scripts, or Select Scripts?" ¬
  with "Exec Summ" or "All Scripts" or "Select Some"
```

It then calls the functions as outlined in Figure 11-7. With the third choice, Select Some, you define which items you want written to the text file. The Executive Summary choice writes the card name and number, background name and number, and number of card buttons, card fields, and background fields to the card field info and then to the file. The All Scripts logic branch calls the `getScripts` function, another three-way tree that you use to select the high-level scripts you want: card, background, script, or all three. The code for this branch shows how easy it is to create a text file:

```
else if it is "Complete" then
  -- get the name of new file, supply a default:
  put the short name of this stack & " CompleteText" into filename
  ask "Export report to what file?" with filename
  if it is empty then exit createReport
    put it into filename
    -- Fill in header for text file
    put "-- Complete Stack Dump of " & the short name of this ¬
    stack & return & return into cd fld info
    -- Get the card, background, and stack scripts
    put getscripts() after cd fld info
    -- Open the file
    open file filename
    -- Write to the file
    write cd fld info to file filename
    -- Repeat for the field and button scripts
    put objectScripts() into cd fld info
    write cd fld info to file filename
    -- Close the file
    close file filename
```

The `GetStats` function is a HyperTalk emulator of the Stack Info menu item. The most interesting line in it is

```
put "Free K in stack: " & round(the freesize of this stack/1000)¬
&& "K" & return after temp
```

The `freesize` function is useful for maintaining compact stacks. To always keep stacks compact, put the following script in your Home stack:

```
on closestack
  put the freesize of this stack into thesize
  if thesize > the size of this stack/10 then
```

continued

```
      divide thesize by 1024
      set numberformat to "0"
      answer thesize & "K free in stack. Compact?" with "no" ¬
      or "yes"
      if it is "yes" then domenu "Compact Stack"
   end if
end closestack
```

Most of the function handlers for extracting object scripts and attributes are straightforward—they consist of nested **repeat** loops to process each button/field/ script of each card. The getCdBtns function is representative. First, you write a header for this section:

```
function getCdbtns
   put "-- CARD BUTTONS:" & return & ¬
   "--------------" & return after theField
```

Then the program loops through each card. (Place **lock screen** at the beginning of the handler and **unlock screen** at the end to avoid actually having the script display the movement about the stack.) The loop first adds a card header, which contains the name, the number of things, and whether it has a card script:

```
repeat with i = 1 to the number of cards -- -1 to skip reporter
   go card i
   set the cursor to busy -- turn the beachball every loop
   put "-- CARD # " & i & "          CARD NAME: " &¬
   the short name of this card & return after theField¬
   put "-- BKGND # " & the number of this bg & ¬
   "                  BKGND NAME: " ¬
   & the short name of this bg & return after theField
   put "--   Number of card buttons:" & the number of btns &¬
   return & return after theField
   -- Is there a card script?
   put the script of this cd into temp
   if the number of lines in temp > 2 then
      put return & "-- CARD SCRIPT: Yes!" & return after theField
   end if
   set the cursor to busy -- keep beachball turning
```

Then you check if there are any buttons, in which case an inner loop extracts the information you want:

```
put the number of btns into num
if num > 0 then
   repeat with j = 1 to num
      put "-- CD BUTTON " & quote & the short name of btn j ¬
      & quote & " :" & return & ¬
      "--------------" & return after theField
      put "-- RECT : " & the rect of btn j & return & ¬
      "-- SHOWNAME : " & the showname of  btn j & return ¬
      after theField
      -- Extract other button attributes here
```

continued

```
      put the script of btn j into temp
      if the number of lines in temp > 2 then -- more than mouseup
        put return & temp & return after theField
      end if
      put return after theField
    end repeat
end if
```

Note that you can get any attribute of the button—the hilite, autohilite, text-size, textalign, loc, visible, icon, and so on—by following the example of showname.

Finally, the outer repeat loop is exited and the program returns theField, which is the container you have been putting all the collected scripts into.

Although the other scripts parallel this model, the headers and object locations are different. Thus, it was just as easy and more readable to create separate functions. A challenging modification would be to pass the object location—card or background—as a parameter and make the functions work for card and background buttons and card and background fields. The button and field listings for the Stack Reporter card were produced by the Stack Reporter and can be found after the listing of the card script handlers.

```
--********************** Description ***************************
-- TYPE:        Index creation and autolinking scripts
-- LOCATION:    Card, background, or stack
-- AUTHOR:      Andrew C. Stone
-- NAME:        Stack Reporter

--****************** Stack Reporter information  ***************
--******** Why have a computer if it won't do the dirty work?
--************************* createReport *******************
--Purpose:    Output selected scripts to a text file
--SYNTAX:     createReport
--Exp Usage:  call createReport" on mouseUp from a button

on createReport
  -- find out which objects to dump to a text file
  answer "Summary (no scripts), All Scripts, or Select Scripts?"¬
  with  "Exec Summ" or "All Scripts" or "Select Some"
  if it is "Exec Summ" then
    put the short name of this stack & " ExecSumText" into filename
    ask "Export report to what file?" with filename
    if it is empty then exit createReport
    put it into filename
    put ExecSummary() into cd fld info -- put it in a container
    open file filename
    write cd fld info to file filename -- write container to a file
    close file filename
  else if it is "All Scripts" then
    put the short name of this stack & " CompleteText" into ¬
    filename
    ask "Export report to what file?" with filename
    if it is empty then exit createReport
```

continued

```
      put it into filename
      put "-- Complete Stack Dump of " & the short name of this ¬
      stack & return & return into cd fld info
      put getscripts() after cd fld info
      open file filename
      write cd fld info to file filename
      put objectScripts() into cd fld info
      write cd fld info to file filename
      close file filename
    else
      put the short name of this stack & " SelectScriptsText" ¬
      into filename
      ask "Export report to what file?" with filename
      if it is empty then exit createReport
      put it into filename
      open file filename
      answer "Write executive summary to report?" with "No" or "Ok"
      if it is "Ok" then
        put ExecSummary() into cd fld info
        write cd fld info to file filename
      end if
      put getscripts() into cd fld info
      -- this contains three-way tree
      write cd fld info to file filename
      answer "Write all btns & flds to report?" with "No" or "Ok"
      if it is "Ok" then
        put objectScripts() into cd fld info
        write cd fld info to file filename
      end if
      close file filename
    end if
    set the scroll of cd fld info to 0
    put "Look in your HyperCard folder for your Text file!"
    wait 3 secs
    hide msg
end createReport


function getStats
  put "Stack:      " & the short name of this stack & return ¬
  into temp
  put "Location:     " & stripPath()  & return & return after temp
put "Number of Backgrounds: " & the number of bgs & return ¬
  after temp
  put "Number of Cards: " & the number of cards & return & ¬
  return after temp
  put "Size of stack: " & round(the size of this stack/1000) ¬
  && "K" & return after temp
  put "Free K in stack: " & round(the freesize of this ¬
  stack/1000) && "K" & return after temp
  return temp
end getStats


-- stripPath takes the long name of the stack and returns
-- just the names of the path above the stack name
function stripPath
  put the long name of this stack into lname
```

continued

```
    delete first word of lname -- <stack >
    delete first char of lname -- <">
    put " " into thechar
    repeat until thechar = ":"
      put last char of lname into thechar
      delete last char of lname
    end repeat
    return lname
end stripPath


--************** DisplayHandlers *****************************
-- This script, and its subroutine, function getHandlers,
-- compiles a list of handlers in the card, background, and
-- stack layer
on displayHandlers
  set cursor to busy
  put quote &"This may take a while!" & quote
  put getHandlers(stack) after cd fld info
  set cursor to busy
  repeat with i = 1 to the number of bgs
    set cursor to busy
    put the name of bg i into temp
    put getHandlers(temp) after cd fld info
  end repeat
  repeat with i = 1 to the number of cards
    set cursor to busy
    put the name of card i into temp
    put getHandlers(temp) after cd fld info
  end repeat
end displayHandlers


function getHandlers what
  put script of what into temp
  put empty into theHandlers
  repeat with i = 1 to the number of lines in temp
    set cursor to busy
    if first word of line i of temp = "on" or ¬
    first word of line i of temp = "function" then
      put line i of temp & return after theHandlers
    end if
  end repeat
  set cursor to busy
  if theHandlers is not empty then -- header only if needed
    put what & ":" & return before theHandlers
    put return after theHandlers
  end if
  return theHandlers
end getHandlers


--********************** function ExecSummary  **************
--Purpose:     Loop through cards and report on number of card
--             buttons and card fields and background buttons and
--             background fields in each
--SYNTAX:      put ExecSummary() into container
--Exp Usage:   put ExecSummary() into card field Info
```

continued

```
function ExecSummary
  push card
  set the cursor to busy
  lock screen
  put empty into theField
  put the short name of this stack into stackName
  put "-- Executive Stack Summary of "  & stackName  & ¬
  return after theField
  put "---------------------------------------" & return ¬
  after theField
  -- Add -1 after the number of cards to exclude
  -- Stack Reporter card
  repeat with i = 1 to the number of cards
    set the cursor to busy
    go card i
    put "-- CARD # " & i & "              CARD NAME: " ¬
    & the short name of this card &  return after theField
    put "-- BKGND # " & the number of this bg & ¬
    "           BKGND NAME: " ¬
    & the short name of this bg & return after theField
    put "-- Number of card fields:" & the number of card flds ¬
     & "            Number of bkgnd fields: " & the number ¬
    of flds & return after theField
    put "-- Number of card buttons:" & the number of btns ¬
    & "            Number of bkgnd buttons: " & the number ¬
    of bg btns & return & return after theField ¬
    set the cursor to busy
  end repeat
  unlock screen
  pop card
  return theField
end ExecSummary


--*********************** function getScripts  ***************
--Purpose:      Loop through cards and backgrounds and stack
--              script and gather the scripts of the selected
--              types in the container
--SYNTAX:       put getScripts() into container
--Exp Usage:    put getScripts() into card field "Info"
--It calls:     function getCards() and function getBkgnds(),
--              which perform the looping through the cards or
--              backgrounds

function getScripts
  push card
  answer "Which Scripts do you want?"  with "Cards" or ¬
  "BackGround" or "All Three"
  lock screen
  if it is "Cards" then
    put getCards() into theField
  else if it is "BackGrounds" then
    put getBgs() into theField
  else
    put "-- STACK SCRIPT:" & return & return & the script ¬
    of this stack & return & return into theField
    put getBgs() after theField
```

continued

```
         put getCards() after theField
      end if
      pop card
      return theField
      unlock screen
end getscripts

function getCards
   put "-- CARD SCRIPTS : " & return & "---------------" & ¬
   return & return into theField
   -- Add - 1  after the number of cards to exclude the
   -- Stack Reporter card
repeat with i = 1 to the number of cards
      go card i
      put the script of cd i into temp
      if the number of lines in temp > 2 then
        put "-- CARDNAME: " & the short name of this card & ¬
        "        CARD #" && i & return & "-- CARD SCRIPT: " ¬
        & return & "---------------------" & return & temp ¬
        & return & return after theField
      end if
   end repeat
   put return & return after theField
   return theField
end getCards

function getBgs
   put "-- BKGND SCRIPTS : " & return & "---------------" ¬
   & return & return into theField
   -- Add - 1  after the number of cards to exclude the
   -- Stack Reporter card
   repeat with i = 1 to the number of bgs
      go first card of bg i
      put the script of this bg into temp
      if the number of lines in temp > 2 then
        put "-- BACKGROUND: " & the short name of this bg & ¬
        "        BKGND #" && i & return & "-- BACKGROUND ¬
        SCRIPT: "
        & return & "---------------------" & return & temp & ¬
        return & return after theField
      end if
   end repeat
   put return & return after theField
   return theField
end getBgs

--*********************** function ObjectScripts  *************
--Purpose:    Put the stack's buttons, field attributes,
--            and scripts into a container
--SYNTAX:     put objectScripts into <container>
--Exp Usage:  put objectScripts into card field "Info"

function objectScripts
   push card
   put "Go for a cup of java! This may take a while!"
   put the short name of this stack into stackName
```

continued

```
        Put "-- Complete Stack Dump of "   & stackName into theField
        put return & "---------------------------------------------" & ¬
        return after theField
        lock screen
        set the cursor to busy
        put "now getting background fields"
        put getBgFlds() after theField
        put "now getting background buttons"
        put getBgBtns() after theField
        put "now getting card fields"
        put getCdFlds() after theField
        put "now getting card buttons"
        put getCdBtns() after theField
        pop card
        return theField
        unlock screen
    end objectScripts


    --***************** ObjectScripts calls these four functions ****
    function getBgFlds
      -- Add - 1  after the number of backgrounds to exclude the
      -- Stack Reporter background
      repeat with k = 1 to the number of bgs
        go first card of bg k
        put "-- BKGND # " & the number of this bg & ¬
        "        Background Fields of background: " ¬
        & the short name of this bg & return after theField
        put "---------------------------------------------" & return ¬
        after theField
        put "--    Number of bkgnd fields: " & the number of flds & ¬
        return after theField
        set the cursor to busy
        put the number of flds into num
        if (num > 0) then
          repeat with j = 1 to num
            put "-- BG FIELD " & quote & the short name of fld j ¬
            & quote & " :" & return & "---------------" & return ¬
            after theField
            put "-- RECT : " & the rect of fld j & return & ¬
            "-- STYLE :" & the style of fld j & return & return ¬
            after theField
            put the script of fld j into temp
            if the number of lines in temp > 2 then
              -- more than mouseup
              put return & temp & return after theField
            end if
            put return after theField
          end repeat
        end if
        set the cursor to busy
      end repeat
      put return after theField
      return theField
    end getBgFlds


    function getBgBtns
```

continued

```
        -- Add - 1   after the number of backgrounds to exclude the
        -- Stack Reporter background
        repeat with k = 1 to the number of bgs
          go first card of bg k
          put "-- BKGND # " & the number of this bg & ¬
          "         BKGND BUTTONS of Background " ¬
          & the short name of this bg & return after theField
          put "------------------------------------------" & return ¬
          after theField
          put "--    Number of bkgnd buttons: " & ¬
          the number of bg btns & return & return after theField
          set the cursor to busy
          put the number of bg btns into num
          if (num > 0)  then
            repeat with j = 1 to num
              put "-- BG BUTTON " & quote & the short name of bg ¬
              btn j & quote & " :" & return ¬
              & "--------------" & return after theField
              put "-- RECT : " & the rect of bg btn j & return & ¬
              "-- SHOWNAME : " & the showname of bg btn j & return ¬
              after theField
              -- Add other qualities here
              put the script of bg btn j into temp
              if the number of lines in temp > 2 then
              -- more than mouseup
                put return & temp & return after theField
              end if
              put return after theField
            end repeat
          end if
        end repeat
        return theField
    end getBgBtns


    function getCdflds
        repeat with i = 1 to the number of cards -- -1 to skip reporter
          set the cursor to busy
          go card i
          put "-- CARD # " & i & "          CARD NAME: " & ¬
          the short name of this card  &  return after theField ¬
          put "-- BKGND # " & the number of this bg & ¬
          "         BKGND NAME: " & the short name of this bg & ¬
          return after theField
          put "--    Number of card fields:" & the number of card ¬
          flds & return after theField
          set the cursor to busy
          put return after theField
          put the number of cd flds into num
          if num > 0 then
            put "-- CARD FIELDS:" & return & "--------------" ¬
            & return after theField
            repeat with j = 1 to num
              put "-- CD FIELD " & quote & the short name of ¬
              cd fld j & quote & " :" & return ¬
              & "--------------" & return after theField
              put "-- RECT : " & the rect of cd fld j & return & ¬
```

continued

```
                    "-- STYLE :" & the style of cd fld j & return & ¬
          return after theField
          put the script of cd fld j into temp
          if the number of lines in temp > 2 then
          -- more than mouseup
            put temp & return after theField
          end if
          put return after theField
        end repeat
      end if
      set the cursor to busy
      put return after theField
    end repeat
    return thefield
  end getCdflds


  function getCdbtns
    put "-- CARD BUTTONS:" & return & "------------" ¬
  & return after theField
    repeat with i = 1 to the number of cards -- -1 to skip reporter
      go card i
      set the cursor to busy
      put "-- CARD # " & i & "          CARD NAME: " & the ¬
      short name of this card & return after theField ¬
      put "-- BKGND # " & the number of this bg & ¬
      "                    BKGND NAME: " ¬
      & the short name of this bg & return after theField
      put "--    Number of card buttons:" & the number of btns ¬
      & return & return after theField
      -- Is there a card script?
      put the script of this cd into temp
      if the number of lines in temp > 2 then
        put return & "-- CARD SCRIPT: Yes!" & return after theField
      end if
      set the cursor to busy
      put the number of btns into num
      if num > 0 then
        repeat with j = 1 to num
          put "-- CD BUTTON " & quote & the short name of ¬
          btn j & quote & " :" & return & ¬
          "---------------" & return after theField
          put "-- RECT : " & the rect of btn j & return & ¬
          "-- SHOWNAME : " & the showname of  btn j & return ¬
          after theField
          put the script of btn j into temp
          if the number of lines in temp > 2 then
          -- more than mouseup
            put return & temp & return after theField
          end if
          put return after theField
        end repeat
      end if
    end repeat
    return theField
  end getCdbtns
```

continued

```
--*********************************************************
--******************** Stack Reporter Card Buttons **************
-- CARD # 9           CARD NAME: Stack Reporter
-- BKGND # 3          BKGND NAME: Stack Reporter
-- Number of card buttons: 14
-- CARD SCRIPT: Yes!

-- CD BUTTON Display All Btn & Fld Scripts:
-- RECT : 293,321,512,341
-- SHOWNAME : true
on mouseUp
  put objectScripts() into cd fld info
  set the scroll of cd fld info to 0
end mouseUp

-- CD BUTTON Display Summary:
-- RECT : 2,317,142,340
-- SHOWNAME : true
on mouseUp
  put ExecSummary() into cd fld info
  set the scroll of cd fld info to 0
end mouseUp

-- CD BUTTON Create Report:
-- RECT : 2,259,141,291
-- SHOWNAME : true
on mouseUp
  createReport
end mouseUp

-- CD BUTTON Display Cd, Bg & Stack Scripts:
-- RECT : 294,300,512,319
-- SHOWNAME : true
on mouseUp
  put getScripts() into cd fld info
  set the scroll of cd fld info to 0
end mouseUp

-- CD BUTTON Help:
-- RECT : 5,142,53,190
-- SHOWNAME : true
on mouseUp
  get the visible of cd fld help
  if it is true then
    hide card picture
    hide  cd fld help
    show cd fld info
  else
    hide cd fld info
    show card picture
    show  cd fld help
  end if
end mouseUp

-- CD BUTTON Install:
-- RECT : 5,203,55,246
```

continued

```
-- SHOWNAME : true
on mouseUp
  domenu "Copy Card"
  go stack "the stack you wish to install"
  if the result is not empty then exit mouseUp
  lock screen
  go last card
  domenu "Paste Card"
  unlock screen with visual iris open
  Answer "Stack Reporter is installed." with "OK"
end mouseUp


-- CD BUTTON Display Stats:
-- RECT : 2,293,142,314
-- SHOWNAME : true
on mouseUp
  put getstats() into cd fld info
end mouseUp


-- CD BUTTON Display Handlers:
-- RECT : 294,281,512,299
-- SHOWNAME : true
on mouseUp
  global clearField
  if clearfield then put empty into cd fld info
  displayHandlers
  set the scroll of cd fld info to 0
end mouseUp


-- CD BUTTON Clear Field:
-- RECT : 299,260,406,281
-- SHOWNAME : true
on mouseUp
  -- insert globals and assignments here
  global clearfield
  put true into clearfield
  set the hilite of me to true
  set the hilite of btn ID 26 to false
end mouseup


-- CD BUTTON Add to Field:
-- RECT : 411,259,511,281
-- SHOWNAME : true
on mouseUp
  -- insert globals and assignments here
  global clearfield
  put false into clearfield
  set the hilite of me to true
  set the hilite of btn ID 25 to false
end mouseup


-- CD BUTTON Display Cd Btns:
-- RECT : 155,263,273,282
-- SHOWNAME : true
on mouseUp
  global clearfield
```

continued

```
      if clearfield then put empty into cd fld "Info"
      put getCdBtns() after cd fld info
      set the scroll of cd fld info to 0
   end mouseUp

   -- CD BUTTON Display Bg Btns:
   -- RECT : 156,283,276,301
   -- SHOWNAME : true
   on mouseUp
      global clearfield
      if clearfield then put empty into cd fld "Info"
      put getBgBtns() after cd fld info
      set the scroll of cd fld info to 0
   end mouseUp

   -- CD BUTTON Display Cd Flds:
   -- RECT : 154,302,276,320
   -- SHOWNAME : true
   on mouseUp
      global clearfield
      if clearfield then put empty into cd fld "Info"
      put getCdFlds() after cd fld info
      set the scroll of cd fld info to 0
   end mouseUp

   -- CD BUTTON Display Bg Flds:
   -- RECT : 153,321,276,341
   -- SHOWNAME : true
   on mouseUp
      global clearfield
      if clearfield then put empty into cd fld "Info"
      put getBgFlds() after cd fld info
      set the scroll of cd fld info to 0
   end mouseUp
```

Fortune for HyperCard

UNIX folks will appreciate the Fortune routine, which demonstrates the use of the random() function, variable parameter lists, and a dynamic field-sizing algorithm. The routine generates a fortune on the screen when you first start a stack or when you click on the fortune button.

The main script, named fortune, goes into a stack's background, preferably the Home stack. If you want a fortune when you quit HyperCard, the calling script, in the Home's stack script, might be:

```
on domenu which
   if which is "Quit HyperCard" then
      go home -- in case you are somewhere else
      fortune
   end if
   pass domenu -- to all other handlers
end domenu
```

Create a new card after your Home card, but in the same background, and name it fortune. Create two scrolling card fields and name them shortFortunes and longFortunes. Fill each with your favorite jokes or pearls of wisdom. Note that HyperCard treats all text between carriage returns as one line, even if that line wraps for several lines. The carriage return is the delimiter between fortune entries.

Finally, create a background field named display and set the font to Geneva Bold, 14, Center. The height and width of the field is handled by the fortune script (see Figure 11-8).

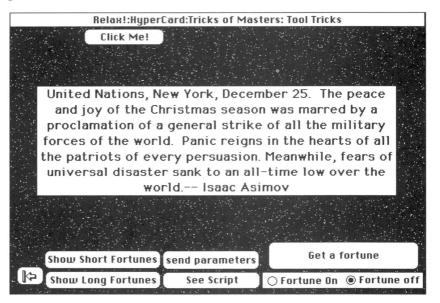

Figure 11-8. The Fortune script produces cards like this one.

The optional parameters, or flags, to the fortune routine are an integer for the time in seconds to display the fortune and either *s* or *l* for a short or long fortune. The parameters can be given in any order, are case insensitive (in keeping with HyperTalk), but must be comma delimited:

```
fortune 5,s -- show a short fortune for 5 seconds
fortune L -- show a long fortune for the default time
fortune 5,s,8,L -- only 8 and L are stored, but all are read
```

Because fortune does not require parameters, the script first initializes `waitCount` (the variable containing the duration to display the fortune) to empty, then randomly selects the long or short scrolling field from which to retrieve the adage:

```
put empty into waitcount -- initialize variable to empty
if random(2) = 1 then -- select default field randomly
  put "shortFortunes" into whichField
```

continued

```
else -- in case there are no flags
  put "longFortunes" into whichField
end if
```

The use of `random` with a parameter of 2 is equivalent to flipping a coin: it returns a 1 or a 2. The `random(number)` function returns an integer between 1 and *number* and can be used to play tricks. Try this: create a new button, name it Click Me!, and give it this script:

```
on mouseWithin
  set loc of me to random(512),random(342)
end mouseWithin
```

the paramcount, the param()

The HyperTalk functions `the paramcount`, `the param of <parameter number>`, and `the params` are similar to argument count and argument vector {argc,argv} in C. The function called `the params` returns the entire message and all of its parameters. The `paramcount` is similar to the argument count: the handler name is assigned 0, the first parameter is 1, and so on. It is used as a looping index:

```
repeat with i = 1 to the paramcount -- loop through custom flags
  put first char of param(i) into test -- put it into a container
  if IsNumeric(test) then -- is it a number?
    put param(i) into waitCount
```

The function `param of <parameter number>` or the syntactically equivalent `param(parameter number)` accesses the *i*th parameter. You check if it is a number with the `IsNumeric` function, which returns true if it is a number and false otherwise. This is an elegant way to use booleans:

```
function IsNumeric what -- in C, isDigit()
  -- in Pascal: in ['0'..'9']
  repeat with i = 1 to the number of chars in the container
    if char i of what is not in "0123456789." then
      return false -- like C, procedure exits on return
    end if
  end repeat
  return true
end IsNumeric
```

If it is a number, the number is saved in the `waitCount` local variable. Otherwise, the parameter is *l*, *L*, *s*, or *S* and the appropriate field name is placed into the `whichField` variable. Or perhaps it contains nothing meaningful, in which case it is ignored. It is important to initialize variables to a default value before entering the parameter testing loop; otherwise, `whichField` and `waitCount` would be unknown variables in latter portions of the script.

```
else if first char of param(i) is "l" or ¬
first char of param(i) is "L" then -- l means long fortune
  put "longFortunes" into whichField
  else if first char of param(i) is "s" ¬
  or first char of param(i) is "S" then -- s means short fortune
  put "shortFortunes" into whichField
```

The main part of the procedure is the single line that fully describes the location of every object so that one card can contain the database scrolling fields and the fortune can appear on any card in the same background. The lack of such an exact specification of an object and the card it is on is a major source of subtle bugs in HyperTalk.

```
put line random(the number of lines in card field whichField of ¬
card "fortune") of card field whichField of card "fortune" ¬
into field "display"
```

The random function is passed the result of the number of function, which returns the total number of distinct lines in whichField. A line in HyperCard is defined by a carriage return, not a text wrap. Thus, you can enter fortunes, jokes, and so on that are as long as you like— only a carriage return delimits the entries in the scrollable fields shortFortunes and longFortunes.

Dynamically Sized Fields

The math to display a field that will hold variable-length strings involves getting the number of characters in the fortune, calculating the number of lines necessary to display all the text, and setting the text field to the appropriate size:

```
put 55 into CharsPerLine -- given the font/width of field
put the number of chars in fld display into numchars
put (numchars div CharsPerLine) + 1 into numlines
-- Now set the rect of "display" to an appropriate size
put 120 into Top -- the top of the display fld
set the rect of fld display to ¬
32,Top,480,(Top + 4 + numlines*(textheight of fld display))
```

The number 55 is an average of how many characters of Geneva Bold 14 fontsize will fit in one line of a field 448 pixels across (480-32). To figure out how many characters can fit in any size field with any font and fontsize, first create and modify a field to the size, location, and font specifications. Set its name to testField. Type a sentence that fills a line exactly. Then type the following into the Message box:

```
put the rect of card field "testField"
-- displays its coordinates in the Message box
```

Use the first and third numbers as your width in the fortune script, where 32 and 480 appear, and the second number as your Top variable. The fourth number, the bottom of the field, is generated dynamically by multiplying the number of lines by the `textheight` of the field and adding the `Top` variable and 4 pixels to account for descenders such as *y* and *j*. You may need to increase it from 4 for very large fonts. Then type:

```
put the number of chars in card field "testField" into msg
```

Use this as the variable `CharsPerLine`.

   The fortune is displayed with a visual effect in HyperCard version 1.2 or greater:

```
show fld display
unlock screen with barn door open slow -- visual effect
```

The `numchars` variable, in addition to helping to size the field, is used to determine the length of time that the fortune is displayed if the user has not specified a display time:

```
if waitCount is empty then
  wait (numchars * 2) Ticks
```

This gives about two seconds of display time per line of text. Adjust this as needed. Finally, the display field is rehidden, and control passes to HyperCard.

```
--*********************Description**************************
-- TYPE:        Displays a random fortune
-- LOCATIONS:   Card, background, or stack
-- AUTHOR:      Andrew C. Stone
-- NAME:        fortune
--******************* Background Script Starts Here ***********
on opencard
  fortune -- call generic function
end opencard
on fortune -- param1,param2 are optional
  lock screen -- lock for later unlock with visual
  put empty into waitcount --initialize variable to empty
  if random(2) = 1 then -- select default field randomly
    put "shortFortunes" into whichField
  else -- if there are no flags
    put "longFortunes" into whichField
  end if
  repeat with i = 1 to the paramcount -- loop through custom flags
    put first char of param(i) into test -- put it in a container
    if IsNumeric(test) then -- is it a number? see below
      put param(i)  into waitCount -- then store it
    else if first char of param(i) is "l" ¬
    or first char of param(i) is "L" then -- l is long fortune
      put "longFortunes" into whichField
    else if first char of param(i) is "s" ¬
    or first char of param(i) is "S" then -- s is short fortune
      put "shortFortunes" into whichField
    end if
```

continued

```
     end repeat

     -- The main part of the procedure
     -- First get a random line of the selected field
     -- This call works on any card of this background
     -- "any" is equivalent to "random"
     put any line ¬
     of card field whichField of card "fortune" into fld display
     -- Change next line if you change "display"'s width or font
     put 55 into CharsPerLine
     put the number of chars in fld display into numchars
     put (numchars div CharsPerLine) + 1 into numlines
     -- Now set the rect of "display" to an appropriate size
     put 120 into theTop -- the top of the display fld
     set the rect of fld display to ¬
     32,theTop,480,(theTop + 4 + numlines*(textheight of ¬
     fld display))
     show fld display
     unlock screen with barn door open slow -- visual effect
     if waitcount is empty then
        wait (numchars * 4) Ticks
        -- increase multiplicand for longer wait
     else
        wait waitcount sec -- a custom specified time was provided
     end if
     hide fld display -- put it away
   end fortune

   --******************* Helper Function, IsNumeric ****************
   function IsNumeric what -- in C, isDigit()
     -- in Pascal: in ['0'..'9']
     repeat with i = 1 to the number of chars in the container
        if char i of what is not in "0123456789." then
          return false -- like C, procedure exits on return
        end if
     end repeat
     return true
   end IsNumeric
```

Chapter **12**

The Quiz Maker

Andrew Stone

Synopsis: How often have you wished you had a way to create quizzes and tests that used the computer's intelligence to perform corrections, generate statistics, and guide learners down a specific path? The Quiz Maker is such a tool. Basically, this stack acts as a master template that generates other stacks. These can contain true-or-false and multiple-choice quizzes that automatically present and grade tests. You can use such a stack for trade show promotion or to test your knowledge.

The stack has two modes: teacher and user. In the teacher mode, all quiz generation and statistics tools are available. Statistics include class average, individual scores, individual question statistics, and a record of each answer that a student gave. New quizzes can be created by pushing a button and typing a question. No knowledge of scripting or HyperCard is needed. In the user mode, all the teacher tools are hidden and students can only travel a predefined path. Many techniques are presented for securing your stack quiz from the prying fingers of students. Text that provides feedback to the student can be typed; if Macintalk is installed, feedback is spoken out loud.

The Quiz Maker

Create Self-Administering and Self-Grading Exams

The Quiz Maker project demonstrates many powerful scripting techniques that give you a new dimension of control over HyperTalk. Basically, the Quiz Maker stack generates other stacks. With this master template, you can create true-or-false and multiple-choice quizzes that automatically present and grade the test. The stack operates in two modes: teacher mode and user mode.

In teacher mode, all quiz generation and statistic tools are available to the teacher. New quizzes can be created and customized without any knowledge of scripting: it is simply a push-the-button and type-in-the-questions operation. In user mode, all tools are hidden, and a student can only "travel" along a predefined path from a sign-in card through the quiz. Although the stack uses the new syntax of HyperCard 1.2 and later versions, it checks the version you are running to prevent errors.

This stack has other possible uses. The stack originated as a trade show promotion tool that gave a test-your-knowledge quiz, replete with sound effects of someone getting slugged on the wrong answer and Handel's "Hallelujah" when the correct answer was chosen. To take the quiz, the person had to fill out a name and address card, thus creating a client database. Hooked up to a Fender amplifier, the Macintosh attracted a lot of people.

In creating the Quiz Maker, the priority was to design a foolproof stack that people with no knowledge of HyperTalk could use to create new quizzes. Defensive coding and error trapping are adequately handled. When the stack is in user mode, a student can travel only a specific route. There is a discussion of securing your stack through trapping menu commands (and a secret that may surprise you).

This chapter explores modifications of the procedure that creates new cards. The procedure automatically creates a self-numbering quiz that is ready to be given the moment the last question is typed in. The following statistics are generated: class average, individual scores, individual question statistics, and a record of each answer that a student gave. The script creates a student index that is sorted by last name with a selection sort. You can view any student's answer to each question by clicking on the student's name.

Another feature of the stack is that the teacher can type in phrases into a field, and the Macintosh will select one randomly and speak encouragement or congratulations depending on the answer. The use of the `speak` XFCN and the MacInTalk driver is presented with caveats regarding a strange bug. Another feature of the Quiz Maker stack is the push-button customization of a number of options: whether special effects will be used, whether all go commands will be trapped, and whether the correct answer will be highlighted in order to teach while the student takes the quiz. The tricks in this stack can be used in any HyperCard development.

The Components of the Quiz Maker Stack

The five backgrounds in the Quiz Maker stack are required given its template nature. Four backgrounds—Welcome, Registry, TorFalse, and Multiple Choice—have only one card each. The last background, Data, has four cards: Preferences, Statistics, Phrases, and the ubiquitous Help.

Welcome, the first background of the stack, is where each student starts and finishes a quiz. Registry is the sign-in background where student information is kept. It is the first stop on the way to taking a quiz. TorFalse and Multiple Choice are the two quiz question template backgrounds.

The Preferences card (Figure 12-1) contains the options for modifying how the quiz operates, including the Teacher Mode and User Mode radio button pair. The Statistics card (Figure 12-2) holds values, such as the number of questions and the number of people who have taken the quiz, as well as all scores arranged by student and by question.

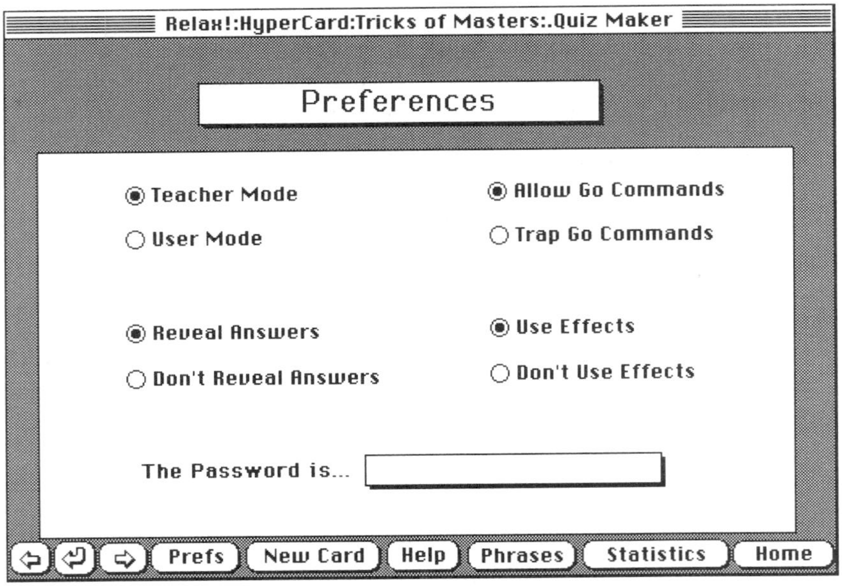

Figure 12-1. The Preferences card contains options for customizing Quiz Maker.

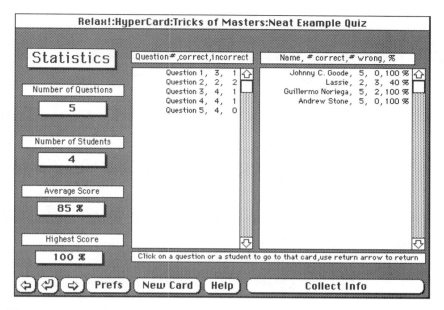

Figure 12-2. The Statistics card accumulates statistics about
the people who take the quiz.

The fields on the Phrases card (Figure 12-3) contain phrases for the Macintosh to speak during the quiz. The Help card contains a scrolling field (Figure 12-4) with instructions for the teacher on how to make a quiz.

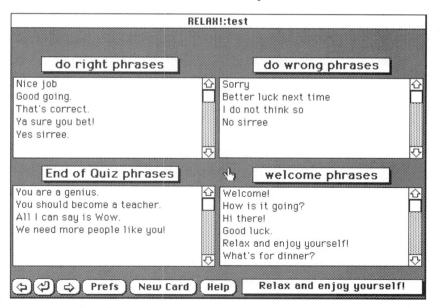

Figure 12-3. The Phrases card contains the words that the
Macintosh will speak.

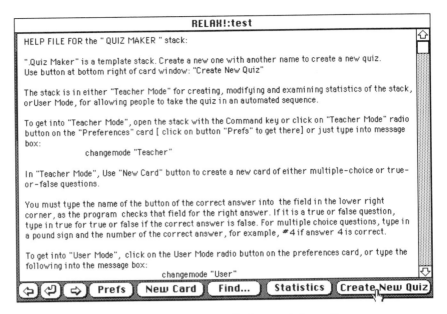

Figure 12-4. The Help card can be scrolled to get information about Quiz Maker.

For those who cannot wait, a complete listing of all scripts and objects is at the end of this chapter—but stick around for a few sentences to find out about shared background buttons.

Six buttons are common to all backgrounds that are part of the teacher mode tool kit. These tools are available only to the teacher and allow the creation of new questions and easy navigation around the stack. Five are navigation buttons: go previous card, go back, go next card, go card Help, and go card Preferences. The sixth is the New Card button, which allows the creation of a new quiz question from anywhere in the stack. See the Welcome card in Figure 12-5.

Creating the Quiz Maker Stack

Create a new stack (without copying the background) and name it .Quiz Maker. Note the period as the first character: this puts the file at the top of the standard file dialog box for ease of selection. It also creates a distinctive name that is checked on openstack to make sure the quiz builder is working on a copy of the template stack and not the original. The code in the openstack handler of the stack script follows. Its job is to present the teacher with three choices:

```
-- This stack is a template; make Teacher create another one
if the short name of this stack is ".Quiz Maker" then
  answer "Create a new Quiz?" with "Help" or "Cancel" or "Ok"
if it is "Ok" then
```

continued

Figure 12-5. The Welcome card illustrates the Quiz Maker buttons that are common to all backgrounds.

```
   createNewQuiz
else if it is "Help" then
   go card "Help"
end if
-- if it is Cancel, you just fall out of handler
```

The CreateNewQuiz handler copies the template stack, then navigates you to it with this file dialog trick:

```
on createNewQuiz -- make a copy of Template
doMenu "Save a Copy..." -- Teacher selects new name
set lockmessages to true
go stack "the stack you just created" -- the great trick
```

We accomplish this navigation in HyperTalk, using the fact that if HyperCard is presented with an unknown stack name in a go command, it displays the standard file dialog box, prefaced by *Where is stack so and so.* So we tell it to go to the stack you just created, and the text *Where is the stack you just created?* is displayed at the top of the dialog box. Having the quiz designer explicitly select the new stack ensures that a new quiz stack is being used.

If you are using version 1.2 or greater, the if statement that hides the Quiz Maker logo with the Hide card picture command will be executed. This further emphasizes that you are not in the template stack any longer:

```
if the short name of this stack is not ".Quiz Maker" then
   if the version >= 1.2 then
```

continued

```
      hide card picture -- the stack maker logo
  end if
end if
```

Name the first card of your stack—and its background—Welcome. Create the six background buttons and fill in their scripts as listed at the end of the chapter (refer to Figure 12-5). Note that the New Card button's script is simply

```
on mouseUp
  doMenu "New Card"
end mouseUp
```

because it is good design to place all fancy handlers at a higher level in the hierarchy.

It is more modular to centralize scripts at the lowest common level to the objects requiring those handlers because you only have to change the script once when you modify it. If a handler is used only by card buttons, it belongs in the card's script. If a handler is called by background buttons and fields, it belongs in the background's script. If multiple backgrounds call the handler, however, it must reside in the stack script. The five backgrounds in Quiz Maker require access to the same handlers, which must reside in the stack script.

Create the remaining four backgrounds, naming the cards and backgrounds as follows:

Card #2	Card Name: MultipleTemplate
Background #2	Background Name: MultipleChoice
Card #3	Card Name: TorFtemplate
Background #4	Background Name: TrueOrFalse
Card #4	Card Name: RegistryTemplate
Background #3	Background Name: Registry
Card #5	Card Name: Preferences
Background #5	Background Name: Data

You can fill the background layer of each background (except Welcome) with gray paint to provide a contrast with the white text fields. But if your quizzes contain many graphics, you may want to leave the backgrounds white. Welcome is the teacher-modifiable background that can display special logos and the like.

To automatically reproduce the shared buttons, create a temporary card button on the first card, Welcome, with this script:

```
on mouseUp
  choose button tool
  repeat with j = 1 to the number of bkgnd buttons
    go first card
    click at loc of bkgnd button j -- select the Jth button
    doMenu "Copy Button"
    repeat with i = 1 to the number of bkgnds - 1 -- first has it
      go next card
      doMenu "BackGround"
      doMenu "Paste Button"
    end repeat
```

continued

```
    end repeat
    go first card
    choose browse tool
end mouseUp
```

This script copies each button, goes to each of the other cards, toggles to the background layer, and pastes the button in. You can surround the body of the script with `lock screen` at the beginning and `unlock screen` at the end, but you might enjoy seeing how much work you are saving!

Now create the remaining three cards in the last background:

Card #6	Card Name: Statistics
Background #5	Background Name: Data
Card #7	Card Name: Phrases
Background #5	Background Name: Data
Card #8	Card Name: Help
Background #5	Background Name: Data

The Preferences Card, Globals, and Radio Buttons

Quiz attributes and customizations are stored on the Preferences card in the form of toggling radio buttons. As you can see from Figure 12-1, the four sets of radio buttons are Teacher Mode and User Mode, Allow Go Commands and Trap Go Commands, Use Effects and Don't Use Effects, and Reveal Answers and Don't Reveal Answers. Each pair turns on or off a global variable that affects the mode and the quiz. To switch to user mode, for example, you simply click on the User Mode radio button. The value true is placed in the `Umode` global variable and a procedure is called to hide the tools, reduce the `userlevel` to 2, and display the Welcome card so you can take a quiz.

Standard Macintosh radio buttons have a "one on and the rest off" operation that is similar to the operation of their namesake, push-button car radio buttons. Special scripts are required to set the `hilite` of the button to true (on) and the `hilite` of the other radio buttons in the group to false (off). On this card there are only two buttons per group, each representing a state of the global boolean container.

Here is where you can apply master thinking to the stack. If you locate the handlers in the card script or a higher script, the button can send a message to the handler with a true or false parameter to set the global. It is a useful trick in any stack.

The most important pair of radio buttons, User Mode and Teacher Mode, toggle the value of the `Umode` global variable, which is true when the User Mode button is highlighted. The code for these buttons follows:

```
-- In button Teacher Mode:
on mouseUp
  changeMode "Teacher"
end mouseUp
```

continued

```
-- In button User Mode:
on mouseUp
  changeMode "User"
end mouseUp
-- In the Stack script:
on changeMode which -- which equals user or teacher
  global Umode, passwd -- needs to check global password
  set the cursor to watch
  if which is "User" then -- go to user mode
    put true into Umode
    set the hilite of btn "User Mode" of card "Preferences" ¬
    to true
    set the hilite of btn "Teacher Mode" of card "Preferences" ¬
    to false
    set the userlevel to 2
    hideTools -- Put away Teacher tools
    go first card -- to begin the quiz
  else if which is "Teacher" then -- go to teacher mode
    ask "What is the password?"
  if it is not passwd then exit changeMode -- protection
    put false into Umode
    set the hilite of btn "User Mode" of card "Preferences" to false
    set the hilite of btn "Teacher Mode" of card "Preferences" to true
    set the userlevel to 5
    showTools -- show all tools & hidden fields
  end if
end changeMode
```

The on `changeMode` `which` handler is called and passed the parameter of `User` or `Teacher` depending on which button called the handler. It alters the state of the `Umode` global variable, highlights the calling button, unhighlights the other button, and calls hideTools and showTools. These two handlers hide and show the buttons and fields that only the teacher can see (discussed later). They also contain the stack's password protection.

You must explicitly set everything about a radio button. But after the button is set, it acts like a variable by holding its state. Thus, on opening the stack, the preferences of the teacher are reestablished—the `hilite` of each radio button is placed in its global variable:

```
on openstack
  global passwd,allowGo,Umode,revealAnswers, ¬
  UseEffects, prevLevel,NumBreakIns
  put the hilite of btn "User Mode" of card "Preferences" ¬
  into Umode --  the user mode
  if Umode then set userlevel to 2 -- reset level if necessary
else set userlevel to 5
  put the hilite of btn "Allow Go Commands" of card ¬
  "Preferences" into allowGo -- allow or trap go commands
  put card field "pword" of card "Preferences" ¬
  into passwd -- the password
  put the hilite of btn "Reveal Answers" of card "Preferences" ¬
  into revealAnswers -- are correct answers shown?
  put the hilite of btn "Use Effects" of card "Preferences" ¬
  into UseEffects -- are phrases spoken?
```

continued

```
put the userLevel into prevLevel -- in order to restore level
put 0 into NumBreakIns -- security checker
```

If the `allowGo` container has a value of true, the arrow keys and menu and keyboard `go` commands can be used. If you do not want students cruising your stack, set the Trap Go Commands button (see the section on "Navigation and Anti-Navigation").

The `revealAnswers` container is the global that controls whether the correct answer "lights up" (by setting its `hilite` to true) when an incorrect answer is chosen. The `UseEffects` global variable controls whether a phrase chosen at random from the appropriate field of the Phrases card will be spoken after each question. It could control other optional effects, such as hiding and showing card pictures and buttons with funny icons. Build the Preferences card by creating the eight radio buttons in the card layer, as shown in Figure 12-1. Fill in their scripts, which consist of the handler name and a parameter as listed under the Preferences card. You have to type in the card script now to get all buttons, except the Mode buttons, to work. Create two shadowed fields: one for the name of the card (Preferences) and one for the password (labeled pword).

Changing Modes

We have to make it impossible for students to break into the stack and cheat. To show how weak even rigorous protection is, however, here is a trick that unlocks any stack. You can create "back doors" into teacher mode if you forget your password, but that further increases the risk of a break in. Suppose that the following happens: you want to get into teacher mode, Trap Go Commands is set, you are in user mode, the `userlevel` is 2 (too low to edit scripts), and you have forgotten your password.

Here is the back door. Simply go home, then choose the menu item Go Back and hold the Command key down. The following lines of code in the openstack handler of the stack script perform this magic:

```
    else if the commandKey is down then --trick to get in
      put passwd into the message box
      -- here it is, because you forgot
      changeMode "Teacher" -- it asks for the password
    end if
end openstack
```

If this seems too simple, you can complicate it by requiring that additional keys (such as the Option key and the Shift key) also be down. Remove these lines entirely if security is crucial.

You can change the mode from any card, if you remember your password, by typing the following into the Message box:

```
changemode "Teacher"
```

You are prompted for your password. If it is correct, the mode is switched:

```
on changeMode which
  global Umode, passwd
  if which is "user" then -- go to user mode
    ...
  else if which is "Teacher" then -- go to teacher mode
    ask "What is the password?"
    if it is not passwd then exit changeMode -- protection
    ...
  end if
end changeMode
```

Suppose that you forget your password after all the students have taken the final exam, and grades are due in an hour, and you removed the Command key back door. Here is the promised trick. From another stack with a userlevel of 5, create a scrolling card field named Hacker. Then type the following into the Message box:

```
put card field passwd of card "Preferences" of stack ¬
"MyQuiz" into card field "Hacker".
```

Even if the MyQuiz stack is protected, this line of code will get the password. You have to use the entire path of the stack, starting with the name of the volume.

Altering Locked Stacks

This trick converts to a more powerful trick: altering locked stacks. From the card containing the Hacker field, type the following into the Message box:

```
put the script of stack "HD90:HyperCard:NeatStack" into ¬
cd fld "Hacker"
```

Then edit out the set userLevel to 2 lines and other protective lines and type:

```
set the script of stack "HD90:HyperCard:NeatStack" to ¬
cd field "Hacker"
```

Voila, you are the master of your fate!

Type into the stack script the on openstack, on createNewQuiz, and on ChangeMode which handlers. Then you arrive at the on showTools and on hideTools handlers. In the on showTools handler, a repeat loop is indexed by the number of backgrounds. The loop contains two inner repeat loops: one shows the background buttons, and one shows the hidden fields.

```
repeat with i = 1 to the number of bkgnds - 1
-- not data background
  set the cursor to watch
  go to card 1 of background i
  repeat with j = 1 to the number of bkgnd btns
```

continued

```
   show bkgnd button j
   if "stats" is in the name of bkgnd btn j then
   -- it is a toggle
     set the name of bkgnd btn j to "Hide Stats"
   end if
 end repeat


 repeat with h = 1 to the number of fields
   show field h
 end repeat
end repeat
```

Hiding selected fields is more difficult. If you create the fields in a certain order, you could hide them by their number, but that is chancy if changes are made. The most compact solution is to look for certain strings in the short name of the object and hide the fields if a match is found.

What is the short name of an object? The name of an object consists of the type of object and either a literal string if you named the object or its ID number. The short name returns an unquoted literal. If you type the following into the Message box:

```
Put the name of this card into msg
```

it returns:

```
card "Welcome"
```

If you type this into the Message box:

```
Put the short name of this card --   into msg is now optional
```

it returns:

```
Welcome
```

The hideTools script checks for each element it needs to hide:

```
repeat with i = 1 to the number of backgrounds - 1
-- not data bkgnd
  go to card 1 of background i
  repeat with j = 1 to the number of bkgnd btns
    if "next" is in the name of bkgnd btn j then hide bkgnd btn j
    else if "Prefs" is in the name of bkgnd btn j then hide bkgnd btn j
    else if "New Card" is in the name of bkgnd btn j then ¬
    hide bkgnd btn j
    else if "Help" is in the name of bkgnd btn j then hide bkgnd btn j
    else if "stats" is in the name of bkgnd btn j then hide bkgnd btn j
    else if "text" is in the name of bkgnd btn j then hide bkgnd btn j
  end repeat
```

continued

```
  repeat with h = 1 to the number of fields
    -- all hidden fields have number in name
    if "number" is in the name of field h then hide field h
  end repeat
end repeat
```

Note that the field names of the special developer's fields hidden from the student are named CorrectNumber, the NumberRight, the NumberWrong, and the StatNumbers. The substring *Number* in each of these makes it easier to hide the fields: if the field has *Number* in its short name, hide the field. Likewise, the go previous card, go back, and go next card background buttons are all named next to ease the burden of the logic of nested `repeat` loops. Because the `ShowName` of these buttons is false (use an appropriate icon to signify the actual direction), their names do not matter; thus, this trick saves some CPU cycles.

on *NewCard* Versus *doMenu "New Card"*

The main part of the automatic sequence generation of quiz question cards (Figures 12-6 and 12-7) and the creation of new Registry cards (Figure 12-8) are handled by first trapping any calls to `doMenu "New Card"`. It checks whether you have selected user mode, which means you require a new Registry card, or teacher mode, which signifies you want a new quiz question.

If you chose teacher mode, you are asked Which type of question: True/False or Multiple Choice? The script leads you to the appropriate template background and creates the new card, thus making a copy of the correct background. So first trap the `doMenu "New Card"`:

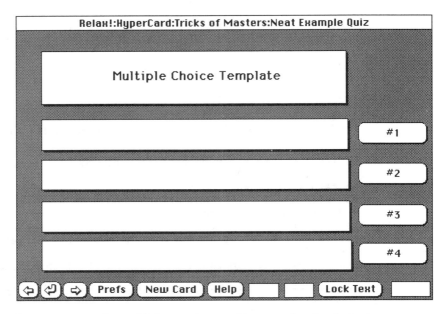

Figure 12-6.   The Multiple Template card is a template for designing a multiple-choice quiz.

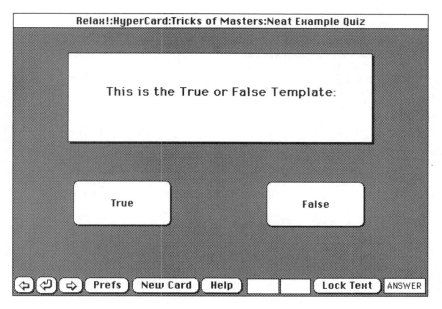

Figure 12-7. The TorFtemplate card makes it easy to design a true-or-false quiz.

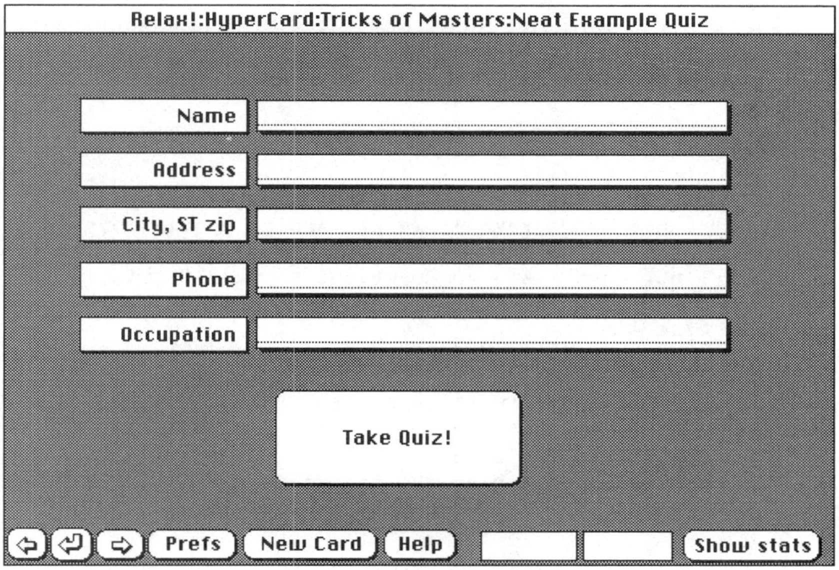

Figure 12-8. The Registry Template card gathers information from the test taker.

```
on doMenu which
  global Umode, AllowGo
  if which is "New Card" then
    lock screen -- matching half in "on newcard"
    if Umode then -- a new student
      go last card of bkgnd "Registry"
    else
      Answer "Which class of question: True/False or Multiple?" ¬
      with "True/False" or "Multiple ??" or "Cancel"
      if it is "True/False" then
        go last card of bkgnd "TrueOrFalse"
      else if it is "Multiple ??" then
        go last card of bkgnd "MultipleChoice"
      else
        exit doMenu
      end if
    end if
    pass doMenu -- create card. Transfer control to "on NewCard"
  else
  -- trap any other menu commands as required
```

The script uses the handy global Umode to determine if it should go to the Registry background or ask Which type of question? (Cancel provides a way out.) Notice that the script must explicitly pass doMenu after going to the correct card. Otherwise, the script would "trap" the command, ending the command's journey up the hierarchical staircase. After passing the handler to HyperCard, the new card is created in the correct background and in the correct order.

After the card is created, HyperTalk looks for the on newCard handler, then performs any requested code: the new card handler does some accounting and housekeeping. If you did not select user mode, the name of the card is set to "Question" & theNumber, where theNumber is a preincremented integer stored in the Num-Questions field on the Statistics card (Figure 12-2).

```
on newcard
  global Umode
  unlock screen -- locking in doMenu "New Card"
  if not Umode then -- we are adding a quiz question
    add one to card field numQuestions of card Statistics
    put card field numQuestions of card Statistics into theNumber
    set the name of this card to "Question" & theNumber
  else
    add one to card field numStudents of card Statistics
  end if
  put 0 into field numberRight
  -- this is better for data aquisition
  put 0 into field numberWrong
  tabkey -- easier on the teacher
end newcard
```

First you unlock the screen that was locked on doMenu "New Card" in order to make the new card appear seamlessly, even though you have gone to a template card in the interim. The numberRight and numberWrong fields are initialized to 0 regardless of the card style—all three backgrounds have these same fields. These fields hold score information with regards to the student in the case of Registry cards or average performance records on the Question cards. Finally, for ease of data entry, the `tabkey` line sets the cursor to blinking in the first field—the Name field on a Registry card and the Question field on the others.

One trick for making handsome titles of fields is to use background buttons (see Figure 12-8). Create one in the background, set the name to `Name:`, set the style to Shadow, and type the following into the Message box:

```
set the textAlign of bkgnd btn "Name:" to right
```

The `textStyle` and `textSize` can likewise be set, thus generating unique buttons. Using the Shift-Option combination, which restrains duplications horizontally or vertically, create clones of the first button and name them as suggested. If you have not already done so, create the background fields on the three template cards and the card fields on the Statistics card. Use the information provided at the end of this chapter for naming conventions. Field styles and text size are a matter of taste and application. A preschool "name the object" quiz might use 18-point Calligraphy, centered; an exam on the theoretical limitations of limits to derive derivatives might require 10-point text size to fit in the allotted space.

One button script worth examining is the script for the Lock Text and Unlock Text background button on the two question backgrounds (similar to the Show stats and Hide stats button on the Registry background). It uses a simple logic toggle that locks and unlocks all fields on the card, then changes the name of itself to reflect the state of the fields' `lockText` attribute:

```
on mouseUp
  get the short name of me -- which state are we in?
  if it is "Lock Text" then
    set the name of me to "Unlock Text"
    repeat with i = 1 to the number of fields
      set the locktext of field i to true
    end repeat
  else
    set the name of me to "Lock Text"
    repeat with i = 1 to the number of fields
      set the locktext of field i to false
    end repeat
  end if
end mouseUp
```

This automates one of the most tedious aspects of HyperCard: the requirement that attributes of objects must be modified individually. This script demonstrates that `repeat` loops can perform this process. You will see extensive use of `repeat` loops in this chapter. HyperCard has changed the debug/recompile/go-get-drunk-because-you-cannot-find-the-bug cycle that plagues compiled language to an instant gratification feedback loop. For those conservatives who argue that HyperTalk is not a "real" language, I just smile and think, "Wait until these folks see version 5.0."

Navigation and Anti-Navigation

This section describes how to protect the integrity of the stack. There is a need to disable keyboard shortcuts to preempt cheating, and other methods are discussed to keep the students on the predetermined course.

User Mode Navigation

 Switching to user mode displays the first card, where the only button present is Would you like to take a Quiz? (Figure 12-9). The button's script is

```
on mouseUp
  global Umode
  if Umode then
    doMenu "New Card"
  else
    answer "Change to User Mode?" with "Ok" and "No"
    if it is "No" then exit mouseUp
    changemode "User"
  end if
end mouseUp
```

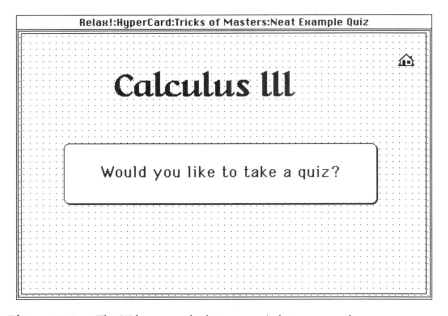

Figure 12-9.   The Welcome card when you switch to user mode.

A doMenu "New Card", which displays a new Registry card, is sent. This is the second link in the quiz path. If you are not in user mode, you are protected from creating another question by accident and provided an option of changing to user mode. The only button which is visible and does anything is the Take Quiz! background button (Figure 12-10).

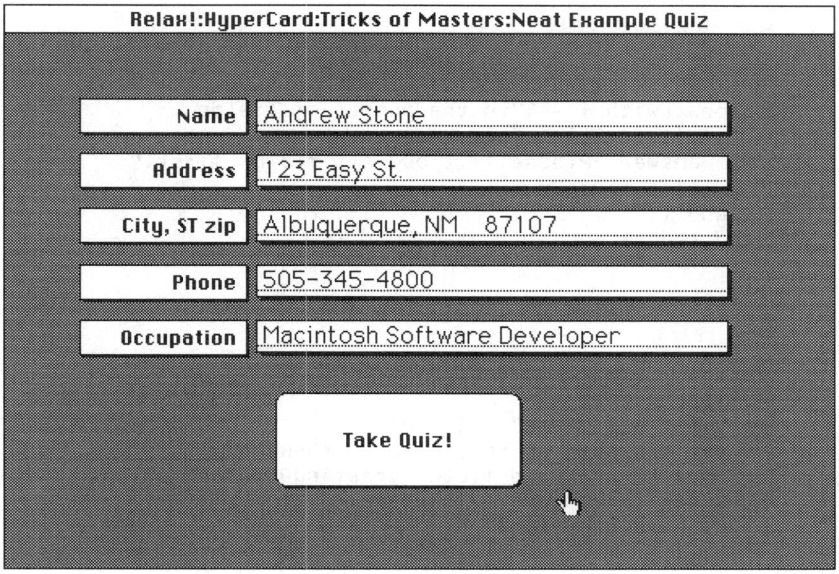

Figure 12-10. In user mode, Take Quiz! is the only visible button.

This script is important to the stack logic because it sets the name of the new Registry card to the name that the quiz taker enters. It demonstrates error-checking, which is the sign of a first-class stack. The first step is to check that you are in user mode; if not, you are offered a chance to switch:

```
on mouseUp
  global theName, Umode
  if not Umode then
    answer "Change to User Mode?" with "Ok" or "Cancel"
    if it is "Cancel" then exit MouseUp -- escape hatch
    changemode "User"
```

Then the script makes sure that you are not on the RegistryTemplate card because the execution of the rest of the script would change the name of the template card. If the name is RegistryTemplate, the script allows processing to continue by sending a mouseUp to the Would you like to take a quiz? button in the Welcome card:

```
else
  if the short name of this card is "RegistryTemplate" then
go card "Welcome"
    send mouseUp to button 1 -- would you like to take a quiz?
```

You must fill in at least the name field because the stack's links are based on the name of the card:

```
else
  if field "Name" is empty then
    answer "Please fill out your name at least" with "Ok"
```

If you want to require that all fields be filled in, you could use

```
repeat with i = 1 to the number of fields
  if field i is empty then
    answer "Please fill out all fields first."
    exit mouseUp
  end if
end repeat
```

Now the script can proceed, because everything must be in order:

```
else
  lock screen
  put field "name" into theName
  set the name of this card to theName
  speakPhrase card field "greetingPhrases" of card "Phrases"
  speak first word of theName
  go card question1
```

Wait, what if there are no questions? Tell the teacher:

```
if the result is not empty then
  answer "Could not find Question 1!"
end if
```

The operation of the result is crucial to understand and may seem backwards at first. If the result is empty, everything went as planned. If the result is not empty, something went wrong—that is, the result contains an error. In the case of a go card command, if the result is not empty, the card does not exist. the result contains "no such card."

The remainder of the navigation logic is in the background scripts of TorFalse and MultipleChoice. Because the scripts for both backgrounds are identical, type the script once and copy it for the other background. These background scripts demonstrate the simplicity of centralized scripts: the User Mode buttons in both backgrounds do not contain scripts! The mouseUps are passed to the background, where they are analyzed and acted upon. First, LockMessages is set to true, which means HyperCard completes this script before recognizing any new mouseUps: this prevents cheating by multiple clicks on the correct answer. Then the script makes sure you are in user mode so that inadvertent mouseUps by the quiz designer are not recognized.

```
on mouseUp
  global theName, Umode
  Set Lockmessages to true -- prevents other mouseDowns
  if Umode then -- prevents designer from sending mouseUps
```

continued

```
if "button" is in the name of the target then
  if field correctNumber is in the short name of ¬
  the target then
    doRight-- in stack script
  else
    doWrong -- in stack script
  end if
```

For the script to continue, *button* must be present in the name (full name as opposed to short name), which means a button was clicked. The name of the button is checked against the contents of the CorrectNumber field, one of the Teacher Mode fields in the bottom right corner where the creator has placed the correct answer (refer to Figure 12-6). If the field is a substring of the button name, the answer is correct and the doRight procedure is called; otherwise, the answer must be incorrect and doWrong is called. More on these handlers later. Then the script determines where to go next: either to the next question or to the student's registry card because the quiz is done.

```
-- Now figure out which card is next:
  put word 2 of the short name of this card into i
    add one to i
    if i < card field "numQuestions" of card "Statistics" then
    -- still more questions
      visual scroll left
      go card "Question" && i
    else -- finished with quiz
      visual iris open
      go card theName
      putTheScore -- in stack script
      wait 2 seconds -- alter if you want more
      go card "Welcome" -- ready for next student
    end if
```

The number of total questions is stored globally in the numQuestions field on the Statistics card. The word2 of the short name of this card is an integer. You add one to this number. If it is less than or equal to the total number of questions, you go card "Question" && <the number>. Otherwise, the quiz is over; you go to the quiz taker's Registry card, call the putTheScore handler, which does just that, wait a bit, and go back to the Welcome card, where the next student can take a quiz. Finally, LockMessages is set to false, which returns control to the user.

There is an important caveat in this simple scheme: if a question is deleted, the order of the rest of the quiz must be maintained by renaming the rest of the questions. This is handled by on doMenu "Delete Card"

```
else if which is "Delete Card" then
  if Umode then exit doMenu -- cannot let students destroy it
    else if "Question" is in the short name of this card then
      put word 2 of the short name of this card into i
      push card
      put "Now renumbering other quiz questions to ¬
      maintain sequence"
```

continued

```
        subtract 1 from card field "NumQuestions" of ¬
        card "Statistics"
        put card field "NumQuestions" of card "Statistics" ¬
        into newNum
        repeat with j = i + 1 to newNum + 1
          go card "Question" && j
          set the name of this card to "Question"&& j - 1
        end repeat
        pop card
        pass doMenu -- cut out that card
      else
        pass doMenu
      end if
```

First, any attempt by a student to delete a card is ignored with the `exit doMenu` statement. Next, if you are currently on a question card, the number of the question, which is the second word of its short name, is put into the `i` variable. Then the number of total questions is decremented and placed into the `newnum` variable. A `repeat` loop renumbers the remaining quiz questions and the card is deleted.

Anti-Navigation: Restricting Travel

You can keep students in the planned card route by trapping any `go` commands other than `Go Home` and `Go Help`. The Trap Go Commands radio button puts a value of false into the global `allowGo` container. The following script is in the multipurpose on doMenu which handler:

```
  else if which = "Back" or which = "First" or which = "Prev" ¬
  or which = "Next" or which = "Last" or which = "Recent" then
    if Umode then
      if not allowGo then
        play boing
      else
        pass doMenu
      end if
    else
      pass doMenu
    end if
  else
    pass doMenu-- to any other menu item
  end if
end doMenu
```

Notice the instances of `pass doMenu`. If you forget these, you cannot do anything because the other menu commands will be stopped.

You could get fancy with what you do if someone tries to use the `go` commands illicitly: create a global called `NumBreakIns`. Put O into this global on openstack. Then increment it after `play boing`:

```
play boing
add one to NumBreakIns
if NumBreakIns > 3 then
  answer "You are being reported by the Mind Police"
  exit doMenu
end if
```

Just the threat of the Mind Police is enough to make people behave! The script checks if any go commands are being called. Then it checks if you are in Umode because the teacher should be able to traverse freely even with this option selected. Finally, the script checks if go commands are being trapped with if not allowGo.

But there is still the issue of go commands created by the arrow keys, so include the following handler:

```
-- Trap arrowKeys
on arrowkey -- which
  global allowGo, Umode, NumBreakIns
  if Umode then
    if allowGo then
      pass arrowKey
    else
      play boing
      add one to NumBreakIns
      if NumBreakIns > 3 then
        answer "You are being reported by the Mind Police"
        exit arrowkey
      end if
    end if
  else
    pass arrowkey
  end if
end arrowkey
```

Several other ways to get into the stack must be plugged. The Message box offers an experienced hacker instant access to scripts by a series of statements:

```
set userlevel to 5
edit script of this stack
```

Therefore, the first precaution is to make the Message box inaccessible in the on doMenu which handler:

```
else if which is "Message" then -- trap Message
  if not Umode then
    pass doMenu
  end if
```

Likewise, the Find... menu item is a hole that must be plugged:

```
else if which is "Find..." then -- trap find
  if not Umode then
    pass doMenu
  end if
```

Finally, printing the stack would give away too much:

```
else if which is "Print Report..." then
  if not Umode then
    pass doMenu
  end if
else if which is "Print Stack..." then
  if not Umode then
    pass doMenu
  end if
```

Note that these commands are trapped by not being passed if the stack is in Umode. This allows the teacher full use of the menu.

Finally, the `BlindTyping` property must be set to false in the HideTools routine, along with a `Hide message` to hide the Message box if it is displayed.

Special Effects

The global variable `UseEffects` is controlled by the radio button pair Use Effects and Don't Use Effects on the Preferences card. It is accessed from the doRight and doWrong stack script handlers. These handlers are called after each question: doRight is called for a correct answer, and doWrong is called for an incorrect one. They handle the accounting first (described in the next section). Then, if `UseEffects` is true, special effects are produced:

```
on doRight
  global UseEffects, theName
    .
    .
    .
  if UseEffects then
    show bkgnd btn "HappyFace" -- custom icon
    speakPhrase card field "correctPhrases" of card "Phrases"
    hide bkgnd btn "HappyFace"
  end if
end doRight

on doWrong
  global UseEffects, theName,revealAnswers
    .
    .
    .
  if UseEffects then
    show bkgnd btn "SadFace"
    speakPhrase card field "incorrectPhrases" of card "Phrases"
    hide bkgnd btn "SadFace"
  end if
```

Two icons were produced with ResEdit: HappyFace and SadFace (see Figures 12-11 and 12-12). These are background buttons on both Question templates. The relevant button is shown and then hidden if `UseEffects` is true.

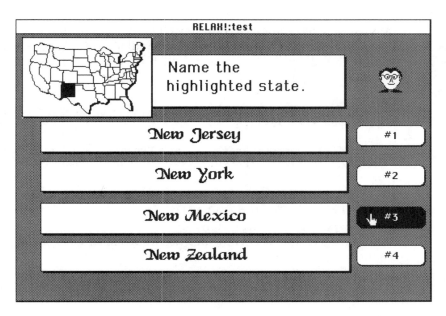

Figure 12-11.   The HappyFace icon special effect shows that the multiple-choice question was answered correctly.

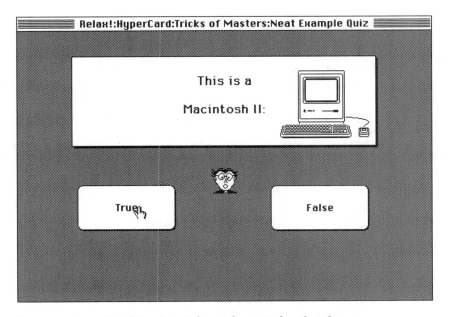

Figure 12-12.   A SadFace icon informs the test-taker that the answer is incorrect.

The next special effect demonstrates the use of text fields to contain easily editable phrases selected at random (refer back to Figure 12-3). You need to install the readily available `speak` XFCN into your stack with Steve Maller's ResCopy or

Apple's ResEdit. The MacInTalk speech driver system file must be in your system folder. The script calls the speakPhrase handler with a parameter of the name of the field where the phrases are kept, which does the work of getting and speaking a phrase:

```
-- Write all quips into the correct field on Phrases card
on speakPhrase theField
  put any line of theField into ¬
  card field currentPhrase of card "Phrases" -- bug discussion
  speak card field "currentPhrase" of card "Phrases"
end speakPhrase
```

It uses the HyperTalk reserved word any to select a line at random from the field that was passed as a parameter.

A bizarre and fascinating bug occurs when you use speak and an element of a container. If you type the following into the Message box:

```
speak line 4 of card field "correctPhrases"
```

it will speak that line, then speak each other line of the field! This may occur because the speak XFCN is being passed a pointer to the field and cannot know when the end of an element is reached. The obvious correction is to create a temporary storage container for the selected phrase, then pass the container to the speak function. Remember, sometimes you need an explicit container for certain operations, and the use of this extra variable or field will solve those mysterious bugs that create unintelligible error dialogs and leave the cursor blinking at the first word of the script.

A welcome phrase is at the beginning of the quiz, and a congratulatory phrase is at the end if the score is over 89 percent. The more phrases that you enter into the Phrases card fields, the less chance of getting the same phrase spoken twice in a row.

Another teacher-modifiable function is the revealAnswers global container, which is controlled by a radio button pair. This script, in the doWrong handler, simply highlights the correct answer if the incorrect answer was chosen:

```
on doWrong
  global
    .
    .
    .
  if revealAnswers then
    set the hilite of bkgnd btn field correctNumber to true
    wait 2 seconds -- adjust as necessary
    set the hilite of bkgnd btn field correctNumber to false
  end if
end doWrong
```

Notice the use of bkgnd btn field correctNumber, which means the background button whose short name is the contents of the correctNumber field. You must spell the answer in the field correctly, although case is unimportant (for example, true or TRUE work if the button's short name is True). Multiple-choice questions require a pound sign, for example, *#4*.

Other special effects include the use of the `flash` command, which takes an integer as a parameter to indicate the number of screen inversions. Type `flash 4` into the Message box for an example.

The use of `"snd "` resources through the HyperTalk `play` command can increase the fun factor of a stack. One place for these effects is at the end of the quiz. You can add scripts to create different effects based on a student's score.

Producing Statistics

The main numerical portion of the Quiz Maker stack is statistics generation. There are several classes of information: student particular, which is stored on each individual's card (Figure 12-13); question particular, which is stored on each question's card, and group statistics, which can be generated dynamically on the Statistics card and updated anytime if more students have taken the quiz by clicking the Collect Info button (Figure 12-2).

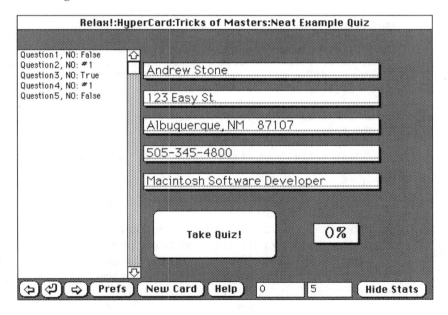

Figure 12-13. The Registry card stores statistics for each quiz taker.

After each question is answered, the doRight and doWrong scripts increment the correct fields on both the question card and the student's card:

```
on doRight
  global UseEffects, theName
  add one to field "numberRight" -- for group stats
```

continued

```
   add one to field "numberRight" of card theName
   put the short name of this card & ", Correct" & return after ¬
   field "statNumbers" of card theName
   .
   .
   .
on doWrong
   global UseEffects, theName,revealAnswers
   add one to field "numberWrong" -- for group stats
   add one to field "numberWrong" of card theName
   put the short name of this card & ", NO: " &  the short name ¬
   of the target & return after field "statNumbers" of ¬
   card theName
   .
   .
   .
```

In addition, the answer selected is placed after the statNumbers field of the student's card, which in effect is the graded paper.

After taking the quiz, the PutTheScore handler is invoked, which places the percent correct in the PercentRight field of the student's card:

```
on putTheScore
   global theName
   put field "NumberRight" of card theName into numRight
   put card field "numQuestions" of card Statistics into total
   put round(((numright/total)*100)) & " %" into field ¬
   "PercentRight" of card theName

   put first word of field "PercentRight" of card theName ¬
   into temp
   if temp > 89 then
      speakPhrase card field "endPhrases" of card "Phrases"
      speak theName
   end if
end putTheScore
```

Note the use of the round function to get an integer grade. The grade is then checked for a high score and congratulatory phrases are spoken. This is the location for inserting different effects given different grades. Hide the PercentRight card field at the beginning of the script if you do not want to reveal the grade; it is shown automatically when teacher mode is selected.

The card script of the Statistics card is the location for the CollectInfo handler. It relies on several repeat loops to gather and process data. It calls two useful functions, FieldSort and addblanks. The FieldSort function is an algorithm that sorts the students field by last name. The addblanks formatting function aligns the items in the field.

The two major receptacles for information, the students card field and the stats card field, are right-aligned scrolling text fields that have lockText set to true. The right alignment allows the fields to look good with a minimum of formatting because the first item of a line is the student's name, a variable-length item. Because you do not know how many words will be in a student's name, the HyperTalk structure of an item is used. An item's structure is a container consisting of a variable number of words separated by commas. This allows the processing of the entire field by getting, for example, item 3 of line 5 of card field students.

The on collectInfo handler places information into the stats and students fields automatically. They are always locked, which allows the use of a modified version of ScrollJump1 (see chapter 5). The two fields provide virtual links to anywhere in the stack and, with the go back button in every background, make stack traversal instantaneous. For example, if no one got Question 6 right, just click on Question 6 and you are looking at the offending question.

The addBlanks function has two parameters, the number of blanks needed and the container that needs blanks added. A typical call to it follows:

```
put field "numberRight" of card i of bkgnd "Registry" ¬
into numRight
put the number of chars in numright into howmany
put addblanks(4 - howmany, numright) into numright
```

The information numberRight is put into the numRight variable. The length of numRight is calculated with the number of chars function, putting this returned integer into howmany. The addblanks function is passed the first parameter of the difference of a constant representing the largest size of the item (4 allows up to 999 answers plus 1 blank for easy viewing) and howmany. The second parameter is the container you want formatted. In this case, it is the numRight variable that is processed and returned.

```
function addblanks num,what
  repeat with i = 1 to num
    put " " before what
  end repeat
  return what
end addblanks
```

The main part of CollectInfo begins by cleaning out any old information in the card fields it will fill. Next is a series of loops exemplified by the following:

```
repeat with i = 2 to the number of cards in background "Registry"
  put the short name of card i of bkgnd "Registry" into theName
  put field "numberRight" of card i of bkgnd "Registry" into ¬
  numRight
  put the number of chars in numright into howmany
  put addblanks(4 - howmany, numright) into numright
  put field "numberWrong" of card i of bkgnd "Registry" into ¬
  numWrong
  put the number of chars in numWrong into howmany
  put addblanks(4 - howmany, numWrong) into numWrong
  put round((numRight/numberQuestions)* 100) into percent
  put the number of chars in percent into howmany
  put addblanks(4 - howmany, percent) into percent
  put theName & ","& numRight &","& numWrong &","&¬
  percent && "%" & return after card field "Students"
end repeat
```

The important data from each card in the Registry background is collected and placed into temporary explicit variables. These variables are formatted, concatenated with the comma item delimiter, and put into the next line of the students card field (in this case). I received the strange error message `No Such Card` when first creating this code because I did not use explicit temporary containers for numeric information. This HyperTalk quirk is worth putting up with in exchange for never having to declare the type of a variable.

The last line of CollectInfo puts the entire field just created through the `FieldSort` line-sorting function:

```
put FieldSort(card field "Students") into card field "Students"
```

The syntax is:

```
put FieldSort(<container>) into <container>
```

This selection sort searches each line to find the alphabetically lowest last name (the last word of item 1) and swaps it with the first line. Although it may not be lightning fast for large fields, it was written entirely in HyperTalk!

```
function FieldSort theField
  -- first strip all blank lines
  put return & return into crcr
  get theField
  repeat
    put offset(crcr,it) into p
    if p = 0 then exit repeat
    delete char p of it
  end repeat
put it into theField
```

After the blank lines are stripped, the nested `repeat` loops continue to find the smallest line and move it to the front of the container.

```
repeat with primary = 1 to the number of lines in theField - 1
  put primary into leastLineNum
  repeat with current = primary + 1 to the number of lines ¬
  in theField
    -- sort by last name
    if last word of item 1 of line current of theField < ¬
    last word of item 1 of line leastLineNum of theField then
      put current into leastLineNum
    -- if last names equal, sort by first name
    else if last word of item 1 of line current of theField = ¬
    last word of item 1 of line leastLineNum of theField then
      if first word of item 1 of line current of theField < ¬
      first word of item 1 of line leastLineNum of theField then
        put current into leastLineNum
      end if
    end if
  end repeat
end repeat
```

continued

```
      if leastLineNum > primary then -- it was out of order
         put line primary of theField into temp -- so swap lines
         put line leastLineNum of theField into line primary of ¬
         theField
         put temp into line leastLineNum of theField
      end if
   end repeat
   return theField --  return the sorted field
end fieldSort
```

The sorted field is then returned and put into the students card field. From the complete listings of the statistics card script, you will get a highly functional model that can be modified as needed.

The Help Card

The last card in the stack is the Help card, which contains instructions for inexperienced quiz designers (Figure 12-4). A sample help file is included at the end of the listing. Note that a Help option on the dialog appears when you open the Quiz Maker stack. This takes a teacher to the Help card, which explains the basics of creating a quiz. Therefore, by including a Create New Quiz card button, you allow someone to begin creating a new quiz if the Help option was selected from the initial dialog. The Create New Quiz card button's script simply calls the CreateNewQuiz stack script handler.

Enhancements

The scripts and techniques in the Quiz Maker can be used in many applications. One suggestion for enhancing the stack is to add the capability to accept short answers to questions. Basically, you would create a hidden background scrolling field with a list of possible answers to the question, then check if the student's answer is in your list. Results might be quite variable and arguments with the students might ensue! Another concept worth exploring is adding an essay question that is stored in a hidden field on the student's card and reviewed by the teacher.

The use of sound can be further developed to create an exciting atmosphere. Special tunes could be played at the end of a successful quiz. The incorporation of card layer pictures on the questions can add to the impact of your quiz.

If all else fails, remember to use explicit variables. But above all, have fun.

```
--***********************Description**************************
-- TYPE:       A template for creating quizzes
-- LOCATIONS:  Card, background, and stack
-- AUTHOR:     Andrew C. Stone
-- NAME:       Quiz Maker script

--******************   Stack Script   ************************
```

continued

```
on openstack
  global passwd,allowGo, Umode,revealAnswers, ¬
  UseEffects, prevLevel
  -- Get globals which are stored as states of radio buttons on
  -- the Preferences card
  put the userLevel into prevLevel -- in order to restore
  put the hilite of btn "User Mode" of card ¬
  "Preferences" into Umode -- the user mode
  put the hilite of btn "Allow Go Commands" of card ¬
  "Preferences" into allowGo -- allow or trap go commands
  put card field "pword" of card "Preferences" into passwd
  -- the password
  put the hilite of btn "Reveal Answers" of card ¬
  "Preferences" into revealAnswers -- are correct answers shown?
  put the hilite of btn "Use Effects" of card ¬
  "Preferences" into UseEffects -- are phrases spoken?
  -- This stack is a template, so make the quiz designer
  -- create another one:
  if the short name of this stack is ".Quiz Maker" then
    answer "Create a new Quiz?" with "Help" or "Cancel" or "Ok"
    if it is "Ok" then
      createNewQuiz
    else if it is "Help" then
      go card "Help"
    end if
  else if the commandkey is down then
  -- user trick to get in
    put passwd into the message box
    changeMode "Teacher" -- still requires password
  end if
end openstack

on createNewQuiz -- make a copy of the template
  global passwd
  doMenu "Save a Copy..." -- teacher selects new name
  set lockmessages to true -- prevents other messages
  go stack "the stack you just created" -- great trick
  -- delete next 3 lines if using version of HyperCard less
  -- than 1.2
  if the short name of this stack is not ".Quiz Maker" then
    hide card picture -- the stack maker logo
  end if
  go to card "Preferences" -- set global variables
  ask "Create a password that you can remember"
  put it into card field "pword"
  put it into passwd
  set lockmessages to false
end createNewQuiz

on changeMode which -- either user or teacher
  global Umode, passwd
  set the cursor to watch
  if which is "User" then -- go to user mode
    put true into Umode
    set the hilite of btn "User Mode" of card "Preferences" ¬
    to true
```

continued

```
      set the hilite of btn "Teacher Mode" of card "Preferences" ¬
      to false
      set the userlevel to 2
      hideTools -- put away teacher tools
      go first card -- to begin the quiz
    else if which is "Teacher" then -- go to teacher mode
      ask "What is the password?"
      if it is not passwd then exit changeMode
      -- password protection
      put false into Umode
      set the hilite of btn "User Mode" of card "Preferences" ¬
      to false
      set the hilite of btn "Teacher Mode" of card "Preferences" ¬
      to true
      set the userlevel to 5
      showTools -- show all tools and hidden fields
    end if
end changeMode


on showTools
  lock screen
  set the blindTyping to true
  push card
  repeat with i = 1 to the number of backgrounds - 1
  -- not data background
    set the cursor to busy
    go to card 1 of background i
    repeat with j = 1 to the number of bkgnd btns
      show bkgnd button j
      if "stats" is in the name of bkgnd btn j then
      -- it is a toggle, so adjust its name
        set the name of bkgnd btn j to "Hide Stats"
      end if
    end repeat
    set the cursor to busy
    repeat with h = 1 to the number of fields -- show all fields
      show field h
    end repeat
  end repeat
  pop card
  unlock screen
end showTools


on hideTools
  lock screen
  set the blindTyping to false -- data security
  hide msg
  push card
  repeat with i = 1 to the number of backgrounds - 1
  -- not data background
    go to card 1 of background i
    set the cursor to watch
    repeat with j = 1 to the number of bkgnd btns
      if "next" is in the name of bkgnd btn j then ¬
      hide bkgnd btn j
      else if "face" is in the name of bkgnd btn j then ¬
```

continued

```
            hide bkgnd btn j
            else if "Prefs" is in the name of bkgnd btn j then ¬
            hide bkgnd btn j
            else if "New Card" is in the name of bkgnd btn j then ¬
            hide bkgnd btn j
            else if "Help" is in the name of bkgnd btn j then ¬
            hide bkgnd btn j
            else if "stats" is in the name of bkgnd btn j then ¬
            hide bkgnd btn j
            else if "text" is in the name of bkgnd btn j then ¬
            hide bkgnd btn j
          end repeat
          repeat with h = 1 to the number of fields
            --  all hidden fields have number in their name
            if "number" is in the name of field h then hide field h
          end repeat
      end repeat
    pop card
    unlock screen
end hideTools


on closestack
  global prevlevel
  set the userlevel to prevlevel
end closestack


--*********************** New Card Routines ***********************
-- Trapping menu commands:
on doMenu which
  global allowGo, Umode, NumBreakIns
  if which is "New Card" then
    lock screen -- Matching half in "on newcard"
    if Umode then -- a new student
      go last card of bkgnd "Registry"
    else
      Answer "Which class of question: True/False or Multiple?" ¬
      with "True/False" or "Multiple ??" or "Cancel"
      if it is "True/False" then
        go last card of bkgnd "TrueOrFalse"
      else if it is "Multiple ??" then
        go last card of bkgnd "MultipleChoice"
      else
        exit doMenu
      end if
    end if
    pass doMenu
    -- create card. Transfer control to "on NewCard"
  else if which is "Delete Card" then
    if Umode then exit doMenu
    -- can't let students destroy stack
    else if "Question" is in the short name of this card then
      put word 2 of the short name of this card into i
      push card
      put "Now renumbering other quiz questions to ¬
      maintain sequence"
      subtract 1 from card field "NumQuestions" of ¬
```

continued

```
            card "Statistics"
            put card field "NumQuestions" of card "Statistics" ¬
            into newNum
          repeat with j = i + 1 to newNum + 1
            go card "Question" && j
            set the name of this card to "Question"&& j - 1
          end repeat
          pop card
          pass doMenu -- cut out that card
        else
          pass doMenu
        end if
        -- trap go commands  Stage 1  See also arrowKey below
      else if which = "Back" or which = "First" or which = "Prev" ¬
      or which = "Next" or which = "Last" or which = "Recent" then
        if Umode then
          if not allowGo then
            play boing
            add one to NumBreakIns
            if NumBreakIns > 3 then
              answer "You are being reported by the Mind Police"
              exit doMenu
            end if
          else
            pass doMenu
          end if
        else
          pass doMenu
        end if
      else if which is "Find..." then -- trap find
        if not Umode then
          pass doMenu
        end if
      else if which is "Message" then -- trap Message
        if not Umode then
          pass doMenu
        end if
      else if which is "Print Report..." then
        if not Umode then
          pass doMenu
        end if
      else if which is "Print Stack..." then
        if not Umode then
          pass doMenu
        end if
      else
        pass doMenu--  to any other menu item
      end if
    end doMenu


    -- This routine automatically numbers the quiz questions
    -- and increments the number of the students
    on newcard
      global Umode
      if not Umode then-- you are adding a quiz question
        add one to card field numQuestions of card Statistics
```

continued

```
      put card field numQuestions of card Statistics into theNumber
      set the name of this card to "Question" && theNumber
    else
      add one to card field numStudents of card Statistics
    end if
    put 0 into field numberRight -- better for data aquisition
    put 0 into field numberWrong
    tabkey -- to move insertion point to field
  end newcard


  --*************** Accounting and Effects scripts ****************
  on doRight
    global UseEffects, theName
    add one to field "numberRight" -- for group stats
    add one to field "numberRight" of card theName
    put the short name of this card & ", Correct" & return after ¬
    field "statNumbers" of card theName
    if UseEffects then
      speakPhrase card field "correctPhrases" of card "Phrases"
    end if
  end doRight


  on doWrong
    global UseEffects, theName,revealAnswers
    add one to field "numberWrong" -- for group stats
    add one to field "numberWrong" of card theName
    put the short name of this card & ", NO: " &  the short name ¬
    of the target & return after field "statNumbers" of ¬
    card theName
    if UseEffects then
      speakPhrase card field "incorrectPhrases" of card "Phrases"
    end if
    if revealAnswers then
      set the hilite of bkgnd btn field correctNumber to true
      wait 2 secs -- adjust as necessary
      set the hilite of bkgnd btn field correctNumber to false
    end if
  end doWrong


  --*************************************************************
  -- patch in all quips and the like in the correct field on
  -- "Phrases" card
  on speakPhrase theField
    put any line of theField into ¬
    card field currentPhrase of card "Phrases"
    speak card field "currentPhrase" of card "Phrases"
  end speakPhrase


  -- Calculating the score
  on putTheScore
    global theName
    put field "NumberRight" of card theName into numRight
    put card field "numQuestions" of card Statistics into total
    put round(((numright/total)*100)) & " %" into field ¬
    "PercentRight" of card theName
    -- congratulations if A score
```

continued

```
    put first word of field "PercentRight" of card theName ¬
    into temp
    if temp > 89 then
      speakPhrase card field "endPhrases" of card "Phrases"
      speak theName
    end if
end putTheScore

--***************** End of stack script ************************
-- The tools that allow easy creation of a quiz.
-- These buttons appear in every background, identically, at
-- the bottom of the screen:
-- Prefs background button
on mouseUp
  go card "Preferences"
end mouseUp


-- New Card background button
on mouseUp
  doMenu "New Card"
end mouseUp


-- Help background button
on mouseUp
  visual iris open
  go card help
end mouseUp


-- Next background button
-- all 3 with same name for hide/show ease
on mouseup -- small next icon
  go next card
end mouseup

on mouseup -- small prev icon
  go prev card
end mouseup

on mouseup -- small return icon
  go back
end mouseup


--************************************************************
-- Background-specific and card-specific scripts.
-- Welcome card. Card 1 of stack; unique card of its background
-- ********** Would you like to take a quiz Button *****
on mouseUp
  global Umode
  if Umode then
    doMenu "New Card"
    tabkey
  else
    answer "Change Mode to User on card Prefs first!"
  end if
end mouseUp
--************************************************************
```

continued

```
-- Background "TorFalse" and background  "MultipleChoice"
-- Background script.
-- It handles all mouseups so that buttons do not require scripts
on mouseup
  global theName, Umode
  Set Lockmessages to true -- prevents other mouseDowns
  if Umode then -- prevents unwanted mouseUps
    if word 2 of the target is "button" then
      if field correctNumber is in the short name of ¬
      the target then
        doRight -- in stack script
      else
        doWrong -- in stack script
      end if
    -- now figure out which card is next
    put word 2 of the short name of this card into i
    add one to i
    if i <= card field numQuestions of card Statistics then
      visual scroll left
      go card "Question" && i
    else -- we are finished with the quiz
      visual iris open
      go card theName
      putTheScore -- in stack script
      wait 2 secs -- alter as necessary
      go card welcome
    end if
  end if
  end if
  Set Lockmessages to false
end mouseup


-- Background button Lock Text in both question backgrounds
on mouseUp
  get the short name of me
  if it is "Lock Text" then
    set the name of me to "Unlock Text"
    repeat with i = 1 to the number of fields
      set the locktext of field i to true
    end repeat
  else
    set the name of me to "Lock Text"
    repeat with i = 1 to the number of fields
      set the locktext of field i to false
    end repeat
  end if
end mouseUp


--***********************************************************
-- Background  "Registry"
--************* button background Take Quiz! ****
-- Note error trapping
-- You must fill out name to proceed
-- You must be in user mode to take the quiz
-- If there are no questions, you are told so
on mouseUp
```

continued

```
      global theName, umode
      if not umode then
        answer "Change to " & quote & "User Mode" &¬
        quote & " on card Prefs first!"
        go card "Preferences"
      else
        if the short name of this card is "RegistryTemplate" then
          go card 1
          send mouseup to button 1--  "would you like to take a quiz?"
        else
          if field name is empty then
            answer "Please fill out your name at least" with "Ok"
          else
            lock screen
            put field "name" into theName
            set the name of this card to theName
            speakPhrase card field "greetingPhrases" of ¬
            card "Phrases"
            speak first word of theName
            go card "Question1"
            if the result is not empty then
              answer "Could not find Question 1!"
            end if
          end if
        end if
      end if
    end if
  end mouseUp


  -- There is a scrolling field, StatNumbers, which records
  -- the student's answers for each question. It is hidden in
  -- user mode. The Show Stats background button accesses it.
  on mouseUp
    get the visible of field "StatNumbers"
    if it is false then
      show field StatNumbers
      set the name of me to "Hide Stats"
    else
      hide field StatNumbers
      set the name of me to "Show stats"
    end if
  end mouseUp


  --****************************************************************
  -- Background Data
  -- Preferences card
  -- It has four sets of radio buttons. Three are
  -- controlled in the card script; teacher/user mode scripts
  -- are handled at stack script
  -- Preferences card script:
  on reveal which
    global revealAnswers
    if which is true then
      set the hilite of btn "Reveal Answers" to true
      set the hilite of btn "Don't Reveal Answers" to false
      put true into revealAnswers
    else
```

continued

```
          set the hilite of btn "Reveal Answers" to false
          set the hilite of btn "Don't Reveal Answers" to true
          put false into revealAnswers
        end if
      end reveal

      on trapGo which
        global allowGo
        if which is false then
          set the hilite of btn "Allow Go Commands" to true
          set the hilite of btn "Trap Go Commands" to false
          put true into allowGo
        else
          set the hilite of btn "Allow Go Commands" to false
          set the hilite of btn "Trap Go Commands" to true
          put false into allowGo
        end if
      end trapGo

      on Seteffects which
        global UseEffects
        if which is true then
          set the hilite of btn "Use Effects" to true
          set the hilite of btn "Don't Use Effects" to false
          put true into UseEffects
        else
          set the hilite of btn "Use Effects" to false
          set the hilite of btn "Don't Use Effects" to true
          put false into UseEffects
        end if
      end Seteffects

      -- Radio button scripts:
      -- Teacher Mode radio button
      on mouseUp
        changeMode "Teacher"
      end mouseUp

      -- User Mode radio button
      on mouseUp
        changeMode "User"
      end mouseUp

      -- Reveal Answers radio button
      on mouseUp
        reveal true
      end mouseUp

      -- Don't Reveal Answers radio button
      on mouseUp
        reveal false
      end mouseUp

      -- Allow Go Commands radio button
      on mouseUp
        trapGo false
      end mouseUp
```

continued

```
-- Trap Go Commands radio button
on mouseUp
  trapGo true
end mouseUp


-- Use Effects radio button
on mouseUp
  Seteffects true
end mouseUp


-- Don't Use Effects radio button
on mouseUp
  Seteffects false
end mouseUp


--***************************************************************
-- Statistics card of background data
-- Card script contains information processing scripts
on CollectInfo
  put card field "numQuestions" into numberQuestions
  if numberQuestions is empty then exit CollectInfo -- just exit
  put card field "numStudents" into numberStudents
  put empty into card field stats
  put empty into  card field students
  -- collect data from each question
  repeat with i = 1 to numberQuestions
    put field "numberRight" of card "Question" && i into numRight
    put field "numberWrong" of card "Question" && i into numWrong
    put "Question" && i & ",   " & numRight & ",    " & numWrong ¬
    & return into line i of card field stats
  end repeat
  -- collect data from each student
  repeat with i = 2 to the number of cards in background ¬
  "Registry"
    put field "numberRight" of card i of bkgnd "Registry" ¬
    into numRight
    put field "numberWrong" of card i of bkgnd "Registry" ¬
    into numWrong
    put the short name of card i of bkgnd "Registry" ¬
    into theName
    put theName & ",  "& numRight &",  "& numWrong &", "& ¬
    round((numRight/numberQuestions)* 100) && "%" & return ¬
    after card field students
  end repeat
  -- figure average
  put 0 into average
  repeat with i = 1 to the number of lines in card field stats
    add item 2 of line i of card field stats to average
  end repeat
  put round((average/(numberQuestions * numberStudents)*100)) ¬
  && "%" into card field "Average"
  -- figure high score
  put 0 into highscore
  repeat with i = 1 to the number of lines in card field students
```

continued

```
      put first word of item 4 of line i of card field students ¬
        into temp -- note use of explicit container****
      if temp > highscore then
        put temp into highscore
      end if
    end repeat
    put highscore && "%" into card field "HiScore"
    --  sort names of students by last name
    put FieldSort(card field students) into card field students
end CollectInfo

--*********************** function FieldSort ********************
-- A selection sort of the lines of a field
-- Syntax:  put FieldSort(<container>) into <container>
-- Copyright Andrew Stone
-- Modified to sort a field by last name

function FieldSort theField
  -- first strip all blank lines
  put return & return into crcr
  get theField
  repeat
    put offset(crcr,it) into p
    if p = 0 then exit repeat
    delete char p of it
  end repeat
  put it into theField
  repeat with primary = 1 to the number of lines in ¬
  theField - 1
    put primary into leastLineNum
    repeat with current = primary + 1 to the number of lines in ¬
    theField -- sort by last name
      if last word of item 1 of line current of theField < ¬
      last word of item 1 of line leastLineNum of theField then
        put current into leastLineNum
      -- if last names are equal, sort by first name
      else if last word of item 1 of line current of theField = ¬
      last word of item 1 of line leastLineNum of theField then
        if first word of item 1 of line current of theField < ¬
        first word of item 1 of line leastLineNum of theField then
          put current into leastLineNum
        end if
      end if
    end repeat
    if leastLineNum > primary then -- it was out of order
      put line primary of theField into temp -- so swap lines
      put line leastLineNum of theField into line primary ¬
      of theField

      put temp into line leastLineNum of theField
    end if
  end repeat
  return theField -- return the sorted field
end fieldSort

-- Collect Info button
```

continued

```
on mouseup
   CollectInfo
end mouseup


--************************************************************** --
Card Field Questions script: similar to ScrollJump1
on mouseUp
   get item 2 of the Clickloc - item 2 of the rect of ¬
   me + scroll of me
   put 1 + it div the textheight of me into LineNum
   set hilite of btn "hiliter1" to false
   get item 2 of rect of me + lineNum * textheight of ¬
   me - scroll of me
   put 1 + it - textheight of me div 2 into v
   show btn "hiliter1" at item 1 ¬
   of loc of btn "hiliter1",v
   set hilite of btn "hiliter1" to true
   set cursor to busy
   hide btn "hiliter1"
   put item 1 of line lineNum of me into cardName
   visual iris open
   go card cardName
end mouseup


-- Card field Students script: similar to ScrollJump1
on mouseUp
   get item 2 of the Clickloc - item 2 of the rect of ¬
   me + scroll of me
   put 1 + it div the textheight of me into LineNum
   set hilite of btn "hiliter" to false
   get item 2 of rect of me + lineNum * textheight of ¬
   me - scroll of me
   put 1 + it - textheight of me div 2 into v
   show btn "hiliter" at item 1 ¬
   of loc of btn "hiliter",v
   set hilite of btn "hiliter" to true
   set cursor to busy
   hide btn "hiliter"
   put item 1 of line lineNum of me into cardName
   visual iris open
   go card cardName
end mouseup


--**************************************************************
-- Help Card "Help" of background data
-- Card buttons:
-- Create New Quiz button
-- In case quiz designer clicked on help at Openstack Dialog
on mouseup
   CreateNewStack
on mouseup


-- Find button
on mouseup
   doMenu "Find..."
end mouseup
```

continued

```
-- button Go Back or use icon
on mouseup
  go back
end mouseup
```

It has a scrolling card field with the following information:
HELP FILE FOR the "QUIZ MAKER" stack:

".Quiz Maker" is a template stack. Create a new one with
another name to create a new quiz. Use button at bottom right of
card window: "Create New Quiz"

The stack is in either "Teacher Mode" for creating, modifying
and examining statistics of the stack, or User Mode, for allowing
people to take the quiz in an automated sequence.

To get into "Teacher Mode", open the stack with the Command key
or click on "Teacher Mode" radio button on the
"Preferences" card [click on button "Prefs" to get
there] or just type into message box:

        changemode "Teacher"

In "Teacher Mode", Use "New Card" button to create a new
card of either multiple-choice or true-or-false questions.

You must type the name of the button of the correct answer into
the field in the lower right corner, as the program checks that
field for the right answer. If it is a true or false question,
type in true for true or false if the correct answer is false.
For multiple choice questions, type in a pound sign and the number
of the correct answer, for example, #4 if answer 4 is correct.

To get into "User Mode", click on the User Mode radio button on
the preferences card, or type the following into the message box:

        changemode "User"

When in "User Mode" (Click on User Mode radio btn on card
"Preferences", or type Changemode "User" into the message
box), all Development tools are hidden, the Userlevel is set to 2.
All go commands, other than go help or go recent, can be disabled
with the "Trap Go Commands" radio button on card
"Preferences". Use the "Prefs" button to get to
"Preferences" card. Use the "Help" button to get here.

Phrases are stored in 4 different fields on the Phrases card.
Change the lines as required. Note: MacInTalk must be present in
the system folder for this to work. Be sure the XFCN "speak" is
in the resource fork of this stack.

HyperAnimals

Joseph F. Buchanan

Synopsis: HyperAnimals is a guessing game that tries to discover the creature that the player is thinking of. This standalone stack is extremely educational for illustrating the use of hidden linkage fields, binary tree relationships, and recursion in a binary tree structure.

The program is useful also because it shows how to write scripts that interact in a way that seems to exhibit intelligence. As the player interacts with the game, the stack learns about animals not stored in its vocabulary. Although a game like this cannot be classified as artificial intelligence, it does exhibit characteristics of AI, especially the capability of increasing knowledge over time by learning from interactions. The game uses a binary tree to hold this knowledge. In addition to these features, the game lets you actually draw the animal if it does not already exist in the HyperAnimals "Zoo," using HyperCard's drawing tools and an "artists" card.

HyperAnimals

A Game That Learns from the Player

HyperAnimals is a HyperCard stack that illustrates the use of hidden linkage fields to define the structure of binary tree data relationships of cards. Through programmed communication with the user, new information can be added to the stack. Essentially, this process "teaches" the HyperCard stack. Also in this chapter is a discussion of the use of recursion in a binary tree structure. Graphics capture and transfer are also described.

The Challenge

The HyperAnimals game is a guessing game that tries to discover the creature that the player is thinking of. As the player interacts with the game, it learns about animals not stored in its vocabulary. A decision-making game like this "learns" from the player, which makes the game more intelligent and varied the more it is played. Although a game like this cannot be classified as artificial intelligence, it does exhibit some characteristics of artificial intelligence—namely, the capability to increase knowledge over time by learning from interactions with the player.

This type of game needs an efficient structure to store the information learned from the person playing the game. The challenge for a script writer is to produce this structure using HyperTalk.

How does HyperAnimals do this? It asks yes-or-no questions from its body of knowledge (its database) and eventually recognizes the player's animal or realizes its lack of knowledge. The structure of this questioning method is called a *binary tree*. An example is shown in Figure 13-1. (See the next section, "Binary Trees and Recursion.") Although HyperAnimals asks only about animals, the technique it uses can be adapted easily to any body of knowledge that can be determined strictly by yes-or-no questions.

Binary Trees and Recursion

A database is a collection of pieces of information, called *records*, within a file. In some databases, such as the database described in this chapter, records have spe-

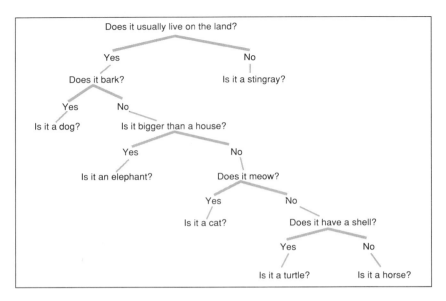

Figure 13-1. HyperAnimals is structured as a binary tree.

cific relationships to other records. These relationships are important to the structure of the database.

In a sequential database, each record is essentially laid end to end in a long line. The relationship between records is minimal and is usually defined by a sorting process. The process of searching for a specific record in a sequential database requires a one-at-a-time, front-to-back examination of the records. The time it takes to find a record in the file depends on the record's location in the file.

In a tree-structured or indexed database, a record can be found quicker (more directly) when its location (index) is known. A binary tree like the HyperAnimals game is a special case of an indexed, tree-structured database because each branch of the tree can search for records in two directions. As the tree is traversed, each decision is either yes or no. Because each level of the binary tree has twice as many branches as the prior level, the number of records that can be contained in such a structure is 2 raised to the Nth power, where N is the number of levels. For example, a binary tree with 6 levels has 64 records.

A record is found by going through the branches. Thus, the maximum number of inquiries necessary to find a record is the number of levels of the tree. A search for a record in a 64-record sequential database could take 64 inquiries. A search for a record in a 64-record binary tree (6 levels) requires at most 6 inquiries.

The HyperAnimals game fits the description of a binary tree. Each question can be answered yes or no. Each question also reduces the size of the database to be considered by half, eventually reaching a point where the animal is found or the animal is not in the database. Because the content of the HyperAnimals binary tree database depends upon the whims of the player, some branches of the tree can be longer than other branches and the number of levels in the binary tree can vary. Also, some animals will take longer to find than others.

To examine the entire binary tree database (not just search for a particular item), you start at the initial point (the first question) and follow each branch to its conclusion. When you program the instructions for following each branch to its conclusion, you need to know how many levels have to be examined for each branch. Because this information differs from tree to tree and branch to branch, it is difficult to program.

A better approach to examining a binary tree is to use recursion. *Recursion* is a process in which a set of instructions for accomplishing a task refers to itself to continue the task. An analogy is a picture of a person holding a picture of himself, which is the same picture of himself holding a picture of himself, ad infinitum.

The recursive command in HyperAnimals analyzes one level of the binary tree to determine where the branches lead. If a branch leads to another level of the tree, the same command is called to examine that next level of the tree, and so on. Instead of the process going ad infinitum, it ends at a level where the branching ends and an end record is found—in HyperAnimals, this end record is an animal.

In a binary tree, each branch has two directions. A yes answer goes to one branch in the path down the tree; a no answer goes to another branch. When you ask if it is a specific animal, an end-of-the-trail question has been reached. At this point a yes answer means a successful guess, and a no answer means the game's knowledge is lacking. If a no answer is given, a process begins so that the game learns from the player.

How is HyperAnimals structured as a binary tree? Every card containing a question is linked to two other cards. Each of these cards is a specific animal or an additional question leading to two more cards. Structuring a HyperCard stack as a binary tree is unusual: cards usually are linked sequentially (a single line of cards in sequence) or linked randomly to buttons according to the design of the creator.

What HyperAnimals Does

In HyperAnimals, the HyperCard stack "learns" from the player. If the animal is not in the stack's vocabulary (the database binary tree), the game script of the stack asks the player for the animal's name and identifying information that distinguishes the animal from animals in the stack's vocabulary. All branching information must be contained in an individual question card. The script within the card must "know" the next question and determine when it has failed to guess the animal, which initiates the process of adding a new animal to its store of information.

How It Works

The player of the game thinks of an animal. Then the player responds to the yes-or-no questions posed by the cards shown by the game script. Eventually, the game either guesses the animal or asks questions so that it can build a new card containing the animal just learned from the player.

When the game knows a new animal (when it has built a new card), the player can add an animal picture from the zoo to the new animal's card. If the picture is not in the zoo, the player can go to an artist's area, draw a picture, and place it on the animal's card. (Or the player can get a picture from another source and paste it onto the animal's card.)

The Game's Structure

HyperAnimals has a simple data structure. Each card is a question or an animal. Each card has two visible fields, four invisible fields, and three buttons that are essential to the function of the card (see Figures 13-2 and 13-3). (The I want to stop! button is not part of the game's binary tree structure.)

Figure 13-2. The game card questions.

Following are descriptions of the relevant fields and buttons:

Question (visible background field): The question posed to the player, for example, Does it swim? or Is it a horse?

Name (visible background field): For game cards containing an animal, this field contains the name of the animal (for example, horse). A picture is usually placed above the name. For game cards containing a question, this field is blank.

Yes (background button): For the player's yes response.

No (background button): For the player's no response.

Delete (background button): For removing an animal from the game.

recurs (invisible background field): A field used when test and report is done from the Title card.

Those were obvious. Now for the more interesting components:

nextAni1 (invisible background field): The card ID number of the card linked to the yes response.

Figure 13-3. The game card with invisible fields shown.

nextAni2 (invisible background field): The card ID number of the card linked to the no response.
prevAni (invisible background field): The card ID number of the card that pointed to this card.
currAni (invisible background field): The card ID number of this card. (This isn't necessary, but it speeds things up a bit.)

The two buttons (Yes and No) are fairly simple. They determine if additional questions need to be asked (for example, Is there a next card?). If the player's animal is correctly guessed, the script makes an appropriate noise and asks if the player wants to play again. If the script guesses the animal incorrectly, the fun begins. A command script named `newAnimal` adds the animal to the game's database.

Behind the Scenes

The logic of the game seems straightforward, but many processes are occurring. For example, the following steps are required to add an animal to the database:

1. Save the information about the current animal (its card ID and what card pointed to it).
2. Find out the name of the player's animal.
3. Request a question from the player that distinguishes the new animal from the current one (the one incorrectly guessed). See Figure 13-4. The question supplied by the player must be one that is answered only yes or no and, in so doing, distinguishes between the player's new animal and the one that the game selected. The yes answer should yield the new animal, and the no answer should yield the animal the game selected. The script of the game cannot detect whether a question is valid; it must accept what the player enters.

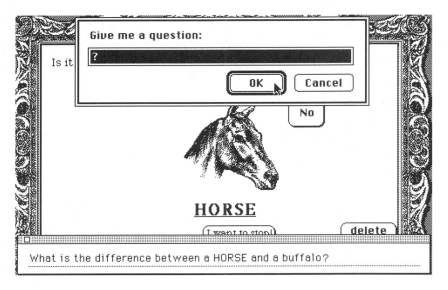

Figure 13-4.   Asking for a distinguishing question.

4. Build a new card containing the new question. Link it back to the card that pointed to the current animal.
5. Enter a link in the previous card pointing forward to the new question (rather than to the current animal incorrectly guessed).
6. Build a new card containing the new animal. Put its name into the name field and enter Is it a...? into the question field.
7. Link the new question to the new animal and to the incorrectly guessed animal. To establish the correct link, the question just entered is posed to the player as it applies to the new animal (as shown in Figure 13-5). For example, if the old animal is a dog and the new animal is a cat, the question might be Does it purr? When that question is posed as it applies to the cat, the answer should be yes. If the question was Does it bark?, the question posed for the cat yields no. This step is important in the process of adding the new animal and the question into the proper place in the database.
8. Set the previous pointers of the two animals to point back to the new question. Make sure the forward pointers are empty.
9. Ask if a picture should be added to the card (see Figure 13-6).
10. Shall you play again? (see Figure 13-7).

Some fundamental problems need to be resolved when an animal is added to the database. Although these problems are not critical to the binary tree structure, they are necessary for the overall value of the game itself. Some examples follow.

Problem
What if the animal is already in the database? For example, the animal may be described in different ways and therefore be in different parts of the tree.
Solution
Include a script that searches for a duplicated animal name in the stack. The

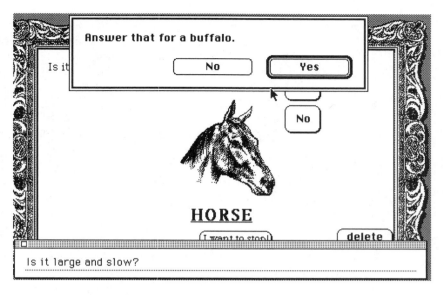

Figure 13-5. Establishing the relationship.

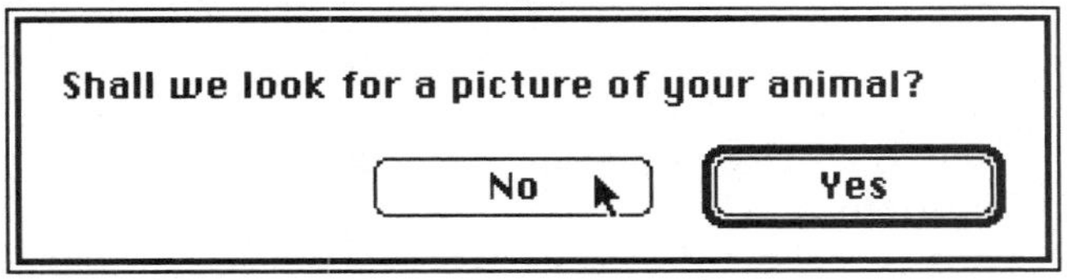

Figure 13-6. Asking if you want to visit the zoo.

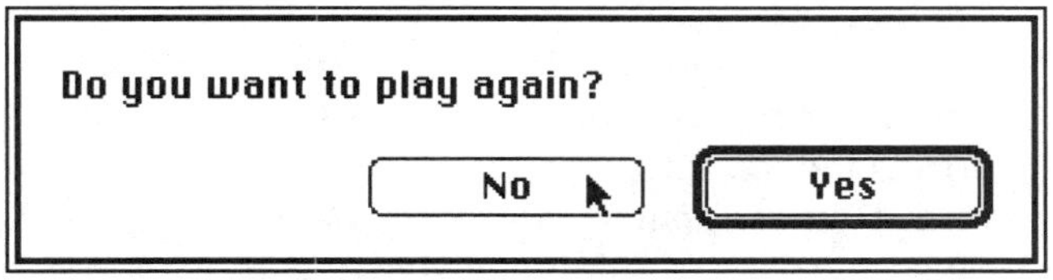

Figure 13-7. Shall you continue?

script shows the location of the duplicate and asks the player if it is correct in its former position. Most likely, the animal was either entered incorrectly the first time or the current entry is in error. Let the player decide. If the animal's position was incorrect originally, the script should then remove the animal from the incorrect location and enter it in its new location in the tree; otherwise, ignore the latest animal response.

Problem
What should you do if the player wants to stop in the middle of constructing the new animal? How can the script prevent links from being lost?

Solution

At any point, the player may respond with Cancel. The script should not make any changes until all the information is entered. If the player cancels, the changes are not made. The exception to this is if a duplicate is found (see the first problem).

Problem

What about proper wording or grammar, for example, Is it *a* elephant? or Is it *an* dog?

Solution

The script should check the text to determine if the animal name begins with a vowel, then add the appropriate indefinite article, if no article has been provided.

Problem

Is the player permitted to add a picture of the animal to the card?

Solution

Yes. Include a set of animal pictures in a portion of the stack named the zoo. Let the player find an animal in the zoo and copy it into the new card. Also let the player use the paint tools and draw an animal. These interactions with the player can be controlled and assisted through script commands.

Problem

Can the player remove an animal?

Solution

Yes. By using the links in each card, the script can adjust the previous questions in the tree and remove the unwanted cards, leaving the tree intact. (See the DropAnimal script.)

Problem

The knowledgeable HyperCard user can delete cards, add cards, or change fields, circumventing the precautions built in the game script. Should tools be provided for the player to check for problems in the binary tree structure of the database (usually for cards that have lost connections to other cards)? Can test and report functions showing the content and structure of the game's knowledge database be provided?

Solution

Yes. These processes are described in the section "Examining the Database Tree."

The Scripts

The HyperAnimals Game stack contains four backgrounds, which correspond to types of cards in the game:

Title card
Game cards
Zoo cards
Artist card

Background scripts and button scripts associated with these backgrounds define commands common to all cards sharing the background. Scripts associated with the stack itself define commands used throughout the entire game.

To build this stack, create the four backgrounds as described in the following sections, *in the order shown*. Only one card is needed initially for each background. After you create the four backgrounds with their buttons, fields, and scripts, all the scripts necessary for building the HyperAnimals stack are in place. When you click on the Purge Stack button in the Title card, all the Game cards are initialized.

Pictures are added manually. Most of the graphics for this stack are from the Clip Art and Art Ideas stacks included with HyperCard. You can copy pictures from graphics files using any paint programs, then paste them into the zoo or onto the beginning animal game cards.

Title Card

The Title card, shown in Figure 13-8, introduces the game and should be named Begin. It plays a little tune ("Old MacDonald Had a Farm") when the stack is opened. On the screen are five buttons: Zoo, Play the Game!, I want to stop!, Test and Report (invisible except at Scripting level), and Purge Stack. Before discussing the buttons on this card, we will describe the concept of database tree analysis (handled by the Test and Report button).

Figure 13-8. The Title card

Examining the Database Tree

There should be a way to check all links in the database structure to discover any "orphans" (cards that cannot be encountered through normal processes). The Test and Report button is included for this function. A player can cause inconsistencies in the game's structure by using HyperCard commands to delete cards or cancel scripts. Although precautions can be built into the script, there is always the possibility that the stack's structure can be changed.

The best way to examine a binary tree structure is to use recursion. (See "Binary Trees and Recursion" at the beginning of this chapter.) The recursive climb-Tree command calls itself as necessary to continually drop down (or climb up, depending on your perspective) each branch in a level until an end is found. As each question is found, it is stored in a line of a text field, with indents as necessary for readability, until each animal at the end of each question line is found. The animal's name is also placed into a line of the text field. The field is then shown on the screen as a complete report. Figure 13-9 shows an example of the treeReport field.

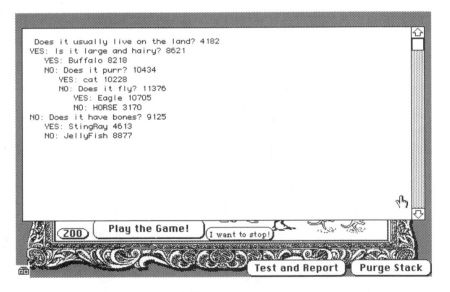

Figure 13-9.   The treeReport field.

During the recursive report process, a flag (an asterisk) is appended to the question field of each card that is encountered. Then the entire stack is examined to see if any cards do not have an asterisk. Because cards without an asterisk were not part of the database tree structure scanned during the recursive process, they are orphans and should be removed.

The Title card's Report hidden field is used in the test and report process. The *recurs* hidden background field is in the background of the Game cards; it is also used by the test and report process to show the current level of recursion in the examination process.

Play the Game! Card Button

The Play the Game! button goes to the first card of the game, then determines whether the Delete button should show on that card. If the player is running at scripting level (userLevel of 5), animals can be deleted from the game.

```
on mouseUp
  go to card "Tree Base" -- the first card of the Game cards
  if the userLevel < 5 then
  -- if the player is running at scripting level, allow delete
    hide bkgnd button "delete"
  else
    show bkgnd button "delete"
  end if
  pass mouseUp -- pass to card script (to stop the silly song)
end mouseUp
```

Zoo Card Button

With the Zoo card button, the player can view animals prior to playing the game.

```
on mouseUp
  go to card "Zoo 1" -- the first Zoo card
  pass mouseUp -- pass on to card script (to stop the silly song)
end mouseUp
```

Test and Report Card Button

The Test and Report button begins the test and report process or hides the Report field if the report has been completed and is visible on the screen. In the test and report process, all Game cards are marked with an asterisk in line 6 of the Question field. Then the treeReport script is initiated, specifying the name of the Report card field as the parameter to the command. (The treeReport script is shown as part of the stack scripts later in the chapter.) The treeReport process includes removing the asterisk from line 6 of all cards encountered when searching the structure. The script then goes through all Game cards sequentially to see if any cards still contain the asterisk. If any asterisks are found, the player is asked whether they should be removed. Finally, the Report field is shown.

```
on mouseUp
  go to card "Begin"
  put the visible of card field "report" into that
  if that then
    hide card field "report"
    exit mouseUp
  end if
  put empty into card field "report"
  set scroll of card field "report" to 0
  go to card "tree base"
  put the short ID of this card into beginID
  set cursor to watch
```

continued

```
      put 1 into cCount
      repeat forever
        go to next card of this bkgnd
        get the short ID of this card
        if it = beginID then exit repeat
        add 1 to cCount
        put * into line 6 of bkgnd field "question"
      end repeat
      treeReport("report")
      go to card ID beginID
      repeat with i1 = 2 to cCount
        put the short ID of this card into saveID
        go to next card of this bkgnd
        get line 6 of bkgnd field "question"
        if it = "*" then
          answer "This card is an orphan, Delete it?" with ¬
          "No" or "Yes"
          if it is "Yes" then
            doMenu "delete card"
            go to card ID saveID
          end if
        end if
      end repeat
      go to card "begin"
      show card field "report"
    end mouseUp
```

Purge Stack Card Button

There are two reasons for using the Purge Stack button. First, the programmer uses it to build the initial game (after setting up the first four cards as described). Second, the player uses it to refresh the game, removing all previous knowledge.

In HyperAnimals, the default (beginning) game has two animal cards (the horse and the stingray) and one question card (Does it live on the land?). The Purge Stack button removes all animals except the horse and the stingray. If the horse or the stingray or both are not in the game, they are put in the game without pictures. Therefore, the only required Game card (as the game is originally constructed) is the tree base initial question card.

The Purge Stack button appears only if the player is using HyperCard at the scripting level. The purge process first verifies that the player wants to take the drastic (unrecoverable) step of purging the stack. Next (unless the process is canceled), all game cards are removed except the original tree base card and the horse and stingray cards (if they are found). If the horse or the stingray is not found, a card for it is created and properly linked. Then the player is returned to the Begin card, and the game is ready to be played.

```
on mouseUp
  answer "Do you really want to purge the stack?" with ¬
  "No" or "Yes"
  if it is "No" then exit mouseUp
  go to card "tree base"
  put the short ID of this card into beginID
```

continued

```
put empty into horseID
put empty into SRID
set cursor to watch
repeat forever
-- get rid of everything except base, horse, and stingray
  go to next card of this bkgnd
  get the short ID of this card
  if it = beginID then exit repeat
  get bkgnd field "name"
  if it is "Horse" then
    put the short ID of this card into horseID
  else if it is "StingRay" then
    put the short ID of this card into SRID
  else
    doMenu "delete card"
    go to prev card -- so you stay within this background
  end if
end repeat
if horseID is empty then -- there wasn't a horse
  doMenu "New Card"
  put the short ID of this card into horseID
  put "Horse" into bkgnd field "name"
  put "Is it a Horse?" into bkgnd field "question"
end if
if SRID is empty then -- there wasn't a stingray
  doMenu "New Card"
  put the short ID of this card into SRID
  put "StingRay" into bkgnd field "name"
  put "Is it a StingRay?" into bkgnd field "question"
end if
go to card ID beginID -- lives on land
put horseID into bkgnd field nextani1
put SRID into bkgnd field nextani2
put 0 into bkgnd field prevani
go to card ID horseID -- horse
put empty into bkgnd field nextani1
put empty into bkgnd field nextani2
put beginID into bkgnd field prevani
go to card ID SRID -- stingray
put empty into bkgnd field nextani1
put empty into bkgnd field nextani2
put beginID into bkgnd field prevani
go to card "begin"
end mouseUp
```

I want to stop! Card Button

When the I want to stop! button is clicked, the player returns to the Home Card.

```
on mouseUp
  visual effect dissolve
  go home
  pass mouseUp
end mouseUp
```

Begin Card

The Begin card scripts do tasks related to the opening tune and the appearance of buttons. Each time the stack is started, the opening tune is played. If the player doesn't want to hear the tune but still wants to see the card, a mouseUp anywhere will stop the sound. If the player is running at scripting level (userLevel of 5) the Test and Report button and Purge Stack button are visible.

```
on mouseUp -- stop the sound
  play stop
end mouseUp

on openCard
  hide menuBar
  hide message box
  if the userLevel < 5 then -- hide buttons
    hide card button "test and report"
    hide card button "purge stack"
  else -- show if at scripting level
    show card button "test and report"
    show card button "purge stack"
  end if
end openCard

on openStack
  dofanfare
  pass openStack
end openStack
```

Game Cards

The Game cards contain background fields and buttons, but the background and cards themselves do not contain scripts. All commands used by the Game cards are defined in the stack scripts. The first Game card is named tree base and should be locked (the Can't Delete Card box should be checked).

The beginning game contains the horse and stingray cards. The Purge Stack button on the Title card puts these Game cards in the tree and makes the appropriate connections. The pictures are added manually. The following sections describe the background buttons and background fields that are needed (see the previous section titled "The Game's Structure").

Yes Background Button

When the player clicks on the Yes button, the player's animal has been correctly identified or the yes branch of the binary tree for this question will be followed.

```
on mouseUp
  get bkgnd field "name"
  if it is not empty then
    put "I GOT IT! I GOT IT! I GOT IT!" -- show some excitement
```

continued

```
      play harpsichord tempo 420 g5 g5 g5 g5 g5 g5 g5 g5 g5 ¬
        g5 g5 g5 g5 g5
      wait 60 ticks
      hide message box
      askRepeat -- does the player want to continue?
    else
      get bkgnd field nextAni1
      -- continue down the line to the next question
      put it into thing
      go to card id thing
    end if
end mouseUp
```

No Background Button

When the player clicks on the No button, the player's animal has not been found in the game's knowledge database or the no branch of the binary tree for this question will be followed. If the player's animal was not found, it needs to be included using the newAnimal command. The picture of the new animal can be added by going to the Zoo cards.

```
on mouseUp
  global novice
  get bkgnd field "name"
  if it is not empty then
    -- this is the last guess and it was wrong
    put "OOPS!  I NEED TO LEARN SOMETHING!"
    play harpsichord tempo 120 g2 -- sound depressed
    wait 60 ticks
    hide message box
    newAnimal -- see the command script in the stack
    if novice is NOT empty then
    -- this is a value containing the ID of the NEW animal card
      answer "Shall we look for a picture of your animal?" with ¬
      "No" or "Yes"
      if it is "Yes" then
        go to card "Zoo 1"
        exit mouseUp
      end if
    end if
    askRepeat
  else
    get bkgnd field nextAni2 -- get the next question
    put it into thing
    go to card id thing
  end if
end mouseUp
```

Delete Background Button

The Delete button gives the player the option to remove an animal from the knowledge database. The script ensures that only an animal is removed; it then removes the animal's card and the question card that pointed to it. The real work is done in the dropAnimal stack script.

```
on mouseUp
  put bkgnd field name into thingg -- get the name of the animal
  if thingg is empty then exit mouseUp
   -- if none, this is not an end, ignore delete
  answer "Do you really want to remove the" && thingg with ¬
  "No" or "Yes"
  if it is "No" then exit mouseUp
  dropAnimal -- this command does the real work
  askRepeat -- shall we play again?
end mouseUp
```

I want to stop! Card Button

When the I want to stop! button is clicked, the player returns to the Home card.

```
on mouseUp
  visual effect dissolve
  go home
  pass mouseUp
end mouseUp
```

Zoo Cards

Although the zoo is an interesting component to the HyperAnimals game, it is not essential to the game's structure and has nothing to do with the knowledge of the game. HyperCard's graphics capabilities make it possible to include pictures of animals on the game cards. Bit-mapped pictures of animals are located on Zoo cards within large buttons. When the player adds an animal to the game's knowledge database, the player has the option of going to the Zoo cards, finding the desired animal picture (if it exists), and adding the picture to the new card. The script detects which animal was clicked on in the Zoo card and places it in an appropriate location.

The first card of the Zoo background must be named Zoo 1 (with a space before the 1). Each animal graphic is positioned within an invisible button. Figure 13-10 shows a possible arrangement for Zoo 1. The Zoo card contains dummy buttons with no scripts and no names. All buttons are transparent; the number of buttons is up to the programmer and depends on the size and position of the animal "cages."

The background script looks for a mouseUp event in one of these buttons. When the player clicks on an animal, a button (with a `roundRect` outline) is shown around the animal and the Take this one! button becomes visible. If the player clicks on the outlined button (named choice) or the Take this one! button, the animal is copied to the new animal card, positioned on the card, and made transparent (as opposed to opaque) so that the buttons are not obscured. The Go back button is always visible; it cancels the process.

The let me draw! button is visible on the Zoo card. It moves the player to the Artist card, where the player can draw the animal.

Note that if the player enters the Zoo from the Title card (just to browse through the animal pictures, not to add a new animal card to the game), the Take this one! and let me draw! buttons are not visible. The `novice` global variable stores the card ID of the new animal's card. It is empty if the Zoo is entered from the Title card.

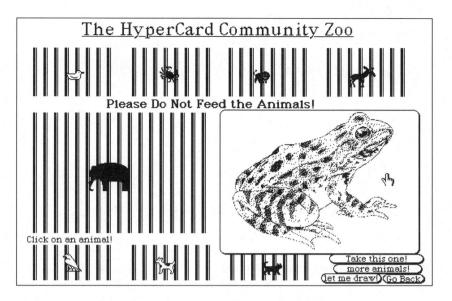

Figure 13-10. The Zoo card.

The background buttons for the Zoo cards follow:

Creatures (background buttons): These have no names and no scripts and are transparent. They are placed where the animal graphic will appear. Bars can be drawn in the background over the area of the buttons, but this is not necessary. You can add as many buttons as you want. Figure 13-10 shows fourteen buttons (the frog has two buttons over it).

Choice (background button): Outlines the player's choice with a `roundRect` outline. The button is originally hidden. It doesn't matter where it goes because the script moves it to the chosen animal.

Take this one! (background button): The player indicates what is wanted.

Let me draw! (background button): Moves to the Artist card.

More animals! (background button): Moves to another Zoo card (if there are any more).

Go Back (background button): Returns to the Title card.

Background Scripts for Zoo Cards

The openCard and closeCard scripts do housekeeping functions for the Zoo cards. The openCard script shows or hides the let me draw! button depending on whether the Zoo was entered to browse or to pick a graphic for a new animal card. The closeCard script hides buttons and unselects the chosen animal graphic.

```
on openCard
  global novice
  if novice is empty then -- see if this is for a new animal
```

continued

```
      hide bkgnd button "let me draw!"
    else
      show bkgnd button "let me draw!"
    end if
end openCard


on closeCard
  global hereRect, thisBtn
  hide bkgnd button "choice"
  put empty into thisBtn
  hide bkgnd button "Take this one!"
end closeCard
```

Background Scripts for Animal Buttons

The animal buttons do not contain script commands. The background script detects mouseUp events and checks to see if they occur within one of the animal buttons by looking at the short name of the button that was clicked on. If the short name is `bkgnd button ID <something>`, it wasn't given a name and is one of the animal buttons. All other background buttons are named. When the animal is identified, the Choice button is placed over the animal graphic and made visible. The Choice button then outlines the animal graphic. The mouseUp event is passed on in case something else was clicked on.

```
on mouseUp
-- this captures any mouseUp in buttons with
-- no scripts (unselected animals)
  global hereRect, thisBtn
  global novice
  get the short name of the target
  if (word 1 of it = "bkgnd") AND (word 2 of it = "button") then
    put the short ID of the target into thisBtn
    put the rect of the target into hereRect
    -- get rectangle that defines the animal
    set the rect of bkgnd button "choice" to hereRect
    -- move the choice button here
    show bkgnd button "choice" -- make it visible
    if novice is not empty then show bkgnd button ¬
    "Take this one!"
  end if
  pass mouseUp
end mouseUp
```

Take this one! Background Button

The Take this one! button is the worker of the Zoo. The rectangular coordinates of the animal graphic are now known because the Choice button outlines it. The paint tools are used to select, copy, and paste the graphic to the new animal card. Calculations determine how the graphic will be centered on the new card; then the graphic is made transparent so that buttons are not obscured. Finally, the player is asked whether the game should start again.

```
on mouseUp
  global hereRect, thisBtn
  global novice
  -- check to see if another one was chosen first
  if thisBtn is NOT empty then ¬
  set the hilite of bkgnd button ID thisBtn to FALSE
  put empty into thisBtn
  if novice is not empty then -- is this a new animal?
    put the userLevel into savLev -- save the mode
    set the userLevel to 3 -- paint level
    choose select tool
    drag from the topLeft of hereRect to the bottomRight ¬
    of hereRect
    -- drag across the button
    doMenu "copy picture"
    go to card ID novice -- go to the new animal's card
    doMenu "paste picture"
    choose select tool
    put the topLeft of hereRect into loc1
    put the bottomRight of hereRect into loc2
    drag from loc1 to loc2 -- select it
    add 1 to item 1 of loc1
    add 1 to item 2 of loc1
    put 325 - item 1 of loc2 into diff
    put item 1 of loc1 + diff into item 1 of loc2
    put 250 - item 2 of loc2 into diff
    put item 2 of loc1 + diff into item 2 of loc2
    drag from loc1 to loc2 -- center it
    doMenu "Transparent" -- make it transparent
    choose browse tool
    set the userLevel to savLev
  end if
  askRepeat
end mouseUp
```

Choice Background Button

Clicking on the outlined choice button (on the selected animal) has the same effect as clicking on the Take this one! button.

```
on mouseUp
  send mouseUp to bkgnd button "Take this one!"
  -- as if the button was clicked on
end mouseUp
```

Let me draw! Background Button

The let me draw! button allows the player to leave the Zoo and go to the Artist card, where an animal graphic can be drawn with HyperCard's paint tools.

```
on mouseUp
  global hereRect, thisBtn
  global novice
```

continued

```
     if thisBtn is NOT empty then ¬
     set the hilite of bkgnd button ID thisBtn to FALSE
     put empty into thisBtn
     if novice is not empty then -- only on a new animal
       go to card "artist card"
     else
       answer "Sorry, draw only from within the game."
       askRepeat
     end if
end mouseUp
```

More Animals! Background Button

The More Animals! button moves the player to another Zoo card.

```
on mouseUp
  go to next card of this bkgnd
end mouseUp
```

Go Back Background Button

The Go Back button gives the player the option to play the game again.

```
on mouseUp
  answer "Do you want to play again?" with "No" or "Yes"
  if it is "Yes" then
    visual effect scroll right
    answer "Think of an animal..." with "Ready!"
    go to card "tree base"
  else
    visual effect dissolve
    go to home
  end if
end mouseUp
```

Artist Card

The Artist Card has its own background, but only one card in the background. See Figure 13-11. The name of the card must be *Artist card*. No buttons or fields are associated with this background or its card. When the Artist Card is opened, the tools are prepared and instructions are given in the message window. When the player has finished drawing, the Return key must be pressed. The background graphic of the game card should be put into the Artist card. This leads the player to draw on the blank part of the card, not into the background frame, so the picture probably will not be too large. Then the entire screen can be selected and copied onto the new animal card.

The openCard script sets up the canvas for the player. The screen is cleared, if desired, and the pencil paint tool is chosen. After a player has finished drawing, the Return key should be pressed. The returnKey script intercepts the Return key from the player. Then, if instructed, the returnKey script selects, copies, and pastes the graphic onto the new animal card.

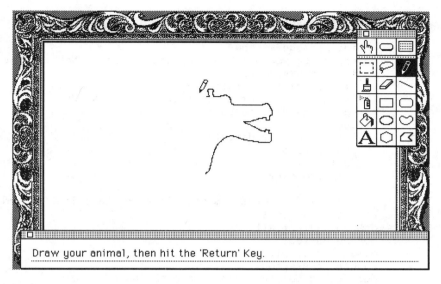

Figure 13-11. The Artist card.

```
on openCard
  global novice,savLev
  put the userLevel into savLev
  if novice is empty then exit openCard
  set the userLevel to 3 -- you need paint tools
  answer "Clear the Screen?" with "No" or "Yes"
  if it is "Yes" then
    choose select tool
    doMenu "Select All"
    doMenu "clear picture"
  end if
  show tool window
  choose pencil tool
  put "Draw your animal, then hit the 'Return' Key."
end openCard


on closeCard -- clean up
  global savLev
  set the userLevel to savLev
  hide tool window
end closeCard


on returnKey
  global novice, savLev
  if novice is empty then
    askrepeat
    exit returnKey
  end if
  answer "Are you finished?" with "Quit" or "No" or "Yes"
  if it is "No" then exit returnKey
  if it is "Quit" then -- bail out
```

continued

```
      set the userLevel to savLev
      choose browse tool
      hide message window
      answer "Do you want to play again?" with "No" or "Yes"
      if it is "Yes" then
        visual effect scroll right
        answer "Think of an animal..." with "Ready!"
        go to card "tree base"
      else
        visual effect dissolve
        go to home
      end if
      exit returnKey
    end if
    -- This is it. Put the masterpiece in the animal's card
    choose lasso tool
    doMenu "select all"
    doMenu "select"
    domenu "copy picture"
    choose browse tool
    put "let's put the animal into the game"
    -- let the player know what is happening
    go to card ID novice
    -- go back to the animal card and put the picture in
    doMenu "paste picture"
    doMenu "select all"
    doMenu "transparent"
    choose browse tool
    set the userLevel to savLev
    hide message window
    askRepeat
end returnKey
```

Stack Scripts

The stack scripts are the general commands that are used throughout the game. These important scripts install, remove, and search for animals. The script that offers the option of playing the game again is also located at the stack script level.

Play Again?

The following displays the dialog asking if the player wants to play again. It is referenced by several buttons in the stack.

```
on askRepeat
  global novice
  put empty into novice
  answer "Do you want to play again?" with "No" or "Yes"
  if it is "Yes" then
    visual effect scroll right
    answer "Think of an animal..." with "Ready!"
    go to card "tree base"
```

continued

```
      else
        visual effect dissolve
        go to home
      end if
end askRepeat
```

Install a New Animal

The following major script is essential to the work of the database. First, it determines the animal that the player was thinking of. Then it establishes the correct indefinite article (*a* or *an*). Throughout communication with the player, the script checks for consistency and allows the player to cancel the action. Two flags, keptAni and retryAni, handle situations such as duplicate animals or animals in the wrong place.

The script searches the database for the animal's name. If a duplicate is found, it asks the player where the error might be and allows the player to cancel if an error has been made. If the animal needs to be moved, the animal's card is copied for later placement and the original card is removed.

If the animal is truly a new one, a question is obtained from the player to distinguish the new animal from the animal that the game script guessed. The new animal is attached (or reattached if it was moved) and the links are set up. See the comments in the following script for a better understanding of each step.

```
on newAnimal
  global novice
  -- What do you have?
  put bkgnd field "name" into aName1
  ask "I Give up! What animal is it?" with "?"
  repeat -- keep going until cancel or a good name is given
    if it is empty then exit newAnimal -- blank response,bail out
    put it into aName2
    put the number of chars of aName2 into i1
    if i1<2 then
      answer "Please type in an animal name or click Cancel." ¬
      with "OK" or "Cancel"
      if it = "cancel" then
        exit newAnimal
      end if
      ask "What animal is it?" with "?"
    else
      exit repeat
    end if
  end repeat
  get word 1 of aName2  -- see if it has an article
  if (it = "a") OR (it = "an") then delete word 1 of aName2
  -- delete it
  put char 1 of aName2 into lettr
  -- see if the first letter is a vowel
  put "a" into arti  -- make an indefinite article
  if letter is in "aeiou" then
    put "an" into arti
  else put "a" into arti
```

continued

```
if aName1 = aName2 then
-- the player is not serious, same name given
  answer "But that is what I said!" with "Just Kidding!"
  exit newAnimal
end if
put FALSE into keptAni
-- flag to guide us through the player's goofs
put FALSE into retryAni -- ditto
-- see if the animal is already there
put bkgnd field "currAni" into cAni
put aniSearch(aName2) into lastAni
if lastAni<>0 then
  answer "But I already know that animal!" with ¬
  "OK, I goofed" or "Show me!"
  if it is "OK, I goofed" then exit newAnimal
  -- try to repair yourself
  go to card ID lastAni
  answer "Is this animal in the wrong place?" with ¬
  "Yes" or "No" or "Forget it!"
  if it is "Forget it!" then exit newAnimal
  if it is "Yes" then
    -- take it out (allowing it to be replaced later)
    put "Removing animal from this place..."
    doMenu "Copy Card"
    put TRUE into keptAni  -- set the flag: you did a COPY
    dropAnimal  -- remove it from the database
    hide message window
    go to card ID cAni
  else -- the former question wasn't definitive enough
    answer "Let's try this question again" with "OK"
    put TRUE into retryAni  -- flag for a redo of the question
    put bkgnd field "prevAni" into pAni
    go to card ID pAni
    -- see what animal you should be comparing against
    put bkgnd field "nextAni1" into thing
    put TRUE into topAni
    if thing<>lastAni then
      put bkgnd field "nextAni2" into thing
      put FALSE into topAni
      -- load the name
      put bkgnd field "name" of card ID thing into aName1
    end if
  end if
end if
-- get the all-important question
put "What is the difference between a " & aName1 into qq
put " and " & arti && aName2 & ". " after qq
repeat  -- keep going until Cancel or a good question
  put qq
  if retryAni then
    ask "Give me a new question:" with "?"
  else
    ask "Give me a question:" with "?"
  end if
  hide message window
  if it is empty then exit newAnimal
```

continued

```
      put it into aQuestion
      put the number of chars of aQuestion into i1
      if i1<2 then
        answer "Please type in a question or click Cancel." with ¬
        "OK" or "Cancel"
        if it = "cancel" then
          exit newAnimal
        end if
      else
        exit repeat
      end if
    end repeat
    get char i1 of aQuestion
    if it <> "?" then put "?" after aQuestion
    put aQuestion
    -- show the player's question and see how it applies
    -- the new animal
    put "Answer that for " & arti && aName2 & "." into qq
    answer qq with "No" or "Yes"
    hide message window
    put it into anAnswer
    if retryAni then
      -- is answer same parity as before?
      if (topAni) AND (anAnswer = "Yes") then exit newAnimal
      -- switch yes and no for this animal
      put bkgnd field "nextAni1" into thing
      put thing into bkgnd field "nextAni2"
      put lastAni into bkgnd field "nextAni1"
      exit newAnimal
    end if
    -- save the ID
    put bkgnd field "currAni" into endAni
    -- save the ID of its predecessor
    put bkgnd field "prevAni" into pAni
    -- make a new card (new end node)
    if keptAni then  -- get it back
      doMenu "Paste Card"
    else
      doMenu "New Card"
      -- make an appropriate question
      put "Is it " & arti &&  aName2 & "?" into bkgnd field "question"
      put aName2 into bkgnd field "name"
      put empty into bkgnd field "nextAni1"
      put empty into bkgnd field "nextAni2"
    end if
    put the short ID of this card into lastAni
    put lastAni into bkgnd field "currAni"
    -- now make a card to distinguish between the old end node
    -- and the new end node
    doMenu "New Card"
    put aQuestion into bkgnd field "question"
    put empty into bkgnd field "name"
    -- get the ID of this new one
    put the short ID of this card into newAni
    put newAni into bkgnd field "currAni"
    -- place it into the prev of the new end node
```

continued

```
      put newAni into bkgnd field "prevAni" of card ID lastAni
      -- place it into the prev of the earlier end node
      put newAni into bkgnd field "prevAni" of card ID endAni
      -- put the prev of this one in as well
      put pAni into bkgnd field "prevAni"
      -- determine the direction and load the right pointers
      if anAnswer is "Yes" then
        put lastAni into bkgnd field nextAni1
        put endAni into bkgnd field nextAni2
      else
        put endAni into bkgnd field nextAni1
        put lastAni into bkgnd field nextAni2
      end if
      -- get the node that points to this newly enlarged branch
      -- and reset the pointer to the new stuff
      put bkgnd field nextAni1 of card ID pAni into thing
      if thing = endAni then
        put newAni into bkgnd field nextAni1 of card ID pAni
      else
        put newAni into bkgnd field nextAni2 of card ID pAni
      end if
      -- show the new end node
      go to card ID lastAni
      put lastAni into novice
    end newAnimal
```

Search for the Animal in the Stack

The following command script searches the game's knowledge database for a dupli-cate animal:

```
    function aniSearch whoAni
      put "searching for another " & whoAni
      set cursor to watch
      push card
      lock screen
      go to card "tree base"
      repeat forever
        go to next card of this bkgnd
        get the short name of this card
        if it is "tree base" then exit repeat
        -- tree base has no animal, you are finished
        put bkgnd field "name" into thisAni
        if thisAni=whoAni then -- you have a duplicate
          put bkgnd field "currAni" into thingg
          pop card
          unlock screen
          return thingg -- return the animal's card ID number
          exit aniSearch -- the end
        end if
      end repeat
      pop card
      lock screen
      return 0 -- all is well
    end aniSearch
```

Remove an Animal

The dropAnimal command script removes an animal from the game's knowledge database. When an animal card is removed, the question card linked to it must also be removed and the links must be adjusted. The question card linked to the animal card is also linked to another animal card. The question card—which poses the question that distinguishes between the two animals—is no longer necessary because one of these animals is removed. Also, the question card being removed was arrived at from a previous question card. That previous question card must now be linked to the one remaining animal card. See the diagram in Figure 13-12.

```
on dropAnimal
  set cursor to watch
  -- see if you are at an end node
  put FALSE into razz
  if bkgnd field "nextAni1" is NOT empty then put TRUE into razz
  if bkgnd field "nextAni2" is NOT empty then put TRUE into razz
  if razz then
    answer "Sorry, can only delete an animal!" -- not a question
    exit dropAnimal
  end if
  -- save current ID and previous ID
  put bkgnd field "currAni" into lastAni
  put bkgnd field "prevAni" into pAni
  doMenu "Delete Card"
  -- the previous node needs to go also
  go to card ID pAni
  -- see which one pointed to the one you just deleted
  -- and save the other ID (the single end node left)
  put bkgnd field "nextAni1" into thing
  if thing=lastAni then
    put bkgnd field "nextAni2" into endAni
  else
    put thing into endAni
  end if
  -- save the ID of this one before deleting.
  put bkgnd field "currAni" into lastAni
  -- save the ID of what pointed to this one
  put bkgnd field "prevAni" into pAni
  doMenu "Delete Card"
  -- Work on the node that pointed to the branches
  -- with deleted nodes. Find which ID pointed to the pruned
  -- branch. Put the good end node ID in the place of the
  -- deleted branch.
  put bkgnd field "nextAni1" of card ID pAni into thing
  if thing=lastAni then
    put endAni into bkgnd field "nextAni1" of card ID pAni
  else
    put endAni into bkgnd field "nextAni2" of card ID pAni
  end if
  -- get the ID of this one
  put bkgnd field "currAni" of card ID pAni into lastAni
  -- place the proper prev node ID of the good end node
  go to card ID endAni
```

continued

```
   put lastAni into bkgnd field "prevAni"
end dropAnimal
```

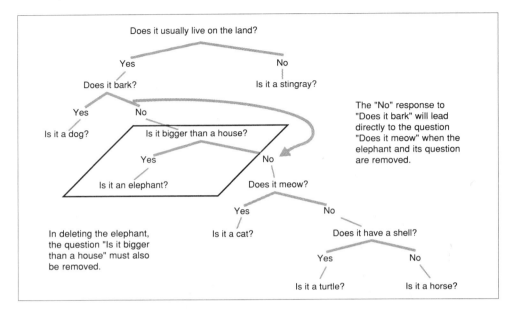

Figure 13-12.   Removing an animal card and its question.

Other Stack Scripts

The three command scripts are simple. The openStack and closeStack scripts show or hide the menu bar. If the menu bar is not visible, the player is not as likely to make changes to the game that could corrupt the structure of the database. The doFanfare script plays the "Old MacDonald" tune. If the mouse is clicked while the song is playing, the music stops. These three scripts are in the Title Card.

```
on openStack
   hide menuBar
end openStack

on closeStack
   show menuBar
end closeStack

on doFanfare -- play "Old MacDonald Had a Farm"
   play harpsichord "ce c c g3 a a gq"
   play harpsichord "e4e e d d ch"
   play harpsichord "g3s c4e c c g3 a a gq"
   play harpsichord "e4e e d d ch"
end doFanfare
```

Other scripts analyze the tree (database). The treeReport and climbTree stack command scripts examine the structure of the binary tree knowledge database. The treeReport script sets up the variables necessary for the recursive progress of climb-

Tree. The nuFld variable contains the main part of the report. The levelDown variable keeps track of how far down into the structure the analysis has gone. The recurs background field shows the progress of the recursion. For a description of recursion, see the section "Binary Trees and Recursion" at the beginning of the chapter.

The climbTree command is recursive; that is, it calls itself. One problem in recursive programming is that global variables and parameters have changing values. Two of these are critical to the working of climbTree: levelDown and cardEIDE. These variables have a different value for each recursive call of climbTree. They need to be saved as local variables so that they won't be changed on subsequent calls. On each call of climbTree, the two branches of the level of the tree are examined. If a branch is to yet another level of the tree (more question cards), climbTree is called again for that question card. The text of the question is put in the nuFld report variable. If the branch of the level contains an animal card, the end has been reached. The information is then added to the nuFld report variable and recursion ends for that branch.

Although HyperTalk supports recursion, there are limits. If the player creates a complex game (an intricate binary tree, more than ten levels deep), the limits of HyperCard might be reached and this command script could fail.

The getHdrStf function script generates the binary tree report to put spaces before the lines of the report as necessary to indicate the level of recursion.

```
on climbTree
-- This recursive command calls itself repeatedly until
-- an end node is found, then it exits. Because it is recursive,
-- the value of the global variables change when you least
-- expect it. Therefore, they are saved as local variables.
-- EIDE (pronounced EYE-DEE) is respectfully named after
-- LeRoy N. Eide, a coworker at the University of Utah.
  global levelDown, cardEIDE, nuFld, tagYN
  global whereFrom, fromLine
  put "Recursion level" && levelDown into bkgnd field "recurs"
  -- show current level
  put cardEIDE into eide
  -- save so that recursion does not change it
  put levelDown into lvlDn -- ditto
  delete line 6 of bkgnd field "question" of card ID eide
  -- a flag area used for the report
  put bkgnd field "nextani1" of card ID eide into thingg
  if thingg is empty then
  -- decide what to put in the report: question or animal name
    put bkgnd field "name" of card ID eide into theLine
  else
    put line 1 of bkgnd field "question" of card ID eide ¬
    into theLine
  end if
  put getHdrStf (lvlDn) into hdrStuff
  put return & hdrStuff && tagYN && theLine && eide after nuFld
  if thingg is NOT empty then -- there is more on this branch
    add 1 to levelDown
    put thingg into cardEIDE
    put "YES:" into tagYN
```

continued

```
          climbTree -- curse and recurs
        end if
        if thingg is NOT empty then -- do the no branch now
          put bkgnd field "nextani2" of card ID eide into thingg
          if thingg is NOT empty then
            add 1 to levelDown
            put thingg into cardEIDE
            put "NO:" into tagYN
            climbTree -- more recursion
          end if
        end if
        subtract 1 from levelDown
        put "Recursion level" && levelDown into bkgnd field "recurs"
      end climbTree


      function getHdrStf n1
      -- This puts indentation into the display for the report.
      -- If HyperCard handled tabs right, you wouldn't need this.
        put empty into thingg
        if n1>1 then
          repeat with n3 = 2 to n1
            put "   " before thingg
          end repeat
        end if
        return thingg
      end getHdrStf


      on treeReport
      -- This calls the recursive command to traverse the tree.
        global levelDown, cardEIDE, nuFld, tagYN
        global whereFrom, fromLine
        set cursor to watch
        show bkgnd field "recurs"
        put param(1) into rFile
        go to card "Tree Base"
        put the short ID of this card into cardEIDE -- beginning card ID
        put 0 into levelDown -- level of recursion
        put empty into tagYN
        put empty into nuFld -- empty the report field
        climbTree -- do the dirty work
        put nuFld into card field rFile of card "begin" -- show report
        put "Recursion level" && levelDown into bkgnd field "recurs"
        go to card "tree base"
        hide bkgnd field "recurs"
        go to card "begin"
      end treeReport
```

Enhancements

HyperCard provides a good basis for organizing information. The tools in fields and buttons give the beginning user ways to collect and relate pieces of information on cards. With the addition of linkage information on each card, sophisticated relationships can be developed between the pieces of information. Utilizing this linkage structure, the HyperCard stack can be programmed to control the addition of new information so that all information is related in the same manner and an "understanding" is developed in the construction of the stack concerning the meaning of the information. When a computer system sets up and follows certain rules in expanding its database, it develops a level of artificial intelligence.

The HyperAnimals game illustrates the construction of a HyperCard stack that uses some basic principles of sophisticated relationships and intelligent information gathering. The basic unit of information used in HyperAnimals is the animal. The format could be changed easily to accommodate another unit. For example, a clinical study of certain physical symptoms could be collected through yes-or-no questions leading to suggested diagnoses. The end product stack could be "frozen" so that the person going though the database always ends up at some diagnosis—the stack would no longer learn. In this type of application, the end cards could be specialized with card buttons and fields giving further options outside the realm of the binary tree data structure, such as links to information stacks or even application programs. The HyperAnimals-type stack could be used as an intermediate stage to producing an online reference work for a professional.

Another expansion on the ideas presented with HyperAnimals is to go beyond two-directional branching to variable branching. Variable branching could be accommodated in the structure by keeping more than two forward links on each card. Rather than separate invisible fields for each link, one invisible field could hold all links with each link on a separate line of the field. The command scripts of this modified version of HyperAnimals would be more complex, but still reasonable.

When using HyperCard to produce database systems, remember that keeping information about the relationships between cards is relatively easy to do with invisible background fields. If the script of a stack controls the entry of information into the stack, the database structure can retain its integrity. Because of the richness of commands in HyperTalk and the tools available, the ability to create sophisticated databases is within the reach of HyperCard users who have never written a computer program.

A Grab Bag of Utilities

by Ted Jones

Synopsis: This chapter contains a collection of five stack tools that can aid your work as a HyperCard developer. HyperBrownie expands on the `go recent` command that only displays the pictures of the last 42 cards you visited. HyperBrownie is more comprehensive and prints names of all the cards a person has visited while using the stack it is installed in. It thus saves a record of how your stack is manipulated and gives a way to analyze the path users follow within the stack.

Script Snooper gathers the scripts in all the cards and backgrounds of a stack and prints them in one listing. The Modem Dialer is a phone number database that shows you how to place regular phone calls using the ATDT dial command in Hyper-Talk. Protecting your stack from inadvertent use is a complicated issue in Hyper-Card. A stack protection section shows how to properly set up password protection in your stacks as well as how to use HyperCard 1.2's `cantModify` and `userModify` commands.

The final script in this chapter shows how to set up a user log to keep up with the new United States Internal Revenue Service tax laws regarding computer usage. Those rules require that you keep track of how long you spend using your computer for business and for pleasure.

A Grab Bag of Utilities

Snapshots, Printing, Dialer, and More

This chapter features five different scripts that can increase the value you get from HyperCard. The first is a HyperBrownie script that saves a record of where you go in HyperCard and lets you print screen dumps of just those cards. The second is a Script Snooper that prints all the scripts in a stack, neatly formatted. The third is a phone number database that lets you dial a number through your modem with a single key or button press. The fourth is a stack password protection scheme. (It can also be used to protect only a background or just a single card, or it can be modified to protect the stack against any modifications from users.) The fifth script is a User Log that records the time you spend using HyperCard.

HyperBrownie

As you browse through HyperCard, the addresses of the cards you visit are saved. By using the Recent command, you can see the last 42 cards you visited, and you can step backwards through all of the cards with the Back command, but you can't easily print a list of just the cards you visit. HyperBrownie saves a record of the cards you visit and then prints them in the format you choose. Even if you use five stacks in one session and visit 150 cards, HyperBrownie remembers them and prints them for you.

What It Does

First, we have to write a handler that gets the ID of each card we visit. If we make our handler an openCard handler, it is activated each time a card is opened (provided there isn't another openCard handler below it in the hierarchy, which refuses to pass on the message). If we put our handler in the Home stack's stack script, it is in the message inheritance path for all stacks. We store the card names in a global variable so that they are available from other stacks.

Next, we create a button to clear out the card names that accumulate in the global variable when we want to start a new collection. This button can also go on the Home card.

And finally, we make another card button named Photo Lab to print the accumulated cards.

How It Works

The Home stack handler is short. It traps the `openCard` message, declares the variable `printList`, and then puts the long ID of the current card into `printList`. (The long ID includes pathname information, as in `card id 2345 of stack "Play Disk:Work Folder:TestStack"`).

```
On openCard -- Home stack script
  global printList
  -- get the long id name of this card -- changed
  put the long id of this card &"," after printList
end openCard
```

The comma is added to separate the new item from the next entry.

The principal handler of the HyperBrownie script is in the Photo Lab button, which actually prints the snapshots.

The opening part of this last handler traps the `mouseUp` message, declares the global variable `printList`, pushes the current card so that you can find your way back, and opens printing. You need to compare the pathname of items you pull from the list to the stack you are in at the moment, so the handler creates a variable named `hereVar` and keeps the current pathname in it. To start, this handler puts the long name (including the pathname) of the current card into `hereVar` and then dumps everything but the pathname with `empty`. Also, the handler gets rid of the final comma in the `printList` variable, because the comma can be misinterpreted as a strange card name. The handler sets `lockMessages` to true so that you don't generate more `openCard` messages and add more items to `printList` as you are printing it, preventing this from turning into a very well-documented closed loop.

```
on mouseUp -- Photo Lab button
  global printList
  push card -- save your starting point
  -- the next 2 lines put the current stack and volume into hereVar
  put the long name of this card into hereVar
  put last word of hereVar into hereVar

  -- get rid of the final comma so it isn't misinterpreted
  put empty into last word of printList
  -- disable messages so cards are not re-added to printList as you ¬
  print
  set lockMessages to true
  set cursor to watch
```

The next section enters the main repeat loop and pulls items one at a time from the global variable `printList` into the local variable `itemVar`. An `if then` structure is used to compare the current pathname (in `hereVar`) to the pathname of the next item to print (in `itemVar`).

```
put item n of printList into itemVar}
if last word of itemVar is not hereVar then
  -- if different stack navigate to new stack and...
  go to last word of itemVar
  -- ... make it the current stack
  put last word of itemVar into hereVar
end if
```

If they are not the same, the handler goes to the new stack, replaces the contents of `hereVar` with the pathname from `itemVar`. In the following section, the pathname information (including "of stack") in `itemVar` is wiped out by putting `empty` into word 4 to 6 of `itemVar`.

The command `print` and the card ID in `itemVar` are concatenated into the variable `printVar`, which is then executed with the `do` command.

```
put empty into word 4 to 6 of itemVar
--put command and card ID into a variable
put "Print" && ItemVar into printVar
do printVar -- use the do command to execute the print command
```

At the end of the handler, the comma is restored to `printList`, the starting card is popped, and printing is closed.

HyperBrownie keeps track of everywhere you go as long as the handlers are in the Home stack. If you go to a card three times, for instance, it prints that card three times. For a sample of HyperBrownie results, see Figure 14-1. These cards were printed at quarter size.

Other Uses for Your Brownie

You can add more cards to your print set by going to them after the first print run finishes, or you can build a new set by first clicking the New List button.

Figure 14-1. Sample HyperBrownie printout.

If this looks like a useful little utility, you might want to improve it on your own. One thing you could do is save the contents of the global variable `printList` to a named field. You could edit the contents of this field or even store it as a text file. Then, you could create a button that would launch the printing session for that set of cards whenever it was pressed. For that matter, you could strip out the `print` commands, write in some `wait` commands (`wait until the mouse is down` or `wait 2 secs`, for example), and have a slide show machine. Don't forget that if you just leave the openCard handler in your Home stack, it is collecting card names all the time. You should disable it when you aren't using it, or you can end up with a huge variable. If you think you will use this routine from time to time, you might use a global variable flag as a safety feature. Put the whole routine inside an `if then` structure that tests the value of a variable like `brownieOn`. If `brownieOn` is true, card names are saved; if it is false, `openCard messages` are ignored.

```
-- ********************** DESCRIPTION **********************

-- TYPE:          Printing tricks
-- AUTHOR:        Ted Jones
-- NAME:          HyperBrownie
-- LOCATIONS:     Script in two buttons and the Home stack
-- RESTRICTIONS:  Won't work with cards, backgrounds, or stacks that
--                have openCard handlers that don't pass the message

-- ***************** SCRIPT STARTS HERE *******************

on openCard -- Home stack script
  global printList
  --get the long id name of this card -- changed
  put the long id of this card &"," after printList
end openCard

on mouseUp -- New List button
  global printList
  put empty into printList
end mouseUp

on mouseUp -- Photo Lab button
  global printList
  push card -- save your starting point
  -- the next 2 lines put the current stack and volume into hereVar
  put the long name of this card into hereVar
  put last word of hereVar into hereVar
  -- get rid of the final comma, so it isn't misinterpreted
  put empty into last word of printList
  -- disable messages, so cards are not re-added to printList as you ¬
  print
  set lockMessages to true
  set cursor to 4 -- watch cursor

  open printing with dialog
  repeat with n = 1 to (the number of items in printList)
    -- if not in the right stack, go to that stack
```

continued

```
      put item n of printList into itemVar
      if last word of itemVar is not hereVar then
        -- if different stack, navigate to new stack and...
        go to last word of itemVar
        -- ... make it the current stack
        put last word of itemVar into hereVar
      end if

    -- Print the card indicated.
    -- First get rid of stack and volume names.
    put empty into word 4 to 6 of itemVar
    -- put command and card ID into a variable
    put "print" && itemVAr into printVar
    do printVar -- use the do command to execute the print command
    end repeat
    close printing

    -- put the comma back at end of list
    put "," after last word of printList
    -- return to starting point
    pop card
end mouseUp
```

Script Printing

Of all of HyperCard's printing capabilities, one of the most important to scriptors is the capability of printing scripts. As scripts get longer, it helps to print them so that you can study them away from the screen. You may also want to print a script to show someone what you've done. Whatever the reason for printing, HyperCard doesn't provide you with the tools to put multiple scripts onto paper easily, but HyperTalk does. What's more, it's easy.

What It Does

Besides being capable of printing an entire script, HyperTalk's editor lets you select, by dragging the mouse cursor down the text, just the lines you want to print before you click the Print button. Suppose, however, that you want more than just one script. Suppose that you want to print all the card scripts in a stack. That is a job for HyperTalk.

At first, it seems that the developers of HyperTalk left out the capability of printing all the scripts in a stack. Actually, the developers made HyperTalk so incredibly flexible that you can write a script that prints all the scripts or just the scripts of the object types you are interested in. We begin with a script that just prints the card scripts. There are actually a number of ways to go about this job. You could manually copy the card scripts one at a time to the Clipboard and then paste them into a field to be printed with the Print Report menu command. You could also write a script that would open every card script one at a time, and then you could manually click all the Print buttons.

The method demonstrated here is a combination of these two approaches.

First, we use the HyperTalk object property the script to gather together all the scripts into a variable (as in get the script of card 1, which returns the entire script of the object specified). While we are at it, we insert an identifying header for each card so that we know where each script came from. Then, we transfer the accumulated scripts in the collecting variable into one object's script (a card field created for the purpose), using the command set with the script property (as in set script of field "Script O'Rama" to it, which inserts the contents of a container into the script of the object indicated). Then, we open the Script Editor and look at the collection of scripts. The user can then click the Print button to actually print the scripts. Because many of the card scripts in the TestStack may be empty, we also provide a little script that gives all the card objects unique scripts.

How It Works

The Script Snooper handler that follows actually gathers scripts card by card and puts them into one place so that you can print them with a single click of the Script Editor Print button.

As usual, the handler is divided into sections by blank lines. The first section sets the cursor to the watch, puts a message into the Message box to explain the delay, locks the screen (to speed up the operation), dumps any scripts previously stored in the Script O'Rama field script, and pushes the card so that you can get back at the end. The next section gets the stack script using a technique that is repeated with slight variations for each object in the stack.

```
-- get the stack script
put "-- The script of" && the name of this stack & ¬
return & return & the script of (the name of this stack) ¬
after hamper
  put 0 & space into bkgndNums
```

The main event here is a put command that places a header and the script (with returns to make things look good) into the variable hamper.

There follows another large repeat loop with two smaller loops inside it. The outer loop cycles through the cards, first going to a card, getting the card script, as explained, and finally, running through the two smaller loops to get the scripts for the other object types. Inside this loop, there is also an if then structure to test whether the card belongs to a new background. If the background hasn't been snooped yet, a getBkgnd message is sent.

```
-- get the card scripts
repeat with n = 1 to the number of cards
  set cursor to busy
  go to card n
  -- check whether the card is part of a new background
  if not (bkgndNums contains the number of this background) then
    put the number of this bkgnd & space after bkgndNums
    getBkgnd
```

continued

```
end if
put "-- The script of" && the name of this card ¬
& "; card number" && n & return & return after hamper
put the script of card n & return & return after hamper
----put return & return after hamper
```

The handler for `getBkgnd` gets the stack script and then uses two repeat loops to get all the background fields and buttons. When all the background scripts are loaded into `hamper`, program flow returns to the main card checking routine.

```
-- get background fields
repeat with o = 1 to the number of background fields
   put "-- The script of" && the name of background field o & ¬
   return & "-- background field number" && o & return & ¬
   return & the script of background field o after hamper
end repeat
```

When all the object types for all the cards have been collected, the card loop ends. At this point, the card pushed at the beginning is popped and you return to the card with the Script O'Rama field. The scripts collected in `hamper` are then inserted into Script O'Rama's script and the Script Editor is opened. You can now print all the scripts in the stack if you choose.

When the Script Editor is closed, the final "clean up" section of the handler commences. Collecting scripts is hard work, and your stack can acquire excessive amounts of free space in the process. As a result, the script does a mandatory Compact Stack with a message to explain the delay and another message to thank users for their patience, followed by the end of the handler. Figure 14-2 shows what you might see after this script has been run.

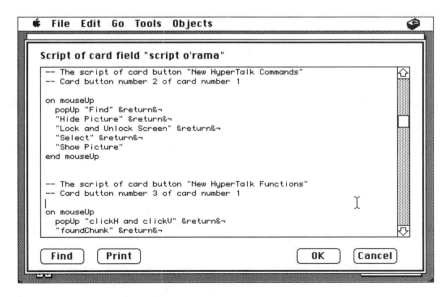

Figure 14-2. Sample Script Snooper printout.

Possible Modifications

Alternatively, the variable could be written to a file and the file printed with TeachText. The next step to take with the Script Snooper idea is to add some code that lets you supply the name of a stack you want snooped. You would probably use an `ask` command, and the script would then go looking for the named stack and snoop it. Also, you might want to skip headings when a script is empty. Have fun.

```
-- ********************** DESCRIPTION **********************

-- TYPE:          Printing tricks
-- AUTHOR:        Ted Jones
-- NAME:          Script Snooper
-- LOCATIONS:     Script in one button
-- RESTRICTIONS:  Because the scripts are combined in a field script,
--                there is a limit of 30,000 characters. If the
--                combined size of all the scripts in a stack is
--                greater than 30,000 characters, save to
--                a file instead.

-- ******************** SCRIPT STARTS HERE ******************

on mouseUp -- Script Snooper button
  global object,hamper,bkgndNums
  set cursor to watch
  put "----------- Now gathering the scripts -----------"
  lock screen
  put empty into hamper
  -- get rid of any previously stored script
  set script of card field "Script O'Rama" to empty
  push card
  -- get the stack script
  put "-- The script of"  && the name of this stack & ¬
  return & return & the script of (the name of this stack) ¬
  after hamper
    put 0 & space into bkgndNums

  -- get the card scripts
  repeat with n = 1 to the number of cards
    set cursor to busy
    go to card n
    -- check whether the card is part of a new background
    if not (bkgndNums contains the number of this background) then
      put the number of this bkgnd & space after bkgndNums
      getBkgnd
    end if
    put "-- The script of" && the name of this card ¬
    & "; card number" && n & return & return after hamper
    put the script of card n & return & return after hamper
    ---- put return & return after hamper

    -- get card buttons
    repeat with o = 1 to the number of card buttons
```

continued

```
      put "-- The script of" && name of card button o & return &¬
      "-- Card button number" && o && "of card number" && n ¬
      & return & return & the script of card button o after hamper
      put return & return after hamper
   end repeat

   -- get card fields
   repeat with o = 1 to the number of card fields
      put "-- The script of" && name of card field o & return & ¬
      "-- card field number" && o && "of card number" && n & ¬
      return & return & the script of card field o after hamper
      put return & return after hamper
   end repeat
end repeat

pop card
-- insert all the scripts stored in "hamper" into the field's script
get the length of hamper
if it > 30,000
then put char 1 to 30,000 of hamper into hamper
set script of card field "Script O'Rama" to hamper
-- open the editor
edit script of card field "Script O'Rama"

-- clean up
put "--------------- Compacting the Stack --------------"
unlock screen
doMenu "Compact Stack"
play "boing"
put "------------ Thanks for your patience ------------"
end mouseUp

on getBkgnd -- Script Snooper button
   -- user command handler to get background information
   global bkgndNums,hamper
   put "-- The script of" && the name of this background ¬
    & "; background number" && word the number of words in bkgndNums ¬
   of bkgndNums & return & return after hamper
   put word the number of words in bkgndNums of bkgndNums
   put the script of background word the number of words in bkgndNums ¬
   of bkgndNums after hamper
   put return & return after hamper

   -- get background fields
   repeat with o = 1 to the number of background fields
      put "-- The script of" && the name of background field o & ¬
      return & "-- background field number" && o & return & ¬
      return & the script of background field o after hamper
   end repeat

   -- get background buttons
   repeat with o = 1 to the number of background buttons
      put "-- The script of" && name of background button o & ¬
      return & "-- background button number" && o & return & ¬
      return & the script of background button o after hamper
```

continued

```
        put return & return after hamper
    end repeat
end getBkgnd
```

Click on the Script Snooper button. The scripts of all the objects in the current stack are displayed together in the Script Editor. To print a copy of these scripts, click the Print button.

Modem Dialer

It's easy to dial a phone number in HyperCard, but it's much harder to pass that dialed number on to the phone company. For people with modems, there is a nice solution to this problem in the `dial with modem` option to HyperTalk's `dial` command. With `dial with modem`, you can pass a phone number to your modem and then on to the phone company from within HyperCard. In the script that follows, we set up a small database with names and phone numbers and provide you with ways to go from field to field and to dial the numbers with the keyboard.

Although you can dial numbers with HyperCard version 1.0.1 and 1.1, we use some of the features of 1.2 to go from a line in one multilined field to a line in another multilined field. In case some of you don't have 1.2, we indicate what lines you can't use with previous versions. Of course, if you don't have a modem, you can't use this script at all.

Note that HyperCard versions through 1.2 can only communicate with a modem through the modem port. If your modem is connected to the printer port, you have to turn off your machine and switch ports before you can dial with your modem.

What It Does

On a card (the Home stack is a convenient place for this card), we create three fields: one for names; one for home phone numbers, and one for work numbers. Figure 14-3 shows how your screen might look. You can either select the numbers with the mouse or with the Tab and Return keys. Once a number is selected, you can dial it by switching on your modem and either clicking on the Dial button or pressing the Enter key.

To disconnect the modem after you have the person on the phone, there is a Disconnect button. For redialing busy numbers, there is a Redial button.

How It Works

The Dial button takes the selection and passes it to the modem. We used the ATDT (Attention dial tone) modem command. If you have pulse service, you can substitute ATDP. The Disconnect button hangs up the line with the ATH modem command (you

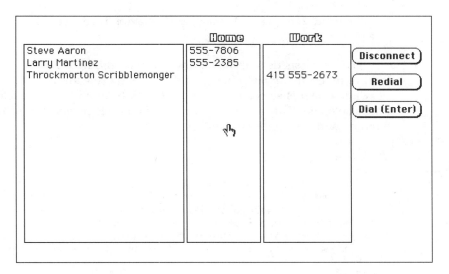

Figure 14-3. Example of Modem Dialer card setup.

can still talk if you pick up the phone). The Redial button sends an AT/ modem command, which repeats the last command issued.

We use the Tab key to move horizontally from field to field and vertically from line to line. The Return key is used to move vertically. Just for fun, we added a Shift key alternative for both the Tab and Return keys. Normally, the tab order is left to right and then down, but when the Shift key is down, the order is right to left and then up. With the Return key, you normally start at the top and go down, but when the Shift key is down, the field above is selected instead.

The tabKey handler is placed at the card script level and performs a number of tasks. First, it determines which line in which field is selected. If nothing is selected, it selects the top line of the lefthand field.

```
on tabKey -- card script
  global fieldNum,lineNum
  get the selectedLine --(requires version 1.2+)
  if it is empty -- nothing is selected
  then put "line 1 of card field 0" into it
```

If the Shift key is also pressed, it tabs backward by subtracting one from the field number. If the left field is already selected, the right-hand field is selected. If the top-left line is selected, a Shift-Tab selects the bottom-right line.

```
-- tabs backwards when Shift key is down
if the shiftKey is down then
  subtract 1 from word 6 of it -- go to previous field
  if word 6 of it < 1 then -- if at first field
    put fieldNum into word 6 of it -- go to last field
    subtract 1 from word 2 of it -- and up one line
    -- if at top line go to bottom line
```

continued

```
      if word 2 of it < 1 then put lineNum into word 2 of it
   end if
```

The next section performs the normal tabbing pattern by adding one to the field number. If the right-hand field is already selected, the left-hand field on the next line down is selected. If the bottom-right line is already selected, the top-left line is selected. The actual selecting of the line is performed in the last line of the handler with the 1.2 command `select`.

```
   -- normal tab pattern
   else
     add 1 to word 6 of it -- go to next field
     if word 6 of it > fieldNum then -- if at last field
       put 1 into word 6 of it -- go to first field
       add 1 to word 2 of it -- and down one line
       -- if at bottom line go to top line
       if word 2 of it > lineNum then put 1 into word 2 of it
     end if
   end if

   select it -- select the line (requires version 1.2+)
end tabKey
```

By trapping the 1.2+ message `returnInField`, we can use the Return key to select the line above or below the current selection. If the Shift key is also pressed, 1 is subtracted from the currently selected line number. There is a check to make sure the number is not smaller than 1; if it is, the line number is set to the number of lines in the field that has been placed in the variable `lineNum`.

```
on returnInField -- card script (requires version 1.2+)
   global lineNum
   get the selectedLine -- what line is selected? (requires version 1.2+)

   -- tabs up in current field when Shift key is down
   if the shiftKey is down then
     subtract 1 from word 2 of it -- go up one line
     if word 2 of it < 1 then -- if at the top line
       put lineNum into word 2 of it -- go to bottom line
     end if
```

Otherwise, the field below the selected field is selected by subtracting one from the line number. As usual, if the bottom field is selected, the top field is selected next.

```
   -- tabs down in current field
   else
     add 1 to word 2 of it -- go down one line
     if word 2 of it > lineNum then -- if at the bottom
       put 1 into word 2 of it -- go to the top line
     end if
   end if
```

continued

```
      select it --(requires version 1.2+)
end returnInField
```

Setup

Because this script requires a number of objects, we included a script to create the objects for you automatically. Make a new card button and name it `Setup`. Enter the following handler into the Setup 2 button:

```
on mouseUp -- Setup button
  doMenu "New Button"
  set the name of button the number of buttons to "Dial"
  set the rect of button "Dial (Enter)" to 421,52,509,74
  doMenu "New Button"
  set the name of button the number of buttons to "Disconnect"
  set the rect of button "Disconnect" to 421,76,509,94
  doMenu "New Button"
  set the name of button the number of buttons to "Redial"
  set the rect of button "Redial" to 421,100,509,122
  edit script of button "Dial (Enter)"
  edit script of button "Disconnect"
  edit script of button "Redial"
  doMenu "New Field"
  set the name of card field the number of card fields to "names"
  set the rect of card fields "names" to 5,47,190,307
  doMenu "New Field"
  set the name of card field the number of card fields to "work"
  set the rect of card fields "work" to 193,47,305,307
  doMenu "New Field"
  set the name of card field the number of card fields to "home"
  set the rect of card fields "home" to 308,47,420,307
  edit script of this card
 choose browse tool
end mouseUp
```

When you click the Setup button, it creates the objects and opens their scripts so that you can type the scripts that follow.

```
-- ********************** DESCRIPTION **********************

-- TYPE:         Dial tricks
-- AUTHOR:       Ted Jones
-- NAME:         Modem Dialer
-- LOCATIONS:    Script in several buttons and in card
-- RESTRICTIONS: Requires a modem and works best with HyperCard
--               version 1.2+

-- ******************** SCRIPT STARTS HERE ******************

on mouseUp -- Dial button
  dial the selection with modem "ATDT" -- use "ATDP" for pulse service
end mouseUp
```

continued

```
on mouseUp -- Disconnect button
  dial empty with modem "ATH"
end mouseUp

on mouseUp -- Redial button
  dial empty with modem "A/"
end mouseUp

on openCard -- card script
  global fieldNum,lineNum
  put the number of card fields into fieldNum
  put the number of lines in card field 1 into lineNum
  select line 1 of card field 1
end openCard

on tabKey -- card script
  global fieldNum,lineNum
  get the selectedLine
  if it is empty -- nothing is selected
  then put "line 1 of card field 0" into it

    -- tabs backward when Shift key is down
    if the shiftKey is down then
      subtract 1 from word 6 of it -- go to previous field
      if word 6 of it < 1 then -- if at first field...
        put fieldNum into word 6 of it -- go to last field
        subtract 1 from word 2 of it -- and up one line
        -- if at top line, go to bottom line
        if word 2 of it < 1 then put lineNum into word 2 of it
      end if

      -- normal tab pattern
    else
      add 1 to word 6 of it -- go to next field
      if word 6 of it > fieldNum then -- if at last field
        put 1 into word 6 of it -- go to first field
        add 1 to word 2 of it -- and down one line
        -- if at bottom line, go to top line
        if word 2 of it > lineNum then put 1 into word 2 of it
      end if
    end if

  select it -- select the line
end tabKey

on returnKey -- card script
  -- Why did user press Return key?
  answer "Start tabbing?" with "Yes" or "No"
  if it is "Yes" then type tab -- select first line of first field
  else pass returnKey -- pass the message on to HyperCard
end returnKey
```

continued

```
on returnInField -- card script

  global lineNum
  get the selectedLine -- what line is selected?

  -- tabs up in current field when Shift key is down
  if the shiftKey is down then
    subtract 1 from word 2 of it -- go up one line
    if word 2 of it < 1 then -- if at the top line . . .
      put lineNum into word 2 of it -- go to bottom line
    end if

    -- tabs down in current field
  else
    add 1 to word 2 of it -- go down one line
    if word 2 of it > lineNum then -- if at the bottom
      put 1 into word 2 of it -- go to the top line
    end if
  end if

  select it
end returnInField

on enterInField
  dial selection with modem "ATDT"
end enterInField
```

Protection: Practicing Safe Stacks

HyperCard comes with a number of protection schemes, but you may not want to depend on the user taking the initiative and selecting the Protect Stack menu item. With HyperTalk, you can offer protection or impose protection, depending on the situation.

One way to protect a stack is to grant access only if the user can provide a password. This next script demonstrates how to offer password protection to the user and then shows how to implement it if the user chooses to.

What It Does

This script is activated each time a stack is opened. First, it checks to see whether a password for the stack exists. If it does, the user is asked to provide the password. If there is no password, the user is given the option of creating one. If the user can't provide the password when asked, the script closes the stack and goes to the Home card.

How It Works

The first step is to go to the first card of the stack you want to protect, create a new card field, name it password, and hide it. This is where the password will be saved and checked.

The first part of the stack level openStack handler checks to see whether the password field is empty. If it is, the second part of the script is executed, which consists of a `repeat` loop that gives the user as many chances as needed to get the password right. If the user doesn't want to protect the stack, the script ends; otherwise, the user is asked to type the password twice. The HyperTalk command `ask password` is used to save and encrypt the user's entry, and the second entry is compared to the first to avoid typographical errors. If the two entries match, the password is saved in the field for future reference and the script ends.

```
on openStack -- stack script

    -- if the stack has not been opened
   if card field "password" is empty then

      repeat forever -- loop so user can try again if an error
         answer "Do you want to password protect this stack?" ¬
         with "Yes" or "No"
         if it is "No" then -- 0 indicates there will be no password
            put 0 into card field "password"
            exit openStack
         end if
         ask password "Enter a password"
         if it is empty then next repeat -- try again
         put it into temp -- store first time
         ask password "Once more, please"
         if it is empty then next repeat -- try again
         if it = temp then exit repeat -- compare first and second times

         -- if fails, go to start of loop
      end repeat

      -- load password into field (encrypted)
      put it into card field "password"
      answer "Thanks"
```

If there is already a password in the field, the user is asked to match it. The user is given two tries to match the password. Here, the input in `ask password` is compared to the encrypted form of the password in the field. If neither attempt matches the real password, the script executes a `go home` command after courteously telling the user `Sorry`.

```
    -- if stack already has a password
   else if card field "password" <> 0 then
      ask password "Enter your password"
      if not (it is card field "password")
      then ask password "One more try" -- if invalid input, try again
      if not (it is card field "password") then
         answer "Sorry" -- if still invalid, bail out to Home
         go home
      end if
   end if
end openStack
```

Alternative Stack Protection (1.2 and Later)

Two new properties, `cantModify` and `userModify`, were introduced in version 1.2. These properties give your stacks another level of protection. The `cantModify` property applies to a particular stack. When it is set to true, it has the effect of locking or write-protecting the stack. This means that you can't do anything that would change the stack: no painting, no editing fields. This may be just what you want if you have a stack you don't want mucked up.

The `userModify` property is global (it affects all stacks), but it really only makes a difference if a stack's `cantModify` property is set to true. With these locked stacks, it has the effect of allowing the user to use the paint tools and to edit fields, but any changes made last only as long as the current card is displayed. When the user goes to another card, all the modifications are lost and the card reverts to its original appearance. This is great for letting a user use a stack without risking undesirable changes.

Using the `cantModify` and `userModify` properties allows the user to browse and use the stack without the chance of the stack being permanently altered or destroyed. In some cases, this is a good alternative to password protection.

Modifications

This script protects an entire stack, but by changing the message handled from `openStack` to `openBackground` or `openCard` and by adjusting the location of the password field, you can use a slightly edited form of this script for protecting parts of a stack. You could also change the script so that when a user can't provide the password, instead of going Home, the `cantModify` and `userModify` properties are set to true, permitting the user to use the stack but preventing it from being permanently changed.

```
-- ******************** DESCRIPTION ********************

-- TYPE:          Protection tricks
-- AUTHOR:        Ted Jones
-- NAME:          Password Protector
-- LOCATIONS:     Script stack script
-- RESTRICTIONS:  Can be circumvented by a knowledgeable scriptor

-- ****************** SCRIPT STARTS HERE ******************

on openStack -- stack script

  -- if the stack has not been opened
  if card field "password" is empty then

    repeat forever -- loop so that user can try again if an error
      answer "Do you want to password protect this stack?" ¬
      with "Yes" or "No"
      if it is "No" then -- 0 indicates there will be no password
        put 0 into card field "password"
        exit openStack
      end if
```

continued

```
        ask password "Enter a password"
        if it is empty then next repeat -- try again
        put it into temp -- store first time
        ask password "Once more, please"
        if it is empty then next repeat -- try again
        if it = temp then exit repeat -- compare first and second times

        -- if fails, go to start of loop
      end repeat

      -- load password into field (encrypted)
      put it into card field "password"
      answer "Thanks"

    -- if stack already has a password
    else if card field "password" <> 0 then
      ask password "Enter your password"
      if not (it is card field "password")
      then ask password "One more try" -- if invalid input, try again
      if not (it is card field "password") then
        answer "Sorry" -- if still invalid, bail out to Home
        go home
      end if
    end if
end openStack
```

A HyperTalk User Log

If you use your computer for business, you can get tax credit for your investment in the computer. Keeping a log is a good way of maintaining your tax records for the IRS. Having to remember to record the starting and ending times of all your computing sessions is a nuisance, but HyperCard can easily save that information for you. Not only does this please the IRS, but if you bill clients, you have an exact record of how much time you spent on a particular job.

The first thing to do is to make HyperCard the startup application so that it starts every time you boot your machine. This is done by selecting HyperCard in the Finder and then pulling down the Special menu and choosing Set Startup. Once you've done that, the script records the time and date each time HyperCard starts and asks you who you are and what you are doing. When you close HyperCard, the closing time is recorded and the elapsed time calculated. A button on your Home card permits you to see the record, or you can open (and print) the text file containing the record by using a word processing program.

How It Works

This user log works by saving data to a text file where it can be accessed either by HyperCard or by a word processing program. A scrolling field is hidden on the Home card and shown when the user presses a button named Show Log. The contents of any saved log information can be viewed in this field, as shown in Figure 14-4.

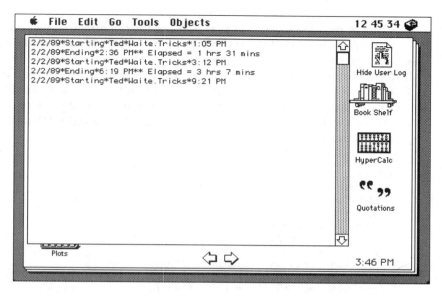

Figure 14-4. Sample HyperTalk User Log.

The session starting script is located in the getHomeInfo handler of the Home stack's stack script. This addition to the usual getHomeInfo handler concatenates the opening entry by reading the clock with the date and the seconds functions and combining that information with the user's name and job (provided by the user through the `ask` command and formatted in a series of `put` statements. The entry is then written to the file named for the current month, which was opened at the beginning of the script. After the file is written to, it is closed and your part of this handler ends.

```
-- fragment to insert into getHomeInfo handler of
-- home stack script just above the pop card command
global startSecs
put "Log." & word 2 of the long date into logVar
open file logVar
read from file logVar until tab
put the short date & "*Starting*" into sessionVar
ask "Who are you?" with "Ted" -- substitute your name
put it & "*" after sessionVar
ask "Doing what?" with card field "lastWhat"
put it into card field "lastWhat"
put the seconds into startSecs
put it & "*" & the time & return after sessionVar
write sessionVar to file logVar
close file logVar
```

When you quit HyperCard, a `quit` message is sent and trapped by a quit handler, again in the Home stack's stack script. This handler is similar, although simpler, than the first one because the session-ending entry is much shorter. The date, the time, and the seconds are all collected and concatenated. The starting seconds, saved in the global variable startSecs in the opening handler, is compared with the closing seconds, and the interval in seconds is then converted into hours, minutes, and seconds. The closing information is written to the text file and saved to disk. Note that just after the file is opened, its entire contents is read into the file buffer with the read from file logVar until tab statement. There are no tabs in the file, so this actually means "read it all out." When the new entry is written to the file at the end of the handler and the file is closed, both the old information and the new is placed into the file.

```
on quit -- home stack script
  global startSecs
  put "Log." & word 2 of the long date into logVar
  open file logVar
  read from file logVar until tab
  put the short date & "*" into sessionVar
  put "Ending" & "*" & the time & "*" after sessionVar
  put (the seconds - startSecs) div 60 into mins
  put mins div 60 && "hrs " into hrs
  put mins mod 60 && "mins" after hrs
  put "* Elapsed = " & hrs & return after sessionVar
  write sessionVar to file logVar
  close file logVar
end quit
```

Setting Up the Log

To make the process of setting up the log a little easier, here is a button script that does most of the work for you. Make a copy of your Home card, add a new card button to the Home card, and give it the following script:

```
on mouseUp -- Setup button
  doMenu "New Field"
  set name of card field the number of card fields to "logField"
  set style of card field "logField" to scrolling
  set rect of card field "logField" to 17,30,413,293
  set textFont of card field "logField" to Monaco
  set textSize of card field "logField" to 9
  set visible of card field "logField" to false
  edit script of card field "logField"
  doMenu "New Button"
  set name of button the number of buttons to "Show User Log"
  set style of button "Show User Log" to transparent
  set rect of button "Show User Log" to 417,30,488,81
  set icon of button "Show User Log" to 1004
  edit script of button "Show User Log"
  go last
  doMenu "New Field"
  set name of card field the number of card fields to "lastWhat"
  set visible of card field "lastWhat" to false
  edit script of stack "Home"
end mouseUp
```

Besides creating the objects you need for the log, this script also opens the scripts so that you can type the scripts that follow.

Once all the scripts are entered, quit HyperCard. You will find a file in the same folder HyperCard is in. The file is called `Log.<month>` where `<month>` is the current month. Throw this file in the trash and launch HyperCard again.

Enter your name and `"Doing HT Tricks Examples"` as you are prompted. Wait a few minutes (or go to the Control Panel and set your clock ahead) and then quit HyperCard again. When you reopen HyperCard, you can click on the Show User Log button and see your first log entry.

Modifications

The most obvious modification would be adding suspend and resume handlers to save the time HyperCard is suspended. If suspend information is still around when HyperCard starts up again, you know that the suspension was not followed by a resumption of HyperCard, and you can use the suspend time as the end of the previous work session before you start a new session. Note that `suspend` and `resume` messages are not sent when HyperCard is running under MultiFinder.

You can also keep track of your total time in another field and add the total to the file at the end of each month.

```
-- *********************** DESCRIPTION ********************

-- TYPE:         File Tricks
-- AUTHOR:       Ted Jones
-- NAME:         User Log
-- LOCATIONS:    Script in several buttons and in Home stack's stack
--               script
-- RESTRICTIONS: Only records time spent in HyperCard

-- ******************** SCRIPT STARTS HERE ******************

on mouseUp -- logField button
   hide card field "logField"
   set name of button "Hide User Log" to "Show User Log"
end mouseUp

on mouseUp -- ...User Log button
   if the visible of card field "logField" is false then
      show card field "logField"
      ask "Show log for which month?" with (word 2 of the long date)
      put "Log." & it into logVar
      open file logVar
      read from file logVar until tab
      put it into card field id 84
      close file logVar
      set name of me to "Hide User Log"
   else
      hide card field "logField"
      set name of me to "Show User Log"
```

continued

```
        end if
end mouseUp

on quit -- home stack script
    global startSecs
    put "Log." & word 2 of the long date into logVar
    open file logVar
    read from file logVar until tab
    put the short date & "*" into sessionVar
    put "Ending" & "*" & the time & "*" after sessionVar
    put (the seconds - startSecs) div 60 into mins
    put mins div 60 && "hrs " into hrs
    put mins mod 60 && "mins" after hrs
    put "* Elapsed = " & hrs & return after sessionVar
    write sessionVar to file logVar
    close file logVar
end quit

    -- fragment to insert into getHomeInfo handler of
    -- home stack script just above the pop card command
    global startSecs
    put "Log." & word 2 of the long date into logVar
    open file logVar
    read from file logVar until tab
    put the short date & "*Starting*" into sessionVar
    ask "Who are you?" with "Ted" -- substitute your name
    put it & "*" after sessionVar
    ask "Doing what?" with card field "lastWhat"
    put it into card field "lastWhat"
    put the seconds into startSecs
    put it & "*" & the time & return after sessionVar
    write sessionVar to file logVar
    close file logVar
```

Part 6

Communications

15 Chauffeur

Chauffeur

Nick Hodge

Synopsis: Bill Atkinson's original vision of HyperCard was a product that would turn a "cold" hard-to-use text based medium into a "warm" graphics-oriented interface that nontechnical people could easily use. To this end, he provided all tools to create such an interface. Unfortunately, designing and setting up such a front end is not a trivial task. For example, a vast amount of data exists in text format on dozens of popular on-line databases, such as Compuserve. HyperCard provides no easy way to manipulate the data on these services.

This chapter presents Chauffeur, a front end that completely insulates you from Compuserve's dry text-based interface. Chauffeur automatically dials Compuserve from anywhere in the world, gets all your waiting EasyPlex electronic mail, talks to people in Forums, delivers any mail you wish to send, scans for messages from users, scans for files to download, and even keeps an address book of all your contacts. The detailed chapter reveals tricks for serial port control, has enhanced serial XCMDs, shows hiding passwords, and much more. You can add sampled sounds so that Chauffeur talks to you as it moves to different areas of Compuserve, and you can learn all the requirements of any general purpose front-end from this chapter. There is a built-in help feature and even an AutoPilot mode that learns and records your manual activities so that Chauffeur can follow them later.

Chauffeur

A HyperCard-to-CompuServe Front End

HyperCard has simplified the creation of easy-to-use information retrieval engines to the point where a stack author can almost transform information into knowledge.

Current electronic information databases are available on CDROMs and in vast electronic networks such as CompuServe and The Source. To use these systems, you need to master a complex set of commands. Or you can use HyperCard to create a *front end*—a user interface that is placed over the front of a less friendly system.

This chapter describes the process involved in creating a front end that interfaces with CompuServe using HyperCard. Bill Atkinson has called HyperCard a "user interface toolkit," and this description can be applied as well to any stack created with HyperCard. Chauffeur is one of the first of many front ends written in HyperCard.

What Is a Front End?

As a user interface, a front end runs in front of another program or system that is usually more difficult to use. One example of a front end is the Finder. It simplifies the tasks of copying files, erasing disks, and renaming directories. Without the Finder, each Macintosh user would have to remember a complex set of commands, such as those used in MS-DOS and UNIX. For example, to create a folder (directory) in DOS, you have to type `mkdir C:\folder`. Then, to copy files to the new directory, you need to type `copy c:\file.dat c:\folder\file.dat` for each file. The Macintosh's interface is much easier to learn, remember, and use.

Why Use HyperCard as a Front End?

HyperCard is a perfect vehicle for front ends. The card and stack structure makes it simple to plan front ends. Each card represents an area that the system that is being front-ended provides. For example, two distinct types of areas are within CompuServe: services and forums. Services include electronic mail, known as EasyPlex, and electronic shopping. Forums are an area where people with similar interests "meet" and exchange files and messages. For example, Apphyper is the forum for HyperCard enthusiasts. In a HyperCard front end, the stack contains separate cards for each service. Each forum shares a common background because they share functionality, but each forum retains its own card for ease of structuring (Figure 15-1).

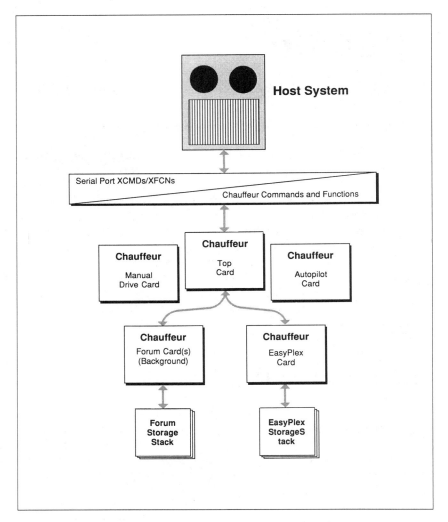

Figure 15-1.   Cards in Chauffeur's stacks represent forums in CompuServe.

Extra cards and backgrounds can be created with a minimum of fuss in Hyper-Card. New services in CompuServe can be accommodated easily in Chauffeur using existing commands and functions. Because HyperCard uses an interpretive language, HyperTalk, Chauffeur can be modified effortlessly at a later stage. This is important when the front end is used in volatile environments where users can request modifications daily.

Graphics and sound form a major part of the HyperCard environment. Graphics can enhance the front-end interface and provide aids to complex tasks. Although sampled sounds require a lot of storage space, they can supply another way to prompt and inform users.

For operations that have to be fast, the advanced author can create XCMDs in Pascal or C. The commands and functions that Chauffeur uses are external, because HyperCard comes with no built-in commands or functions for communication through the serial port. Harry Chesley, Apple employee and author of The Waite Group's *Supercharging C* (Addison-Wesley, 1987) has written a set of XCMDS and XFCNS for serial port communication.

Because HyperTalk can be sluggish in handling text, you must be careful when you design the text aspects of front ending. Many algorithms and scripts that Chauffeur uses were refined several times. Front ends for communications systems should be fast because the user is paying for connect time.

General Front End Design

Chauffeur is a CompuServe-specific front end. By using the basic techniques described in this chapter, you can simplify the process of developing communications system front ends. Before you begin, however, there are a few important considerations.

First, the users of the system are the center of the developmental process. What they request is what you will try to deliver. Talk to the users and make a list of their requests. Because HyperCard is designed for instant, "on-the-fly" modification, you can make changes as you develop your stack.

Almost as important as what the user requests is the hallowed user interface. If users are intimidated by what is happening when they try to use your stack, your front end hasn't improved the situation. Sit several end users down with your stack and let them play. Watch their reactions to alerts; take note of their criticisms. Be receptive to requests for changes in design. Chauffeur passed through five iterations before reaching its current state, and I don't consider it finished yet.

You also must become familiar with the target or host system in its native environment. The target system for Chauffeur is CompuServe. You can get to know most communications systems by using standard communications packages such as Red Ryder or Microphone. It is essential to know the structure of the host system's menus and prompts and the different responses that may be returned. In becoming familiar with the host system, you may discover options, such as stringing commands together, that will enhance the speed of your front end.

While you are becoming familiar with the system, capture a transcript of the communications sessions. These transcripts are invaluable in the testing stages of your front end: the transcript can be used to emulate the host system without running up a hefty bill. Also, you can use a second Macintosh connected with a simple printer cable and communications package to the Macintosh that is running your stack to simulate the process and debug your stack without running up expensive bills.

What Is Chauffeur?

Chauffeur, written in HyperCard, is an interactive and self-running front end to CompuServe. Chauffeur derives its name from the idea that to get anywhere with a luxury vehicle, a chauffeur will add an atmosphere of opulence.

Figure 15-2 illustrates CompuServe running under Chauffeur. If you are familiar with CompuServe's interface (and we assume that you are), you see what an improvement this is!

The Chauffeur system consists of multiple stacks. The main controlling stack, called Chauffeur, holds all the scripts, cards, and buttons that facilitate the communications session. Chauffeur requires Hypercard version 1.2.1 or later.

There are also associated storage stacks. Various stacks contain all the accumulated messages to be sent and received. Each forum and the EasyPlex electronic mail system "owns" its own storage stack. Because it is difficult to remember the numbers assigned to each CompuServe user, Chauffeur also has a special stack where the user can store commonly used CompuServe addresses.

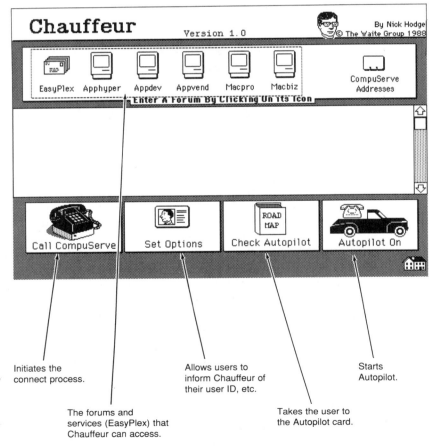

Figure 15-2. Running under Chauffeur, the CompuServe interface becomes easy to use.

The Chauffeur Help stack contains an easy-to-use help system that ties in with the main controlling stack. By holding down the Option key while clicking on an item in the Chauffeur stack, you are presented with a card displaying help information on that item.

The first card presented is the Top card (Figure 15-2), the home card of the Chauffeur system. From this card, the user can access each forum and service that Chauffeur enters.

Setting Options

Before you log on to CompuServe, you set options that you want to use. By clicking on the Set Options button, Chauffeur presents you with a set of questions: user name, user ID, phone number, and so forth.

After the options are set, you can log on to CompuServe. During this process, Chauffeur supplies CompuServe with your name and password and enters the Top menu. While you are online, Chauffeur changes the gray background with a more noticeable white background. This background, accompanied with a button flashing *online*, reminds you that you are spending money!

Using Chauffeur as a normal HyperCard stack is called *manual drive*. Users are in total control of where they are heading. They can respond interactively with CompuServe at any stage. On Autopilot, Chauffeur takes control of the communications session and follows a script taught by the user.

With Chauffeur's Autopilot option, you can program an Autopilot script for Chauffeur to follow. From the Top card, just put the Autopilot into operation and go and have coffee. Chauffeur handles all the work of logging on, entering EasyPlex, and reading and sending messages (Figure 15-3).

Another button that appears on all cards while you are online is the Hangup button. This button permits you to log off CompuServe at any time.

CompuServe Services

When you click on an icon, Chauffeur advances to that card. For example, if you click on the EasyPlex mail system icon, Chauffeur takes you to EasyPlex, both on-screen and in the transmission that is going on in the background.

At the EasyPlex card, you can send or read mail (Figure 15-4). If there are pending messages for you in EasyPlex, Chauffeur displays the number of unread messages underneath the read messages button. You can return to the Top card by clicking on the Top Menu button.

Forums

At the Top card, you can click on one of the forum icons and be presented with a forum (Figure 15-5). If there are any messages for you in that forum, Chauffeur places a message under the read messages button.

When entering a forum, Chauffeur first checks if you have joined the forum

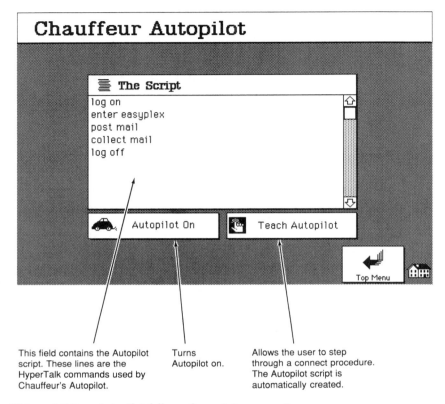

Chauffeur Autopilot

The Script

```
log on
enter easyplex
post mail
collect mail
log off
```

Autopilot On   Teach Autopilot   Top Menu

This field contains the Autopilot script. These lines are the HyperTalk commands used by Chauffeur's Autopilot.

Turns Autopilot on.

Allows the user to step through a connect procedure. The Autopilot script is automatically created.

Figure 15-3. Autopilot follows the scripts you write.

previously. If so, it continues; otherwise, Chauffeur gives you the option of joining the forum as a full member.

Next, Chauffeur checks if there are any members in conference. Again, Chauffeur supplies all of the responses to the menus that CompuServe presents.

There are more things to do than read messages sent to you and send messages to others. You also can read messages left in the forum for other people. You can get a listing of all messages in that forum and choose which ones you want to read.

Within a forum are different subtopics. From a pop-up field, you can set the subtopics that interest you. Only message headings from those subtopics are returned. The scanned listing is contained in the forum's storage stack and can be used to select messages to be read the next time you are online. You can read either an individual message or a thread from a message. (A thread contains the message itself plus any replies left in that forum.)

Modes

The transparency of the user interface is a major feature of Chauffeur. When Chauffeur is offline, all buttons that you use when online are still functional, except they show the stored data or allow you to compose messages to send. By using the buttons offline, users can learn the system's basics at their leisure--and much more cheaply than experimenting online.

Chauffeur's Internals

Chauffeur has been written to be open ended, because CompuServe is a varying system that is always being updated. Many functions can be changed with the end user noticing little.

But HyperTalk Has No Serial Port XCMDs

In HyperCard 1.2.1, there are no commands or functions that allow serial port communication to the outside world. These serial ports, called the printer and modem

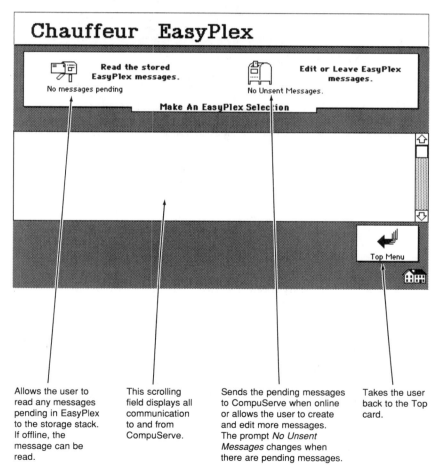

Allows the user to read any messages pending in EasyPlex to the storage stack. If offline, the message can be read.

This scrolling field displays all communication to and from CompuServe.

Sends the pending messages to CompuServe when online or allows the user to create and edit more messages. The prompt *No Unsent Messages* changes when there are pending messages.

Takes the user back to the Top card.

Figure 15-4. With Chauffeur's EasyPlex card, you can send and read electronic mail.

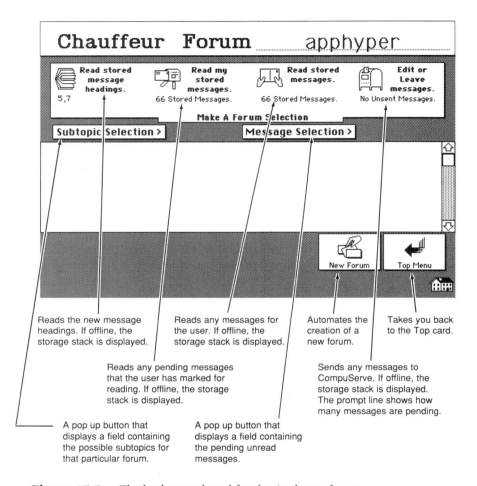

Figure 15-5. The background card for the Apphyper forum.

ports, are used by modems and are used by AppleTalk for network communication and printer connections.

The serial port works like a file. The file must be opened before any work can begin. After the file is opened, the program can send data out the serial port just like writing data to a file on disk. Likewise, data can be read from the serial port.

Harry Chesley has written a set of XCMDs that allow HyperTalk programmers to send characters into and out of the serial port. These XCMDs are available from the Apple Programmers and Developers Association and are contained in a stack called HyperTerm.

The following XCMDs and XFCNs are used in Chauffeur:

openSPort <port>

This XCMD opens the serial port for use by Chauffeur before communication can start. The *port* variable is the serial port to use. It should be 1 for the modem port or 2 for the printer port.

resetSPort <port,configuration>
This XCMD resets the serial port *port* with the settings as defined in the *configuration* variable. Refer to *Inside Macintosh*, volume II, pages 250-51 for a full description of the settings for *configuration*.

sendSPort <port,addLineFeeds,string>
An XCMD that sends a string of characters held by *string* out of serial port *port*, adding line feeds after carriage returns if *addLineFeeds* is true. This command is used to take a command or message from HyperCard and send it out through the serial port.

SPortHasChar <port>
This XFCN returns true if serial port *port* has an unread character waiting. This is used as a check to see if there are pending characters before interrupting the flow.

recvSPort <port>
This XCFN returns the next character from serial port *port* if available or waits for the next available character.

recvUpTo <port,termCharacter,timeOut,echo,edit>
An XCFN that returns characters available up to *termCharacter* from serial port *port* or waits for *timeOut* 60ths of a second and returns those characters. If *echo* is true, *recvUpTo* echoes the characters out the serial port, adding line feeds after carriage returns. If *edit* is true, *recvUpTo* deletes the last character in the buffer.

bufferSPort <port,oldBuffer,newBufferSize>
This XCFN is used to change the size of the serial port *port* buffer. The *oldBuffer* is the global variable of the old serial port buffer. The *newBufferSize* is the new buffer's size in bytes.

closeSPort <port>
This XCMD closes the serial port.

Two of these externals, openSPort and closeSPort, were written by the author in LightSpeed C.

```
/*
openSPort XCMD
Written by Nick Hodge for Chauffeur.
Translated APDA MPW Pascal XCMD, except for the use of RAM serial
drivers and handshake setting.
Takes one parameter: the serial port to open. It then sets up the serial
port to do XON/XOFF flow control, both in and out.
*/

#include <SerialDvr.h>
#include <HyperXCMD.h>
#include <OSUtil.h>

void Failed (paramPtr,theError)
XCmdBlockPtr paramPtr;
int theError;
{
  Str255 tmpStr;
```

continued

```
      SysBeep (5);
      NumToString(theError,tmpStr);
      paramPtr->returnValue =
PasToZero(paramPtr,(StringPtr)tmpStr);
      /* mayday code! */
   } /* Failed */

   pascal void
   main(paramPtr)
   XCmdBlockPtr  paramPtr;
   {
      short serialPort;
      int sPortInDvr,sPortOutDvr,OSError;
      Str31 str;
      SerShk *handShake;
      Handle firstPart;

      firstPart = paramPtr->params[0];    /* Grab first parameter */

      ZeroToPas(paramPtr,*(unsigned char **)firstPart,str);
        /* convert to Pascal string */
      serialPort = StrToNum(paramPtr,str);
        /* convert to number that is serial port # */

      if (serialPort == 2) {
        sPortInDvr = -8;
        sPortOutDvr = -9;
        OSError = RAMSDOpen(sPortB);    /* open the printer port */
      } else {
        sPortInDvr = -6;
        sPortOutDvr = -7;
        OSError = RAMSDOpen(sPortA);    /* open the modem port */
      } /* if */

      if (OSError != 0) {
        Failed (OSError);         /* whoops, something is wrong */
      } else {
        handShake->fXON = (char) true;
        handShake->fInX = (char) true;
        handShake->xOn = 0x11;    /* hex for XON character */
        handShake->xOff = 0x13;   /* hex for XOFF character */
        handShake->fCTS = (char) false;
        handShake->fDTR = (char) false;
        handShake->errs = 0;
        handShake->evts = 0;
        OSError = SerHShake (sPortInDvr,handShake);
      /* using the structure, set handshake */
        OSError = SerHShake (sPortOutDvr,handShake);
       /* for both incoming and outgoing comms.*/
        if (OSError != 0) {
        Failed (OSError);        /* whoops, something is wrong */
      } /* if */
      } /* if */
   } /* main */
```

Next, the CloseSPort XCMD:

continued

```
/*
closeSPort XCMD
Written by Nick Hodge for Chauffeur.
Translated APDA MPW Pascal XCMD, except for the use of the RAM serial
drivers.
Takes one parameter: the serial port to open. It then simply closes it.
*/

#include <SerialDvr.h>
#include <HyperXCMD.h>
#include <OSUtil.h>

#define nil 0

void Failed (paramPtr,theError)
XCmdBlockPtr paramPtr;
int theError;
{
  Str255 tmpStr;
  SysBeep (5);
  NumToString(theError,tmpStr);
  paramPtr->returnValue = PasToZero(paramPtr,(StringPtr)tmpStr);
    /* mayday code! */
} /* Failed */

pascal void
main(paramPtr)
XCmdBlockPtr  paramPtr;
{
  short serialPort;
  int OSError;
  Str31 str;
  Handle firstPart;

  OSError = 0;
  firstPart = paramPtr->params[0]; /* Grab the first parameter */
  ZeroToPas(paramPtr,*(unsigned char **)firstPart,str);
    /* convert to Pascal string */
  serialPort = StrToNum(paramPtr,str);
    /* convert to number that is serial port # */

  if (serialPort == 2) {
    RAMSDClose(sPortB);   /* close the printer port */
  } else {
    RAMSDClose(sPortA);   /* close the printer port */
  } /* if */

  if (OSError != 0) {
    Failed(paramPtr,OSError); /* whoops, something is wrong */
  }  /* if */
} /* main */
```

Why rewrite these two externals, you may ask? During the testing phase of
Chauffeur, there were problems with losing characters. This was blamed on the fact
that the serial port was not handshaking—a technique used in communications to
ensure that data is being received correctly. If the guest is running behind in collecting incoming characters, it tells the host to hold on for a minute while it catches up.

An XOFF character (Control-S) is sent to the host to tell it to halt for a while. After the guest has caught up, an XON character (Control-Q) is sent to reinitiate the communications session.

These externals open the serial port for use and set up the port to handshake. The `closeSPort` external closes the opened serial port driver. For further explanation, refer to *Inside Macintosh*, volume II, pages 250 and 251.

Using XCMDs and XFCNs as foundations, the structure of the front end can be built. These extra commands and functions can be written in HyperTalk or in a lower-level language such as Pascal or C. To facilitate easier understanding, HyperTalk is the preferred method. Although this results in slower execution, the script and structure are easier to decipher. Chauffeur uses many multifunctional scripts, all of which handle the communication that occurs between the front end and the host system.

The Three Types of Data in Communications

Essentially, there are three types of incoming data: prompts, menus, and messages. *Prompts* are lines of text sent out by the host that require the guest to read and type some sort of command. A *menu* contains lines of text that inform the user of the possible commands that can be typed at a prompt line. Sometimes a menu contains data that the front end must extract and use on the currently visible card. A *message* is any data that the front end must collect for the user to read at some later time.

Let's look at the case in which the front end is waiting for a prompt line before continuing. Chauffeur must read each line of data coming in and examine its contents against a set of expected values. Incoming data up to that line is discarded. A function handler called WaitFor waits a certain amount of seconds for possible prompts. The WaitFor handler can compare multiple prompts to the incoming data.

WaitFor is based on another function called IncomingChars. This handler is written in HyperTalk, but in the future it may be rewritten in C to increase the execution rate. Because this handler is a time-critical part of Chauffeur, it is optimized for maximum throughput. (Numbers in the listing relate to the author's comments in the text.)

```
function IncomingChars timeOut
   -- This procedure discards incoming text until it gets a match to
   -- "string" and returns the captured text and returns from
   -- back...
   global connected,searchString,returnString
   put 0 into whichMatch -- no match yet
   put false into ending -- no, we are not ending yet
   put 0 into ticksTaken -- and we haven't started yet
   multiply timeOut by 60 -- change to ticks, not seconds
   put empty into returnString
   put space into lastChars
   repeat with i = 1 to the number of items in searchString
      put last char of item i of searchString after lastChars
   end repeat
   repeat while not ending
```

continued

```
1    put recvUpTo(1,return,60,false,true) into incoming
     BeachBall
     if incoming is not empty then
2      put incoming after returnString -- and store for the return
       if lastChars contains last char of last line of ¬
       returnString then
         repeat with i = 1 to the number of items in searchString
              -- look for the matches
              if last line of returnString contains item i of ¬
              searchString then
3                 put true into ending -- found one!
                  put i into whichMatch -- we found this one (i)
                  exit repeat
              end if
         end repeat
       end if
4      else
5        if not SPortHasChar (1) then -- no, just a slow comms speed
         add 60 to ticksTaken -- not found, so increment timeOut
              if ticksTaken > timeOut then
                  put true into ending -- waiting too long
                  -- now you do advanced checking, just in case
                  get the number of lines in returnString
                  get line it - 1 to it of returnString
                  -- if no more chars, must be prompt
6                 if lastChars contains last char of it then
                      -- you have a prompt character, must be garbled prompt
                      put 0 into whichMatch -- doesn't recognize the prompt
                      CommProblems searchString -- tell user what is happening
                  end if
7                 if it contains "NO CARRIER" then -- CompuServe dumped us
                      Hangup
                      answer "The next message will cancel all scripts." with "OK"
                      do "get the hilite of card field comms"
                      -- force error to exit all
                  end if
              end if
         end if
       end if
     end repeat
8 Display returnString  -- display incoming text
  if whichMatch is not 0 then delete last line of returnString
  return whichMatch  -- return what is found
end IncomingChars
```

IncomingChars reads the serial port and captures any incoming data up until a return (1) or for one second, whichever comes first. See Figure 15-6. If the incoming data returned by the recvUpTo XFCN is not empty, the script starts to check the lines of text it just received (2). If there is a match (3) with the desired list of responses, IncomingChars returns back to the calling handler. All data received in this process is stored into a global variable that any level handler can examine.

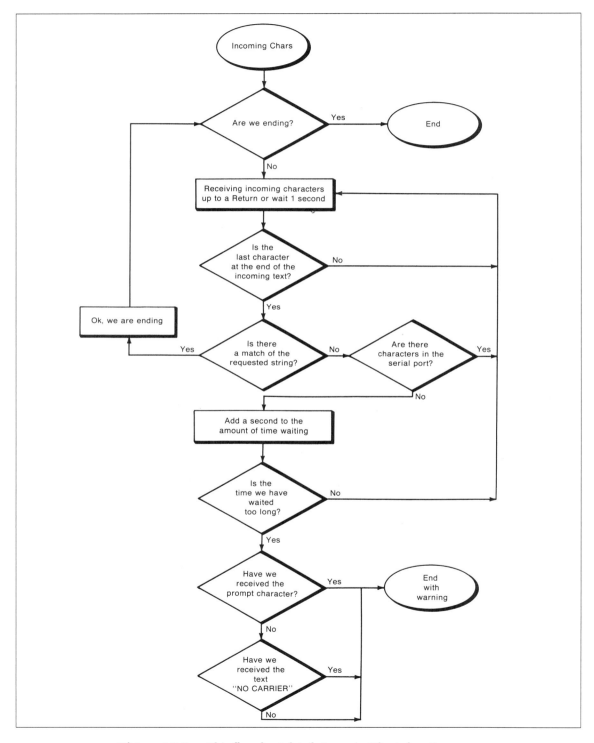

Figure 15-6. This flowchart details IncomingChar's functions.

Is Chauffeur Still Online?

In addition to looking for a match in the incoming data, the IncomingChars handler must make sure that the host is still talking to Chauffeur. The `ticksTaken` variable is incremented each time the `recvUpTo` function waits without any captured data (4).

Chauffeur first checks to see if the serial port was too slow in receiving some characters (5). It also checks the last three lines of captured data and looks for the prompt character (6), which is the last character in the line that is being searched for. In CompuServe, the prompt character is usually an exclamation mark or a colon. Chauffeur then uses a handler called CommProblems to inform the user that there may be a problem in the communications session. There is the possibility that CompuServe "dumped" or hung up. This is checked at 7. Finally, at 8, the incoming data is displayed in a scrolling field.

Receiving Data

Now let's look at receiving messages and real data. In CompuServe, data can be sent in two ways: paged and unpaged. Paged data is usually divided by prompt lines such as *Press Enter to continue!* Chauffeur automatically sends out a Return character when it detects this occurrence.

For paged data, a function handler called StoreUntilPaged is used. It takes three parameters: `continueString` is the prompt line that divides the message, and `timeOut` and `endString` both function in the same fashion as the WaitFor handler. StoreUntilPaged uses IncomingChars to save time at some later date.

Unpaged data is collected through the StoreUntil handler. Instead of using a `continueString` to indicate when to press Return, StoreUntil takes another parameter: `cancelString`. This parameter is a line that Chauffeur checks for when testing the incoming data to see if the host has finished sending messages. For example, when you are reading a threaded message in the forums, if there are no more messages in the thread, CompuServe returns to the *Function:* prompt. In the scripts for reading messages in forums, the line reads

```
put StoreUntil ("Function:",20,"Read action:") into forumMessages
```

The method that CompuServe uses to send out the messages follows. (What the CompuServe user types is underlined.)

```
Function: rt onl 12345
-- Message number 12345
Read Action: n
-- Message number 12347
Read Action: n
Function:
```

Upon receiving the word *Function:*, Chauffeur issues the CompuServe command `rt onl 12345`, which means read only the thread of message 12345. Following this, StoreUntil is called and returns the contents of message 12345 back to the calling script, which issues the n response (read next message in thread). StoreUntil is called again. It returns message 12347 to the calling script, and again the calling script issues the n response. This time, when StoreUntil is called, it returns the word `canceled`, signaling that there are no more messages.

Sending Data

Higher-level handlers are used to control incoming data, but manipulating outgoing data is easier. From a front end, two types of data go out: commands and messages. To send commands in Chauffeur, a command handler called SendLine sends a line of text out through the serial port to CompuServe.

The SendMessage handler sends whole messages out to CompuServe. These messages are either EasyPlex mail being sent to other users or messages in the forums. Luckily, CompuServe has a standard editor that is similar in both EasyPlex and the forums. This editor takes a line of text, or 80 characters, at a time. Inside the editor, a prompt stating the current line number of the message is always displayed with a colon prompt. Part of the SendMessage handler algorithm divides the outgoing data into 80-character pieces. These 80 characters are only sent after receiving the colon prompt.

Using these six handlers, the process of writing the communications sections of the script is greatly simplified. All that is needed are the prompt lines and responses that the host system will return.

How Does Chauffeur Log On?

Before any of your scripts can work, Chauffeur must log on to the CompuServe network. This process requires some knowledge of modems and how they work.

Modems have a "language," and one of the most popular languages is the Hayes command set. This command set has been adopted as an industry standard.

From the computer connected to the modem, the communications software sends a command prefixed with the two characters *AT*, which stand for *attention* (get ready for a command). The body of the command is followed by a Return character. After the connection is made, the modem sends a response—usually, *OK*—back to the connected computer.

The Hayes commands that Chauffeur uses are simple. Depending on what options you set up, Chauffeur sends a string of AT commands to the modem (Figure 15-7).

The autologon handler in the script of the Top card uses the set options to set the modem with these different Hayes commands. After a connection is established, Chauffeur gets the attention of the computer host at the other end and checks for the response. If the text line received by the `WaitFor` command is not a standard CompuServe *User ID:* prompt, it sends out the line *cis*, informing the gateway to "log me into CompuServe, please." (Gateways, such as TymeNet and satellites, usually redirect any communications to another system.)

When Chauffeur detects the *User ID:* prompt, it gives your user identification

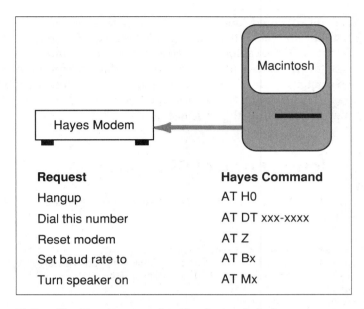

Figure 15-7. The Hayes command set has been adopted as an industry standard.

to CompuServe. This is retained on disk after setting your user options. Following this, it provides your password at the *Password:* prompt.

Chauffeur has now logged onto CompuServe. It passes through the normal introductory messages and enters the Top menu. If you have set an autologon procedure within CompuServe itself, Chauffeur traps this and manually reenters the Top menu. At the Top menu, Chauffeur sets the CompuServe options to *set terminal other,* which makes sure that only the text is sent. Other terminal command set control characters are not sent; these control characters are used by special terminals such as Digital VT100s and other front ends for special formatting on the screen. After this, Chauffeur is online to CompuServe.

Removing Spurious Characters

In most communications hosts there are excess characters such as prompt lines, unwanted messages, headings, menu listings, and page numbers. These spurious chunks of text are detected by Chauffeur and removed by two special handlers.

The DeleteLFs handler takes a string of characters with linefeed characters and returns it without linefeed characters. Linefeed characters, sent by CompuServe at the beginning of each line, tell the guest communications program to advance by one line. For the technically minded, a linefeed character is a Control-J, ASCII 10. Almost every handler in Chauffeur dealing with raw incoming data calls DeleteLFs.

The other handler, DeleteUnWanted, has many purposes. It takes four parameters: `messageString`, `onlyAfter`, `mustContain`, and `addThis`. The `MessageString` container is the raw data. The `OnlyAfter` variable is a chunk of text that

DeleteUnWanted looks for. Only after this line appears will the DeleteUnwanted handler start to collate the lines in `messageString` and return them to the calling script. The characters defined in `mustContain` must be contained in a line before DeleteUnWanted will return it to the calling script. DeleteUnWanted adds `addThis` characters to the beginning of each line to be returned.

This handler refines the captured data. It is used when a captured message may be surrounded by irrelevant lines of text.

Deleting Control Characters

Another method of deleting control characters used in Chauffeur is a sly trick. Here is the script:

```
-- store the incoming message
set the lockText of field "forum In" to false
click at the loc of field "forum In"
choose button tool
choose browse tool
set the lockText of field "forum In" to true
-- and continue
```

This script utilizes a little-known anomaly in HyperCard: if you are editing a field and change from the browse tool to the button tool and back, all control characters in the active field are deleted. The script accomplishes the same under Hyper-Talk control.

Keeping the User Aware

Keeping the user informed is an important part of writing front ends. Experienced users want to know that the system is working. Likewise, inexperienced users require feedback to reflect what is going on. Chauffeur uses five methods to keep the user aware; sound, central scroll fields, alerts, a problems handler, and a background change indicator.

Sound

Sound is an interesting method Chauffeur uses to keep the user informed. Different functions have a set of two tones, indicating that a process has been completed. A double tone indicates reaching a certain section: a service or the Top menu. A rising set of tones indicates logging onto CompuServe, and several sets of falling tones signal a finished task. (These tones were chosen by a frustrated musician, not a human interface expert.) The scripts use the `SoundAlert` command to handle using the sounds for user feedback.

Central Scroll Fields

Second, Chauffeur displays all incoming data in a scrolling field in the center third of each card. You can examine this field at any stage of the online session to review what has happened in that session. To control the fields, the Display handler is in the script of the stack. Chauffeur automatically rescrolls the field to its lowest position. The script, called reScroll, is common among all Chauffeur scrolling fields that take incoming characters:

```
on reScroll
  put textHeight of me into textHite
  put round ((the height of me)/textHite) into visLines
  put the number of lines in me + 1 into numLines
  if numLines > visLines then
    set the scroll of me to textHite * (numLines – visLines)
  end if
end reScroll
```

Alerts

The third method of user feedback is a shadow field called Alert. This field is usually hidden, but it is displayed when required. A line or two of text is put into this field informing the user that the current process may take a while and is still working. This field is also used by the `SendMessage` command to show the percentage of the current message that has been sent.

Problems

The CommProblems handler provides necessary feedback apparatus in Chauffeur. This procedure is called if Chauffeur misses a prompt or times out. CommProblems is usually called by the IncomingChars handler when it has trouble with the communications session with CompuServe. The user can manually bail out of trouble, continue regardless, or hang up.

Card Background Change

Finally, Chauffeur changes the background color of each card in synchronization with the connect status. When Chauffeur is connected to CompuServe, the background is white. If Chauffeur is not connected, the background is standard gray. This trick is achieved by displaying a gray pattern on the background. When Chauffeur is online to CompuServe, the script through the `ShowConnectStatus` command shows an opaque white field called Dummy Background. This field is over the entire card, thereby changing gray to white. The HyperTalk `hide background` command could not be used because any graphics on the background would also be hidden.

Chauffeur's Overall Structure

When Chauffeur changes the current card, it sends commands to CompuServe to switch the primary section. The obvious place to contain this initial communication is in the openCard handler.

Each CompuServe function, such as sending mail and reading mail within a service, is associated with a button. In Chauffeur, scripts that automate CompuServe functions are in mouseUp handlers. This structure is used in all openCard handlers and mouseUp handlers on the Top, EasyPlex, and forum background cards. Each of the handlers that deal with CompuServe has a similar structure:

```
on handler
if the optionKey is down then go to help system
if learnMode is on then add me to Autopilot Script
if connected then communicate to CompuServe
  else just update the screen
```

The learnMode global variable is set true when users teach Chauffeur the path they want the Autopilot to follow when automatically logging on. Each handler adds a line of Autopilot Script to a field on the Autopilot card corresponding to its function. The connected global variable is an important variable that is set true when Chauffeur is communicating with CompuServe.

Structure of EasyPlex

EasyPlex is CompuServe's electronic mail system. Chauffeur has an entire card for EasyPlex functions: reading EasyPlex messages and sending EasyPlex messages.

The EasyPlex card has an openCard handler that is executed each time the card is opened. If connected, Chauffeur sends the CompuServe command: go easyplex. When you are connected to CompuServe, this command changes the current section to EasyPlex. Upon entering EasyPlex, Chauffeur checks to see if there are any pending messages for you and displays the number of messages in a field under the read messages icon.

The following script completes these tasks:

```
get WaitFor (20,"Enter Choice !","EasyPlex!","or HELp!")
  put DeleteLFs(returnString) into EasyPlexMenu
    if it is 1 then
      if EasyPlexMenu contains "READ mail" then
        repeat with i = 1 to the number of lines in EasyPlexMenu
          if line i of EasyPlexMenu contains "READ mail" then
            put offset ("READ mail",line i of EasyPlexMenu) + 10 ¬
            into starting
            put offset ("pending",line i of EasyPlexMenu) + 8 into ending
            put char starting to ending of line i of EasyPlexMenu ¬
            into card field "Read EasyPlex Count"
          end if
        end repeat
```

continued

```
        end if
    else
        repeat with i = 1 to the number of lines in EasyPlexMenu
            if line i of EasyPlexMenu contains "message" then
                put line i of EasyPlexMenu into card field ¬
                "Read EasyPlex Count"
                exit repeat
            end if
        end repeat
    end if
SendLine "set mode command" & return
get WaitFor (10,"EasyPlex!")
```

The script must accommodate three types of menus and prompts that may be set. This is accomplished by using multiple results to look for in the `WaitFor` line. Following this, the resulting value is tested to check which prompt was found: Enter Choice!, EasyPlex! or Help!

There are two styles for showing the number of unread messages. The resulting value is displayed in the Read EasyPlex Count card field. Finally, Chauffeur sends the command `set mode command` to CompuServe, which tells EasyPlex to display the one-line prompt. This shortened prompt line increases speed. The last `WaitFor` contains that one-word prompt, EasyPlex!.

The EasyPlex storage stack is examined by the openCard handler of the EasyPlex card to see if there are any unsent messages. The number is placed into the field below the Send EasyPlex icon.

At this point, Chauffeur is into the EasyPlex section of CompuServe. From here, you can read messages that are waiting for you or send messages out to any other user. It is important to note that Chauffeur creates messages only offline and allows you to read messages only offline.

When you click on the Read EasyPlex button, Chauffeur reads pending messages that you will respond to later when you are disconnected. The script sends out options to set page off—that is, to display the entire message and not break it up with Press Enter to Continue! prompt lines. Using the `read all` command, CompuServe displays each message, one after the other. The script works like this:

```
SendLine "set page off" & return
get WaitFor (30,"!")
SendLine "read all" & return -- read the message
repeat while not ending
  put StoreUntil("EasyPlex!",15,"Action!") into EasyPlexIn
  if EasyPlexIn is "canceled" then
    put true into ending
  else
    put DeleteUnWanted(EasyPlexIn,"Date:",empty) into EasyPlexIn
    -- and store them in the EasyPlex Storage stack
```

Using the `StoreUntil` command, Chauffeur can read all the messages in EasyPlex and store them in your EasyPlex storage stack. DeleteUnWanted takes away any spurious lines of text before the *Date:* line contained in all messages.

The Send EasyPlex button is on the EasyPlex card. It reads the pending message from the storage stack and sends it to EasyPlex. Chauffeur sets the `set edit line` option to on to use the line-number-prompt method.

```
-- get the pending unsent message...
SendLine "set edit line" & return
get WaitFor (30,"EasyPlex!")
SendLine "compose" & return  -- tell CS you are composing
get WaitFor (15,"(/EXIT when done)")
put "From:" && userName & return before EasyPlexOut
put "To:" && whoto & return before EasyPlexOut
put "Subject:" && subject & return before EasyPlexOut
SendMessage EasyPlexOut,30,"card field alert"
-- okay, go for it again
```

Generally, after you create a message, CompuServe displays a range of prompts such as Send Message To:. Waiting for each of these prompts uses valuable time. To increase efficiency, CompuServe allows the user to add the subject matter, who the message is for, and who it is from at the beginning of each message to avoid these prompts. Chauffeur adds these lines to the head of each message sent:

```
To:  who to
From: who from
Subj: the subject
```

After sending and reading messages, you can log off using the Hangup button or reenter the Top menu.

Structure of Forums

The structure of forums is similar to the structure in the EasyPlex section of Chauffeur. Because functions in forums are shared across all CompuServe forums, Chauffeur has a single background for all forums.

All scripts for forums are also in the background. This includes the scripts for the four functions used in forums: reading scanned message headings, reading individual messages, reading your pending messages, and sending messages. This allows you to modify and improve the stack at different stages.

Again, the openCard handler sets up the initial communication to each forum. The forum that Chauffeur addresses depends on the name of the card. For example, the card that deals with the Apphyper forum is called Apphyper.

When entering the forum, the openCard handler checks to see if the forum is "unjoined" and lets you join it. Each forum in CompuServe gives you the option of joining the group after reading certain disclaimers and laws governing its use. The forum is unjoined and you are a visitor or guest until you supply the forum with your name. The process here is a simple matter of examining the returned text for the string of text VISITORS MENU. This text only appears if the forum is unjoined.

As you saw previously, Chauffeur also checks if there are messages left for you by other members in that forum. If so, the script places prompting text under the appropriate icon on the screen. A similar check is applied to see if there is a conference in progress within that forum. If so, you are given the opportunity of joining the conference.

Finally, the pop-up field that contains a listing of the forum's subtopics is also checked. If this field is empty, Chauffeur gets the latest listing of subtopics by using the UpDateSubTopics handler, which executes the following script:

```
-- okay, let's read the listing
-- subtopics field is empty
SendLine "op" & return -- going into options
get WaitFor (20,"Enter choice !","Function:")
SendLine "su" & return -- subtopic selection
get WaitFor (12,"SUBTOPIC SELECTION")
put StoreUntilPaged ("<CR> for more !",30,¬
"Enter choice  ","Function:") into subTopics
SendLine "t" & return -- return to top menu
get WaitFor (20,"Function:","Enter choice !")
-- and return
```

As in in the EasyPlex section of CompuServe, Chauffeur sets the options upon entering the section. Chauffeur sends out the following:

```
-- this sets the options (only S - this session)
SendLine "op;sm n;re l;ed linedit;um off;s" & return
get WaitFor (12,"Function:")
-- and also sets the subtopics to view
```

The line can be interpreted as follows:

sm n;re l	stop at the end of message number re 1
ed linedit	set the editor to line-number-prompted editor for the SendMessage command
um off	set menus off; just use single-line prompts
s	for this session only

By setting options for the session only, the user is not inconvenienced at a later stage by not getting a familiar response from CompuServe. This is an important point to remember.

When you click on the read message headings button, a *qsn*, or quick scanned listing, is returned. This scanned listing is stored in the forum's storage stack for later perusal. The script for this is uncomplicated:

```
-- warn user
SendLine "qsn" & return -- do CompuServe qsn
put StoreUntil ("Press <CR>",60,"Function:") into ScanListing
put DeleteUnWanted (scanListing,empty,":",space) into scanListing
-- and store it
```

DeleteUnWanted cleans up the resultant text before storing it in the storage stack.

Reading selected messages is also a simple task, as is reading messages left for you. After you have selected the messages you want to read by clicking on the read messages button, Chauffeur reads and stores them. There are two methods of reading messages: individual and threaded. Chauffeur uses the same script for both methods, but sends two different commands:

```
-- set options; warn user
if char 1 of it is "o" then
  put "ri" into readType
else
  put "rt onl" into readType
end if
-- make the screen look nice
SendLine readType && thisMessage & return
repeat while not ending
  put StoreUntil ("Function:",20,"Read action:") into forumMessages
  if forumMessages is not "canceled" then
    put DeleteUnWanted (forumMessages,"#:") into forumMessages
    -- and store the messages
```

By economizing on scripts, execution and maintenance are more efficient.

Sending Messages

Sending messages to the forum is a simple task. The only anomaly is that a message may be a reply to an existing message. It is important from a CompuServe point of view that a reply be sent to CompuServe as a reply, not as a separate message. This helps other users in the forum read a thread of a particular message trail. The script follows:

```
-- get the message first
if word 1 of whoto is "reply" then -- is it a reply?
  SendLine "re" && word 2 of whoto & return
  -- this is a reply
  get WaitFor (15,"to end message.")
  SendMessage forumOut,30,"card field alert"
  -- fix the other prompts that follow
else
  SendLine "l" & return
  -- this time you are just leaving a message
  -- fill in some prompts first here
  get WaitFor (15,"to end message.")
  SendMessage forumOut,30,"card field alert"
  -- it is all done
```

So, after the message is sent into the forum, the thread is still intact because Chauffeur has replied to a specific message in that forum. Like using the EasyPlex card, after sending and reading messages, you can log off using the Hangup button or reenter the Top menu by clicking on the appropriate buttons.

Autopilot: How Does It Work?

A major feature of Chauffeur is the Autopilot. This interesting set of scripts allows Chauffeur to run the front end virtually by itself. This process can be implemented easily into any front end.

The central part of the Autopilot is the idle loop in the script of the stack. This loop executes a line of the Autopilot script if the Autopilot is turned on. The status of the Autopilot is contained in the `selfRunning` global variable. Here is the idle handler:

```
on idle
  global connected,selfRunning,executeLine,learnMode
  -- some modal button stuff
  if selfRunning then
    get line executeLine of card field "Chauffeur script" of ¬
    card "Chauffeur"
    if it is not empty and (char 1 of it ≠ "-") and ¬
    (char 2 of it ≠ "-") then
      do it
      put 1 + executeLine into executeLine
    else
      if connected then
        log off
      end if
    end if
  end if
  -- some other script stuff here
  pass idle
end idle
```

This handler contains the line `do it`. The HyperTalk `do` command is a powerful command. In this case, it is used to execute a line of a field of text as if it were a HyperTalk script. A set of commands that describe a particular task can be created: log on, collect mail, post messages, and so on. Chauffeur has a collection of these commands:

```
log [on|off]
enter [forum name|service name]
collect [mail|headings|messages]
post [mail]
```

Using these new commands, you can build an Autopilot script that is easy to read and maintain.

The scripts that handle the four commands are as follows:

```
on log onOff
  global selfRunning,csPosition,connected
  if onOff is "Off" then
    send mouseUp to bkgnd button "Hangup"
    enter "Top"
    put false into selfRunning
```

continued

```
      else
        enter "Top"
        send mouseUp to card button "Connect"
      end if
end log


on enter serviceName
  global csPosition
  visual effect dissolve
  go to card serviceName
  put the short name of this card into item 1 of csPosition
  put the short name of this background into item 2 of csPosition
end enter


on collect typeMessage
  global selfRunning,csPosition
  if selfRunning then
    if item 1 of csPosition is "EasyPlex" then
      send mouseUp to card button "Read EasyPlex"
    else if item 2 of csPosition is "forums" then
      repeat with pCount = 1 to the paramCount
        get param (pCount)
        if it is "headings" then
          send mouseUp to card button "QSN"
        else if it is "mail" then
          send mouseUp to card button "Read Mine"
        else if it is "messages" then
          send mouseUp to card button "Read These"
        end if
      end repeat
    end if
  end if
end collect


on post typeMessage
  global selfRunning,csPosition
  if selfRunning then
    if item 1 of csPosition is "EasyPlex" then
      send mouseUp to card button "Send EasyPlex"
    else if item 2 of csPosition is "forums" then
      send mouseUp to card button "Send Pending"
    end if
  end if
end post
```

Using the HyperTalk send command, you can simulate the user clicking on buttons and entering different cards. The scripts that handle the communications side of Chauffeur just check the selfRunning global variable to verify the self-running status before putting prompts on the screen.

The post and collect commands are context sensitive—that is, in different sections of CompuServe, they are required to send disparate commands to Chauffeur. Therefore, another global variable, csPosition, has been defined to allow each handler to check the context.

User Selections in Scrolling Fields

Each forum first supplies a quick scan listing of the messages it holds. After the listing is collected, Chauffeur allows you to select a message to be read when you are next online. The listing is in a scrolling field in the forum storage stack. Following is the script behind the field that allows you to click on a particular message. (Numbers relate to the author's comments in the text.)

```
on mouseUp
  global forumName,storageName
  lock screen
  set lockmessages to true
  set the cursor to watch
1 get item 2 of the clickLoc
  subtract the top of me from it
  divide it by the textHeight of me
  add (the scroll of me/ the textHeight of me) + 1 to it
  put line trunc (it) of me into messageNumber
  put trunc(it) into lineNumber
  if messageNumber is not empty then
    get word 1 of messageNumber
    if first character of it is not space then
      delete first character of it
    end if
    if last character of it is ":" then
      delete last character of it
    end if
    push card
    go to first card in background "Messages In"
2   find it in field "Message Number"
    if the result is "not found" then
      pop card -- return to listing
      pop card -- return to controller stack
      push recent card -- push the listing card
      if char 1 of messageNumber is space then
        delete first character of messageNumber
3       answer "Read in which manner?" with "Threaded" ¬
        or "Only"
        if it is "Threaded" then
          put "t" before messageNumber
        else
          put "o" before messageNumber
        end if
4       put messageNumber && return after card field ¬
        "Read These" of card forumName
        pop card -- return to listing
        push recent card
        -- this is the controller stack return place
        do "put messageNumber into line lineNumber of" && the ¬
        target
      else
5       delete first character of messageNumber
        go to card forumName
        repeat with i = 1 to the number of lines in card field ¬
```

continued

```
      "Read These"
         if messageNumber is in line i of card field ¬
         "Read These" then
            delete line i of card field "Read These"
            exit repeat
         end if
      end repeat
      pop card -- return to listing
      push recent card
      -- this is the controller stack return place
      do "put space & messageNumber into line lineNumber of" ¬
      && the target
    end if
  end if
 end if
 set lockmessages to false
 unlock screen
end mouseUp
```

Chauffeur first calculates the line number of the mouseClick (1). This line is extracted from the field and used by Chauffeur to derive a message number. Subsequently, Chauffeur attempts to find that message in the existing database of messages (2). If the result is not found, Chauffeur realizes it must be a message to be read when next online or a message you want to delete from the read list when next online.

If the message is being added to the read list, an answer alert box (3) allows you to specify if you want to read the message threaded or individually. The character *o* indicates only, or individual, and the character *t* indicates threaded. This message number is added to the pop-up field that appears on the forum card in Chauffeur (4). Otherwise, the message is deleted from the read list in Chauffeur (5).

These messages can now be read by Chauffeur when next online to CompuServe, using the first character, *o* or *t*, to indicate only or threaded.

Exploring Your Messages

After data is accumulated in the storage stacks, what then? Data by itself is simply a collection of words: what we need is a system in which correlations are obvious to the user.

In the forum storage stacks, Chauffeur has an interesting "hypermedia"-like technique of reviewing the messages. The script of the forum field follows:

```
on mouseUp
  lock screen
  get the clickLoc
  set the lockText of me to false
  click at it
  click at it
  put the selectedText into findThis
  put the short id of this card into currentCard
  set the lockText of me to true
  if it is not empty then
```

continued

```
      repeat
        find whole findThis in me
        if the result is not empty then
          beep
          exit repeat
        end if
        if not(the short id of this card is currentCard) then
          exit repeat
        end if
      end repeat
    end if
end mouseUp
```

This script monitors mouseUp messages. After getting a mouse click, it uses a devious method to find the word that was clicked on. It first sets the lockText property to false, allowing the text within the field to be edited, then double-clicks at the mouse position to return a single word within the selectedText property. This word is searched for elsewhere in the storage stack.

The concepts and techniques in this handler have been in the HyperCard community for some time. If your front end deals with mountains of incoming messages, it may be advantageous to include similar scripts.

Replying to messages can also be greatly simplified. Why retype the subject and recipient when it is already in the original message? In the EasyPlex stack, the following script is found in the Reply to this Message button:

```
on mouseUp
   repeat with i = 1 to the number of lines in field "EasyPlex In"
     get offset ("From:",line i of field "EasyPlex In")
     if it > 0 then
       put char it + 7 to length(line i of field "EasyPlex In") ¬
       + 1 of line i of field "EasyPlex In" into whoto
       put i+1 into i
       put line i of field "EasyPlex In" into subject
       delete first word of subject
       exit repeat
     end if
   end repeat
   LeaveMessage whoto,subject
end mouseUp
```

This script searches the inbound message line by line for the characters *From:*. In the structure of the incoming message, this line is followed by the line containing the subject. These two containers are passed to the LeaveMessage handler, which uses these two values to create a new outbound message, automatically inserting the subject and receiver.

Hiding Password Input

Some interesting handlers in the script of the Top card set options before Chauffeur connects to CompuServe. The SetOptions handler asks a series of questions regarding user name, user ID, and so forth, and stores the responses in an options file. This file is used thereafter by Chauffeur to connect to CompuServe.

The EnterPassword handler is a little different. In communications systems, it is common to hide the entry of passwords. In HyperCard, a password entry cannot be hidden unless `blindTyping` is implemented so that you can type into a hidden Message box. Chauffeur uses this technique for blind input of a password. The scripts follow:

```
on EnterPassword
  global returnCount,firstPass,oldBlindTyping
  show card field "alert"
  put return & "Please type your CompuServe password." into ¬
  card field "alert"
  put the blindTyping into oldBlindTyping
  set blindTyping to true
  hide msg
  put 0 into returnCount
  put empty into firstPass
end EnterPassword

on returnKey
  global returnCount,firstPass,oldBlindTyping
  if returnCount is empty then
    pass returnKey
    exit returnKey
  end if
  if returnCount is 0 then
    put msg into firstPass
    put empty into msg
    put 1 into returnCount
    put return & "Please type your password in again to check." ¬
    into card field "alert"
    hide msg
    exit returnKey
  end if
  if returnCount is 1 then
    if msg is firstPass then
      hide msg
      hide card field "alert"
      set blindTyping to oldBlindTyping
      put empty into msg
      WriteOption firstPass
      close file "Chauffeur Options"
      put empty into firstPass
      put empty into returnCount
      hide msg
    else
      answer "Sorry, the password did not check out." with "OK"
      EnterPassword
    end if
  end if
end returnKey
```

First, the EnterPassword handler stores the old `blindTyping` setting in a global variable. There is nothing worse for HyperCard users than to have something changed without their knowledge. Always reset values like this to their original setting. A prompt is placed into the alert field to ask the user to type the password. After the Return key is pressed, the returnKey handler is called into action. It checks the number of times the Return key is pressed. If it is the first time, Chauffeur prompts the user to type the password in again to double check the original entry. The second time the Return key is pressed, if all is well, the password is saved to the options file.

Help!

Implementing the help system for Chauffeur was a simple task. In Chauffeur, the user just holds down the Option key and clicks on an item to display a help card.
A handler in the script of the Chauffeur stack channels all help calls:

```
on ChauffeurHelp object
  global connected
  if not connected then
    lock screen
    go to stack "Chauffeur Help"
    find object in field "keywords"
    unlock screen with dissolve
  else
    ConnectedWarning
  end if
end ChauffeurHelp
```

This handler is called from almost every script of an object in Chauffeur. The command takes one parameter, `object`, and opens the Help stack to the card displaying help. Nothing could be simpler.
In the script of the Chauffeur stack, another handler traps a mouseUp call in case the user wants help on a card or background:

```
on mouseUp
  if the optionKey is down then
    get the short name of this bkgnd
    if it is not "forums" then
      get the short name of this card
    end if
    ChauffeurHelp it
  end if
end mouseUp
```

Implementing a help system is as easy as typing text on some cards in a separate stack. If you establish a help system, your users will feel more comfortable with your front end.

HyperCard to the Rescue

HyperCard is a perfect environment for creating front ends for communications systems. One major deficiency in many communications services is the lack of graphics, which results in a user interface that is inferior to the Macintosh user interface. It is like giving people the user interface of the Macintosh, yet forcing them to use MS-DOS style commands.

With a little work, you can overlay a set of complex commands with a familiar interface. With a HyperCard front end, the users of your stack will be more at ease, more efficient, and more productive with your communications system. By using HyperCard and the methods described in this chapter, you can give a familiar Macintosh interface to the coldest communications system.

Part

Performance

Benchmarking HyperTalk

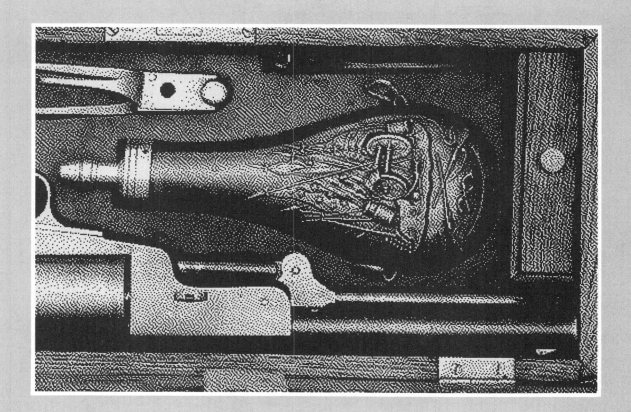

Mark ^Zimmermann

Synopsis: If you consider yourself a top notch HyperCard developer, you should know the answers to these questions: When you are working on a script, should you embed comments in the code or avoid them? Is there a penalty for packing many operations into a single line, or should they be spread out across several lines? Where is the best place to put message handlers from a speed standpoint—in the button, card, background, or card layer? What style of looping and control is most efficient? Are all mathematical operations equally slow, or is it worth avoiding some in favor of others? These and other provocative questions are answered in this chapter on benchmarking HyperCard. Every language keyword and process is subjected to the scrunity of a standard speed and response test.

You'll discover that HyperTalk performance diverges significantly from what you would expect from common interpreted languages. There are many cases where understanding HyperTalk's strengths can make the difference between slow and fast code. The chapter explores everything of importance, including the speed of mode changes, comments and blank lines, numerical and text operations, multi-line formulas, searching and stack compaction, repeat loops, if-then structures, and more. As new versions of HyperCard come to market, you can run this stack and quickly find out how much each command has been speeded up.

Chapter **16**

Benchmarking HyperTalk

Unveiling HyperTalk Performance

HyperTalk benchmarks are small (and not-so-small) test routines that you can run to measure, in a consistent and reproducible fashion, the performance of your programs. With a set of comprehensive scripts, arranged in a test configuration, you can determine the speed advantages and disadvantages of various commands, operators, and functions. This can lead to higher performance from your own stacks and also helps you avoid common mistakes in designing efficient scripts. You also can recognize when alternative approaches are equally fast, and pick the one that is cleaner and easier to write and revise.

The Value of Benchmarks in HyperTalk

Throughout this chapter on benchmarks, the central theme is a practical one—making your stacks run faster and better. Benchmarks are also of intellectual interest, of course. It's fun to be able to boast that your supercomputer executes 500,000,000 floating-point arithmetic operations per second, for example, or that your LISP machine can make 500,000 logical inferences per second. It's also important to be able to compare different hardware and software systems, to see which is the most cost-effective solution for a particular task. But given a Macintosh and a problem to be solved in the HyperCard environment, what really counts is solving that problem efficiently and elegantly. (Efficiency and elegance almost always go together.) A working knowledge of HyperTalk benchmark results can help you do just that.

Our benchmarks answer many questions that are constantly coming up: When you're working on a complex HyperTalk script, should you embed comments in the code, or should you avoid them because they slow down execution too much? Should you work hard to pack as many operations into each line of the script, or is there no penalty for spreading them out (each on its own line)? Given a choice from the standpoint of speed, where should you put message handlers—at the button, card, background, or stack level? Which styles of looping and control-flow management are most efficient? Are all mathematical operations equally slow, or is it worth avoiding some in favor of others?

The root question is which scripting issues are worth worrying about and which ones produce negligible differences in performance? This chapter helps you find the answers. Along the way, you also see how to develop the tools to answer new performance questions as they arise. That is more important than the specific results we'll derive here.

Summary of Major Benchmark Results

Here, for those who are too busy or impatient to wait any longer, are the main conclusions from the benchmarks developed and analyzed in the remainder of this chapter. The individual sections that follow derive and explain each of these key results in much more detail and discuss the implications for actual scripting.

Mathematical Operations

➤ Addition, subtraction, and multiplication are equally fast, whether the numbers being used are integers or floating-point values.

➤ Division is 30–60 percent slower than the other ordinary arithmetic operations.

➤ Trigonometric functions take about as long as four ordinary arithmetic operations.

➤ Generating a random number takes about as long as three ordinary arithmetic operations.

➤ Overall, mathematical operations in HyperTalk are run at about the same speed as the slowest (highest precision, floating-point) mathematical operations in other computer languages on the Macintosh.

Numerical Operations

➤ Transferring a number from one container to another is about 10 percent slower than using a literal value embedded in a script.

➤ Getting a value from a container and then putting it into another container takes almost twice as long as a single-statement `put` operation that does the same thing.

➤ The `add <source> to <target>` construction is about 10 percent faster than `put <source> + <target> into <target>`. Similar small speed differences hold for analogous mathematical operators such as `multiply <number> by <multiplier>`.

➤ In general, moving numbers in HyperTalk is exceedingly slow compared to the same processes in compiled languages; the speed of HyperTalk is comparable to or a bit slower than that of interpreted languages such as standard BASIC.

Text Operations

➤ Moving text characters from one container to another takes longer when more characters are being transferred, but the extra time is only significant when thousands of characters are involved.

▶ It takes about 20 percent longer to put characters `before` or `after` the contents of a container than it does to put the same characters `into` that container.

▶ Testing for a string in a container typically takes about 30 percent less time if the string is found than if it is not.

▶ The `offset` function takes about four times longer to execute than an `is in` test. Counting the words in a container takes about six times longer than an `is in` test.

▶ Overall, character movement in HyperTalk is similar in speed to numerical data movement—very slow compared to compiled languages.

Loops and Conditional Structures

▶ The fastest looping structure is `repeat N times`, which actually is faster than writing N copies of the statements to be repeated!

▶ Running `repeat with` using a counter is about 10 percent slower than an equivalent `repeat N times` loop.

▶ Other repeat-loop structures are about 40 percent slower to execute than the equivalent `repeat N times`.

▶ HyperTalk if-then tests take about the same length of time regardless of whether the test is true or false.

▶ Single-line if-then structures are only about 5 percent faster than the multi-line indented equivalent form.

▶ Generally, for looping and conditional structures, HyperTalk is comparable in speed to other interpreted languages—slower by a factor of 10 to 100 than a fully compiled language.

Message Handlers and Functions

▶ Message handlers and function definitions execute equally fast (within a few percentage points) whether placed at the button, card, background, or stack level of the HyperTalk hierarchy.

▶ Sending a message to an explicit target (overriding the usual HyperTalk inheritance hierarchy) is highly inefficient—from 40 to 250 percent slower than letting the message flow via normal channels.

▶ Although messages in HyperTalk are only loosely analogous to subroutines in non-object-oriented languages, their general speed of execution in HyperTalk is comparable to that of function and subroutine calls in standard interpreted languages.

Mode Changing

▶ Mode changing, especially into painting modes, is exceedingly slow, though more recent releases of HyperCard have made significant improvements.

▶ If the screen display is locked, operations to show and hide entities such as fields or buttons execute three to ten times faster than they do with the screen unlocked.

Comments and Blank Lines

▶ Comments, even long ones extending over many lines, add very little to script execution time.

➤ A blank line inside a loop can slow down script execution by about 40 percent.

Multiline Formulas and Recursion

➤ Mathematical operations execute significantly faster if they are written in single-line formulas rather than spread out over many separate HyperTalk statements on different lines or executed inside a `repeat` loop.

➤ Recursion is relatively fast and efficient for function definitions and evaluation if the number of recursive calls is reasonable (that is, if the number of levels of recursion is limited to a few dozen, and the algorithm avoids unnecessary recalculation of partial results).

Searching and Stack Compaction

➤ Stack compaction and sorting based on a field's contents typically take roughly 100 ms per card on a 68020-based Macintosh and 3–4 times longer on a 68000-based Macintosh, for stacks of less than a few thousand cards. The operations seem to grow slower logarithmically, however, so time spent per card will be longer in huge stacks.

➤ The `find` command in a kilocard stack typically takes a few seconds or less to find common words.

➤ Worst-case searching for strings shorter than three characters (such as `find "ab"`), or for longer strings that begin with three characters common to many words (such as `find "thex"`) takes roughly 20 ms per card on a 68020-based Macintosh and 3–4 times longer on 68000-based Macintosh.

➤ HyperCard `find word` operations are generally fast, with execution times less than a second, but `find chars` operations are frequently as slow as the worst-case generic `find` command discussed previously.

Framework for HyperTalk Benchmarks

In this section, we begin to get into the details of benchmarking. Specifically, we start by building some frameworks: scripts with slots for HyperTalk statements that we want to compare.

Our Standard Macintosh Testbeds

Before describing the HyperTalk scripts, however, it's important to establish some foundations. For a benchmark to be useful, it has to be reproducible, and for it to be reproducible, the environment in which it runs has to be solidly defined. Thus, throughout this chapter, we have chosen to quote results for two factory-standard "testbed" systems, not enhanced or accelerated: a Macintosh Plus and a Macintosh II. (The results for these two systems will, in general, scale straightforwardly to other machines or to modified systems.) Unless otherwise stated, the version of HyperCard being used is 1.2.1, with no additional scripts or handlers or external functions added to the program or to the Home stack.

The operating system used is version 6.0, run as-is and not under MultiFinder or with any special continuously active INITs installed (such as clocks or screen blankers). At the Control Panel, no RAM cache is turned on. All software resides on a single 40-ms average seek time SCSI hard drive. (Note, however, that except for the stack compaction and searching tests, none of our benchmarks are sensitive to the specifics of the disk drive being used.) Each Macintosh testbed system has 1 megabyte of installed memory.

These are simple, realistic, conservative operating environments that probably match the largest possible base of currently installed hardware. Except in a few places where absolute benchmark timing numbers are necessary, we always state important results in a machine-independent way, as a percentage relative to other ways of doing the same operation. Percentage comparisons are useful no matter what kind of machine your scripts run on. Where timings vary with the size of the problem to be solved, we provide formulas or rules to let you estimate how long operations will take in your specific circumstances. We also compare the absolute performance of HyperTalk with that of other interpreted or compiled languages for executing specific tasks on the Macintosh.

The Benchmark Template

With those preliminaries out of the way, how do you begin to benchmark? Because most HyperTalk commands execute in a fraction of a second, when you want to see how fast a particular operation is, you have to repeat it over and over again to get an accurately measurable interval. You have to set up automatic timers to record the elapsed time. In addition, you must remove the "overhead" of the scripts involved in setting up and performing the repetitions themselves (unless you're comparing different ways to loop and repeat). Finally, you have to present the results of the benchmark in a useful form. The first script does just that:

```
--Benchmark Template #1
on mouseUp
  global z, overhead, timing
  set the cursor to watch
  put 0 into z
  put the ticks into startTicks
  repeat with i = 1 to 166
  -- do the standard "overhead" operation here
  end repeat
  put the ticks into endTicks
  put endTicks - startTicks into overhead
  put 0 into z
  put the ticks into startTicks
  repeat with i = 1 to 166
  -- do the operation being benchmarked here
  end repeat
  put the ticks into endTicks
  put endTicks - startTicks into timing
  -- do a test for correct value of z here
  put (timing - overhead) / 10000 into line 1 of¬
```

continued

```
        card field "timing results"
        -- compute & put the results wherever they belong
end mouseUp
```

There are some simple but important points to notice about this script. It responds to a mouseUp message, so it can be put behind a button and executed with a click—handy for debugging a benchmark or for testing a function on a new system without running through a long complex series of operations. The template has two sections: a part to measure the overhead involved with (but not including) setting up for the critical operation and a second part to time that operation itself. The overhead section is identical to the second part except that it eliminates the single statement being measured. Thus, to get the added time associated with a given HyperTalk command, subtract the overhead time from the timing measurement.

The HyperTalk statement or command being benchmarked is repeated 166 times. This number gives the highest accuracy without taking too long so that the test is practical. On an American-model Macintosh, the internal clock (read by the HyperTalk ticks function) increments 60.15 times every second (not the 60 times per second which is frequently assumed). To get clean timings with good consistency between tests, an operation must execute many times. The test computes the average time, in seconds/operation, required to do a particular task. The results are reported to a reasonable number of significant figures, to avoid giving a false impression of precision which isn't there. If the number of ticks that elapse during 166 executions of a function are divided by 10,000, all of the requirements are satisfied.

An Aside

If you are using a Macintosh with a different tick rate, the *relative* results of all your benchmark calculations will be correct but the *absolute* timings displayed on the cards will not be right. If this bothers you, and if you are using a European-model Macintosh (which increments the ticks 50 times/second for European current, which is 50 cycles/second) you have two choices. You may change all occurrences of 166 in our benchmark scripts to 200; alternatively, you may change the divisor 10,000 in the benchmark calculation to 8,300 (which is 166 * 50), then add the statement set the numberFormat to "0.####" to your scripts. (If your Macintosh has been modified to change the vertical retrace interval (to interface with a nonstandard video system, for instance), you will have to change the value 166 (or the benchmark divisor) to something else. For scripts that involve 16 repetitions of functions, change 16 to 20 or change the benchmark divisor from 1,000 to 800 (which is 16 * 50). To reiterate, *these changes are not necessary* for the scripts to execute correctly and to give you useful information about HyperTalk operation speeds. They are only required to convert the ticks into seconds/operation for those who care about absolute measurements.

It is important to include some test for correctness of benchmark execution whenever possible. Ideally, a benchmark should actually calculate something nontrivial—something that requires HyperTalk to do some real problem solving. (After all, you do plan to write scripts that are nontrivial themselves, don't you?) Besides realism, there are two major reasons for making your benchmarks calculate a quantity that you can then check for accuracy:

▶ A future version of HyperCard, perhaps with a clever compiler or global optimizer, might notice that you never really "did anything" with the results of a benchmark calculation; it then could simply skip execution of the benchmark statement—leading to nonsensical infinite speed results! (Real-world optimizing compilers do this for other computer languages.)

▶ A correctness test protects against hardware failures, software failures, and most importantly typographical errors in entering a benchmark script.

One final item to note: In our benchmark scripts, we avoid any comments or annotations inside the critical overhead or timing loops, except for benchmarks that check the speed of HyperTalk comment statements themselves. A comment inside the inner loops might add inaccuracy to the measured operation speeds. Good programming style says "Comment Thy Code," but because these benchmarks are generally so short and simple, and because the risk exists of affecting performance measurements, it's better to break that rule.

Mathematical Operation Benchmarks

In the following sections, we look at benchmarks for basic mathematical operations.

Addition Benchmark

The most fundamental benchmarks deal with the procedures of mathematics: adding, subtracting, multiplying, and dividing numbers. To begin, consider the problem of addition for whole numbers. Here is the script to compute the average amount of time required to add integers:

```
-- Integer Addition Benchmark
on mouseUp
  global z, overhead, timing
  set the cursor to watch
  put 0 into z
  -- overhead loop follows...
  put the ticks into startTicks
  repeat with i = 1 to 166
    put   i   into z
  end repeat
  put the ticks into endTicks
  put endTicks - startTicks into overhead
  put 0 into z
  -- timing loop follows...
  put the ticks into startTicks
  repeat with i = 1 to 166
    put z + i into z
  end repeat
  put the ticks into endTicks
```

continued

```
    put endTicks - startTicks into timing
    if z <> 13861 then
      beep
      answer "Error in integer addition benchmark!" with "OK"
      exit mouseUp
    end if
    put (timing - overhead) / 10000 into line 1 of¬
    card field "timing results"
end mouseUp
```

As you can see, this script follows the general framework of the template. First we time a HyperTalk statement, in this case the line put   i   into z. Then we time the same operation modified to include the operation we want to benchmark, which here results in the line put z + i into z. The lines only differ in "z + *i*" versus " *i* ". Note that we design the script so the lines are exactly the same length, thus avoiding any possible speed advantage that a shorter line might have. Note also that both lines perform similar operations involving a put operation on a loop index and a global variable. The only significant difference is the presence of an integer addition— which is the quantity we want to measure.

The numerical result of this benchmark is 0.0047 second = 4.7 ms per operation on a Macintosh Plus using the standard benchmark configuration specified earlier; it is 1.3 ms/operation on a similarly configured Macintosh II. We'll analyze this and other mathematical benchmark results in detail in the next section of this chapter.

Subtraction and Multiplication Benchmarks

The benchmark for integer subtraction is essentially the same as the one for addition, only inverted. Instead of adding the numbers from 1 to 166, we start out with the total and subtract integers until we finish with 0.

A nontrivial integer multiplication benchmark is a bit tougher to devise. Multiplying together all of the numbers from 1 through 166 would be an interesting test, but it would result in a final result too large to be contained in a standard precision integer and in fact would be more of a test of the floating-point multiplication capabilities of HyperTalk.

So, how do we test integer multiplication? From here on, instead of repeating all constant parts of our benchmark template (initialization, setting the clock, testing the results, and so on), we just show the critical overhead and timing loops. You can simply insert this code into the framework to get the complete script:

```
-- Integer Multiplication Benchmark--key loops

  -- the OVERHEAD loop:
repeat with i = 1 to 166
  put    i    into z
  put z mod 173 into z
end repeat

  -- the TIMING loop:
repeat with i = 1 to 166
  put z * i into z
```

continued

```
    put z mod 173 into z
end repeat
```

Every time two integers are multiplied together in this script's critical timing loop, the result is reduced to a small integer value by putting the remainder when divided by 173 into z (in the statement `put z mod 173 into z`). The value 173 was chosen because it's larger than any multiplier in the range 1 through 166. The result varies pseudo-randomly in the range 1 through 172. (This makes sure that the numbers multiplied are a typical crossection of the small integers.) You might worry that the modular arithmetic reduction could take more or less time in the overhead and the timing loops. But a little experimentation shows that it doesn't vary significantly, so this benchmark is a valid one.

Division Benchmarks

Integer division opens another can of worms, because dividing one number by another frequently results in a fraction. To ensure that division always results in an integer, we use the following tactic:

```
-- Integer Division Benchmark--key loops

  -- the OVERHEAD loop:
repeat with i = 1 to 166
  put z + (i*i)    into z
end repeat

  -- the TIMING loop:
repeat with i = 1 to 166
  put z + (i*i)/i into z
end repeat
```

In this benchmark, each integer is divided into its own square—so it always results in a unique division problem with an integral outcome. We could worry that a future compiling/optimizing dialect of HyperTalk might recognize that $(i*i)/i$ algebraically reduces to just i, but for now this benchmark is fine.

The scripts for our other HyperTalk mathematical benchmarks (covering floating-point operations, trigonometric functions, and pseudo-random number generation) can be summarized quite simply. Each computes the results of a simple mathematical operation, averaged over typical values for the inputs. They follow precisely the same patterns as the integer benchmark tests. The floating-point arithmetic tests use numbers with a fractional part. The tests of the trig functions and random number generator, as their names imply, perform the chosen operation repeated inside timing loops.

Running the Benchmarks

Our benchmark stack is designed to make it easy to run any or all of the test scripts. Each benchmark sits behind its own button, so it can be executed by itself with a single mouse click. Each cluster of benchmarks on a given theme (for example, Mathematical Operations, or Numerical Data Movement) has a button that sends mouseUp messages to the individual benchmarks, so they can be run as a group. Finally, a button on the first card of the benchmark stack sends mouseUp messages to all of the separate thematic collections of benchmarks—which lets you execute the entire suite of benchmarks on request.

There is one desirable user action after clicking the Run All Benchmarks button: Do nothing! If you move the mouse while a benchmark is running, you generate interrupts to the Macintosh operating system that move the cursor around the screen. That takes processor power, and it slows down the benchmark unfairly and unpredictably. To get consistent results, avoid mousing during a benchmarking session. Also avoid running benchmarks while other unusual processes are executing in the background (downloading files over the phone, for instance). On the other hand, if your system typically is run with some background programs installed (perhaps a screen dimmer or the infamous Talking Moose), you may want to keep them around during benchmarking—to give you a personalized set of timings that match your normal operating environment.

Analysis of Mathematical Operation Benchmarks

The outcome of our benchmarks for numerical operations, shown in Figure 16-1, may be somewhat surprising. In Figure 16-1, results are in units of seconds per operation being tested (s/op) with the overhead of the testing framework removed. Addition, subtraction, and multiplication take about the same length of time, regardless of whether they are applied to integers or to floating-point numbers! *It's not necessary to avoid using numbers with a decimal part or to avoid multiplication in favor of addition and subtraction in your HyperTalk scripts.* (Here and throughout the chapter, major conclusions are italicized to highlight them in the analysis.)

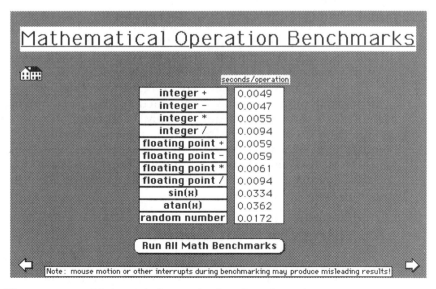

	seconds/operation
integer +	0.0049
integer −	0.0047
integer *	0.0055
integer /	0.0094
floating point +	0.0059
floating point −	0.0059
floating point *	0.0061
floating point /	0.0094
sin(x)	0.0334
atan(x)	0.0362
random number	0.0172

Run All Math Benchmarks

Note: mouse motion or other interrupts during benchmarking may produce misleading results!

Figure 16-1. Mathematical operation benchmark results.

What is happening is that integers are converted to floating-point numbers by HyperTalk before it works on them. The mathematical operations are executed by the SANE (Standard Apple Numeric Environment) routines to achieve maximum precision results. (In tests run on Macintosh systems with special floating-point mathematical coprocessor chips, the increase in speed is dramatic for all these operations, as you might expect. However HyperCard still goes through SANE, and SANE then uses the floating-point processor.) The procedure of converting all integers to floating-point values is a standard one for other interpreted languages such as BASIC. It simplifies the interpreter and it gives guaranteed good results, but at a price of slower execution speed. Many compiled languages such as C or FORTRAN, on the other hand, treat integers as a special data type; they thereby can do faster integer arithmetic.

Unlike other arithmetic operations, division is a different animal—it takes 30–60 percent longer, on the average, than adding, subtracting, or multiplying. *For a time-critical task, instead of dividing by a constant, it is wise to multiply by the precalculated reciprocal of that constant. Try multiplying by 0.25 instead of dividing by 4, for example. As with the other operations, there is no significant difference between integer and floating-point division timings.*

All of the ordinary arithmetic operations take only a few milliseconds—about the same time as in most other languages on the Macintosh. This turns out (as you will see later) to be less time than it takes to execute a typical multiline HyperTalk statement. *Extensive efforts to avoid common arithmetic operations will not save a lot of time in typical HyperTalk scripts. Arithmetic is "cheap"—almost "free."*

Trigonometric functions take about four times as long to evaluate as a simple arithmetic operation. This begins to be significant, especially if a trig function is used to compute the same value many times in an inner loop of a script. *If possible, call a trig function outside the loop and store its value in a container; then in the inner loop use that container instead of the function itself.*

When doing a repetitive series of trig operations (for example, moving around a circle, where sines and cosines repeat every cycle), you may want to consider creating a look-up table of precalculated values that you can then refer to. One way to do this is to pre-compute and store one value in each line of a container—call it `tabula`—giving you the equivalent of a one-dimensional array of numbers. When you need the Nth value, just ask for `line N of tabula`. But be sure that the process of building the look-up table and retrieving values from it doesn't take longer than doing the trigonometric functions themselves! It's not possible to predict which approach is more efficient in all cases—it depends on how many values you need to tabulate and how often you use them.

The last mathematical operation benchmarked, random number generation, is not cheap either; it takes about as long to execute as three common arithmetic operations. Be aware of this penalty when using pseudo-random values. Unfortunately, a reliable HyperTalk algorithm or external function (XFCN) to generate your own random integers will probably take more than three arithmetic operations to program; if you really need an unpredictable number, HyperTalk's built-in `random` function is the most efficient route. *Don't generate more random deviates than you really need, and avoid algorithms that require you to throw away a significant fraction of the values generated.*

Conclusions

The bottom line for all our mathematical operation benchmarks is that HyperTalk is sluggish in performing these operations, but no more so than BASIC or other interpreted languages. For high-precision floating-point arithmetic computations, HyperTalk does about as well as anything else. Compared to other tasks in HyperTalk that we will investigate, arithmetic is not an overwhelming concern when optimizing your stacks for high performance. Avoid frivolous arithmetic inside loops that execute hundreds or thousands of times, but don't worry about it otherwise.

Numerical Data Movement Benchmarks

After an arithmetic operation, something has to be done with the results. The answer has to be stored, and other numbers have to be moved to prepare for further calculations. Numerical data movement refers to the fundamental tasks of fetching and storing numbers. (In HyperTalk, the distinction between different types of variables is blurred or nonexistent; thus, there also may be similarities between different types of textual data movement operations.)

Most of the time, programmers don't have to think much about data movement. In non-HyperTalk programming languages, you write a statement such as z = 1, which hides the fact that internally a number is being retrieved from one place in memory and transferred to another. In HyperTalk, when you write put 1 into z the processor does the same thing—moves a value from one location to another. Because the minute details of data movement are hidden (unlike in assembly language programming), you can devote more attention to higher-level concepts as you develop scripts, but those hidden details need to be checked when performance is crucial.

Questions and Answers

Benchmarking can answer a variety of performance-related issues associated with numerical data movement. Does it take less time to put a smaller number, 1, into a container than it takes to put 1234 in there? Is it more efficient to write π as the HyperTalk constant pi or typed out as 3.14159 . . . ? In many varieties of BASIC, it's faster to define constants that hold frequently used values such as 0, 1, 10, and so on, and then use those constants in programs; does the same speed advantage occur in HyperTalk when using containers instead of literal values? Is a two-step get i followed by put it into z faster than simply put i into z? And how do HyperTalk operators that combine data movement with arithmetic, such as add i to z perform relative to the alternative?

In compiled languages such as C or FORTRAN, the answer to almost all of these questions is, It doesn't matter! The compiler scans the program to be executed and automatically sets up each operation in the fastest, most efficient way. Internally, that is in sharp contrast to classical interpreted languages such as BASIC. A typical BASIC interpreter is faster at fetching values from variables (the non-HyperTalk equivalent of containers) than at accepting them as in-line literal numbers in a program's source code statements. When a standard version of BASIC (such as Microsoft's interpreter) encounters the statement LET Z = 1234, it has to literally multiply and add the decimal string of characters 1234 to achieve the binary representation: ((((1 *10) + 2) * 10) + 3) * 10 + 4 in decimal equals 1 00110 10010 in binary. This takes a little longer when the number is larger (or has more digits in its decimal representation), because more arithmetic must be done to go from decimal to binary.

HyperTalk is anything but a classical interpreted language. To find out how well it does, we have to benchmark it. As with our benchmarks to evaluate and compare mathematical operations, benchmarking numerical data movement problems is the same straightforward matter of timing two sections of a HyperTalk script: one part with the operation of interest included and the other part without. Here, for example, is the script for the put pi into z benchmark:

```
-- Put pi into z Benchmark
on mouseUp
  global z, overhead, timing
  set the cursor to 4
  put 0 into z
  -- overhead loop follows...
  put the ticks into startTicks
  repeat with i = 1 to 166
  end repeat
  put the ticks into endTicks
  put endTicks - startTicks into overhead
  put 0 into z
  -- timing loop follows...
  put the ticks into startTicks
  repeat with i = 1 to 166
    put pi into z
  end repeat
  put the ticks into endTicks
  put endTicks - startTicks into timing
  if z <> pi then
    beep
    answer "Error in put π into z benchmark!" with "OK"
    exit mouseUp
  end if
  put (timing - overhead) / 10000 into line 5 of¬
  card field "timing results"
end mouseUp
```

As you can see, it's a very simple script that follows our template quite slavishly. The two loops compare the execution time for a single extra statement, put pi into z.

The rest of the benchmark scripts for numerical data movement are similar. (We don't list all the scripts here because they would occupy too much space; the benchmark stack is available on the *Tricks of the HyperTalk Masters* companion disk from Heizer Software as well as from many public bulletin boards.) The only possibly puzzling button title, put π... into z, runs a script to test the effect of extra blank space on an assignment statement. (In other words, does a number with lots of space around it take longer for HyperTalk to use?) It isn't possible to put all that extra space in the name of the button, hence, the ellipsis.

Analysis of Numerical Data Movement Benchmarks

The results of the numerical data movement benchmarks (shown in Figure 16-2) are quite interesting. First and most surprisingly, *there is little or no correlation between the length of the decimal representation of a number and the time required to put it into a container.* On a standard configuration Macintosh Plus, any of the `put <number> into z` operations takes about 19 ± 1 milliseconds; on a standard Macintosh II, the corresponding time is 5.1 ± 0.2 ms. It also doesn't matter if the numbers being moved are integers or floating-point values.

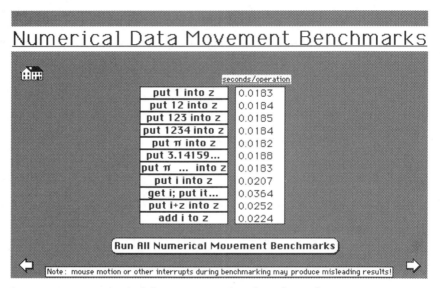

Numerical Data Movement Benchmarks	seconds/operation
put 1 into z	0.0183
put 12 into z	0.0184
put 123 into z	0.0185
put 1234 into z	0.0184
put π into z	0.0182
put 3.14159...	0.0188
put π ... into z	0.0183
put i into z	0.0207
get i; put it...	0.0364
put i+z into z	0.0252
add i to z	0.0224

Run All Numerical Movement Benchmarks

Note: mouse motion or other interrupts during benchmarking may produce misleading results!

Figure 16-2.   Numerical data movement benchmark results.

On the other hand, the length of a number makes a difference if you want to fetch a value from a container rather than use a literal number embedded in a script. *Retrieving a number from a container takes about 10 percent longer.* Worse still is separating a fetch-and-store operation into two parts; `get i` *followed by* `put It into z` *takes almost twice as long as the equivalent* `put i into z`. Another significant timing difference occurs when you have a choice between `add i to z` and `put i+z into z`. *Using the* `add` *command with a container is about 10 percent faster than using the plus operator.*

Conclusions

In sharp contrast to BASIC and other interpreted languages, in HyperTalk it's not worthwhile avoiding the presence of literal numerical strings in your scripts. For example, `put 365.24 into daysPerYear` is fine. Choose the method of expression which is clearer and easier to understand (and easier to debug), because there is no performance penalty. It is, however, profitable to avoid `get` statements followed by the use of the container `it`, in favor of a simpler and faster direct `put` statement. And it is slightly advantageous to use specialized arithmetic commands, such as `add <source> to <destination>`, when appropriate, rather than more common equivalents, such as `put <source> + <destination> into <destination>`.

Text Operation Benchmarks

We do arithmetic with numbers, but we talk and write with words made up of letters. Text operations (such as moving strings of characters from one container to another or finding a string inside a container) are the important analogs to the mathematical operations and numerical data movement benchmarks discussed in the previous sections.

Key Questions

How fast is HyperTalk in shuttling characters between containers as compared to other languages? Is it better to put characters `before`, `into`, or `after` the contents of a container? Does it take longer to check if a string is present, or if it is absent, in a large body of text? Is it cheaper time-wise to get a yes/no answer for a string's presence than to find out the actual offset of that string inside some text? And how many milliseconds does it take to ask HyperTalk to count the words or other items inside a container? These are some of the questions we'll be designing our text operation benchmarks to answer.

The Scripts

As you've already seen, after a problem is defined it's usually straightforward to write a HyperTalk script, based on our template, to measure the quantitative performance of HyperCard for a given task. The only additional complexity in benchmarking string operations is that in many cases we want hundreds or thousands of characters in a string, to time large-scale data movement. Thus, we need a simple, efficient way to build up the data for these tests. It's not hard to figure out how to generate such a long string, as the script to time the operation `put 1000 chars` shows:

```
-- Put 1000 chars benchmark script
on mouseUp
  global z, overhead, timing
  set the cursor to watch
  put "" into z
  -- overhead loop follows...
  put the ticks into startTicks
  repeat with i = 1 to 166
  end repeat
```

continued

```
        put the ticks into endTicks
        put endTicks - startTicks into overhead
        put "" into z
        put "" into s
        -- build long string for benchmark test...
        repeat with i = 1 to 40
          put "abcdefghijklmnopqrstuvwxy" after s
        end repeat
        -- timing loop follows...
        put the ticks into startTicks
        repeat with i = 1 to 166
          put s into z
        end repeat
        put the ticks into endTicks
        put endTicks - startTicks into timing
        if z <> s then
          beep
          answer "Error in put 1000 chars benchmark!" with "OK"
          exit mouseUp
        end if
        put (timing - overhead) / 10000 into line 4 of¬
        card field "timing results"
      end mouseUp
```

As you can see, to build a string of length 1000 without laboriously typing it out in full, you just concatenate, end-to-end, 40 strings of length 25.

You will need to build up some similarly big strings for the upcoming ...is in... and offset benchmarks. For those, just create the first half of the test string, then either insert or don't insert the actual word to be searched for (Hello). The test string has a target buried deep inside, in a typical place (halfway through) for a good test of the string searching commands in HyperTalk.

Results and Analysis

The major results of the text movement benchmarks are not too startling. (See Figure 16-3.) First, putting a few characters into a container is faster than putting many characters into it. A least-squares fit to the data indicates that the time in milliseconds to put N characters is approximately $21 + N/170$ on a standard configuration Macintosh Plus; on a standard Macintosh II, the best-fit formula is approximately $6 + N/600$ milliseconds. Those formulae aren't as useful as a good rule of thumb: *The time to do text movement operations doubles at 4,000 characters, triples at 8,000, quadruples at 12,000, and so on.*

It's therefore not worth worrying much over simple character movement when fewer than a thousand or so characters are being transported. On the other hand, the benchmarks show that it is noticeably more costly (20 percent or so) to put characters before or after the current contents of a container than it is to put them into a container. This makes sense—HyperCard does more shifting of values when inserting letters than when it simply discards or overwrites a previously existing string.

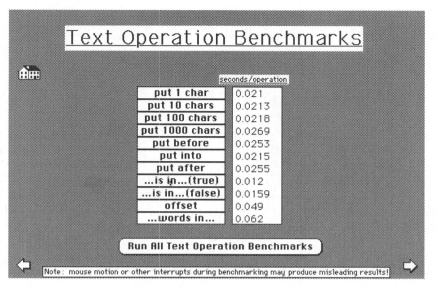

Figure 16-3. Text operation benchmark results

A similar small difference occurs in the time it takes to check for the presence or absence of a character string in a container using is in. (Note that this is *not* the HyperTalk find command, which searches through a stack; here, we are benchmarking an operator that returns true or false if a string is in a single chosen container.) If the string is in that container in a random location, it will on the average be found halfway through a scan of the container. A smart scanner will stop looking and return the answer true at that point. If the string isn't there, the entire contents of the container have to be examined. Not surprisingly, therefore, *it takes a bit longer (30 percent or so) to execute an* ...is in... *test that returns false as compared to one that returns true.*

A real surprise comes when we look at the offset benchmark. It tests the function which returns the distance from the start of the string to where the source string is located. Logically, this shouldn't take any longer than an ...is in... test because both involve scanning through exactly the same string, looking for exactly the same target. The only difference between the two functions is that ...is in... returns a true or false result, and offset returns the position in the string where the substring was found (if it was found; if not, offset returns 0).

So if the operations are similar, why does offset take four times longer to execute than ...is in...? Even though the reason isn't known, you should certainly *avoid using* offset *to test for a true/false answer to a string's presence.* The offset command is so slow that, it sometimes pays to do some checking and branch to avoid executing it unnecessarily. *If there is more than a 20 percent chance that a string will not be found by the* offset *command, it will on the average save time to first do an* ...is in... *check and, only if the answer is* true, *then ask for the offset.*

A final text-oriented benchmark test evaluates the ...words in... command, which counts the number of words in a chosen container. *Counting words is quite slow—it takes roughly three times longer than a* put *and six times longer than an*

...is in... *test*. Similar results arise from asking for the number of lines, items, or characters. Clearly, in time-critical inner loops don't ask for word (or other) counts unless necessary.

Conclusions

There are several important results you should remember from studying text operations in HyperTalk. Moving characters from one container to another is relatively fast until many thousands of characters are involved. Checking for the presence of a string using ...is in... is also very efficient. In contrast, operations such as offset or ...words in..., which return numerical results, are much slower and should be avoided when possible in time-critical parts of a script.

Conditional Structure Benchmarks

All our HyperTalk benchmarks thus far have been deterministic (even the pseudo-random number function). Each point in the programs' flow was predictable. But real programs have to respond to events in the outside world, and they have to redirect their flow of execution according to computed and changing values. Such decision-making is handled by if-then conditional command structures. Loops, which contain a section of a script to be repeated for a while, are another example of a conditional command. (In more conventional programming languages, with explicit goto syntax available, it's easy to write a repeat loop explicitly in terms of if-then tests and goto statements. In HyperTalk, without a goto, it's still possible to craft such a loop, but it takes recursion or other tricks with message handlers.)

Conditional structures are among the most important things to benchmark in HyperTalk because many scripts spend most of their time executing conditional structures in critical inner loops. Inner loops are simply the most active parts of a script—they consist of the statements that get executed the most often. In Hyper-Talk, given the way messages are created and sent to handlers of one type and another, it isn't always obvious where the inner loops of a script are hidden. But if you are experiencing slow performance of an important script, you'll need to locate the inner loops and fix them.

Key Questions

Important questions that arise concerning conditional operations are centered on repeat loops and upon if-then structures. What is the penalty for using a loop as opposed to writing out the operations over and over again? In a more conventional interpreted programming language, such as BASIC, loops usually take some time to set up and control. Thus, it is faster and more efficient in those languages (albeit somewhat tiresome) to repeat a statement by hand—in-line coding. Instead of writing X=Y(1): FOR I=2 TO 4: X=X+Y(I): NEXT I, for instance, write the equivalent

X=Y(1): X=X+Y(2): X=X+Y(3): X=X+Y(4), which runs much faster. Does in-line coding have the same speed advantages for HyperTalk?

How do the varieties of `repeat` structures that HyperTalk provides compare in efficiency? Is `repeat N times` better or worse than `repeat with i = 1 to N`? Going back to the simpler `if-then` statements, does it make any difference if the tested clause is normally true versus normally false? If readability is not a factor, is it faster to have an `if-then` statement on a single line, as opposed to spread out in a nicely indented, multiline format?

repeat Loop Scripts

Our scripts to benchmark these conditional structure issues are quite simple. They differ from the earlier benchmark scripts, however, in an important way. Earlier scripts always measured the difference between executing an overhead loop and a timing loop, which contains the operation under investigation. That approach was necessary to avoid confusing the effects of the `repeat` loop structure itself with the function being timed.

In this section, we don't want to subtract that kind of overhead—we want to see the effects of different forms of `repeat` structures themselves. So, we compare the elapsed time for the same standardized operation (`add 1 to z`) repeated 166 times, where the repetition is controlled by different means.

Thus, the benchmark script for `repeat N times` (which turns out to be the most efficient approach) is simply:

```
-- repeat N times benchmark
on mouseUp
  global z, timing
  set the cursor to watch
  put 0 into z
  -- timing loop follows...
  put the ticks into startTicks
  repeat 166 times
    add 1 to z
  end repeat
  put the ticks into endTicks
  put endTicks - startTicks into timing
  if z <> 166 then
    beep
    answer "Error in repeat N times benchmark!" with "OK"
    exit mouseUp
  end if
  put timing / 10000 into line 2 of¬
  card field "timing results"
end mouseUp
```

The script for the first conditional structure we will test is no structure at all but rather in-line coding, consisting of 166 repetitions of the statement `add 1 to z`. You can enter it by using the HyperCard script editor's cut and paste tools to save typing the statement that many times. The other benchmarks to test `repeat` loops are much more compact. The `repeat` and `exit` approach uses this core loop:

```
repeat
  add 1 to z
  if z = 166 then exit repeat
end repeat
```

The `repeat until` method is done with

```
repeat until z = 166
  add 1 to z
end repeat
```

The `repeat while` uses the tactic

```
repeat while z <> 166
  add 1 to z
end repeat
```

The `repeat with` uses

```
repeat with i = 1 to 166
  add 1 to z
end repeat
```

Finally, the `next repeat` structure relies upon

```
repeat with i = 1 to 166
  add 1 to z
  next repeat
  beep
end repeat
```

This last kind of `repeat` loop is actually testing the cost of prematurely jumping out of a `repeat with` loop structure to begin the next cycle; if all goes well, there are no beeps and the loop acts identically to all the other ways to count up to 166.

if-then **Scripts**

The benchmark scripts to test variations of the `if-then` structure are similarly simple affairs. They consist of 166 explicit, in-line coded repetitions of a cluster of statements. In every case, if the benchmark is executing properly, the global `z` container counts from up to 166; a `beep` statement in the alternative branch of the `if` should never be executed. For the `if true then else` test, the core benchmark structure is

```
if true then
  add 1 to z
else
```

continued

```
    beep
  end if
```

and, conversely, the `if false then else` test consists of 166 instances of

```
  if false then
    beep
  else
    add 1 to z
  end if
```

The `if true` in-line test is 166 repeats of `if true then add 1 to z else beep`; its mirror image is the `if false` in-line test, which is just 166 repetitions of `if false then beep else add 1 to z`.

Results, Analysis, and Conclusions

The set of conditional structure benchmarks are variations on a single theme. What is the outcome? As shown in Figure 16-4, a surprise awaits script writers from a conventional interpreted computer language setting (such as most versions of BASIC). Counter-intuitively, *it is actually slower to write out a tight loop than it is to execute it using a* `repeat N times` *structure*. The penalty is only a few percent, but considering the inconvenience and illegibility of written out in-line style coding, there's no reason to resort to it when you want a fixed number of loop repetitions.

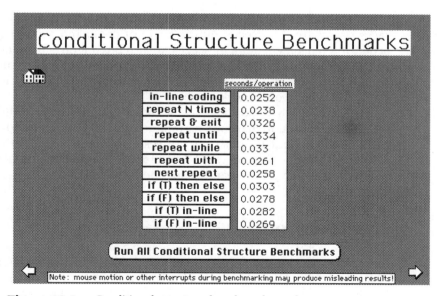

	seconds/operation
in-line coding	0.0252
repeat N times	0.0238
repeat & exit	0.0326
repeat until	0.0334
repeat while	0.033
repeat with	0.0261
next repeat	0.0258
if (T) then else	0.0303
if (F) then else	0.0278
if (T) in-line	0.0282
if (F) in-line	0.0269

Run All Conditional Structure Benchmarks

Note: mouse motion or other interrupts during benchmarking may produce misleading results!

Figure 16-4. Conditional structure benchmark results

On the other hand, *there is a small (less than 10 percent) but noticeable speed sacrifice when going from the straightforward* `repeat N times` *construction to an equivalent implementation using a* `repeat with` *syntax*. The `repeat with` is required when you need a counter inside the loop. But if you never use that counter, you can save a little time by not asking HyperTalk to provide it. *The other three major ways to control a loop,* `repeat until`, `repeat while`, *and* `repeat and exit`, *all take about 40 percent longer to do their job than the simplest* `repeat N times`. But they all are more flexible and are required when a loop has to be iterated for an unpredictable number of times.

Finally, looking at the simpler conditional structures, *there are no significant differences between if-then computational rates if the test returns true rather than false. There is a small speed enhancement, about 5 percent, when the if-then statement can be written in a single line rather than in a multiline indented form*. But the time gained by squeezing a complex statement into a single line is usually more than lost when the script has to be debugged or revised. Single-line `if-then` structures are only appropriate in handling very simple choices.

Handler Structure Benchmarks

HyperTalk's uniqueness as a programming language appears most prominently in the concept of message handlers. Handlers, as detailed in *The Waite Group's Hyper-Talk Bible*, are program entities that respond to specific kinds of messages. They are defined by scripts that begin with `on....` A handler can be located in almost any place in the HyperCard hierarchy: button (or field), card, background, stack, Home stack, or in the HyperCard program itself.

HyperTalk messages convey information between objects in HyperCard. Messages usually travel directly up the chain of command according to the standard order of inheritance, but a message can also be sent directly to an entity anywhere else in the hierarchy. Thus, a message can go sideways as well as vertically. Hyper-Talk's `send` command allows a programmer to control message routing and send a command wherever it needs to go.

A particularly important type of HyperTalk message handler is the programmer-defined function that returns a value to its caller; other handlers perform other sorts of actions but do not return a result. Functions are defined by HyperTalk scripts that begin with the word `function...` and include the word `return` somewhere in the body of the handler for the function.

Key Questions

In complex stacks and scripts, many vital performance questions have to be answered regarding handler placement. For maximum speed, where should a message handler be put in the hierarchy? Is there a difference between storing handlers at the button, card, background, or stack levels? Should messages be addressed to specific recipients or allowed to percolate by default up the chain of command? Does it matter where functions are defined and called? Our benchmarks can help answer such questions.

Handler Benchmarks

For uniformity as well as simplicity, we take again our standard operation of add 1 to z as a starting point. For the first benchmark button, named on . . . (button), the script is

```
-- on ... (button) benchmark
on buttonIncrementZ -- define a button-level handler
  global z
  add 1 to z
end buttonIncrementZ

on mouseUp
  global z, timing
  set the cursor to watch
  put 0 into z
  -- timing loop follows...
  put the ticks into startTicks
  repeat 166
    buttonIncrementZ
  end repeat
  put the ticks into endTicks
  put endTicks - startTicks into timing
  if z <> 166 then
    beep
    answer "Error in on ... (button) benchmark!" with "OK"
    exit mouseUp
  end if
  put timing / 10000 into line 1 of¬
  card field "timing results"
end mouseUp
```

This script has a new feature: a separate handler, buttonIncrementZ, adds 1 to the global z variable. Similarly, at the card, background, and stack levels of the HyperCard pyramid, the script defines the cardIncrementZ, backgroundIncrementZ, and stackIncrementZ handlers. They have identical definitions and only differ in their locations and names.

The scripts associated with the benchmarks on . . . (card), on . . . (background), and on . . . stack are thus identical to the script for on . . . (button), except they call handlers that won't be found until higher levels of the hierarchy. Thus, benchmark tests do not do send messages explicitly; they rely on the default inheritance of messages.

To test the ability of HyperTalk to send a message to a specific recipient, the scripts for send (button), send (card), send (background), and send (stack) take charge and direct their requests to the level containing the handler. For example, the script for the send (stack) benchmark is

```
-- send (stack) benchmark
on mouseUp
  global z, timing
  set the cursor to watch
```

continued

```
      put 0 into z
      -- timing loop follows...
      put the ticks into startTicks
      repeat 166
        send stackIncrementZ to this stack
      end repeat
      put the ticks into endTicks
      put endTicks - startTicks into timing
      if z <> 166 then
        beep
        answer "Error in send (stack) benchmark!" with "OK"
        exit mouseUp
      end if
      put timing / 10000 into line 8 of card field "timing
results"
end mouseUp
```

Finally, to test the capability of programmer defined HyperTalk functions to respond automatically to callers, we define function-type handlers at the button, card, and stack levels. Our functions are very simple; they each return a value one greater than the value that they were called with. For instance, the card-level function is simply:

```
function fcnCardIncrement n
  return 1 + n
end fcnCardIncrement
```

It is called by a script with the following core loop:

```
      repeat 166
        put fcnCardIncrement(z) into z
      end repeat
```

This script causes the fcnCardIncrement function to be called 166 times. Each time, the current value in the z container is passed to the function, and the function adds 1 to that value and returns the result. Like our previous benchmarks, this is another way to count up to 166, using a function call.

Analysis and Conclusions

What conclusions can we draw from the handler structure benchmarks? Figure 16-5 displays the numbers for a standard Macintosh Plus. First, and most unexpectedly, *it makes almost no difference at what level of the HyperCard hierarchy the on...* *message handler is located.* You can put the handler wherever it is most logical, with negligible performance penalty. If all other considerations are equal, a handler at the stack level may execute 1–2 percent faster—not an effect worth worrying about, in general, compared with other factors in script execution speed.

One might think that sending a message directly to a target would be faster and more efficient than simply letting it bubble up through the HyperCard system, getting rejected or passed along at every previous level. That natural expectation

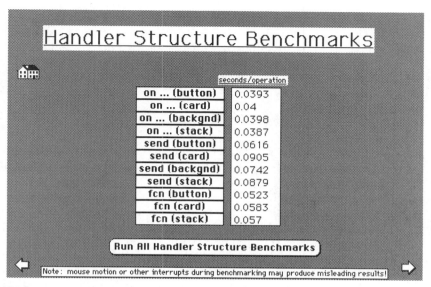

Figure 16-5. Handler structure benchmark results

would be wrong! *Sending a message to circumvent or override the default HyperCard order of inheritance is slow.* An explicit `send` to a card button takes 40-50 percent longer to execute than simply letting the button get the message automatically. Sending a personalized message to a chosen card, background, or stack is even slower—execution takes as much as 2.5 times longer than you might expect. Clearly, time-critical tasks should send a message only when there is some desperate need to override the normal inheritance order.

After being surprised by HyperTalk's message sending inefficiencies, it is a relief to benchmark function-definition handlers. *It tends to take a little longer to get an answer back from a function at a higher level of the hierarchy (such as the stack level) than it does at the button or card rank.* But the differences are not consistent and are at most one or two percent—as with on handlers, not worth losing sleep or programming time over.

Mode-Changing Benchmarks

HyperCard diverges from the standard Macintosh style of doing things in various ways. One of the ideals of the Mac micro-universe is "modelessness"—an ugly word for the concept that the user should be in charge, not the computer. A modal program, which you may have experienced in programs that run on many other computer systems, has a variety of internal states, such as typeover mode, insertion mode, page preview mode. To get from one place to another, you have to manually change modes. And because one mode may be entered from a previous mode, it can become quite daunting to maneuver through the invisible maze that such systems trap the user in.

It's a frustrating and archetypically un-Macish experience to be trapped in a mode that you don't want, especially if you're unable to get out without consulting the instruction book. (If you write a program that has modes, you also have to be prepared to be strung up by the Macintosh Thought Police, self-appointed Keepers of the One True Way.)

Modes in HyperCard

HyperCard has modes. But at least its modes are usually obvious to the user and are reflected by which tool is in use. You may be in a browsing mode with the pointing hand cursor, ready to push a control button or select text in a field. Or you may be in button or field editing mode or in a painting mode with one of the many picture-drawing tools. A single HyperCard object can have modes as well. A button can be visible or invisible, highlighted or unhighlighted, for instance. These are sometimes called properties, but the end result is that the button is in a mode.

In sophisticated HyperTalk scripting, it's occasionally necessary to change modes to get a job done. Unfortunately, in all early versions of HyperCard, mode changing from a script is one of the most time-consuming operations around. Internally, a lot of program code segments and data structures have to be activated or deactivated to turn a hypertext-browsing system into a bit map-painting system or a button or field toolkit. The sluggishness that is documented by our mode-changing benchmarks in this section is likely to be high on the list of things to improve in future editions of HyperCard. (Version 1.2.1 already shows significant improvement over its predecessors.)

Key Questions and Scripts

Meanwhile, how bad is the mode-switching problem? Our benchmarks for this set of tasks fall into two major categories: tool-choosing tasks (such as `choose brush tool`), and show/hide tasks (such as `hide card button 5`). In each case, we test the speed of these operations in two modes: with the screen display free to update itself (`lockScreen` set to false) so that you actually see all the changes and with the visible image frozen (`lockScreen` set to true) so that only the final result is displayed. Our first benchmark is simply a null test that involves repeatedly choosing the browse tool, which is already selected—a no-operation benchmark that provides something to compare the other results to. The scripts for the rest of the tests are exceedingly simple. For example, the benchmark for going into and out of painting (with the brush tool) mode is performed by

```
-- choose brush benchmark (default, with unlock screen)
on mouseUp
  global timing
  set the cursor to watch
  -- timing loop follows...
  put the ticks into startTicks
  repeat 16
```

continued

```
    choose brush tool
    choose browse tool
  end repeat
  put the ticks into endTicks
  put endTicks - startTicks into timing
  put timing / 1000 into line 4 of card field "timing results"
end mouseUp
```

Note that we only repeat the loop 16 times rather than 166 times (we then divide the timing in ticks by 1,000 instead of 10,000 to compute seconds/operation). Mode changing is so slow that you would have to wait for several minutes to do the standard number of cycles through the benchmark `repeat` loop.

For the show/hide benchmarks and for tests with `lockScreen` true, the hide field benchmark script is nicely representative:

```
-- hide field benchmark (with lock screen)
on mouseUp
  global timing
  set the cursor to watch
  lock screen
  -- timing loop follows...
  put the ticks into startTicks
  repeat 16
    hide card field 1
    show card field 1
  end repeat
  put the ticks into endTicks
  unlock screen
  put endTicks - startTicks into timing
  put timing / 1000 into line 11 of card field "timing results"
end mouseUp
```

Analysis and Conclusions

The main conclusions from benchmarking HyperCard mode changing are depressingly obvious (see Figure 16-6). Choosing a nonbrowsing tool of any type is a slow and painful operation; it takes over 1.5 seconds on a Macintosh Plus running HyperCard version 1.2.1 to go from browsing mode to painting mode and back again. Mode changing should be done from a HyperTalk script only after careful consideration, if at all. *Change modes as infrequently as possible, and do as much as you can in a given mode before going to another one.* Consider alternative ways to control the appearance of the screen (for instance, jump to a different card rather than draw something new on the current card). Or buy a faster processor.

Animation of very simple shapes can be done in a painting mode of HyperCard. You can draw simple objects, select them with the lasso or select tools, move them around, and so forth. But the speed and visual jerkiness of these effects, especially on machines such as the Mac Plus and Mac SE, makes complex animation difficult or impossible. If you can pre-compute the sequence of images that you want to display, a `show cards` kind of command can produce a flip-book style of animation that

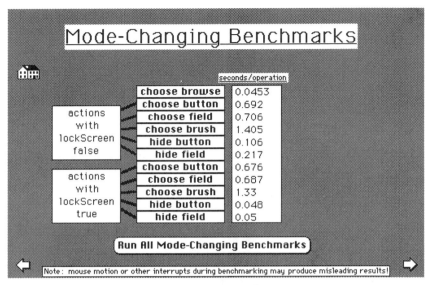

Figure 16-6. Mode changing benchmark results

works well for some purposes. But even that tends to be expensive in terms of disk storage space.

There is a single ray of hope in this gloomy vista. When the screen display is frozen by the HyperTalk statement `lock screen`, show/hide operations execute several times faster than they do with the screen unlocked. That's a major effect for a trivial price and worth keeping in mind when you have several buttons and fields that appear or vanish at one time.

Comment and White Space Benchmarks

Now we move into one of the most cosmetic of subjects— benchmarking features that make absolutely no difference to the execution of a script. Comments and white space are there solely for the developer of a program; they are ignored by the computer. In a compiled language, there would be no question of the irrelevance of comments, at least as far as their effect on execution time. (A heavily commented program might compile more slowly, but after it is translated into machine-executable code, the comments are gone, never to return.)

Key Questions and Scripts

In an interpreted language, such as HyperTalk, there is reason to be concerned about including comments and extra blank lines (white space) in a script. How much of a penalty does one have to pay to adequately comment code? Are short comments better than longer ones? Do extra empty lines take much time for the HyperTalk interpreter to skip over?

Benchmarking comments and white space can be done with scripts that are very similar to those we used to test conditional structures previously in this chapter. We take a standard operation, add 1 to z, and try various approaches to annotating or embellishing it. With no comments, it measures the raw execution time of the loop containing the single add 1 to z statement. A comment can be placed either above the statement (labeled *a* in Figure 16-7) or below that statement (labeled *b*) in the inner program loop. Multiple comments can be distributed in either place equally. For example, the four comments benchmark looks like the following

```
-- 4 comments benchmark
on mouseUp
  global z, timing
  set the cursor to watch
  put 0 into z
  --  timing loop follows...
  put the ticks into startTicks
  repeat 166 times
    -- let's add the number one to the value in variable z
    -- let's add the number one to the value in variable z
    add 1 to z
    -- let's add the number one to the value in variable z
    -- let's add the number one to the value in variable z
  end repeat
  put the ticks into endTicks
  put endTicks - startTicks into timing
  if z <> 166 then
    beep
    answer "Error in 4 comments benchmark!" with "OK"
    exit mouseUp
  end if
  put timing / 10000 into line 5 of card field "timing results"
end mouseUp
```

For 100 comments, just repeat the comment line 50 times above and below the only executable statement in the loop. To compare a short and a long comment, substitute -- ++z or -- let's go ahead and try to add the number one to the value in variable z for the default medium-length comment in one of the 1 comment benchmark loops. To benchmark the effect of white space, replace the comment lines with blank statements.

Analysis and Conclusions

The results of these tests? Somewhat surprisingly (and unlike in many interpreted versions of BASIC), *comments are almost "free" as far as HyperTalk speed is concerned.* Figure 16-7 shows results for a standard Mac Plus.) The comment lines beginning with -- are skipped so rapidly that in some benchmark runs their effect is impossible to measure. On the average, each line of comment adds 0.1 millisecond (100 microseconds) to execution time on a standard Mac Plus and roughly a quarter as much to timings on a Mac II. And if you really like to write essays in your scripts, things get better: 100 lines of commentary add less than 1 ms to the benchmark execution time. That's a few percent extra overhead, which is quite negligible compared to other effects such as mouse movement by the user or input-output delays depending on disk drive properties.

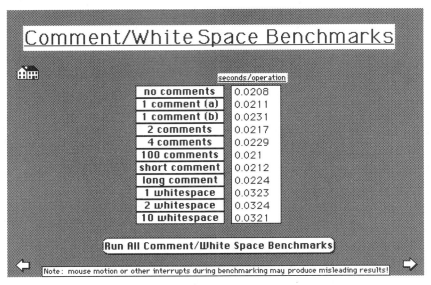

Figure 16-7.   Comment and white space benchmark results.

Adding blank lines within a critical inner loop is a different matter altogether. *Even a single blank line in a script can slow down execution speed by 30–40 percent.* Additional blanks don't make much difference. Why the current HyperTalk interpreter dislikes blank lines but is happy to skip over comments that begin with -- is a mystery. But *when execution time is critical, don't put in white space; use empty comments instead, if you must.*

Multiline and Recursive Benchmarks

When you write a complex formula in HyperTalk, you have to decide when to take a break and start a new line, just as when you write prose you have to choose when to end a sentence and start another, because it may be all very well to act literary and continue with a single sentence until the reader is gasping for breath (or crying for mercy), and it may be unaesthetic in scripting to define a temporary container to hold a partial result from a long equation when, with just a few more characters, the entire thing could have been computed in one fell swoop, but on the other hand— you get the idea: long HyperTalk lines are possible but hard to follow.

Short sentences are nice. So are short HyperTalk lines. But at what price? Break up a simple equation? Speed may suffer. So may readability. How about string operations? Costs versus benefits? Answer: benchmark. Evaluate the results. Don't go overboard. Be concise. Think.

Beyond questions of style in programming, there are always choices in designing and scripting algorithms. Sometimes a function can be written very simply and explicitly as a straightforward equation with no further function calls. For instance, the factorial function 10! is by definition $1*2*3*4*5*6*7*8*9*10$. Alternatively, you could write a program to compute N! by successively multiplying together the numbers 1 through N; this is an iterative or `repeat` loop approach. A third method would rely upon recognizing that N! is just (N-1)! *N, along with the definition 1! = 1. This is known as *recursion*—a function is defined in terms of simpler cases of itself, eventually "bottoming out" in a definition. All three approaches yield the same result mathematically, but in some cases one method is simpler to program or to understand.

Key Questions and Scripts

Does HyperTalk encourage or discourage any particular style of programming? We can benchmark both multiline and recursive programming styles quite simply, using extensions of some of our earlier benchmarks. Consider first the question of time costs associated with breaking up mathematical statements into multiple parts on separate lines. You might suspect that HyperTalk, as an interpreted language, would slow down on a many-line equation when it had to move more data around and fetch and store it repeatedly. We can begin to test this hypothesis with the following single-line arithmetic script:

```
-- 1 line math benchmark
on mouseUp
  global z, timing
  set the cursor to watch
  put 0 into z
  -- timing loop follows...
  put the ticks into startTicks
  repeat 166 times
    add (1 + 2 + 3 + 4) to z
  end repeat
  put the ticks into endTicks
  put endTicks - startTicks into timing
  if z <> 1660 then
    beep
    answer "Error in 1 line math benchmark!" with "OK"
    exit mouseUp
  end if
  put timing / 10000 into line 1 of card field "timing results"
end mouseUp
```

We can rewrite the core of this script equivalently as the following for a 2-line math benchmark:

```
repeat 166 times
  add (1 + 2) to z
  add (3 + 4) to z
end repeat
```

or as the following for a four-line math benchmark:

```
repeat 167 times
  add 1 to z
  add 2 to z
  add 3 to z
  add 4 to z
end repeat
```

Similarly, a string-oriented script with the following core HyperTalk statements makes our one-line string benchmark:

```
repeat 166 times
  put "abcdefgh" after z
end repeat
```

Obvious variations with the string broken into two or four lines make up other string benchmark routines.

Computing 10! can be done in several ways, as explained. The explicit in-line approach and the looping methods are simple, but to do it recursively takes a few moments of thought:

```
-- recursive 10! benchmark
function fact N
  if N = 1 then return N
  return fact(N-1)*N
end fact

on mouseUp
  global z, timing
  set the cursor to watch
  put 0 into z
  -- timing loop follows...
  put the ticks into startTicks
  repeat 16 times
    put fact(10) into z
  end repeat
  put the ticks into endTicks
  put endTicks - startTicks into timing
  if z <> 3628800 then
    beep
    answer "Error in recursive 10! benchmark!" with "OK"
    exit mouseUp
  end if
  put timing / 1000 into line 9 of card field "timing results"
end mouseUp
```

The Fibonacci numbers are defined recursively (or iteratively) as $F(0) = 0$, $F(1) = 1$, and $F(N) = F(N-1) + F(N-2)$. Thus, each Fibonacci number is the sum of the previous two numbers in the list: 0, 1, 1, 2, 3, 5, 8, 13, 21, 34, 55, and so on. Given the definition, you can easily write out looping formulae (iterative, moving from $F(0)$ and $F(1)$ upwards) and recursive (moving from $F(10)$ downwards) formulae for evaluating $F(10) = 55$. The Fibonacci scripts, in fact, look quite similar to the benchmark scripts for the 10! evaluation.

But unlike evaluating a factorial function, evaluating a Fibonacci number by recursion is a much tougher problem, in terms of computer work required, than doing it iteratively. Working backwards to evaluate F(10), we ask HyperTalk to give us F(9) + F(8); to compute F(9) it must calculate F(8) + F(7). Unless we work very hard to restructure our algorithm, you can see that F(8) will be derived twice during the computation of F(10). F(7) will have to be evaluated three times, F(6) will be computed five different times, and so forth, getting worse as it recurses down to F(1) and F(0). That's wasted effort, so you shouldn't be surprised that a recursive Fibonacci evaluation takes longer than an iterative one.

Analysis and Conclusions

What are the results of the multiline and recursive benchmarks? Alas for good programming style, *it tends to be bad to break complex operations into multiple lines of HyperTalk code.* In the benchmarks, splitting simple problems such as additions or string concatenations into two lines adds about 50 percent to the average execution time; splitting the same problems into four lines costs even more, up to 250 percent or more over the single-line implementation. Figure 16-8 shows these results on a standard Macintosh Plus, a worst case scenario. The problems are admittedly artificial and are much simpler than the usual equations or string manipulations that you would want to split. In real cases, the penalties for using a multiline style would probably be less.

Looping algorithms are slower than in-line implementations. The iterative 10! calculation took about five times longer than the single line implementation. Some of the slowness can be explained by the need to use a repeat with structure, with its own overhead, and some is due to the extra lines in the script that have to be interpreted as compared to the one line method. But clearly it is not advantageous to use a general algorithm to compute a single, easily specified value.

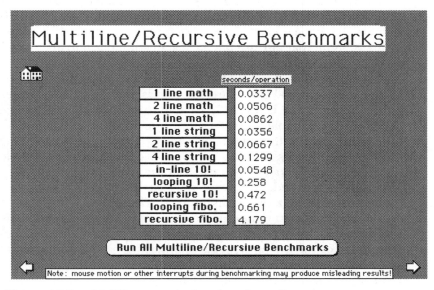

Figure 16-8. Multiline recursive benchmark results.

The recursive algorithms used to compute 10! and F(10) are slower than their looping counterparts, but not as slow as one might expect. HyperTalk seems relatively efficient in doing recursion—as long as you don't try too much recursion. (More than a few dozen levels of a function calling itself may create memory problems on many systems.) So, when an algorithm calls for it, recursive implementations aren't something to be feared—within limits.

Stack Compaction, Sorting, and Searching Benchmarks

Setting up to benchmark the HyperTalk `compact stack`, `sort`, and `find` commands is a difficult task. With a reasonably small HyperCard stack, the time required for each of these commands to execute is too short to measure reliably. Small stacks, a few tens of kilobytes long, also may give deceptively good performance because they fit entirely in the Macintosh's internal (RAM) memory. When such a stack grows just a little, or when available memory is tight, radically different timings result.

Even on a multimegabyte Macintosh system, HyperCard may be forced to go to the disk more often than you might expect. You may want to run HyperCard under MultiFinder, or with a beefed-up System file that occupies large amounts of memory, or with a large RAM cache enabled to compensate for a slow disk drive. How can you find a consistent, reproducible, widely available test stack that has half a megabyte (or more) of text and can be expanded if necessary to test larger memory systems?

The Benchmark Stack

The best solution is to use a large public-domain document and make stacks from that. We selected the King James Version of the Bible and created two HyperCard stacks from the first three books (Genesis, Exodus, and Leviticus): a stack with a single chapter per card, called Chapters, and a stack with a single verse per card, Verses. (Note that our use of Old Testament biblical material is not meant to imply religious belief or disbelief in this or any other theological system!) In our standard test configurations with a Macintosh Plus and Macintosh II, 1 MB of RAM, no RAM cache, and a typical (40 ms average access time) hard disk, any test stack of greater than about 200 kB is probably enough to exhaust internal free memory.

We used simple HyperTalk scripts to create the Chapter and Verse stacks. The raw input text of the stacks consisted of about 10,000 lines, or 100,000 words, or 530,000 characters. The stacks had a single background, with fields to hold the card number, the total number of cards in the stack, the name of the book from which the card originated, and the actual text (chapter or verse) itself. Table 16-1 gives some important size information for each stack:

The tabulated values for words per card and characters per card are for the average number of benchmark text words and characters, not including HyperCard overhead or the (small) contents of other fields besides the main one on each card. Note that one extra card is in each stack, the first card, which is a title introduction card; thus there are 117 chapters and 3605 verses in the benchmark text.

Table 16-1. **Biblical Stacks for Benchmarking Compaction, Sorting, and Searching**

	Chapters	Verses
stack size	0.56 MB	1.07 MB
number of cards	118	3606
average words per card	850	30
average characters per card	4,500	150

Results and Analysis for Compaction and Sorting

Compacting the benchmark Chapters stack took 50 seconds on a standard configuration Macintosh Plus; compacting the Verses stack required 530 seconds. *The approximate compaction time is a few tenths of a second per card, and the time required per card increases slowly as the number of cards grows.* Stack compaction times, more than any operation, are highly dependent on the specific characteristics of your disk drive. Even a compaction on the same drive might take more or less time, depending on the fragmentation of the files on the drive and the layout of the available sectors.

Because of its slowness and I/O dependence, stack compaction is something that you should think seriously about before starting on a multikilocard stack. It's necessary to compact a stack occasionally, in particular as it grows or is edited, or before attempting to search with the find command when speed is critical. But, compaction should never be attempted without warning (and getting permission from) the user.

Sorting the cards in the Chapters stack by the first word in the main field took about 30 seconds on the Macintosh Plus; the same sort on the Verses stack ran for 500 seconds before completion. The similarity between the times required to sort and compact stacks is probably not a coincidence. Compacting a stack involves reading in its cards and rewriting them to disk in an optimal order for speedy retrieval, much the same as sorting.

In general theoretical limits on sorting efficiency demand that a sort of N objects requires at least $K*N*log(N)$ operations, where K is some fixed value depending on the details of the sort. However, additional time may be required proportional to the number of objects, and it's not possible to accurately estimate the sorting time for very large stacks based on only the limited data that we have. (See chapter 17, "Large Stacks.") *We speculate that sorting a stack with N cards on our standard configuration Macintosh Plus should require approximately $0.03*N*log(N)$ seconds for very large N* (with the logarithm taken to base 10, a common logarithm). A Mac II will, as usual, perform roughly three to four times faster than a Mac Plus. Thus, a sort on a Macintosh Plus of a 10,000 card stack should take about 20 minutes, a 100,000 card stack about 4 hours, and a 1,000,000 card stack about 2 days! The same rough time estimates hold for compacting such a stack.

Results and Analysis for Searching

Searching a stack for a chosen string is, fortunately, a much faster operation than sorting or compacting—most of the time. On our standard system, HyperCard's find command typically took only one to three seconds to locate many words that occurred few or no times in the Chapters or Verses stacks— words such as *lament* and *diligently*. When a search is begun for a common word, the elapsed time to display the first hit is even less.

But in the worst cases, searches for unusual or bizarre strings took much longer. For example, see the wide variation among timings for the searches in Table 16-2; all searches used the standard find command, and none came up with any occurrences of the word being searched for. The tests used standard configuration Macintoshes and HyperCard version 1.2.1.

Table 16-2.   **HyperTalk Timings (in seconds)
for the *find* Command**

Word	Verses Stack		Chapters Stack	
	Mac Plus	*Mac II*	*Mac Plus*	*Mac II*
thex	30	13	3	2
xhet	2	1	9	4
mosesq	13	5	6	2
tx	255	92	16	7
thx	4	2	10	4
lm	270	92	16	5
lme	10	2	6	2

Unlike the regular find operation, the find word HyperTalk command always took less than 5 seconds (on a Mac Plus) to either locate or confirm the absence of a term in the benchmark stacks. But the find chars command performed as slowly as find for many rare strings (such as *lame* within the word *lament* or *ligent* within *diligently*), taking up to 145 seconds to answer a request.

What do these strange timings indicate about the HyperTalk find command and its variants? Clearly, for many searches HyperCard is not looking at every word on every card; information is associated with each card that tells the find command when the card can be skipped. That extra overhead for our Verses benchmark stack explains why the stack is 1.07 MB long rather than the 0.56 MB of the Chapters stack.

The extra storage space corresponds to about 150 bytes per card. It's enough room to store information about which three-letter character groups begin words that are in fields on that card. Other authors have called it "surrogate coding"—the extra space serves as a compressed surrogate or replacement for the actual words on a card, for purposes such as rapid searching. Until more information about HyperCard's file structure is made public, however, we cannot understand or explain the inner workings of the algorithm any further.

Whatever the details of find, it is clear that the search acceleration system does sometimes break down, especially when looking for rare sequences of letters or for characters embedded in a word (in the find chars variant). When the find command can't figure out how to skip over cards, it is reduced to sequentially scanning through the stack—a necessarily slow operation. What does this mean for practical problems? For small stacks that can fit into available memory, problems should be rare. The initial search for a term may take extra time (especially when working from a slow device such as a floppy disk), but thereafter searches will be very fast. But if you are working with a large stack (such as our benchmarks), if you need real-time responsiveness, or if a user has the freedom to search for an arbitrary string, be prepared for occasional slow (multiminute) delays.

The ultimate solution is to avoid using HyperTalk's find command entirely when you must have rapid, flexible responses to unpredictable requests for data from a large file. A sequential search is not the answer. The best alternative is an inverted index approach, where you invest time and storage space in building an ordered (for example, alphabetized) set of pointers to the words you need to find quickly.

Final Impressions

When we started this odyssey through HyperTalk benchmarks, we expected some surprises, and we got them. In many cases, HyperTalk performance diverges significantly from what we thought we would see based on other, more ordinary interpreted computer languages. The major results of our benchmarks are summarized at the beginning of this chapter and in Figure 16-9. But the final impression, after all the details, is amazement at the strengths of HyperTalk as a whole. Where it falls short of the ideal in speed, we can look forward to enhancements in future releases or in extensions by independent programmers. HyperTalk is a powerful yet simple language, capable of performing almost any programming task with elegance.

Summary of Benchmark Results

Summarize Results	Stadndard Mac Plus	Standard Mac SE	Accel'd. Mac SE with math.	Standard Mac II
Math Ops.	0.0126	0.0103	0.0027	0.0027
# Movement	0.0212	0.0162	0.0061	0.0057
Text Ops.	0.0275	0.0215	0.0078	0.0072
Conditionals	0.0285	0.0224	0.0088	0.0074
Handlers	0.0581	0.0455	0.0205	0.0148
Modes	0.542	0.4694	0.4819	0.1723
Comments	0.0246	0.0192	0.0076	0.0067
Recursion	0.548	0.445	0.2051	0.1523
Grand Total	1.2625	1.0494	0.7407	0.369

Figure 16-9. Summary of Benchmark Results.

Large Stacks

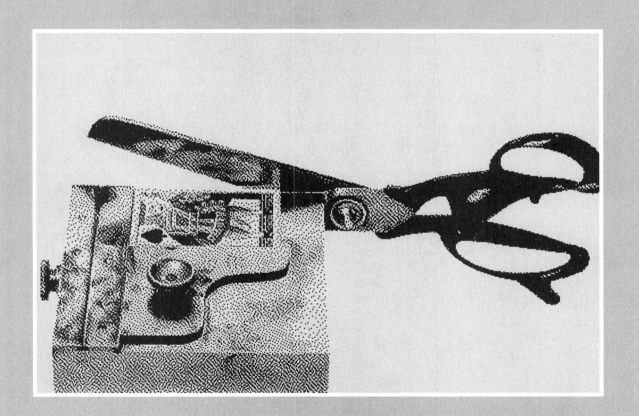

Steven F. Martin

Synopsis: The idea of using HyperCard as a simple database becomes less practical as the size of the database grows. A `go` or `find` command used on a stack that is 800K or less takes only seconds to search, but as soon as the data exceeds several megabytes, HyperCard shows significant degradations in search times. Although more RAM can improve these times, and a faster hard disk can certainly help, these are items that the stack developer can't control. There are, however, dozens of tricks you can employ to speed up large stacks and this chapter reveals them.

Here you will learn ways around the limitations of HyperCard. General tips, such as locking the screen, using the RAM cache, placement of scripts, and stack switching problems, are revealed. You'll learn how to manage large stacks on small floppy disks, the two techniques for splitting up stacks, and how to employ the powerful binary search technique. An insertionPoint function is given. Finally, information on extracting data from large stacks, with a complete script, and details on using virtual stacks (a stack spread out across several disks) are explained.

Large Stacks

Speeding Up Large Stacks

HyperCard is a wonderful tool for managing data. The user interface is easy to manipulate, so you can examine data in your own customized environment. Because HyperCard provides such a rich environment for collecting and browsing data, many people use it to manage varying amounts of information, from small collections of notes to very large databases of business names and accounts. Unfortunately, when stacks become too large, you often have to trade power and flexibility for efficiency and speed.

This chapter is concerned with what happens when so much data is collected in one stack that operations such as going to a different card cause appreciable delays. As stack sizes increase and exceed the size of available RAM, special attention is needed to select the most efficient scripts to achieve the best possible performance.

We will look at ways around the limitations of HyperCard when working with large stacks, the most efficient use of scripting to avoid unnecessary memory consumption, and tricks to make the most of your Macintosh's available RAM. You will also learn tricks that help you quickly move between different cards in large stacks and avoid waiting for time-consuming sorting and compacting operations.

What Is a Large Stack?

What each person calls a large stack depends on several factors. A stack should be considered large when operations such as go and find take more than 1 or 2 seconds. This slowdown becomes an issue with smaller stacks for someone with a Macintosh Plus, 1MB of RAM, and a floppy disk. It takes a larger stack for the slowdown to be apparent on a Macintosh II with 8MB of RAM and a hard disk.

Of all these factors, the access time of the disk you are using has the greatest effect on the performance of large stacks. Access time is how long it takes for the disk to move from one location to another. For many Macintosh hard disks, this access time is around 28 milliseconds; a floppy can have an access time of more than 100ms. A stack on a hard disk can be searched and manipulated much faster than one that is on a floppy disk. Because HyperCard automatically saves updates to disk, the speed of any modifications of the stack is impacted greatly by the disk access time. Searches (by find or go, for example) are also affected by disk speed, even though some searching information can be temporarily stored in RAM. This is why the amount of RAM in your Macintosh can be crucial. If there is not enough RAM for HyperCard to temporarily store searching information, performance will be adversely affected.

Due to the nature of HyperCard (RAM is consumed based on the number of objects used), it is difficult to know how many cards or what size stack will start to cause speed problems. A large stack may be comprised of mostly scripts and only few cards. A database stack may have no scripts but many cards, or it may have few cards and hundreds of fields. Performance is most often a problem when there are many cards. When there are so many cards that searching becomes slow, the scripting techniques in this chapter will help speed up many operations.

General Tips

This section provides general tips that will help you deal with large stacks. We look at how to set the Macintosh RAM cache, how much memory to give the HyperCard application when running under MultiFinder, and how to access card data quickly.

Memory—RAM Cache Versus HyperCard Size

When an application is run under the Finder, it uses all available memory. All Macintosh applications have a size property that controls how much memory is allocated for the application when it is launched under MultiFinder. The size property of an application can be modified by selecting it and choosing Get Info from the File menu or typing Command-I.

Setting the size of the RAM cache from the Control Panel is another way to affect memory allocation under MultiFinder or the Finder. The RAM cache is application independent and can speed up many applications by holding data in memory that would otherwise require disk accesses. When you have more than 750K available to run HyperCard, you have a choice about how you allocate that memory.

If you do a Get Info on the HyperCard application itself, you will see that it preselects a RAM size of at least 1000K. The documentation for HyperCard states that it will function properly with a RAM size of as little as 750K, but with some limitations (for example, paint tools won't be available). Performance can be greatly improved by increasing the size property for HyperCard to as large as possible. This allows the caching of search information and other data, reducing the amount of disk activity.

A large RAM cache would seem to be a good alternative to increasing the RAM size of the HyperCard application, but it actually is not. A large RAM cache slows down many HyperCard operations and cache can also adversely affect other applications (the Macintosh Programmers Workshop, for example, recommends a small RAM cache). Furthermore, it is cumbersome to change the RAM cache; you must reboot the machine for a change to take effect. It is usually best to run with a small (32K or 64K) RAM cache for all your applications. This way, you get the benefit with applications that take advantage of the RAM cache without seriously degrading the performance of applications that are encumbered by it.

When dealing with large stacks and using MultiFinder, allocate as much memory as possible to HyperCard by adjusting its size in the Get Info dialog. Remember that if you want to run other applications at the same time, you must leave enough RAM available for them also. Consider what other tools you may want to use with HyperCard and adjust the RAM size of HyperCard so that it is as large as possible while still leaving room for those other applications.

Locking the Screen

When you have to search through many cards or collect information from lots of different cards in a stack, access time is very important. One simple way to speed up these operations is to lock the screen when moving among a large number of cards. HyperTalk provides the lock screen command for this purpose. Every time you go to a card, all the card data must be updated on the screen. If this information is not currently in memory, it has to be retrieved from disk. By locking the screen, you prevent screen updates and increase the speed of your search.

For example, suppose you have an address stack that contains two background fields called state and area code that appear on every card. The following script searches the stack and returns a list of all area codes for a given state. The state that you want to find area codes for is passed as the only argument.

```
function CollectAreaCodes State--State is passed by the ¬
calling procedure
  find whole State in field "state"
  if the result is empty then
    put field "area code" into AreaCodes
    -- save the ID of the first card so that we know when
    -- we are finished.
    put the id of this card into FirstOne
    go next card
    repeat until the id of this card is FirstOne
      find State in field "state"
      put "," & field "area code" after AreaCodes
    end repeat
    return AreaCodes
  -- the state was not found, return an error message
  else return "Error--State" && State && "not found"
end CollectAreaCodes
```

As this function executes, the find command takes you to each card that State is on. HyperTalk has two commands, lock screen and unlock screen, that can help in this situation. The lock screen command freezes the display of the current card and does not update the screen until an unlock screen command is executed. With the lock screen and unlock screen commands, you can avoid the time it takes for the display of each card. You simply place lock screen at the front of your handler and unlock screen at the end.

Note that the lock and unlock commands are features of HyperCard version

1.2 or greater. They are shorthand for the commands that would be used to set the global `lockscreen` property. If you have an older version of HyperCard, substitute `set the lockscreen to true` for `lock screen` and substitute `set the lockscreen to false` for `unlock screen`.

Unlike setting the `lockscreen` property, however, the `lock` command is cumulative. If you use `lock screen` twice, you will need two `unlock screen` commands to unlock it. For this reason, take care to balance the use of `lock screen` and `unlock screen` commands. Because the `lock` command is cumulative, you should put an `unlock screen` before each `return` command when you modify the previous script to lock the screen.

Don't Go to a Card Unless You Have To

The script in the previous section uses the `find` command to quickly find all the cards containing a certain word. The `find` command, like `go`, takes you to a different card. If you are unable to use the `find` command (perhaps you need to test the sum of several numeric fields on a card) you will end up going to every card in the stack. This is unnecessary and time consuming. Even though the screen is locked, it takes more work to go to a card than to access selected data from it. This section shows you how to avoid going to cards for better performance.

Here is a simple script that totals the values of a numeric field on every card of a stack. It demonstrates an inefficient use of the `go` command.

```
-- inefficient use of go example
function Total fieldname
  put 0 into total
  lock screen
  repeat (the number of cards)
    go next card
    add field fieldname to total
  end repeat
  unlock screen
  return Total
end Total
```

A much faster way to do the same thing is to take advantage of a feature of the HyperTalk `field` command that allows you to bypass going to a different card. Instead of going to each card to get a value from a field, you can write `get field amount of card x`, which is much faster and does not cause any card movement. Here is a new version of the previous script that does not use the `go` command.

```
function Total fieldname
  put 0 into total
  repeat with x = 1 to the number of cards
    add field fieldname of card x to total
  end repeat
  return Total
end Total
```

There is no longer any need to lock the screen because this script always stays on the same card.

Sometimes, it is necessary to change cards (if you are using the find command you have no choice), but in general avoid going to different cards whenever possible. If you know the name, ID, or number of a card, use that to access the field directly. Going to each card and testing for some condition is the slowest technique.

Placing Scripts in Long Stacks for Optimal Performance

You are probably familiar with the hierarchy that HyperTalk uses to find a command or function. It looks first in the script of the object that references the command or function, then works its way back up, looking in the card, background, and stack scripts, and finally the Home stack script. You therefore have a choice to make about where to place a function or command. Scripts placed toward the bottom of the hierarchy (in buttons and fields, for example) are found first and therefore executed slightly (but not significantly) faster. On the other hand, if a function is placed in a card script, it may only be used from that card and not from other cards in the stack.

We'll sidetrack for a moment to build an example that shows one of the more complicated aspects of script placement.

To keep the structure of a stack simple, it helps to have only one background for the entire stack. If there is more than one background, you must be careful about how you search through the stack. When you write a script that collects data from a stack with one background, however, you often want to be able to present the result on a different background than that in the database stack.

To achieve both these goals, you have to create a second stack that displays the results of database searches in the desired fashion and provides buttons to perform different kinds of database searches. The scripts for these buttons switch stacks, collect data, return to the search stack, and present the data. Here is a simple script that does just that.

```
on MouseUp
  put 0 into total
  lock screen
  -- switch stacks to collect data
  go to "Database Stack"
  repeat with x = 1 to the number of cards
    -- UpperCase is a function that converts a string to uppercase
    put UpperCase(field "data" of card x) into item x of result
  end repeat
  -- back to the result stack
  go back
  put result into field "Result"
end MouseUp
```

The hierarchy that HyperTalk uses to find commands in fields, buttons, cards, and so on is well documented. When the script is in one stack and the current card is in another, however, it is not clear exactly where HyperTalk will look first for function and command handlers. In this example, you need to decide where to place the script for the UpperCase function. As it turns out, HyperTalk looks first in the stack where the currently executing script resides, then at the current card, if that card is in a different stack. Figure 17-1 shows the hierarchy HyperTalk uses when searching for commands and functions in scripts.

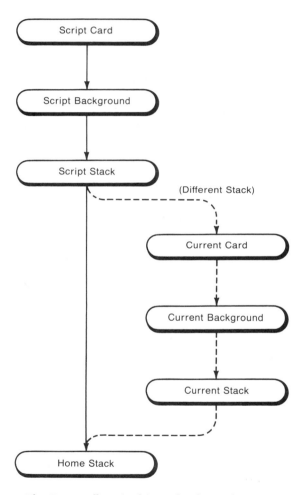

Figure 17-1.   The HyperTalk script hierarchy shows the script and current card in different stacks.

For the best speed, then, keep functions needed by a script in the same stack as the script that uses them. This is also better from a programming point of view, because it is easier to keep track of the location of scripts for functions if they are kept in the stack they are called from.

The Stack Switching Problem

Although the previous UpperCase example is simple, often you will want to perform more complicated operations inside a repeat loop. Surprisingly, such actions will cause HyperCard to perform what we will call "stack switching": HyperCard's title bar (which identifies the filename of the current stack) jumps back and forth between the two stacks (unless you lock the screen). This stack switching slows things down and can be avoided with proper script placement. Stack switching occurs when HyperTalk has to access the calling script's stack temporarily, even though your script is running over a second stack, as shown in Figure 17-2.

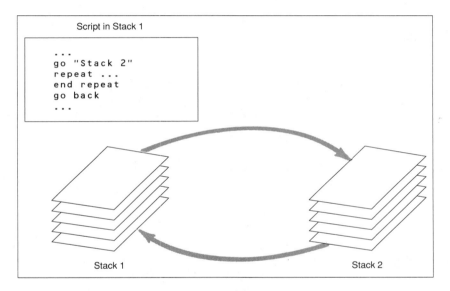

```
          Script in Stack 1

    . . .
    go "Stack 2"
    repeat ...
    end repeat
    go back
    . . .
```

Stack 1   Stack 2

Figure 17-2.   Stack switching can slow down stack performance.

A trick to avoid stack switching uses the HyperTalk **send** command. If you place all the scripts needed to perform your search in the database stack's stack script, you can send the stack a message to perform the search. HyperCard will not have to refer to the original stack in order to fetch the next HyperTalk statement and therefore will not switch back and forth. Here is how the previous UpperCase example would have to be restructured to use the **send** command.

```
-- database stack script
on UpperCaseData--located in the database stack script
  put empty into the result
  repeat with x = 1 to the number of cards
    put UpperCase(field "data" of card x) into item x of ReturnValue
  end repeat
  return returnValue
end UpperCaseData
```

continued

```
-- search button script
on MouseUp--located in another stack in a button script
  send UpperCaseData to "Database Stack"
  put the result into field "Result"
end MouseUp
```

Note that you can use the send command like a function call. The only difference is that the result returned is accessed by the HyperTalk statement the result
immediately following the send. Using send may seem somewhat inconvenient, but it
is often worth the effort in order to avoid stack switching.

Managing Stacks on Floppy Disks

Unless you have a hard disk, you are limited with regard to the size of stack you may
use. A two-sided floppy disk can hold about 779K. Unfortunately, this does not mean
that you can use a stack that large if you have a floppy disk drive. This section tells
you what the size limitations are and how to work within them.

An 800K Disk, a 400K Stack

There are many reasons why you occasionally will want to compact your stacks.
Because the size of a stack grows gradually as the stack is manipulated by the user,
you will certainly want to compact stacks that are modified every once in a while.
Also, version 1.2 of HyperCard suggests that you compact your stacks (actually it
says to compact them twice) to take advantage of some of its performance improvements. Because later versions may also require you to compact your stacks, it is a
good idea to have the capability to do so. Unfortunately, HyperCard needs enough
disk space to make a copy of a stack in order to compact it. To compact a 100K stack
requires about 100K of additional free space on the same disk as the stack. This
means the largest stack that can be compacted on an 800K floppy disk is about 390K
after you take into account the space allocated for the invisible desktop file.

This does not mean that you cannot use larger stacks if you have only a floppy
disk. Some stacks that you never modify can fill the entire disk without causing
problems. Other stacks grow relatively slowly when simple modifications are performed. But even if you do not add new cards or buttons, editing scripts and changing the values in fields can cause HyperCard to allocate more memory for the stack.
If your stack accidentally becomes too large, you can ask a friend with a hard disk to
compact your stack. The next section shows you a way to avoid getting into that
situation.

Automatic Compaction for Floppy Disk Systems

After a stack becomes more than half the size that your floppy disk has available,
you cannot compact it. It is therefore very important to monitor stack size and

compact a stack when it starts to approach this limit. Although you could do this manually, it is much more convenient to have the stack monitor its own size and let you know when it needs to be compacted.

The following script allows you to use a large stack without constantly worrying that it will become too large to compact. The idea is to monitor the size of the stack and the amount of free space on the disk and automatically compact the stack when things are getting tight.

```
-- We need to initialize the CheckSize variable when the
-- stack is opened.
-- CheckSize is true unless the user has declined compaction
-- during this session.
on OpenStack
  global CheckSize
  put true into CheckSize
end OpenStack

-- If only field values are modified, this script could be
-- placed in an "on CloseField"
-- handler to prevent constant checking
on Idle
  global CheckSize
  -- If the user has not declined compaction, check to
  -- see if it is necessary
  if CheckSize then
    put the size of this stack into StackSize
    put the DiskSpace - Stacksize into FreeOnDisk
    -- If the stack is 90% of the amount of free space (and there
    -- is still room), compact it
    if StackSize > .9 * FreeOnDisk and StackSize < FreeOnDisk then
      answer "Stack is near size limit. Compact it?" with ¬
      "Cancel" or "OK"
    end if
    if it is "OK" then DoMenu "Compact Stack"
    -- If the user does not want the stack compacted, stop checking
    -- its size.
    else put false into CheckSize
  end if
end Idle
```

This method is not foolproof. A script could create several new cards or add a great deal of new data to a stack that make the stack grow too large before the idle handler can check the size. When this happens, you have to split your stack into two smaller ones and keep them on different disks.

Splitting and Combining Stacks

Sometimes, you want to split a large stack or join several small stacks together. For example, you may have a large stack on your Macintosh II at work and then want to take part of it home for perusal. Although HyperTalk does not provide any simple way to do this, with a little bit of scripting and some scripts provided with Hyper-

Card, these operations can be performed relatively quickly. This section describes several ways of dealing with splitting and merging stacks.

Suppose, for example, you need some way to deliver a 2MB stack. Because 1MB will not fit on a floppy disk, the most obvious solution for copying a large stack like this from one machine to another is to use a backup application such as HDBackup, which comes with the Macintosh system software, or one of several commercial products (such as FastBack, Redux, or DiskFit). These applications split large files onto several floppies and restore them by putting the pieces back together.

Splitting a Stack by Card Copying

For our example, we will create a subset of a large stack by looping through all the cards in our stack and creating a new stack that consists of all cards that satisfy a fictional predicate called "CardMeetsCriteria". You could use this to split a stack into several pieces by rewriting CardMeetsCriteria each time to select a different group of cards.

```
on CopyCards
  domenu "New Stack"
  ask "What is the name of the new stack that you just created?"
  put it into NewStack
  repeat with x = 1 to the number of cards
    if CardMeetsCriteria(x) then
      go card x
      DoMenu "Copy Card"
      push card
      go last card of NewStack
      DoMenu "Paste Card"
      pop card
    end if
  end repeat
  go first card of NewStack
  domenu "Delete Card"
end CopyCards
```

This copying approach has a hidden problem. Backgrounds in the new stack that had the same ID in the original stack will not always share IDs in the new stack. So if the script is used on a stack with only one background, the new stack will have several backgrounds. This means that if you modify the background of a card in the new stack, those changes are not reflected everywhere you would expect. This is unacceptable and will have to be worked around. This method is also quite slow because there is a lot of overhead in switching from one stack to the other and creating new cards.

Another method would be to go through every field on every card and copy it to the other stack. This requires so much stack switching that it is much too slow except for the smallest of stacks. It may be acceptable if you want to copy just one card from one stack to another stack with the same background.

Avoiding the Card Copying Problem

The biggest problem in copying data from one stack to another is that you have to keep going back and forth, getting the data from one stack and putting it into the other one. The next two methods for splitting a stack or creating a subset of a stack avoid this problem.

Using the Delete Card Command

The first method uses the HyperCard menu command Delete Card. It is quite straightforward. Imagine that you have a name and address stack that you want to split, putting all cards in which the names begin with A–L in one stack and all cards beginning with M–Z in another. First, assuming you have a hard disk, make a copy of the stack you want to split (either from the Finder or by using the Save Copy command from the File menu). Now you can use a script that goes through the cards in the new stack and deletes the cards in which the name starts with M–Z. Here is an example of such a script:

```
on DeleteCards
   lock screen
   repeat with x = the number of cards down to 1
     if field "Name" of card x >= "M" then
       go card x
       DoMenu "Delete Card"
     end if
   end repeat
   unlock screen
end DeleteCards
```

You can go to the new stack and type DeleteCards into the Message box. The resulting stack contains all cards whose name field starts with A–L. A variation of the DeleteCards script would be used to remove all the A–L cards from the second stack.

Notice that for speed this script locks the screen and does not go to every card that it tests. Be sure to compact this stack when you are done because the space taken up by the stack is reclaimed not as the cards are deleted but only when the stack is compacted.

The key to the efficiency of this method is that the two operations it employs are quite fast. Copying a stack is fast whether you use the Save a Copy command from HyperCard or use the Finder (although Save a Copy is faster). The Delete Card operation is much faster than the New Card operation because HyperCard does not have to allocate more memory for the stack as it does when a new card is created.

Using Export and Import Scripts

The second method uses the Export and Import scripts provided with HyperCard version 1.2 or greater. Switching between the two stacks is avoided by first writing the data out to a file using a modified Export script, then reading it back in to a different stack using the Import script. It is best to test the cards for inclusion in the new stack at Export time, because it is easier to look at field values than to test the data as it is read in from the disk. Also, the size of the data file will be smaller because you won't be writing out the entire contents of the original stack.

Here is the GetFieldData handler from the original Apple Export Button script, which we have modified to allow for the selective exportation of cards.

```
on GetFieldData
  global FIELDNAMES,CONTENTS,FILENAME
  set cursor to watch
  put empty into CONTENTS
  if FIELDNAMES is empty then CleanExit
  put id of this background into backtemp
  lock screen
  go first card of this background
  put id of this card into cardtemp
  repeat
    if id of this background is backtemp ¬
    and CardMeetsCriteria(the number of this card) then
      repeat with count = 1 to the number of lines in FIELDNAMES
        do "put" && line count of FIELDNAMES && "& return ¬
        after CONTENTS"
    if number of chars in CONTENTS > 50000 then
        write CONTENTS to file FILENAME
        put empty into CONTENTS
    end if
      end repeat
      go next card of this background
    end if
    if id of this card is cardtemp then exit repeat
  end repeat
  write CONTENTS to file FILENAME
  unlock screen
end GetFieldData
```

The only difference is that instead of exporting data from every card, you are just exporting cards from the subset that you want to be in your new smaller stack. Now you can create a new stack using the same background as your original stack and use the Import button to get the exported data.

The three methods have their own advantages and disadvantages in different situations. If you want to modify the data as you transfer it, you may be better off with the export/import method. If you are just copying a few cards, you may want to copy the data field by field. Of the three methods, the Delete Card method is the fastest and simplest in most cases.

Finding a Card in a Large Stack

One of the problems with a very large HyperCard stack is finding a particular card quickly. HyperCard provides many different methods for doing this. The find command is very fast at searching for an occurrence of a word or phrase anywhere in a stack. The go command is also very flexible and usually quite fast. When stacks become full of cards and other objects, the access times for these commands can start to slow down, depending on how they are used. This is especially true of the go command.

There are three ways to use the `go` command to randomly access a card in a stack. You can go to a card based on its number, its card ID, or its name. Using the card number is the fastest way to go to a card, giving the card ID is next, and using the name is the slowest. Unfortunately, it is not as easy for a user to manipulate card numbers and IDs as it is to manipulate card names. Because the ID is a unique number, it is good for buttons that act as links, but you certainly would not want to present the user with a list of IDs from which to choose. In addition, the number of a card can change if cards are inserted or deleted before the card.

In a HyperCard application such as a database, usually a key field uniquely identifies the card. This would be the title for a database of movies or books or the name for an address stack. It would seem natural to use the value of the key field as the name of each card so that you can simply use the HyperTalk `go` command to go to a particular card based on the value of that key field, for example, `go "Casa-blanca"`. When stacks are small, this method works quite well. Unfortunately, with stacks that are much larger than available RAM, the `go` command can become quite slow when used this way.

Another problem with using the `go ⟨name⟩` command is that you are limited to 31-character names. Strangely, HyperCard allows you to set the name of a card to a longer string but when you use the `go` command with the card's full name, Hyper-Card complains that it cannot find a card with that name.

Also, by setting the name of each card to the value of one of its fields, you increase the size of the stack because of redundant information. In the movie database example, the title is stored twice for each card. It is in the title field and is also the name of the card. This is not desirable in stacks that are already so large that they are causing performance problems.

Another alternative is to use the `find` command to search for the key value in the key field. By using the `find whole` command (version 1.2 or greater), only correct values are found in most cases (although *word1 word2* would be found within *word1 word2 word3*). Although fast, the `find` command is usually much slower than the `go` command when used to locate one particular card and so is still not acceptable.

A much better way to find a card in a very large stack is to use a binary search. A binary search is one in which a divide-by-two algorithm helps speed the search. If you sort the stack on some field, you can use this efficient search method to quickly find any card. Furthermore, if you use this same method to find the appropriate location to insert each new card, you can keep the stack sorted without time-consuming sort operations.

What the Binary Search Does

The BinarySearch script implements a binary search on a sorted stack to vastly improve search time for large stacks. A binary search works by dividing the search space in half repeatedly until the desired value is found. This search is quite efficient in terms of speed: $O(\log_2 n)$, where *n* is the number of cards in the search space. Because the search time varies logarithmically with the number of cards, for 10 cards it may take $\log_2 10$ or about 3 seconds, and for 100 cards it is about 6 seconds. Access time doubles only when the number of cards goes up by 10 times.

How It Works

When you tell HyperCard to go card <cardname>, it appears to perform a linear search from the beginning to the end of the stack, looking for a card with that name. This search is quite fast if all card names are in RAM, but when disk accesses are required because RAM is not sufficient to store the names of all the cards, the linear search slows down substantially. With the linear search method, when the stack is twice as big, it takes twice as long to find a card near the end of the stack. The speed of this search is O(n).

The binary search works by dividing the stack in half over and over until the card is found. It does, however, require that the stack is sorted on the field whose value you use to find the card.

Let's work through an example. Suppose you want to find the movie *Star Wars* in your movie stack of cards. If your stack has 5,000 cards and Star Wars is the 4,700th, the go command has to look through the names of 4,700 cards. The binary search instead starts by looking at the 2,500th card. Let's suppose that it contains the movie *Dog Day Afternoon*. You know that *Star Wars* is later in the stack than that, so you can eliminate 2,500 cards from the search by looking at just 1. This process can be repeated by dividing the remaining search space until we narrow in on *Star Wars*. With 5,000 cards, the most accesses that could be required is 12. With 15 accesses, you can locate 1 card in a stack of up to 32,768 cards! So even though your script is written in HyperTalk and doesn't use the compiled go command, you can get much better performance because you don't look at nearly as much data.

Here is the script that returns the number of the card you are looking for, given the field to perform the search on (title in the movie example) and the key value for that field (such as Star Wars). The stack must be sorted on the field specified by FieldName. Field FieldName must be on every card in the stack.

```
-- ************************ DESCRIPTION **************************
-- TYPE:        Searching stack
-- AUTHOR:      Steve Martin
-- NAME:        BinarySearch
-- LOCATIONS:   Put the script in the stack or background (if there is
                only one background) script.
-- ************************ SCRIPT STARTS ************************
-- pass name of bkgnd field the stack is sorted on and the value to be
-- searched for in this field
function BinarySearch FieldName, Value
  -- initialize the start and finish variables
  put 0 into start
  put the number of cards into finish
  -- the main loop, we are done when start = finish - 1
  repeat until start = finish - 1
    -- get the midway point between start and finish
    put trunc((finish - start)/2+start) into n
    put background field FieldName of card n into CardNValue
    -- if we hit the card, return its number
    if Value = CardNValue then return n
    -- the card is later in the stack; move start to the midpoint
    if Value > CardNValue then put n into start
    -- the card is earlier in the stack; move finish to the midpoint
```

continued

```
      else put n into finish
    end repeat --the loop is finished; either card finish contains the ¬
    result
or
    -- we didn't find it
    if Value = background field FieldName of card finish then
      return finish
    else return "not found"
end BinarySearch
```

Timing Comparisons

Table 17-1 compares the average amount of time required to go to a card using the BinarySearch function versus using the standard method of just going to the name of the card. The values for this table were computed using a 3.2MB stack on a Macintosh II with 2MB of RAM and a Rodime hard disk with a 28ms access time. The RAM cache was set to 32K. HyperCard was run under MultiFinder with its Get Info RAM size set to 1000K. A random list of card names was generated. For each timing, HyperCard was restarted so that no cached data would influence the timings. The test function then looped a number of times, checking the time only before and after each card change. All times are in ticks.

Table 17-1.   BinarySearch Versus *go*

	BinarySearch			Card Name		
Number of Cards	*Average*	*Minimum*	*Maximum*	*Average*	*Minimum*	*Maximum*
5	107	82	131	427	60	796
50	98	73	137	507	41	1877
100	103	61	152	484	31	484

You can see from Table 17-1 that on average the BinarySearch is about four times as fast as using card names. In some cases going by card name is faster, but the range of times is much wider. Under some circumstances you may have to wait up to 30 seconds. The BinarySearch method is much more consistent, never taking more than 3 seconds (or 180 ticks).

In Table 17-2, the same tests were done, but this time HyperCard was run under the Finder instead of MultiFinder so that it would use as much memory as possible on a 2MB machine. You can see from Table 17-2 that both methods benefit from the availability of more memory. With almost 2MB to work with, the BinarySearch method is only about twice as fast as the card name method for a stack of this size.

Table 17-3 was computed the same way as Table 17-1, except that this time the screen was locked. Although this does not reflect the interactive use of Bi-

Table 17-2. BinarySearch Versus *go* with Finder

Number of Cards	BinarySearch			Card Name		
	Average	*Minimum*	*Maximum*	*Average*	*Minimum*	*Maximum*
5	106	76	127	280	55	633
50	83	60	127	152	19	1332
100	79	47	126	125	21	1182

narySearch, it better illustrates the time taken by the search without the card display. Table 17-3 shows that the card name method can be almost instantaneous (9 ticks is less than 1/6th of a second.) Still, the BinarySearch method performs best on average; this timing demonstrates that it is about five times as fast when you only compare search times.

Table 17-3. BinarySearch Versus *go* Under MultiFinder with Locked Screen

Number of Cards	BinarySearch			Card Name		
	Average	*Minimum*	*Maximum*	*Average*	*Minimum*	*Maximum*
5	100	72	120	432	41	682
50	80	49	117	466	9	1862
100	81	42	122	449	24	2139

Table 17-4 compares the speeds under Finder with the screen locked. Once again you can see that the card name method starts to catch up as more memory is available, but on average, it is about half as fast.

Table 17-4. BinarySearch Versus *go* Under Finder with Locked Screen

Number of Cards	BinarySearch			Card Name		
	Average	*Minimum*	*Maximum*	*Average*	*Minimum*	*Maximum*
5	94	68	118	244	42	506
50	73	49	115	139	7	1057
100	66	29	113	110	8	1230

These tables demonstrate that the BinarySearch method is the best choice when dealing with large stacks. With smaller stacks, the overhead associated with the BinarySearch method (it is written in HyperTalk which is evaluated, not compiled) makes it slower than go, but when go becomes noticeably slow, BinarySearch provides a consistent improvement.

Table 17-5 is the same as Table 17-4, except the stack is smaller. This version of the test stack has only 1,500 cards and is about 1.1MB. Table 17-5 demonstrates that when the stack is smaller, the card name method is faster, especially when used repeatedly. The key factor is that there is enough RAM for HyperCard to store most of the stack data off the disk. You can see that the maximum search time for the card name method has gone way down. There was much less disk activity because most of the data was eventually pulled into RAM.

Table 17-5. **Smaller Stack BinarySearch Versus *go* Under Finder with Locked Screen**

	BinarySearch			Card Name		
Number of Cards	*Average*	*Minimum*	*Maximum*	*Average*	*Minimum*	*Maximum*
5	61	45	77	66	56	80
50	48	20	77	47	7	174
100	47	20	77	45	6	176

Sorting—The InsertionPoint Function

You now have a quick way to find any card in a large stack as long as the stack is sorted. However, this method is useless if you add new cards without maintaining order on the stack. HyperCard has a built-in sorting command called (believe it or not) sort. For small stacks it may be Okay to sort the stack every time you add a new card, but with large stacks, sorting the stack frequently takes too much time. This section shows how you can keep the stack sorted without having to sort the stack every time you add new cards.

The next script we will look at is a modification of the BinarySearch function that allows you to maintain the stack without having to sort it. The concept is simple: use a binary search to find the appropriate location for each new card before it is created with New Card. Here is the new function that returns the number of the card you should go to before performing the New Card operation.

```
--   *********************** DESCRIPTION ***************************
-- TYPE:      Finding location for new card in a stack
-- AUTHOR:    Steve Martin
-- NAME:      NewCardLocation
-- LOCATIONS: Put the script in the stack or background (if there
--            is only one background) script.
```

continued

```
-- *********************** SCRIPT STARTS ***********************
function NewCardLocation FieldName, Value
  -- initialize the start and finish variables
  put 0 into start
  put the number of cards into finish
  -- the main loop, we are done when start = finish - 1
  repeat until start = finish - 1
    -- get the midway point between start and finish
    put trunc((finish - start)/2+start) into n
    put background field FieldName of card n into CardNValue
    -- if we hit the card, return its number
    if Value = CardNValue then return "exists"
    -- the card is later in the stack, move start to the midpoint
    if Value > CardNValue then put n into start
    -- the card is earlier in the stack, move finish to the midpoint
    else put n into finish
 end repeat --the loop is finished, either card finish contains the ¬
 -- result
or
  -- we didn't find it
  if Value = background field FieldName of card finish then¬
    return "exists"
  else return start
end NewCardLocation
```

This script can be supplemented with the following script, which asks the user for the key value for a card and inserts it at the correct location when New Card is selected from the File menu:

```
on newcard
  -- the InNewCardScript variable prevents recurison when the
  -- new card is actually created
  lock screen
  -- get the value of the key field
  ask "Key value of card to insert:"
  put it into key
  -- go to the location where the new card belongs
  go to card NewCardLocation ("Key Field",key)
  send newcard to Hypercard
  put key into field "Key Field"
  unlock screen
end newcard
```

With this message handler in the background script, cards are automatically inserted in the proper order. You will never have to sort the stack because the cards will be in order from the start. Because the scripts will not function properly if the value of the Key Field is later changed, you need to deal with that possibility. You could simply set the locktext property of the field so that it cannot be modified by typing. You could also write a closeField handler that would cut the card and paste it into its new position.

Extracting Data from a Large Stack

After you have a large stack, you undoubtedly will want to search it for a specific phrase or string. This section looks at how to use the HyperTalk find command to search a stack for all the cards that contain a string.

The Cross-Reference Script Example

This section presents an example that demonstrates many of the scripting techniques discussed in this chapter to search a stack and collect information about it. The motivation for this script was a database of motion picture cast and credit information. Each card contains a field for the movie's cast, director, writer, and so on. The stack is sorted by the title field and at publishing time contained 5300 movies and used about 3.5Mb of disk space. Variations on these scripts are used to quickly find all the credits for a given actor, director, and so on.

The setup consists of two stacks. One contains cards for all the movies, and one is an index containing one card for each person mentioned in the movie stack, listing their movies. Because the complete index stack would be too large (and take forever to generate), the index cards are created on demand and therefore must be generated as quickly as possible.

The Problems

The problems are how to quickly retrieve all the credits for any person and how to find any movie quickly. The stack to be searched is quite large, and the goal is to provide an interactive (that is, fast) interface to the data. Originally, the name of each card was the title of the movie that it contained. As the stack grew, it became apparent that a faster method would be necessary to find a movie. Also, the method of going to a card based on its name did not work for movie titles that were longer than 31 characters.

What It Does

This set of scripts provides two major functions. First, the custom goto command allows a user to find a movie or person quickly by typing a command into the Message box. For example, in the movie stack you would simply type goto "Casablanca" to see the credits for that movie. Similarly, in the credit stack you would type goto "Alfred Hitchcock" to see all of his credits.

How It Works

These scripts use the BinarySearch script and the locking and unlocking techniques to find cards and quickly retrieve data from the movie stack. The following scripts are located in the Movie Stack script:

```
-- This is the script that you use to interactively find a movie by
-- typing a command such as: goto "Casablanca"
on goto movie
  go card BinarySearch("title",movie)
end goto
-- The GetArray script searches the entire movie stack, collecting movie
-- titles into an array that tells where the person was found.
on GetArray
  -- Searchname is the name of the person to be searched for
  -- ReturnArray is the global array that will contain the result
  -- of the search
  -- Found is a flag that tells whether or not the person was found
  global SearchName,ReturnArray,Found
  find whole SearchName
  if the result is not empty then
    put empty into ReturnArray
    put false into Found
    exit getarray
  end if
  put the FoundChunk into FChunk
  put the FoundField into FField
  put field "title" & FChunk into FirstOne
  repeat forever
    set the cursor to busy
    if IsGoodFind(FChunk) then
      put true into found
      put word 3 of FField into FieldNumber
      put field "title" into movie
      get line x of ReturnArray
      if it is empty then put movie into line FieldNumber of¬
      ReturnArray
      else
          get posofinsert(movie,it)
          if item 1 of it is "at" then
            if item 2 of it is 1 then put movie into item (item2 ¬
            of it) of line fieldnumber of ReturnArray
            else put " " & movie into item (item 2 of it) ¬
            of line fieldnumber of ReturnArray
          else
            if it is 1 then put movie & ", " before line fieldnumber ¬
            of ReturnArray
            else put " " & movie & "," before item it of line ¬
            fieldnumber of ReturnArray
          end if
      end if
    end if
    find whole SearchName
    put the foundchunk into FChunk
    put the foundfield into FField
    if field "title" & FChunk is firstone then exit repeat
  end repeat
  pop card
end getarray
```

continued

```
function BinarySearch FieldName, Value
  put 0 into start
  put the number of cards into finish
  repeat until start = finish - 1
    put trunc((finish - start)/2+start) into n
    put background field FieldName of card n into CardNValue
    if Value = CardNValue then return n
    if Value > CardNValue then put n into start
    else put n into finish
  end repeat
  if Value = background field FieldName of card finish then
    return finish
  else return start
end BinarySearch


-- The IsGoodFind script determines if the foundchunk
-- constitutes an entire item. This prevents finding "Harry Carey"
-- inside the item "Harry Carey Jr."

function IsGoodFind FChunk
  -- FChunk is of the form "char x to y of background/card field z"
  -- word 6 to 8 of FChunk describes the field it was found in
  put the value of word 6 to 8 of FChunk into FField
  put word 2 of FChunk into StartChar
  put word 4 of FChunk into EndChar
  if (StartChar is 1) or¬
  (char max(StartChar-2,0) to StartChar-1 of FField) is ", " then
    if (the length of FField) is endchar then return true
    if char endchar + 1 of FField is "," then return true
  end if
  return false
end IsGoodFind


function posofinsert Movie, List
  put the number of items of List into NumOfItems
  repeat with Item = 1 to NumOfItems
    put stripspace(item x of list) into TitleOfItem
    if Movie = TitleOfItem then return "at," & Item
    if Movie < TitleOfItem then return Item
  end if
  end repeat
  return "at," & noi+1
end posofinsert


function stripspace string
  repeat while char 1 of string is " "
    delete first character of string
  end repeat
  repeat while last char of string is " "
    delete last character of string
  end repeat
  return string
end stripspace
```

The following scripts are in the Cross Index Stack script

```
on goto name
  go card BinarySearch("Name",name)
end goto

function nameinsertionpoint name
  global start,finish
  put sortname(name) into name
  put 0 into start
  put number of cards into finish
  repeat until (start = finish)
    put trunc((finish - start)/2+start) into n
    put field "sort name" of card n into sortn
    if name > sortn then put n into start
    else put n into finish
    if start = finish - 1 then
      if name >= (field "sort name" of card finish) then return finish
      else return start
    end if
  end repeat
  if start > finish then return finish
  else return start
end nameinsertionpoint

function sortname string
  put number of words of string into len
  get last word of string
  if it is "jr." or it is "ii" or it is "sr." or it is "iii" then
    put word len-1 of string & " " before string
    delete word len of string
  else
    put last word of string & " " before string
    delete last word of string
  end if
  return string
end sortname

function stripspace string
  repeat while char 1 of string is " " or char 1 of string is "["
    delete first character of string
  end repeat
  repeat while last char of string is " " or last char of string is "]"
    delete last character of string
  end repeat
  return string
end stripspace
```

The following script is the script for the Cross Reference background button

```
on mouseUp
  global SearchName, ReturnArray, Found
  put false into Found
  ask "Find credits for whom?"
  put it into SearchName
  set the cursor to busy
  lock screen
  push card
```

continued

```
      go "Movie Stack"
      send GetArray to "Movie Stack"
      pop card
      repeat with x = 1 to number of lines of return array
        put line x of return array into field x
      end repeat
      if Found is false then
        ask SearchName && "not found, delete this card?" with "Yes"
        if it is "yes" then domenu "Delete Card"
      end if
      unlock screen
    end mouseUp
```

The Virtual Stack

This section shows you some tricks that allow you to keep one large stack spread out over several disks. Except for the fact that you have to swap disks, the stack has the appearance of one large stack even though it is distributed among several disks.

The first step is to modify the next card and previous card buttons. Instead of just going to the next or previous card, you must first check if you need to jump to the other stack. Here are the modified scripts:

```
-- The NEXT CARD button script of "Stack 1"
on mouseUp
  if the number of this card is the number of cards then
    go to the first card of "Stack 2"
  else go next card
end mouseUp

-- The PREV CARD button script of "Stack 1"
on mouseUp
  if the number of this card is 1 then
    go to the last card of "Stack 2"
  else go previous card
end mouseUp

-- The NEXT CARD button script of "Stack 2"
on mouseUp
  if the number of this card is the number of cards then
    go to the first card of "Stack 1"
  else go next card
end mouseUp

-- The PREV CARD button script of "Stack 2"
on mouseUp
  if the number of this card is 1 then
    go to the last card of "Stack 1"
  else go previous card
end mouseUp
```

Now, if you browse the stack using the next and previous buttons, you automatically jump to the other stack when you go "off the edge" of the current stack. Well, not quite automatically. The first time you do this, HyperCard presents you with the Where is Stack 2 dialog. You then have to insert the appropriate disk and swap disks two or three times. After both disks have been inserted once, you are presented with the standard Insert Disk XXXX messages at the appropriate times. Unfortunately, the Macintosh operating system asks you to swap disks twice each time you cross a stack boundary.

This works fine if you are just using the next and previous buttons. Now let's look at how we can use the BinarySearch script. Basically not much is changed, except that you go to the appropriate stack before you perform the BinarySearch. Here is a modified version of the goto script that works in our two-stack environment:

```
-- This script should be placed in the stack script of both stacks
on goto movie
  if movie >= "M" then go "Stack 1"
  else go "Stack 2"
  go card BinarySearch("title",movie)
end goto
```

Now you can use the goto command just as before, even though the stack is split between two disks. The important thing that you can't do as easily is search using the find command. Because there is no way to get find to jump from one stack to another automatically, you have to perform the search once for each stack, collecting the data into one array, as was done before. Here is the modified script for the Cross Reference background button from the Search stack:

```
on mouseUp
  global SearchName, ReturnArray, Found
  put false into Found
  ask "Find credits for whom?"
  put it into SearchName
  set the cursor to busy
  lock screen
  push card
  go "Stack 1"
  send GetArray to "Stack 1"
  go "Stack 2"
  send GetArray to "Stack 2"
  pop card
  repeat with x = 1 to number of lines of array
    put line x of array into field x
  end repeat
  if Found is false then
    ask SearchName && "not found, delete this card?" with "Yes"
    if it is "yes" then domenu "Delete Card"
  end if
  unlock screen
end mouseUp
```

Because the GetArray command does not reinitialize ReturnArray but simply adds data to it, this modification is quite simple. All you have to do is send a GetArray to each stack. You are asked to insert the appropriate disks, but apart from that it is transparent.

Stretching HyperCard

As we move into the age of CD-ROM and other large storage devices, HyperCard will be stretched to its limits. It is up to Apple to make sure that HyperCard continues to be a useful tool with such large amounts of data. The tips in this chapter provide a bridge to the time when HyperCard itself deals with large stack issues better.

Extending HyperTalk
with Externals

David P. Sumner

Synopsis: One of the smartest things that Bill Atkinson did was allow developers to extend the capability of HyperCard by adding external commands and functions written in other languages. This feature makes it easy for someone with little experience to swap and trade powerful software extensions that improve and enhance HyperCard's performance. The only problem with this feature is knowing what external commands and functions are available and finding out how to use them.

    This chapter provides all you need to use external commands and functions and to pick the best ones for your particular application. You'll find a complete tutorial on resources, including how to use ResEdit and ResCopy. Then, a special reference section provides a collection of the most popular externals organized into Resources, Graphics and Special Effects, Input/Output Enhancements, Menus, File Handling, Communications, Printing, Peeking into the Macintosh from HyperCard, and determining the running environment. You'll find out about such popular externals as `HyperSnd`, `FontSize`, `Zoomrect`, `Copybits`, `MulitScroll`, `MarchingAnts`, `Inkey`, `AskDialog`, `ShowMenu`, `Files`, `ChangeFileType`, `CommRead`, `PrintField`, `Peek-Byte`, `ScreenSize`, `SortReals`, and many more.

Extending HyperTalk with Externals

Filling "Holes" with XCMDs and XFCNs

Some theories maintain that dinosaurs became extinct because they could not adapt to changing circumstances. Conversely, the flexibility provided to HyperTalk by its external routines suggests a long life for HyperCard. With these external routines, the HyperTalk language can be extended to meet your special needs.

When HyperCard first appeared on the scene, some people complained about its shortcomings. It didn't support much of the Macintosh interface, such as menus, and printing capabilities were lacking. Now, thanks to a number of XCMDs and XFCNs developed by talented individuals from around the world, HyperTalk has all these capabilities and more.

What Are XCMDs and XFCNs?

An external command (XCMD) or external function (XFCN) is a special kind of code resource. It is effectively a new command or function that can be used from inside a HyperTalk script. Although most XCMDs and XFCNs are written in Pascal or C, they are used just like any HyperTalk command or function. You don't have to know anything about any language other than HyperTalk to use such external routines.

External routines vary greatly in complexity. Some may represent simple extensions to HyperTalk, and others may be essentially complete programs in themselves. It is not at all unreasonable to let HyperCard provide the graphics interface for a program, with the program itself cast as an XFCN. The `DisAsm` XFCN in the Memory Tools stack, for example, is a disassembler in a single external function.

What's the Difference?

The primary distinction between XCMDs and XFCNs is that XFCNs are functions that return a value, and XCMDs are commands that "do something." However, this distinction is somewhat blurry in reality. XCMDs can return values, too, in the HyperTalk variable `the result`, but usually the response from an XCMD is an error message. Moreover, XFCNs can perform operations in addition to returning a value.

Several popular XFCNs would have been more appropriately called as XCMDs and vice versa. You could argue that XFCNs would be enough; that XCMDs are as redundant as the latter part of this sentence.

From the point of view of the HyperTalk programmer, the most important distinction is that XFCNs are used differently than XCMDs.

XCMDs are used by just typing their name followed by appropriate parameters. Usually, error conditions are returned in the HyperTalk variable `the result`. For example, the XCMD `DeleteFile` takes the name of a file as its only parameter and then deletes it. If anything goes wrong, the result contains an error number. Therefore, you would see the `DeleteFile` XCMD used in a script like this:

```
DeleteFile TheFileName
if the result is not empty then CheckError
```

On the other hand, the XFCN `FileName` takes a file type as its only parameter and returns the name of a user-selected file as a functional value. `FileName` used in a script looks like this:

```
put FileName("TEXT") into UserChoice
```

Notice that the parameters for an XFCN are enclosed in parentheses. Also, because an XFCN returns a value, you must do something with it. Usually, an XFCN is preceded by a HyperTalk connective such as `put`, `get`, or `if`, indicating what is to be done with the value returned by the function.

Human Error

Occasionally, when you try to use XFCNs and XCMDs, you get the message, `Can't Understand` followed by the name of the XFCN or XCMD. This all-too-common occurrence can have a number of causes. You may have simply forgotten to place the XCMD or XFCN into your stack or Home stack. You may have misspelled the name. However, there are other possibilities.

If you leave off the parentheses around the parameters of an XFCN or if you don't try to do something with the value of the XFCN, HyperCard gets confused. It thinks you are trying to use an XCMD rather than an XFCN, and when it finds that there isn't any XCMD with the name of your XFCN, it displays an error message.

Similarly, if you put parentheses around the parameters of an XCMD or if you preface the XCMD with something like `put`, HyperCard is again confused and attempts to find an XFCN with the name of your XCMD.

Where Do They Come From?

XFCNs and XCMDs are resources just like icons, cursors, and fonts. Many stacks contain XFCNs and XCMDs and all you have to do in order to use them is to move them from the stack they are in to your stack. You can do this with `ResEdit` or with the `ResCopy` XCMD. We discuss both of these options later in this chapter.

All the stacks and XCMDs-XFCNs discussed in this chapter are public domain unless specified otherwise. See the individual stacks or the Developer stack for any restrictions on distribution. Most of the authors ask only that they be given credit whenever their XCMDs and XFCNs are used in publicly distributed stacks. Please give credit where much credit is certainly due and acknowledge the use of these external routines whenever you use them. All of the external routines described in this chapter are in stacks available on Compuserve and on other on-line databases and bulletin boards.

Public bulletin boards, particularly large on-line databases, such as Compuserve, Genie, and Delphi, have numerous stacks that you can download onto your own disk. You can try out the XCMDs and XFCNs in their native environment and then if you like what you see, you can use `ResCopy` to move them into your own stack.

The Developer Stack

The Developer Stack by Steve Dzarga contains a large number of XCMDs and XFCNs and is a must for anyone wanting to use external functions in their own stacks. It is available on all the major on-line databases and many local bulletin boards as well. Most of the XCMDs and XFCNs discussed in this chapter can be found in this single source.

Watch for Associated Resources

Many XCMDs and XFCNs require special additional resources such as dialog boxes, fonts, cursors, or strings to be in the stack. You must be aware of these resources and be sure to move them to any stack in which you place the associated XFCN or XCMD. Also, you may want to modify some of the associated resources so that their effect is more appropriate for your special purposes. In the next section, we take a closer look at resources in general and discuss how to create and modify them with `ResEdit`.

Resources in HyperCard Stacks

Resources include cursors, icons, pictures, strings of characters, dialog boxes, windows, menus, and even program code itself. In particular, the XCMDs and XFCNs that make HyperTalk so extendable are resources.

Why Resources?

After you program the Macintosh for a while, you really begin to appreciate the value of resources. They make programs easier to modify and more modular. In addition, the resources belonging to one program can easily be transferred and used by another.

For example, suppose that you have a program that prints an error message you find annoying. You can change the resource that produces that string without knowing anything at all about how the program works. You can similarly change the titles of menu items, alter the appearance of icons or cursors, move buttons to different locations in dialog boxes, and in general, make cosmetic changes to a program without any knowledge of how it works. On most other computers, such changes to a program necessitate recompiling the entire program, so you can see how flexible Macintosh programs are due to the resource concept.

As another example (Apple likes to make a point of this one), if all the strings used by your program are saved as resources, it is a snap to make a version of the program that runs in any foreign language.

Moreover, resources used by one program can be used by another one. All you have to do is to use one of the resource moving or editing tools that we mention shortly.

Resource Fundamentals

Every resource must reside in the resource fork of some file. You identify a resource by the file it is in, its resource type, and its resource ID. A resource type (or ResType) is a four-character ASCII string. For example, `"ICON"` is the type for an icon resource, `"XCMD"` is the type for an external command, and `"STR "` is the type for a string resource. Notice that the string resource type has a space as its fourth character. That's significant; all resource types are precisely four characters long. Sound resources have a type of `"snd "`; again. The last character is not missing but is a space. Also, you cannot use `"SND "` for a sound resource, or `"icon"` for an icon resource. Resource types are case-sensitive.

Using Resources in HyperCard

Some resource types are more important to the HyperCard programmer than others. The most important ones include `"ICON"`, `"snd "`, and the XCMDs and XFCNs.

When you create a transparent button in HyperCard, you are allowed to assign an icon to it. These icons are stored as resources either in your own stack, the Home stack, or HyperCard itself. You will notice that all the icons assigned to buttons have different ID numbers. These ID numbers serve to distinguish one icon from another. In fact, every resource that you use must have an ID number associated with it, and no two resources of the same type can have the same resource ID. It's okay if an icon and a cursor resource have the same ID, but no two icons can have the same ID.

You can also distinguish resources by name. For example, you can script something like `set the icon of button 4 to Ewa` where `Ewa` is the name of icon 10334.

Moving Resources into HyperCard

Okay, so resources are great, and there are lots of them readily available for you to use in your own stacks. Now, how do you go about actually getting them in there?

There are several options. The simplest is to use the `ResCopy` XCMD developed by Apple's Steve Maller.

ResCopy

Syntax: `ResCopy`

The Result: Unknown

Author: Steve Maller, Apple Computer

Remarks: Copyright Apple Computer, Inc. Commercial Licensing Available

Description: `ResCopy` is modeled on the Font/DA Mover application you use to put fonts and desk accessories into your system file.

Note: Be sure to use version 4.0 or higher of `ResCopy`.

To illustrate, create a new stack in HyperCard and call it `ResExample`. Now, go to the Developer stack and enter `ResCopy` in the message window. You see a dialog box appear that is reminiscent of that of Font/DA Mover (see Figure 18-1). The left-hand window contains all the resources in the stack you were in when you executed `ResCopy` (in this example, that's the Developer Stack). Click the right Open button, and you see a somewhat unusual File Dialog box. Notice that at the bottom of this dialog box, you have the option of using just stacks or arbitrary resource files. If you opt for files other than stacks, you are only able to copy resources from them. This is true even if the file you select is a stack.

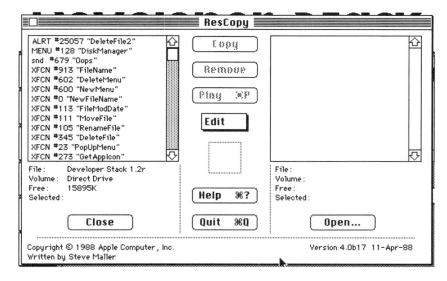

Figure 18-1.   ResCopy's main dialog window.

Locate your ResExample stack and click on the open button. You see the right window become active. Because the new stack doesn't contain any resources, the right window is empty. Let's move an XCMD over to our new stack. Scroll around if necessary in the left window and locate the XCMD `ResCopy`. Select `ResCopy` with the mouse. The copy button becomes active, and the arrows on it point toward the stack receiving the new resource. Click copy, and after a brief pause, you see `ResCopy` appear in the right window. It is now a bona fide resource in your new stack.

If there is already a resource in your stack having the same ID as the one you are copying, ResCopy displays a dialog box that lets you choose to cancel the operation, replace the resource, or save the resource with a new ID.

Be careful about changing the ID of any resource you move from one stack to another. You may later want to copy some scripts from the original stack. If any of these scripts use this resource and refer to it by ID, you will have a problem. If you change the ID of any resource, therefore, also be sure to edit any scripts that refer to it.

You can delete a resource by first selecting it and then clicking the Remove button.

You may select more than one resource at a time by holding down the Shift key as you make your selections. Thus, you can move or delete whole groups of resources at once.

Some Nice Extras

`ResCopy` is an exceptionally well-done XCMD. Not only can you use it to save a great deal of effort in moving resources from place to place, but it also provides a few nice fringe benefits. You can examine certain types of resources to see what they are like before deciding to copy them. For example, if you select an icon, you see the icon displayed in the lower-middle of the `ResCopy` window. If you select a `"CURS"` resource, the cursor changes shape accordingly. Finally, if you select a `"snd"` resource (a sound), the Play button becomes active, and you can click it to hear the sound.

The Edit button produces a pop-up menu with options that allow you to change either the name or the ID of the resource.

As if this were not enough, `ResCopy` also provides the option of copying resources directly from file to file without the use of the dialog window. From within a script, use

```
ResCopy "fromFileName", "ToFileName","ResourceType","ResourceID"
```

You may optionally use the name of the resource (rather than its ID) as the fourth parameter. The filenames here refer to the full pathnames of the files. See the file handling section of this chapter for details on pathnames.

If you only want to move resources from one file to another, `ResCopy` is all you need. It's quick and powerful enough to do the job. What if you are more ambitious, however, and want to either create your own resources or modify already existing ones?

For several types of resources, special purpose editing and creating tools are available. However, we concentrate here on the use of `ResEdit`, the most general purpose resource editor currently available.

Using *ResEdit*

ResEdit, available from APDA, is a powerful resource editing tool. With it, you can edit and create resources such as cursors, icons, dialog boxes, menus, and others. You can even create new types of resources of your own design.

There is one golden rule to follow when using ResEdit on a file. Make a backup! Otherwise, you are at risk of mangling the file, thereby making it unusable; without a backup, you have no way of getting back to the original. If you use a hard disk, I would suggest that you work with a copy of the file on a floppy in the internal drive.

Make sure you work on the backup of any file that you modify. You are doing delicate brain surgery on your file, and if you slip, you could destroy it.

Making Resources with *ResEdit*

As an example, we will make a "DLOG" resource that will produce the dialog box shown in Figure 18-2. This "DLOG" can then be used with any external routines that can display dialog boxes. In the process, we'll create a "PICT" resource, too. You could use ResEdit to create any kind of resource used by the Macintosh.

First, go to the Art Ideas stack and locate the picture of the book shown in Figure 18-2. Actually, you can use another picture of a book if you like. Use the select tool to select the book picture, copy the picture, and paste the picture into the scrapbook. Then, make a new stack called Test stack. Place your dialog box and picture resources into this stack.

Good! Now, open ResEdit. You see one or more small scrollable and moveable windows appear in the upper-left side of the screen (one window for each mounted volume). Locate your newly made Test stack and open it by double-clicking it.

Because your Test stack has no resources in it, you get a dialog box telling you

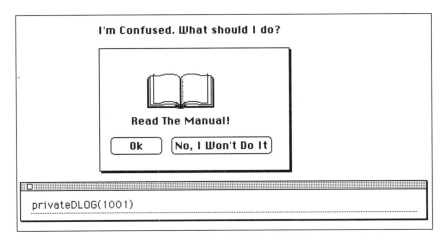

Figure 18-2.   DLOG displays custom made dialog box.

that your stack has no resource fork and asking whether you really want to create one. Click Yes in this box. If you cheated and moved some resources into Test stack with ResCopy before doing this example, you won't see this dialog box at all.

You should be looking at an empty scrolling window titled Test stack. Choose New from the File menu. You see a thin scrolling window containing a lot of four-letter resource types. The first thing you want to do is to get the picture of the book into your stack. Scroll down until you find "PICT", select that type with the mouse, and click the OK button (Figure 18-3).

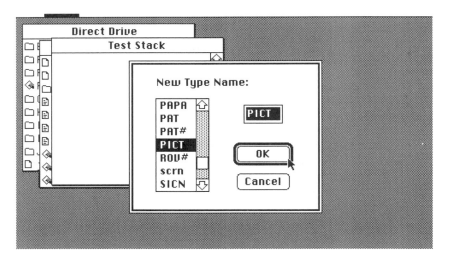

Figure 18-3.　Resource types listed on screen.

A window appears that has the title PICTures from Test stack. Go to the scrapbook and copy the picture of the book you made earlier. Return to ResEdit and select Paste from the Edit menu. You should see the picture appear in the window (Figure 18-4). Choose Get Info from the File menu. In the dialog box that appears, locate the edit field titled ID and change the number there to a 0 (zero). If you like, you can give the "PICT" resource a name like Book as in Figure 18-5. Now, close the windows until you are again looking at the Test stack window, which now contains the word PICT.

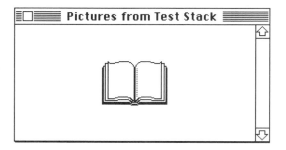

Figure 18-4.　Picture as resource in Test stack.

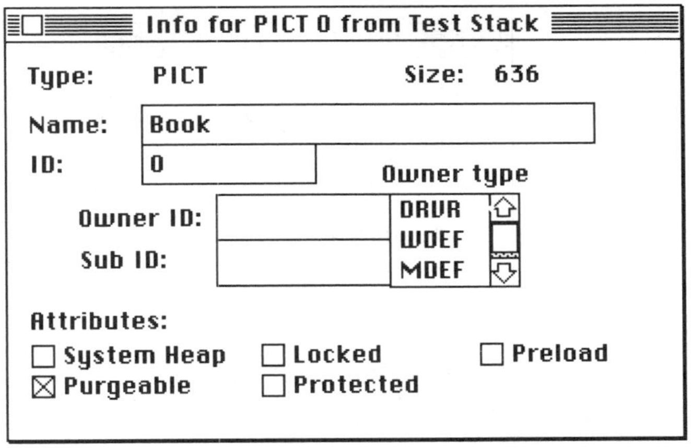

Figure 18-5. The Info box for the "PICT" resource.

Again, choose New from the File menu. When the scrolling window of Resource types appears, select "DLOG" and click OK. You see an empty window titled DLOGs from Test stack. Proceed to make your dialog by first choosing New (again!) from the File menu. What happens next is that you see a new window appear with a title something like DLOG ID=12345 from Test stack. This window contains a picture of a small dialog box.

Choose Display as Text from the DLOG menu, and another dialog box appears (see Figure 18-6). In this box, first clear the checkbox called goAwayFlag; you don't want your dialog box to have a close box. Now change the edit field named ProcID to 3. This produces a standard shadow dialog. Finally, change the Items ID value to 1001. This last step is for uniformity; you could use the ID chosen for you by ResEdit. Now, close this window.

Next, choose Get Info from the File menu. In the dialog box that appears, change the ID to 1001 (to be consistent with the choice you made for the Items ID in the last step). In case you ever want to refer to this dialog by name, enter the name Manual into the edit field called Name. (See Figure 18-7.)

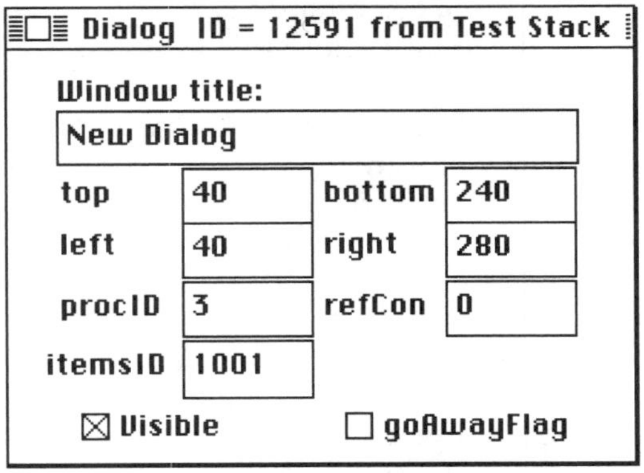

Figure 18-6. Dialog box used to set basic attributes.

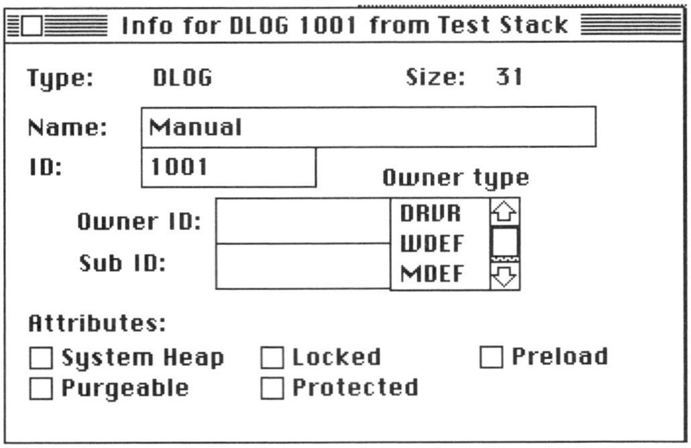

Figure 18-7. Information box in which you provide a name for the dialog box.

Close this window and also close the DLOGs from Test stack window. At this point, you should be looking at the Test stack window.

To make the DITL (Dialog Item List) for your dialog box, choose New from the File menu. Select DITL in the resulting window, and click OK. Finally, choose New again, and a window titled something like Dialog Item List ID=12345 from Test stack appears. Choose Get Info from the File menu. In the dialog box that appears, change the ID to 1001 (so that this becomes the items list for the dialog box you just made) and close this window. Your front window should be titled DITLs from Test stack.

At last you are set up to really do something. You can actually place the items you want into the dialog box. You will find that the rest of this example has a lot of the feel of making a card in HyperCard.

Choose New from the File menu. In the dialog box that appears (see Figure 18-8), click the radio button called PICT. You have told ResEdit that you want to create a PICTure resource. Next, click the radio button called Disabled so that your picture will not cause a response if the user clicks it. Finally, change the ID (at the bottom of the dialog box) to a 0. Remember that you put a "PICT" resource with ID 0 into your stack just a few minutes ago. ResEdit gets this picture and uses it as one of the items in your dialog. Close this window. You see the picture of the book in the middle of the Items box. You can move this picture around with the mouse and resize it, very much the same way as from within HyperCard. Go ahead and fix this picture the way you want it.

Choose New again from the File menu, and this time, click the radio button called Static text. Choose the Disabled option here, too. Enter Read the Manual! into the Text field. Close the box, and you see a small rectangle that includes the text you just typed. Move and resize this box to suit yourself.

Choose New from the File menu again, and this time, leave all the radio buttons set as they are; just change the title of the button to Ok, and then close the window. You see a small button named Ok in the Items window. As before, move and resize it much like you would in HyperCard. Finally, make the second button named No, I Won't Do It and situate it as you like.

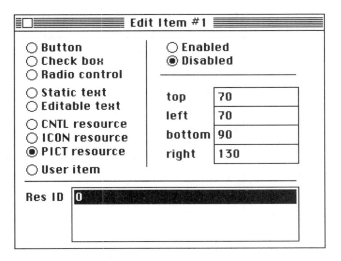

Figure 18-8. Dialog box in which you set attributes of first items.

When everything looks good to you, close the Dialog Items List window. That's it. You just made a complete dialog box that you can later use with a dialog XFCN. You will use the **"PICT"** resource in a later example as well.

Close all the windows until you get the message `Save Test stack?` Click Yes to save all your work. For another example using `ResEdit`, see the discussion of the `MarchingAnts` XFCN.

Useful Resource External Functions

There are several XFCNs and XCMDs that make it easier to deal with specific types of resources in HyperCard stacks. The most versatile of these is the `Resources` XFCN. It provides you with a list of all the available resources of a given type.

Resources

Syntax: `Resources (ResType, ResourceFileName)`

Returns: A list of all named resources of a given type

Author: Steve Maller, Apple Computer, Inc.

Description: The first parameter is required and must be a legitimate resource type. Types such as **"snd "** and **"STR#"** may not be recognized unless you enclose them in quotes. If the optional second parameter is not included, Resources returns a list of all the named resources of that type in your stack, the Home stack, Hyper-Card, and the system. (That's the natural inheritance path for available resources.)

If you include the second parameter, it should be the full pathname for some resource file. In this case, you get back a list of all the named resources of the specified type that reside in just that resource file.

For example, `Resources("FONT")` returns the names of all the fonts stored in the system, HyperCard, Home, and the stack from which `Resources` was called. On the other hand, `Resources("FONT","Hard Drive 1:HyperCard")` returns the names of all the fonts (if any) that are stored specifically in the copy of HyperCard on Hard Disk 1.

There are a few fine points about the `Resources` XFCN worth mentioning. First, it ignores resources of type `"snd"` in your system file (the idea being that they are not generally the right type of sounds for HyperCard). Also, `"DRVR"` resources whose names begin with a period are skipped. The reason for this is that it is assumed that if you ask about DRVRs, you really want to know about desk accessories and not hardware drivers (whose names begin with a period) like .Printer.

ChangeCurs

Syntax: `ChangeCurs CursorID`

The Result: Unknown

Author: Jay Hodgdon

Description: The XFCN `ChangeCurs` XCMD by Jay Hogdon is a godsend for changing cursors in the middle of a script. "What's that?" you say. "HyperTalk already has the `set cursor` command." That's right, it does. Unfortunately, the command isn't always reliable.

Example: Try the following script in a button:

```
on MouseEnter
  set cursor to watch
end MouseEnter

on MouseLeave
  set cursor to arrow
end MouseLeave
```

If you move the cursor over this button, you will be lucky if you notice anything at all.

However, if you replace the `set cursor` commands with corresponding calls to `ChangeCurs`, this script behaves as advertised. The cursor changes on entering and leaving the button. Once you specify a cursor with `ChangeCurs`, that cursor remains in effect until another call to `ChangeCurs` or HyperCard resets it to indicate a particular HyperCard situation, such as being in an editable field.

HyperSND

Syntax: `HyperSND`

The Result: Unknown

Author: Matthias Urlichs, West Germany

Description: This XCMD takes no parameters. It simply attempts to change all sound data found in the current stack into a HyperCard-playable format.

FontSize

Syntax: `FontSize(FontName)`

Returns: A comma-separated list of all available sizes for the given `"FONT"`

Author: Guy de Picciotto

Description: For example, `FontName(Geneva)` on some systems would return the list `9,10,12,14,18,20,24`.

Graphics and Special Effects

XFCNs and XCMDs also let you create graphics and special effects in your stacks.

The next XFCN makes it possible to move fields around much the same way as you would move windows in ordinary Macintosh applications.

DragRect

Syntax: `DragRect(left,top,right,bottom)`

Author: Clyde O. Taylor

Returns: The displacement for moving the rectangle

Description: `DragRect` allows you to drag fields in much the same way as you would drag a window. You pass the coordinates of a rectangle to `DragRect` with the mouse down, and it keeps control until you release the mouse button. While it is in control, it draws a dotted outline of the rectangle on the screen. When you release the button, it returns the current offset needed to set the rectangle to the location of the dotted rectangle.

One effect of `DragRect` is to allow you to produce fields that can be moved with the mouse at any time without leaving browse mode! It really is a nice effect. See Figure 18-9.

Example: Put the following script, from Taylor's stack, into the script of any field that you want to become a moveable field.

```
on mouseDown
  put item 1 of the loc of me into x
  put item 2 of the loc of me into y
  get the rect of me
  put "put DragRect(" before it
  put ") into delta" after it
  do it
  set the loc of me to (x + item 1 of delta), (y + item 2 of delta)
end mouseDown
```

If you want the field to be fully portable, you must also set the field's `LockText` property to true so that you get a `MouseDown` message when the user clicks on the

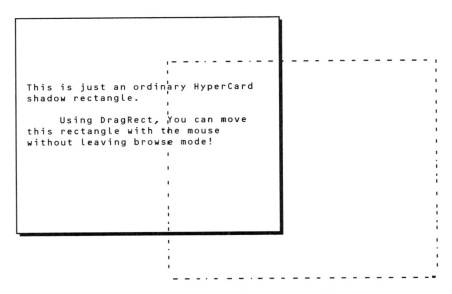

Figure 18-9. `DragRect` used to drag a dotted outline of the field.

field. If you don't set `LockText` to true, you can still move the field by holding down the Command key when you click and drag with the mouse.

This is such a nice effect that you may want to place the previous handler into virtually every field you create. Particularly during the development of a stack, it is nice to be able to just grab the field and move it without having to first choose the field tool.

The next XCMD, `ZoomRect`, has a visually pleasing effect. It causes one rectangle to appear to move to another location, much as if it were being transported there by the Starship Enterprise.

ZoomRect

Syntax: `ZoomRect l1,t1,r1,b1,l2,t2,r2,b2`

The Result: None

Author: Clyde O. Taylor

Description: This XCMD's primary value is to draw attention to buttons, fields, and other HyperCard objects in a visually appealing way.

Example: Working with a stack that contains the `ZoomRect` XCMD, first create two card fields named **A** and **B**, respectively. Put the following script into a button named `Swap`. When you click the Swap button, you see the effect of the two fields interchanging places by zooming from one to the other.

```
on MouseUp
  put the rect of card field A into RectA
  put the rect of card field B into RectB
```

continued

```
      do "ZoomRect" && RectA & "," & RectB
      do "ZoomRect" && RectB & "," & RectA
      set the rect of card field A to RectB
      set the rect of card field B to RectA
end MouseUp
```

Another nice effect possible with `ZoomRect` is to have a very small button zoom open when the user clicks it.

The next XCMD makes the `CopyBits` toolbox trap routine available to Hyper-Talk programmers.

CopyBits

Syntax: `CopyBits (l1,t1,r1,b1,l2,t2,r2,b2,EraseFlag)`

The Result: Unknown

Author: Clyde O. Taylor

Description: `CopyBits` allows you to make a copy of any portion of the card window and display the resulting picture inside any rectangle you like. The portion of the card being copied can include text in a field or any portion of background and card graphics. `CopyBits` literally copies what is on the screen.

The parameters l1, t1, r1, and b1 are the left, top, right, and bottom coordinates of the rectangle enclosing the material you wish to copy. The parameters l2, t2, r2, and b2 are the corresponding coordinates of the rectangle that holds the copy. The last parameter is either 0 or 1. If it is 1, `CopyBits` erases from its original rectangle the image being copied.

You can perform some neat effects with `CopyBits`, but you need to be aware of one crucial point: The image that `CopyBits` displays does not become a part of the card itself. Any operation that causes an update of the card window erases any images copied using `CopyBits`.

Moreover, any image erased by `CopyBits` that was part of the card window is restored by any action that causes an update. Some things that can cause an update of the card window include choosing a painting tool and then choosing the browse tool, any `OpenCard` message, and the statement `go to this card`.

You can produce some nice animation using `CopyBits`. All you need to do is to set up a series of rectangles into which successive copies of an image will appear. Then, use `CopyBits` with the erase flag set to move the image from rectangle to rectangle.

TitleBar

Syntax: `TitleBar`

The Result: Unknown

Author: Chris Knepper, Apple Computer, Inc.

Description: `TitleBar` is a simple but useful XCMD. It toggles HyperCard's Title bar from shown to not shown. This is particularly useful on a Macintosh II.

There are several XFCNs available that provide the ability to display pictures, including gray scale and color, from within a HyperCard stack.

DispPICT

Syntax: DispPICT fileName, windowing, 0, left, top ,right, bottom, delay, 0,0

The Result: Coordinates at which the user clicked the mouse

Author: David Fry

Description: The DispPICT XCMD displays a full-screen picture; it is not limited to the HyperCard window. This can be of significant value on a Macintosh II. It is also capable of displaying color (on a Macintosh II) and gray scale files as well as MacPaint files and "PICT" files. DispPICT also shows any file that contains a "PICT" resource with ID 0.

If the windowing parameter is 1, DispPict shows the picture inside moveable and resizeable scrolling window; if windowing is 0, a fixed borderless window is used.

The delay parameter allows you to specify a number of seconds for the picture to appear before automatically going away. Thus, you could use DispPICT to briefly show a picture in an OpenStack handler.

The other parameters provide even greater flexibility, but for most purposes, it is probably sufficient to use the default values of 0 as shown.

GetPicture

Syntax: GetPicture ResID,left,top,right,bottom

The Result: Unkown

Author: Clyde O. Taylor

Description: GetPicture lets you display any picture, including those with color, that you have stored in your stack as a resource. You simply provide the resource ID of the picture as the first parameter and the coordinates of the rectangle that is to hold the picture as the remaining four parameters. It's really that simple. Of course, as with the CopyBits XCMD, the picture does not become a part of the card window. Any action that causes HyperCard to update the card results in the picture's disappearing.

Color

If you have access to a Macintosh II, you may have wished that you could use color in your stacks. Well, with the help of some nifty XFCNs, you can.

RGBForeColor

Syntax: `RGBForeColor RedPart,GreenPart,BluePart`

The Result: None

Author: Clyde O. Taylor

Description: This simple XCMD allows you to set the foreground color on a Macintosh II color monitor to whatever color you like. The three parameters are all integers between 0 and 65535. They represent a mixture of the colors red, green, and blue. The XCMD displays on the screen the color corresponding to the indicated mixture.

Because it is awkward to write something like `RGBForeColor 63229,4500,341` every time you want to use this XFCN, Taylor uses a nice technique of assigning each color that will appear in a stack to a global variable. For instance, you could assign `4584,65535,64910` to `LightBlue`. Then, whenever you want to set the Foreground color to light blue, you execute the statement

```
do "RGBForeColor" && LightBlue
```

If you want to figure out what mixtures of Red, Blue, and Green to use for a particular color, simply use the Color CDEV in the Control Panel Desk Accessory. This utility not only lets you easily compose your own colors, but also tells you the appropriate numbers that produce the color as well.

There is a corresponding XCMD to set the background color.

RGBBackColor

Syntax: `RGBBackColor RedPart,GreenPart,BluePart`

The Result: None

Author: Clyde O. Taylor

Description: This works in essentially the same way as `RGBForeColor`, except that it sets the background color. Moreover, the effect of this command is immediate; you do not have to first cause an update of the card window.

MungeMCTB

Syntax: `MungeMCTB Red,Green,Blue`

The Result: Error

Author: Chris Knepper, Apple Computer, Inc.

Description: `MungeMCTB` sets the color of the Menu bar and all pull-down menus to the color specified by the mixture of red, green, and blue supplied in the parameters. The parameters are all integers between 0 and 65535; their interpretation is the same as for `RGBForeColor`.

MultiScroll XCMD

Another interesting XCMD is MultiScroll by Oscar Hill. The concept behind this nicely done XCMD is to provide the Dueling Scroll Fields effect described by Mitchell Waite and Ted Jones in chapter 4 of this book.

It's a bit too complicated to explain the details here, but you can find a complete description in Hill's stack Multiscroll XCMD available on Compuserve. You will find that the speed advantage provided by this XCMD is not so super on a Mac Plus or Mac SE. However, noticeable improvements occur using a Macintosh II.

Input/Output Enhancements

One of the most wonderful things about the Macintosh is the versatility and simplicity of the user interface. This interface—with its buttons, pull-down menus and dialog boxes, among other features—is not fully supported by HyperTalk. Fortunately, many XCMDs and XFCNs are available to bring these capabilities to the HyperTalk programmer.

Inkey

Syntax: Inkey()

Returns: The ASCII code for key

Author: Guy de Picciotto

Description: The computer uses a code for every keypress and every combination of keypresses. The Inkey XFCN scans the keyboard and returns the ASCII code corresponding to any keypress that produces an ASCII value.

Note that Option, Shift, and Command do not produce an ASCII value but serve to modify other keypresses.

Inkey provides the same capabilities to HyperTalk as the corresponding Inkey BASIC command. You can place Inkey anywhere in a script to watch for keypresses.

Examples: The next script shows you the ASCII value of the various keys on the keyboard. Put it in a button and try it!

```
on MouseUp
  put "Press Enter Key to Exit"
  put empty into ch
  put NumToChar(3) into EnterKey
  -- 3 is the ASCII value for the Enter Key

  repeat until ch = EnterKey
    put Inkey() into ch
    if ch is not empty then put CharToNum(ch)
  end repeat
```

continued

```
      put "Finished "
end MouseUp
```

To use the next example script, you must first create a transparent button called `star`. This example script lets you move the button star all over the screen by pressing the appropriate cursor keys. Press the left arrow and the button moves left, the up arrow moves the button up, and so on. You shouldn't have any trouble seeing some practical applications for this idea!

```
on MouseUp
  put "Press Enter Key to Exit"
  put empty into ch
  put NumToChar(3) into EnterKey
  put NumToChar(28) into LeftArrow
  put NumToChar(29) into RightArrow
  put NumToChar(30) into UpArrow
  put NumToChar(31) into DownArrow

  put the loc of button "star" into where
  repeat until ch = EnterKey
    put Inkey() into ch
    if ch is empty then next repeat
    put the loc of button "star" into where
    if ch=RightArrow then add 10 to item 1 of where
    if ch=LeftArrow then subtract 10 from item 1 of where
    if ch=UpArrow then subtract 10 from item 2 of where
    if ch=DownArrow then add 10 to item 2 of where

    lock screen
    set the loc of button "star" to where
    unlock screen
  end repeat

  put "Finished "
end MouseUp
```

MarchingAnts

Syntax: `MarchingAnts()`

Returns: Rectangle selected by user

Author: George Coyne

Description: This is a nice XFCN.

When a HyperTalk script executes the command,

```
put MarchingAnts() into MyRect
```

the cursor becomes a crosshair, and when you click and drag the mouse, a rectangle with rotating dashed-line sides appears (the sides resemble marching ants, hence the name). When you release the mouse, an answer dialog box appears and asks, `Plot This Region?` You have the option of canceling or trying again. The XFCN then returns the coordinates of the rectangle you produced, or it returns `empty` if you click the Cancel button.

`MarchingAnts` is very useful when you want the user to select a portion of the card (say, to place a field or paste a picture in that part of the card). The only annoying thing about `MarchingAnts` is that the dialog box has a fixed message. It would have been better if the dialog box's message had been one of the parameters. Because the author was nice enough to include the source file for his XFCN, you can modify it for your own purposes if you can program in Pascal.

Even if you are not a Pascal programmer, you can modify `MarchingAnts` so that it displays a different message in the answer dialog box. You see, the dialog message is produced by a callback to HyperCard, and as a consequence, the dialog message is actually part of the `MarchingAnts` code. All you have to do is change the characters directly. The big question is how?

Let's work through using `ResEdit` to change `MarchingAnts` to display the more generic message `Use This Rect?` rather than `"Plot this Region?"` You should work through this example using a copy of your stack to avoid losing the original.

First, go to the Finder and open `ResEdit`. When `ResEdit` appears, you see one or more windows containing files/folders that look much like those in the Finder. Locate the stack that has the *copy* of `MarchingAnts` that you want to modify. Then, open this stack by double-clicking its name. A window appears that contains a list of the stack's resources. Because `MarchingAnts` is an XFCN, double-click on the word `XFCN` and you see a list of all the XFCNs stored in your stack. Locate `MarchingAnts` and open it (either by double-clicking or by selecting it and choosing Open from the File menu).

From the Edit menu choose item Get Info. After you do so, you see a display of the raw code for `MarchingAnts` in hexadecimal. It doesn't matter whether the code means anything to you. All you want to do is to change some text, and if you're careful enough, that won't require any knowledge of what this hexadecimal stuff is all about.

Choose the Find Ascii . . . command from the Search menu, and search for `"Plot this Region?"`, or just scroll down until you see this phrase on the right side of the window, as shown in Figure 18-10. Either use the replace option or carefully change the phrase `"Plot this Region?"` to `"Use this Rect?  "`

Note the spaces at the end of the replace string. You must not change the overall length of the XFCN. In particular, you can't replace `"Plot This Region?"` with any longer string, such as, `"Select This Rectangle?"`. If the new string is shorter or longer than the original, you could overwrite, or change the location or position, of the machine code, which could likely cause a crash. Compare your work with that of Figure 18-11.

Check `MarchingAnts` to make sure that it matches its pre-edit length. If the length is different, you made an error; close `ResEdit` without saving the changes to `MarchingAnts` and try again. Otherwise, close and save the changes. Now, try your new copy of `MarchingAnts`.

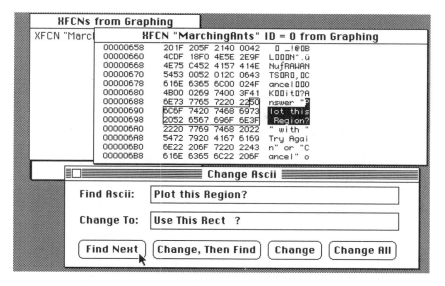

Figure 18-10. Window used to locate **"Plot this Region"** in the MarchingAnts code.

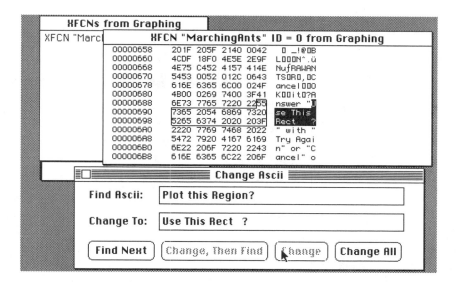

Figure 18-11. MarchingAnts code after the change.

DoList

Syntax: Mode 1: DoList ResourceID,TheList,Flag

Mode 2: DoList SelectButtonName,CancelButtonName,TheList,Flag

Mode 3: DoList SelectButtonName,CancelButtonName,TheList,¬

Flag,H,V

The Result: List of items chosen by user

Author: James L. Paul

Description: `DoList` is an essential XCMD for every category of HyperTalk programming. It brings basic list handling capabilities to HyperTalk and its applications are endless.

Notice that you can use `DoList` in any of three different ways. In all of these, the variable `TheList` represents a list of strings, the items of which are separated by commas. The variable `Flag` must be `ONE`, `DIS`, or `CON`.

All three modes operate in much the same way. A dialog window shows a scrolling field with `theList`'s items displayed one per line. The user makes a selection from these items and clicks the Select button or the Cancel button. The results of the user's choice are returned in `the result`. It seems more natural to use something like `put DoList...`, so you may justifiably wonder why `DoList` is not an XFCN rather than an XCMD.

The `Flag` values determine whether the user can choose just one item (`Flag=ONE`), any number of consecutive items (`Flag=CON`), or any number of items not necessarily contiguous (`Flag=DIS`).

See Figure 18-12 for an illustration of `DoList` in Mode 3 with `Flag=DIS`, `SelectButtonName=Choose`, and `CancelButtonName=Quit`.

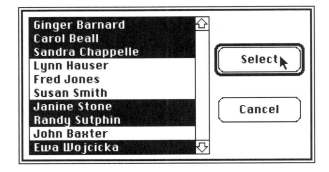

Figure 18-12.   DoList's Mode 3 used to select names from a mailing list.

Mode 3 allows you to specify also the location of the list window by providing the horizontal (H) and vertical (V) coordinates of the upper-left point of the window. Mode 1 is the most flexible, but requires the most effort because it needs a special dialog window.

If the user clicks the Cancel button, `the result` will be `empty`. Otherwise, the result will contain the number of elements selected followed by a comma and a list of the selected items separated by commas.

It is almost too easy to think of examples for `DoList`. A teacher writing a grading stack could use it to display a list of students, stack developers could use `DoList` to provide lists of all the fields in the current background, and then the chosen fields could all be operated on simultaneously.

Example: This illustration asks the user to select a group of background fields and then proceeds to set them all to the same font. You can easily see how to generalize this idea to produce numerous development aids. This example assumes that each background field has a distinct name.

```
put empty into FieldList
-- Make a list of all background fields
repeat with i=1 to number of fields
put (short name of field i) & "," after FieldList
end repeat

delete last char of FieldList -- get rid of trailing comma

-- Ask user to select some of these fields
DoList "Choose","Cancel",FieldList,"DIS"
put the result into TheseFields
if TheseFields is empty then exit to HyperCard

answer "Use What Font?"
if it is empty then exit to HyperCard
put it into TheFont

repeat with i= 1 to item 1 of TheseFields
set font of field (item i+1 of TheseFields) to TheFont
end repeat
```

BarButton

Syntax: BarButton [direction], [maximum], [minimum], [default value]

The Result: Value of button when user releases mouse

Author: Lloyd Maxfield, Infosynthesis

Description: This neat little XCMD provides a simple way to obtain a range of values from a HyperTalk script. You almost have to see this one work to appreciate what it does. When the user clicks in a (usually rectangular) button that contains a script using BarButton, the cursor changes to a crosshair, and a portion of the button's rectangle becomes black. The darkened portion of the button's rectangle follows the movements of the mouse, and when the user releases the mouse, BarButton returns a value corresponding to the percentage of the rectangle that is darkened. (See Figure 18-13.)

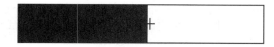

Figure 18-13.   BarButton's visual input technique.

All of its parameters are optional. If you don't include any parameters, it always operates from bottom to top if the rectangle is higher than it is wide, and from right to left otherwise.

It appears that the HyperTalk variable it must contain the rectangle of the button at the time `BarButton` is called (or there is a system crash!).

Example: A typical use of `BarButton` contains lines such as the following three inside a MouseDown handler of a rectangular button.

```
get the rectangle of me
BarButton
put the result into ButtonValue
```

Warning: Do not use `BarButton` in any stack that is displaying color. The system bombs if you do.

ThumbBtn

Syntax: `ThumbBtn(Left, Right, Minimum, Maximum, Direction)`

Returns: The value of the button when the user releases the mouse

Author: Ian Summerfield, England (Shareware)

Description: This is a nifty XFCN that emulates the behavior of the thumb buttons in the MacWrite scroll bars (see Figure 18-14). The first parameter is the left edge of the thumb button's movement area, the second parameter is the right edge of the thumb button's movement area, the third and fourth parameters are the first and last values in the thumb button's range of values, and the last parameter is a Boolean that is true if the button is to scroll horizontally and false if it is to scroll vertically.

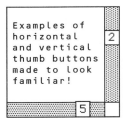

Figure 18-14.   `ThumbBtn` provides extra input options.

To use `ThumbBtn`, you must first design the scrolling rectangle that is to enclose it. The button itself is just an ordinary HyperCard rectangular button. The value that shows in the button as the user drags it is just the button's name. All `ThumbBtn` does is monitor the movement of the mouse and set the location and name (value) of the button accordingly.

`ThumbBtn` is a little deceptive. Although it is a nice XFCN, it is not really a thumb button in the sense that it could be used to replace one of the thumb buttons in a HyperCard scrolling field. All that the button does is change value as it is moved. Any effects that you want to accompany the changing values must be provided by your own scripts.

Dialog Boxes

HyperTalk programmers are familiar with the answer and ask dialog boxes, but are also painfully aware that more versatile support of dialog boxes is lacking in Hyper-Talk. However, there are a few external routines that provide much of what is lacking. The simplest approach is provided by `AskDialog`, an extension of the ask dialog box of HyperTalk.

AskDialog

Syntax: `AskDialog(text,DefaultReply,top,left,font)`

Returns: `empty` if user clicks on Cancel, otherwise text typed by user

Author: Ian Summerfield, England

Description: This XFCN is an extension of the standard HyperTalk ask dialog box. `AskDialog` provides the option to place the dialog window anywhere on the screen and the ability to alter the dialog's font.

It is important to note that this XFCN does not require any resources to be present in the stack because it uses HyperCard's own ask dialog window.

Example: Executing the following statement from a HyperTalk Script (or the message window) produces the dialog box shown in Figure 18-15.

```
put AskDialog("How are you?","Just Fine", 10,10,"Cartoon")
```

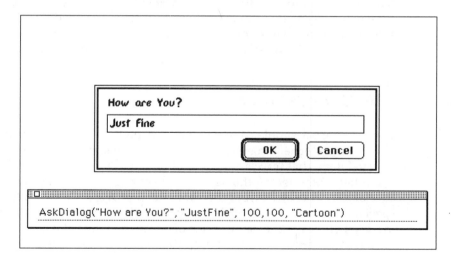

Figure 18-15.   `AskDialog` box.

PrivateDLOG

Syntax: `PrivateDLOG(DialogID)`

Returns: Item number of button selected by the user

Author: Tom Pittman

Description: This XFCN provides the ability to use custom-made dialog boxes in your stacks, but it suffers from the severe shortcoming of not being able to return the contents of any text edit fields that the dialog box contains.

The only difficulty with using `PrivateDLOG` is the creation of a dialog resource. This is easy to do with `ResEdit`. In the section on Resources, we created an example dialog box that can be used with `PrivateDLOG`. See Figure 18-2 for an example of our dialog box displayed by the `PrivateDLOG` XFCN.

Adding Menus to HyperCard Stacks

When designing stacks, you may find some cards cluttered with buttons. One way out of this mess is to allow the user to make choices from a menu. Menus provide an excellent way for users to send commands to your stack, to select appropriate values for parameters, or select from a group of options. Moreover, menus are an essential part of the Macintosh interface. Although HyperTalk does not support menus, a number of XCMDs do.

Standard Menus

Adding a menu or two to the main Macintosh menu is perhaps the most natural choice. It's easy to do with the external routines provided by Michael Long of Nine-To-Five Software. These menu externals are a package deal; they must be used together to provide the standard menu interface familiar to all users.

The General Idea

The idea here is simple. Whenever any menu item is selected from a menu, Hyper-Card sends a `DoMenu` message. This message has one parameter, the name of the selected item, that travels along with it. It doesn't matter who put the menu into the Menu bar; the effect is the same. We first put a menu into the Menu bar using a special XFCN (`NewMenu`), and then we intercept HyperCard's `DoMenu` message with a special DoMenu handler inside our stack script. This handler checks the parameter to see whether it is the name of one of our menu items. If it is, we act on it, otherwise we pass the `DoMenu` message on up the message hierarchy.

NewMenu

Syntax: `NewMenu("Title","Item 1","Item 2",...,"Item n")`

Returns: ID for the newly created menu

Author: Michael Long, Nine-To-Five Software

Description: You supply a menu title as the first parameter to `NewMenu` and then provide each of the items in the menu as a separate parameter. Notice that this means that you are limited to a maximum of 15 items in each menu. `NewMenu` returns the ID number of the menu, and it is imperative that you maintain the value of this number in a global variable for use with the other menu commands and in particular for disposing of the menu when you close your stack.

DeleteMenu

Syntax:	`DeleteMenu(menuNumber)`
Returns:	`empty`
Author:	Michael Long, Nine-To-Five Software

Description: You must use this XFCN when you are ready to dispose of a menu. Never leave a stack without disposing of all the menus it created; other stacks don't expect these menus, and the results are unpredictable. However, don't try to dispose of a menu more than once. This can also have undesirable effects (like system bombs).

ShowMenu

Syntax:	`ShowMenu(menuNumber)`
The Result:	Unknown
Author:	Michael Long, Nine-To-Five Software

Description: Under certain adverse conditions, your menus may suddenly disappear from the Menu bar. You can make them reappear by using the `ShowMenu` XCMD.

ChangeMenu

Syntax:	`ChangeMenu menuNumber, itemNumber, Item`
The Result:	Unknown
Author:	Michael Long, Nine-To-Five Software

Description: This XCMD makes it possible to change the text of any of your menu items. However, note that you can't use it to change the title of any menu.

EnableMenu

Syntax:	`EnableMenu menuNumber, itemNumber, TRUE/FALSE`
The Result:	Unknown
Author:	Michael Long, Nine-To-Five Software

Description: Sometimes you may want to disable some of the items in your menu. For instance, if you have a file-saving routine that is accessed through a menu, you don't want anyone to select that item if there is a file currently available to save. When the third parameter is true, EnableMenu enables the designated item; otherwise the item is disabled.

CheckMenu

Syntax:　　　CheckMenu menuNumber, itemNumber, TRUE/FALSE

The Result:　Unknown

Author:　　　Michael Long, Nine-To-Five Software

Description: Some menu items represent a selection of options for the user. You can indicate which options are active at any given time by appending a checkmark to the item. CheckMenu adds a checkmark to the given itemNumber if the third parameter is TRUE and removes a checkmark if that parameter is FALSE.

As an example, suppose that you want to create a menu to help you make fields for a stack you are developing. For simplicity, assume that you want to create fields that have a style of scrolling, shadow or rectangle. Suppose, too, that each field will have Geneva, Monaco, or Chicago as its textfont. You could create the menus shown in Figure 18-16 to help you produce these fields.

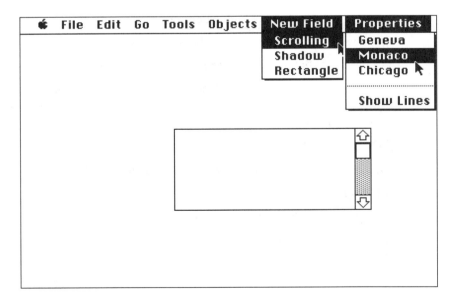

Figure 18-16.　　New menus added to HyperCard's Menu bar.

Try the following example scripts in a stack that contains the menu XCMDs and XFCNs. You will find that they create the indicated menus and maintain them as advertised. These scripts are fully documented, and you should be able to use them as generic examples of menus in HyperCard.

First, you need to create your menu(s). Usually you will do this in an OpenStack handler as shown below.

```
on OpenStack
  global NewFieldMenu,PropertiesMenu

  -- We must create our menus when the stack first opens.
  put "New Field" into MenuTitle

  put NewMenu(MenuTitle,"Scrolling","Shadow","Rectangle") ¬
  into NewFieldMenu

  put "Properties" into MenuTitle

  put NewMenu(MenuTitle,"Geneva","Monaco","Chicago","(-","Show Lines") ¬
  into PropertiesMenu

end OpenStack
```

What gets opened must be closed. You must dispose of your menus when you are finished. The CloseStack handler is a logical place to do this. Notice the global variables in all these examples.

```
on CloseStack
  global NewFieldMenu,PropertiesMenu

  put DeleteMenu(NewFieldMenu) into NewFieldMenu
  put DeleteMenu(PropertiesMenu) into PropertiesMenu
end CloseStack
```

Now, without warning and without your being able to detect it, your menus could disappear from time to time. Using `ShowMenu` every so often makes sure that your menu stays in the Menu bar. The next example shows an idle handler that performs this function.

```
on idle
-- Every so often (120 ticks), we use ShowMenu to make sure that
-- our menus are still visible in the Menu bar.
 global NewFieldMenu,PropertiesMenu, lastTick

  if (the ticks-lastTick)>120 then
    put the ticks into lastTick
    ShowMenu NewFieldMenu
    ShowMenu PropertiesMenu
  end if
  pass idle  -- pass idle in case something else is going on.
end idle.
```

Now, when the user selects one of our menu items, we have to be able to detect it and take appropriate action. All of this is done with a HyperTalk DoMenu Handler.

```
-- This is the heart of our menu handling
-- here is where we intercept DoMenu and take action in case
-- one of our items was selected.

global NewFieldMenu,PropertiesMenu

if MenuItem is "Scrolling" then
  MakeField "Scrolling"    --  Look at the MakeField handler.

else if MenuItem is "Shadow" then
  MakeField "Shadow"

else if MenuItem is "Rectangle" then
  MakeField "Rectangle"

else if MenuItem is "Geneva" then
  SetFont Geneva       -- Look at the SetFont handler.

else if MenuItem is "Chicago" then
  SetFont Chicago

else if MenuItem is "Monaco" then
  SetFont Monaco

else if MenuItem is "Show Lines" then
  set ShowLines of last card field to true
  ChangeMenu PropertiesMenu,5,"Hide Lines"
-- Since the lines are showing we change the menu item to
-- Hide Lines so that the user can undo the choice.

else if MenuItem is "Hide Lines" then
  set ShowLines of last card field to false
  ChangeMenu PropertiesMenu,5,"Show Lines"
-- Toggle the Hide Lines and Show Lines items.
else

    pass DoMenu  -- VERY IMPORTANT!! Don't forget to pass DoMenu.

  end if

end DoMenu
```

The Main HyperTalk Functions needed for this example are in the following script.

```
on SetFont WhichOne
  global FieldFont,PropertiesMenu
  put WhichOne into FieldFont
  set TextFont of last card field to FieldFont
  -- After setting the font of our field correctly
  -- we make sure that only the selected font has a
  --checkmark. First, we uncheck all three items.
  repeat with i=1 to 3
    CheckMenu PropertiesMenu,i,FALSE
  end repeat

  -- Now, we put a check mark in front of the selected font.
```

continued

```
      if FieldFont = "Geneva" then put 1 into i
      if FieldFont = "Monaco" then put 2 into i
      if FieldFont = "Chicago" then put 3 into i
      -- Now i contains the item number of the selected font.
   CheckMenu PropertiesMenu,i,TRUE
end SetFont

on MakeField FieldStyle
global PropertiesMenu

   DoMenu "New Field"
   set style of last card field to FieldStyle

-- Because all our fields have no lines showing as a
-- default, we make sure the user has an option
-- of making them visible.

   ChangeMenu PropertiesMenu,5,"Show Lines"
   choose browse tool -- Remember that New Field selects the field tool.

end MakeField
```

You will discover that it is not difficult to elaborate on this example and create some really useful tools for stack development.

Other Alternatives

Although using standard menus is much better than cluttering up your cards with a zillion buttons, there are some drawbacks, too. First, you must have an idle handler in the stack in order to be able to put your menus back into the Menu bar in case they are inadvertently removed by some other operations in your stack. There is also the limitation of only being able to use 15 items at most in a menu. (This could be fixed by rewriting the NewMenu XFCN.) Finally, there is the problem that a user may not expect to find your menus in the Menu bar. HyperCard already has a lot of menus of its own there, and yours could go unnoticed.

What's the alternative? Pop-up menus. You've undoubtedly seen them before. Put a pop-up menu on a card, and it takes up no more space than a single button. When clicked, however, a menu appears that can contain many items. Moreover, it is possible to create hierarchical pop-up menus. In these menus, items may have submenus attached to them, making some snazzy effect possible.

Several external routines produce pop-up menus. We discuss just one of them, HPopUp by Roland Mailleux of Belgium. This XFCN provides not only pop-up menus but hierarchical ones as well.

HPopUp

Syntax: HPopUp(Left,Top,MainList,Submenu1,SubMenu2,...SubMenu13)

Author: Roland Mailleux, Belgium

Description: First, be aware that HPopUP requires four "VEPP" resources to function, so be sure that you copy these along with HPopUp itself.

The first two parameters to HPopUp give the horizontal and vertical coordinates for where you want the pop-up menu to appear. MainList is a list of the main menu items separated by semicolons. These first three parameters are required. If you do no more than this, you will get a standard pop-up menu. However, HPopUp also allows you to produce a hierarchical pop-up menu by adding up to 13 additional submenu lists. Each submenu list begins with a # followed by the number of its associated main menu item.

Place the HPopUp XFCN inside a button. It is essential that you use a Mouse-Down handler inside this button—not the usual MouseUp handler.

One of the nice features of HPopUp is that it returns the text of the selected item and not just a number. This makes it particularly easy to use. If you decide later to add more options to a menu, you do not have to worry about any renumbering.

File Handling XCMDs and XFCNs

Most file handling on the Macintosh uses the Standard File Package that is part of the Macintosh system. The most important part of this package consists of two routines called SFGetFile (generally used for opening a file) and SFPutFile (generally used for saving a file). These routines display standard dialog boxes and allow the user to select a file from a scrolling list of filenames. The user can cancel at any time or can change drives, move around from folder to folder, and eject disks, all under the control of these routines. Although HyperCard does not provide any access to these routines from within HyperTalk, there are external routines that do (see Figure 18-17).

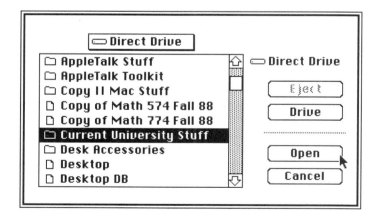

Figure 18-17.   Standard file dialog window produced by FileName XFCN.

The Nature of Macintosh Files

Before discussing the nature and use of the file XFCNs, it is appropriate to explain a few things about Macintosh files. First, you must understand that every Macintosh file consists of two parts, called forks, one for data and one for resources. One of the forks may be empty. Text files, for example, usually consist entirely of data, whereas most applications contain resources only.

You need to understand several properties of files. A file has a file type and a creator signature. The file type tells you what kind of file it is; is it a text file, an application, or what? The creator signature, on the other hand, tells you what file created this one. Both of these properties consist of a four-letter word, the case of which matters. For example, the type of a text file is `TEXT` and not `text`), the type of an application is `APPL`. A text file created by MacWrite has a file type of `TEXT` and a creator signature of `MACA`. Although a text file created by Microsoft WORD also has a file type of `TEXT`, its creator signature is `MSWD`.

Next, you must appreciate the idea of the full pathname of a file. For instance, if a file named `Patches` is located inside a folder named `Desk Accessories`, which, in turn, is inside a folder named `Misc Stuff`, and this latter folder lies in the main directory of the hard disk named `Hard Drive 1`, the full pathname for this file is `Hard Drive 1:Misc Stuff:Desk Accessories:Patches`. Because the system limits strings to a maximum of 255 characters, not all files can be identified by a full pathname. This is a limitation for some of the XFCNs we will discuss, but not generally a serious one.

What HyperTalk Provides

HyperTalk isn't entirely devoid of file handling capabilities. It provides commands to open and close files and to read and write data to text files. You must provide the full pathname of any file you use with these functions.

Just as HyperTalk's file functions do, so most of the XFCN-XCMD utilities require the full pathname of the file you wish to use. That raises the most crucial question of them all. How do you conveniently get the full pathname of a file from within a script?

The Heart of File Handling—*FileName* and *NewFileName*

The most essential XFCNs for file manipulation are `FileName` and `NewFileName`. `FileName` is an XFCN that, when invoked, produces the usual SFGetFile dialog box (see Figure 18-17) and lets the user search for the desired file. `NewFileName` puts up a standard SFPutFile dialog box (see Figure 18-18) and lets the user provide a name to use for saving the file.

FileName

Syntax: `FileName(FileType)`

Returns: Full pathname of the file chosen by the user

Author: Steve Maller, Apple Computer, Inc.

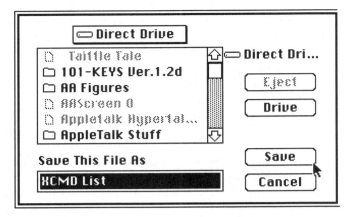

Figure 18-18.   Access to SFPutFile added to HyperTalk by `NewFile`.

Description: The `FileName` XFCN takes one parameter at most. If you just use `FileName()` with nothing in the parentheses, the resulting Standard File Dialog box displays all files at each level— even those that are invisible in the Finder. However, you may include a file type as a parameter to `FileName`. In that case, only the files of that type appear in the dialog box. For instance, `FileName("STAK")` only allows the user to select a HyperCard stack; `FileName("APPL")` only allows the user to select an application.

Although `FileName` does a tremendous amount of work for you, it's only the beginning of file handling (in HyperCard). When you use `FileName`, you get back the full pathname of the selected file, but nothing, absolutely nothing, has yet happened to that file. The whole point of using `FileName` is to conveniently (and conventionally) get the pathname of the file and that's it. You have to pass this pathname to other routines to actually do anything with the file.

Typically, a script containing `FileName` has two lines that look like this:

```
put FileName("STAK") into UserChose
if UserChose is empty then exit to HyperCard
```

It is important to check whether the value returned by `FileName` is `empty`. If it is, the user clicked the Cancel button in the dialog box, and you should probably not continue with any file manipulations.

`FileName` is the bread and butter of file handling in HyperCard. Still, it does have a limitation. Most notably, it only allows you to specify one type of file for display in the Standard File Dialog box. The next XFCN overcomes this.

CustomFileName

Syntax: `CustomFileName(FileTypes)`

Returns: Full pathname of the file chosen by the user

Author: Oscar F. Hill

Description: `CustomFileName` works pretty much like `FileName`, but it allows you to specify more than one type of file for display. Moreover, a modified file dialog box is used in this XFCN, thereby allowing the user to make selections with command key equivalents rather than the mouse.

Also, `CustomFileName` provides more information than does `FileName`. The result returned by `CustomFileName` consists of three lines. The first line is the full pathname of the file that the user selected. The second line is the type of the file, and the third line is the creator of the selected file. If you want to use `CustomFileName` to place the full pathname of a user-selected text file into a container called `WhichFile`, you write

```
put line 1 of CustomFileName("TEXT,APPL") into WhichFile
```

If you want the creator of the file to be placed into the container `FileMaker`, you write

```
put line 3 of CustomFileName("TEXT,STAK,APPL") into FileMaker
```

NewFileName

Syntax: `NewFileName(Prompt,DefaultFileName)`

Returns: A new file's full pathname as chosen by the user

Author: Andrew Gilmartin, Brown University

Description: Although `FileName` and `CustomFileName` provide HyperTalk programmers with easy access to the SFGetFile dialog box and associated routines, `NewFileName` provides the same access to SFPutFile. You will want to use this XFCN to allow the user to conveniently save a file. Just as with `FileName`, so `NewFileName` provides only the dialog box mechanizations and simply returns the full pathname of the file the user types into the dialog box. It does not actually save anything or create any file or anything else.

The syntax for `NewFileName` is a bit different from that of `FileName`. You may include a prompt (such as `Save as`) as the first parameter and a default filename as the second parameter. Usually, the second parameter is a null string.

Example: You could place the following script in a button named `Save` to allow the user to save the contents of any field to a text file.

```
on MouseUp
  ask "Save Which Field " with ""
  put it into WhichField
  if it is empty then exit MouseUp
    put NewFileName("Save as ","") into NameToUse
  if NameToUse is empty then exit MouseUp
    open file NameToUse
-- Note that open creates a new file if one with
-- the given name does not already exist.
    put NameToUse
```

continued

```
        write field WhichField to file NameToUse
        close file NameToUse
end MouseUp
```

A corresponding script to read from a file would be

```
on MouseUp
        ask "Place text into Which Field?" with ""
        if it is empty then exit MouseUp
        put it into WhichField

        put FileName("TEXT") into FileToRead
        if FileToRead is empty then exit MouseUp

        open file FileToRead
        read from file FileToRead
        put it into field WhichField

        if FileLength(FileToRead)>16384 then
        beep
        answer "File too long - only 16K bytes read" with "OK"
        end if

        close file FileToRead
end MouseUp
```

The *PathParts* Function

Often, while using these file-handling routines, you will find it necessary to use only some portion of a full pathname. Although it is easy to write a simple HyperTalk script to handle this problem, a few XFCNs help a lot. The one-line function PathParts, defined in the following text, takes a full pathname as a parameter and returns the component parts as a comma-separated list. You may then access the parts of the full pathname as items in this list.

```
function PathParts FullPathName
        return Substitute(":", ",", FullPathName)
end PathParts
```

Here, Substitute is a simple XFCN that is surprisingly useful for a number of tasks.

Substitute

Syntax: Substitute(ToReplace,ReplaceBy,Target)

Returns: Each occurrence of ToReplace in Target is replaced by ReplaceBy

Author: Eric Celeste

Description: Substitute replaces every occurrence of a particular string in a target string by a second string.

DeleteFile2

Syntax: `DeleteFile2`

The Result: OSErr

Author: David Conger

Description: This XCMD lets you conveniently delete files. It is a fully contained routine. Execute `DeleteFile2` from within a script or the message window, and it does everything else. It brings up a standard dialog window and lets the user select a filename. It then asks the user to confirm deleting the file. If the user confirms, the file is erased.

DeleteFile

Syntax: `DeleteFile(FullPathName)`

Author: Dewi Williams

Description: Although `DeleteFile2` does it all, `DeleteFile` takes a single parameter equal to the full pathname of the file to delete. It then simply deletes the file. This is a better XCMD for deleting files under the control of a HyperTalk script.

Example:

```
put FileName() into ToDelete
put last item of PathParts(ToDelete) into TheName
Ask "Really Delete " & TheName with "Yes" or "No"
If it is "No" then exit to HyperCard
DeleteFile(ToDelete)
```

CopyFile

Syntax: `CopyFile(OldFile,NewFile)`

Returns: 1 if all is OK, otherwise an OSErr

Author: Brad J. Hicks

Description: This XFCN copies a given file. Here, the first parameter is the full pathname of the original file, and the second parameter is the simple name for the copy.

Example: A typical use of `CopyFile` might be

```
put FileName("TEXT") into UseThisFile
if UseThisFile is empty then exit to HyperCard
put "Copy of " & UseThisFile into DeFault
ask "Save a copy of " & UseThisFile & " as " with DeFault
if it is empty then exit to HyperCard
put it into NewName
CopyFile ( UseThisFile,NewName)
```

Note that the copy of the original file resides in the same folder as the original file. You cannot use this XCMD to directly copy files to other folders or volumes.

RenameFile

Syntax: `RenameFile(OldName,NewName)`

Returns: 0 if successful, 1 if parameter error, or OSErr otherwise

Author: Dewi Williams

Description: This XFCN lets you rename your files. The first parameter is the full pathname of the file, and the second parameter is the new name of the file.

Example:

```
RenameFile("Hard Drive 1: Text Stuff: New Letter", "Letter to Ewa")
```

Files

Syntax: `Files(FullPathName,FileTypes)`

Returns: A list of all files in the folder specified by `FullPathName`

Author: Guy de Picciotto

Description: This is a wonderful XFCN. Used in conjunction with the `DoList` XCMD, it provides some super capabilities. If you send the `Files` XFCN a full pathname, it returns a list (delimited by carriage returns) of all files of the indicated types residing in the same folder as the file you specified. That is, the value returned by `Files` consists of a bunch of simple filenames, one per line.

Example: The following script puts a list in a card field named `All Stacks` of all the stacks in the file hierarchy, beginning at a selected folder and tracing back to the root directory.

```
on MouseUp
  put empty into card field "All Stacks"
  put fileName("STAK") into UseLevel
  if UseLevel is empty then exit MouseUp
  put PathParts(UseLevel) into UseParts

  put (item 1 of UseParts) &":" into CurrentLevel
  repeat with i=2 to number of items of UseParts
    put return & CurrentLevel & return &return¬
    after card field "All Stacks"
    put return & Files(CurrentLevel,"STAK") after card field "All Stacks"
    put return & return & return after card field "All Stacks"
    put (item i of UseParts) & ":" after CurrentLevel
  end repeat
end MouseUp
```

You could also use the `Files` XCMD to search each text file in a particular folder for a specific phrase, or you could use it with the `Resources` XFCN and `ResCopy` XCMD to move all the resources from all the stacks in some folder into another stack.

Another suitable use would be returning a list of all the files in some folder, then using the `DoList` XCMD to allow the user to select any number of those files, and then using the `DeletFile` XCMD to delete each selected file one by one.

Getting and Changing Properties

Several XFCNs and XCMDs provide easy ways to change some important properties of files. You have already seen that the `CustomFileName` XFCN also provides the creator and type of a file. Other XFCNs that allow you to manipulate file properties are

FileModDate

Syntax: `FileModDate(FullPathName,"")`

Returns: Creator and last modified date for the file

Author: Dewi Williams

Description: Given a full pathname for a file, this XFCN returns in ticks the date the file was created and the date it was last modified. To change the date to human-readable form, use the HyperTalk function `convert`.

FileLength

Syntax: `FileLength(FullPathName)`

Returns: Number of bytes in the file

Author: Jeff Fischer

Description: This XFCN takes a full pathname as its only parameter and returns the length of the file in bytes. This can also be conveniently used directly from the Message box. Just try typing

        `FileLength(NewFile())`

into the message window and press return.

ChangeFileType

Syntax: `ChangeFileType(FullpathName,FromType,ToType)`

Author: Larry Wolfarth

Description: This neat little XFCN lets you change the type of any file.

Example: The next script could be used to let a user change a Microsoft Word file into a standard text file so that it could be read by HyperCard. Suppose that the next script is in a button titled `Word to Text`

```
on MouseUp
put FileName("WDBN") into UseThis
if UseThis is empty then exit MouseUp
put empty into theFile

put UseThis into temp

repeat until last char of temp = ":"
put last char of temp before theFile
delete last char of temp
end repeat

answer "Really change "& theFile & " to text?" with "Yes" or "No"
if it is "Yes" then put ChangeFileType(UseThis,"TEXT","MSWD")
end MouseUp
```

What If There's a Problem?

The file-handling XCMDs we've been talking about usually work just fine, but sometimes there may be unexpected errors in the operating system and the XCMDs may fail. In this case, most of them return an error number in the HyperTalk variable the result. If there is an error, the result will contain a negative integer representing the operating system error.

Communications

HyperCard has a number of facilities that would make it a natural choice for running a bulletin board. Its major shortcoming is a lack of communications support from within HyperTalk. However, several XFCNs make serial communications possible from within HyperCard.

The Developer stack contains serial external routines that make the transmission and reception of simple ASCII text an easy matter.

CommInit

Syntax: CommInit

The Result: None

Author: BIAP Systems/Chuck Shotton

Description: CommInit initializes the serial port for transmission and reception of data at 1200 baud, 8 bit characters, no parity, and 1 stop bit.

CommWrite

Syntax: CommWrite TheString

The Result: None

Author: BIAP Systems/Chuck Shotton

Description: CommWrite transmits the ASCII string in TheString out the serial port using the terminal settings determined by CommInit.

CommRead

Syntax: CommRead()

Returns: Empty if no data is available; otherwise, serial data received

Author: BIAP Systems/Chuck Shotton

Description: CommRead returns any string of ASCII text that is available in the serial buffer.

Example: The three external routines, CommInit, CommWrite, and CommRead, form the basis for simple communications from within HyperTalk. The following script asks the user for the name of a card field, and then proceeds to transfer the contents of the field out the serial port. Assume this script is contained inside a button called transmit.

```
on MouseUp
  ask "Send Which Field?"
  if it is empty then exit MouseUp
  put it into TheField

  repeat with i = 1 to number of lines of card field TheField
    CommWrite(line i of card field TheField)
  end repeat

end MouseUp
```

On the other hand, the next script receives serial transmissions from another source and stores the incoming text in a card field. The variable EOF is used to denote an end-of-transmission character. This script assumes that a control-Z (ASCII 26) character is sent by the source to terminate the transmission. You may have to change this for your special needs. Assume this script is inside a button named Receive.

```
on MouseUp
  put NumToChar(26) into EOF
  ask "Store Data in What Field?"
  if it is empty then exit MouseUp
  put it into TheField
  repeat
    put CommRead() into Data
    if Data is not empty then
    put Data after card field TheField
    if last char of data is EOF then exit to HyperCard
    end if
  end repeat
end MouseUp
```

Before either of the two previous examples will work, you must initialize the serial port by using the XCMD `CommInit`. A natural place to put this XCMD is inside an OpenStack handler. Thus,

```
On OpenStack
CommInit
-- other stuff too if you like
end OpenStack
```

Printing

Although HyperCard makes it easy to print cards, stacks, and scripts, it does not provide a great deal of printing capabilities. A simple XCMD helps.

PrintField

Syntax: `PrintField FieldName, FontName, FontSize, Text Styles`

The Result: Unknown

Author: Mark Scherfling

Description: Only the field name is required. No printing dialog box appears, and the current printer settings are used. Printing is not formatted to conform with the appearance of the text in the field.

Example: If you wanted to print using the characteristics of the field being printed, you could use,

```
ask "Print What Field?"
put it into TheField
put textFont of field TheField into TheFont
put textSize of field TheField into TheSize
put textStyle of field TheField into TheStyle
put Field && quote & TheField & quote into FieldName
PrintField  FieldName, TheFont, TheSize, TheSize
```

The Power of Peeking

The Memory Tools stack, available on Compuserve, contains a collection of XFCNs that make it possible to access the contents of specific locations in the Macintosh memory and, if desired, to change them. The `Peek` XFCN shows you the value stored at any particular memory location, and the `Poke` XCMD lets you change the contents of any memory location in RAM.

These external routines provide a great deal of power to the HyperTalk programmer. It may surprise you to learn just how much you can do with the `Peek` XFCN. In fact, peeking into memory can be just as effective as a specially designed XFCN or XCMD.

There are numerous ways that peeking into memory can of value in a Hyper-Card stack. The examples in this section are not meant to be exhaustive, but rather suggestive of the possibilities. A full understanding of this material requires some familiarity with the hexadecimal system. However, even if you are not familiar with hexadecimal numbers and the concepts of computer memory, read on. You will discover that you can still do a lot with some of this information.

There are some reasonable arguments against using peeks in a stack, particularly if the significance of a memory location could change at some time in the future. Note that Apple Computer discourages peeking and poking. Although the locations of some globals are documented in *Inside Macintosh*, all compilers and assemblers reference them by name, not by number.

PeekByte

Syntax: `PeekByte(Address)`

Returns: The value of the byte stored at the given address

Author: David P. Sumner, University of South Carolina

Description: Given a hex address, `PeekByte` tells you the value stored at that location. Similarly, the `PeekWord` XFCN returns the value of the word stored at a given (hex) address, and `PeekLong` returns the long integer stored at a given address.

The Macintosh stores a number of useful pieces of information in low memory locations from 0 to DA0 (in hexadecimal). What kinds of things can you accomplish by peeking into these locations?

You Can Obtain Status Information

For example, the memory location 260 (hex) contains the value of the volume setting (as set in the control panel). If you want to get the value of the current setting of the volume, use

```
put PeekByte("260") into VolumeSetting
```

Location 2D0 contains a flag that indicates whether the cursor is visible or invisible. If the byte stored there is 1, the cursor is invisible; otherwise, it is visible. Thus, you could check to see whether the cursor is visible from within a script by checking the value returned by `PeekByte("2D0")`.

What Keyboard Are You Using?

You can tell what kind of keyboard is attached to the Macintosh by peeking into location 21E. Thus, if `PeekByte("21E")` is 0, there isn't any keyboard attached at all. If the value of the byte at 21E is 0B, the keyboard is the standard MacPlus keyboard with a numeric keypad. If the value in 21E is 03, the keyboard is the old classic keyboard with no numeric keypad. You can determine the value returned for another keyboard by simply hooking it to the Macintosh and checking the value of `PeekByte("21E")`.

Detecting foreign keyboards is a bit trickier. An excellent reference to the low-level details of Macintosh keyboards can be found in a pair of articles by Joel West entitled "Be a Keyboard Sleuth" in *MacTutor Magazine*. The first of these articles appeared in the August, 1986, issue of *MacTutor*.

Peeking at Keypresses

You have already learned about the `Inkey` XFCN that allows you to monitor the keyboard from within a HyperTalk script. By peeking into the right places, you can do many of the same things that `Inkey` does, and much more. In fact, peeking can provide information that `Inkey` can't.

For example, the location (hex) 185 contains the ASCII code for the most recent keypress. Thus, the following loop continues to execute until the user presses the Esc key (the Clear key on many keyboards).

```
repeat until PeekByte("185") = 27
-- body of the loop here
end repeat
```

Moreover, by peeking into the keycode memory location at hex 184, you can distinguish between the keys on the numeric keypad and the keys on the main keyboard. For example, if `PeekByte("184")` = 0D, the / key on the numeric keypad is being pressed. Checking for specific keys is not as reliable an operation as checking for characters by looking at the ASCII value, because the value of the keycode is dependent on the keyboard that is attached to the Macintosh.

Another way to check for keypresses is to peek into the keymap memory locations starting at hex 174. To see what happens to these memory locations when someone presses a key, try using the following loop in any button of a stack containing the `PeekLong` XFCN.

```
on MouseUp
repeat until the MouseClick
 put PeekLong(174) & PeekLong(178) & PeekLong(17C)
end repeat
end MouseUp
```

Now click this button and watch the values in the Message box as you press various keys. You will observe that even though the Option key, Command key, Shift key, and Caps Lock key produce no ASCII value, they all produce an effect in the keymap memory location. In fact, you can tell if the Shift key is down by checking memory location 17B. If the value stored there is odd, the Shift key is down. If the value at 17B is 2, Caps Lock is down and Shift and Option are up.

By peeking into memory location (hex) 186, you can get the tick count at the time of the last keypress. You could use this to measure the time interval between keypresses, or to detect a long period of inactivity. Don't forget that the HyperTalk function `convert` changes the number of ticks in location 186 into a human-readable form.

Another useful location is (hex) 16A. The long integer stored here is the number of ticks since the computer was turned on. By peeking into this location, you can tell how long the computer has been on.

Finally, you could check to see whether HFS is active by peeking into (hex) 3F6. If this is -1, only MFS is supported.

Where Am I? What Am I Doing Here?

Some stacks ask questions of the user when they first open. "Are you running on a Mac II?," "Do you have a large monitor?", "Are you running under MultiFinder?"

It is generally not necessary to ask such intrusive questions. You can determine this information by use of appropriate XFCNs and other means.

As you saw in the previous section, you can determine a great deal about the current environment by peeking into appropriate portions of the Macintosh's memory. You could determine the current volume level, the type of keyboard being used, how much memory is available, and more.

You can determine whether the user's system contains a particular `"FONT"` or `"FONT"` size by using the `Resources` XFCN and the `FontSize` XFCN described in the section on resources.

The next few XFCNs and XCMDs provide further information to your stacks about the environment in which they reside.

MultiFinder

Syntax: `MultiFinder()`

Returns: True if MultiFinder is running and false otherwise

Author: Unknown

Description: This simple XFCN requires no parameters, but the parentheses must be there anyway because it is an XFCN.

ScreenSize

Syntax: `ScreenSize("1988SDrazga")`

Returns: Large if a large screen monitor is being used and Small otherwise

Author: Steve Dzarga

Description: This XFCN requires a parameter only to reassure its owner that his copyright is being protected. Because it is frequently desirable to know whether your stack is operating on a large monitor, this is a useful XFCN.

Several useful XCMDs and XFCNs don't fall into any of the preceding categories.

DeProtect

Syntax: `Deprotect(FullPathName)`

The Result: Unknown

Author: Ned Horvath and Allan Foster

Description: `Deprotect` removes the password protection from any stack.

RandPerm

Syntax: `RandPerm(n)`

Returns: A list of the integers 1,2,...n arranged in a random order

Author: David P. Sumner

Description: `RandPerm` is a useful XFCN for simulations and game playing stacks. It returns a permutation of the numbers 1,2,..n almost instantly—hundreds of times faster than HyperTalk.

ShutDown

Syntax: `ShutDown`

The Result: Unknown

Author: Will Cate

Description: Performs a standard Macintosh shutdown from within HyperCard. Use with care. This can corrupt a stack, so you should always return to the Home card before shutting down your Macintosh.

doRestart

Syntax: `doRestart`

The Result: Unknown

Author: Jim Henderson

Description: Performs a standard Macintosh restart from within HyperCard. Use with care; like the preceding XCMD, this is not suggested by Apple because it can potentially corrupt the stacks.

SortReals

Syntax: `SortReals(AnyContainer)`

Returns: A sorted list of contents of `AnyContainer`

Author: George Coyne

Description: `SortReals` takes any list of real numbers, separated by spaces, and returns a similar list of the same numbers sorted in descending order.

Part

Reference

The Complete HyperTalk Reference

The Complete
HyperTalk Reference

Ted Jones

Synopsis: Once you know how to write scripts in HyperTalk, your main problem becomes one of remembering the exact syntax for each command and function, as well as properties. Unfortunately, HyperCard's Help stack is primitive and devoid of useful examples. Even Apple's official script guide book provides few details on using the various commands. This section is an exhaustive compendium of all the keywords in the HyperTalk language. A complete definition is provided for each keyword, command, function, property, operator, constant, menu item, tool, and message. Most items contain one or several examples of their usages in HyperTalk. As appropriate, each entry also contains Syntax, Notes, Cautions, and See Also entries.

The reference differentiates concepts and ideas from keywords so that you can use it as a master glossary, in addition to as a reference. Version differences and reserved words are indicated. A stack version of the reference is also available so that you can have the information available as you are developing your stacks.

The Complete
HyperTalk Reference

Everything to Script With and More

Using the HyperTalk Reference Guide

The material in these pages is organized in alphabetical order with all the symbols listed first. A complete definition is provided for every keyword, command, function, property, operator, constant, menu item, tool, and message. Most items contain one or several examples of their usages in HyperTalk scripts or from the Message box. As appropriate, entries also contain Syntax, Notes, Cautions, and See Also sections.

This reference includes definitions for HyperTalk concepts and ideas, so it serves also as a glossary of terms. If you are unclear about terms used in Hyper-Talk—such as abbreviations, variables, or messages—you can find an explanation here. Words that are used several ways often have multiple listings, so if the first listing isn't what you want, keep looking. The See Also heading gives you names of related concepts and keywords. This guide also contains an ASCII character code table and other information you might need.

Every word listed here that is not actually used in the HyperTalk language is labeled Concept or Utility with the warning *(not a reserved word)*. Otherwise, all listings indicate how the term is used in HyperTalk.

HyperTalk Reserved Words

A HyperTalk reserved word is a predefined word that has meaning to HyperTalk independent of the user. These words are the basic vocabulary of HyperTalk. The user can add new words to the HyperTalk vocabulary by creating variables and messages, but these words do not become reserved words.

HyperTalk operators are evaluated in a set order. The precedence of these operators is defined in the operator precedence listing. The lower the precedence number, the higher the precedence and the sooner the operation is executed. Parentheses can be used to override the natural precedence of operators.

Syntax Conventions

A syntax listing takes the following form:

```
command <container> [preposition modifier]
```

or

```
the function of <expression>
```

The text between the angle brackets, such as `<container>`, indicates what value is appropriate for the situation. In the case of `<container>`, any of HyperTalk's containers could be used: `field id 3`, `the message box`, `variableA`. In the case of `<expression>`, a text, numeric, or logical expression might be appropriate. Everything between square brackets, `[preposition modifier]`, is optional. When several arguments are possible, the alternatives are separated by vertical bars, `[preposition1 | preposition2 modifier]`.

A case in point is the `put` command:

```
put <content> [before | into | after <container>]
```

The following `put` commands are possible.

`put "Hello"` displays Hello in the Message box.
`put "Hello" into field "Salutations"` puts Hello into the field specified.
`put field "Salutations" after the archiveVar` places the contents of the field, `Hello`, after the contents of the variable `archiveVar`.

In the Examples category, notes can either be on the same line as the HyperTalk code, following a — comment operator, or they can be on the next line following a comment indicator. Words appearing in examples that end in `...Var` are variables, for example, `brushVar`, `numVar`, `thisVar`, or `thatVar`.

See the index for all the pages in this book on which any referenced word can be found.

The Reference

" String Delimiter

Notes Quote. Characters between quotation marks or interpreted as a unit (a text string) and not as HyperTalk.

Examples
```
put "Hello Fred" into msg
-- Line above displays Hello Fred in Message box
put "put" && quote & "Hello Fred" & quote && ¬
"into msg" into doVar
-- Puts put "Hello Fred" into msg in variable doVar
do doVar
-- Hello Fred displayed in Message box
```

See Also   **&, &&, quote**

& **String Operator**

Notes   Concatenate. The concatenation operator joins one string or constant to another string or constant. Precedence = 6.

Examples
```
put "Hello" & "Fred" into the message box
-- Line above displays HelloFred in message box
put "Good morning, it's " & the long date into msg
put card field 1 & the time into card field 2
put "This" & "&" & "that" into msg
-- This&that displayed in message box
not(4>3 and 3<4) -- a logical nand
dial "(415)" & "555-1212"
```

See Also   **&&**

&& **String Operator**

Notes   Concatenate with a space. The concatenate and space operator joins one string or constant to another string or constant and inserts a space between them. Precedence = 6.

Examples
```
put "Hello" && "Fred"
-- Line above displays Hello Fred in message box
put "Good morning, it's" && the long date
put card field 1 && the time into card field 2
put "This" && "&" && "that"
-- This & that displayed in message
go to card "Graphics" && var
-- If 1 is in var then goes to card Graphics 1
```

See Also   **&**

( ) **Logical Operator**

Notes   Parentheses. A precedence controller that forces HyperTalk to evaluate the enclosed expression first. Also used with functions to indicate the arguments passed with the function name. Precedence = 1.

Examples
```
2-6*3-1 -- Returns -8
2-(6*3)-1 -- Returns -17
2-(6*3-1) -- Returns -10
2*3+5/3 -- Returns 7.666667
2*(3+5)/3 -- Returns 5.333337
trunc(average(2-(6*3)-1, 2-(6*3-1),the number of cards))
-- Demonstates uses of parentheses with functions
```

See Also   **Precedence**

✱ **Math Operator**

Notes   Times. Multiplies numbers. Precedence = 4.

Examples
```
4*5 -- Returns 20
3*numVar
```

continued

*

```
numVar*card field 2
card field 2*the number of cards
2-6*3-1 -- Equivalent to 2-(6*3)-1 returns -17
```

See Also   **multiply, Precedence**

+ Math Operator

Notes   Plus. Adds numbers. Precedence = 5.

Examples
```
4+5 -- Returns 9
3+numVar
numVar+card field 2
card field 2+the number of cards
2+6*3+1 -- Equivalent to 2+(6*3)+1 returns 19
```

See Also   **add, Precedence**

- Math Operator

Notes   Minus. Subtracts numbers. Precedence = 5.

Examples
```
4-5 -- Returns -1
3-numVar
numVar-card field 2
card field 2-the number of cards
2-6*3-1 -- Equivalent to 2-(6*3)-1 returns -17
```

See Also   **subtract, Precedence**

-- Operator

Notes   Comment. Indicates that the following text is a comment and not code. Can be used either on a line by itself or at the end of a command. Every non-HyperTalk line in a script should be commented.

Examples
```
-- HyperTalk poem follows
on poem -- poem user command
```

/ Math Operator

Notes   Divided by. Divides numbers. Precedence = 4.

Examples
```
4/5 -- Returns .8
1/0 -- Returns INF for infinity
3/numVar
numVar/card field 2
card field 2/the number of cards
2-6/3-1 -- Equivalent to 2-(6/3)-1 returns -1
```

See Also   **divide, div, mod, Precedence**

< Logical Operator

Notes   Less than. Returns true if the expression on the left is less than the expression on the right. Precedence = 7.

Examples
```
4<5 -- Returns true
-12 < -20 -- Returns false
3<numVar
numVar<card field 2
card field 2<the number of cards
2-6<3-1 -- Equivalent to (2-6)<(3-1) returns true
```

See Also **Precedence**

$<=$ Logical Operator

Notes Less than or equal to. Returns true if the expression on the left is larger than or equal to the expression on the right. Precedence = 7.

Examples
```
4<=5 -- Returns true
-12<=-20 -- Returns false
abs(-5)<=abs(5) -- Returns true
3<=numVar
numVar<=card field 2
card field 2<=the number of cards
2-6<=3-1 -- Equivalent to (2-6)<=(3-1). Returns true
```

See Also **Precedence**

$<>$ Logical Operator

Notes Not equal to. Returns true if the expression on the left does not equal the expression on the right. Precedence = 8.

Examples
```
4<>5 -- Returns true
-12<>-20 -- Returns true
3<>numVar
numVar<>card field 2
card field 2<>the number of cards
2-6<>3-1 -- Equivalent to (2-6)<>(3-1) returns true
```

See Also **Precedence, ≠**

$=$ Logical Operator

Notes Equal to. Returns true if the expression on the left is equal to the expression on the right. Precedence = 8.

Examples
```
4=5 -- Returns false
-12=-20 -- Returns false
3=numVar
numVar=card field 2
card field 2=the number of cards
2-6=3-1 -- Equivalent to (2-6)=(3-1) returns false
```

See Also **Precedence**

$>$ Logical Operator

Notes Greater than. Returns true if the expression on the left is larger than the expression on the right. Precedence = 7.

>

Examples
```
4>5 -- Returns false
-12>-20 -- Returns true
3>numVar
numVar>card field 2
card field 2>the number of cards
2-6>3-1 -- Equivalent to (2-6)>(3-1) returns false
```

See Also **Precedence**

>=   Logical Operator

Notes Greater than or equal to. Returns true if the expression on the left is larger than or equal to the expression on the right. Precedence = 7.

Examples
```
4>=5 -- Returns false
-12>=-20 -- Returns true
3>=numVar
numVar>=card field 2
card field 2>=the number of cards
2-6>=3-1
-- Equivalent to (2-6)>=(3-1) returns false =
```

See Also **Precedence**

^   Math Operator

Notes Raised to the power of. The exponential operator raises a number to the power of another number. Precedence = 3.

Examples
```
4^5 -- Returns 1024
-12^-20 -- Returns 0
3 ^ numVar
numVar ^ card field 2
card field 2^ the number of cards
2-6^3-1 -- Equivalent to 2-(6^3)-1. Returns -215
(2-6)^(3-1) -- Returns 16
```

See Also **Precedence**

≠   Logical Operator

Notes Not equal to. Returns true if the expression on the left does not equal the expression on the right. Precedence = 8.

Keyboard Option-= (equal)

Examples
```
4≠5 -- Returns true
-12≠-20 -- Returns true
3≠numVar
numVar≠card field 2
card field 2≠the number of cards
2-6≠3-1 -- Equivalent to (2-6)≠(3-1). Returns true
```

See Also **Precedence**, $<$, $>$

≤ Logical Operator

Notes   Less than or equal to. Returns true if the expression on the left is smaller than or equal to the expression on the right. Precedence = 7.

Keyboard   Option-, (comma)

Examples
```
4 <= 5 -- Returns true
-12 <= - 20 -- Returns false
6 <= 6 -- Returns true
3 <= numVar
numVar <= card field 2
card field 2 <= the number of cards
2-6<=3-1 -- Equivalent to (2-6)<=(3-1). Returns true
```

See Also   **Precedence**

≥ Logical Operator

Notes   Greater than or equal to. Returns true if the expression on the left is larger than or equal to the expression on the right. Precedence = 7.

Keyboard   Option- (hyphen)

Examples
```
4>=5 -- Returns false
-12 >= -20 -- Returns true
3>=numVar
numVar >= card field 2
card field 2 >= the number of cards
2-6 >= 3-1 -- Equivalent to (2-6)>=(3-1). Returns false
```

See Also   **Precedence**

¬ Editor Character

Notes   Soft return. Indicates that the HyperTalk command line is continued on the next line.

Keyboard   Option-Return

Example
```
put "This and that happened" ¬
into stringVar -- Same as put "This and that" into stringVar
```

abbr date / abbrev date / abbreviated date — Date Format

Notes   Converts the date to a shorter format. Format = abbreviated day of week + abbreviated month + day + year.

Examples
```
-- if the date is Monday, December 21, 1987...
put the long date into dateVar
convert dateVar to the abbrev date
-- Returns Mon, Dec 21, 1987
put the abbrev date
-- Puts Mon, Dec 21, 1987 into the message box
```

See Also   **abbrev date, date**

Abbreviations

Concept (*not a reserved word*)

Notes Short forms of and alternatives to common HyperTalk words.

Word	1.0.1	1.2 +
abbreviations	abbr/abbrev	
background	bkgnd	bg
backgrounds	bkgnds	bgs
button	btn	
buttons		btns
card		cd
cards		cds
commandKey	cmdKey	
field		fld
fields		flds
grey		gray
picture		pict
second (1.2 + only)		sec
second (1.2 + only)		second
tick (1.2 + only)		tick

See Also (*Listing for each word*)

abs **Math Function**

Syntax
```
the abs of <number>
abs(<number>)
```

Notes Returns the absolute value of the number. Ignores a negative sign.

Examples
```
the abs of 5 -- Returns 5
abs(- 5) -- Also returns 5
put the abs of numVar into message box
abs(the mouseV - 100) -- Returns 90 if mouseV is 10
```

add **Command**

Syntax
```
add <source> to <destination>
```

Notes Adds the numeric value of the source to the numeric value of the destination container. The source can be a literal, but the destination must be a container. All containers used with the **add** command must contain a numeric value before the statement executes.

Examples
```
add 5 to numVar -- Returns 9 if numVar was 4
add numVar to card field "Subtotal"
```

continued

```
add the number of cards to char 1 of line 1 of ¬
card field "Index"
add numVar to numVar
-- Same as multiplying numVar by two
```

See Also   **+, subtract**

after   Preposition

Notes   A put command preposition that causes the source string to be appended to the end of any strings in the destination container.

Examples
```
put "Now it's time" into textVar
put " to say good-bye." after textVar
-- result = Now it's time to say good-bye
```

See Also   **before, into, put**

all   Adjective

Notes   Used with show command to specify all the cards in a stack.

Example
```
show all cards
```

and   Logical Operator

Syntax
```
<expression1> and <expression2>
```

Notes   Boolean operator that returns true if both expressions are true and false if either or both expressions are false. There is not a built-in nand, but you can simulate one with not(<expression1> and <expression2>).

Examples
```
if 4>3 and 3<4 then beep -- Beeps
if trueVar and (the mouseV > 100) then go Home
if showLines of field 1 and textFont of ¬
field 1 is "geneva"
then type "Hello"
if trueVar and trueVar2 and not falseVar then beep
if not(4>3 and 3<4) then beep -- No beep
```

See Also   **or**

annuity   Math Function

Syntax
```
annuity(<interest rate>, <number of payments>)
```

Notes   annuity = (1 - (1 + rate) ^ (- periods)) / rate returns the amount you must invest per dollar of periodic payment. Investment = annuity() * payback. Payback = investment / annuity(). To calculate a mortgage, use the formula loanSize = annuity() * payment

Examples
```
annuity(0.2,12) -- Returns 4.439217
annuity(rateVariable,field "periods")
-- To get $20,000 per year at 8% for 20 years
-- your cost =
20000*annuity(.08,20) -- Returns 196362.948149 or
-- $196,362.95
-- If you borrow $115,000 at 9.875% for 30 years your
```

continued

annuity

```
-- payments =
115000/annuity(.09875/12,30*12)
-- Returns 998.600945 or $998.60
```

answer   Command

Syntax   answer <prompt> [with <reply> [or <reply> [or <reply>]]]

Notes   HyperTalk's alert box and button response dialog box generator. Maximum three options with last option being the default. The default option can be selected by clicking or by pressing the Return or Enter keys. Prompt and reply strings should be quoted or placed in containers. The answer box stays on the screen and the user can do nothing else until one of the reply buttons is clicked. The content of the button selected is placed into the variable it. The prompt string can be approximately 46 characters long.(See Figure R-1.) The reply strings can be approximately 13 characters long. On a small screen Mac, the left top of alert box is at 84,92; right bottom at 427,181. Position on larger screens varies but box is centered horizontally and 181 pixels below the top of the screen. (See Figure R-2.) Position of the box can't be changed.

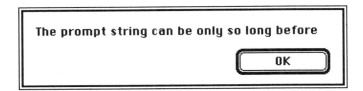

Figure R-1.   The answer box's prompt string.

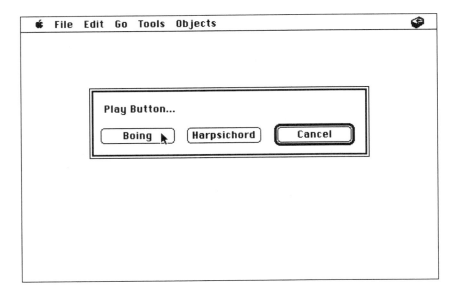

Figure R-2.   The answer box's position on the screen.

Examples
```
answer "Shall we Continue?" with "OK" or "Cancel"
on mouseUp
    put "The prompt string can be only" into promptVar
    put space & "so long before it's cut off" after promptVar
    answer promptVar
end mouseup
answer field 3 with "200,200" or the mouseLoc
on mouseUp
    answer "Play Button..." with "Boing" or ¬
    "Harpsichord" or "Cancel"
    if it is "Boing" then -- Action based on value of it
      click at the loc of button "Boing"
      else if it is "Harpsichord" then
        click at the loc of btn "Harpsichord"
    else
      beep
    end if
end mouseUp
```

See Also **ask**

any Ordinal

Notes Specifies a random element of a group of similar objects or chunks. Most often used with the **go**, **show**, **get**, and **put** commands.

Examples
```
go any card of this bkgnd
put "SURPRISE" into any word of any field of any card
```

Argument Concept *(not a reserved word)*

Notes A value passed as a parameter with a message. In the statement **beep 3**, **beep** is the command and message name; **3** is the argument that is passed with the message as a parameter to HyperCard.

See Also **Message, Parameter**

arrow Cursor

Notes The usual Macintosh pointer cursor. Not available before version 1.2.

1.2 + New version 1.2 feature.

Example `set cursor to arrow`

See Also **cursor, set**

arrowKey Command

Syntax `arrowKey <keyName>`

Notes Has the same effect as pressing one of the arrow (cursor) keys. The **keyName** options are: **up**, **down**, **right**, and **left**. If the **textArrows** property is false (or if you are using version 1.0.1), **arrowKey right** is the same as **go next card** and **arrowKey left** is the same as **go previous card**. If the **textArrows** property is true, the arrow keys move the insertion point cursor in field or Message box text.

Caution The words **right** and **left** can't be quoted in commands.

arrowKey

Example
```
arrowKey right
-- Yet another way of going to the next card
on arrowKey which
  if which is up then pop card
  if which is "right" then go home -- Quotes mandatory
end arrowKey
on mouseUp -- Put insertion point in field, move it 4
  -- characters to the right and down 1 line
  select before text of field 5
  -- Version 1.2+ command
  set textArrows to true
  -- so arrowKey doesn't go next card
  repeat 4
    arrowKey right -- move right 4 characters
  end repeat
  arrowKey down -- move down one line
end mouseUp
```

See Also   **arrowKey** *(Message)*, **Messages**

ASCII   Character Codes *(not a reserved word)*

Notes   American Standard Code for Information Interchange. The numbers that computers use to represent characters. Some Apple fonts have special characters. Chicago 12 has the characters shown in Figure R-3, which can be used in fields but not in Paint. Figure R-4 shows ASCII and non-ASCII character codes for Geneva 9 point.

⌘	**Chicago 12**	`put numToChar(17) into line 1 of field 1`
✓	**Chicago 12**	`put numToChar(18) into line 2 of field 1`
◆	**Chicago 12**	`put numToChar(19) into line 3 of field 1`
🍎	**Chicago 12**	`put numToChar(20) into line 4 of field 1`

Figure R-3.   Chicago 12-point font character codes.

See Also   **numToChar, charToNum**

ask   Command

Syntax   `ask <question> [with <default-reply>]`

Notes   Generates a dialog box and allows the user to type a reply. (see Figure R-5.) Prompt and reply strings should be quoted or placed in containers. Returns either the reply or **empty** (if no reply or if Cancel clicked) in the variable **it**. Pressing the Return or Enter keys is the same as clicking the OK button. On a small-screen Mac, the top left of alert box is at 87,100; bottom right at 424,205. Position on larger screens varies but is centered horizontally and 100 pixels below the top of the screen. The position of the box on the screen can't be changed.

Examples
```
ask "What is your name?"
on openCard
  ask "Enter your hourly rate :" with 25
  if it is empty then exit openCard
  Put it into card field "hourRate"
end openCard
```

continued

582

ASCII Control Character Codes (Geneva 9)

VALUE	ABBREV	MEANING	VALUE	ABBREV	MEANING	VALUE	ABBREV	MEANING
000	NUL	empty	011	VT	Vertical tab	022	SYN	Synchronous idle
001	SOH	Start of heading	012	FF	formFeed	023	ETB	End of transmission block
002	STX	Start of text	013	CR	return	024	CAN	Cancel
003	ETX	End of text	014	SO	Shift out	025	EM	End of medium
004	EOT	End of transmission	015	SI	Shift in	026	SUB	Substitute
005	ENQ	Enquiry	016	DLE	Data link escape	027	ESC	Escape
006	ACK	Acknowledge	017	DC1	Device control 1	028	FS	File separator
007	BEL	Bell	018	DC2	Device control 2	029	GS	Group Separator
008	BS	Backspace	019	DC3	Device control 3	030	RS	Record separator
009	HT	tab	020	DC4	Device control 4	031	US	Unit separator
010	LF	lineFeed	021	NAK	Negative acknowledge			

ASCII Character Codes (Geneva 9)

032	space	046	.	060	<	074	J	088	X	102	f	115	s
033	!	047	/	061	=	075	K	089	Y	103	g	116	t
034	"	048	0	062	>	076	L	090	Z	104	h	117	u
035	#	049	1	063	?	077	M	091	[	105	i	118	v
036	$	050	2	064	@	078	N	092	\	106	j	119	w
037	%	051	3	065	A	079	O	093	]	107	k	120	x
038	&	052	4	066	B	080	P	094	^	108	l	121	y
039	'	053	5	067	C	081	Q	095	_	109	m	122	z
040	(	054	6	068	D	082	R	096	`	110	n	123	{
041	)	055	7	069	E	083	S	097	a	111	o	124		
042	*	056	8	070	F	084	T	098	b	112	p	125	}
043	+	057	9	071	G	085	U	099	c	113	q	126	~
044	,	058	:	072	H	086	V	100	d	114	r	127	DEL
045	-	059	;	073	I	087	W	101	e				

Non-ASCII Character Codes (Geneva 9–varies by font and size especially beyond 167)

128	Ä	140	å	152	ò	163	£	174	Æ	185	π	196	ƒ	207	œ
129	Å	141	ç	153	ô	164	§	175	Ø	186	∫	197	≈	208	–
130	Ç	142	é	154	o	165	•	176	∞	187	ª	198	∆	209	—
131	É	143	è	155	õ	166	¶	177	±	188	º	199	«	210	"
132	Ñ	144	ê	156	ú	167	ß	178	≤	189	Ω	200	»	211	"
133	Ö	145	ë	157	ù	168	®	179	≥	190	æ	201	…	212	'
134	Ü	146	í	158	û	169	©	180	¥	191	ø	202	SP	213	'
135	á	147	ì	159	u	170	™	181	µ	192	¿	203	À	214	÷
136	à	148	î	160	†	171	´	182	∂	193	¡	204	Ã	215	◊
137	â	149	ï	161	°	172	¨	183	Σ	194	¬	205	Õ	216	ÿ
138	a	150	ñ	162	¢	173	≠	184	Π	195	√	206	Œ		
139	ã	151	ó												

Figure R-4. The ASCII and non-ASCII character codes for Geneva 9 point.

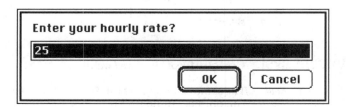

Figure R-5. The ask command dialog box.

ask

```
ask line 4 of field id 2 with item 3 of replyVar
```

See Also **answer**

ask password Command

Syntax `ask password <question> [with <default-reply>]`

Notes Use this command to provide password protection for a stack. Ask the user for a password (which is returned in encrypted form in the variable `it`), store this password in a field, and when the stack (or background or card) is opened again, use the `ask password` command to ask the user for the password. If you click the Cancel button, the variable `it` contains the constant `empty` rather than the value in the dialog box field.

Examples
```
ask password "Enter secret number:"
ask password "The code again please:" with " 5 Characters"
on openCard -- Handler to save and check passwords
   if card field "Password" is empty then
     ask password "Enter a password for this stack."
     if it is not empty
     then put it into card field "Password"
     else go home
   else
     ask password "Enter your Password"
     if not (it is card field "Password") then go home
   end if
end openCard
```

atan Math Function

Syntax
```
the atan of <number>
atan(<number>)
```

Notes Short for arctangent. Returns the angle in radians when given the two short sides of a right triangle. The number is the length of the side opposite the angle divided by the length of the other short side. To convert to degrees, multiply the result by $180/\pi$.

Examples
```
the atan of 45 -- Returns 1.548578
atan(1.0) -- Returns 0.78
the atan of numVar
atan(field 1 * numVar2)
round((atan(50/60)*180/pi)*10)/10
-- Returns 39.8 degrees
```

See Also **sin, cos, tan**

Author Level Concept *(not a reserved word)*

Notes The same as `userLevel` 4. Permits the user to browse, write, paint, and manipulate objects but doesn't permit scripting.

See Also **userLevel**

autoHilite Button Property

Syntax `[the] autoHilite of <button>`

Notes Gives the `autoHilite` value of the specified button. Can use a literal name or a name in a container. True means the button highlights when pressed and flashes when clicked. False means there is no visual feedback. Use with the `set` command to change a button's `autoHilite` property.

Examples
```
the autoHilite of button 1 -- Returns true or false
if autoHilite of button id 5 is true then beep
if the autoHilite of button id 5 is true then beep
if autoHilite of button id 5 then beep
-- Previous 3 are equivalent
get autoHilite of bkgnd button 5
put the autoHilite of button 1 into butValue
set autoHilite of butVar to true
set autoHilite of btn 3 to not the autoHilite of btn 3
```

autoTab Field Property

Syntax `[the] autoTab of <field>`

Notes Determines what happens when the Return key is pressed and the cursor is in the bottom visible line of a nonscrolling field. If `autoTab` is true, the cursor moves to the top line of the next field in relative order. If `autoTab` is false, the cursor goes to the next, invisible line of the same field.

1.2+ New version 1.2 feature.

Examples
```
the autoTab of field id 3 -- Returns true or false
set autoTab of card field 3 to true
```

average Math Function

Syntax `average(<number list>)`

Note The maximum number of elements in the `number list` is 64.

Examples
```
average(4,8) -- Returns 6
average(10,field 2,numVar,the number of cards)
average(numVar)
-- If numVar contains 4,5,6 returns 5
```

back Reserved Word

Note Used for navigation. Goes to the most recently displayed card.

Example `go back`

See Also **go**

Back Menu Command

Notes Used for navigation. Goes to the most recently displayed card. Use `go back` instead. Going back always generates `closeCard` and `openCard` messages, sometimes generates `closeBkgnd` and `openBackground` messages, and sometimes generates `closeStack` and `openStack` messages.

Back

Example   `doMenu "Back"`

See Also   **go**

Background   **Menu Command**

Notes   Toggles between card and background graphic layers. Use `set editBkgnd` instead.

See Also   **editBkgnd**

Background   **Concept**

Notes   A collection of objects, graphics, and scripts that may be common to one card, all the cards, or a subset of all the cards in a stack. The background has a script, a picture layer, and may have buttons and fields. The background object is between the stack and the card in the object hierarchy. When a background is added to a stack, it gets the number following the number of the background before it. Any backgrounds with the same or higher numbers are renumbered. The minimum background size is 64 bytes. The actual size of your backgrounds will depend on the number of objects, the size of the scripts, and the complexity of the graphics they hold.

> ▶ Properties: `cantDelete`, `id`, `name`, `number`, `script`, `showPict`
> ▶ All messages can be handled in the background script.

1.2 +   Starting with version 1.2, you can open the background script with Option-Command-B.

background   **Object**

Notes   Specifies a class of objects (background 1) or identifies other objects as belonging to a background (background button 1). Abbreviation is `bkgnd`.

1.2 +   New abbreviation is `bg`.

Examples
```
get the name of background 1
put "Hello" into bkgnd button 1
go to cd 1 of bg 2 -- version 1.2
```

Background Button   **Object**

Notes   Buttons belonging to a background and present on all cards sharing that same background. Abbreviation is `bkgnd button`.

1.2 +   New abbreviation is `bg btn`.

See Also   **background, button**

Background Field   **Object**

Notes   Fields belonging to a background and present on all cards sharing that same background. Abbreviation is `bkgnd field` or just `field`.

1.2 +   New abbreviation `bg fld` or `fld`.

See Also   **background, field**

Background Picture

Concept

Notes   A picture—created with the Paint tools, or with another application and copied in through the Clipboard—that is shared with all cards with the same background. The background picture can be edited when the `editBkgnd` property is set to true. Can be concealed by the card picture.

1.2+   Picture can be hidden with `hide background picture` and `show background picture`. New abbreviation is `bg pict`.

See Also   **Copy Picture, Cut Picture, Graphics, hide picture, Paste Picture, show picture, showPict**

background picture

Noun

Notes   Any graphics belonging to the background.

1.2+   In version 1.2 and higher, you can `show` or `hide` the background picture. Abbreviations include `bkgnd pict` and `bg pict`.

Examples   `hide bg pict`

See Also   **Background Picture, hide picture, show picture, showPict**

backgrounds

Object Type

Notes   Designates a type of object. Used with `the number` function. Abbreviation is `bkgnds`.

1.2+   New abbreviation is `bgs`.

Example   `put the number of backgrounds into msg`

See Also   **background**

barn door

Visual Effect

Notes   Like a double wipe. `barn door open` starts at the middle and wipes left and right to the sides; `barn door close` starts at the sides and wipes to the middle.

Example   `visual effect barn door open fast to black`
`go to card id 3484`

See Also   **visual**

beep

Command

Syntax   `beep <count>`

Notes   Activates the Macintosh beep sound for the number of times indicated in the count parameter.

Examples   `beep`
`beep 5`
`beep beeptimes`
`if card field 1 > 1 then beep card field 1`

See Also   **play, dial**

before

before	**Preposition**
Notes	A put command parameter that causes the source string to be appended to the front of any strings in the destination container.

Examples	`put " to say good-bye." into textVar`
	`put "Now it's time" before textVar`
	`-- Result = Now it's time to say good-bye.`

See Also	**after, into, put**

bg **bgs** **bkgnd** **bkgnds**	**Abbreviation**
Note	Abbreviations for background and backgrounds.
1.2 +	**bg** is new abbreviation.

Example	`set name of bkgnd 2 to "Perspective"`
	`go to card 1 of bkgnd "Sunset"`
	`go to cd 1 of bg "Sunset"a`
	`put the number of bkgnds into msg`
	`put the number of bgs into msg`

See Also	**background, backgrounds**

Bkgnd Info	**Menu Command**
Notes	Displays the Background Info dialog box. (See Figure R-6.) Found on the Objects menu when the `userLevel` is 4 (Authoring) or higher. The three dots are three periods and not an ellipsis.

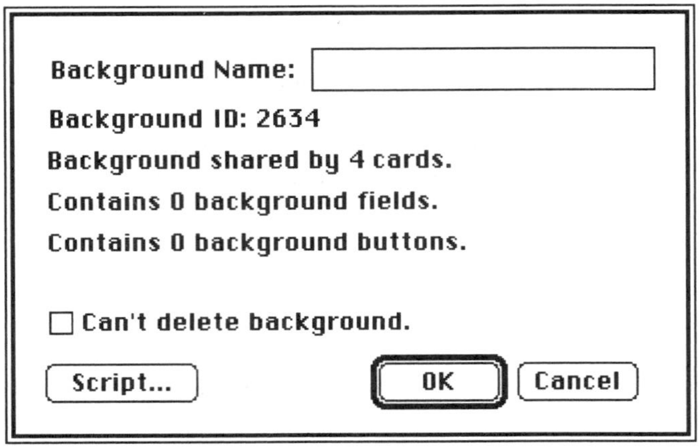

Figure R-6. The Background Info dialog box.

Examples	`doMenu "Bkgnd Info..."`

blindTyping — Global Property

Syntax [the] blindTyping

Notes Blind typing means typing into the Message box when it is hidden. If true you can blind type, if false you can't.

Examples
```
the blindTyping
-- Returns true or false (the required)
set blindTyping to true
set the blindTyping to propVar -- propVar contains
true or false
```

Boolean Algebra — Concept *(not a reserved word)*

Notes A system of algebra created by George Boole that compares logical values (true and false) rather than numbers. What computers do.

See Also **Keywords, Operators**

botRight — Button/Field/Window Property

Notes Abbreviation for bottomRight

1.2+ New version 1.2 feature.

Example `get the botRight of the message box`

See Also **bottomRight**

bottom — Button/Field/Window Property

Syntax [the] bottom of <object/window>

Notes Returns in pixels the distance between the top of the screen and the bottom of the object or window. Equivalent to item 4 of the rect of <object or window>. Changing the bottom does not change the height but does change the top. Can be used with buttons, fields, and windows (card window, tool window, pattern window, message window). Not available before version 1.2.

1.2+ New version 1.2 feature.

Example
```
bottom of button 1
set the bottom of card field 1 to 300
set bottom of btn 1 to bottom of cd window/2
-- Places bottom of button halfway down window.
on mouseUp
  put "the message window" into field 1
  put bottom of field 1 into msg
  -- Displays bottom of field
end mouseUp
```

See Also **bottomRight, cursor, height, left, right, set, top, topLeft, width, Windows**

bottomRight — Button/Field/Window Property

Syntax
```
[the] bottomRight of <object/window>
[the] botRight of <object/window>
```

Notes Returns in pixels the x and y coordinates for the bottom right corner of a field,

bottomRight

button, or window (card window, tool window, pattern window, message window). Equivalent to `item 4 of the rect of <object or window>` and `item 3 of the rect of <object or window>`. Changing the `bottomRight` does not change the `height` or the `width`, but it does change the `top` and the `left`. Not available before version 1.2.

1.2 +   New version 1.2 feature.

Example
```
bottomRight of button 1
set the bottomRight of card field 1 to 200,300
set botRight of btn 1 to ¬
bottom of cd window/2,right of cd window/2
```

See Also   **bottom, cursor, height, left, right, set, top, topLeft, width, Windows**

Bring Closer   Menu Command

Notes   Brings the selected object one layer closer to the top. Background objects can't be brought closer than the bottom card object. Available when `userLevel` is 4 (Authoring) or higher and a button or field is selected.

Keyboard   Command- + (plus)

1.2 +   You can now bring an object all the way to the top in one step regardless of its starting position. At the keyboard, this is done with Shift-Command- + (plus); in a script, you can use `type "+" with shiftKey,commandKey`.

Example   `doMenu "Bring Closer"`

See Also   **Send Farther**

Browse   Concept

Notes   Navigating around a stack or several stacks without changing the stack in any way.

See Also   **userLevel**

browse tool   General Tool

Notes   This is the tool with which you browse the stack. You must also use the browse tool to activate buttons and enter or edit text in a field.

Short Cut   You can select the browse tool from the keyboard with Command-Tab.

Example   `choose browse tool`

See Also   **choose, Tool Palette**

brush   Painting Property

Syntax   `[the] brush`

Notes   Gives you the current pattern and lets you change it with the `set` command. Default brush setting is 8. (See Figure R-7.)

Examples
```
the brush
-- Returns current brush setting (the required)
set brush to 10
```

continued

```
if the brush <> 8 then set brush to brushVar
put brush into brushHolder
```

See Also   **pattern, choose, set**

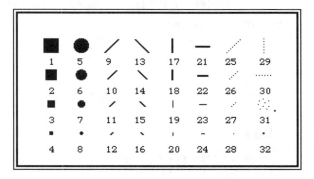

Figure R-7.   The default brush setting.

Brush Shape   **Menu Command**

Notes   Displays the dialog box in the brush listing without numbers. The three dots are three periods and not an ellipsis.

Example   `doMenu "Brush Shape..."`

brush tool   **Painting Tool**

Notes   Use with the `drag` command to draw lines with the current pattern and shape. Use with the `click` command to make "dots." The default brush is a 4-pixel circle. The default pattern is black.

Example   `choose brush tool`

See Also   **drag, click, set, choose, Tool Palette**

btn   **Abbreviation**

Notes   Abbreviation for button.

Example   `send mouseUp to btn 3`

See Also   **buttons**

btns   **Abbreviation**

Notes   Abbreviation for buttons.

1.2 +   New version 1.2 + feature.

Example   `get the number of cd btns`

See Also   **button**

bucket tool

bucket tool   Painting Tool

Notes   Use with the `click` command to pour the pattern on the screen. If the pixel at the location clicked is white, the pattern fills the white area until a black border is reached. If the pixel is black, the black is filled until a white border is reached.

Example
```
on mouseUp
   choose bucket tool
   set pattern to 4
   click at 268,42
end mouseUp
```

See Also   **click, pattern, choose, Tool Palette**

Bug   Concept *(not a reserved word)*

Notes   An error in a computer program. Probably your fault unless your machine is possessed by a demon (not covered by Apple Care). Many HyperTalk bugs result from confusion in referring to objects. Reread the `Naming` listing if you have a persistent error in a script.

See Also   **Debugging**

busy   Cursor

Notes   The beach ball cursor HyperCard uses when it compacts a stack. Each time `busy` is set, the ball rotates one-eighth of a turn, so you can make the ball spin by calling `busy` repeatedly.

1.2+   New version 1.2 feature.

Example   `set cursor to busy`

See Also   **cursor, set**

Button   Concept

Notes   A HyperCard object used for initiating actions. Belongs to either a card or a background. HyperCard does not provide either double outlined default buttons or dimmed buttons. The minimum button size on disk is 30 bytes. The maximum script size is 30,000 characters.

> ▶   Properties: autoHilite, bottom (1.2+), botRight (1.2+), height (1.2+), hilite, icon, id, left (1.2+), loc, name, number, rect, right (1.2+), script, showName, style, textAlign, textFont, textHeight, textSize, textStyle, top (1.2+), opLeft (1.2+), visible
> ▶   Only mouse messages go directly to the button script, but any other message can be handled if it is sent to the button with the `send` command.

button   Object

Notes   Designates a type of object. Assumed to belong to a card unless background is specified. Abbreviation is btn.

Example   `set the name of button 1 to "Go Home"`

continued

```
if the name of bkgnd btn 1 is "Gone"
then doMenu "Quit HyperCard"
```

Button Info   Menu Command

Notes   Accessible when the userLevel is 4 (Authoring) or higher. Displays the Button Info dialog box. (See Figure R-8.)

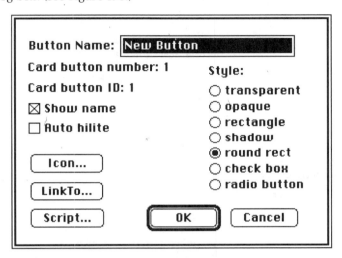

Figure R-8.   The Button Info dialog box.

Short Cut   Double click a button with the button tool.

Example   `doMenu "Button Info..."`

button tool   General Tool

Notes   Available from the authoring (4) and scripting (5) userLevels. Used with the click and drag commands to select, reposition, clone, and resize buttons. Used with doMenu command to copy, cut, paste, and clear buttons.

Short Cut   With versions 1.2 +, you can select the button tool from the keyboard with Command-Tab-Tab.

Examples   `choose button tool`
`if the tool is not "button tool" then choose button tool`

See Also   **click, drag, doMenu, choose, Tool Palette**

buttons   Object Type

Notes   Designates a type of object. Used with the number function.

1.2 +   Abbreviation is btns.

Example   `put the number of background buttons into msg`

See Also   **button**

Byte

Byte
Concept *(not a reserved word)*

Notes Eight binary bits that can store a number value up to decimal 255.

See Also **Kilobyte**

cantDelete
Background/Card/Stack Property

Syntax `[the] cantDelete of <object>`

Notes When `cantDelete` is set to true, the object can't be deleted from the stack. When it is false, the object can be deleted. The same as checking the Can't delete... box in the Info dialog box. To change the value, use the statement `set the cantDelete of <object> to <value>`.

1.2 + New version 1.2 feature.

Examples
```
the cantDelete of this card -- Returns true or false
set the cantDelete of bkgnd 3 to false
```

cantModify
Stack Property

Syntax `[the] cantModify of stack <name>`

Notes When `cantModify` is true, the stack is locked or write protected, and the user can't alter a stack in any way. Similar to Browsing mode. Setting this property to true is the equivalent of working on a locked disk, as indicated by the little padlock image that appears on the Menu bar. `cantModify` is set to true if the stack is on a CD-ROM disc, on a floppy with the write protect tab open, or if Locked is checked in the Finder's Get Info dialog box. In any of these cases, you are unable to change the `cantModify` property value from inside HyperTalk.

1.2 + New version 1.2 feature.

Examples
```
the cantModify of this stack -- Returns true or false
set cantModify of stack "Art Ideas" to true
on openStack -- Handler to check for locked media
  set cantModify of this stack to false
  if cantModify of this stack is true
  -- Stays true if the media is locked
  then answer "This stack is locked."
end openStack
```

See Also **userModify, Write Protect**

Card
Concept

Notes Basic unit of a HyperCard stack. An object that can contain graphics, buttons, and fields. Looking at a card, you also see the graphics, buttons, and fields that belong to the background shared by the particular card. The minimum card size is 64 bytes.

> ▶ Properties: `cantDelete` (1.2 +), `id`, `name`, `number`, `script`, `showPict` (1.2 +)
> ▶ All messages can be handled in the card script

See Also **Backgrounds, Messages, Objects, Properties**

card Object

Notes Designates a card object.

1.2+ Abbreviation is cd.

Example
```
go to card id 3456
get the name of card 4
go to cd "Home"
```

Card Button Concept

Notes Buttons unique to a particular card. Buttons are presumed to be card buttons unless you specify background button.

1.2+ Abbreviation is cd btn or just btn.

Example `send mouseUp to button id 2`

See Also **Background Button, Button, button**

Card Field Concept

Notes Fields unique to a particular card. Fields are presumed to belong to the background unless you specify card field.

1.2+ Abbreviation is cd fld.

Example `get card field id 2`

See Also **Background Field, Field, field**

Card Info Menu Command

Notes Displays the Card Info dialog box as shown in Figure R-9.

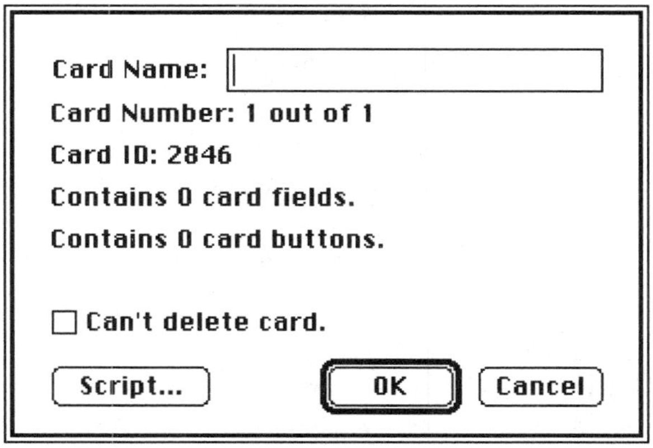

Figure R-9. The Card Info dialog box.

Found on the Objects menu when the userLevel is 4 (Authoring) or higher. The three dots are three periods and not an ellipsis.

Examples `doMenu "Card Info..."`

See Also **doMenu**

Card Picture

Card Picture Concept

Notes A picture–created with the Paint tools, or with another application and copied in through the Clipboard–that is unique to one card. A card picture can conceal a background picture.

See Also **Copy Picture, Cut Picture, hide picture, Paste Picture, show picture, showPict**

card picture Noun

Notes Any graphics belonging to the card.

1.2 + In version 1.2 and higher, you can show or hide the card picture. Abbreviations include card pict and cd pict.

Examples show cd pict

See Also **Card Picture, hide picture, show picture, showPict**

card window Window

Notes The main HyperCard window that displays the current card. The card window completely fills a small screen Macintosh and is centered on a larger screen. The window can be repositioned, moved off the screen, or even hidden.

Example
```
set loc of card window to -600,0 -- Moves window off screen
hide card window -- Makes card disappear
```

cards Object Type

Notes Designates a type of object. Used with the number function.

Example put the number of cards into msg

See Also **card**

cd
cds Abbreviation

Notes Short for card and cards in version 1.2 and higher.

1.2 + New version 1.2 feature.

Examples
```
go to cd id 3456
put the number of cds into field 3
```

See Also **card**

centered Paint Property

Syntax [the] centered

Notes If true, paint shapes are drawn from the center; if false, shapes are drawn from the corner. The default value is false. The regular polygon tool automatically draws centered.

Examples
```
the centered -- Returns true or false (the required)
get centered
-- Returns true or false in the variable it
```

continued

```
set centered to true
set the centered to centeredVar
-- Puts the value into a variable
set centered to not the centered
```

char
character
Chunk

Syntax   `char <number> [to <number>] of <string>`

Notes   A character. For the string `Hello`, char 1 is H; char 2 to 4 is ell. The string can be quoted, or it can be the contents of a container.

Examples
```
put char 5 of "Macintosh" into the message box
-- Displays n
put message box into char 4 of field 1
if char 1 of var1 is empty then exit repeat
put char var1 to var2 of message box into card field 1
```

See Also   **line, item, word, do**

chars
characters
Chunk Type

Notes   Way of referring to characters as individual entities not grouped into words.

Examples
```
the number of chars in field 1 -- Returns a number
on MouseUp
  put "Hello Fred" into field 2
  find chars "llo" in field 2
end MouseUp
```

See Also   **Containers, find, number**

charToNum
String Function

Syntax
```
[the] charToNum of <character>
charToNum(<character>)
```

Notes   Returns ASCII code for the character. Strings must be quoted. Can also convert constants like `return`, `tab`, etc.

Example
```
charToNum("A") -- Returns 65
charToNum(var1)
-- Returns the value of the character in the variable
charToNum(return) -- Returns 13
get the charToNum of it -- Where it is a variable
put charToNum(8) into field 1
if the charToNum(char 3 of var1) is 13 then beep
on mouseUp -- Script to change all characters to lowercase
  repeat with i = 1 to the number of chars in field 1
    get charToNum of char i of field 1
    if it > 64 and it < 91 then
    add 32 to it
    put numToChar(it) into char i of field 1
    end if
```

continued

charToNum

```
        end repeat
    end mouseUp
```

See Also   **numToChar, ASCII**

checkbox   **Button Style**

Notes   A little box with text to the right. You can check the box by clicking. If you want to set the `textFont` and `textStyle` with buttons, you use radio buttons for the font (only one at a time) and check boxes for the style (can be a combination of elements).

Examples   `set the style of button id 3 to checkbox`

See Also   **Buttons, style**

checkerboard   **Visual Effect**

Notes   An effect that changes the card to the new card, to an image, in separate offset squares rather than all at once. Requires a contrasting image or card to go to.

Example
```
visual effect checkerboard slow
go next
```

See Also   **visual**

choose   **Command**

Syntax   `choose <tool>`

Notes   Used to select a tool from the Tool Palette. Tools available depend on `userLevel` property, as shown in Figure R-10.

Keyboard   Command-Tab chooses the browse tool.

1.2 +   Command-Tab-Tab chooses the button tool; Command-Tab-Tab-Tab chooses the field tool.

Examples
```
choose button tool
choose var1 -- Tool name in variable
choose field 1 -- Tool name in field
on enterKey
   -- Stack handler to cycle through General tools
   if the tool is "browse tool"
   then choose button tool
   else if the tool is "button tool"
   then choose field tool
   else choose browse tool
end enterKey
```

See Also   **individual tools**

Chunk   **Concept**

Notes   A component (char, word, item, line) of a string. Usually from a container.

Example
```
get char 2 of item 3 of line 1 of field "Example"
put any char of "abcdefg" into noteVar
```

See Also   **char, chars, Containers, item, line, word**

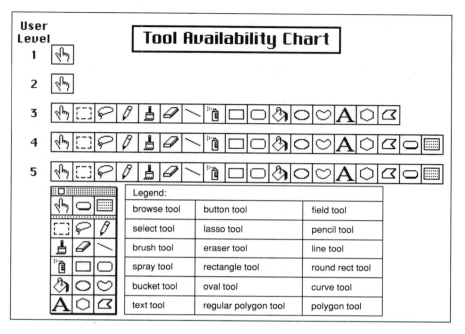

Figure R-10. The Tool Palette.

Clear Button Menu Command

Notes Erases the selected button. Can't be undone.

Example
```
doMenu "Clear Button"
on mouseUp -- Handler to delete a button
  choose button tool
  click at the loc of button 1
  doMenu "Clear Button"
end mouseUp

on mouseUp -- 1.2+ alternative to the previous handler
  select btn 1
  doMenu "Clear Button"
end mouseUp
```

Clear Field Menu Command

Notes Erases the selected field. Can't be undone.

Example `doMenu "Clear Field"`

Clear Picture Menu Command

Notes Erases the selected picture. Can be undone with the Undo menu command.

Example `doMenu "Clear Picture"`

Clear Text

Clear Text   Menu Command

Notes   Erases the selected text. Can't be undone.

Example   doMenu "Clear Text"

click at   Command

Syntax   click at <h>,<v> [with modKey [,modKey2 [,modKey3]]]

Notes   Simulates the user clicking at the specified coordinates. The first coordinate is the distance in pixels from the left edge of the screen. The second coordinate is the distance from the top of the screen. The coordinates can be in separate literals or containers separated by a comma, or they can be combined in one container. The coordinates can also be supplied by a function or property. You can simulate pressing up to three modifier keys (commandKey, optionKey, shiftKey) at the same time as the click.

1.2 +   Clicking a Paint tool when the picture is hidden (showPict is false) generates an error message. Do a show card picture or show bkgnd picture before clicking.

Examples
```
click at 100,100
click at hVar,vVar
click at loc of button 4
-- Coordinates from a property
click at mouseLoc with commandKey
-- Function coordinates
click at locVar with keyVar -- locVar = 50,250, keyVar = ¬
shiftKey
on mouseUp -- Select text in locked field
  set lockText of me to false -- Unlock field
  click at the clickLoc
  click at the clickLoc -- Simulate a double click
  find the selection in field id 2
  -- Do find on selection
set lockText of me to true -- Re-lock field
end mouseUp
```

See Also   **bucket tool, select tool, lasso tool, pencil tool, brush tool, text tool, drag**

clickH   System Function

Syntax
```
the clickH
click()
```

Notes   Returns the x coordinate of the mouse cursor as of the last time the mouse button was down prior to the start of a script. Does not return the current cursor location.

1.2 +   New version 1.2 feature.

Examples
```
the clickH -- the mandatory
put clickH() into the message box
```

See Also   **clickLoc, clickV, mouseLoc**

clickLoc   System Function

Syntax
```
the clickLoc]
clickLoc()
```

Notes
Returns the location of the mouse cursor as of the last time the mouse button was down prior to the start of a script. Does not return the current cursor location.

Examples
```
the clickLoc -- the mandatory
-- Returns a coordinate pair (h,v> requires the
put clickLoc() into var1
set the loc of button 1 to the clickLoc
if item 2 of the clickLoc > 200 then exit
mouseDown
```

See Also   **clickH, clickV, mouseClick, mouseLoc**

clickV   System Function

Syntax
```
the clickV
clickV()
```

Notes
Returns the y coordinate of the mouse cursor as of the last time the mouse button was down prior to the start of a script. Does not return the current cursor location.

1.2 +   New version 1.2 feature.

Examples
```
the clickV -- the mandatory
if clickV() is > numVar then exit to hypercard
```

See Also   **clickH, clickLoc, mouseLoc**

Clipboard   Utility *(not a reserved word)*

Notes
A place to store text and pictures temporarily. The Clipboard is accessible from all applications and is a good way to transport small amounts of data. The contents of the Clipboard remain the same until something else is copied or the Macintosh is shut down. To preserve the contents of the Clipboard between sessions or to avoid accidentally overwriting it, paste it into the Scrapbook.

See Also   **Copy..., Cut..., Paste...**

close file   Command

Syntax
```
close file <name>
```

Notes
Closes a text file. Generates an error if there isn't an open file. You may have to give a pathname if the file is not at hand. Files are closed automatically when you quit HyperCard, execute the `exit to hypercard` statement, or use the Command-. (period) key combination.

Examples
```
close file "NamesFile"
close file var1 -- File name in variable
close file card field 1 -- File name in field
-- File name with full pathname
close file "MovieDrive:GangsterFldr:ItalianFldr:Godfather"
```

See Also   **Pathname, open file, write, read, Text Files**

close printing

close printing	**Command**
Syntax	*close printing*
Notes	Ends a printing session.
| Examples | ```
on mouseUp -- Handler to print 2 cards
   open printing
   print card 3
   print card 8
   close printing
end mouseUp
``` |
| See Also | **open printing, print** |

closeBackground	**Message**
Notes	Sent when you navigate from one background to another unless lockMessages is true. closeBackground handlers should be in background object or higher scripts.
| Examples | ```
send closeBackground to this bkgnd
on closeBackground
   play "Harpsichord"
end closeBackground
``` |
| See Also | **Handlers, Hierarchy** |

closeCard	**Message**
Notes	Sent when you navigate from one card to another unless lockMessages is true. closeCard handlers should be in card object or higher scripts.
| Examples | ```
send closeCard to this card
on closeCard
   set scroll of card field 1 to 0
end closeCard
``` |
| See Also | **Handlers, Hierarchy** |

closeField	**Message**
Notes	Sent when you leave a field if the contents of the field have been changed.
Caution	Don't depend on closeField. There are several circumstances in which this message won't actually be sent.
| Examples | ```
send closeField to field 3
on closeField
   beep
end closeField
``` |
| See Also | **Handlers, Hierarchy** |

closeStack	**Message**
Notes	Sent when you leave one stack and go to another stack unless lockMessages is true. Also sent when you quit or suspend HyperCard. closeStack handlers should

be in stack object or higher scripts (can be as low as the card level in a stack with only one card).

Examples
```
send closeStack to this stack
on closeStack
   -- Handler to let user compact a stack when closing
   answer "Stack contains" && ¬
   round(the freeSize of this stack/1024) && ¬
   "K free space" with "Compact" or "Ok"
   if it is "Compact" then doMenu "Compact Stack"
end closeStack
```

See Also   **Handlers, Hierarchy**

commandKey   System Function

Syntax
```
the commandKey or the cmdKey
commandKey()
```

Notes   Returns down if the Command key is currently pressed or up if the Command key is not pressed.

Examples
```
put the commandKey into cmdKeyVar -- Requires the
if commandKey() is down then send mouseUp to button1
if the cmdKey is down and the optionKey is down then beep
```

See Also   **commandKey** *(reserved word)*

commandKey   Modifier

Notes   Simulates the user pressing the Command key. Abbreviation is **cmdKey**.

Examples
```
drag from 10,10 to 90,90 with commandKey
click at 10,10 with commandKey
type "n" with cmdKey -- Alternative to doMenu "New Card"
```

See Also   **commandKey** *(function)*, **Modifier Keys**

Commands   Concept *(not a reserved word)*

Syntax   `command/message name [ parameter1 parameter2 etc.]`

Notes   Commands are actually handlers that are built into HyperCard. What the scriptor types are statements composed of message names and the associated arguments that are passed to HyperCard as parameters. A command and its associated arguments can be up to 254 characters long.

HyperTalk Commands

(name) = undocumented

(1.2) = available starting with version 1.2.

add	answer	ask
beep	choose	click
close file	close printing	convert
delete	dial	divide
do	doMenu	drag

Commands

edit script	find	get
global	go	hide
lock screen (1.2)	multiply	open
open file	open printing	play
pop card	print... with	print card
push card	put	read
reset paint	select (1.2)	send
show	show cards	sort
subtract	type	unlock screen (1.2)
visual	wait	write

Example   play "Boing" "a b c"

See Also   **Handlers, Messages**

Comment (--)   **Operator** *(not a reserved word)*

Notes   Comment. Indicates that the following text is a comment and not code. Can be used either on a line by itself or at the end of a command. Every non-HyperTalk line in a script should be commented.

Examples
```
-- HyperTalk poem follows
on poem -- poem user command
```

Compact Stack   **Menu Command**

Notes   Removes all free space and otherwise optimizes the stack. Compacting requires free disk space equal to the size of the stack. Trying to compact when there isn't enough space on the disk generates an error message.

Example
```
doMenu "Compact Stack"
on closeStack
   -- Script lets user compact stack on closing
   answer "Stack contains" && ¬
   round(the freeSize of this stack/1024) ¬
   && "K free space" with "Compact" or "Ok"
   if it is "Compact" then doMenu "Compact Stack"
end closeStack
```

See Also   **freeSize, size**

compound   **Math Function**

Syntax   compound(<rate per period>,<number of periods>)

Notes   Returns what one dollar would turn into at the end of the time specified. To figure what an investment will produce, multiply the result by the original principal. The rate is decimal (.10 = 10%).

Examples
```
compound(0.10,10)
-- 10% compounded yearly for 10 years results in 2.593742
compound(.02,4)
```

continued

```
-- 8% compounded quarterly for a year returns 1.082432
compound(0.10,10) * 100
-- Multiplying by principal of 100 gives 259.3742
round(compound(0.10,10)*100*100)/100
-- Multiplying rounding and dividing gives 259.37
compound(rateVar,card field "Periods")
on mouseUp
  put 100 into investmentVar -- Starting principal
  repeat for 10 -- Repeat for 10 years
    multiply investmentVar by compound(.00029,365)
    -- 8% compounded daily
  end repeat
  set the numberFormat to .00
  -- Change to dollar format
  put "$" & investmentVar into message box
-- Displays $288.16
end mouseUp
```

Concatenation

Concept *(not a reserved word)*

Notes The concatenation operator (&) joins one string or constant to another string or constant. To join strings and put one space between them, use the && operator.

Caution Do not use more than two &s at a time. &&& is not valid.

See Also **&, &&** *(at beginning of Reference)*

Constants

Concept *(not a reserved word)*

Notes A constant is a string of characters that stands for something other than those characters. Constants differ from variables in that they always stand for the same thing.

HyperTalk Constants:

zero	one	two
three	four	five
six	seven	eight
nine	ten	first
second	third	fourth
fifth	sixth	seventh
eighth	ninth	tenth
return	tab	space
lineFeed	formFeed	up
down	true	false
quote	empty	pi

Examples
```
put "Cats have" & return & nine & return & "lives" ¬
into field 3
```

See Also **Values,** *(individual constant listings)*

Containers

Containers **Concept** *(not a reserved word)*

Notes Things that can hold a value. HyperTalk containers include local and global variables, fields, `the message box`, and `the selection`. HyperTalk chunks (lines, items, words, and chars) also have most of the characteristics of containers. All values are stored as character strings but can be interpreted by HyperTalk as numbers, dates, or text. Fields are the only containers that can maintain a value between HyperCard sessions (but see also **Text File**). To specify the contents of a container when the container designator would also make sense, use `the value of <container>`.

Example
```
put char 1 to 4 of word 2 of item 3 of line 9 of ¬
field 2 into chunkVar
on mouseUp
  put "The thing contained" into field id 3
  put "field id 3" into containerVar
  put the value of containerVar into msg
  --Display = The thing contained
end mouseUp
```

See Also **char, field, global, get, item, line, message box, put, selection, Text File, value** *(function)*, **Values, Variables, word**

contains **Logical Operator**

Syntax `<textA> contains <textB> | <textB> is in <textA>`

Notes Returns true if the string `textB` can be found in the string `textA`. Returns false if `textB` is not in `textA`. Precedence = 7.

Examples
```
"password" contains "pass" -- Returns true
if field 1 contains stringVar then exit repeat
if "pass" is in the selection
then put the selection into var1
```

See Also **is in, is not in**

Control Structures **Concept** *(not a reserved word)*

Notes Arrangements of keywords that control the way a program flows. There are three kinds of control structures in HyperTalk: `on... end` or `function... end` handler structures, `if... then` structures and `repeat... end` structures.

▶ If Then Structures:

Syntax 1 `if <expression> then <command statement>`

Example `if the optionKey is down then go home`

Syntax 2 `if <expression>`
`then <command statement>`

Example `if the mouse is up`
`then put "Press the mouse button" into the msg`

Syntax 3 `if <expression> then <statement> else <statement>`

Example `if var1 < var2 then add 1 to var1 else add 1 to var2`

continued

Syntax 4
```
if <expression> then <command statement>
else <command statement>
```

Example
```
if not the mouseClick then put "No click yet" into msg
else put "We have a click" into msg
```

Syntax 5
```
if <expression> then <command statement>
else
  <command statements> -- Multiple statements OK
end if
```

Example
```
if the centered then put "Draw from center" into msg
else
  play "boing"
  put "Will draw from corner" into msg
end if
```

Syntax 6
```
if <expression>
then <command statement>
else if <expression>
then <command statement>
else if <expression>
then <command statement>
```

Example
```
if the tool is browse
then choose button tool
else if the tool is button
then choose field tool
else if the tool is field
then choose select tool
```

Syntax 7
```
if <expression> then
  <command statements> -- Multiple statements OK
else
  <command statements> -- Multiple statements OK
end if
```

Example
```
if the centered then
  play "harpsichord"
  put "Will draw from center" into msg
else
  play "boing"
  put "Will draw from corner" into msg
end if
```

Syntax 8
```
if <expression> then
  <command statements> -- Multiple statements OK
else if <expression> then
  <command statements> -- Multiple statements OK
else if <expression> then
  <command statements> -- Multiple statements OK
end if
```

Example
```
if the mouseV < 75 then
  play "harpsichord"
  put "Get down from there!" into msg
else if the mouseV > 290 then
  play "boing"
  put "What are you doing down there?" into msg
else if the mouseV < 290 and the mouseV > 200 then
```

continued

Control Structures

```
            play "beep"
            put "You're still pretty low." into msg
         else
            put "How dull, right in the middle." into msg
         end if
```

▶ Repeat Loop Structures:

Syntax 1 `repeat [for] <number> -- For a set number of iterations`

Example
```
repeat for 5
on mouseUp -- Number of beeps determined by field
   repeat for field 1 -- field 1 contains an integer
      beep
   end repeat
end mouseUp
```

Syntax 2 `repeat forever -- Requires an internal exit`

Example
```
repeat forever
   if the mouse is down and the shiftKey then next repeat
   -- Stays in loop but no beep
   if the mouse is down and the commandKey then exit repeat
   -- Exit from repeat loop
   if the mouse is down and the optionKey then exit mouseUp
   -- Exits entire handler
   if the optionKey is down and the commandKey is down
   then exit to HyperCard
   -- Exits nested handlers
   beep
end repeat
```

Syntax 3 `repeat until <condition> -- Until the condition is met`

Example
```
repeat until the commandKey is down
repeat until var1 > 5
on mouseUp -- Handler to inform or annoy the user
   repeat until the mouse is down
      put "Hit the mouse, big guy." into the message box
      beep
   end repeat
end mouseUp
```

Syntax 4 `repeat while <condition> -- As long as condition is met`

Example
```
on mouseUp -- Handler to play ever higher notes
   put 10 into var1
   repeat while the mouse is up
      play "harpsichord" var1 * 5
      add 1 to var1
   end repeat
   play stop
end mouseUp
```

Syntax 5 `repeat with <variable> = <number> to <number>`

Example
```
repeat with i = 1 to 10
repeat with n = 5 to 30
repeat with i = var1 to item 1 of card field 2
   play "harpsichord" i * 5
end repeat
```

Syntax 6   `repeat with <variable> = <number> down to <number>`

Example   `repeat with i = 20 down to 1`
`  set the loc of button 1 to i,i`
`end repeat`

> ▶ The `exit` keyword can be used to leave a `repeat` loop, or it can be used in either of the control structure types to leave the entire handler. There is even an `exit to hypercard` version that lets you escape from nested handlers. `exit` is demonstrated in `repeat` example 2.
>> ▶ The `next` keyword can be used to skip the rest of the current loop and start the next one. `next` is demonstrated in `repeat` example 2.

See Also   **exit, Functions, Handlers, if then, next, repeat, User Defined Functions, User Defined Messages**

controlKey   Command

Syntax   `controlKey <argument>`

Notes   Sent automatically when the Control key and another key are pressed. The second key pressed is identified in the argument passed along as a parameter of the `controlKey` message. You can also execute `controlKey` from the Message box or from your scripts. The argument values for all the keys are listed in the following table.

Argument		Keyboard Equivalent	
1	a, Home	19	s
2	b	20	t
3	c, Enter	21	u
4	d, Enter	22	v
5	e, Help	23	w
6	f	24	x
7	g	25	y
8	h, Delete	26	z
9	i, Tab	27	Esc, Clear, Left bracket ([)
10	j	28	Backslash (\\), Left arrow
11	k, Page Up	29	Right bracket (]), Right arrow
12	l, Page Down	30	Up arrow
13	m, Return	31	Hyphen (-), Down arrow
14	n	39	Single quotation mark (')
15	o	42	Asterisk (*)
16	p, all function keys	43	Plus (+)
17	q	44	Comma (,)
18	r	45	Minus (−)

controlKey

46	Period (.)	54	6
47	Slash (/)	55	7
48	0	56	8
49	1	57	9
50	2	59	Semicolon (;)
51	3	61	Equal (=)
52	4	96	Tilde (~)
53	5	127	Forward Delete

Examples
```
controlKey 19 -- Used as command in a script
-- The handler below would react to several key combos
on controlKey which
  -- Argument value in variable which
  if which = 20 then -- Letter t
    go "HyperTalk Tricks" -- A named stack
  else if which = 4 then -- Letter d
    go "Developer Stack 1.2 r" -- A named stack
  else if which = 19 then -- Letter s
    go card id 12133 of stack ¬
    "StackDisk:NewStacks:Stack Starter ß.972"
    -- ß = Option-s
    -- A card of an exceptional pathnamed stack
  else if which = 21 then -- Letter u
    set userLevel to 5 -- Change the userLevel
  end if
end controlKey
```

See Also   **enterKey, functionKey, returnKey**

convert   Command

Syntax   convert <container> to <format> [and <format>]

Notes   Converts a date or time in a container into one of the following formats:
seconds returns 2662133495 (seconds since 1/1/04)
    or 2662133460 (if time or short time,
      gives the seconds to the last full minute)
    or 2662069380 (if any date, gives seconds to the first second of the day)
dateItems returns 1988,5,10,17,31,35,3 (Y,Mo,D,H out of 24, Min,S,D of W)
    or 1988,5,10,17,31,0,3 (if time or short time, gives dateItems to the last
      minute)
    or 1988,5,10,0,0,0,3 (if any date, gives dateItems to the first second of day)
long date returns Tuesday, May 10, 1988
short date returns 5/10/88
abbreviated date returns Tue, May 10, 1988
long time returns 5:31:35 PM
short time returns 5:31 PM
Use the two formats option to get both the date and the time in one step (see last example).

Caution   Note different results based on amount of information originally saved. Best to work with the long time, which saves every date item.

Examples

```
put the date into dateVar -- 5/10/88
convert dateVar to abbrev date -- Tue, May 10, 1988
convert dateVar to long date -- Tuesday, May 10, 1988
convert dateVar to short date -- 5/10/88
convert dateVar to dateItems -- 1988,5,10,0,0,0,3
convert dateVar to seconds -- 2662069380
put the long time into field 1 -- 5:31:35 PM
convert field 1 to short time -- 5:31 PM
convert field 1 to long time -- 5:31:35 PM
convert field 1 to dateItems -- 1988,5,10,17,31,35,3
convert field 1 to seconds -- 2662133495
convert field 1 to short date and short time
-- 7/8/88 5:31 PM
```

See Also   **abbreviated date, date, Format, seconds, time**

Copy Button   **Menu Command**

Notes   Places the selected button onto the Clipboard. Copying a button with an icon into a stack also moves the icon resource.

Keyboard   Command-C, Function-3

Example
```
doMenu "Copy Button"
on mouseUp -- Handler to copy a button
  choose button tool
  click at the loc of button 1
  doMenu "Copy Button"
end mouseUp
```

See Also   **Clear Button, Cut Button, Paste Button**

Copy Card   **Menu Command**

Notes   Places the current card onto the Clipboard.

Example   `doMenu "Copy Card"`

See Also   **Clear Card, Cut Card, Paste Card**

Copy Field   **Menu Command**

Notes   Places the selected field onto the Clipboard.

Keyboard   Command-C, Function-3

Example   `doMenu "Copy Field"`

See Also   **Clear Field, Cut Field, Paste Field**

Copy Picture   **Menu Command**

Notes   Places the selected picture onto the Clipboard.

Keyboard   Command-C, Function-3

Example   `doMenu "Copy Picture"`

See Also   **Clear Picture, Cut Picture, Paste Picture**

Copy Text

Copy Text — Menu Command

Notes   Places the selected text onto the Clipboard.

Keyboard   Command-C, Function-3

Example   `doMenu "Copy Text"`

See Also   **Clear Text, Cut Text, Paste Text**

COS — Math Function

Syntax
```
the cos of <angle/radians>
cos(<angle/radians>)
```

Notes   Returns the cosine of an angle. To convert degrees to radians, multiply the angle in degrees by `pi/180`. Cosine values range between -1 and 1. As shown in Figure R-11, the cosine of an acute angle (A) = the adjacent side (b) divided by the hypotenuse (c). If you know the angle and any one of these two sides, you can get the other side: `b/cos(A*pi/180) = c`, `c*cos(A*pi/180) = b`. If you know sides b and c only, you can find side a with `sqrt(c*c-b*b)`. Once you have all three sides, you can find the angle of the acute angle with `atan(a/b)*180/pi = A`.

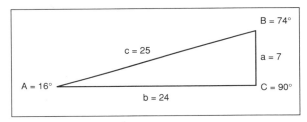

Figure R-11.   The `cos` function.

Examples
```
cos(75) -- The cosine of 75 radians returns 0.921751
the cos of radianVar
cos(50*pi/180) -- Cosine of 50 degrees 0.642788
round(24/cos(16*pi/180)) -- Returns 25
round(25*cos(16*pi/180)) -- Returns 24
sqrt(25*25-24*24) -- Returns 7
round(atan(7/24)*180/pi) -- Returns 16
```

See Also   **atan, sin, tan**

cross — Cursor

Notes   The crosshair cursor. Can also be referred to as cursor 2.

1.2 +   Starting with version 1.2, can be referred to by name as cursor `cross`.

Example   `Set cursor to cross`

See Also   **cursor**

Current — Concept *(not a reserved word)*

Notes   The card, background, or stack on the screen at the moment.

See Also   **this**

cursor   Global Property

Syntax   [the] cursor to <value>

Notes   Controls the appearance of the mouse cursor. This property can only be used to set the cursor, not to get the current value. You can control the cursor only while a handler is running. Besides the cursors included with HyperTalk, you can make custom cursors using ResEdit or some other resource editor and then refer to the custom cursor by ID number or name. Required cursor resources must reside in a stack you are distributing. A cursor is a 16-pixel by 16-pixel graphic image with a mask of the same size and a 1-pixel hot spot (see Figure R-12) that determines the actual pixel coordinate for mouseDown messages or mouseLoc functions. HyperTalk's built in cursors: iBeam = 1 (text), cross = 2, plus = 3, watch = 4.

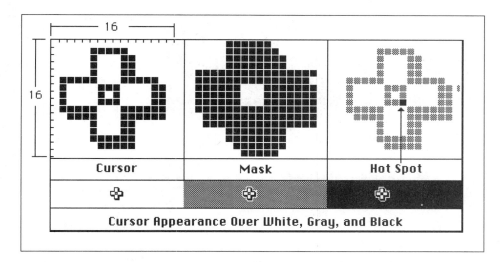

Figure R-12.   Cursor size.

1.2+   New cursors: arrow, busy, none. All cursors can now be designated by name. arrow is the standard Macintosh cursor pointer. busy is the beach ball that rotates 1/8th turn each time it is called. Setting the cursor to none clears the screen so that the user is not distracted by the cursor.

Examples
```
set the cursor to 4 -- Shows the wrist watch
set the cursor to item n of numVar
set the cursor to none
on mouseUp -- Beach ball exercising handler
  repeat until the mouse is down
    set cursor to busy
  end repeat
end mouseUp
```

curve tool   Painting Tool

Notes   The curve tool can't be simulated in a script.

Custom Messages

Custom Messages

Concept *(not a reserved word)*

Notes   Another name for user defined commands and functions. These are messages you create and then write handlers for.

See Also   **User Defined Commands, User Defined Functions, User Defined Messages**

Cut Button   Menu Command

Notes   Removes the selected button from the card and places it on the Clipboard. Sends a `deleteButton` message.

Keyboard   Command-X, Function-2

Example
```
doMenu "Cut Button"
on mouseUp
  choose button tool
  click at the loc of button 1
  doMenu "Cut Button"
end mouseUp
```

See Also   **Clear Button, Copy Button, Paste ButtonG**

Cut Card   Menu Command

Notes   Removes the current card from the stack and places it on the Clipboard. Sends a `deleteCard` message. To give a card a new background, cut and paste it to another stack, change it slightly (rename it, for instance), and then cut it again and paste it back where it started.

Keyboard   Command-X, Function-2

Example   `doMenu "Cut Card"`

See Also   **Copy Card, Paste Card**

Cut Field   Menu Command

Notes   Removes the selected field from the card and places it on the Clipboard. Sends a `deleteField` message.

Keyboard   Command-X, Function-2

Example   `doMenu "Cut Field"`

See Also   **Clear Field, Copy Field, Paste Field**

Cut Picture   Menu Command

Notes   Removes the selected picture from the card and places it on the Clipboard.

Keyboard   Command-X, Function-2

Example   `doMenu "Cut Picture"`

See Also   **Clear Picture, Copy Picture, Paste Picture**

Cut Text — Menu Command

Notes — Removes the selected text from the card and places it on the Clipboard.

Keyboard — Command-X, Function-2

Example — doMenu "Cut Text"

See Also — **Clear Text, Copy Text, Paste Text**

Darken — Menu Command

Notes — Scatters random black pixels in the selected graphic area.

Example —
```
doMenu "Darken"
on mouseUp -- Handler to make a speckled square
  choose select tool
  drag from 50,50 to 100,100
  doMenu "Darken"
end mouseUp
```

See Also — **Lighten**

date — System Function

Syntax — the [short | abbreviated (abbrev) | long] date

Notes — Returns the current date (assuming the clock in your Macintosh is set correctly and working).
The different formats are
the long date returns Tuesday, February 10, 1988
the date and the short date return 2/10/88
the abbrev date returns Tue, Feb 10, 1988

Examples —
```
the date -- Returns 5/10/88
put the abbrev date into dateVar
if word 2 of item 2 of the long date > 10 then beep
```

See Also — **convert, dateItems, time**

Decrement — Concept *(not a reserved word)*

Notes — Repeatedly reducing a numeric value by a set amount. HyperTalk's **repeat** loops don't offer a step feature to let you easily decrement a number by more than 1 at a time.

Examples —
```
on mouseUp
  repeat with i = 20 down to 1
    set name of button 1 to i
  end repeat
end mouseUp
```

See Also — **repeat**

delete — Command

Syntax — delete <chunk> of <container> [of card <designator>]

Notes — Removes the text in the specified chunk of the specified container. In the case of words, items, and lines, **delete** removes the spaces, commas, and returns, as

delete

well as the text. Deleting a line leaves one fewer lines rather than an empty line. You can specify the card if the container is not on the current card. Doesn't work on whole containers (delete field 2).

Example
```
delete word 1 of the selection
delete char 2 of line 1 of card field 3
delete line 1 to the number of lines of field "Notes" of ¬
field "Notes" of card "Things to do"
on mouseUp
  put "one,two,three" into listVar
  delete item 2 of listVar -- listVar now = "one,three"
end mouseUp
```

See Also   **empty**

Delete Card   **Menu Command**

Notes   Removes the current card from the stack. Sends the following messages in the following order: deleteCard, closeCard, openCard. Available when the userLevel is 2 (Typing) or higher.

1.1 +   Can be undone with doMenu "Undo". Also, the closeCard and openCard messages are no longer sent.

Example   `doMenu "Delete Card"`

Delete Stack   **Menu Command**

Notes   Removes the current stack, after the user confirms the alert box, and takes you Home. Sends the following messages in the following order: closeCard, closeBackground, closeStack, deleteStack, (to Home stack) openStack, openBackground, openCard. Available when the userLevel is 2 (Typing) or higher.

Example   `doMenu "Delete Stack"`

deleteBackground   **Message**

Notes   Sent to a background before it is deleted.

Example
```
on deleteBackground -- Background, stack, or Home handler
  answer "Curses! Deleted again."
end deleteBackground
```

deleteButton   **Message**

Notes   Sent to a button before it is deleted.

Example
```
on deleteButton
  play "Boing"
end deleteButton
```

deleteCard   **Message**

Notes   Sent to a card before it is deleted.

Example   `on deleteCard`

continued

```
    answer "You will regret this."
end deleteCard"
```

deleteField   Message

Notes   Sent to a field before it is deleted.

Example
```
on deleteField
   global rescueVar
   put the value of the target into rescueVar
   -- Saves text in field to a variable
end deleteField
```

deleteStack   Message

Notes   Sent to a stack before it is deleted.

Example
```
on deleteStack
   put "Good-bye" into message box
end deleteStack"
```

dial   Command

Syntax   `dial <number> [with modem [<modemParameters>]]`

Notes   Causes your Macintosh to generate touch tone sounds. Used for sound effects or for dialing a phone. Hold mouthpiece of phone up to speaker or buy a device to connect the sound output to the phone. Pick up the phone and get a dial tone before you execute the command. Enclose phone numbers in quotation marks so that hyphens are not interpreted as minus signs.

Modems   To dial with a modem, make sure the modem is connected to the modem port (won't work through printer port). If you have tone service use the ATDT modem argument; for pulse service use ATDP. These are standard modem commands: AT means attention, D is the dial command, T is for touch tone dialing, and P is for pulse dialing. See your modem manual for other commands. There is a default modem parameter, but it tends to cut off calls. The modem stays on the line with ATDT unless you force a disconnect (see the last example).

Example
```
dial "408-555-1212"
dial "(415)" && "555-1212"
dial "1-408-996-1010" with modem "ATDT -- Tone dialing
dial "1-408-996-1010" with modem "ATDP" -- Pulse
dial empty with modem "A/"-- Re-dials last number
dial empty with modem "ATH" -- Disconnects modem
```

diskSpace   System Function

Syntax
```
the diskSpace
diskSpace()
```

Notes   Returns the number of unused bytes on the disk that holds the current stack. To convert this number to kilobytes, divide by 1,024.

Examples
```
on doMenu what
-- Handler to check to see if you have room to compact
```

continued

diskSpace

```
if what is "Compact Stack" or what is "Copy Stack" then
  put (the size of this stack - the freeSize of this ¬
  stack * 2) div 1024 into needVar
  put the diskSpace div 1024 into haveVar
  answer needVar && "K needed to compact;" && ¬
  haveVar && "K available" with "Compact" or "Cancel"
  if it is Cancel then exit doMenu else pass doMenu
end if
pass doMenu
end doMenu
```

See Also **freeSpace**

dissolve   Visual Effect

Notes   Looks like the current card dissolves into the next card or into the specified image.

Example
```
visual effect dissolve slowly to inverse
go home
```

See Also **visual**

div   Math Operator

Syntax   `<dividend> div <divisor>`

Notes   The divide and truncate operator divides the first number by the second and returns an integer. Any remainder is ignored.

Example
```
10 div 3 -- Result = 3
get 49 div 5 -- Puts 9 into the variable it
if the number of cards div it > 10 then beep
on mouseUp -- Handler to format a dollar amount
  put trunc(450056.6789*100) into amount
  -- amount = 45005667
  put amount div 100 into dollars
  -- dollars = 450056
  put "$" & dollars  & "." & (amount mod 100) in msg
  -- $450056.67
  get the number of chars of dollars -- 6
  if it is > 3 then put "," after char it - 2 of msg
  -- $450,056.67
end mouseUp
```

See Also **/, divide, mod**

divide   Command

Syntax   `divide <dividend-destination> by <divisor>`

Notes   Divides the first number by the second and puts the result into the container holding the first number. The divisor can be an unquoted numeric value. Division by 0 gives an INF result.

Example
```
divide numVar by 9 --If number was 48 it will be 5.333333
divide numVar by field 1
divide the selection by numVar * 3
```

continued

```
       put 45 into dividendVar
       divide dividendVar by 0 -- dividendVar is INF
```

See Also   **/, div, mod, numberFormat**

do **Keyword**

Syntax   do <container>

Notes   Executes one HyperTalk statement previously placed in the container. Gives you the option of using different commands on the same line of a handler. If a command that should work doesn't, try putting it into a variable and doing it.

Example
```
on mouseUp
   put "go home" into field 1
   do field 1 -- Goes to card 1 of the Home stack
end mouseUp
on mouseUp
   put "button 1" into var2
   put "set loc of" && var2 && "to" && the clickLoc into it
   do it -- it contains set loc of button 1 to 250,200
end mouseUp
do line 3 of commandsVar
-- Executes a command on that line
on mouseUp -- Handler to flash text in the Message box
   put "Card field 3" into fieldVar -- Text is in the field
   repeat with i = 1 to 5
      do "get line" && i && "of" && fieldVar
      -- Same as get line 1 ( up to 5) of card field 3
      put it into msg
   end repeat
end mouseUp
```

doMenu **Command**

Syntax   doMenu <name>

Notes   Simulates selection of the named menu item. The **doMenu** command is used to execute all the menu commands. To execute a menu command, the menu item must be available (see Menu Commands), and you must provide the exact name of the item.

Caution   If you write a handler for the **doMenu** message to prevent or alter the use of some menu command, be sure to include a **pass** command for other **doMenu** options or the Menu bar will be disabled.

Example
```
doMenu "New Card" -- Creates a new card
doMenu "Button Info..."
doMenu itemVar
-- Where itemVar contains the name of a menu item
doMenu "Control Panel" -- Desk accessories are selectable
on doMenu what
   if what is "New Card" then go last -- Adds to end
   pass doMenu
end doMenu
on mouseUp -- Handler to make a miniature card image
   doMenu "Copy Card"
```

continued

doMenu

```
            type "v" with commandKey,shiftKey
          end mouseUp
```

See Also **Menu Commands, pass**

down Constant

Notes Describes the pressed state of keys and buttons. While the mouse button is pressed, the function `the mouse` returns down; consequently the statement, `the mouse is down` is true. The same is true for the modifier keys: `shiftKey`, `optionKey`, and `commandKey`.

Example `if the optionKey is down then go home`

See Also **commandKey, Constants, Functions, mouse, optionKey, shiftKey**

drag Command

Syntax `drag from h,v to h,v [with modKey1 [,modKey2 [,modKey3]]]`

Notes Simulates dragging the cursor with the mouse. The first h,v coordinates are the starting point and the second coordinates are the ending point. The coordinates can be literal numbers, each number can be in a separate container, or the two coordinate pairs can each be in a two-item container. See the individual tool listings for the modifier keys available and their effects. The speed of the `drag` is determined by the `dragSpeed` setting. The tool that is dragged is chosen with the `choose` command.

Caution You can't use the `drag` command to simulate the lasso tool, the curve tool, or the polygon tool.

1.2+ Dragging a paint tool when the picture is hidden (`showPict` is false) generates an error message. Do a `show card picture` or `show bkgnd picture` before dragging.

Example
```
drag from 55,100 to 200,250
drag from varH,varV to the mouseLoc with optionKey
on mouseUp -- Handler to move a button slowly
   choose button tool
   set dragSpeed to 75
   drag from the loc of button id 3 to the clickLoc
end mouseUp
```

See Also **choose, click, dragSpeed,** *(individual paint tools)*

dragSpeed Global Property

Syntax `[the] dragSpeed`

Notes Determines how fast, in pixels per second, a `drag` command drags. For a slow `drag`, try 72 (an inch per second); for a fast `drag`, use 1440 (20 inches per second) or higher. The `dragSpeed` is reset to 0 on `idle` (when no handlers are running), so it can't be set in the Message box. Confusingly, 0 is the maximum speed.

Example
```
set dragSpeed to 75
set dragSpeed to card field 1
on mouseUp -- Draws graphic bullets across the screen
   choose pencil tool
   set the dragSpeed to 500
```

continued

```
      repeat until the mouse is down
        get random(340)
        drag from 1,it to 510,it
        drag from 1,it to 510,it
      end repeat
    end mouseUp
```

See Also   **drag**

Draw Centered   **Menu Command**

Notes   Sets the `centered` property to true. Instead, use `set centered to true` or `false` for greater control.

Example   doMenu "Draw Centered"

See Also   **centered**

Draw Filled   **Menu Command**

Notes   Sets the `filled` property to true. Instead, use `set filled to true` or `false` for greater control.

Example   doMenu "Draw Filled"

See Also   **filled**

Draw Multiple   **Menu Command**

Notes   Sets the `multiple` property to true. Instead, use `set multiple to true` or `false` for greater control.

Example   doMenu "Draw Multiple"

See Also   **multiple**

Edit Pattern   **Menu Command**

Notes   Shows the pattern editing dialog box (see Figure R-13.), with the current pattern ready for editing. You can edit any of the 40 patterns, and the edited patterns are saved with the stack.

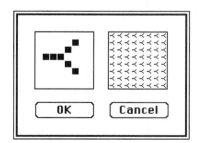

Figure R-13.   The pattern editing dialog box.

Example   doMenu "Edit Pattern"

edit script Command

Syntax `edit script of <object>`

Notes Opens the Script Editor and shows the script of the specified object. Program flow halts until the Script Editor is closed.

Example
```
edit script of button 1
edit script of card field id 2
edit script of card "Home"
edit script of me
-- Shows the script that contains the statement
edit script of target
-- The object that first received the message
edit script of this stack
-- The current stack. Also this card, this background
on mouseDown -- Put in card or higher script
   -- Handler to show script of all buttons & field & cards
   -- If Option key down and no mouseDown handler in target
   if the optionKey is down
   then edit script of target -- Show script of target object
end mouseDown
```

See Also **me, Naming, Script Editor, target**

editBkgnd Global Property

Syntax `[the] editBkgnd`

Notes If the `editBkgnd` is set to true, the results of using the painting tools go into the background graphic layer, and any buttons or fields pasted belong to the background. If the `editBkgnd` is set to false, the graphics, buttons, and fields go into the card layer.

Example
```
set editBkgnd to true
set editBkgnd to not the editBkgnd
```

See Also **multiple**

eight Constant

Notes Stands for the number 8.

See Also **Constants**

eighth Ordinal Constant

Notes Specifies the 8th object or chunk in an enclosing object or container.

Example `get eighth word of eighth field of eighth card`

See Also **Constants**

else Keyword

Notes Used in an `if then` control structure to indicate an alternative to the primary action.

Example   if the shiftKey is down then play "Boing" else beep

See Also   **Control Structures**

empty   Constant

Notes   Stands for the null character, ASCII code number 0. Putting empty into a container is the same as removing all value from the container. Same as "".

Example
```
put empty into card field 2
put empty into the selection
put empty into char 1 of item 2 of line 3 of variable1
if the message box is empty then answer "Wake up out there!"
```

See Also   **Constants, delete**

end   Keyword

Notes   Used to mark the end of a control structure.

Example
```
on beep howMany
   if howMany > 3 then
      answer "Give me a break!"
   end if
   repeat howMany
      play "harpsichord"
   end repeat
end beep
if the mouse is down then play "Boing" else beep
```

See Also   **Control Structures, else, if, on**

enterInField   Message

Notes   Sent when the Enter key is pressed or the enterKey command is executed and a field is open. If you don't use this message for some special purpose, it passes on to HyperCard and closes the field.

1.2 +   New version 1.2 feature.

Examples
```
on enterInField
   -- Put in card script or higher in several fields
   dial the selection -- Converts selected numbers to tones
   put the selection into field "PhoneLog" -- Records call
end enterInField
```

See Also   **Messages, returnKey, tabKey, enterInField, returnInField**

enterKey   Command

Syntax   enterKey

Notes   Executing this command is the equivalent of pressing the Enter key. If a field is open when an enterKey command is executed, no message is sent, but the field is closed without a closeField message being sent. Subsequent commands/keypresses send messages that can be trapped. The message is sent initially to the card object.

enterKey

1.2 + See `enterInField` for the new message sent when the `enterKey` command is executed and a field is open.

Examples
```
on mouseUp -- Button handler
  -- This is destructive of the field's contents
  tabKey -- Opens the first field on the card
  type "Isn't it time for you to go to bed"
  enterKey -- Closes the field
end mouseUp
on enterKey
  choose button tool
end enterKey
```

See Also **enterInField, Messages, returnKey, tabKey**

equals Logical Operator

See Also = *(at beginning of Reference)*

eraser tool Paint Tool

Notes A 16-pixel by 16-pixel square that turns everything it touches to white on the background layer (`editBkgnd` is true) or to transparent on the card layer (`editBkgnd` is false).

Example
```
on mouseUp
  choose eraser tool
  drag from 100,100 to clickLoc
end mouseUp
```

See Also **choose, Tool Palette**

Error Message Concept *(not a reserved word)*

Notes When HyperCard can't interpret something in a script, it interrupts the script and displays an alert box with a message explaining (in theory) the problem. There is no way to intercept these messages. This is annoying to the scriptor and can be very confusing to the casual user.

exit Keyword

Syntax `exit <messageName | repeat> | exit to HyperCard`

Notes Used to short circuit a repeat structure or a handler. With the `to hypercard` option, it can even get out of nested handlers.

Example
```
on mouseUp
  send subroutineMessage
end mouseUp
on subroutineMessage
  repeat forever
    if the optionKey is down then exit repeat
    -- Exits loop but finishes both handlers
    if the commandKey is down then exit subroutineMessage
    -- Finishes first handler
    if the shiftKey is down then exit to hypercard
```

continued

```
        -- Skips both handlers
    end repeat
end subroutineMessage
```

See Also   **Control Structures, Messages, Handlers**

exp   Math Function

Syntax
```
the exp of <number>
exp(<number>)
```

Notes   Returns e to the **<number>** power where e is 2.7182818.

Examples
```
exp(9) -- Returns 8103.083928
round(exp(9) -- returns 8103
exp(numVar)
```

See Also   **exp1, exp2**

exp1   Math Function

Syntax
```
the exp1 of <number>
exp1(<number>)
```

Notes   Returns 1 less than e to the **<number>** power where e is 2.7182818.

Examples
```
exp1(9) -- Returns 8102.083928
round(exp1(9) -- returns 8102
exp1(card field2)
```

See Also   **exp, exp2**

exp2   Math Function

Syntax
```
the exp2 of <number>
exp2(<number>)
```

Notes   Returns 2 to the **<number>** power.

Examples
```
exp2(9) -- Returns 512
exp2(9)/2 -- returns 256
exp2(the selection)
```

See Also   **exp, exp1**

Export Paint   Menu Command

Notes   Takes a picture of the current screen and stores it as a MacPaint document that the user can name by typing into a dialog box. Graphics, buttons, and fields, but not windoids, are shown in the picture. Available when any painting tool is chosen.

Example
```
choose select tool
doMenu "Select All"
doMenu "Export Paint..."
```

See Also   **Screen Dump, Select All**

Expression

Expression   **Concept** *(not a reserved word)*

Notes   A source of value composed of literals, constants, containers, functions, properties, operators, and other expressions.

Example
```
6*3 -- Expression results in a value of 18
6*3^numberVar+three
6*round(cos(50*pi/180)+ the lineSize
```

Externals   **Concept** *(not a reserved word)*

Notes   Units of compiled computer code added to HyperCard or to HyperCard stacks to increase the functionality of HyperTalk. Can be either commands (XCMDs) or functions (XFCNs).

See Also   **Resources, XFCN, XCMD**

false   **Constant**

Notes   Not true. Result of some properties and of the logical operators.

Example
```
the autoHilite of button 1
-- Returns false (if the button is a default button)
6<3 -- Returns false
not the visible of button1
-- Returns false (if the button is visible)
put false into truthValue
-- Variable truthValue contains false
if truthValue then beep
-- No beep as truthValue = false
```

See Also   **true**

FatBits   **Menu Command**

Notes   Enlarges a portion of the active graphic layer. A painting tool must be selected for this item to be available. Enlarged area centers on the last changed pixel. `drag` and `click` command coordinates in FatBits apply to the enlarged area, not the entire card.

Example
```
choose pencil tool
doMenu "FatBits"
```

Field   **Concept**

Notes   A HyperTalk container that is usually visible on the screen (but see `visible` property) and that the user can usually type text into (but see `lockText` property). Fields can contain up to 30,000 characters or 2,000 lines of text and can belong to either a particular card or to all the cards of a given background. You can access a field on another card in the same stack (`get field 2 of card 34`) without going to the card. If the field is in another stack, you must navigate to that stack before you can access it. Text in fields is editable and searchable. The minimum field size on disk is 30 bytes.

> Properties: `autoTab` (1.2 +), `bottom` (1.2 +), `botRight` (1.2 +), `height` (1.2 +), `id`, `left` (1.2 +), `loc`, `lockText`, `name`, `number`, `rect`, `right` (1.2 +), `script`, `scroll`, `showLines`, `style`, `textAlign`, `textFont`,

textHeight, textSize, textStyle, top (1.2 +), topLeft (1.2 +), visible

▶ Only mouse location messages (mouseEnter, mouseWithin, mouseLeave) are normally handled by fields, but when lockText is true, the other mouse messages can be handled. Any message can be sent to a field to be handled.

See Also **Containers, field** *(reserved word)*, **Properties, style**

Field Info **Menu Command**

Notes Shows the Field Info dialog box. (See Figure R-14.) Available when the userLevel is 4 (Authoring) or higher and a field is selected.

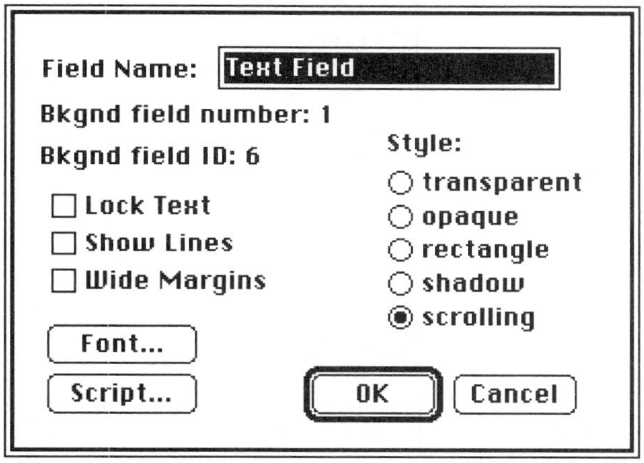

Figure R-14. The Field Info dialog box.

Example doMenu "Field Info..."

field **Object**

Notes Designates a text container that is usually visible on the screen. Fields are presumed to belong to the background unless you specify card.

Example
```
put "Hello" into field 1
-- Puts the quoted literal into the first background field
put field 1 into card field 3 of card 4
-- The card field on card 4 contains Hello
put char 2 of word 1 of card field 3 of card 4 into msg
-- Displays e in the message box
```

See Also **Field** *(concept)*, **Containers, Properties, style**

field tool **General Tool**

Notes Used to select, resize, reposition, clone, make a new field, and delete fields. Available when the userLevel is 4 (Authoring) or higher.
To reposition, drag from the middle.
To resize, drag from a corner.
To clone a copy, drag from center with optionKey. Copies inherit all proper-

field tool

ties of the original but not the text in the field container. Sends a `newField` message.
To delete, doMenu "Field Delete" (or doMenu "Cut Field" to preserve a copy). Sends a `deleteField` message.
To make a new transparent field, drag with `commandKey`. Also sends a `newField` message.

Example
```
on mouseUp
   set dragSpeed to 50
   choose field tool
   drag from 10,10 to 40,40 with commandKey
   -- Creates new transparent field
   drag from the loc of card field 1 to 100,100
   -- The center of card field 1 moved to 200,100
   drag from topLeft of card field 1 to 50,50
   --Resizes field from the top left corner, 1.2+ only
   drag from the loc of card field 1 to 300,200 with optionKey
   -- Clones a copy
   doMenu "Clear Field" -- Deletes the clone
end MouseUp
```

See Also   **choose, drag, Tool Palette**

fields   Object Type

Notes   Used with `the number` function to indicate the object of the inquiry.

Example   `put "Not Empty" into field the number of fields`

See Also   **field**

fifth   Ordinal Constant

Notes   Indicates the fifth instance of a specified object or chunk type in an enclosing object or container.

Example   `put "Number 9" into fifth line of fifth field`

See Also   **Constants**

File   Concept

Notes   An area on a disk outside HyperCard stacks where text can be stored. Files are opened with the `open file` command. Once files are opened, you can put new text in with the `write` command and take text out with the `read` command. Use `close file` when finished. There is a memory buffer associated with open files that can hold up to 16,384 characters.

Example
```
on mouseUp -- Handler to read from a file to a field
   open file "textFile"
   read from file "textFile" until return
   put it into card field 1
   close file "textFile"
end mouseUp
```

See Also   **close file, open file, read, write**

file   Reserved Word

Notes   Identifies a name as belonging to a file as opposed to an object or container.

Example
```
open file "textFile"
read from file "textFile" until return
put it into card field 1
close file "textFile"
```

See Also   **close file, File, open file, read, write**

Fill   Menu Command

Notes   Fills a graphic selection with the current pattern.

Example
```
choose lasso tool
click at the clickLoc with commandKey
-- Selects an enclosed area plus all black touching it
doMenu "Fill"
-- Fills entire selection with pattern
```

filled   Painting Property

Syntax   `[the] filled`

Notes   If true, shapes are drawn filled with the current pattern. If false, shapes are drawn with transparent insides.

Example
```
on mouseUp
    choose rectangle tool
    set filled to true
    drag from 100,200 to 1,1
end mouseUp
```

See Also   **Choose, pattern**

Find   Menu Command

Notes   Shows the Message box with `Find""` displayed. (See Figure R-15.)

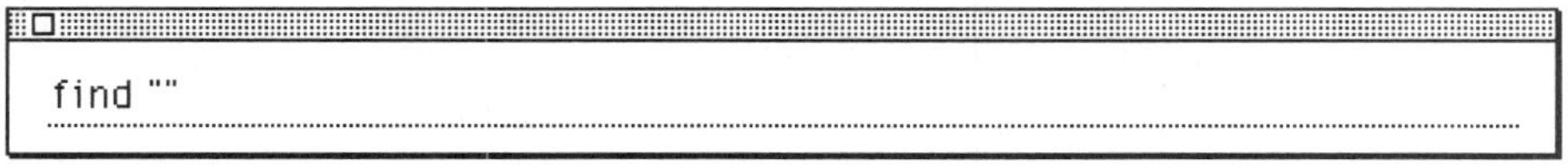

```
find ""
```

Figure R-15.   The `find` command Message box.

In most cases, you will want to use some version of the `find` command instead.

Keyboard   Command-F

Example   `doMenu "Find"`

find   Command

Syntax
```
find [chars | word] <source> [in field <designator>]
find [whole | string] <source> [in field <designator>]
```

Notes   Searches the current stack for a string literal or a string in a container. To look in

find

another stack, you must go to that stack. You can specify a background field to search in (find "Hello" in field id 3) but be careful. If you specify background field id 3, HyperCard determines the relative number (1, say) of that field and looks in field 1 of all the backgrounds of the stack. If the find command executes when the current background does not contain background field id 3, HyperCard does its usual unlimited search. Use chars to look for a string of characters anywhere in a word. Use word if you are looking for a whole word. The function the result returns not found after a find if nothing was found and empty if something was found. The find command works fastest when the source contains at least three characters. find word is the default setting.

Caution The find command looks in hidden fields as well as visible fields. If a word is found in a hidden field on another card, that card is opened but the field is not shown. You can't use find on variables.

1.2 + Two new options are find whole and find string. The find whole option is like find word but allows spaces (multiple words) in the source string. The find string option is like find chars but permits spaces in the source string.

Example
```
find word "Needle" in field "Haystack"
find word "back" -- Finds back but not backwards
find card field 2 in var1
-- Field contains search string, field designator in
-- variable
if the result is not empty then put "Sorry, no luck"
-- is not empty = is "not found"
put "Amanda Harry,Steve Cohen, Harry Cohen" into field 1
find "Harry Cohen" -- Will box Harry in Amanda Harry
find chars "rry Co" -- Will box rry in Amanda Harry
find whole "Harry Cohen" -- Boxes Harry Cohen
find string "rry Co" -- Boxes just those characters
on mouseUp
   -- Handler to find multiple occurrences of a word
   ask "Find what?"
   type "Find word" && quote & it & quote & return
end mouseUp -- Press return key for the next occurrence
```

See Also **foundChunk, foundField, foundLine, foundText, result**

Finder System Software *(not a reserved word)*

Notes The application you launch when you first start your Macintosh. The Finder is the home of the desktop metaphor and the place you go to open applications and sort files. A recent addition to the Finder is MultiFinder, which allows you to switch back and forth between multiple applications that are maintained in memory at the same time.

See Also **MultiFinder**

First Menu Command

Notes Goes to the first card in the current stack. Use go to first card or go first instead.

Keyboard Command-1

Example `doMenu "First"`

See Also **go**

first Constant

Notes Used in naming to indicate that the chunk, container, or object that follows is the first of its type.

Example
```
go to first card
go first card of this bkgnd
get name of first button of first card
put "M" into first char of field 2
```

See Also **Containers, Naming, Objects**

five Constant

Notes Stands for the number 5.

Example `go to card five`

See Also **Constants**

flash XCMD

Syntax `flash <number>`

Notes An example XCMD included with HyperCard that inverts the screen and then reinverts it to normal the number of times specified. Don't forget the `<number>` argument or your Mac will hang. You can get a nicer effect with `visual plain fast to inverse` and `go to card`. Vary the speed to taste.

Example
```
flash 2
flash numVar
```

fld
flds Abbreviations

Notes Short for field and fields respectively.

1.2+ New version 1.2 feature.

Example `put numVar into cd fld the number of cd flds`

See Also **Constants**

Flip Horizontal Menu Command

Notes Flips the current graphic selection so that the right becomes the left.

Example
```
choose select tool
drag from 10,10 to 100,100
doMenu "Flip Horizontal"
```

See Also **choose, doMenu, Flip Vertical**

Flip Vertical

Flip Vertical **Menu Command**

Notes Flips the current graphic selection so that the top becomes the bottom.

Example
```
choose select tool
drag from 10,10 to 100,100
doMenu "Flip Vertical"
```

See Also **choose, doMenu, Flip Horizontal**

formFeed **Constant**

Notes Used with text files. If a text file is formatted with formFeeds (ASCII 10's) between pages, you can use the `formFeed` constant to import one page of the file at a time into HyperCard.

Example
```
read from file "textFile" until formFeed
```

See Also **Files, read, write**

foundChunk **String Function**

Syntax
```
the foundChunk
```

Notes Returns the chars of the string boxed by the `find` command in the format `chars <number> to <number> of (card | bkgnd) field <number>`. If the `find` is unsuccessful, `foundChunk` returns `empty`. This function can be used to build a search and replace utility.

1.2+ New version 1.2 feature.

Caution The result of a `foundChunk` function is `empty` if it is not part of the script that executed the successful `find`. It must be executed immediately after the `find`.

Examples
```
put "This is HyperTalk" into field 1
find word "HyperTalk" in field 1
put the foundChunk into msg
-- chars 9 to 17 of field 1
put "fun" into the foundChunk -- "This is fun"
on mouseUp -- A search and replace handler
  ask "Find what?"
  put it into findVar
  ask "Replace with"
  put it into replaceVar
  put "Find whole" && quote & findVar & quote into msg
  put false into flagVar
  repeat forever
    returnKey
    if the foundChunk <> empty then
      put "put" && replaceVar && "into" && ¬
      the foundChunk into commandVar
      do commandVar
    else
      exit repeat
    end if
    answer "This is card" && the number of this card &¬
    ", continue searching?" with "Stop" or "Continue"
    if it is "Stop" then exit repeat
```

continued

```
          end repeat
        end mouseUp
```

See Also   **find, foundField, foundLine, foundText**

foundField   **String Function**

Syntax   `the foundField`

Notes   Returns the designator of the field containing the string boxed by the `find` command in the format `(card | bkgnd) field <number>`. This function can be used to show hidden fields containing found text.

1.2+   New version 1.2 feature.

Caution   The result of a `foundField` function is `empty` if it is not part of the script that executed the successful `find`. It must be executed immediately after the `find`.

Examples
```
        on mouseUp
          put "This is HyperTalk" into field 1
          find word "HyperTalk" in field 1
          put the foundField into msg -- Returns bkgnd field 1
          if the visible of the foundField is false
          then show the foundField
        end mouseUp
```

See Also   **find, foundChunk, foundLine, foundText**

foundLine   **String Function**

Syntax   `the foundLine`

Notes   Returns the line number and the designator of the field containing the string boxed by the `find` command in the format `line <number> (card | bkgnd) field <number>`. This function can be used to capture the context of a found string.

1.2+   New version 1.2 feature.

Caution   The line number is derived from the number of return characters in the field and does not necessarily match what the user would see on the screen. If a field is resized, forcing a word wrap, the return characters won't be at the end of the lines. As with the other `found...` functions, `foundLine` must be executed as part of the `find` script.

Examples
```
        on mouseUp
          put "What is this?" & return into field 1
          put "This is HyperTalk" after field 1
          find word "HyperTalk" in field 1
          put the foundLine into msg -- line 2 of bkgnd field 1
          put the value of the foundLine into msg
          -- This is HyperTalk
        end mouseUp
```

See Also   **find, foundChunk, foundField, foundText**

foundText   **String Function**

Syntax   `the foundText`

Notes   Returns the text found by the `find` command.

foundText

1.2 + New version 1.2 feature.

Caution The result of a foundText function is empty if it is not part of the script that executed the successful find. It must be executed immediately after the find.

Examples
```
on mouseUp
   put "This is HyperTalk" after field 1
   find word "HyperTalk" in field 1
   put the foundText into msg -- HyperTalk
end mouseUp
```

See Also **find, foundChunk, foundField, foundLine**

four   Constant

Notes Stands for the number 4.

Example `put it into field four of card four`

See Also **Constants**

fourth   Ordinal Constant

Notes Used in naming to indicate that the chunk, container, or object that follows is the fourth of its type.

Example
```
go to fourth card
get the name of fourth button of fourth card
put "M" into fourth line of fourth field
```

See Also **Constants**

Free Space   Concept

Notes Disk space occupied by a HyperCard stack but no longer needed. This wasted space accumulates in various ways and can be eliminated by compacting the stack.

See Also **diskSpace, freeSize**

freeSize   Global Property

Notes Returns the number of bytes of free space that have accumulated in the stack. Compact the stack to get rid of the free space.

Example
```
the freeSize of this stack
if the freeSize of this stack div 1024 > 20
then doMenu "Compact"
```

See Also **Compact**

from   Preposition

Notes Preposition added to HyperTalk to make statements read more like English.

Example
```
subtract 3 from numVar
read from file fileName until delimiterVar
```

function   Keyword

Syntax   `function <functionName> ([<parameterList>])`

Notes   Equivalent in a function handler of `on` in a message handler. `function` is followed by the function name and a list of parameters passed with the function. The parentheses are required even when no arguments are passed with the function. The handler ends with `end <functionName>`. The most important line in a function handler is the one that starts with the keyword `return` and actually returns the value of the expression following `return` to the statement that originally executed the function.

Example
```
on mouseUp -- Handler that executes a user function
  ask "Enter a number between 2 and 10"
  -- Put numeric value into it
  put exponentiate(it) into msg
  -- exponentiate is a user defined function that passes
  -- the value of it as a parameter and displays the
  -- result of the function in the Message box
end mouseUp
function exponentiate var -- Handler for user function
  return var ^ var -- Returns value of expression
end exponentiate
function diskspace -- Returns diskSpace in K
  global flag
  if flag is true then pass diskSpace
  if flag <> true
  then put true into flag -- Set flag first pass
  put diskSpace() into var -- Recursive call
  put false into flag -- Reset flag
  return var div 1024 -- Return adjusted value
end diskspace
```

See Also   **Argument, Functions, Parameter, return**

functionKey   Command

Syntax   `functionKey <keyNumber>`

Notes   Simulates pressing one of the 15 function keys on the extended keyboard. Function keys with assigned values are 1 (Undo), 2 (Cut), 3 (Copy), and 4 (Paste). The other 11 keys can be given any meaning you wish, and you can even redefine the first four keys. Whether or not you have the extended keyboard, you can use this command from the Message box and in scripts.

Examples
```
functionKey 6 -- Sends message with 6 as argument
functionKey numberVar -- Argument in variable
-- Handler for the functionKey message follows
on functionKey which -- Key number in variable which
  if which is 6 then -- User defined Function key
    doMenu "Compact Stack"
    go home
  else if which is 2 then -- Alter built-in function key
    answer "are you sure you want to cut me?" with ¬
    "Yes" or "Cancel"
  if it is "Cancel" then exit functionKey
  end if
```

continued

functionKey

```
pass functionKey -- Lets HyperCard do its usual thing
end functionKey
```

See Also **Messages, returnKey, tabKey, enterInField**

Functions

Concept *(not a reserved word)*

Notes A function is like an instrument that reports on the status of the mouse, certain keys, or the clock, or it reports the results of calculations, etc. Functions always return a value of one kind or another that can then be used in the same way any other value is used. Like commands, when a function is executed, its name is sent up the object hierarchy. You can intercept these functions and change the usual result of a function with a function handler. You can also make your own functions. The syntax for user defined functions is

```
functionName (<argument list>)
```

The `functionName` can be any alphanumeric string that is not a HyperTalk reserved word. The argument list can be empty, although the parenthesis are required, or it can be up to 64 comma-separated values. Numeric values must be less than 1 billion. As explained in the **function** KEYWORD and **return** KEYWORD listings in this Reference, a function handler is needed to get a value or to process the parameters. The resulting value or values are returned in the function.

HyperTalk Functions

(name) = undocumented

(1.2) = for use with versions starting with 1.2.

abs	annuity	atan
average	charToNum	clickH (1.2)
clickLoc	clickV (1.2)	commandKey
compound	cos	date
diskSpace	exp	exp1
exp2	foundChunk(1.2)	foundField (1.2)
foundLine (1.2)	foundText (1.2)	(heapSpace)
length	ln	ln1
log2	max	min
mouse	mouseClick	mouseH
mouseLoc	mouseV	number
numToChar	offset	optionKey
pram	paramCount	params
random	result	round
screenRect (1.2)	seconds	selectedChunk (1.2)
selectedField (1.2)	selectedLine (1.2)	selectedText (1.2)
shiftKey	sin	sound
sqrt	(stackSpace)	target
ticks	time	tool
trunc	value	version

See Also **function, return,** *(individual listings)*

636

General Tools   Concept *(not a reserved word)*

Notes   The top three tools in the Tool Palette. These tools—browse, button, and field—are available when the userLevel is 4 (Authoring) or higher.

See Also   **browse tool, button tool, choose, field tool, Tool Palette**

get   Command

Syntax   `get <source>`

Notes   Puts the value of the source expression, container, function, or property into the variable `it`.

Examples
```
get 5 * 9 / 3
get card field x
get the long date
get the short name of the target
get card field x * the number of cards
```

global   Keyword

Syntax   `global <variableName>`

Notes   Declares a variable to be global. The value in a global variable is available in any handler that also declares that variable to be global. The values in global variables are preserved throughout a HyperCard session but are lost when HyperCard is suspended or when you quit. To preserve values between sessions, save them to fields.

Caution   Global is a keyword and can't be executed from the Message box or as part of a do statement.

Examples
```
global globalVar
global singles,doubles,triples,homeRuns
```

See Also   **Variables**

Global Variable   Concept *(not a reserved word)*

Notes   A HyperTalk container accessible from any handler in which it is declared (`global variableName`). Global variables are used to share values between handlers or to save values between one execution of a given handler and another. Global variable values are preserved until HyperCard is shut down or suspended.

Example
```
on mouseDown
   global start -- Declaration of global variable
   put the ticks into start -- Value into variable
end mouseDown
on mouseUp
   global start -- Variable declared, value shared
   put "Time elapsed:" && start - the ticks && "ticks" ¬
   into message box
end mouseUp
```

See Also   **global, Local Variable, Variables**

go

go   **Command**

Syntax   `go [to] [stack]<[pathname]designator>`
`go [to] background <designator>[of[stack]<designator>]`
`go [to] card<designator>[of<bkgnd/stack designator>]`

Notes   Navigates from the current card to the object (stack, background, or card) designated in `<destination>`. Any of the naming options can be used. If a stack,
without a particular card named, is the destination, the first card in the stack is
opened: `go [stack]"Dreams"`. If a background is the destination, the first card
of the background is opened: `go bkgnd 2`. You can go to any card in the current
stack: `go card id3454`, or you can limit navigation to a specified background: `go
next card of bkgnd 2`. You may have to provide a pathname for distant stacks.
Use `set lockScreen to true` to prevent the trip from being displayed on the
screen. To prevent messages from being sent, use `set lockMessages to true`.
You can add a visual flourish by adding a visual effect or two before the `go`
command if the screen is not locked and the browse tool is chosen. `go` generates
different messages depending on the situation: almost always `closeCard` and
`openCard`, sometimes `closeBackground`, `openBackground`, `closeStack`, and
`openStack`. If you attempt to go to a nonexistent card, `the result` returns `No
Such Card`. If the card is found, `empty` is returned. Special `go` options:

> `any` goes to a random card in the current stack or background.
> `back` goes to last card visited.
> `first` goes to the first card in the current stack or background.
> `help` goes to the first card of the Help stack (generates a `help` mes-
> sage).
> `home` goes to the first card of the Home stack.
> `last` goes to the last card in the current stack or background.
> `mid` goes to the middle card in the current stack or background.
> `next` goes to the next card, in relative order, of the current stack or
> background.
> `prev` goes to the previous card in relative order of the current stack or
> background.
> `recent` shows the Recent cards dialog box.

Examples
```
go to card 34
go to card "Herman" of stack "Jake"
put the result into msg -- No Such Card or empty
go last of this bkgnd
on mouseUp
  lock screen
  set lockMessages to true
  set lockRecent to true
  go card 3 of "HyperDisk:NewStacks:PowerStacks:ShopList"
  go third card of bkgnd id 3873
  unlock screen -- optional
end mouseUp
```

See Also   **lockMessages, lockRecent, lockScreen, Pathnames, visual**

Graphics   Concept *(not a reserved word)*

Notes   Pictures created with the Paint tools or with another application and copied in
through the Clipboard. All graphics are bit-mapped (no draw objects). Two
graphic layers are available at all times: the card layer, which is unique to a particular card, and the background layer, which is shared by all cards with the same
background. The maximum size on disk of a bit-mapped graphic is 44 K.

See Also   Copy Picture, Cut Picture, hide picture, Painting, Paste Picture, show picture, showPict

gray   **Image Modifier Argument**

Notes   Not a constant, but used with the `visual` command to specify a gray screen as an interim step between the current screen and the destination card.

Example   `visual effect dissolve fast to gray`

See Also   **visual**

grey   **Image Modifier Argument**

Notes   Alternative spelling for gray in HyperTalk versions starting with 1.2.

1.2+   New version 1.2 feature.

Example   `visual effect dissolve fast to grey`

See Also   **visual, gray**

grid   **Painting Property**

Syntax   `[the] grid`

Notes   If true, the snap grid is active; if false, the snap grid is inactive. The snap grid is an invisible 8-pixel by 8-pixel grid that prevents some tools (line, select, text, rectangle, round rect, oval, polygon, regular polygon, and curve) from starting or ending drags on any point but a snap point. (See Figure R-16.) `grid` has no effect on the pencil, brush, lasso, bucket, spray, or eraser tools.

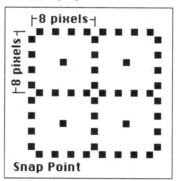

Figure R-16.   The snap grid.

Example   `put the grid into message box`
`set grid to true`

Handler   **Concept** *(not a reserved word)*

Notes   The basic unit of HyperTalk code. A handler starts with the keyword on or `function` followed by a message name and possibly some parameters. Command and function statements follow, and the handler ends with a line that starts with the keyword **end** and the message name again. Handlers can't be nested physically inside each other, although one handler can call another with the **send**

Handler

command or, in the case of user defined and redefined commands/functions, using the command in a handler activates the new handler.

Example
```
on mouseUp
  go to home
end mouseUp
function driveSpace
  return round(diskSpace() / 1024)
end driveSpace
```

See Also **end, Messages, on**

heapSpace **Undocumented System Function**

Syntax
```
the heapSpace
heapSpace()
```

Notes Reports on the status of the memory heap. Useful if you are working on XCMDs or if you are overly interested in what is happening inside your Macintosh.

Examples `put "The heap = " && heapSpace() div 1024 && "K" into msg`

See Also **diskSpace, freeSpace, size, stackSpace**

height **Button/Field/Window Property**

Syntax `[the] height of <designator>`

Notes Returns the height in pixels of a specified field, button, or windoid. When used with `set`, `height` preserves the mid point and extends or retracts the top and bottom.

1.2+ New version 1.2 feature.

Example
```
put the height of message box into message box -- 35
set height of card field id 3 to 56
on idle
  -- Handler to make sure your push buttons are standard
  put the number of buttons into tempVar
  if style of button tempVar is "roundRect" and height ¬
  of button tempVar <> 22 then -- 22 is the standard height
    answer "Naughty! The interface police are on the way."
    set height of button tempVar to 22
  end if
end idle
```

See Also **visual, gray**

Help **Menu Command**

Notes Normally opens the Help stack. Generates a `help` message that can be trapped. Use `go help` instead.

Keyboard Command-?

Example `doMenu "Help"`

See Also **go**

help   Command

Syntax   help

Notes   Can be executed in a script or from the Message box or sent by HyperCard as a result of a go help command or a Help menu command. If not trapped, causes the first card of the Help stack to open. Usually causes closeCard, closeBackground, closeStack, openStack, openBackground, and openCard messages to be sent.

Example
```
help -- In Message box or in a handler to go to Help stack
on help -- Adds a step to the usual procedure
   put "What does Carol Kaehler say?" into the message box
   pass help
end help
```

help   Reserved Word

Notes   Used with the go command to send a help message and, normally, to go to the Help stack.

Example   go help

See Also   **go**

hide   Command

Syntax
```
hide <object or window>
hide (card | bkgnd) picture
hide picture | pict of (card | bkgnd) <designator>
```

Notes   Used to make buttons, fields, windoids (message window, tool window, pattern window), and the Menu bar vanish from the screen. Hidden fields drop out of the tab order, but you can find text in a hidden field, although nothing shows on the screen.

1.2+   Starting with HyperCard 1.2, you can hide and show the graphic layers independently of the objects on a card or background. Each card now offers the following options: no graphics, card graphic only, background graphic only, both card and background graphics. You don't need to designate the card if it is the current card/background. To hide the graphics of any other card/background, you must provide a name of the card or background including the pathname if the card is in a distant stack. For cards and backgrounds, there is now a related showPict property that is true if the graphic layer is shown and false if it is hidden.

Examples
```
hide card button 1
hide menuBar
hide pattern window
on mouseUp
   put "button id 3" into something -- Or "message box"
   hide something -- Designator in variable
end mouseUp
hide bkgnd picture
hide picture of first card
hide picture of bkgnd 2
hide pict of layerVar of whatVar
```

See Also   **show, visible, message box, show picture, shopPict**

Hierarchy

Hierarchy

Concept *(not a reserved word)*

Notes HyperCard objects have a natural hierarchy that regulates the way messages flow through them. The lower a handler is positioned, the less the chance of its being preempted by another handler. The higher the handler is positioned, the more widely it can be shared with other objects.

Complete Object Hierarchy (top to bottom)
1. HyperCard
2. HyperCard XCMDs & XFCNs
3. Home stack XCMDs & XFCNs
4. Home stack handlers
5. stack XCMDs & XFCNs
6. stack handlers
7. background handlers
8. card handlers (some messages enter here)
9. button and field handlers (other messages enter here)

See Also **Messages, Handlers**

highlight
highlite
hilite

Button Property

Syntax `[the] hilite of <buttonDesignator>`

Notes If true, most buttons are inverted with black pixels turned white and enclosed white pixels turned black. Unenclosed white areas of an icon are not affected. False is the normal value. To make an `autoHilited` button permanently inverted requires a `set hilite of me to true` statement at the top of the mouseUp handler. When a `checkBox` style button is highlighted, it is checked. When a `radio-Button` is highlighted, its circle is filled with black.

Example
```
set the hilite of button id 4 to true
set hilite of button 3 to not hilite of button 3
-- Operates a checkBox style button
on mouseDown -- Card handler for one set of radio buttons
  if style of target is "radioButton" then
  get the short name of target -- Puts Radio 2 in it
    set hilite of button id 5 to it = "Radio 1" -- false
    set hilite of button id 6 to it = "Radio 2" -- true
    set hilite of button id 7 to it = "Radio 3" -- false
  end if
end mouseDown
```

Home

Stack Concept

Notes Goes to the first card of the Home stack. Use `go home` instead.

Keyboard Command-H

Example `doMenu "Home"`

See Also **go**

home   Reserved Word

Notes   Used with the go command to go to the Home stack.

Example   go home

See Also   **go**

Home Card/Stack   Concept

Notes   A special stack required to run HyperCard. Contains user information about preferences setting and path information for the stacks you use. The Home Card is like a HyperCard Finder that you can get to at anytime with Command-H.

See Also   **go**

hypercard   Reserved Word

Notes   Used for two things. First, to bypass objects if you are sending a message that you don't want trapped by intervening handlers. Second, to bail out of a handler without executing any more statements, especially with nested handlers.

Example
```
send help to hypercard
exit to hypercard
```

See Also   **Control Structures, exit, Handlers, repeat, send**

ibeam   Cursor

Notes   The ibeam cursor, normally associated with text fields, can be referred to by name or as cursor 1.

1.2+   New version 1.2 feature.

Example   set the cursor to ibeam

See Also   **cursor**

icon   Button Property

Syntax   [the] icon of <buttonDesignator>

Notes   Returns the resource ID number of the icon of the designated button. If a button has no icon, it returns a 0 value. Most often used with the **set** command to change the icon. Icons can be set by ID number or by name. Icons are 31-pixel by 31-pixel graphic images stored as resources in stacks or applications. (See Figure R-17.) Besides the icons included with HyperCard, you can create your own icons with **ResEdit** or Icon Factory.

Example
```
set the icon of button id 4 to 0 -- No icon
set icon of target to 19162 -- Large next hand
set icon of me to "sml Next Hand" -- Icon name
on mouseDown -- Handler to animate button
   put "6179,29484,19162,32650" into iconsVar
   put 1 into i -- Initialize counter
   repeat while the mouse is down
     set icon of me to item i of iconsVar -- Cycle icons
```

continued

icon

```
    if i < 4 then add 1 to i else put 1 into i
  end repeat
end mouseDown
```

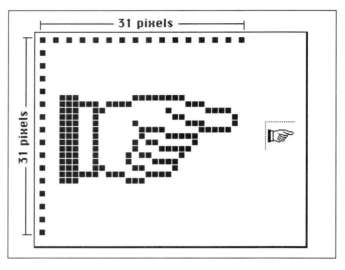

Figure R-17.   Icon stored as resource.

id Object Property

Syntax [the] id of <objectDesignator>

Notes Returns the ID number of the designated object. Often used with this, target, or me as object designator. With cards, you can get the short id (2343), the abbreviated id (card id 2343), or the long id (card id 2343 of stack "HyperStack: PowerFolder:ShoppingListStack"). The default adjective is abbreviated. The id property can't be set.

Example
```
the id of card field "TimeODay"
the id of me
-- Get the id of object holding executing statement
put the id of target into idVar
-- Get the id of the message entry point
if the short id of this card is 3434 then go next
```

idle Message

Notes This message is sent when nothing else is being sent. On a Mac +, idle messages are sent every 5 ticks. idles are sent between mouseWithin messages. idle message handlers can slow performance, so use them sparingly if at all. The only reason to handle the idle message is if you need to check on some condition that doesn't generate its own message.

Example
```
on idle
  if the mouseH > 500 then beep
  -- Beeps when mouse is near right edge
end idle
```

See Also **Messages, Handlers**

if   Keyword

Notes   Indicates the start of an `if then` control structure. `if` is short for "if the follow-ing is true." When testing to see whether a variable contains true or a function or property returns true, you can use `if flagVar` or `if visible` rather than `if flagVar is true` or `if visible is true`.

Example   `if 3>2 then beep -- Results in a beep`

See Also   **Control Structures, then, else, exit**

Increment   Concept *(not a reserved word)*

Notes   Repeatedly increasing a numeric value by a set amount. HyperTalk's repeat loops don't offer a step feature to let you easily increment a number by more than 1 at a time.

Examples
```
on mouseUp
   put 10 into var
   repeat until var > 100
     put var into field "display"
     add 10 to var
   end repeat
end mouseUp
```

See Also   **repeat**

into   Preposition

Notes   A `put` command parameter that causes the source string to replace the contents of the destination container or chunk.

Examples
```
put "Now it's time blah" into textVar
put " to say good-bye." into word 4 of textVar
-- Result = Now it's time to say good-bye.
```

See Also   **after, before, put**

Invert   Menu Command

Notes   Changes all the white pixels in a graphic selection to black and all the black pixels to white. Nice way to get white text on a black background.

Example
```
doMenu "Invert"
on mouseUp -- Handler to create inverted text
   choose text tool
   click at 100,100
   type " Hello "
   doMenu "Select"
   doMenu "Invert"
end mouseUp
```

iris   Visual Effect

Notes   Comes in two versions: `iris open`, which starts at the center of the screen and causes a rectangle of the destination card or image to expand until it fills the screen, and `iris close`, which causes the destination card or image to sweep in from all sides and converge on the center.

iris

Example visual effect iris open fast to grey
go last card

See Also **visual**

is Logical Operator

Notes   Synonym for = . Returns true if the expression on the left is equal to the expression on the right. Precedence = 8.

Examples   4 is 5 -- Returns false
if the mouse is down then beep
-- if the mouse function returns down expression is true

See Also   =

is in String Operator

Syntax   `<textB> is in <textA>`

Notes   Returns true if the string **textB** can be found in the string **textA**. Returns false if **textB** is not in **textA**. **textB** can be a multiline string. Precedence = 7.

Examples   if "pass" is in "password"
then beep -- Returns true then beeps
if field 1 is in textVar then exit repeat
if the selection contains "pass"
then put the selection into textVar

See Also   **contains, is not in**

is not in String Operator

Syntax   `<textb> is not in <textA>`

Notes   Returns false if the string **textB** can be found in the string **textA**. Returns true if **textB** is not in **textA**. **textB** can be a multiline string. Precedence = 7.

Examples   if "pass" is not in "password"
then beep --Returns false
if field 1 is not in textVar then exit repeat
if the selection contains "pass"
then put the selection into textVar

See Also   **contains, is in, is not in**

is not within Logical Operator

Syntax   `<point> is not within <rectangle>`

Notes   Returns true if the point is outside the rectangle and false if it is inside. The point can be a coordinate pair as a quoted literal, in a container, the result of a property (**loc**), or the result of a function (**mouseLoc**, **clickLoc**). Similarly, the rectangle can be four comma-separated numbers quoted, in a container, or the result of a property (**rect**). When you want to know when a point is within a rectangle, use **is within**.

1.2+   New version 1.2 feature.

Examples
```
if "45,100" is not within "40,50,90,150
then choose pencil tool -- Returns false
if clickLoc is not within rectVar then flash 2
on mouseWithin
   set the cursor to plus -- Plus cursor while within
   wait until the mouse is down or ¬
   the mouseLoc is not within the rect of target
   if the mouse is down then beep -- Beep if click within
end mouseWithin
```

is within   Logical Operator

Syntax   `<point> is within <rectangle>`

Notes   Returns true if the point is inside the rectangle and false if it isn't. The point can be a coordinate pair as a quoted literal, in a container, the result of a property (`loc`), or the result of a function (`mouseLoc`, `clickLoc`). Similarly, the rectangle can be four comma-separated numbers quoted, in a container, or the result of a property (`rect`). When you want to know when a point is not within a rectangle, use `is not within`.

1.2 +   New version 1.2 feature.

Examples
```
if "45,100" is within "40,50,90,150
then choose pencil tool -- Returns true and chooses pencil
if clickLoc is within rectVar then flash 2
on mouseWithin
   set the cursor to plus -- Plus cursor while within
   wait until the mouse is down or ¬
   the mouseLoc is not within the rect of target
   if the mouse is down then beep -- Beep if click within
end mouseWithin
```

it   Container

Notes   A local variable HyperTalk uses to store the results of the commands `get`, `answer`, `ask`, and `read`. `it` can be made global by declaring `it` with the `global` command, but this is not a good idea because the value can change unexpectedly. `it` is used in much the same way the Clipboard is used for temporarily storing data. Moving the value of `it` into another variable (or even a field) is like pasting the Clipboard into the Scrapbook.

Examples
```
get the date -- The date is placed into the variable it
put it into msg
-- The date is displayed in the message box.
```

See Also   **answer, ask, get, read**

item   Chunk

Notes   A chunk of a larger container set off by commas.

Examples
```
on mouseUp
   put "Parsley, sage, rosemary, and thyme." into field 1
   put item 1 of field 1 into message box -- Displays Parsley
   put empty into item 2 to 4 of field 1
```

continued

item

```
-- Leaves "Parsley,, and thyme."
put " garlic, onions," into item 2 of field 1
-- "Parsley, garlic, onions, and thyme."
delete item 2 of field 1 -- Removes text and comma
-- "Parsley, onions, and thyme."
end mouseUp
put replaceVar into item which of field id idVar"
```

See Also   **char, Containers, line, word**

items   Chunk Type

Notes   Used with the number function to specify the chunk type being inquired about.

Examples   `put return after item the number of items`

See Also   **item**

K   Abbreviation *(not a reserved word)*

Notes   Short for kilobyte.

See Also   **Byte, Kilobyte**

Keep   Menu Command

Notes   Saves changes to the graphic layer to disk. After changes are "kept," you can't undo them with the Revert menu command.

Example   `doMenu "Keep"`

See Also   **Revert**

Keyboard Messages   Concept *(not a reserved word)*

See Also   **Messages**

Keywords   Concept *(not a reserved word)*

Notes   Words that mark control structures or otherwise control program flow in scripts. Also global. which is used to declare global variables. Keywords can't be used in the Message box or in do statements because they are not sent as messages when they execute in a script. An exception to this rule is the send keyword, which can be executed in the Message box—go figure!

do	end	exit	function
global	if	next	on
pass	repeat	return	send

See Also   **Functions**

Kilobyte Concept *(not a reserved word)*

Notes One kilobyte equals 1,024 bytes. One byte equals 8 bits and can express numbers up to decimal 255 or hexadecimal FF. Used for measuring disk and memory (RAM) space.

language Global Property

Syntax [the] language

Notes Reports the current HyperTalk language translator in use. The default is English, but if you have other translator resources in your copy of HyperCard, you can set this property to other languages.

Example
```
the language -- Probably returns English
set language to "Italian"
```

lasso tool Painting Tool

Notes Used to select all the black pixels on the screen or to select an enclosed area by clicking inside it. Use cautiously. The select tool is usually a better choice. Available when the userlevel is 3 (Painting) or higher. Graphics can also be lasso selected with the drag... with optionKey command with the select tool and with the doMenu "Select" command after an object is first created. In any case, the following manipulations of the selection are possible:
To reposition a lasso selection:
```
drag from <start> to <finish>
```
To close a selection:
```
drag from <start> to <finish> with optionKey
```
To smear the trailing edge:
```
drag from <start> to <finish> with commandKey
```

Example
```
choose lasso tool
click at 60,60 with commandKey
-- Selects all black pixels or an enclosed area
drag from 60,60 to 200,200 with optionKey
-- Clones a copy
drag from 200,200 to 30,300 with commandKey
-- Smears the selection across the screen
```

See Also **Select, select tool**

last Ordinal Constant

Notes Used with the go command to specify the last card of a stack.

Example
```
go last
go last card of this bkgnd
```

See Also **go**

Last Menu Command

Notes Opens the last card of the current stack. Better to use the go last command.

Example doMenu "Last"

See Also **go**

Layer

Layer Concept *(not a reserved word)*

Notes   There are two graphic layers and any number of field and button layers above a HyperCard screen. Layers are a way of referring to the priority of similar objects. Objects (buttons or fields) that have message priority over other objects have a higher relative number and are conceptually and visually above the other objects. Card graphics can conceal, and are thought of as being above, background graphics.

See Also   **Bring Closer, Graphics, Send Farther**

left Property

Syntax   [the] left of <rectangle>

Notes   Returns in pixels the distance between the left of the screen and the left of the object or window. Equivalent to `item 1 of the rect of <object or window>`. Changing the left does not change the `width` but does change the `right`. Can be used with buttons, fields, and windows (card, tool, pattern, message).

1.2+   New version 1.2 feature.

Example
```
left of button 1
set the left of card field 1 to 300
set left of btn 1 to right of cd window / 2
on mouseUp -- Background handler to line up fields
  repeat with i = 1 to the number of fields
    set the left of field i to the mouseH
  end repeat
end mouseUp
```

See Also   **bottom, bottomRight, cursor, height, right, set, top, topLeft, width, Windows**

length String Function

Syntax
```
the length of <string>
length(<string>)
```

Notes   Gives the number of characters in a quoted string literal or in a container (the contents of all containers are stored as character strings. All characters except `empty` are counted by `the length` function. Equivalent to `the number of characters in <string>`.

Examples
```
the length of "HyperCard" -- Returns 9
put length("HyperCard") into charCount
if the length of word 3 of line 2 of field 1 is 4 then beep
get the length of line 2 of card field "Notes"
```

Lighten Menu Command

Notes   Scatters random white pixels in the selected graphic area. Available when a Painting tool is selected.

Example
```
doMenu "Lighten"
on mouseUp -- Button handler to create a white speckled box
  choose select tool
  drag from 100,100 to 300,200
```

continued

```
    doMenu "Lighten"
end mouseUp
```

See Also **Darken**

line Chunk

Notes A character string ending with a return character. The number of lines visible on the screen may not match the number of strings ending with a return character, especially when fields are resized.

Examples
```
get line 3 of field 1
put empty into line 1 of textVar -- Leaves the return
delete line 1 of textVar -- Removes the return
if the length of line 3 card field 1 > 30
then put return after char 30
put line 1 to 5 of field 3 into field 2 of card "Summary"
```

See Also **char, Containers, delete, item, line**

Line Size Menu Command

Notes Displays a dialog box that lets user set the lineSize property. (See Figure R-18.) Available when a Painting tool is selected.

Figure R-18. The Line Size dialog box.

Example
```
on mouseUp -- Button handler draws with line selected by user
    choose line tool
    doMenu "Line Size"
    drag from 1,1 to 511,340
end mouseUp
```

See Also **lineSize**

line tool Painting Tool

Notes Used to draw lines. Normally dragging with line tool makes a 1-pixel-wide black line, but you can use patterns with **draw... with optionKey** and you can change the **lineSize** with **set lineSize to <number>**. You can also let the user choose a line size by showing the Line Size dialog box with **doMenu "Line Size"**. Available when the **userlevel** is 3 (Painting) or higher.

Example
```
on mouseUp
    choose line tool
    drag from 60,60 to 20,200
    -- Draws a 1-pixel wide black line
    set lineSize to 3
    set pattern to 20
    -- To draw with 3 pixel wide patterned line
```

continued

line tool

```
                drag from 200,200 to 30,300 with optionKey
            end mouseUp
```

See Also   **brush tool, drag, lineSize, pattern, pencil tool**

lineFeed   Constant

Notes   Used with text files. When importing text that is formatted with lineFeeds (ASCII 10) at the end of lines or records, use `lineFeed` to capture one line or record at a time.

Examples   `read from file "textFile" until linefeed`

See Also   **Constants, Files, return, write**

lines   Chunk Type

Notes   Used with the `number` function to specify the class of objects you are interested in.

Caution   Lines are strings separated by return characters and don't necessarily match the screen display.

1.2+   Convert the example to a returnInField handler and set `autoTab` to false to create fields that transform themselves as you type.

Examples
```
on closeField -- Card handler detects too many lines in a field
    if the number of lines of field 1 > (the bottom of field 1 ¬
    - the top of field 2) / the text height of field 1
    then set the style of field 1 to scrolling
end closeField
```

See Also   **char, Containers, delete, item, line**

lineSize   Painting Property

Syntax   [the] lineSize

Notes   Gives you the current line size (applies to the line tool and the shape tools). Change it with the `set` command. The `lineSize` options are 1 (default), 2, 3, 4, 6, and 8.

Examples
```
the lineSize -- Normally returns 1
set lineSize to 8
put lineSize into lineSizeHolder
if lineSize is > 3 then add lineSize to compensatorVar
```

See Also   **Line Size**

LinkTo   HyperCard Button Option *(not a reserved word)*

Notes   One of the few HyperCard options not available to scriptors. Used to automatically write a script to link one card to another. The script goes into a button.

Literal Concept *(not a reserved word)*

Notes A string of characters that are interpreted as themselves. "Hello", "Hello, Dolly", and "H" are examples of quoted literals. This entire sentence is an example of an unquoted literal.

See Also **String, Values**

ln Math Function

Syntax
```
the ln of <number>
ln(<number>)
```

Notes Returns the log to the base e of the number.

Examples
```
ln(10) -- Returns 2.302585
the ln of numVar
put the ln of cos(8*pi/180) into msg -- Returns -.00978
```

See Also **ln1, log2**

ln1 Math Function

Syntax
```
the ln1 of <number>
ln1(<number>)
```

Notes Returns the log to the base e of the number plus 1.

Examples
```
ln1(10) -- Returns 2.397895
the ln1 of numVar
```

See Also **ln, log2**

loc Abbreviation

See Also **location**

Local Variable Concept *(not a reserved word)*

Notes A HyperTalk container that is only accessible from one handler and that loses its value when its handler ends. Local variables are used in situations where you only need to store a value temporarily or where you want to use variable names that are used for other purposes elsewhere in the script. To create a local variable, assign it a value with the **put** command.

Examples
```
on mouseDown -- Button handler lets you drag button around
    -- Assign value to a local variable
    put the loc of me into localVar
    tracker -- Calls a subroutine handler
    -- Restore button to starting position;
    -- the value in the tracker variable is ignored
    set the loc of me to localVar
end mouseDown
on tracker -- Handler in button, card or higher object
    put the mouseLoc into localVar
    -- Assign value to a different local variable
```

continued

Local Variable

```
      repeat while the mouse is down -- Stops when button up
        put the mouseLoc into newVar
        if newVar <> localVar then
      set the loc of target to the mouseLoc -- Move button
      put newVar into localVar
        end if
      end repeat
    end tracker
```

See Also **Global Variable, Variables**

location Button/Field/Window Property

Syntax [the] location or [the] loc

Notes Returns the screen position of the center of buttons and fields or of the left-top corner of windows and windoids. The position is expressed as a coordinate point x,y. The location can be changed with the set loc of <object/window> to <value> statement or by dragging the object/window with the mouse. If the location of buttons or fields is outside the card window, they are not visible, although their visible property is still true.

Examples
```
the location of field 1 -- Returns a coordinate pair
-- like 123,78 (the required)
set loc of message box to 22,100
-- Button handler that makes the button follow the cursor
on mouseStillDown -- Button handler
  set loc of me to mouseLoc
end mouseStillDown
-- The following script places HyperCard's windoids
-- around the card window on startup. These windoids are
-- not visible on a small screen Mac
on startup -- Home stack script (add to existing handler)
  set loc of tool window to 513,-8
  set loc of pattern window to 517,132
  set loc of message window to 0,353
  show tool window
  show pattern window
  show message window
end startup
```

See Also **rectangle**

lock screen Command

Syntax lock screen

Notes Functionally, the same as the statement set lockScreen to true. Prevents the screen from being updated while a card is being changed or during a transition to another card. Often associated with lockMessages. Use unlock screen to refresh the screen.

1.2 + New version 1.2 feature.

Caution As with lockScreen, if you set the value to true twice in the same script, you must set it to false twice if you want to show the screen before the handler ends.

Examples lock screen

continued

```
if the lockScreen is false then lock screen
-- To avoid the double trues problem
on mouseUp -- Button handler
  lock screen
  push card
  go to stack "Address" -- Navigate somewhere
  get field 2 of card 34 -- Get a value
  pop card -- Return to starting point
  put it into field id 3 -- Put value into container
  unlock screen with dissolve -- Show the changed card
end mouseUp
```

See Also   **lockMessages, unlock screen**

Locked Media   **Concept** *(not a reserved word)*

Notes   Media you can't write or copy to. Also called write-protected media. There are five ways a stack can be locked: if it is on a CD-ROM disc: if the write-protect tab on a floppy is open, if it is in a read-only folder on a network, if the Locked box in the Finder's Get Info dialog box is checked, or if the `cantModify` property is set to true. The example shows how to test for locked media.

Examples
```
on mouseUp
  set cantModify to false
  if the cantModify is true then answer "This baby is locked"
end mouseUp
```

See Also   **cantModify**

lockMessages   **Global Property**

Syntax   [the] lockMessages

Notes   No `open...` or `close...` messages are sent while `lockMessages` is true. Permits going to a card without triggering `closeCard`, `openCard`, etc., messages. The default value is false. Setting `lockMessages` to true is a good idea before navigating to another stack to get the contents of a field. Also speeds up navigation. Usually associated with `lockScreen`.

Examples
```
the lockMessages -- Returns true or false (the required)
set lockMessages to true
```

See Also   **lockRecent, lockScreen**

lockRecent   **Global Property**

Syntax   [the] lockRecent

Notes   If the `lockRecent` is true, HyperCard does not save the miniature representation of each card you visit, saving RAM. The card identification is saved on the back stack as usual so that you can press the ~ (tilde) key to retrace your steps. If `lockScreen` is false, the miniature representation is saved as usual. The default value is false. Setting `lockRecent` to true speeds up navigation. Usually associated with `lockScreen` and `lockMessages`.

Examples
```
the lockRecent -- Returns true or false (the required)
set lockRecent to true
```

See Also   **lockMessages, lockScreen**

lockScreen

lockScreen   Global Property

Syntax   [the] lockScreen

Notes   The screen is not updated as long as lockScreen is true. Permits going to a card or changing the current card without the user seeing anything. The screen is automatically refreshed at the end of a script.

Caution   If you set lockScreen to true twice, you must set it to false twice to reveal the new screen before the end of the script.

Examples
```
the lockScreen -- Returns true or false (the required)
set lockScreen to true
if lockScreen is false then set lockScreen to true
-- Prevents multiple true settings
```

See Also   **lock screen, lockMessages, lockRecent, unlock screen**

lockText   Field Property

Syntax   [the] lockText

Notes   If a field's lockText property is true, the text can't be edited but the field can receive mouseDown and mouseUp messages just like a button. The default value is false. You can temporarily lock the text by pressing the Command key while clicking the mouse button.

Examples
```
the lockText of field 1 -- Returns true or false (the required)
set lockText to true
on mouseUp
  -- Card handler to get the word clicked on in a locked field
  set lockText of target to false -- Unlock the field
  click at the clickLoc
  click at the clickLoc -- Select the word clicked on
  put the selection into field 2 -- Put into another field
  set lockText of target to true -- Relock the field
end mouseUp
```

log2   Math Function

Syntax
```
the log2 of <number>
log2(<number>)
```

Notes   Returns the log to the base 2 of the number.

Examples
```
log2(10) -- Returns 3.321928
log2(numVar)
```

See Also   **ln, ln1**

Logical Operators   Concept *(not a reserved word)*

Notes   Operators that return true or false rather than numeric or text values.

Examples   `if 9 > 5 then answer "It's true"`

See Also   **Boolean Algebra, Operators**

Math Functions

Concept *(not a reserved word)*

Notes   Functions used in mathmatical expressions:

abs	annuity	atan	average
compound	cos	exp	exp1
exp2	ln	ln1	max
min	random	round	sin
sqrt	tan	trunc	value

See Also   **Functions**

Math Operators

Concept *(not a reserved word)*

See Also   **Operators**

max   Math Function

Syntax   `max(<numbers>)`

Notes   Returns the largest number in a list of up to 64 numbers separated by commas. The numbers can be in a container, but containers and functions can't be mixed with literals. The statement `max(3,5,it)` causes an error.

Caution   If a multiline container is the source of the numbers, only the numbers in the first line are evaluated.

Examples
```
max(10,4,8,2,8.36) -- Returns 10
max(numVar)
max(the mouseV,the mouseH)
```

me   Object Designator

Notes   Returns the name of the object containing the statement that includes me. Not only is it shorter than other forms of naming, but it can be used in any object without alteration.

1.2+   Starting with version 1.2, me can refer to the contents of a field as well as the name of the field. If there is any ambiguity, use the name of me to refer to the name or the value of me to refer to the contents.

Examples
```
put the name of me into msg -- Displays card button "Button" ¬
if in that button
set hilite of me to true -- Hilites a button
on mouseUp -- Field handler using new me
  put me into card field "Collector"
end mouseUp
```

See Also   **Naming, target**

Menu Commands

Concept *(not a reserved word)*

Notes   Every HyperCard menu item is also a command that you can use in a script. Menu commands are accessed with the doMenu command. The menu commands avail-

Menu Commands

able to you depend on the user level and whether or not a printing tool is selected.

▸ **When** userLevel **is 1**
Back, Find..., First, Help, Home, Next, Last, Message, Open Stack..., New Stack..., Page Setup..., Prev, Print Card, Print Report..., Print Stack..., Quit HyperCard, Recent, Save a Copy..., Undo

▸ **When** userLevel **is 2**
The items above and Clear Text, Copy Text, Cut Text, Delete Card, New Card, Paste Text

▸ **When** userLevel **is 3 and a General tool is selected**
The items above and Background, Compact Stack, Copy Card, Cut Card, Delete Card, Delete Stack..., New Card, Open Stack..., Protect Stack..., Text Style... (when insertion point is in a field)

▸ **When** userLevel **is 4 or 5 and a General tool is selected**
The items above and Bkgnd Info... (when button or field is selected), Bring Closer (when button or field is selected), Button Info (when a button is selected), Card Info..., Clear Button, Clear Field, Copy Button, Copy Field, Cut Button, Cut Field, Field Info... (when a field is selected), New Background, New Button, New Field, Paste Button, Paste Field, Send Farther, Stack Info...

▸ **When** userLevel **is 3+ and a Painting tool is selected**
Back, Background, Brush Shape..., Clear Picture, Copy Picture, Copy Card, Cut Picture, Cut Card, Darken, Delete Card, Draw Centered, Draw Filled, Draw Multiple, Edit Pattern..., Export Paint..., FatBits, Fill, Find..., First, Flip Horizontal, Flip Vertical, Grid, Help, Home, Import Paint..., Invert, Keep, Last, Lighten, Line Size..., Message, Opaque, Paste Picture (if a picture is on the Clipboard), Paste Text (if text is on the Clipboard), Paste Button (if a button is on the Clipboard), Paste Field (if a field is on the Clipboard), Pickup, Polygon Sides..., Power Keys, Prev, Quit Hyper-Card, Recent, Revert, Rotate Left, Rotate Right, Select, Select All, Text Style... (when the text tool is selected), Trace Edges, Transparent, Undo

See Also   **doMenu,** *(listings for individual menu commands)*

Message   Menu Command

Notes   Toggles the Message box. Better to use show the message box or hide the message box.

Examples   doMenu "Message"

Keyboard   Command-M

See Also   **hide, message box, show**

message
message box   Container

Notes   The one line windoid that appears on the screen when you press Command-M or Command-F. A place to send messages to HyperCard (starting with the card level) or to display messages to the user. Abbreviations and variations are the message box, message box, the message window, message window, the message, message, the msg, and msg. The Message box is the default container for the put command and is also shown, if hidden, by put. Otherwise use show and hide to reveal or conceal the Message box. Because a return character causes the Message box to execute its contents, it can only contain one line, but that line can be of any length. The default location of the Message window is 22,300 and its rectangle is 22,300,494,335. It can be repositioned by setting its `loc` property to a new coordinate.

Caution   Can't be used to execute keywords like `if`, `then`, `else`, `global`, `pass`, or `do`. `send` can be executed.

Examples
```
put "Hello" into the message box
put the message window into textVar
put word 3 of message box into word 5 of field 2
on mouseUp
  global findVar
  put "Find whole" && findVar && "in field 3" into msg
  returnKey -- Executes find command
end mouseUp
on mouseUp
  hide the message box
set the loc of message to 10,150 -- Center of screen
  put "Here I am" into the message
end mouseUp
```

message window   Container

Notes   Variation of the message box.

See Also   **Containers, message box**

Messages   Concept *(not a reserved word)*

Notes   Method of communication between HyperCard, HyperCard objects, and Hyper-Talk scripts. Besides the system messages listed here, every HyperTalk command is sent as a message when executed. In addition, you can turn any word into a message by making a handler for it. The Messages are

All commands and functions,
arrowKey (left,right,up,down),
closeBackground, closeCard, closeField, closeStack,
deleteBackground, deleteButton, deleteCard, deleteField, deleteStack,
enterKey, help, idle,
enterInField, returnInField,
mouseDown, mouseEnter, mouseLeave, mouseStillDown, mouseUp,
mouseWithin,
newBackground, newButton, newCard, newField, newStack,
openBackground, openButton, openCard, openField, openStack,
quit, resume, returnKey, startup, suspend, tabKey.

See Also   *(listings for individual messages)*

min   Math Function

Syntax   `min(<numbers>)`

Notes   Returns the smallest number in a list of up to 64 numbers separated by commas. The numbers can be in a container, but containers and functions can't be mixed with the literals. The statement `min(3,5,it)` causes an error. If a multiline

min

container is the source of the numbers, only the numbers in the first line are evaluated.

Examples
```
min(10,4,8,2,8.36) -- Returns 2
min(numVar)
min(the mouseV,the mouseH)
min(5*6,10-2,sqrt(5))
```

See Also   **max**

Misc Functions Concept *(not a reserved word)*

Notes   Functions that don't fit into any convenient catagory:

param	paramCount	params	result
sound	target	tool	value

See Also   **Functions,** *(individual listings)*

mod   Math Operator

Syntax   `<numberA> mod <numberB>`

Notes   Stands for modulus. Returns the remainder after `numberA` is divided by `numberB`. Use `div` to get the truncated result of dividing `numberA` by `numberB`. The following example handler shows how `mod` can be used to keep incrementing numbers within a range of 0 to `numberB`.

Examples
```
7 mod 2 -- Returns 1
11 mod 4 -- Returns 3
on mouseUp
  repeat with i = 1 to 8
    put i mod 4 & "," after field 1
    -- Puts 1,2,3,0,1,2,3,0 into the field
  end repeat
end mouseUp
```

See Also   **div, /**

Modifier Keys   Concept *(not a reserved word)*

Notes   Keys that can be pressed to modify the behavior of Painting tools or the `type` command. The three modifier keys are `commandKey`, `optionKey`, and `shiftKey`.

Examples
```
drag from 50,50 to 100,100 with optionKey,shiftKey
type "q" with commandKey
```

See Also   **click, commandKey, drag, optionKey, shiftKey, type**

mouse   Function

Syntax
```
the mouse
mouse()
```

Notes   Returns the current state of the mouse button—**down** if it is pressed or **up** if it is not pressed.

Examples
```
the mouse -- Normally up
if mouse() is down then play "harpsichord"
wait until the mouse is down
```

mouseClick Function

Syntax
```
the mouseClick
mouseClick()
```

Notes Returns true if the mouse button has been clicked since the script started and false if the button has not been clicked. If you test for mouseClick once and get true, the value is then reset to false, and you can test it again later to see whether the mouse has been clicked again. You can also use the wait until the mouse is up statement to test for a click while a script is running.

Examples
```
the mouseClick -- Normally returns false
if mouseClick() then play "Harpsichord"
wait until the mouseClick
on mouseUp -- Button handler distinguishes single clicks from
-- double clicks
  wait 5 ticks
  if the mouseClick
  then beep 2 -- Double-click action
  else beep 1 -- Single-click action
end mouseUp
```

See Also **clickLoc, mouseH, mouseLoc, mouseV**

mouseDown Message

Notes Sent to the object (button, field, or card) under the cursor when the user presses the mouse button. Usually used to warn that something will happen if the button is released.

Examples
```
on mouseDown
  set the hilite of the target to true
end mouseDown
```

See Also **mouseEnter, mouseLeave, mouseStillDown, mouseUp, mouseWithin**

mouseEnter Message

Notes Sent to a button or field when the cursor enters the object's rectangle. Usually used to change the object or to provide more information to the user.

Examples
```
on mouseEnter
  show card field "Instructions"
  set the name of me to "Quit?"
end mouseEnter
-- Next handler changes cursor while inside an object
on mouseEnter -- In button or field
  set the cursor to pointer
  wait until the mouse is down or the mouseLoc is ¬
  not within me
end mouseEnter
```

See Also **mouseDown, mouseLeave, mouseStillDown, mouseUp, mouseWithin**

mouseH

mouseH	**System Function**

Syntax
```
the mouseH
mouseH()
```

Notes   Returns the current x coordinate of the mouse cursor; x is the distance from the left edge of the screen in pixels. Equivalent to `item 1 of the mouseLoc`.

Examples
```
the mouseH
if the mouseH <10 then put "Move to the right, please" ¬
into the message box
wait until the mouseH > 100
on idle -- Another navigation scheme. Handler at card level
-- or higher
  if the mouseH < 1 then go prev
  else if the mouseH > 512 then go next
end idle
```

See Also   **clickLoc, mouseClick, mouseLoc, mouseV**

mouseLeave   Message

Notes   Sent to a button or field when the cursor leaves the object's rectangle. Usually used to change the object.

Examples
```
on mouseLeave
   hide card field "Instructions"
   set the name of me to "Mystery"
end mouseLeave
```

See Also   **mouseDown, mouseEnter, mouseStillDown, mouseUp, mouseWithin**

mouseLoc   System Function

Syntax
```
the mouseLoc
mouseLoc()
```

Notes   Returns the current x,y coordinates of the mouse cursor; where X is the distance from the left edge and y is the distance from the top edge of the screen in pixels. Use `the clickLoc` to get the location of the last mouse click.

Examples
```
the mouseLoc
put mouseLoc() into locVar
on mouseStillDown -- Button handler that drags button around
-- the screen
  set the loc of button 1 to the mouseLoc
end mouseStillDown
```

See Also   **clickLoc, mouseClick, mouseLoc, mouseV**

mouseStillDown   Message

Notes   Sent to the object (button, field, or card) under the cursor when the mouse button is pressed down for longer than three ticks. Can be used to make a pseudo `repeat` loop. No other system message can be sent until the mouse button is released.

Examples   `on mouseStillDown`

continued

```
    add 1 to card field "Days"
end mouseStillDown
-- Two handler mouseStillDown timer follows
on mouseDown -- Put both in button and press it
  global startVar -- Get starting time
  put the ticks into startVar
end mouseDown
on mouseStillDown
  global startVar
  put the ticks into stopVar -- Get ending time
  put stopVar - startVar into msg -- Display
end mouseStillDown
```

See Also **mouseDown, mouseEnter, mouseLeave, mouseUp, mouseWithin**

mouseUp Message

Notes Sent to the object (button, field, or card) under the cursor when the user releases the mouse button. The most commonly handled message. Used in buttons and elsewhere to make things happen.

Examples
```
on mouseUp
  hide card field "Instructions"
  set the name of me to "Mystery"
  doMenu "Quit HyperCard
end mouseUp
```

See Also **mouseDown, mouseEnter, mouseLeave, mouseStillDown, mouseWithin**

mouseV System Function

Syntax the mouseV

Notes Returns the current y coordinate of the mouse cursor; y is the distance from the top edge of the screen in pixels. Equivalent to item 2 of the mouseLoc.

Examples
```
the mouseV
wait until the mouseV > 100
on idle -- The shy Menu bar handler
  if the mouseV < 20 then hide menuBar
  else if mouseV() > 20 then show menuBar
end idle
```

See Also **clickLoc, mouseClick, mouseLoc, mouseV**

mouseWithin Message

Notes Sent to a button or field when the cursor is inside the object's rectangle. Alternates with idle messages. Can be used to increment a variable or to otherwise make gradual changes.

Examples
```
on mouseWithin -- Card handler to make objects hop right
  put item 1 of the loc of the target + 5 into var
  set the loc of the target to var, item 2 ¬
  of the loc of the target
end mouseWithin
```

See Also **mouseDown, mouseEnter, mouseLeave, mouseStillDown, mouseUp**

msg

msg — Container

Notes   Abbreviation for the message box.

Examples   `put "Hello" into msg`

See Also   **Containers, message box**

MultiFinder — System Software *(not a reserved word)*

Notes   An extension of the normal Macintosh Finder that lets the user switch back and forth between several applications, each of which is allocated a section of memory. Only useful if you have lots of RAM or very small applications.

Caution   Using MultiFinder can cause problems with using the `print... with` or `open` (application) commands. Also, the `suspend` and `resume` system messages are not sent when HyperCard is running under MultiFinder.

See Also   **Finder**

multiple — Painting Property

Notes   Used with Painting tools. If true, dragging with line or shape tools causes multiple lines or shapes to be drawn. Actual appearance depends on the `centered` and `multiSpace` properties. If false (default), only one line or shape is drawn.

Examples   `the multiple`
`set the multiple to true`

See Also   **centered, multiSpace**

multiply — Command

Syntax   `multiply <numberA> by <numberB>`

Notes   Multiplies `numberA` by `numberB` and puts the result into the `numberA` container. The second number can be either a literal or a number in a container, but the first number must be in a container. Containers must contain numeric values before execution.

Examples   `put 5 into numVar`
`multiply numVar by 4 -- Returns 20`
`multiply item 3 of card field 2 by ¬`
`the number of card buttons`

See Also   ***, divide, numberFormat**

multiSpace — Painting Property

Syntax   `the multiSpace`

Notes   The minimum number of pixels between multiple images of a shape. The range of possible settings is 1 (default) to 9. To avoid accidentally getting more than the minimum spaces when drawing larger shapes, try setting a slow `dragSpeed`.

Examples   `on mouseUp`
`    choose rectangle tool`
`    set multiple to true`
`    set the multiSpace to 3`

continued

```
                    set the dragSpeed to 10
                    drag from startVar to finishVar
                  end mouseUp
```

See Also   **centered, multiple**

name   Object Property

Syntax   `[the] [short | abbreviated | long] name`

Notes   Returns the name of the object. In the case of objects without a name, `name` returns the ID number. In the case of cards, `the long name` is prefaced with the object type, the name is quoted, and the pathname (`card "Harvey" of stack "HyperDisk:PowerStacks:ShoppingList"`) is included. `the short name` is just the unquoted name (`Harvey`), whereas `the abbreviated name` (the default) gives a quoted name and an object type (`card button "Harvey"`). The maximum length of a HyperCard object name is 31 characters

Examples
```
the name of field 3
-- Returns field <name> or field id <number>
the long name of this card
-- card id 8102 of stack "Copies:Hyper:Experiments"
set the name of button id 3 to "Wallbanger"
set the name of me to "Script"
```

See Also   **Naming, number, id**

Naming   Concept *(not a reserved word)*

Notes   HyperCard objects can be referred to in a number of ways. All objects can have names, (`card "Eureka"`) and stacks must have names. All objects except stacks have ID numbers (`background id 2343`) and relative numbers (`field 1`). To refer to a distant stack, you need to include the pathname (`go to card 3 of stack "HyperDisk:FluffFolder: QuantumTheory"`). You can also refer to the object containing the statement that is currently executing with **me** (`hide me`), the object that first received the initiating message with `target` (`hide the target`), and the current card, background, and stack with `this` (`get the number of cards in this stack`). String chunks in a container also have to be referred to, as in `get char 1 of word 2 of item 3 of line 4 of field 3`. See the **send** listing for message-naming rules and **variable** for variable-naming rules.

See Also   **Containers, id, me, name, number, Objects, pathname, send, target, this, variable**

New Background   Menu Command

Notes   Inserts a new card with a new, blank, and empty background. Sends `closeCard`, `closeBackground`, `newCard`, `newBackground`, `openCard`, and `openBackground` messages.

Keyboard   Command-9

Example   `doMenu "New Background"`

See Also   **Background, editBkgnd**

New Button

New Button   **Menu Command**

Notes   Adds a new roundRect button to the current layer with the name New Button. Sends a newButton message.

Keyboard   Command-7

Example   doMenu "New Button"

See Also   **Buttons**

New Card   **Menu Command**

Notes   Adds a new card to the current background after the current card. Sends closeCard, openCard, and newCard messages. Available when the userLevel is 2 (Typing) or higher.

Keyboard   Command-N

Example   doMenu "New Card"

See Also   **Cards**

New Field   **Menu Command**

Notes   Adds a new transparent field to the current card. Sends a newField message. Available when the userLevel is 4 (Authoring) or higher.

Keyboard   Command-8

Example   doMenu "New Card"

See Also   **Cards**

New Stack   **Menu Command**

Notes   Creates a new stack that the user must name by typing into a dialog box. (See Figure R-19.)

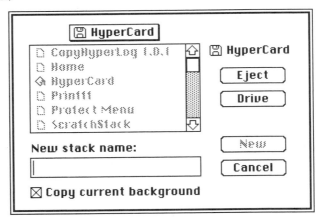

Figure R-19.   The New Stack dialog box.

The current background graphics, fields, buttons, properties, and the stack script (but not the card script) are copied unless the Copy Background checkbox is deselected. Sends `closeCard`, `closeBackground`, `closeStack`, `openCard`, `newStack`, `openBackground`, and `openStack` messages. Available when the `userLevel` is 2 (Typing) or higher.

1.2+   If the Copy current background button is not checked, the stack resource fork is not copied.

Example   `doMenu "New Stack"`

newBackground   Message

Notes   Sent to the card after a New Background menu command or after a new background is pasted into a stack. Best to trap at the stack level or higher.

Examples
```
on newBackground
   answer "There are now" && the number of bkgnds && ¬
"backgrounds"
end newBackground
```

See Also   **Messages, Handlers**

newButton   Message

Notes   Sent to the button after a button is created (includes cloning).

Examples
```
on newButton
   global cardButtons
   -- cardButtons value also set in openStack and
   -- deleteButton handlers
   if the number of card buttons > cardButtons then
      answer "Put new button in background?" with ¬
"Yes" or "No"
      if it is "Yes" then
       add 1 to cardButtons
       doMenu "Cut Button"
       set editBkgnd to true
       doMenu "Paste Button"
       set editBkgnd to false
      end if
   end if
end newButton
```

See Also   **deleteButton, Messages, Handlers**

newCard   Message

Notes   Sent to the card after a card is created. To check before the card is added, trap the `doMenu` message and look for the New Card argument.

Examples
```
on newCard
   put the number of cards into field "cards in stack"
end newCard
```

See Also   **Messages, Handlers**

newField   Message

Notes   Sent to the field after a field is created.

newField

Examples
```
on newField
    global bkgndFields,cardFields
    -- bkgndFields value also set in openStack and
    -- deleteFields handlers
    put " Click where you want the field centered "
    wait until the mouse is down
    get the mouseLoc

    if the number of bkgnd fields > bkgndFields then
      add 1 to bkgndFields
      set the loc of field the number of fields to it
    else if the number of card fields > cardFields then
      add 1 to cardFields
      set the loc of card field the number of card fields ¬
      to it
      -- Card field outline
    end if
end newField
```

See Also   **Messages, Handlers**

newStack   Message

Notes   Sent to the card after a stack is created. Best trapped in the Home stack.

Examples
```
on newStack
    -- Handler to put linking button in Home card
    answer "Link to Home stack?" with "Yes" or "No"
    if it is "Yes" then
      get the short name of this stack
      go to home
      doMenu "New Button"
      set the name of button the number of buttons to it
      put "on mouseUp" & return & "go" && it & return & ¬
      "end mouseUp" into tempVar
      set script of button the number of buttons to tempVar
      go back
      choose browse tool
    end if
end newStack
```

See Also   **Handlers, Messages**

Next   Menu Command

Notes   Opens the next card in the stack. If the current card is the last card in the stack, the first card is opened. Use **go next** instead. Sends **closeCard** and **openCard** messages and possibly **closeBackground** and **openBackground** messages.

Keyboard   Command-3

Example   doMenu "Next"

See Also   **go**

next Keyword

Notes Used in a `repeat` loop to skip part of a loop cycle and start a new one.

Example
```
go next card
go next card of this bkgnd
```

See Also **Control Structures**

next Modifier

Notes Used with the `go` command to navigate to the next card. Goes from the last card to the first card. Sends `closeCard` and `openCard` messages and possibly `closeBackground` and `openBackground` messages.

See Also **go**

nine Constant

Notes Stands for the number 9.

Example `put nine into word nine of field nine of card nine`

See Also **Constants**

ninth Ordinal Constant

Notes Refers to the ninth object or chunk of a specified type in an enclosing object or container.

Example `put nine into ninth word of ninth field of ninth card`

See Also **Constants**

none Cursor

Notes A blank or invisible cursor.

1.2+ New version 1.2 feature.

Example `Set cursor to none`

See Also **cursor**

not Logical Operator

Notes Means its not the case that. Switches the logical value of an expression. Not true is false and not false is true.

Examples
```
not the visible of button 1 -- false if the visible is true
if not the mouse is down then beep -- Beeps if mouse is up
```

number String/System Function

Syntax
```
[the] number of <object-type>
[the] number of <chunk> in <container>
[the] number of cards in <background designator>
```

Notes Returns the number of objects of a specified type (2 card fields on this card, 3

number

background fields in this background, 20 cards in this stack) or the number of string chunks (chars, items, lines, words) in a specified container (field, variable, selection, message box, line, item, word).

1.2+   Can tell you the number of cards in a specified background as well as the number of cards in a stack.

Examples
```
the number of card fields
the number of buttons
repeat for the number of cards
if the number of lines in field 3 is 3
then answer "Three lines"
put number of cards in this bkgnd && "cards this bkgnd" ¬
into field "bkgndInfo"
```

See Also   **id, name, Naming**

number   Object Property

Syntax   `[the] number of <object descriptor>`

Notes   Can return the relative number of an object (button 1, field 2, card 3, background 4). The number value can't be changed with the **set** command. Background numbers can only be changed by copying and pasting. Card numbers can be changed by copying and pasting or sorting. The order of buttons and fields can be changed with the Send Farther and Bring Closer menu commands.

Examples   `the number of field "Tax" -- Returns a number like 3`

numberFormat   Global Property

Syntax   `[the] numberFormat`

Notes   Controls the way numbers look. The result of every math operation while the `numberFormat` is `.00` contains two decimal places even if they are filled with zeros. This is the usual format for working with money. If the format is `.####`, up to four digits result from math operations, but the digits are not padded with zeros. You can even combine #s and 0s, as in `.00###`, to get a number that has at least two decimal places and can show up to five decimal places. The maximum number of digits you can specify is 31. The `numberFormat` is reset to the default `.######` on `idle`, so it can't be set in the Message box. Changing the `numberFormat` has no effect on numbers already in containers.

Examples
```
45/30 -- Returns 1.5
4/3 -- Returns 1.333333
set the numberFormat to ".00"
45/30 -- Returns 1.50
set the numberFormat to "00.00"
45/30 -- Returns 01.50
set the numberFormat to "00.00######"
4/3 -- Returns 01.33333333
```

numToChar   String Function

Syntax
```
the numToChar of <number>
numToChar(<number>)
```

Notes   Returns the character an ASCII number represents.

Example	`the numToChar of 65 -- Returns A`
	`numToChar(variable)`
	`if numToChar(13) is return then beep -- beeps`
	`get the numToChar of it -- Where it is a variable`
	`put the numToChar(119) into field 1`
	`if the numToChar(item 3 of field 2) is return`
	`then put "End of line" into msg`

See Also	**charToNum, ASCII**

Object Descriptor

Concept *(not a reserved word)*

Notes	A way of referring to a particular object. Composed of the object type plus a specific relative number, ID number, or name (designator).
Example	`-- Object type is card, id 3432 is specific designator` `go to card id 3432`
See Also	**id, name, Naming, number, Objects**

Object Hierarchy

Concept *(not a reserved word)*

Notes	The natural order of HyperCard objects that controls the order in which objects receive messages. Lower objects get messages first, but higher objects get messages from more places. If the flow of messages is a river, buttons and fields are the creeks near the headwaters, the Home stack is where the river meets the sea, and HyperCard is the ocean.
See Also	**Hierarchy, Objects**

Objects

Concept *(not a reserved word)*

Notes	The building blocks of HyperCard, consisting of stacks, backgrounds, cards, fields, and buttons.
See Also	**background, button, card, field, stack**

offset

String Function

Syntax	`offset(<textA>,<textB>)`
Notes	If the string `textA` is found in the string `textB`, `offset` returns the first char of the match. If the string is not found, `offset` returns 0.

Example	`offset("stein","Springstein") -- Returns 7`
	`offset("Hol","Springstein") -- Returns 0`
	`put offset(findVar,card field 2) into whereVar`
	`on mouseUp`
	`    put "Springstein" into textVar`
	`    put offset("stein",textVar) into startVar`
	`    put "er" into char startVar to startVar + ¬`
	`    the length of textVar -- Returns Springer`
	`    put textVar -- Displays Springer`
	`end mouseUp`

See Also	**contains, is in**

on

on Keyword

Syntax on <messageName>

Notes Starts a message handler and indicates which message is being handled. The maximum length of a message with parameters is 254 characters. A handler ends with the keyword **end** followed again by the message name (no parameters). You can place any number of statements between these two keywords, up to the script maximum of 30,000 characters. Function message handlers start with **function** rather than on.

Example
```
on mouseUp -- Button handler
   put "Ow! You clicked me." into the message box
end mouseUp
```

See Also **function, Handler, end**

---

one Constant

Notes Stands for the number 1.

Example put one into word one of field one of card one

See Also **Constants**

Opaque Menu Command

Notes Turns transparent pixels in a card graphic layer selection to white. Available when a graphic is selected.

Example
```
on mouseUp
   choose select tool
   drag from 0,0 to 200,200
   doMenu "Opaque"
end mouseUp
```

---

opaque Button/Field Style

Notes A rectangular area you can't see through. The button name and icon (if any) or field text stands out on a white mask regardless of the background.

Examples set the style of button id 3 to opaque

See Also **Buttons, Fields, style**

---

open Command

Syntax open [<document> with] <application>

Notes Suspends HyperCard and opens another application. Optionally, you can open a document belonging to another application. Sends a **suspend** message and then a **resume** message when the user quits the other application and HyperCard starts again.

Caution Global variable values and push/pop stack information are lost when HyperCard is suspended, so save these first if you need them. **suspend** and **resume** messages are not sent when HyperCard is running under MultiFinder.

Example open "MacWrite"

continued

```
open "Dear John" with "MacWrite"
open docVar with appVar
```

See Also **resume, suspend**

open file   Command

Syntax   `open file <fileName>`

Notes   Opens a new or existing text file. A text file must be opened before it can be read from or written to. Because filenames must be referred to frequently when reading and writing, it is a good idea to put the name into a container. To open a file that is not at the top level of the file hierarchy, you must provide a complete pathname, including the disk and all folders. If even one character of your pathname is incorrect, you get an error − 120. You also get an error message if the file is already open, the file is locked, or the disk is full. Trying to open a file without a pathname can result in a new file being created accidentally. To overcome this problem, use Steve Maller's `Filename` XFCN, which shows a dialog box and lets the user click through the folders to the desired file.

Caution   If HyperCard can't find a file of the name provided, it doesn't prompt you to find the file but assumes that the file doesn't exist and creates a new one.

Example
```
open "dataFile"
open "HyperDisk:FilesFolder:TopSecret:dataFile" -- Pathname
put "dataFile" into fileNameVar
open fileNameVar -- Opening a name in a variable
-- Next button handler fragment requires Filename XFCN
on mouseUp
   put Filename("TEXT") into fileName -- Gets pathname
   if fileName is empty then exit to HyperCard
   open fileName -- and etcetera
end mouseUp
```

See Also   **close file, read, write**

open printing   Command

Syntax   `open printing [with dialog]`

Notes   Informs the printer driver that you are going to start sending some printing requests. The `with dialog` option displays the Print Stack dialog box. Be sure to use the `close printing` command when you are through printing. Navigation and other commands can also be located between the `open printing` and `close printing` commands.

Example
```
open printing
open printing with dialog
on mouseUp
   open printing
   print 4 cards
   go to stack "ClipArt"
   print card 8
   close printing
end mouseUp
```

See Also   **close printing, print**

Open Stack

Open Stack Menu Command

Notes Displays a dialog box that allows the user to click to and open any stack. (See Figure R-20.) Sends `closeCard`, `closeBackground`, `closeStack`, `openStack`, `openBackground`, and `openCard` messages.

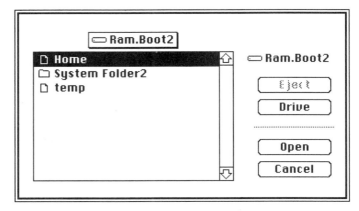

Figure R-20. The Open Stack dialog box.

Example `doMenu "Open Stack"`

Keyboard Command-O

See Also **go**

openBackground Message

Notes Sent to the card after the `startUp` message and every time a card of a background other than the current background is opened. Best to trap at the stack level or higher.

Examples
```
on openBackground
   answer "This is background" && the short name of this ¬
background
end openBackground
```

See Also **closeBackground, Messages, Handlers**

openCard Message

Notes Sent to the card every time a card is opened. Trapping this message at the card level makes the card treatment unique. Place a handler in a higher object for it to be shared by more cards.

Examples
```
on openCard
   put the number of cards into field "CardNum"
end openCard
```

See Also **closeCard, Messages, Handlers**

openField Message

Notes Sent to the field when the insertion point cursor appears in a field.

Examples
```
on openField
  beep
end openField
```

See Also **closeField, Handlers, Messages**

openStack Message

Notes Sent to the card when a stack is opened. Best trapped in the stack or the Home stack.

Examples
```
on openStack
  hide the message box
  hide the menuBar
end openStack
```

See Also **closeStack, Handlers, Messages**

Operators Concept *(not a reserved word)*

Notes Words or symbols used in expressions.
Math operators: $+$, $-$, $*$, $\wedge$, div, mod, /
String operators: &, &&, is in, contains, is not in
Grouping: ( )
Logical operators: $<$, $>$, $<=$, $>=$, , , $=$, $<>$, , and, or, not, is, is not

1.2+ is within, is not within

See Also **Operator Precedence,** *(listing for individual operators)*

Operator Precedence Concept *(not a reserved word)*

Notes When operators are combined in an expression, the order in which they are performed is determined by their precedence value. The lower the number in the following table, the sooner the operation is performed. When operators have equal precedence, they are evaluated from left to right except for exponentiation, which is evaluated from right to left, so 2^3^4 = 2^(3^4). Nested parenthetical expressions are evaluated from the inside out.

Precedence	Operators
1	( )
2	not $-$ (minus sign)
3	$\wedge$
4	$*$ / div mod
5	$+$ $-$
6	& &&
7	$<$ $>$ $<=$ $>=$ is in contains is not in is within is not within
8	$=$ is is not $<>$
9	and
10	or

optionKey

optionKey — System Function

Syntax the optionKey

Notes Returns down if the Option key is pressed down. Otherwise, returns up.

Example the optionKey
wait until the optionKey is down

See Also **commandKey, optionKey** *(reserved word)*, **shiftKey**

optionKey — Modifier

Notes Used to refer to the Option key.

Example drag from 100,100 to 200,200 with optionKey

See Also **commandKey** *(modifier)*, **optionKey** *(function)*, **shiftKey** *(modifier)*

or — Logical Operator

Syntax <expression1> or <expression2>

Notes Returns true if one or both of the expressions bracketing it are true. There is no built-in XOR, but you can simulate one with (<expression1> or <expression2>) and (not(<expression1> and <expression2>)).

Examples
```
if 3>5 or 5>3 then beep -- Beeps, second expression is true
if 3<5 or 5>3 then beep -- Beeps, both true
if the mouseClick or optionKey is down or variable = 5
then exit to HyperCard
if (3<5 or 5>3) and (not(3<5 and 5>3)) then beep
-- XOR, no beep because both are true
```

See Also **and, is**

oval tool — Tool

Notes Used, along with the **drag** command, to draw round or oval shapes. Normally drawn with a one-pixel-wide black line but the **drag... with optionKey** variation lets you substitute the current pattern for black. The line size can be changed with the **lineSize** property. Ovals can be constrained to circles with the **drag... with shiftKey** command. Ovals can be lasso selected immediately after creation with the **doMenu "Select"** command.

Example
```
on mouseUp
  choose oval tool
  drag from 50,50 to 100,100
  set centered to true
  drag from 150,150 to 200,170 with shiftKey -- From center
  -- Last is equivalent to drag from 150,150 to 170,170
  set lineSize to 4
  set pattern to 5
  drag from 300,50 to 350,100 with optionKey
  -- To draw centered with thick, patterned line
end mouseUp
```

See Also **centered, choose, drag, lineSize, pattern, Tool Palette**

Page Setup Menu Command

Notes Displays the Page Setup dialog box so that the user can change the settings. (See Figure R-21.)

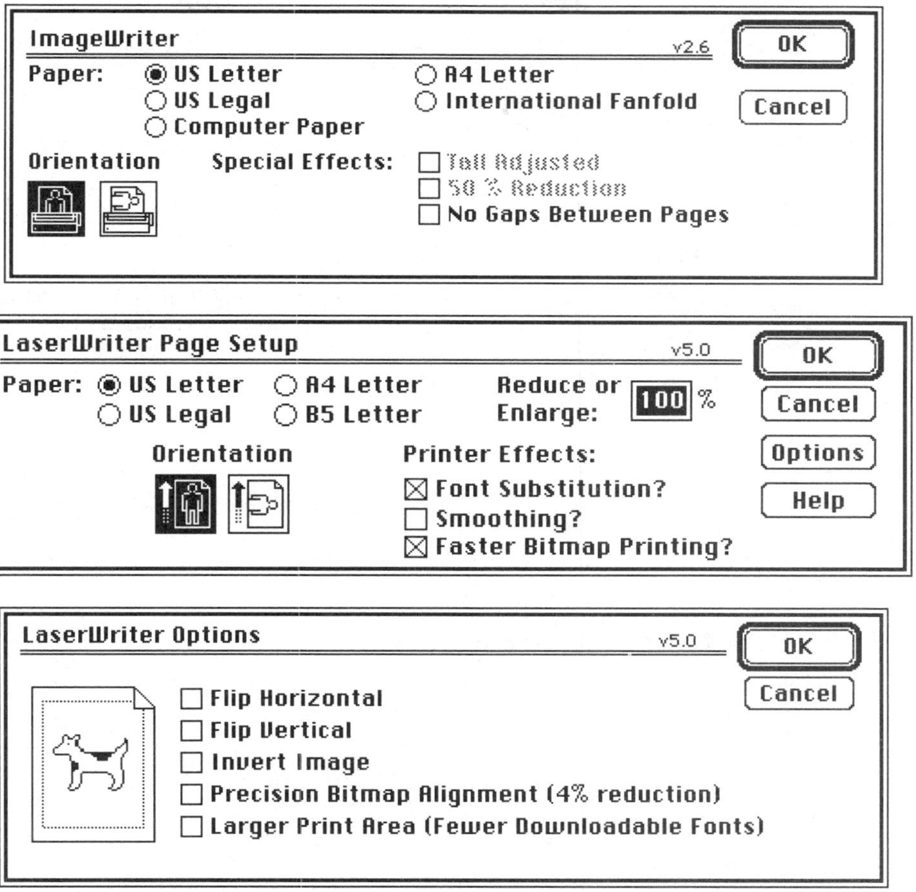

```
┌─────────────────────────────────────────────────────────────────┐
│ ImageWriter                              v2.6      ┌─────────┐    │
│                                                    │   OK    │    │
│ Paper:    ● US Letter          ○ A4 Letter         └─────────┘    │
│           ○ US Legal           ○ International Fanfold            │
│           ○ Computer Paper                         ┌─────────┐    │
│                                                    │ Cancel  │    │
│ Orientation    Special Effects: ☐ Tall Adjusted   └─────────┘    │
│  ┌──┐ ┌──┐                       ☐ 50 % Reduction                │
│  │  │ │  │                       ☐ No Gaps Between Pages          │
│  └──┘ └──┘                                                        │
└─────────────────────────────────────────────────────────────────┘
```

```
┌─────────────────────────────────────────────────────────────────┐
│ LaserWriter Page Setup                   v5.0     ┌─────────┐     │
│                                                   │   OK    │     │
│ Paper: ● US Letter   ○ A4 Letter  Reduce or ┌───┐%└─────────┐     │
│        ○ US Legal    ○ B5 Letter  Enlarge:  │100│ ┌─────────┐     │
│                                             └───┘ │ Cancel  │     │
│         Orientation        Printer Effects:       └─────────┘     │
│          ┌──┐ ┌──┐         ☒ Font Substitution?   ┌─────────┐     │
│          │  │ │  │         ☐ Smoothing?           │ Options │     │
│          └──┘ └──┘         ☒ Faster Bitmap Printing? └───────┘    │
│                                                   ┌─────────┐     │
│                                                   │  Help   │     │
│                                                   └─────────┘     │
└─────────────────────────────────────────────────────────────────┘
```

```
┌─────────────────────────────────────────────────────────────────┐
│ LaserWriter Options                      v5.0     ┌─────────┐     │
│                                                   │   OK    │     │
│  ┌─────────┐   ☐ Flip Horizontal                  └─────────┘     │
│  │         │   ☐ Flip Vertical                    ┌─────────┐     │
│  │   🐕    │   ☐ Invert Image                     │ Cancel  │     │
│  │         │   ☐ Precision Bitmap Alignment (4% reduction)        │
│  └─────────┘   ☐ Larger Print Area (Fewer Downloadable Fonts)     │
└─────────────────────────────────────────────────────────────────┘
```

Figure R-21. Page Setup dialog boxes.

Example doMenu "Page Setup..."

Painting Tools Concept *(not a reserved word)*

Notes Tools that are used for painting. (See Figure R-22.)

See Also **choose, editBkgnd, Graphics, Tools,** *(individual tools)*

Paint Text Concept *(not a reserved word)*

Notes Text produced by the text tool in the Painting Palette. Paint text is actually a bit-mapped part of one of the two graphic layers. It can't be edited or searched, and it does not benefit from the higher resolution available on the LaserWriter.

See Also **Fields, Graphics, Pictures, text tool**

Paint Text

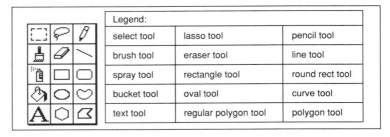

Legend:		
select tool	lasso tool	pencil tool
brush tool	eraser tool	line tool
spray tool	rectangle tool	round rect tool
bucket tool	oval tool	curve tool
text tool	regular polygon tool	polygon tool

Figure R-22.   Painting tools.

Painting   Concept *(not a reserved word)*

Notes   Using the Painting Tools from the Tool Palette to create bit-mapped graphics on one of the two graphic layers. Painted graphics are not like the object graphics in MacDraw, which are not supported by HyperCard.

See Also   **Fields, Graphics, Tool Palette, text tool**

Palette   Concept

Notes   A tear-off menu, especially after it has been torn off. HyperCard's palettes let you choose tools or patterns by clicking icons or pattern samples.

See Also   **Painting, Tool Palette**

param   System Function

Syntax
```
the param of <number>
param(<number>)
```

Notes   Returns the parameter specified by the number. Allows you to use selected parameters when you don't need all of them. Can be used in handlers that trap any message that passes parameters.

Example
```
on play
   -- To play the notes passed in a different voice
   if param(1) is "boing" -- True
   then play "harpsichord" param(2)
   else pass play
end play
play "boing" "a b" -- Type into message box
```

See Also   **Parameters, paramCount, params**

paramCount   System Function

Syntax   `the paramCount`

Notes   Returns the number of parameters passed with the message trapped by the current handler.

Example
```
on play
   get the paramCount
   if it is 1 then put "Playing a simple" && param(1) into ¬
```
continued

```
     message box
     else if it is 4 then
        put "Playing" && param1 && "notes" && quote & param(4) & ¬
        quote && "at tempo" && param(3) into message box
     end if
     pass play
  end play
  play "boing" -- Type into the message box
  play "boing" tempo 150 " a b" -- Type into the message box
```

See Also **param, Parameters, params**

Parameters **Concept** *(not a reserved word)*

Notes Parameters are units of information, or arguments, passed along with a message name when a command or function is executed. HyperCard's internal handlers pull messages apart to interpret them, and your user defined handlers can do the same.

See Also **Argument, Handlers, Messages, param, paramCount, params**

params **System Function**

Syntax `the params`

Notes Returns the entire message, including the message name and all parameters.

Example
```
-- If the message is play "boing" tempo 150 "a b"
on play
 put "Now executing" && the params into message box
 pass play
end play
```

See Also **param, paramCount, Parameters**

pass **Keyword**

Syntax `pass <messageName>`

Notes Passes the handled message on so that other handlers higher in the object hierarchy or in HyperCard can trap it. Also ends the current handler.

Example
```
on beep
   flash 1
   pass beep -- A screen flash precedes every beep
   play "boing" -- Not executed
end beep
```

See Also **Handlers, Messages, send**

Password **Concept**

Notes A string of characters that only you know. Password protection is one of several ways to protect or limit access to a stack.

See Also **ask password, Protect Stack, Protection**

Paste Button

Paste Button   **Menu Command**

Notes   Places a copy of the button on the Clipboard into the current object layer (card or background). Sends a `newButton` message.

Keyboard   Command-V, Function-4

Example
```
doMenu "Paste Button"
on mouseUp -- Button handler to paste a button to the bkgnd
--assumes that a button is on the Clipboard
  set editBkgnd to true -- Open background layer
  doMenu "Paste Button"
end mouseUp
```

Paste Card   **Menu Command**

Notes   Places a copy of the card on the Clipboard after the current card. Sends `close-Card` and `openCard` messages. A pasted-in card doesn't register as a new card.

Example   `doMenu "Paste Card"`

Paste Field   **Menu Command**

Notes   Places a copy of the field on the Clipboard into the current object layer (card or background). Sends a `newField` message.

Keyboard   Command-V, Function-4

Example   `doMenu "Paste Field"`

Paste Picture   **Menu Command**

Notes   Places a copy of the picture on the Clipboard into the current graphic layer (card or background).

Keyboard   Command-V, Function-4

Example   `doMenu "Paste Picture"`

Paste Text   **Menu Command**

Notes   Places a copy of the text on the clipboard after the insertion point.

Keyboard   Command-V, Function-4

Example   `doMenu "Paste Text"`

Pathname   **Concept** *(not a reserved word)*

Notes   Information that permits HyperCard to find a stack, application, document, or file not in the immediate vicinity. The pathname consists of a disk or server followed by any folders (there may be several) and then the destination file.

Example
```
go to stack "HyperDisk:TopFolder:InnerFolder:PlayStack"
open "HD80:Applications:Graphic:MacPaint"
open file "OtherDrive:HyperStuff:Complaints"
go to card 4 of stack "BackupDisk:Files"
```

See Also   **go, open, open file, print**

pattern   Painting Property

Syntax   `the pattern`

Notes   Used to change the pattern to something other than the default black. You can choose among 40 numbered patterns. Each stack has its own pattern palette, which can be edited in the Edit Pattern dialog box (show with `doMenu "Edit Pattern..."`). The default patterns are shown in Figure R-23.

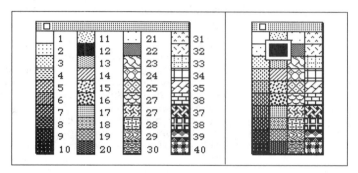

Figure R-23.   The Pattern Palette and the Edit Pattern dialog box.

Example
```
the pattern -- Returns a number representing the current
-- setting
set pattern to 30
set pattern to newPatternVar
put the pattern into prevPattern -- Save before changing
```

See Also   **pattern window**

Pattern Palette   Window *(not a reserved word)*

Notes   A HyperCard windoid (shown in the pattern listing) that displays the available patterns. Also known as the pattern window.

See Also   **pattern**

pattern window   Window

Notes   A HyperCard windoid (shown in the pattern listing) that displays the available patterns. Also known as the Pattern Palette. Show with a `show pattern window` command to let the user choose a pattern and hide with a `hide pattern window` command. The default location of the pattern window is 300,70, and its rectangle is 300,70,371,199. It can be repositioned by setting its `loc` property to a new coordinate. The `loc` of a window is the top left corner and not the center. Use the `pattern` property to change the current pattern.

Keyboard   Tab key, when any Painting tool is selected, is equivalent to `show pattern window`.

Example
```
show the pattern window
set the loc of pattern window to 100,100
```

See Also   **location, pattern, show**

Peeking

Peeking   **Concept** *(not a reserved word)*

Notes   Version 1.2 introduced several new techniques for quickly opening an object's script. This is called peeking and simply means that the Script Editor is quickly opened for the specified object. To close the Script Editor, in addition to the usual techniques, you can now press Option-Command and click the mouse or press any key. You can peek at the card script by pressing the Option-Command-C key combination. To see the background, press Option-Command-B and to see the stack script press Option-Command-S. Peeking at buttons and fields varies with the tool selected.

> When the browse tool is selected, all visible buttons can be peeked by clicking them while the Option and Command keys (or Shift-Option-Command keys) are pressed. Visible fields are peeked by clicking with the Shift-Option-Command key combination. Peeking at a script has no effect on the tool selected, so you can edit a button or field without having to choose browse tool again afterwards.

> When the button tool is selected, you can peek at both visible and hidden buttons by clicking with Option-Command.

> When the field tool is selected, you can peek at both visible and hidden fields by clicking with Option-Command.

1.2 +   New version 1.2 feature.

pencil tool   **Painting Tool**

Notes   Used to make one-pixel-wide lines. If a drag or click starts with a white pixel, the line is black; if the pixel is black, the line is white. This tool is available when the `userlevel` is 3 (Painting) or higher. You can use an XFCN like `Pixel()` to determine in advance whether a pixel is white or black.

Example
```
choose pencil tool
drag from 50,50 to 100,100 -- Draws a line
click at 75,75
-- Put a white dot at the halfway point of the line
```

pi   **Constant**

Notes   Stands for the ratio of the circumference of a circle to its diameter (or π). HyperTalk's pi is precise to 20 decimal places.

Example
```
set format to ".####################"
-- 20 decimal places
put pi into msg -- Returns 3.14159265358979323846
cos(50*pi/180) -- Cosine of 50 degrees is 0.642788
```

Pickup   **Menu Command**

Notes   Transfers the graphic behind a selection to the selection, something like an iron-on decal. Available when a picture (graphic element) is selected.

Example   `doMenu "Pickup"`

pict   **Abbreviation**

Notes   Short for picture.

Pictures   Concept *(not a reserved word)*

Notes   Graphics created with the Paint tools or with another application and copied in through the Clipboard. See Graphics.

See Also   **Copy Picture, Cut Picture, hide picture, Painting, Paste Picture, show picture, showPict**

picture   Reserved Word

Notes   Refers to a bit-mapped graphic image.

1.2   You can also use the abbreviation `pict`.

Example
```
show card picture
hide background pict
```

See Also   **Graphics, hide, show**

play   Command

Syntax
```
play <"voice"> [tempo <number>] [<"notes">]
play stop
```

Notes   Plays notes through the Macintosh speaker or audio jack. Uses the specified voice at the default (120) or specified tempo. If no notes are specified, middle C is played.

▶ Voice: Three voices are included with HyperCard (boing, harpsichord, and silence). The silence voice is used to play long rests. These voices are Format 2 **"snd "** resources that can be copied and pasted into your stacks or into HyperCard with **ResEdit, ResMover, ResCopy**, or similar utilities. Other sound resource voices can be obtained from third parties. You can make your own **play** resources with Faralon's MacRecorder.

▶ Tempo: The normal tempo range is from 42-66 (largo) to 69-152 (presto). Try tempi below 42 and above 1000 for special effects. The complete range is 32 to 32,767. Fast tempi can interfere with long duration notes. The default tempo is 120.

▶ Letter Notes: Use the letters A through G to specify the note you want. Use the letter R for a rest. Notes should be separated by spaces and set off by quotes. The default note is middle C (261.63 Hz). Maximum 75–80 notes per statement.

▶ Accidentals: Append a # to the number for sharps or a b for flats (**A A# C bb**).

▶ Octave: The default octave is 4 (middle A at 440 Hz), but you can change the octave for the current note and all subsequent notes with a number following the note (**A3 A#4 C Bb5**). The highest note is B7 (3951.1 Hz) and the lowest note is C0 (16.352 Hz).

▶ Duration: The default length is a quarter note q, but you can change the length for the current note and all subsequent notes with a letter after the note and octave. **w** = whole note, **h** = half note, **e** = 8th note, **s** = 16th note, **t** = 32nd note, and **x** = 64th note (**A3t A#4 Cw Bb5e**).

▶ Dotted notes: You can also put a period after a note to increase its length, and the length of notes of the same duration that follow it, by approximately 50 percent. A dotted quarter note is like a 3/8th note (**gq.**). A dotted half note is like a 3/4th note (**Gh.**). The notes continue dotted until another duration modifier is encountered. In **A3t. A A A#4**

play

Cw Bb5e, the first 4 notes are 3/64th notes and the last two are normal whole and normal eighth notes.

▶ Triplets: Put a 3 after the duration letter to squeeze 3 notes into the time it normally takes to play 2. Whether the note is a whole note or a 64th note, it and all subsequent notes of the same duration play a third faster until another duration modifier is encountered. In A3q3 A A A#4 Cq Bb5e, the first 4 quarter notes are played 1/3 faster than normal, the next note is a normal quarter note, and the last a normal eighth note.

▶ Number Notes: The alternative to letter notes and octave numbers are note numbers. The number 60 is middle C with C sharp at 61 and C flat at 59. The D above middle C is 62 (56t. 71 60w 85e3).

▶ Relationship Between Notations:

Note	Frequency	HyperTalk Note	HyperTalk Number
C	261.63 Hz	C	60
C sharp-D flat	277.18 Hz	C#-Db	61
D	293.66 Hz	D	62

The play stop version of the command cuts off any previous play commands that are queued to be played.

Caution To prevent scratchy sound and to keep your sound in synch with other actions, use the wait until the sound is "done" statement after a play command.

Example
```
play "boing"
play "harpsichord" tempo 150 "a b"
play "harpsichord" tempo 50 "60 65"
play "boing" tempo 32767 ¬
"c6w c c c c c c c c c c c c c"
-- Laser sound effect
play "harpsichord" "ce3 cc cc ab3w bbe3 bb bb gw"
play "silence" "cw c" -- Long rest
play boing" "a b c r g g r f" -- Short rests
play voiceVar tempoVar field "Notes"
on mouseUp
   play "boing" tempo 100 "cw c c c c c c c c"
   wait 3 secs
   play stop -- Cuts off play after two boings
end mouseUp
```

See Also **beep, dial, sound, wait**

plus Cursor

Notes The big plus cursor shown in Figure R-12. Can also be referred to as cursor 3.

1.2 + New version 1.2 feature.

Example Set cursor to plus

See Also **cursor**

Polygon Sides Menu Command

Notes Displays the Polygon Sides dialog box so that the user can choose the regular polygon desired. Normally, you use the `polySides` property to determine the type of polygon drawn. Available when a Painting tool is selected.

Example `doMenu "Polygon Sides"`

See Also **polySides, regular polygon tool**

polygon tool Painting Tool

Notes Not usable from HyperTalk.

See Also **regular polygon tool**

polySides Painting Property

Syntax `the polySides`

Notes Used to determine the number of sides the regular polygon tool draws with. (See Figure R-24.) The range is 3 to 8 and the default is 4.

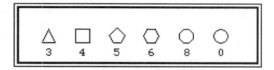

Figure R-24. Choices for `polySides` command.

Caution The 0 sided polygon is available only from the Poly Sides dialog box. `set poly-Sides to 0` does not work.

Example
```
on mouseUp
   choose regular polygon tool
   set polySides to 3
   set polySides to numVar
   drag from 100,100 to 200,200
end mouseUp
```

See Also **Polygon Sides**

pop card Command

Syntax `pop card [before | into | after <container>]`

Notes Retrieves the card ID and pathname for the last card pushed onto the push/pop stack. If no container is specified, the pop card navigates to the last card pushed. If a container is specified, the pathname is stored there without navigating to the card.

Example
```
on mouseUp
   go to card id 6464
   push card
   go to card id 3474 of stack "Help"
   push card
   go to card 2836 of stack "Home"
```

continued

pop card

```
pop card -- Goes to card id 3474 of the Help stack
pop card into bypassVar
-- card id 6464 etc in variable
go bypassVar -- Goes to card id 6464
end mouseUp
```

See Also   **Pathname, push card**

Power Keys   **Menu Command**

Notes   When Power Keys are active, the user can substitute a single keystroke for a menu selection. The scriptor is better advised to use the `powerKeys` property for this purpose. Power Key shortcuts are also available for use in scripts, but they don't save that much effort, and they make scripts harder to read. The menu command is available when a Painting tool is selected.

Example   `doMenu "Power Keys"`

powerKeys   **Paint Property**

Syntax   `the powerKeys`

Notes   When `powerKeys` is true, the user can substitute a single keystroke for a menu selection. Power Key shortcuts are also available for use in scripts, but they don't save that much effort, and they make scripts harder to read. The `powerKeys` options are

Black pattern	B	Opaque	O
Darken	D	Pickup	P
Draw Centered (toggle)	C	Revert	R
Draw Multiple (toggle)	M	Rotate Left	[
Fill	F	Rotate Right	]
Flip Horizontal	H	Select	S
Flip Vertical	V	Select All	A
Grid (toggle)	G	Trace Edges	E
Invert	I	Transparent	T
Lighten	L	White pattern	W
Line size	1–4,6,8		

Example   `set the powerKeys to true`

Precedence   **Concept** *(not a reserved word)*

See Also   **Operator Precedence**

Prev   **Menu Command**

Notes   Opens the previous card in the stack. If the current card is the first card in the stack, the last card is opened. Use `go prev` instead. Sends `closeCard` and `open-Card` messages and possibly `closeBackground` and `openBackground` messages.

Keyboard	Command-2
Example	doMenu "Prev"
See Also	**go**

prev
previous
Modifier

Notes Used with the go command to navigate to the previous card. Goes to the last card from the first card. Sends `closeCard` and `openCard` messages and possibly `closeBackground` and openBackground messages.

Example
```
go prev
go prev card of this bkgnd
```

See Also **go**

print
Command

Syntax
```
print card | <card designator>
print <number> cards
```

Notes Prints the designated card or cards. If `print` is by itself, it is the equivalent of doMenu "Print Card", except that it can print several cards at a time. When located between `open printing` and `close printing` commands, several `print` commands can specify particular cards or a range of cards to be printed. These printing instructions are saved until the `close printing` command is executed.

Example
```
print card
print card id 3454
print last
print all cards
print numberVar cards
on mouseUp
  open printing with dialog
  print 4 cards
  print card 8
  go stack "Card Ideas"
  print card 4
  close printing
end mouseUp
```

See Also **close printing, Naming, open printing**

print (with)
Command

Syntax `print <document> with <application>`

Notes Similar to `open with`, in that it suspends HyperCard, launches another application, and then opens a document. In this case, it also starts the printing process by showing the Print dialog box. A `suspend` message is sent before the other application is launched and a `resume` message is sent when HyperCard takes back control (except when you are running under MultiFinder). You can even use this command to print HyperCard's text files with the TeachText application that comes with system software. Remember that if the application or document is not at the top of the file hierarchy, you either have to provide complete pathname information, or the user has to click through the folders to the files. See the

print (with)

suspend listing for advice on saving global variables and push/pop stack values before suspending HyperCard.

Caution   Through version 1.2, if you attempt to launch an application and there isn't enough RAM, nothing happens: no printing, no alert, no beep. Unlike the simple print command, this command should not be executed between open printing and close printing commands.

Example
```
print "Letter to Mom" with "MacWrite"
print docVar with field selectVar
-- Names in containers
print "HyperCardData" with "TeachText"
print "Disk1:Folder2:FldrC:Notes" with ¬
"Disk2:Folder1:Write"
```

See Also   **open, Pathname, suspend**

Print Card   Menu Command

Notes   Prints the current card at full size.

Keyboard   Command-2

Example   doMenu "Print Card"

See Also   **Print Stack, Print Report, print, print (with)**

Print Report   Menu Command

Notes   Prints the contents of specified fields of the current stack. A dialog box is displayed and the user can choose from a number of different formats and options. Figure R-25A shows the dialog box when the Columns format is selected, and

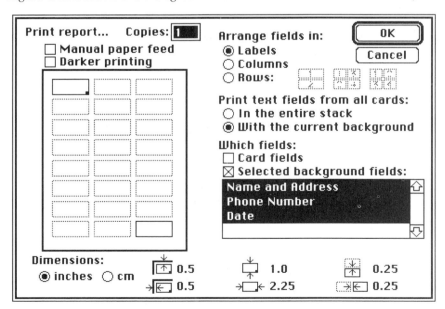

A. Columns format.

Figure R-25.   Row and column options provided by Print Reports.

Figure R-25B shows it when Labels is selected. Print Reports can be used to print the contents of a single field if the field is the only one of its description in the background specified (you may have to create a new background and copy in the field and the contents of the field.)

Example `doMenu "Print Report..."`

See Also **print, Print Card, Print Stack**

Print Stack   Menu Command

Notes Prints all the cards of the current stack. A dialog box is shown, and the user can choose from a number of different options and formats. The ImageWriter box is shown in Figure R-26.

The paging sequence for full size printing is shown in Figure R-27A, for half size printing in Figure R-27B, and for quarter size printing in R-27C.

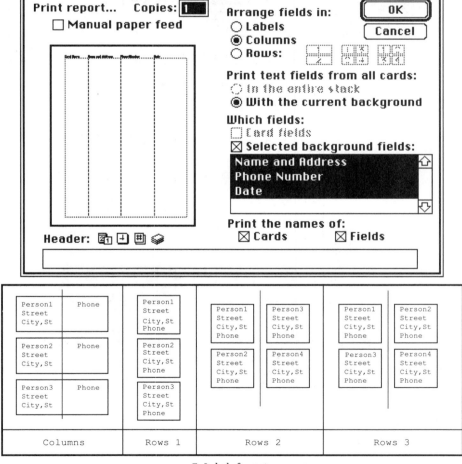

B. Labels format.

Figure R-25.   (cont)

Print Stack

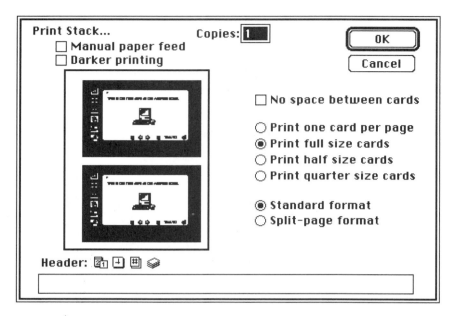

Figure R-26. The ImageWriter box for the Print Stack command.

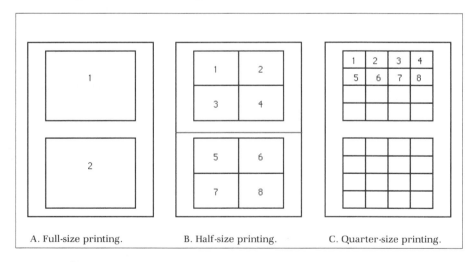

A. Full-size printing.   B. Half-size printing.   C. Quarter-size printing.

Figure R-27. Printing paging sequences.

Example   doMenu "Print Stack..."

See Also   **print, Print Card, Print Report**

Properties

Concept *(not a reserved word)*

Notes   Properties are the attributes of objects, of windows, of the Painting mode, or of HyperCard itself (global properties). An object's properties determine how it looks and acts. All properties can be read and many can be set. To read a prop-

690

erty, use it like a function (the userLevel) or in a get command statement (get the userLevel). To set a property, use the set command (set the userLevel to 5). Many object properties can also be set in Info dialog boxes, and most Painting properties can be set with dialog boxes opened from the Options menu. In the table that follows, (CS) means the property can't be set, (CG) means you can't get it, (1.1) means it is available for versions of HyperCard starting with 1.1, and (1.2) means it is available starting with 1.2.

▶ Background Properties

cantDelete (1.2)	name	number
id(CS)	script	showPict (1.2)

▶ Button Properties

autoHilite	bottom (1.2)	botRight (1.2)
height (1.2)	hilite	icon
id (CS)	left (1.2)	loc
name	number	rect
right (1.2)	script	showName
style	textAlign	textFont
textHeight	textSize	textStyle
top (1.2)	topLeft (1.2)	width (1.2)
visible		

▶ Card Properties

cantDelete (1.2)	name	number
id (CS)	script	showPict (1.2)

▶ Field Properties

autoTab (1.2)	bottom (1.2)	botRight (1.2)
height (1.2)	id (CS)	left (1.2)
loc	lockText	name
number	rect	right(1.2)
script	scroll	showLines
style	textAlign	textFont
textHeight	textSize	textStyle
top (1.2)	topLeft (1.2)	visible
wideMargins	width (1.2)	

▶ Global Properties

blindTyping	cursor (CG)	dragSpeed
editBkgnd	language	lockMessages
lockRecent	lockScreen	numberFormat
powerKeys	textArrows (1.1)	userLevel
userModify (1.2)		

Properties

▶ **Painting Properties**

brush	centered	filled
grid	lineSize	multiple
multiSpace	pattern	polySides
textAlign	textFont	textHeight
textSize	textStyle	

▶ **Stack Properties**

cantDelete (1.2)	cantModify (1.2)	FreeSize(CS)
name	script	size (CS)

▶ **Window Properties**

bottom (1.2)	botRight (1.2)	height (1.2)
left (1.2)	loc	rect
right (1.2)	top (1.2)	topLeft (1.2)
visible	width (1.2)	

See Also **reset paint,** *(listings for each property and for object types)*

Protect Stack

Menu Command

Notes Opens the Protect Stack dialog box. (See Figure R-28.) As a scriptor, you are more likely to use the **ask password** command to protect a stack, but you can give the user the option of setting his or her own level of protection with a simple **doMenu** "**Protect Stack...**" command. Available when the **userlevel** is 2 (Typing) or higher.

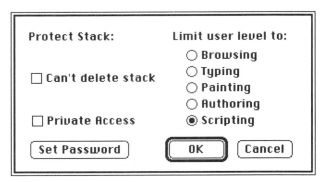

Figure R-28. The Protect Stack dialog box.

Example doMenu "Protect Stack..."

See Also **ask password**

push Command

Syntax push card | <card descriptor>

Notes Pushes a card identification onto the push/pop stack so that it can be "popped" off at a later time with the **pop card** command. Use **push card** to save the current card. By providing a card descriptor, you can save any card in the current stack (**push card id 34**). You can also push the recent card (the **recent** feature uses another LIFO stack like the push/pop stack) with **push recent card. push** and **pop** are usually used to provide a bread crumb trail through the stacks, but they can also be used to save a record of your travels for later reference if you **pop** the pushed cards into a container.

Caution If you **pop** more often than you **pushp**, you end up at the Home Card. When the push/pop stack is empty, a **pop card** command always gives you the card ID of the Home card.

Example
```
on mouseUp
  push card
  go to card 4 of stack "Help"
  push card
  go to card 2 of stack "Home"
  pop card into holderVar
  -- ID of last card saved in variable
  pop card
  -- Skips card 4 of Help and goes to first card
end mouseUp
```

See Also **pop card**

put Command

Syntax put <content> [before | into | after <container>]

Notes Takes a literal string or the value of a container and puts it into another container. The default **put** container, if no destination container is specified, is the Message box. **put** is also used to place a starting value into a variable before it is used in mathematical operations. HyperTalk variables don't have to be declared prior to use, so simply putting a value into a new variable is sufficient to create it. Use **into** to replace the existing contents of the container with the new contents, **before** to place the new contents in front of the old, or **after** to place the new contents at the end of the old. To delete the contents of a container, but not the container, put the constant **empty** into it.

Caution Putting an expression like **"4+9"** into a container results in the text value 4 + 9 rather than the numeric 13 being assigned to the container. To get the numeric value, put **the value of** 4 + 9 into the container. A long **put** statement can be broken into several lines with a soft return (Option-Return), but don't use a soft return between quotation marks.

Example
```
on mouseUp
  put "4+9" into expressionVar
  -- expressionVar holds 4+9
  put expressionVar into msg
  -- 4+9 displayed in message box
  wait 2 secs
  put the value of expressionVar into msg
  -- 13 in msg
```

continued

put

```
end mouseUp
on mouseUp
  put ", Groucho" into field 2
  put "I must be going"
  -- Displays I must be going in the message box
  put "Hello, " before msg -- Note space after comma
  -- Displays "Hello, I must be going" in the message box
  put the message box after field 2
  -- Displays "Hello, I must be going Groucho" in field 2
end mouseUp
put word 2 of textVar into word 3 of ¬
card field textVar2
put empty into fullVar
-- Previous content of fullVar dumped
put the mouseLoc into coordVar
-- Getting a function value
-- Type the following lines into the message box
doMenu "New Button"
put the number of card buttons into buttonVar
put "Put the name of button" && buttonVar into msg
-- Displays "put the name of button 3" (number varies)
-- Press the Return key
-- Displays the card button "New Button"
```

See Also   **get**

quit   Message

Notes   Sent to the card just before HyperCard quits. Best trapped at the stack or the Home stack levels.

Example
```
on quit
  global referenceVar
  put referenceVar into field "reference" of card 1
  -- Saves value for next time
  answer "Quitting now will fry your memory board" ¬
  with "Go ahead" or "Please Stop"
  if it is "Please Stop" then answer "Too late!"
end quit
```

See Also   **Messages, Handlers**

Quit HyperCard   Menu Command

Notes   Choosing this item shuts down HyperCard and restarts the Finder. Always available. Sends closeCard, closeBackground, closeStack, and quit messages.

Keyboard   Command-Q

Example   doMenu "Quit HyperCard"

See Also   **ask password**

quote   Constant

Notes   Stands for the ASCII double quote character (34). Used when you need quotation marks inside quotation marks. You can also substitute smart quotes (" produced by Option-[and " produced by Shift-Option-[) if you need to show only quotation marks. If you are building a script and need to have the quotes interpreted as the quote character by HyperTalk, you must use the quote constant to replace the quotation marks stripped away when a quoted literal is evaluated.

Example
```
put "card field" && quote & "Verbatim" & quote into msg
-- Puts card field "Verbatim" into the message box
put "card field ""Verbatim""" into msg
-- Puts card field "Verbatim" into the message box
on mouseUp
   put "put" && quote & "card field ""Verbatim""" & ¬
   quote && "into msg" into it
   do it -- it = put "card field ""Verbatim""" into msg
   -- message box displays card field "Verbatim"
end mouseUp
```

See Also   **Constants, do**

radioButton   Button Style

Notes   A little circle with text to the right that you can highlight by clicking, which unhighlights the previously highlighted button. If you want to set the textFont and textStyle with buttons, use radio buttons for the font (only one at a time) and check boxes for the style (can be a combination of elements).

Example
```
set the style of button id 3 to radioButton
on mouseUp -- Card handler to operate set of radio buttons
   global lastButton -- Load value in openCard handler
   set hilite of button lastButton to false
   put short name of target into lastButton
   set hilite of button lastButton to true
end mouseUp
```

See Also   **Buttons, style**

random   Math Function

Syntax
```
the random of <number>
random(<number>)
```

Notes   Returns a random number between 1 and a positive number. You can't use random(-20).

Example
```
random(20)
-- Returns numbers between 1 and 20 inclusive
random(20)+5
-- Returns numbers between 6 and 25 inclusive
random(NumVar)
repeat 20
   play "Harpsichord" random(100)+30
end repeat
```

read   Command

Syntax
```
read from file <fileName> until <delimiter character>
read from file <fileName> for <number of characters>
```

Notes   Pulls the contents of a text file from the disk and places it into the variable it. The two options are to pull everything until a delimiting character or to pull a set number of characters. The next read statement pulls the contents starting

read

where the last read left off. Files must be opened prior to a read command and should be closed after, though several files can be open at the same time. Tab characters are commonly used to delimit fields, and return characters commonly delimit records in a database. Return characters can mark the end of a line or a paragraph in a word processor file. Commas are frequently used between cells of a spreadsheet. In addition, any ASCII or non-ASCII character can be used as a delimiter. If you supply more than one character as the delimiter, HyperTalk takes the first and ignores the rest. Data read from a file is placed in a memory buffer as well as in the variable it. Subsequent write commands add new data to this buffer and the combined contents replace the previous file when the file is closed. Following a write command, it is impossible to read a file until it has been closed and reopened. The maximum number of characters you can read in one chunk is 16,384.

Caution As of the summer of 1988, read loops can mysteriously fail when you are running under MultiFinder. To be safe, access files when running under the Finder.

Example
```
read from file "data" until return
read from file fileName until tab
read from file fileName until delimiterVar
read from file fileName until numToChar(3)
read from file "HyperDisk:dataFile" until delimiterVar
read from file fileName for 10 -- 10 characters
on mouseUp
  open file "data"
  read from file "data" for 2
  -- Get field count in header
  put it into fieldsVar -- Store count in variable
  repeat while i = 1 to fieldsVar
    -- Repeat for number of fields
    read from file "data" until tab
    -- Get a field value
    put it into field i -- Put value into field
    put last char of field i -- Strip tab
  end repeat
  close file "data"
end mouseUp
on mouseUp
  -- Read part or all of file into one container
  put "Combined Reference:HCFile:dataFile2" ¬
  into fileName
  open file fileName
  read from file fileName until "@"
  put it into field 2
  close file fileName
end mouseUp
-- The next example presumes a stack with 3 cards with
-- 5 background fields per card.
-- Reads tab & returns delimited text into
-- separate containers
on mouseUp
  put "Combined Reference:HCFile:dataFile2" ¬
  into fileName
  open file fileName
  repeat 3 -- The number of records or cards
    repeat with i = 1 to 4
```

continued

696

```
                    -- The number of fields per record or card
                    read from file fileName until tab
                    -- Read one field
                    put it into field i
                    -- Put into the appropriate container
               put empty into last char of field i -- Strip tab
                 end repeat
                 read from file fileName until return
                 -- Read the last field in the record
                 put it into field 5
                 put empty into last char of field 5
                 -- Strip return
                 go next -- Go to another card for the next record
               end repeat
               close file fileName
           end mouseUp
```

See Also   **close file, open file, write**

Recent   Menu Command

Notes   Displays the Recent dialog box with miniature images of up to 42 of the last cards visited. The user can go to a card by clicking on its image. The scriptor should use `go recent` instead. Sends `closeCard` and `openCard` messages, possibly `closeBackground` and `openBackground`, and maybe even `closeStack` and `openStack` messages.

Keyboard   Command-R

Example   `doMenu "Recent"`

See Also   **go**

recent   Reserved Word

Notes   Displays the Recent dialog box with miniature images of up to 42 of the last cards visited.

Example   `go recent`

See Also   **Recent, back**

rect   Abbreviation

See Also   **rectangle**

rect tool   Abbreviation

See Also   **rectangle tool**

rectangle   Button/Field Style

Notes   A rectangle with a simple one-pixel-wide border. Abbreviation is `rect`.

Example   `set the style of button id 3 to rectangle`

See Also   **Buttons, Fields, style**

rectangle

rectangle — Button/Field/Window Property

Syntax
```
[the] rectangle of <object | window>
[the] rect of <object| window>
```

Notes
Returns the coordinates of the top left corner and the bottom right corner of the designated object (button, window, or field) separated by commas (L,T,R,B). The rectangle can be changed with the `set rectangle of <object> to <value>` statement. If `right` is smaller than `left` and `bottom` is smaller than `top`, the button or field will be invisible, regardless of its `visible` property value. Abbreviation is `rect`.

1.2+
With version 1.2, there are eight new functions for working with rectangles. `left`, `top`, `right`, and `bottom` return items 1, 2, 3, and 4 of the rectangle, respectively. `topLeft` and `bottomRight` return the coordinate pairs for those points. `height` returns `bottom` and `top`; `width` returns `right` and `left`. There is also a new logical operator, `is within`, that tests whether a point is inside a rectangle.

Example
```
the rectangle of field 1
put the rect of button id 3
set the rect of button 1 to "100,100,150,150"
set item 1 of rect of me to item 1 of rect of target
```

See Also
bottom, bottomRight, height, is within, left, loc, right, top, topLeft, width

rectangle tool — Painting Tool

Notes
Used with the `drag` command to make square-cornered rectangles. Drawn with a 1-pixel-wide black line unless the `lineSize` or `pattern` properties are changed. The first coordinate pair in the `drag` command is the corner unless the `centered` property is set to true. This tool is available when the `userlevel` is 3 (Painting) or higher.

> Thicker borders: `set lineSize to (1 to 8)`.
> Patterned rectangles: `drag... with the optionKey`.
> Change pattern: `set pattern to (0 to 40)`.
> Filled: `set filled to true`.

Example
```
on mouseUp
    choose rectangle tool
    drag from 50,50 to 100,100 -- draws a rectangle
    set pattern to 10
    set lineSize to 5
    drag from 100,100 to 200,200 with optionKey
    -- A thick, patterned rectangle
    set filled to true
    drag from 100,100 to 200,200
    -- A thick, black bordered rectangle filled with a pattern
end mouseUp
```

See Also
draw, multiple, oval, regular polygon, round rect

Recursion — Concept *(not a reserved word)*

Notes
Repeatedly calling a message handler from that message handler. HyperTalk does not permit very much recursion and gives you a `Too much recursion` error if you push its limits (see first example). If you are careful, you can skate at the edge of the recursive ice with a handler like the second example.

Example
```
on mouseUp
   beep
   send mouseUp
end mouseUp
function diskspace -- Card handler that returns diskSpace in K
-- global flag
  if flag is true then pass diskSpace
  if flag <> true
  then put true into flag -- Set flag first pass
  put diskSpace() into var -- Recursive call
  put false into flag -- Reset flag
  return var div 1024 -- Return adjusted value
end diskspace
```

See Also   **convert, dateItems, time**

reg poly tool regular polygon tool

Painting Tool

Notes   Use with the `drag` command to make polygons with equal sides. The default number of sides is 4, but you can change the number from 3 to 8 by setting the `polySides` property. Drawn with a 1-pixel-wide black line unless the `lineSize` or `pattern` properties are changed. Always drawn centered. This tool is available when the `userlevel` is 3 (Painting) or higher.

- ▶ Change number of sides: `set polySides to` (3 to 8).
- ▶ Thicker borders: `set lineSize to` (1 to 8).
- ▶ Patterned rectangles: `drag with the optionKey`.
- ▶ Change pattern: `set pattern to` (0 to 40).
- ▶ Filled: `set filled to true`.
- ▶ Concentric: `set multiple to true`.
- ▶ Evenly spaced concentric: `set multiSpace to` (1 to 9) and set a low `dragSpeed` for large shapes. Shapes can be lassoed on creation with `doMenu "Select"` and then repositioned, cloned, cut, copied, etc.

Caution   The 0-sided polygon can be selected only from the Polygon Sides dialog box and not with a `set polySides...` command.

Example
```
choose regular polygon tool
drag from 50,50 to 100,100 -- draws a 4 sided polygon
set pattern to 37
set lineSize to 5
set polySides to 3
drag from 100,100 to 200,200 with optionKey
-- Draws a thick, patterned triangle
set filled to true
drag from 100,100 to 200,200
-- Draws a thick, pie lattice filled triangle
```

See Also   **draw, round rect tool, oval tool, rectangle tool**

repeat   **Keyword**

Syntax
```
repeat [for] <number>
repeat forever
```

continued

repeat

```
repeat with <variable> = <number> to | down to <number>
repeat until | while <condition> <logical operator> <value>
```

Notes Signals the start of a repeat loop. Use to with repeat with to increment the variable counter or use down to to decrement it. Both the conditional loops (repeat while... and repeat until...) are entry condition loops. This means the test is made before the loop starts. If the condition is met the first time, the contents of the loop won't be executed. The example handler demonstrates a technique for making an exit condition loop that always runs at least once. repeat loops can be nested a theoretical maximum of 32 deep.

Example
```
repeat for 5
repeat with i = 10 to numVar
repeat until the mouse is down
on mouseUp -- Repeat loop in a button handler that must be
-- executed once
   repeat forever
     answer "Shall we continue?" with "Yes" or "No"
     if it is "Yes" then exit repeat
   end repeat
end mouseUp
on mouseUp
   repeat with n = 1 to 10
     show button ("Perspective" && n)
   end repeat
end mouseUp
```

See Also **Control Structures, exit**

Reserved Word   Concept *(not a reserved word)*

Notes Any word that has inherent meaning for the HyperTalk interpreter. Names, variables, and user messages become meaningful only after they are introduced by the user.

See Also **Commands, Constants, Functions, Keywords, Operators**

reset paint   Command

Syntax `reset paint`

Notes Restores the default values of all the Painting properties. The painting properties and their default values are

Property	Default Value	Property	Default Value
brush	8	pattern	12
centered	false	polySides	4
filled	false	textAlign	left
grid	false	textFont	geneva
lineSize	1	textHeight	16
multiple	false	textSize	12
multiSpace	1	textStyle	plain

See Also **Properties,** *(individual listings)*

Resources   Concept *(not a reserved word)*

Notes Pieces of Macintosh code stored in the resource fork of the System, an application, or a document. Common HyperCard resources include icons (**"ICON"**), fonts (**"FONT"**,**"FOND"**), cursors (**"CURS"**), sounds (**"SND "**), external commands (**"XCMD"**), and external functions (**"XFCN"**). If a stack that you distribute requires resources not included with HyperCard, you can copy fonts into the stack's resource file with Apple's Font/DA mover, and you can copy other resources (and edit them or create new resources) with Apple's ResEdit. Perhaps the easiest way to move resources (except **FONT**s) into and out of stacks is with Steve Maller's ResCopy XCMD (aka ResMover).

See Also **Fonts, Icons, Cursors, Sounds, XCMDs, XFCNs**

result   Misc. Function

Syntax `[the] result`

Notes When some commands result in errors, `the result` returns an explanation. Otherwise, it is empty. Following a `go` command, `the result` is either `empty` if the card exists, or "No Such Card" if it doesn't exist. After a `find` command, `the result` either returns `empty` if successful or "not found" if unsuccessful.

Example
```
on mouseUp
    find "Rumplestiltskin"
    put the result into resultVar
    if resultVar <> empty then answer "Sorry," && resultVar
end mouseUp
```

resume   Message

Notes Sent when HyperCard resumes, following the launching of another application (except when running under MultiFinder). If the values of global variables were stored into fields or files on the `suspend` message, you will want to restore them to their global variables on the `resume` message. Handlers for the `resume` message can be in the card or higher object scripts.

Example
```
on resume
    global globalVar
    put card field "Storage" into globalVar
    play "Harpsichord"
end resume
```

See Also **Handlers, Hierarchy, Messages, suspend**

return   Constant

Notes Stands for the ASCII carriage return character (13). Signals the end of a line in a field, the end of a statement in a script, and causes contents of the Message box to be transmitted as a message up the object hierarchy if it appears in a Message box. Used as a delimiter in `read` and `write` commands.

Example
```
put "beep" & return into msg -- beep executed in message box
put return after word 2 of field 1 -- Breaks line
```

continued

return

```
read from file "Constant Trouble" until return
on mouseUp
  open file "Constant Trouble"
  put field 3 & return into writeVar
  write writeVar to file "Constant Trouble"
  close file "Constant Trouble"
end mouseUp
on mouseUp
  -- Button handler to build a script to make a button beep
  put "on mouseUp" & return & "beep" & return & ¬
  "end mouseUp" into scriptVar
  set script of button "Beep" to scriptVar
end mouseUp
```

See Also **Constants, tab**

return **Keyword**

Syntax `return <expression>`

Notes Used in function handlers to direct back to the handler that called the function the value or values the expression evaluates to. See the **Functions** and **function** (Keyword) listing for more on function handlers and the use of user defined or user redefined functions in HyperTalk.

Example
```
return round(cos(50*pi/180)^paramVar
-- User function in a statement and the
-- handler it calls
put "This stack cluster has" && ¬
cardCount(stack1,stack2) ¬
&& "cards" into prompt -- cardCount() is the function
answer prompt
-- The function handler that calculates
-- this value follows
function cardCount stack1,stack2
  -- Parameters in variables
  set lockMessages to true -- Avoids other handlers
  put the number of cards into counter
  push card
  go to stack1 -- Variable contains name of a stack
  add the number of cards to counter
  go to stack2
  add the number of cards to counter
  pop card
  return counter -- Variable contains number of cards
end cardCount
-- Or
function cardCount
  set lockMessages to true -- Avoids other handlers
  put the number of cards into counter
  push card
  repeat with i = 1 to the paramcount
    go param(i)
    add the number of cards to counter
  end repeat
  pop card
```

continued

```
      return counter
    end cardCount
```

See Also   **function, Functions, Messages**

returnInField   Message

Notes   Sent when the Return key is pressed or the `returnKey` command is executed and a field is open. If you don't use this message for some special purpose, it passes on to HyperCard and adds a carriage return character to the field, or if the `autoTab` property is true, `returnInField` tabs from the last line of a field to the first line of the next field.

1.2+   New version 1.2 feature.

Example
```
on returnInField
  go next card
end enterInField
```

See Also   **enterInField, Messages, returnKey, tabKey,**

returnKey   Command

Syntax   `returnKey`

Notes   Executing this command is the equivalent of pressing the Return key. If a field is open when a `returnKey` command is executed, no message is sent, but the field is closed without a `closeField` message being sent. Subsequent commands/keypresses send messages that can be trapped. The message is sent initially to the card object.

1.2+   See **returnInField** for the new message sent when the `returnKey` command is executed and a field is open.

Example
```
on mouseUp
  put "play boing" into message box
  returnKey -- Executes message box playing boing
end mouseUp
-- Handler to replace message box with
-- multiline container. Click outside field
--   to close it before pressing Return
on returnKey
  -- message box replaced by multiline container
  put the number of lines in field "script" into ¬
  linesVar
  repeat with i = 1 to linesVar
    do line i of field "script"
  end repeat
end returnKey
on returnKey
  -- Handler lets you trap message and
  -- use the message box
  if the msg <> empty then pass returnKey
  go next
end returnKey
```

See Also   **enterInField, enterKey, Messages, returnInField**

Revert

Revert **Menu Command**

Notes Returns the current graphic to the way that it was last saved to disk. The Keep menu command saves the current image to disk, replacing the previous picture.

Example doMenu "Revert"

See Also **Keep**

right **Button/Field/Window Property**

Syntax [the] right of <rectangle>

Notes Returns in pixels the distance between the left of the screen and the right of the object or window. Equivalent to item 3 of the rect of <object or window>. Changing the right does not change the width but does change the left. Can be used with buttons, fields, and windows (card, tool, pattern, message).

1.2+ New version 1.2 feature.

Example
```
right of button 1
set the right of card field 1 to 300
set right of btn 1 to left of cd window / 2
on mouseUp -- Card handler to line up fields
   repeat with i = 1 to the number of fields
      set the right of field i to the mouseH
   end repeat
end mouseUp
```

See Also **bottom, bottomRight, cursor, height, left, set, top, topLeft, width, Windows**

Rotate Left **Menu Command**

Notes The current graphic selection is rotated counter-clockwise 90 degrees. Available when a graphic is selected.

Example doMenu "Rotate Left"

See Also **Flip Horizontal, Flip Vertical, Rotate Right**

Rotate Right **Menu Command**

Notes The current graphic selection is rotated clockwise 90 degrees. Available when a graphic is selected.

Example doMenu "Rotate Right"

See Also **Flip Horizontal, Flip Vertical, Rotate Left**

round **Math Function**

Syntax
```
the round of <number>
round(<number in container>)
```

Notes Rounds off the number to the nearest integer. In the case of .5s, the number is rounded to the nearest even integer: both round(45.5) and round(46.5) = 46.

Example
```
round(45.89) -- Returns 46
round(45.23) -- Returns 45
round(45.5) -- Returns 46
```

continued

```
beep the round of numVar
-- If variable is 2.3333, beeps twice
```

See Also   trunc

round rect tool
round rectangle
tool

Painting Tool

Notes   Used with the **drag** command to make round-cornered rectangles. Drawn with a 1-pixel-wide black line unless the **lineSize** or **pattern** properties are changed. First, coordinate pair in the **drag** command is the corner unless the **centered** property is set to true. This tool is available when the **userlevel** is 3 (Painting) or higher.

▶ Thicker borders: set **lineSize** to (1 to 8).
▶ Patterned rectangles: **drag** with the **optionKey**.
▶ Change pattern: set **pattern** to (0 to 40).
▶ Filled: set **filled** to true.

Example
```
choose round rect tool
drag from 50,50 to 100,100 -- Draws a round rectangle
on mouseUp
   -- Button handler to draw a round rectangle with a thick,
   -- patterned border . . .
   set pattern to 37
   set lineSize to 5
   drag from 100,100 to 200,200 with optionKey
   -- . . . and a thick, black patterned round rectangle
   -- filled with the pie lattice pattern.
   set filled to true
   drag from 200,200 to 300,300
end mouseUp
```

See Also   **draw, oval, rectangle tool, regular polygon**

roundRect

Button Style

Notes   A standard Mac style button. Unfortunately, there is no easy way to do a double bordered default button, though you can simulate one with the paint tools.

Example   `set the style of button id 3 to round rect`

See Also   **Buttons, Fields, style**

Save a Copy

Menu Command

Notes   Saves a copy of the current stack to disk. The user has to name the copy. The copy becomes a backup, so the original stack remains the current stack.

Example   `doMenu "Save a Copy"`

Screen Dump

Concept *(not a reserved word)*

Notes   An exact copy of what you see on a regular Macintosh screen. A screen dump gives you windoids and the cursor in addition to graphics and objects. About the only thing you can't record is pulled down menus. A screen dump to the printer is performed with the Shift-Command-4 keyboard combination. Shift-Command-

Screen Dump

3 saves the dump to a numbered MacPaint document that you can open with the Import Paint menu command.

See Also   **Export, Graphics, Paint, Select All**

screenRect   Global Property

Syntax   `the screenRect`

Notes   Returns the screen size of the user's Macintosh. The `screenRect` of the original Mac is 0,0,512,342. If the `screenRect` is larger than that, you won't need to hide the `menuBar` to show the whole screen and you can place the palettes and the Message box around the card window where they are handy but out of the way. The `screenRect` can't be set.

1.2+   New version 1.2 feature.

Example
```
on startUp -- Add to startup handler in Home stack
    if the screenRect <> 0,0,512,342 then -- Big screen
        -- Save normal position
        put the loc of card window into tempVar
        repeat 10 -- Make the window jump around screen
            put width of card window / 2 into aVar
            put right of the screenRect + aVar into bVar
            put height of card window / 2 into cVar
            put bottom of the screenRect + cVar into dVar
            set loc of card window to ¬
            random(bVar) - aVar,random(dVar) - cVar
        end repeat
    end if
    set the loc of card window to tempVar -- Restore
end startUp
```

See Also   **Properties, rectangle** *(property)*, **Windows**

Script   Concept

Notes   Used in two ways. Refers to all the handlers in one object (the `script` property), and refers to all the interrelated handlers needed to perform a given task, regardless of their locations.

See Also   **Handlers, Script Editor**

script   Object Property

Syntax   `script of <objectDesignator>`

Notes   Returns the specified object's script. The current script can be put into a variable or field and modified. The modified script or a totally new script can then be put into the object with a `set` command statement. The maximum size of a script is 30,000 characters.

Caution   Setting a script destroys the previous script. Avoid using `the` with this property.

Example
```
on mouseUp
    put script of card 3 into scriptVar
    put return "visual effect dissolve slowly" after ¬
    line 4 of scriptVar
```

continued

```
      set script of card 3 to scriptVar
    end mouseUp
```

Script Editor   **Utility** *(not a reserved word)*

Notes   Place where scripts are edited. Takes the form of a modal dia┐
R-29.)

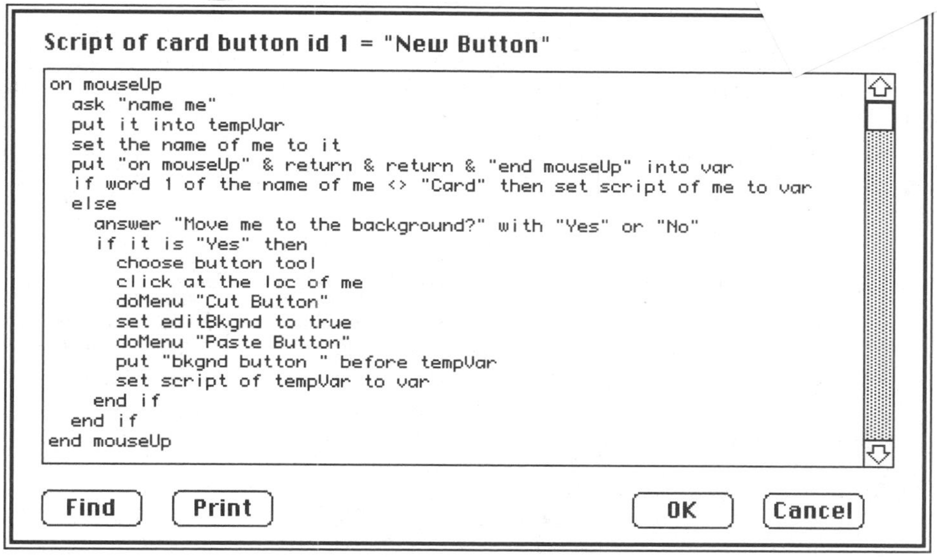

```
┌─────────────────────────────────────────────────────────┐
│ Script of card button id 1 = "New Button"               │
│ ┌─────────────────────────────────────────────────────┐ │
│ │on mouseUp                                        △  │ │
│ │  ask "name me"                                      │ │
│ │  put it into tempVar                                │ │
│ │  set the name of me to it                           │ │
│ │  put "on mouseUp" & return & return & "end mouseUp" into var│
│ │  if word 1 of the name of me <> "Card" then set script of me to var│
│ │  else                                               │ │
│ │    answer "Move me to the background?" with "Yes" or "No"│
│ │    if it is "Yes" then                              │ │
│ │      choose button tool                             │ │
│ │      click at the loc of me                         │ │
│ │      doMenu "Cut Button"                            │ │
│ │      set editBkgnd to true                          │ │
│ │      doMenu "Paste Button"                          │ │
│ │      put "bkgnd button " before tempVar             │ │
│ │      set script of tempVar to var                   │ │
│ │    end if                                           │ │
│ │  end if                                             │ │
│ │end mouseUp                                       ▽  │ │
│ └─────────────────────────────────────────────────────┘ │
│  ( Find )  ( Print )              ( OK )  ( Cancel )     │
└─────────────────────────────────────────────────────────┘
```

Figure R-29.   The Script Editor modal dialog box.

Scripts are automatically formatted with two space indentations inside each on, if, and **repeat** control structure. If the bottom line of a handler is not flush left, check your control structures. Make sure the message names agree in the on, end, and any exit statements. Press the Tab key to test the formatting. Hyper-Talk is case-insensitive (a and A are the same). It preserves upper- and lowercase letters in quoted literals, however. Use soft returns (Option-Return) to create multilined statements when lines are too long for the screen. Soft returns can't be used between quotation marks or after the then keyword. HyperTalk usually doesn't mind blank lines but won't tolerate them in multilined statements.

Options

Command-A	Select the entire script
Command-C	Copy the selection to the Clipboard
Command-F	Show the Find dialog box
Command-G	Go to the next occurrence of the Find text
Command-H	Copy the selection into the Find field and go to the next occurrence
Command-P	Print the selection or the entire script
Command-V	Paste the contents of the Clipboard into the selection

Command-X	Cut the selection to the Clipboard
Enter	Same as clicking OK (closes the Script Editor)
Tab	Automatic formatting of the script

Example See Figure R-29.

See Also **Control Structures, Peeking**

Scripting Level

Concept *(not a reserved word)*

Notes The most advanced and powerful HyperCard User Level. Allows access to scripts as well as to everything available at the lower levels.

See Also **userLevel**

scroll **Field Property**

Syntax
```
the scroll of <objectDesignator>
```

Notes Returns the number of pixels that the specified field is scrolled from the top. The starting scroll value is 0 and the bottom scroll value depends on the number of visual lines (not necessarily lines ending with a return character) and the height of the text.

Example
```
the scroll of card field "TimeODay"
put the scroll of me
-- Returns scroll of the field that holds the executing
statement
on mouseUp
   -- Button handler to scroll all bkgnd fields to the top
   repeat with n = 1 to the number of fields
     set the scroll of field n to 0
   end repeat
end mouseUp
```

See Also **Properties**

scroll **Visual Effect**

Notes An effect that looks like a card is sliding in from off the screen. The `scroll` options include `up`, `down`, `left`, and `right`.

Example
```
visual effect scroll left very fast
go next
```

See Also **visual**

scrolling **Field Style**

Notes A nearly standard Mac vertical scrolling field. Unfortunately, the elevator area remains grey even when there is nothing to scroll.

Example
```
set the style of field id 3 to scrolling
```

See Also **Buttons, Fields, scroll, style**

searchScript — User Message

Syntax `searchScript <string>`

Notes An example of a user defined command included in the stack script of the Home stack. If executed in the Message box, `searchScript` looks in every script in the stack for an occurrence of the string. If it finds the string, it opens the Script Editor but doesn't box the string. Use the Script Editor's Find feature to locate the string in the Script Editor.

Example `searchScript "on openBackground"`

See Also **Script Editor, User Defined Messages**

sec — Abbreviation

Notes Short for `second` (time modifier).

1.2+ New version 1.2 feature.

See Also **second, seconds, wait**

second — Ordinal Constant

Notes Indicates the second instance of a specified object or chunk type in an enclosing object or container.

Example `put "Number 9" into second line of ¬`
`second field`

See Also **Constants**

second — Time Modifier

Notes Specifies a second when a unit of time is required.

1.2+ New version 1.2 feature.

Example `wait 1 second`

See Also **seconds, wait**

seconds secs — System Function

Syntax `the seconds  or  the secs`
`seconds()  or  secs()`

Notes Returns the number of seconds since January 1, 1904. The best way to figure the interval between two times or dates is to compare the `seconds`. The exception is very short intervals that can be found by comparing `ticks`.

Examples
```
the seconds -- Returns something like 2668471080
on closeStack
  global startTime -- Saved previously
  convert startTime to seconds
  put seconds() into finishTime
  put (finishTime - startTime) div 60 into elapsedMins
  put (finishTime - startTime) mod 60 into elapsedSecs
```

continued

seconds, secs

```
      put "Elapsed time:" & elapsedMins && "Minutes &" ¬
      && elapsedSecs && "Seconds" into message box
   end closeStack
```

See Also   **convert, date, time, ticks**

Select   Menu Command

Notes   If a graphic element has just been created, this command lassos it (except for Paint text, which gets the marching ants treatment). If a select tool selection already exists, this command reduces it to a lasso selection.

Example   `doMenu "Select"`

See Also   **Graphics, lasso tool, select tool**

select   Command

Syntax
```
select <button designator> | <field designator>
select [before | after] text of <field designator>
select [before | after] <chunk> of <field> | msg
select empty
```

Notes   A great new feature. Lets you select buttons and fields by name rather than by clicking on them with the proper tool. (If you select a button, the button tool becomes active.) Also lets you select any chunk (character, word, item, line) of a field or the whole field. Specified chunks in the Message box can be selected. To select the entire message, use `select line 1 of msg`. You can also place the insertion point anywhere in a field with the `select before | after` syntax. Finally, you can deselect the selection or remove the insertion point from a field with `select empty`.

1.2 +   New version 1.2 feature.

Caution   To place the insertion point in a field or to show a text selection, the screen must be unlocked when the `select` statement is executed.

Example
```
select bkgnd button id 3
doMenu "Copy Button"
select line lineVar of field fieldVar
select after text of field 2
put "Did you notice this message?" into msg
select line 1 of msg
on mouseUp
  select button 3
  doMenu "Copy Button"
  go last
  doMenu "Paste Button"
  choose browse tool
end mouseUp
on mouseUp
  lock screen
  show cd fld id 30
  show cd fld id 31
  unlock screen
  select char 1 of cd fld id 31
end mouseUp
```

See Also   **selectedChunk, selectedField, selectedLine**

Select All   Menu Command

Notes   Selects all picture elements of the current graphic layer (card or background). Copying the results of this command puts a copy of the picture onto the Clipboard. To get a MacPaint picture of the screen that includes buttons and fields, use the Export Paint command. To get windows, the menu bar, and the cursor, do a screen dump.

Example   `doMenu "Select All"`

See Also   **EditBkgnd, Export Paint, Screen Dump**

select tool   Painting Tool

Syntax   `choose select tool`

Notes   Use the `drag` command to select area, `drag... with commandKey` for tight selection, or `drag... with optionKey` for shrink-to-fit selection. Reposition selections with the `drag` command; clone with `drag... with optionKey`; stretch with `drag... with commandKey`. Selections can also be copied, cut, pasted, or cleared with the `doMenu "Copy Picture"`, `doMenu "Paste Picture"`, etc. commands.

Examples
```
choose select tool
drag from 100,100 to 200,200 -- Select area
drag from 150,150 to 300,300 with optionKey
-- Drag off a clone
doMenu "Copy Picture" -- Put a copy on the Clipboard
```

See Also   **lasso tool, Select All**

selectedChunk   String Function

Syntax   `the selectedChunk`

Notes   Returns the chars of the selection in the format `chars <number> to <number> of (card | bkgnd) field <number>`. If there is an insertion point, the `selectedChunk` returns its location: `char 38 to 37 of bkgnd field 2`. If no field is open and the Message box is not in use, the `selectedChunk` returns `empty`.

1.2 +   New version 1.2 feature.

Examples
```
on mouseUp
  select text of bkgnd field 2
  put the selectedChunk into msg
  wait 2 secs
  -- Displays something like char 1 to 73 of
  -- bkgnd field 2
  select word 4 of bkgnd field 2
  put the selectedChunk into msg
  wait 2 secs
  -- Displays char 12 to 19 of bkgnd field 2
  select after word 4 of bkgnd field 2
  put the selectedChunk into msg
  wait 2 secs
  -- Displays char 19 to 20 of bkgnd field 2
  select empty
  put the selectedChunk into msg
```

continued

selectedChunk

```
                          -- message box empty
                        end mouseUp
```

See Also   **selection, selectedField, selectedLine, selectedText**

selectedField   **String Function**

Syntax   `the selectedField`

Notes   Returns the designator of the field containing `the selection` in the format `(card | bkgnd) field <number>`.

1.2 +   New version 1.2 feature.

Examples
```
put the selectedField into msg
-- Shows something like bkgnd field 2
on returnInField
  put the selectedField into nextVar
  if word 3 of nextVar = the number of fields
  then select text of field 1
  else
    add 1 to word 3 of nextVar
    select text of nextVar
  end if
end returnInField
```

See Also   **selectedChunk, selectedLine, selectedText, selection**

selectedLine   **String Function**

Syntax   `the selectedLine`

Notes   Returns the line number and the designator of the field containing `the selection` in the format `line <number> (card | bkgnd) field <number>`. This function can be used to capture the context of a selected string.

1.2 +   New version 1.2 feature.

Examples
```
put the selectedLine into msg
-- Displays something like line 1 of bkgnd field 2
put the value of the selectedLine into msg
-- Displays the actual text
```

See Also   **selection, selectedChunk, selectedField, selectedText**

selectedText   **String Function**

Syntax   `the selectedText`

Notes   Returns `the selection`.

1.2 +   New version 1.2 feature.

Examples   `put the selectedText into field 2`

See Also   **selection, selectedChunk, selectedField, selectedLine**

selection   **Container**

Notes   Any text selected by the browse tool becomes `the selection` and can be manipulated like any other container.

Caution	Selected text is unselected if the user clicks on an autohighlighted button. Before using a button handler to manipulate a selection, set the `autohilite` property of the button to false.
Examples	`put the selection into card field 1` `put line 2 of defaultVar into line 2 of the selection`
See Also	**Containers, select, selectedChunk, selectedField, selectedLine**

send Keyword

Syntax	`send <message> [to <object>]`
Notes	Sends the specified message to the current object and then on up the hierarchy or to a specified object. Unless there is an `exit to hypercard` statement in the specified object's handler, program flow returns to the line after the `send` keyword after the message is handled. Messages can be sent directly to any object in the current stack or to any other stack object. To send a message to an object belonging to another stack, like a button, you must first go to the other stack. Besides the built-in system messages and command messages, you can also send **User Defined Messages,** as explained in that listing. A user defined message can be any collection of alphanumeric characters and underscores (_) starting with a letter. The name can't include spaces or punctuation. There must also be a handler for the message in the object the message is sent to (or above it in the Object Hierarchy), otherwise the user gets an error alert. Function messages can't be sent with `send`.

Example
```
send mouseUp
send mouseUp to button "Print"
send printingSubroutine to stack "Utilities"
on mouseUp
  go to stack "Utilities"
  send printingSubroutine to bkgnd button "Print"
  go back
end mouseUp
```

See Also	**Messages, Pass**

Send Farther Menu Command

Notes	Sends the selected button or field one level farther to the back (makes the relative number smaller). Card buttons and fields can never go farther down than the top background button or field. Because button and field layers are intermixed, an object's relative number may not change with each Send Farther command if an object of the other type is behind it.
1.2 +	You can now send an object all the way to the bottom in one step regardless of its starting position. At the keyboard, this is done with Shift-Command— (hyphen). While in a script, use `type "-" with shiftKey,commandKey`.

Example
```
doMenu "Send Farther"
on mouseUp
  select me
  repeat until the number of me is 1
    doMenu "Send Farther"
  end repeat
end mouseUp
```

See Also	**Bring Closer**

set

set   Command

Syntax   `set <property> [of <object> | <window>] to <value>`

Notes   Changes the value of the specified property. Not all properties can be set; see **Properties** for a complete listing. Many properties belong to objects that also must be specified. Some properties must be preceded by `the`, others can't be preceded by `the`, and with most, it doesn't matter.

Example
```
set userLevel to 5
set the name of card field 1 to "Cupertino"
set script of button 1 to scriptVar -- Where scriptVar contains
a script
set visible of field 1
```

See Also   **Properties, get, put**

seven   Constant

Notes   The number 7.

Examples
```
put seven into line seven of field seven of card
seven
```

See Also   **Constants**

seventh   Ordinal Constant

Notes   Indicates the seventh instance of a specified object or chunk type in an enclosing object or container.

Example
```
put "Number 9" into seventh line of ¬
seventh field
```

See Also   **Constants**

shadow   Button/Field Style

Notes   A drop shadowed rectangle that seems to rise above the card.

Example   `set the style of button id 3 to shadow`

See Also   **Buttons, Fields, style**

shiftKey   System Function

Syntax
```
[the] shiftKey
shiftKey()
```

Notes   Returns up if the Shift key is not pressed and down if it is pressed.

Example
```
wait until the shiftKey is down
if shiftKey() is down then add 1 to numVar
```

See Also   **commandKey** *(function)*, **optionKey** *(function)*, **shiftKey** *(modifier)*

shiftKey   Modifier

Notes   Used to refer to the Shift key.

Example   `choose rectangle tool`
`drag from 100,100 to the mouseLoc with shiftKey`

See Also   **commandKey** *(modifier)*, **optionKey** *(modifier)*

short   Adjective

Notes   Used with `the name`, `the number`, `the date`, and `the time` to limit the value returned to the shortest possible representation. Also used with the `convert` command.

See Also   **convert, date, name, number, time**

ShortCuts   Concept *(not a reserved word)*

Notes   Techniques that make working with HyperTalk and HyperCard a little easier.

▶ See **Peeking.**
▶ Open Button Info dialog box by double clicking on button with Button tool.
▶ Toggle Message box with Command-M.
▶ Toggle Menu bar with Command-Space.
▶ Toggle Painting Tool Palette with Command-Tab.
▶ Toggle Pattern Palette (when a Painting tool is selected) with Tab.
▶ See Power Keys
▶ Clone a button by dragging it with the button tool while the Option key is pressed.
▶ Clone a field by dragging it with the field tool while the Option key is pressed (the text isn't copied).
▶ Drag a field with the Option and Shift keys pressed to clone the field and its text (1.2.2 +).
▶ Choose the browse tool with Command-Tab.
▶ Choose the button tool with Command-Tab,Tab (press the Tab key twice) (1.2 +).
▶ Choose the field tool with Command-Tab,Tab,Tab (1.2 +).
▶ Shift-Command- + (plus) brings an object all the way to the top of the card or background layer (1.2 +).
▶ Shift-Command— (hyphen) sends an object all the way to the back of the card or background layer (1.2 +).

show   Command

Syntax   `show menuBar`
`show <object or window> [at <location>]`
`show card | bkgnd picture`

Notes   Makes the indicated object or window visible if it is invisible and does nothing if it is already visible. This is the same as `set the visible of <object> to true`. The optional location consists of a coordinate pair (x,y). With objects, the location is the center of the object and with windows, it is the left-top corner.

1.2 +   As of version 1.2, you can show and hide the graphic layers of each card and background.

Example   `show field 1`
`show tool window at 100,100`

continued

show

```
show whatVar at whereVar
-- whatVar contains an object name,
-- whereVar contains the location coordinates
on openStack
  show message box
  hide card window
  hide tool window
  hide pattern window
  put "Never underestimate the power of the Force"
  -- into the message box
  wait 2 secs
  show card window
end openStack
on mouseUp
  show card picture
end mouseUp
```

See Also **Buttons, Fields, Objects, showPict, Windows**

show (cards) Command

Syntax `show <number> cards`

Notes Shows the specified number of cards starting with the current card. If you sub-stitute the adjective `all` for the number, `show` shows all the cards in the stack starting with the next card and ending back at the starting card. Can be used for animation or to "warm up" the cards so that they open faster later. No visual effects are possible, and the `openCard` and `closeCard` messages are not sent. On a Mac Plus, a sample 34-card stack took 1029 ticks to show cold, 936 ticks to show when prewarmed with the screen locked (which took 193 ticks to do), and 912 ticks to show when prewarmed with the screen unlocked. To run through the prewarmed cards with the screen locked took 88 ticks.

Example
```
show 5 cards
show numVar cards
on openStack
  show all cards
end openStack
```

See Also **go**

showLines Field Property

Syntax `the showLines of <field>`

Notes If true, the specified field is lined. If false, the field is unlined. Scrolling fields can't be lined.

Example
```
set the showLines of field 1 to true
set the showLines of nameVar to true
-- Where nameVar contains the name of a field
if the style of field n <> scrolling
then set the showLines of field n to true
```

See Also **Properties**

showName Button Property

Syntax `the showName of <button>`

Notes If true, the specified button displays its name. If false, the name is not displayed.

Example
```
set the showName of button 1 to true
set the showName of nameVar to true
-- Where nameVar contains the name of a button
```

See Also **Properties**

showPict Card/Background Property

Syntax `the showPict of <object designator>`

Notes If true, the specified card or background graphic is shown (same as `show <type> picture`). If false, it is hidden (same as `hide <type> picture`). Pictures can be shown and hidden from other cards and backgrounds, but you must be in the same stack.

Example
```
set the showPict of this card to true
set the showPict of bkgnd 2 to false
set showPict of card 4 to not (showPict of card 4)
```

See Also **hide, Properties, show**

sin Math Function

Syntax
```
the sin of <angle/radians>
sin(angle/radians)
```

Notes Returns the sine of an angle. The angle must be provided in radians rather than degrees. (See Figure R-30.) To convert degrees to radians, multiply by pi/180. The value of the sine will vary between 1 and -1. The sine of an acute angle (A in Figure R-30) = the opposite side (a in the Figure R-30) divided by the hypotenuse (c in the figure). If you know the angle and any one of these two sides, you can get the other side: a/sin(A*pi/180) = c, c*sin(A*pi/180) = a. If you know sides a and c only, you can find side b with sqrt(c*c $-$ a*a) = b. Once you have all three sides, you can find the angle of the acute angle with atan(a/b)*180/pi = A.

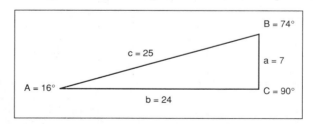

Figure R-30. Figuring angles.

Examples
```
sin(1) -- The sine of 1 radian returns 0.841471
the sin of radianVar
sin(30*pi/180) -- Sine of 30 degrees returns 0.5
round(7/sin(16*pi/180)) -- Returns 25
round(25*sin(16*pi/180)) -- Returns 7
```

continued

sin

```
sqrt(25*25-7*7) -- Returns 24
round(atan(7/24)*180/pi) -- Returns 16
```

See Also   **atan, cos, tan**

six   Constant

Notes   The number 6.

Examples   `put six into line six of field six of card ten`

See Also   **Constants**

sixth   Ordinal Constant

Notes   Indicates the sixth instance of a specified object or chunk type in an enclosing object or container.

Example   `put "Number 9" into sixth line of sixth field`

See Also   **Constants**

size   Stack Property

Syntax   `the size of <stack designator>`

Notes   Returns the size of the designated stack in bytes. Divide by 1024 to get the kilobytes.

Example   `the size of this stack div 1024`

See Also   **Properties**

sort   Command

Syntax   `sort [ascending | descending] [text | numeric | international | dateTime] by <expression> [of field | <chunk of field>]`

Notes   Sorts the cards in a stack by applying a specified criteria to the value of a specified field, the value of a chunk of that field, or the value of a characteristic of the card. The default criteria is ascending text, but the stack can also be sorted in descending order using the numeric value of a field or any of the date and time values. If the field to be sorted contains text with international characters from the non-ASCII character set, choose the international criteria. If the criteria is numeric, HyperTalk finds the number even when it is mixed with alphabetic characters.

Caution   If you refer to a field by its relative number, make sure there aren't backgrounds that use that numbered field differently. You can say field 1 of bkgnd id 2345 but HyperTalk ignores the restriction. Also, let HyperCard insert the date and time values or mimic the short time and short date formats.

Example
```
sort by field 1
-- Assumes the field is text and sorts
-- the stack in ascending order
sort by char 1 of field 2
sort descending numeric by numVar
-- Where numVar contains a field name
sort dateTime by card field n.
```

continued

```
-- Alphabetical by card name
sort by the name of card
-- In random order
sort numeric by random(the number of cards))
sort by the name of card
sort by the number of card
sort by the number of bkgnd
sort by the name of bkgnd
on mouseUp
   put "Henry James" into card field 1
   put "card field 1" into fieldVar
   sort by word 2 of the value of fieldVar
   -- Sorts by James not by field
end mouseUp
```

See Also   **go**

Sound Concept

Notes   Using the computer to play music, speech, or special effects.

See Also   `play`

sound Misc. Function

Syntax   `the sound`
        `sound()`

Notes   Returns the voice of the sound playing or "done" when the current `play` command is finished (done is a string, not a constant, and must be quoted in a logical expression). Used with the `wait` command to keep sounds and other actions in sync and to prevent the disk drive from operating during `play` commands (causes breaking up of the sound). It is possible to load one `play` command while another is playing if you have a SCSI drive. This technique is called double buffering and makes it easier to synchronize sounds with visual actions (see the following example handler).

Caution   Double buffering does not work if the `play` commands are loading from a floppy drive or if you want to play the same sound over and over and keep the sound and screen action in sync.

Examples
```
play "Boing" "a b c d f"
the sound -- Returns Boing
wait until sound() is "done"
-- Stops program flow until the current sound ends
on mouseUp
   play "sound1" -- Where "sound1" is a long sound
   go to card "one" -- sound1 playing
   play "sound2"
   -- Load sound2 while sound1 is playing
   wait until the sound is "done" or ¬
   the sound = "sound2"
   go to card "two" -- sound2 playing
   play "sound3"
   -- Load sound3 while sound2 is playing
   wait until the sound is "done" or ¬
```

continued

sound

```
      the sound = "sound3"
      go to card "three" -- sound3 playing
end mouseUp
```

See Also **play, wait**

space Constant

Notes Stands for the ASCII space character (32). Used when you need a space in a string, although you can always use a space inside quotation marks " " or **"space age "**, and there is also a concatenate and space operator && (see the beginning of this Reference).

Examples `put "card field" & space & numberVar into msg`

See Also **Constants, &&**

space,free System Function

See Also **freeSpace**

space,heap System Function

See Also **heapSpace**

spray tool Painting Tool

Notes Used with the **drag** and **click** commands to apply scattered pixels of the current pattern. The spray tool is turned into an eraser by the **commandKey** modifier. To simulate dragging, you must set the **dragSpeed** to something other than the default setting (100 to 500 works well). (See Figure R-31.) This tool is available when the **userlevel** is 3 (Painting) or higher.

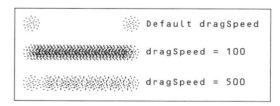

Figure R-31. Spray paint effect.

Examples
```
choose spray tool
set the dragSpeed to 100
drag from 50,50 to 50,100 -- Draws a sprayed line
drag from 50,50 to 50,100 with commandKey
-- Erases sprayed line
```

sqrt Math Function

Syntax
```
the sqrt of <number>
sqrt(<number>)
```

Notes Means the square root of. Returns the square root of the specified number. If <number> is an expression, it must be inside parentheses. Without parentheses, the sqrt of 3 * 8 − 4 = sqrt(3) * 8 − 4.

Example
```
sqrt(49) -- Returns 7
sqrt(variable)
sqrt(variable/the number of cards)
sqrt(25*25-7*7) -- Returns 24
the sqrt of (25*25-7*7) -- Returns 24
```

Stack   Concept *(not a reserved word)*

Notes The principal metaphor that HyperCard is built around. A stack is a grouping of data screens called cards that can have their own fields for holding text, buttons for carrying out actions, and graphics for displaying visual information.

▶ Properties: canDelete (1.2), cantModify (1.2), freeSize, name, script, size.
▶ All messages can be handled in a stack script.

See Also **Containers, field** *(reserved word)*, **Properties, style**

stack   Object

Notes Designates a Macintosh file. Stacks are collections of cards, each of which can have its own background, fields, buttons, and graphics. The minimum size of a stack is 4,896 bytes, and the theoretical maximum is 512 megabytes.

Example
```
go to stack "Address"
go to card 3 of stack "Help"
```

See Also **Objects, Properties**

Stack Info   Menu Command

Notes Displays the Stack Info dialog box. (See Figure R-32.) Available when the userLevel is 4 (Authoring) or higher.

Keyboard Command-S

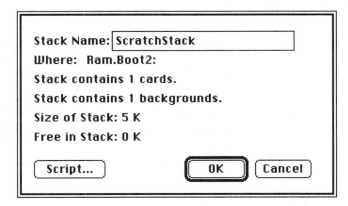

Figure R-32.   The Stack Info dialog box.

Stack Info

1.2 + The Size of Stack now includes the resource fork as well as the data fork of the stack.

Example `doMenu "Stack Info..."`

stackSpace **Undocumented System Function**

Syntax `the stackSpace`
`stackSpace()`

Notes Reports on the status of the memory stack, not the HyperCard stack. Useful if you are working on XCMDs.

Examples `put "The stack = " & stackSpace() div 1024 into msg`

See Also **diskSpace, freeSpace, heapSpace, size**

startUp **Message**

Notes Sent when HyperCard is launched. Handlers for this message should be in the Home stack's stack script.

Examples
```
send startUp -- sends message up object hierarchy
on startUp
  play "Harpsichord" "60 61 62 63 64 65"
  hide menuBar
end startup
```

See Also **Handlers, Hierarchy, Messages**

String **Concept** *(not a reserved word)*

Notes Same as a literal. A group, or string, of characters that are interpreted as themselves. This sentence is an example of a string.

See Also **Containers, Literal, Value**

String Functions **Concept** *(not a reserved word)*

Notes Functions used to manipulate strings:

charToNum	foundChunk (1.2)	foundField (1.2)
foundLine (1.2)	foundText (1.2)	length
number	numToChar	offset
selectedChunk (1.2)	selectedField (1.2)	
selectedLine (1.2)	selectedText (1.2)	

See Also **Functions**

String Operators **Concept** *(not a reserved word)*

See Also **Operators**

style **Button/Field Property**

Syntax `the style of <button or field>`

Notes Determines how a button or field looks on the screen. (See Figure R-33.) The appearance of the contents of a field is also affected by the `showLines` and the `wideMargins` properties. The appearance of a button is also affected by the `icon` property.

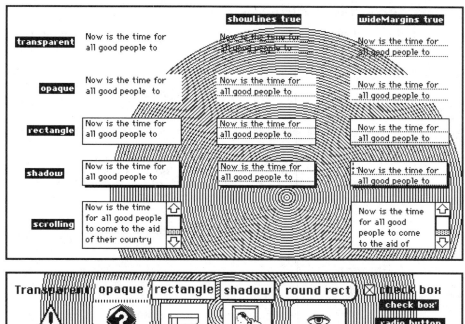

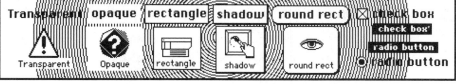

Figure R-33. Button and field appearance options.

Caution When setting styles for buttons, use `radioButton` rather than radio button, `checkBox` rather than check box, and `roundRect` rather than round rect.

Example
```
set style of button 1 to radioButton
set style of card field 1 to scrolling
if not the style of field 2 is scrolling
then set showLines of field 2 to true
```

See Also **icon, showLines, wideMargins**

subtract **Command**

Syntax `subtract <number> from <destinationContainer>`

Notes Reduces the value of the `destinationContainer` by the value of the number. The number can be a literal or a value in a container. The `destinationContainer` must start off containing a number.

subtract

Example
```
put 10 into numberVar
subtract 4 from numberVar -- Changes numberVar to 6
put 3 into number2Var
subtract numberVar from number2Var -- number2Var = -3
subtract item 3 of field 3 from item 2 of the msg box
```

See Also   − (minus)

suspend   System Message

Notes   Sent just before HyperCard launches another application, except when running under MultiFinder. Handlers for **suspend** should be in the stack or in the Home stack's stack script.

Caution   Global variables and the card address stacks used with **back**, **recent**, and **pop** do not survive the suspension of HyperCard. If you need to save this data, trap the **suspend** message and move the data into fields or files.

Examples
```
send suspend -- sends message up object hierarchy
on suspend
   global numberVar -- Variable holds important value.
   play "Harpsichord" "60 61 62 63 64 65"
   put numberVar into field "toolBox" of card 1
   -- Stores value needed later
end suspend
```

See Also   **Handlers, Hierarchy, Messages, resume**

System Functions   Concept *(not a reserved word)*

Notes   Functions used to get information about the mouse and keyboard.

(1.2) = available for versions starting with 1.2:

clickH (1.2)	clickLoc	clickV (1.2)
commandKey	date	diskSpace
heapSpace	mouse	mouseClick
mouseH	mouseLoc	mouseV
number	optionKey	screenRect (1.2)
seconds	shiftKey	stackSpace
ticks	time	version

See Also   **Functions**

System Messages   Concept *(not a reserved word)*

Notes   Messages sent by HyperCard.

See Also   **Messages**

tab   Constant

Notes   Stands for the ASCII tab character (9). Used primarily when you need a tab delimiter to separate field values when writing to or reading from text files. Also used to format text going to a word processor.

Examples
```
write "card field" & tab to file "newData"
read from file "newData" until tab
```

See Also   **Constants, return**

tabKey   Command

Notes   Sent when the Tab key is pressed or when the command `tabKey` is executed in the Message box or in a script. One `tabKey` opens the first unlocked field on the current background and selects up to 30,000 characters of text. If no background fields exist, `tablKey` looks for card fields. If no text is in the field, the insertion point is placed on the top line of the field. Subsequent `tabKey` messages close the open field and open the next one in relative order going from background fields to card fields. The `tabKey` usually signals a move from one field to another but can be used to trigger a handler on a card with no unlocked fields.

1.2+   The `select` command offers greater control over selections, which gives you the option of selecting a chunk of a field or placing the insertion point anywhere in the text you wish.

Examples
```
send tabKey -- sends message up object hierarchy
on tabKey
   type space && space & space -- Inserts 4 spaces into your
text
end tabKey
```

See Also   **Handlers, Hierarchy, Messages**

tan   Math Function

Syntax
```
the tan of <angle/radians>
tan(<angle/radians>)
```

Notes   Returns the tangent of an angle given in radians. To convert degrees to radians, multiply by pi/180. Tangent values range from $-$INF to INF. The tangent of an acute angle (A) = the opposite side (a) divided by the adjacent side (b). If you know the angle and any one of these two sides, you can get the other side: a/tan(A*pi/180) = b, b*tan(A*pi/180) = a. Once you have both side a and b, you can find the angle of the acute angle with atan(a/b)*180/pi = A. If you know sides a and b, you can also find side c with sqrt((a*a) + (b*b)) = c.

Examples
```
tan(1) -- The tangent of i radian returns 1.557408
the tan of radianVar
tan(30*pi/180) -- Tangent of 30 degrees returns 0.57735
round(7/tan(16*pi/180)) -- Returns 24
round(24*tan(16*pi/180)) -- Returns 7
round(atan(7/24)*180/pi) -- Returns 16
```

See Also   **atan, cos, sin**

target

target   Misc. Function

Syntax
```
the [short] target
target()
```

Notes   Returns the object type (stack, bkgnd, card, bkgnd field, card field, bkgnd field, or card field) and the name of the object that was the point of entry for the message that initiated this script. In the case of a mouse click on a button, the button is the target even if the mouseUp handler is in the card script (button "Hit Me"). If the object is not named, an ID number is returned (button id 4378). If you add the short modifier, the object type is not returned (Hit Me). If you have a button send the initial message to another button, the second button becomes interpreted as the target. A mouseDown handler in the stack script can use the target to identify every button, field, or card that is clicked and that either has no mouseDown handler of its own or that passes the message.

1.2+   As of version 1.2, the target can also refer to the contents of a field as well as to the container. Where there is ambiguity, you can force an interpretation with the value of the target, when you want to refer to the contents, or the name of the target, when you want to refer to the container. Usually HyperCard can figure which you want. Fields must be locked (lockText = true) for fields to receive mouseUp messages.

Example
```
-- When the target is a card button
the target -- returns card button "up" (if named) or card
-- button id 2 if not
the short target -- Returns "up" or id 2
on mouseWithin -- Card level handler
  set the loc of target() to the mouseLoc
  -- Buttons and fields try to center themselves on the cursor
end mouseWithin
on mouseUp -- Card level handler
  -- Assumes 2 locked, scrolling card fields named dodad and
  -- thingy
  -- Click on either field to execute the script
  put "This is dodad" into cd fld "dodad"
  put "This is thingy" into cd fld "thingy"
  put "•" & the target into line 2 of the target
  put "••" & the name of the target into line 3 of the target
  put "•••" & the value of the target into line 4 of the target
end mouseUp
```

See Also   **me, this**

tempo   Reserved Word

Syntax   `tempo <number>`

Notes   A play command parameter that controls the interval between notes. The default parameter is 120. Below 50 is slow and above 1000 is fast. If tempo is set too high, long duration notes are clipped.

Example   `play "Boing" tempo 1000 "a b g f d"`

See Also   **play**

ten   Constant

Notes   The number 10.

Examples   `put line ten of field ten into card field ten of card ten`

See Also   **Constants**

tenth Ordinal Constant

Notes   Indicates the tenth instance of a specified object or chunk type in an enclosing object or container.

Example   `put "Number 9" into tenth line of tenth field`

See Also   **Constants**

Text File Concept *(not a reserved word)*

Notes   A storage file created under script control that lets you store and retrieve ASCII data outside HyperCard stacks. Text files are saved to disk so that they are preserved between HyperCard sessions. HyperTalk only supports sequential files (accessed sequentially like audio tape); there are no random access files.

See Also   **close file, open file, read, write**

Text Style Menu Command

Notes   Displays the Text Style dialog box. (See Figure R-34.) Changes apply to either the selected field, the open field, or the text tool and any paint text created since the last mouse click.

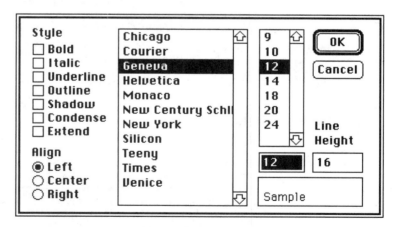

Figure R-34.   The Text Style dialog box.

Useful if you want the user to select the text characteristics; otherwise, it's better to set the `textFont`, `textStyle`, `textSize`, `textAlign`, and `textHeight` properties directly. Available when the `userLevel` is 3 (Painting) or higher and either the text tool is selected, the field tool and a field is selected, or the browse tool is selected and the insertion point is in a field.

Examples   `doMenu "Text Style"`

Keyboard   Command-T

text tool

text tool   Painting Tool

Notes   Used in conjunction with the `type` command to paint text on either of the graphic layers. The resulting text is bit-mapped, which means that it is not editable and does not give high resolution results on the LaserWriter. The default text properties are 12-point plain Geneva with a line height of 16 pixels aligned to the left. You can change text characteristics by setting the `textFont`, `text-Style`, `textSize`, `textAlign`, and `textHeight` properties, but these changes affect all the text typed since the last `click at` command. There is no HyperTalk equivalent for the HyperCard feature that lets you press the Enter key to start a new text string that can have characteristics different from the preceding text. This tool is available when the `userlevel` is 3 (Painting) or higher.

Examples
```
on mouseUp
  choose text tool
  click at 50,50
  type "Painted text has its advantages"
  doMenu "Select"
  doMenu "Invert"
end mouseUp
```

textAlign   Field/Button/Painting Property

Syntax   `[the] textAlign [of field]`

Notes   Determines whether text is centered, right justified, or left justified. Applies to either the specified field or button, the selected field, or the text tool and any paint text typed since the last mouse click or `click at`. The default value is `left`. The other options are `right` and `center`. Text is usually left justified, although it is sometimes centered. Numbers, especially in tables, are often right justified. It is easiest to place the insertion point in a small field if the text is centered.

Examples
```
textAlign of field 1 -- Returns left, right, or center
set textAlign to center
```

See Also   **textFont, textHeight, textSize, textStyle**

textArrows   Global Property

Syntax   `[the] textArrows`

Notes   This property applies to HyperCard version 1.1 + . If `textArrows` is true, pressing the arrow (cursor) keys repositions the insertion point if a field or the Message box is open. When `textArrows` is false, pressing the right arrow key opens the next card and pressing the left arrow key opens the previous card. Pressing the up arrow key takes you to the first card you visited and then forward through the cards, repeating your travels. Pressing the down arrow key takes you backwards through the cards, retracing your earlier travels. Even when `textArrows` is true, you can still use the arrow keys for navigation if you press the Option key at the same time.

Examples
```
the textArrows -- Returns false or true
set textArrows to false
```

textFont   Field/Button/Painting Property

Syntax   `[the] textFont [of field]`

Notes Determines the typeface of the specified field or button, the selected field, or of the text tool and any paint text typed since the last mouse click or `click at` command. The default value is Geneva. The range of possible font values depends on what font resources are available.

Examples
```
textfont of field 1 -- Returns a font name
set textFont to Chicago
```

See Also **textAlign, textHeight, textSize, textStyle**

textHeight Field/Painting Property

Syntax `[the] textHeight [of field]`

Notes Returns the height of a line including the space between it and the line above. Applies to either the specified field, the selected field, or to the text tool and any paint text typed since the last mouse click or `click at` command. The default value is 16. The `textHeight` can't be less than the `textSize` but can be as large as you wish.

Examples
```
the textHeight of field 1 -- Returns a number (16, 18, etc.)
set textHeight to 30
```

See Also **textAlign, textFont, textSize, textStyle**

textSize Field/Button/Painting Property

Syntax `[the] textSize [of field]`

Notes Determines the size of the text. Applies to either the specified field or button, the selected field, or to the text tool and any paint text typed since the last mouse click or `click at` command. The default value is 12. The range of possible sizes depends on what size resources are available.

Examples
```
the textSize of field 1 -- Returns a number (12, 14, etc.)
set textSize to 9
```

See Also **textAlign, textFont, textHeight, textStyle**

textStyle Field/Button/Painting Property

Syntax `[the] textStyle [of field]`

Notes Determines the style of the text. Applies to either the specified field or button, the selected field, or to the text tool and any paint text typed since the last mouse click or `click at` command. The default value is `plain`. The range of possible values in addition to `plain` are `bold`, `italic`, `underline`, `condense`, `extended`, `outline`, `shadowed`, and any combination of these.

Examples
```
the textStyle of field 1 -- Returns a style or list of styles
set textStyle to outline
set textStyle to bold,underline,expand
```

See Also **textAlign, textFont, textHeight, textSize**

then Keyword

Notes Precedes the action in an `if then` control structure.

then

Example   if optionKey is down
         then answer "Your sitting on my Option key."

See Also   **Constants**

third   Ordinal Constant

Notes   Indicates the third instance of a specified object or chunk type in an enclosing object or container.

Example   put "Number 9" into third line of third field

See Also   **Constants**

this   Object Modifier

Notes   Used in object designators to indicate the current card, background, or stack. Because it is so general, this is especially useful in scripts that are to be shared widely; an openCard handler in the Home stack for example.

Example
```
on mouseUp
   put the name of this card into msg
   wait 3 secs
   put the name of this stack into msg
   wait 3 secs
   put the number of cards in this bkgnd into msg
end mouseUp
```

See Also   **Constants**

three   Constant

Notes   The number 3.

Examples   put three into line three of field three of card three

See Also   **Constants**

tick   Time Modifier

Notes   Specifies a tick when a unit of time is required.

1.2 +   New version 1.2 feature.

Example   wait 1 tick

See Also   **ticks, wait**

ticks   System Function

Syntax   the ticks
         ticks()

Notes   Returns the number of ticks (each tick is 1/60th of a second) since the Macintosh was last restarted. Used to measure short intervals of time or to measure longer periods of time very accurately.

Example   the ticks -- Returns a number (18927)

continued

```
on mouseUp
-- Button handler to time the interval between a beep and a
-- mouse click
  wait random(200)
  beep
  put ticks() into startingVar
  wait until the mouse is down
  put the ticks into endingVar
  put endingVar - startingVar into the message box
end mouseUp
```

See Also   **seconds, time**

time   System Function

Syntax
```
the [long | abbrev | short] time
time()
```

Notes   Returns the time according to the Macintosh clock chip in one of two formats. hh:mm AM/PM if the adjectives `short`, `abbreviated`, `abbrev`, or `abbr` are used (also if no adjective is used). If the adjective `long` is used, the format is hh:mm:ss AM/PM. Adjectives can't be used with the `time()` syntax, so it always returns the shorter format.

Example
```
time() -- Returns 3:23 PM
the long time -- Returns 3:23:10 PM
on mouseUp
   -- Handler assumes an earlier time was put into
   -- startTime and converted to seconds
   global startTime
   put the long time into finishTime
   convert finishTime to seconds
   put finishTime - startTime into interval
   put interval div 3600 into hrsVar
   put interval mod 3600 into remainder
   put remainder div 60 into minVar
   put remainder mod 60 into secVar
   put "Elapsed ="  && hrsVar & ":" & minVar & ¬
   ":" & secVar into msg
end mouseUp
```

See Also   **dateItems, seconds, ticks, time**

Tool   Concept

Notes   A mode that determines what effect mouse events have. See the **choose** listing for the possible tools.

tool   Misc. Function

Syntax
```
the tool
tool()
```

Notes   Returns the name of the current tool. See the **choose** listing for the possible tools.

tool

Example
```
the tool -- Returns browse tool
if tool() is oval tool then set filled to true
put the tool into saveTool
-- Stores the name of current tool for later reference
choose saveTool -- Restores the previously stored tool
```

See Also   **choose, Tool Palette, Tools**

Tool Palette   Window

Notes   A HyperCard windoid displaying the available tools. (See Figure R-35.) Also known as the tool window. Only the General tools in the top row are available when the **userLevel** is less than 3 (Painting).

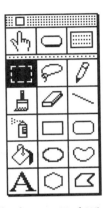

Figure R-35.   The Tool Palette or Tool Window.

See Also   **choose**

tool window   Window

Notes   A HyperCard windoid displaying the available tools. Also known as the Tool Palette. Show with **show tool window** to let the user choose a tool and hide with **hide tool window**. The default location of the tool window is 200,70 and its rectangle is 200,70,268,199. It can be repositioned by setting its **loc** property to a new coordinate. The **loc** of a window is the left-top corner, not the center. Use the **choose** command to change the current tool.

Keyboard   Option-Tab toggles the tool window.

Example
```
show the tool window
set the loc of tool window to 100,100
```

See Also   **choose, Properties**

Tools   Concept *(not a reserved word)*

Notes   Eighteen HyperCard modes that determine what effect mouse events (clicks and drags) have. Use the **tool** function to learn the current tool and the **choose** command to change the tool.

See Also   **choose, Tool Palette, tool window, tool**

top   Button/Field/Window Property

Syntax [the] top of <object/window>

Notes Returns the distance between the top of the screen and the top of the object or window in pixels. Equivalent to item 2 of the rect of <object or window>. Changing the top does not change the height but does change the bottom. Can be used with buttons, fields, and windows (card, tool, pattern, message).

1.2+ New version 1.2 feature.

Example
```
top of button 1
set the top of card field 1 to 100
set top of btn 1 to bottom of cd window/2
on mouseUp
  put "the message window" into field 1
  put top of field 1 into msg
  -- Returns top of the field
end mouseUp
```

See Also **bottom, bottomRight, cursor, height, left, right, set, topLeft, width, Windows**

topLeft   Button/Field/Window Property

Syntax [the] topLeft of <object/window>

Notes Returns the x and y coordinates in pixels for the left-top corner of a field, button, or window (card, tool, pattern, message). Equivalent to item 1 of the rect of <object or window> and item 2 of the rect of <object or window>. Changing the topLeft does not change the height or the width but does change the bottom and the right.

1.2+ New version 1.2 feature.

Example
```
topLeft of button 1
set the topLeft of card field 1 to 200,300
set topLeft of btn 1 to ¬
bottom of cd window/2,left of cd window/2
```

See Also **bottom, bottomRight, cursor, height, left, right, set, top, width, Windows**

Trace Edges   Menu Command

Notes Puts a ring of black pixels around every black pixel or grouping of black pixels in the current selection and turns the originally black pixels white. Available when a picture (graphic element) is selected.

Example doMenu "Trace Edges"

Transparent   Menu Command

Notes Turns all the white pixels in the current selection to transparent pixels. Available when a picture (graphic element) is selected.

Example doMenu "Transparent"

transparent   Button/Field Style

Notes   With buttons, you can see only the name and icon (if any); with fields, you can see only the text (if any). Transparent fields can be used where you would otherwise use paint text but need to edit the text. Transparent buttons can cover graphics and make any rectangular area of the screen a clickable region.

Examples   `set the style of button id 3 to transparent`

See Also   **Buttons, Fields, style**

true   Constant

Notes   Used in logical expressions to indicate that a condition is met. The same as the literal value "true." All Boolean expressions evaluate to either true or false.

Examples
```
put true into flag
put the mouse is down into flag -- true or false
if flag is true then beep
```

See Also   **Constants, Control Structures, if**

trunc   Math Function

Syntax
```
the trunc of <number>
trunc(<number>)
```

Notes   Returns the integer of the number, disregarding anything to the right of the decimal point. Parentheses are sometimes required to correctly interpret an expression: `the trunc of var1 * var2 - var3` would equal `(the trunc of var1) * var2 - var3`.

Example
```
the trunc of 4.89 -- Returns 4
trunc(numVar)
trunc(numVar*the number of cards)
```

See Also   **round**

two   Constant

Notes   The number 2.

Examples   `put two into line two of field two of card two`

See Also   **Constants**

type   Command

Syntax   `type <string> [with modKey [,modKey2 [,modKey3]]]`

Notes   Used to simulate the user typing to a field with the browse tool or to the current picture layer with the text tool. Can also simulate the user making keyboard alternative selections of the Menu Commands. The modifier keys, principally `commandKey`, are used to simulate the user making keyboard alternative menu selections.

Caution   The modifier keys are not used to reproduce the characters they would produce if you were typing into a field from the keyboard. To produce an uppercase A, you must put an uppercase A into the `type` command string.

1.2 +   In a locked stack, you can't use `type` unless the `userModify` property is set to true.

Examples
```
type "Hello"
on mouseUp
  -- Button handler. Requires a wide field with two lines
  put "It's really the thing" into textVar
  choose text tool
  click at 50,50
  type textVar
  -- Content of variable typed on screen at 50,50
  type "x" with commandKey
  -- Cuts the text to the clipboard
  type tab with commandKey -- Select browse tool
  type tab -- Selects the text in the first field
  type "This is the spirit of your Macintosh"
  -- Replaces the text in the field
  type return -- Starts a second line in the field
  type textVar
  type "q" with commandKey -- Quits HyperCard
end mouseUp
```

See Also   **put**

Typing Level   Concept *(not a reserved word)*

Notes   The second of HyperCard's five user levels. Allows the user to type into fields but prevents any other modifications of the stack.

See Also   **userLevel**

Undo   Menu Command

Notes   Restores changes to pictures, text, buttons, and fields since the last mouse click or Clipboard operation. Text and picture deletions can be restored but not button or field deletions. Card deletions can be undone in versions after 1.1.

Keyboard   Command-Z

Example
```
doMenu "Undo"
on mouseUp
  choose button tool
  drag from loc of button 1 to 100,100
  drag from loc of button 1 to 200,200
  doMenu "Undo" -- Button returned to 100,100
end mouseUp
```

unlock screen   Command

Syntax   `unlock screen [with [visual] [effect] <name> [<speed>] [to ¬ <image>]]`

Notes   Equivalent to the statement `set lockScreen to false`. Shows the screen after it has been locked to prevent updating during changes or transitions. The command adds the option of unlocking with a visual effect. See the *visual* listing for details.

1.2 +   New version 1.2 feature.

unlock screen

Caution   As with `lockScreen`, if you set the value to true twice in the same script, you must set it to false twice if you want to show the screen before the handler ends. The `speed` and `image` parameters for the `visual effect` option cannot be provided in a container; they must be literals (but see the `do` command). Visual effects work only when the browse tool is selected and the screen is unlocked. On the Mac II, you must also set the Characteristics in the Monitor section of the Control Panel to "2 colors" or to "2 grays".

Examples
```
unlock screen
unlock screen with venetian blinds fast to inverse
on mouseUp
   lock screen
   choose oval tool
   set centered to true
   set filled to true
   set pattern to 5
   drag from 256,156 to 400,300 with shiftKey
   choose browse tool
   -- Visual effects in Browse mode only
   unlock screen with dissolve slow to card
   -- Show the changed card
end mouseUp
```

See Also   **lock screen, lockMessages, visual**

until   Reserved Word

Notes   Used with `repeat` loop statements that test a specified value before each iteration of the loop. The loop continues in effect until the condition is met. Also used in `wait` statements that wait for a value to meet a condition before continuing.

Examples
```
repeat until the mouse is down
wait until the shiftKey is down
```

See Also   **repeat, wait**

up   Constant

Notes   A value returned by the functions `commandKey`, `mouse`, `optionKey`, and `shiftKey` and as a parameter by the `arrowKey` command. The same as the literal value "up." Used to evaluate the state of the mouse button or selected keyboard keys.

Examples
```
wait until the mouse is up -- Program flow holds here
on arrowKey which
   if which is up then go home
   else pass arrowKey
end arrowKey
```

See Also   **arrowKey, Constants,** *(individual function listings)*

User Defined Commands   Concept *(not a reserved word)*

Notes   See **User Defined Messages** for introductory material. User defined commands are just like the built-in commands, except that you make up their names and determine what they will do.

Example
```
-- User Command to restore usual values, etc.
userCommand
-- Command name used on a line of a handler or in message box
on userCommand
  reset paint
  choose browse tool
  show message box
  show menuBar
end userCommand
on mouseUp
  put "field 1,field 2,field 3" into var1
    -- Field list
  put 50 into var2 -- The left side
  userCmd2 var1,var2
    -- User command with parameters
end mouseUp
on userCmd2 var1,var2
  -- User command handler that lines up the
  -- left sides of fields
  repeat with i = 1 to the number of items in var1
    set left of item i of var1 to var2
  end repeat
end userCmd2
```

See Also **Commands, Messages, User Defined Functions, User Defined Messages**

User Defined Functions

Concept *(not a reserved word)*

Notes See **User Defined Messages** for introductory material. User defined functions are more complicated than user defined commands. The syntax for the function is

```
functionName (<argument list>)
```

The (**<argument list>**) can be empty, although the parentheses are required, or it can be any number of comma-separated values. The function handler starts with the keyword **function** instead of **on** but is otherwise like other message handlers. As with built-in functions, a function is replaced in the statement that executed it by the value it returns. In a user defined function handler, the keyword **return** is used to send the value back to the statement.

Examples
```
function userFunction
  return "This is version" && the version
end userFunction -- "This is version 1.2" goes in msg
put userFunction() into msg -- Enter in message box
```

See Also **function** *(keyword)*, **Functions, Messages, return** *(keyword)*, **User Defined Commands, User Defined Messages**

User Defined Messages

Concept *(not a reserved word)*

Notes HyperTalk gives you the ability to create your own messages by making up a message name and writing a handler for it. The message name can be any combination of alphanumeric characters and the underscore character (_). The name must start with a letter and can't include spaces or any punctuation marks. User

737

User Defined Messages

defined messages can pass parameters just like the built-in messages. There are three types of user defined messages: user defined commands, user defined functions, and subroutine/handlers. The first two have their own listing, so we cover only subroutine/handlers here. Besides commands and functions, you can use the send keyword to run subroutine/handlers. The message that starts a subroutine/handler is like a user defined command except that it can't pass parameters. Subroutine/handlers are a good way to break up long and complicated handlers. Also used to isolate elements that would benefit from having local variables that are not shared with the rest of the handler. You must use global variables to share values between a subroutine/handler and the handler that called it.

Examples
```
send subroutineMessage to button "Print"
-- Statement in a handler that launches a subroutine
on subroutineMessage
   -- Card handler for user defined subroutine message
   global cardNum
   open printing with dialog
   print card cardNum
   close printing
end subroutineMessage
```

See Also   **Commands, Functions, Parameters, Variables**

User Preferences

Concept *(not a reserved word)*

Notes   A selection of properties that can be set with buttons located on the last card of the Home stack. These properties include: userLevel, powerKeys, and blindTyping.

1.1 +   A button to set the textArrows property was added to version 1.1.

userLevel

Global Property

Syntax   [the] userLevel

Notes   Returns the current userLevel setting. The possible values are 1 (Browsing), 2 (Typing), 3 (Painting), 4 (Authoring), and 5 (Scripting). The higher the number, the more the user, and your scripts, can do.

Caution   The userLevel can be restricted by settings in the Protect Stack dialog box.

Examples
```
the userLevel -- Returns a number between 1 and 5
put userLevel into userWas
-- Preserves starting userLevel
set userLevel to 4 -- Change userLevel
doMenu "Stack Info..." -- Show dialog box
set the userLevel to userWas
-- Restore previous userLevel
```

userModify

Property

Syntax   [the] userModify

Notes   When userModify is true, the user can make changes to a card even if cantModify is true. The Painting tools can be used, text can be edited, and objects can be edited, but the changes are not saved when the card is closed. The

738

combination of `cantModify` and `userModify` gives the user a chance to actually use a stack without allowing the stack to be altered. Although `userModify` is called a global property, it is set to false each time a stack is closed, so it must be set to true on a stack by stack basis.

1.2+   New version 1.2 feature.

Examples
```
the userModify  -- Returns true or false
set userModify to true
```

See Also   **cantModify**

Value   Concept

Notes   The raw material of data processing. In HyperTalk, a value can be a number, a text string, a date, or the time. The sources of value, besides the numbers and literals input by users, include functions, properties, expressions, and containers. Values of all types are stored in containers as text strings and reinterpreted as needed.

See Also   **Constants, Containers, Literals**

value   Math/Misc. Function

Syntax
```
[the] value of <expression>
value(<expression>)
```

Notes   Returns the value of the expression. The expression can be an expression in a container or a literal string between quotation marks. `value` is also used with `me` and `target` to force the return of the contents of a field rather than the name of the field.

Example
```
the value of sin(7*9/3) -- Returns 0.836656
put "sin(7*9/3)" into numVar -- sin(7*9/3)
put the value of numVar into card field 2
-- 0.836656
put "3*9+2" into expressionVar
put expressionVar into msg -- Displays 3*9+2
put value of expressionVar into msg -- 39
on mouseUp
   put 4 into var1
   put var1 & " + 10" into var2
   -- var2 contains 4 + 10
   put value of var2 & " * " & var1 into var3
   -- var3 contains 14 * 4
   put the value of var3 into msg -- Returns 56
end mouseUp
on mouseUp
   put "card field 3" into target
   set the lockText of the value of the target to false
   -- Locks card field 3
end mouseUp
```

Variable   Concept *(not a reserved word)*

Notes   A variable is a reference to a value (of any length) stored in RAM. Variables and control structures are the two essential elements of all computer languages.

Variable

HyperTalk has global and local variables (plus several other kinds of containers that have some of the same features usually associated with variables). The default variable type is local except in the Message box where all variables are global. Both local and global variables can contain a string of any length (limited only by memory) and can be accessed more quickly than fields or files saved to disk. Variables also vanish when HyperCard is interrupted, so keep values you don't want to lose in fields or transfer them into fields on `suspend`, `quit`, or `closeStack` messages. The theoretical maximum number of variables that can be active at one time is 512, but actual limits are determined by the size of the variables and the amount of RAM available. Naming: Variable names must start with an alphabetic character and can contain any combination of alphanumeric characters and the underscore character (_). They must start with a letter and can't contain spaces or punctuation marks. Variables are commonly written in all lowercase letters except for the first letters of words after the first (`myVar`, `yourVar`, `varContainerBob`). You can also separate words with the underscore character (`my_var`, `your_var`, `var_container_bob`). You might also consider capitalizing the first letter of global variables to distinguish them from local variables. To avoid conflicts with global variables of different stacks, you might give all the globals of a given stack a distinctive prefix or suffix.

See Also   **Containers, Global Variables, Local Variables, Values**

venetian blinds   Visual Effect

Notes   An effect in which the card changes to the destination card or image in horizontal bars.

Example
```
visual effect venetian blinds very slow to black
go prev
```

See Also   **visual**

version   System Function

Syntax
```
[the] version
the [long] version [of hypercard]
the version of <stackDescriptor>
```

Notes   The simple version of `version` returns the version of HyperCard in use. If your scripts take advantage of features introduced with 1.2 or later versions, you should use the `openStack` message to make sure the required version is running. The `long` modifier returns the standard Macintosh version resource format as explained in *Inside Macintosh*. The stack version returns a list of five numbers (01228000,012280000,01208000,01208000,2687277481). The first number tells which version of HyperCard created the stack; 01228000 is version 1.2.2. The second number tells which version last compacted the stack. The third number reports the oldest version of HyperCard that has changed the stack since it was last compacted. The fourth number tells which version of HyperCard last changed the stack. The fifth number is the number of seconds between midnight, January 1, 1904, and the time the stack was last modified and closed. If the stack was created, modified, or compacted by a version of HyperCard prior to 1.2, the number in the list will be 00000000.

1.2 +   New version 1.2 feature.

Example
```
the version -- Returns 1.2
the long version -- Returns 01208000
```

continued

```
the version of this stack
-- Returns 01228000,01228000,01208000,01208000,2687277481
on openStack -- Stack handler
  if the version < 1.2 then
    answer "Sorry, this stack requires version 1.2"
    go home
  end if
end openStack
```

visible   Button/Field/Window Property

Syntax   [the] visible of <button or field>

Notes   Returns true if the specified object is not hidden and false if the object is hidden. Changing the visible property hides or shows the object.

Caution   Just because the visible of an object is true doesn't mean that the user can necessarily see it. An object can be visible on the screen but concealed under graphics or other objects. You can't see buttons and fields that are located off the card window. Neither can you see a button or field if its rectangle property is set with the bottom right corner above or to the left of its top left corner.

Examples
```
the visible of field 1-- Returns true or false
set the visible of button 2 to false -- Hides button
set visible of objectVar to not visible of objectVar
-- The variable holds the name of a button or field
```

See Also   **hide, Properties, show**

visual   Command

Syntax   visual [effects] <effect name> [<speed>] [to <image>]

Notes   When used with a go command, visual causes a visual effect during the transition from one card to the next. Several visual commands can be executed in succession for complex effects. Besides the simple effects, you can also control the speed of the transition with the **speed** parameter and specify what the screen will look like at the end of an effect with the image parameter (best used in a sequence of effects). Visual effects are ignored if they are not followed by a go command. Can be used without actually going to another card with the go to this card option.

▶ **Visual Effects**

barn door	barn door		
close	open		
checkerboard			
dissolve			
iris close	iris open		
plain			
scroll down	scroll left	scroll right	scroll up
venetian blinds			
wipe down	wipe left	wipe right	wipe up

visual

zoom close   zoom in   zoom open   zoom out

  ▶ **Speed Modifiers**

fast   very fast   slow

slowly   very slow   very slowly

  ▶ **Image Modifiers**

black   card   gray

inverse   white

Caution   The `speed` and `image` parameters cannot be provided in a container; they must be literals (but see the **do** command). Visual effects work only when the browse tool is selected and the screen is unlocked. On the Mac II, you must also set the Characteristics in the Monitor section of the Control Panel to "2 colors" or "2 grays".

Examples
```
visual effect dissolve
visual effect wipe left slowly
visual checkerboard fast to black
put "checkerboard" into effectVar
do "visual" && effectVar && "slowly to inverse"
on mouseUp
   -- Handler showing effect sequence on one card
   visual effect iris open slowly to black
   visual effect barn door open fast to card
   go to this card
end mouseUp
```

See Also   **go**

wait   Command

Syntax
```
wait [for] <number> [seconds | ticks]
wait until <condition>
wait while <condition>
```

Notes   Stops program flow for a specified period of time, until a condition is met, or as long as a condition is met. If a number follows `wait`, the default unit of time is ticks (1/60th of a second), although you can also specify seconds. A condition can be anything that evaluates to true. Examples of conditions include `the mouse is down`, `the optionKey is down`, `not the ticks < 45899`, `the sound is "done"`, `the sound is "boing"`, or `the mouseClick`.

Examples
```
wait 5 -- Waits 5 ticks
wait 4 secs -- Waits 4 seconds
wait timeVar -- Waits for time value in the variable
wait until the mouseClick
-- Waits for the mouse button to be clicked
wait while the mouseH is < 450 and the mouseV < 250
wait until the sound is "done" or the sound is "boing"
```

watch   Cursor

Notes   The little watch you see whenever you have to wait. Can also be referred to as cursor 4.

742

Example   `Set cursor to watch`

See Also   **cursor**

wideMargins   Field Property

Syntax   `[the] wideMargins of <field>`

Notes   Returns true if the specified field has `wideMargins` and false if it doesn't. A field with `wideMargins` set to true has more space between the text and the field border than it would if `wideMargins` was set to false.

Examples
```
the wideMargins of field 1 -- Returns true or false
set the wideMargins of card field 2 to false
-- Narrower margins
set wideMargins of fieldVar to true
-- The variable holds the name of a field
```

width   Button/Field Property

Syntax   `[the] width of <designator>`

Notes   Returns the width in pixels of a specified field, button, or windoid. When used with `set`, it preserves the mid point and extends or retracts the right and left sides.

1.2+   New version 1.2 feature.

Example
```
put the width of message box into message box -- 472
set width of card field id 3 to 200
on closeCard
-- Handler to re-size fields to same width
  repeat with i = 1 to the number of fields
    put the width of field i & "," after maxVar
  end repeat
  put max(maxVar) into maxVar
  repeat with i = 1 to the number of fields
    set the width of field i to maxVar
  end repeat
end closeCard
```

See Also   **visual, gray**

Windoids   Concept *(not a reserved word)*

Notes   Little windows with close boxes and drag bars but no other window controls. See individual listings.

See Also   **hide, message box, Pattern Palette, Properties, show, Tool Palette, Windows**

Windows   Concept *(not a reserved word)*

Notes   HyperCard has one main window, called the card window, and three special purpose windows, also known as Windoids: the tool window, pattern window, and message window. See individual listings.

See Also   **hide, message box, Pattern Palette, Properties, show, Tool Palette, Windoids**

wipe

wipe   Visual Effect

Notes   An effect in which the card changes to the destination card or image in a wave from one side to the opposite side. The `wipe` options include `up`, `down`, `left`, and `right`.

Example
```
visual effect wipe left to black
visual effect wipe right
go next
```

See Also   **visual**

with   Reserved Word

Notes   Used with `drag` and `type` commands to simulate the pressing of modifier keys.

Examples
```
drag from 50,50 to 100,100 with the optionKey
type "q" with commandKey
```

See Also   **repeat, wait**

within   Logical Operator

Notes   See listing for **is within**.

word   Chunk

Syntax   `word <number>`

Notes   Use `word` to specify a particular word in a container. A word is any group of characters set off by spaces.

Examples
```
get word 3 of field 2
put "HyperTalk" into word 2 of line 1 of selection
get word numberVar of field nameVar
```

See Also   **char, Chunks, Containers, field, item, line, wait**

words   Object Type

Notes   Used with `the number` function to indicate the object of the inquiry.

Example   `put "Not Empty" into word the number of words`

See Also   **field**

write   Command

Syntax   `write <container> to file <fileName>`

Notes   Sends the contents of the container to a buffer for the specified file. The file must already exist and have been opened with the `open file` command. If a `write` command follows a `read` command, the written data is appended to the read data in the buffer. Subsequent writes append more data to the buffer until a `close file` command replaces the previous contents of the file with the contents of the buffer.

Examples   `write textVariable to file "textFile"`

continued

```
write card field n to file stash
on mouseUp -- Button handler to write text to a file
  put "Combined Reference:HCFile:dataFile2" into ¬
  fileName
  open file fileName
  write field 1 to file fileName
  close file fileName
end mouseUp
on mouseUp -- Button handler to append text to a file
  put "Combined Reference:HCFile:dataFile2" into ¬
  fileName
  open file fileName
  -- Save old contents to buffer
  read from file fileName until "@"
  -- No @ in file so reads all
  write field 1 to file fileName -- Append to buffer
  close file fileName -- Replace file with buffer
end mouseUp
```

See Also **close file, open file, read**

zero Constant

Notes The number 0.

Examples
```
on mouseUp
  repeat until the number of fields is zero
    click at the loc of field the number of fields
    doMenu "Clear Field"
  end repeat
end mouseUp
```

See Also **Constants**

zoom Visual Effect

Notes An effect that causes rectangles to radiate from the click location (zoom open) or rectangles to collapse to the center of the card (zoom close). The zoom options include open or out and close or in.

Example
```
visual effect zoom out
go next
```

See Also **visual**

Index

The Waite Group

100 Shoreline Highway, Suite 285   Mill Valley, CA 94941   (415) 331-0575

Compuserve: 74146,3515   usernet: bplabs!well!mitch   AppleLink: D2097

Dear Reader:

Thank you for considering the purchase of our book. Readers have come to know products from **The Waite Group** for the care and quality we put into them. Let me tell you a little about our group and how we make our books.

It started in 1976 when I could not find a computer book that really taught me anything. The books that were available talked down to people, lacked illustrations and examples, were poorly laid out, and were written as if you already understood all the terminology. So I set out to write a good book about microcomputers. This was to be a special book—very graphic, with a friendly and casual style, and filled with examples. The result was an instant best-seller.

Over the years, I developed this approach into a "formula" (nothing really secret here, just a lot of hard work—I am a crazy man about technical accuracy and high-quality illustrations). I began to find writers who wanted to write books in this way. This led to co-authoring and then to multiple-author books and many more titles (over seventy titles currently on the market). As The Waite Group author base grew, I trained a group of editors to manage our products. We now have a team devoted to putting together the best possible book package and maintaining the high standard of our existing books.

We greatly appreciate and use any advice our readers send us (and you send us a lot). We have discovered that our readers are detail nuts: you want indexes that really work, tables of contents that dig deeply into the subject, illustrations, tons of examples, reference cards, and more.

I think you will find that **The Waite Group's Tricks of the HyperTalk Masters** is a good example of The Waite Group formula for a computer book. You'll find exciting and informative applications of HyperCard, tricks, facts, tips, projects, warnings, and much more. If you like this book, you may want to take a look at its companion title, **The Waite Group's HyperTalk Bible**. That book provides beginning to intermediate tutorials on the syntax of HyperTalk and teaches scripting using an object-oriented, hands-on approach.

If you'd like to extend your programming experience into the fast and powerful C language, you'll want to study our book **C Primer Plus**. This book teaches you generic ANSI C and prepares you for the next step of learning the complex Macintosh Toolbox. Watch for future Waite Group books in the Macintosh Library. A list of all our titles can be found in the back of this book. In fact, let us know what you want and we'll try to write about it.

Thanks again for considering the purchase of this title. If you care to tell me anything you like (or don't like) about the book, please write or send email to the addresses on this letterhead.

Sincerely,

Mitchell Waite
The Waite Group

The Waite Group Library

If you enjoyed this book, you may be interested in these additional subjects and titles from **The Wa** **Group** and Howard W. Sams & Company. Reader level is as follows: ★ = introductory, ★★ = intermedia ★★★ = advanced. You can order these books by calling 800-428-SAMS.

Level	Title	Catalog #	Price	
	C and C++ Programming Language			
Tutorial, UNIX & ANSI				
★	C Primer Plus, Revised Edition, Waite, Prata, & Martin	22582	$24.95	
★★	C++ Programming, Berry	22619	$24.95	
★★★	Advanced C Primer ++, Prata	22486	$24.95	
Tutorial, Product Specific				
★	Microsoft C Programming for the PC, Revised Edition, Lafore	22661	$24.95	NEW
★	Turbo C Programming for the PC, Revised Edition, Lafore	22660	$22.95	NEW
★★	Inside the Amiga with C, Second Edition, Berry	22625	$24.95	
Reference, Product Specific				
★★	Microsoft C Bible, Barkakati	22620	$24.95	NEW
★★	Quick C Bible, Barkakati	22632	$24.95	NEW
★★	Turbo C. Bible, Barkakati	22631	$24.95	NEW
★★	Essential Guide to ANSI C, Barkakati	22673	$7.95	NEW
★★	Essential Guide to Turbo C, Barkakati	22675	$7.95	NEW
★★	Essential Guide to Microsoft C, Barkakati	22674	$7.95	NEW
	DOS and OS/2 Operating System			
Tutorial, General Users				
★	Discovering MS-DOS, O'Day	22407	$19.95	
★	Understanding MS-DOS, O'Day & Angermeyer	27067	$17.95	
Tutorial/Reference, General Users				
★★	MS-DOS Bible, Second Edition, Simrin	22617	$22.95	
Tutorial/Reference, Power Users				
★★	Tricks of the MS-DOS Masters, Angermeyer & Jaeger	22525	$24.95	
Tutorial, Programmers				
★★	MS-DOS Papers, Edited by The Waite Group	22594	$26.95	
★★	OS/2 Programmer's Reference, Dror	22645	$24.95	NEW
★★★	MS-DOS Developer's Guide, Revised Edition, Angermeyer, Jaeger, et al.	22630	$24.95	NEW
	UNIX Operating System			
Tutorial, General Users				
★	UNIX Primer Plus, Waite, Prata, & Martin	22028	$22.95	
★	UNIX System V Primer, Revised Edition, Waite, Prata, & Martin	22570	$22.95	
★★	UNIX System V Bible, Prata and Martin	22562	$24.95	
★★	UNIX Communications, Henderson, Anderson, Costales	22511	$24.95	
★★	UNIX Papers, Edited by Mitchell Waite	22570	$26.95	
Tutorial/Reference, Power Users and Programmers				
★★	Tricks of the UNIX Masters, Sage	22449	$24.95	
★★★	Advanced UNIX—A Programmer's Guide, Prata	22403	$24.95	
	Macintosh			
Tutorial, General Users				
★	HyperTalk Bible, The Waite Group	48430	$24.95	NEW
Tutorial/Reference, Power Users and Programmers				
★★	Tricks of the HyperTalk Masters, Edited by The Waite Group	48431	$24.95	NEW

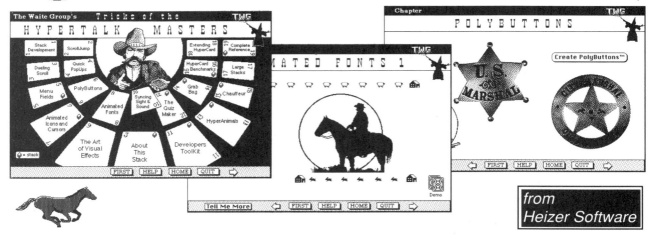

Please send me Tricks of the HyperTalk Masters: The Stacks

Name_____Office Use Only:_____

Daytime Phone   (_____)_____

Diskette Order Form

Set of Four Disks (30283)	$	50.00
Disk #1—Main Tricks (30279)	$	15.00
Disk #2—Sound & Front Ends (30280)	$	15.00
Disk #3—Developer's Tools (30281)	$	15.00
Disk #4—Complete HyperTalk Ref. (30282)	$	15.00
CA residents add 6.5% sales tax	$	
Shipping and Handling *US/Canada - $3 / Foreign - $7*	$	3.00 or 7.00
Heizer Software Catalog	$	**FREE**
Total	$	

Payment:

Check enclosed (payable to Heizer Software) #_____

VISA   VISA   MasterCard   MasterCard   AMERICAN EXPRESS   American Express

Card #_____ Exp. Date_____

Signature _____
(we cannot process credit card orders without your signature)

PLEASE PRINT:

Name_____

Organization_____

Address_____

City_____ State_____ Zip_____

Heizer Software

P.O. Box 232019
Pleasant Hill, CA 94523

USA

Tricks of the HyperTalk Masters: The Stacks

Please fold along line and tape closed. Do not staple.